Simon de La
Loube

re

A new historical relation of the Kingdom of Siam

Simon de La
Loube

re

A new historical relation of the Kingdom of Siam

ISBN/EAN: 9783742812674

Manufactured in Europe, USA, Canada, Australia, Japa

Cover: Foto ©Thomas Meinert / pixelio.de

Manufactured and distributed by brebook publishing software
(www.brebook.com)

Simon de La
Loube

re

A new historical relation of the Kingdom of Siam

A NEW

Historical Relation

OF THE

KINGDOM

OF

SIAM,

BY

Monsieur *DE LA LOUBERE*,

Envoy Extraordinary from the *FRENC[H]* KING, to the KING of *SIAM*, i[n] the years 1687 and 1688.

Wherein a full and curious Account is given of the *Ch[i]nese* Way of Arithmetick, and Mathematick Learnin[g]

In Two TOMES

Illustrated with SCULPTURES

Done out of *French*, by *A. P.* Gen. R. S. S.

LONDON,

Printed by *F. L.* for *Tho. Horne* at the *Roy[al] Exchange*, *Francis Saunders* at the *New E[x]change*, and *Tho. Bennet* at the *Half-Moon* i[n] St. *Pauls* Church-yard. M DC XCIII.

A TABLE OF THE CHAPTERS.

The Occasion and Design of this Work.

PART I.

Of the Country of Siam.

PART II.

Of the Manners of the Siameses *in general.*

A 2 XIII. Of

The CONTENTS.

PART III.

Of the Manners of the Siameses *according to their several Conditions.*

A NEW

HISTORICAL RELATION OF THE KINGDOM OF SIAM.

The Occasion and Design of this Work.

At my return from the Voyage I made to Siam, *in quality of his Most Christian Majesties Envoy Extraordinary, they whose right it is to command, requir'd me to render them an exact account of the things, which I had seen or learnt in that Country; which will be the whole matter of this work. Others have sufficiently informed the Public of the Circumstances of this long Voyage: But as to what concerns the Description of a Country, we cannot have too many Relations, if we would perfectly know it; the last always illustrating the former. But that it may be known from what time I write, I shall declare only that we set Sail from* Brest *on the First of* March, Anno 1687. *That we cast Anchor in the Road of* Siam *the* 27th *of* September, *in the same Year. That we departed thence for our return the* 3d *of* January, 1688. *And that we landed at* Brest *the* 27th *of* July *following.* The Occasion of this work.

My Design is therefore to treat first of the Country of Siam, *its Extent, Fertility, and the qualities of its Soil and Climate: Secondly, I will explain the manners of the* Siameses *in general, and then their particular Customs according to their various Qualities. Their Government and Religion shall be comprehended in the last part; and I flatter my self that the further the Reader shall advance in the perusal of this work, the more he will find it worthy of Curiosity; by reason that the Nature and Genius of the* Siameses, *which I have every where endeavoured to penetrate into, will be discovered more and more. In fine, not to stay on things, which would not please every one, or which would interrupt my Narrative* too *much, I will at the end insert several Memoirs which I brought from this Country,* The Design of this work.

and which I cannot ſuppreſs without injuring the Curioſity of the Public. But if notwithſtanding this precaution, I do yet enlarge on certain matters beyond the reliſh of ſome, I intreat them to conſider that general expreſſions do never afford juſt Idea's; and that this is to proceed no farther than the ſuperficial Knowledge of things. 'Tis out of this deſire of making the Siameſes *perfectly known, that I give ſeveral notices of the other Kingdoms of the* Indies *and of* China: *For though rigorouſly taken, all this may appear foreign to my Subject, yet to me it ſeems that the Compariſon of the things of Neighbouring Countries with each other, does greatly illuſtrate them. I hope alſo that a pardon will be granted me for the* Siameſe *names, which I relate and explain. Theſe remarks will make other relations intelligible as well as mine, which without theſe Illuſtrations might ſometimes cauſe a doubt concerning what I aſſert.*

In a word, thoſe with whom I am acquainted do know that I love the Truth; but it is not ſufficient to give a ſincere relation to make it appear true: 'Tis requiſite to add clearneſs to ſincerity, and to be thoroughly informed of that wherein we undertake to inſtruct others. I have therefore conſidered, interrogated, and penetrated, as far as it was poſſible; and to render my ſelf more capable of doing it, I carefully read over, before my arrival at Siam, *ſeveral Antient and Modern Relations of divers Countreys of the Eaſt. So that in my opinion this preparation has ſupplied the defect of a longer reſidence, and has made me to remark and underſtand in the three Months I was at* Siam, *what I could not perhaps have underſtood or remark'd in three Years, without the aſſiſtance and peruſal of thoſe Diſcourſes.*

PART

A MAPP of the KINGDOME of SIAM
Golfe of Siam
Golfe of Bengale
Upper Siam
Siam
Pegu
Martaban
Cap of Camboya
Cap of Singapura
Part of Sumatra
The Streights of Malacca
Golfe of Cochinchina
Pulo Cornoro
Patane
Bintang I.

PART I.

Of the Country of Siam.

CHAP. I.

The Geographical Description.

NAvigation has sufficiently made known the Sea Coasts of the Kingdom of *Siam*, and many Authors have described them: but they know almost nothing of the Inland Country, because the *Siameses* have not made a Map of their Country, or at least know how to keep it secret. That which I here present is the work of an *European*, who went up the *Menam*, the principal River of the Country, to the Frontiers of the Kingdom; but was not skilful enough to give all the Positions with an entire exactness. Besides he has not seen all; and therefore I thought it necessary to give his Map to Mr. *Cassini*, Director of the Observatory at *Paris*, to correct it by some Memorials which were given me at *Siam*. Nevertheless I know it to be still defective; but yet it fails not to give some notions of this Kingdom which were never heard of, and of being more exact in those we already have. *How much this Kingdom is unknown.*

Its Frontiers extend Northward to the 22d Degree, or thereabouts; and the Road which terminates the Gulph of *Siam*, being almost at the Latitude of 13 degrees and a half, it follows, that this whole extent, of which we hardly have any knowledge, runs about 170 Leagues in a direct Line, reckoning 20 Leagues to a degree of Latitude, after the manner of our Seamen. *Its Frontiers Northward.*

The *Siameses* do say that the City of *Chiamai* is fifteen days journey more to the North, than the Frontiers of their Kingdom, that is to say at most, between sixty and seventy Leagues; for they are Journeys by water, and against the Stream. 'Tis about thirty years since their King, as they report, took this City, and abandon'd it, after having carried away all the People; and it has been since repeopled by the King of *Ava*, to whom *Pegu* does at present render Obedience. But the *Siameses* which were at that expedition, do not know that famous Lake, from whence our Geographers make the River *Menam* arise and to which, according to them, this City gives its Name: which makes me to think either that it is more distant than our Geographers have conceived, or that there is no such Lake. It may also happen that this City adjoyning to several Kingdoms, and being more subject than another to be ruined by War, has not always been rebuilt in the same place: And this is not difficult to imagine of the Cities which are built only with wood, as all in these Countreys are, and which in their destruction leave not any Ruines nor Foundations. However it may be doubted, whether the *Menam* springs from a Lake, by reason it is so small at its entrance into the Kingdom of *Siam*, that for about fifty Leagues, it carries only little Boats capable of holding no more than four or five Persons at most. *The City of Chiamai and its Lake.*

The Kingdom of *Siam* is bounded from the East to the North by high Mountains, which separate it from the Kingdom of *Laos*, and on the North and West by others, which divide it from the Kingdoms of *Pegu* and *Ava*. This double Chain of Mountains (inhabited by a few, savage, and poor, but yet free People, whose Life is innocent) leaves between them a great Valley, containing in some places between fourscore and an hundred Leagues in breadth, and is wa- *The Country of Siam is only a Valley.*

tered

tered from the City of *Chiamai* to the Sea, that is to say from the North to the South, with an excellent River which the *Siamese* call *Me-nam*, or *Mother-water*, to signifie, *a great water*, which being encreased by the Brooks and Rivers it receives on every side, from the Mountains I have mentioned, discharges it self at last into the Gulph of *Siam* by three mouths, the most navigable of which is that toward the East.

Cities seated on the River. On this River, and about seven Miles from the Sea, is seated the City of *Bancok*: and I shall transiently declare, that the *Siamese* have very few habitations on their Coasts, which are not far distant from thence; but are almost all seated on Rivers navigable enough to afford them the Commerce of the Sea. As to the names of most of these places, which for this reason may be called Maritime, they are disguised by Foreigners. Thus the City of *Bancok* is called *Fon* in *Siamese*, it not being known from whence the name of *Bancok* is derived, altho there be several *Siamese* Names, that begin with the word *Ban*, which signifies a Village.

The Gardens of *Bancok*. The Gardens which are in the Territory of *Bancok*, for the space of four Leagues, in ascending towards the City of *Siam* to a place named *Talacoan*, do supply this City with the Nourishment which the Natives of the Country love best, I mean a great quantity of Fruit.

Other Cities on the *Menam*. The other principal places which the *Menam* waters, are, *Me-Tac* the first City of the Kingdom to the North North-West, and then successively *Tian-Tong*, *Campeng-pet* or *Campeng* simple, which some do pronounce *Campingpet*, *Laconcevan*, *Tchainat*, *Siam*, *Talacoan*, *Talaquiat*, and *Bancok*. Between the two Cities of *Tchainat* and *Siam*, and at a distance, which the Meanders of the River do render almost equal from each other, the River leaves the City of *Louvo* a little to the East, at the 14 d. 42 m. 32 S. of Latitude, according to the observations which the Jesuites have published. The King of *Siam* does there spend the greatest part of the year, the more commodiously to enjoy the diversion of Hunting: but *Louvo* would not be habitable, were it not for a channel cut from the River to water it. The City of *Me-Tac* renders obedience to an Hereditary Lord, who, they say, is a Vassal to the King of *Siam*, whom some call *Paya-Tac*, or Prince of *Tac*. *Tian-Tong* is ruin'd, doubtless by the Ancient Wars of *Pegu*. *Campeng* is known by the Mines of excellent Steel.

Another River likewise called *Menam*. At the City of *Laconcevan* the *Menam* receives another considerable River which comes also from the North, and is likewise called *Menam*, a name common to all great Rivers. Our Geographers make it to spring from the Lake of *Chiamai*; but it is certain that it hath its source in the Mountains, which lye not so much to the North as this City. It runs first to *Meuang-fang*, then to *Pitchiai*, *Pitsanoulouc*, and *Pitchit*, and at last to *Laconcevan*, where it mixes, as I have said with the other River.

Pitsanoulouc, which the *Portugueses* do corruptly call *Porselouc* has formerly had hereditary Lords, like the City of *Me-Tac*: and Justice is at present executed in the Palace of the Ancient Princes. 'Tis a City of great commerce, fortified with fourteen Bastions, and is at 19 degrees and some minutes Latitude.

Laconcevan stands about the mid-way from *Pitsanoulouc* or *Porselouc* to *Siam*, a distance computed to be Twenty five days Journey, for those that go up the River in a Boat or *Balon*; but this voyage may be performed in twelve days when they have a great many Rowers, and they ascend the River with speed.

Cities of Wood. These Cities, like all the rest in the Kingdom of *Siam*, are only a great number of Cabbins frequently environ'd with an enclosure of Wood, and sometimes with a Brick, or Stone Wall, but very rarely of Stone. Nevertheless as the Eastern people have ever had as much magnificence and pride in the figures of their Language, as simplicity and poverty in whatever appertains to Life, the names of these Cities do signifie great things; *Tian-Tong*, for instance, signifies *True Gold*; *Campeng-pet*, *Walls of Diamond*; and 'tis said that its Walls are of Stone: and *Laconcevan* signifies the *Mountain of Heaven*.

The superstition of the *Siamese* at *Meuang-fang*. But as for what concerns *Meuang fang*, the word *Fang* being the name of a Tree famous for dying, and which the *Portugueses* have called *Sapan*; some in-

terpret

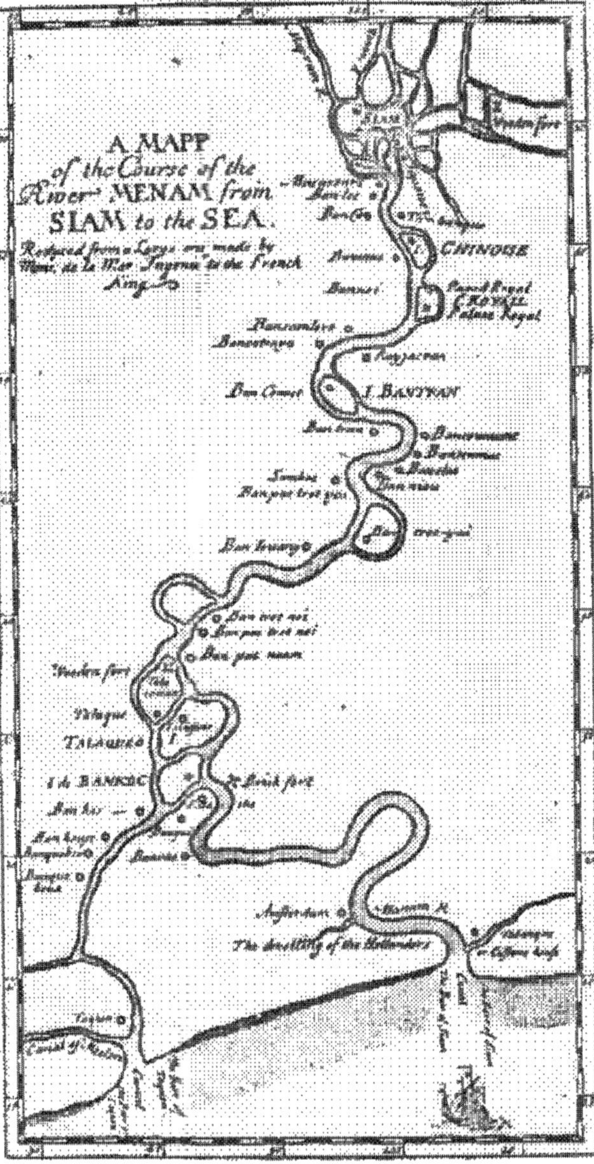

A MAPP of the Course of the River MENAM from SIAM to the SEA.
Reduced from a Large one made by Mons. de la Mar Ingenier to the French King
I. CHINOISE
Palais Royal
I. BANTYAN
Wooden fort
TALAQUEO
I. de BANKOC
Brick fort
Amsterdam
The dwelling of the Hollanders

terpret it the *City of the word of Sapan.* And because that there is kept a Tooth, which is pretended to be a Relick of *Sommona-Codom,* to whose Memory the *Siameses* do erect all their Temples; there are some who call not this City *Mouang-sang,* but *Mouang-leou,* or the *City of the Tooth.* The superstition of these people continually draws thither a great number of Pilgrims, not *Siameses* only, but from *Pegu,* and *Laos.*

Such another Superstition prevails at a place named *Pra bat,* about five or six leagues to the East-North-East of the City of *Louvo*; the superstition is this; In the *Balie* Language, which is the learned tongue of the *Siameses,* or the Tongue of their Religion, *Bat* signifies a *Foot,* and the word *Pra,* of which it is not possible exactly to render the signification, signifies in the same tongue whatever may be conceived worthy of veneration and respect. The *Siameses* do give this title to the Sun and Moon, but they do also give it to *Sommona-Codom,* to their Kings, and some considerable Officers. *Another Superstition at Prabat.*

The *Prabat* is therefore the print of a mans foot, cut by an ill Graver upon a Rock; but this impression containing about 13 or 14 inches in depth, is five or six times as long as a man's Foot, and proportionably as broad. The *Siameses* adore it, and are perswaded that the Elephants, especially the white ones, the Rhinoceros, and all the other Beasts of their Woods, do likewise go to worship it when no person is there; And the King of *Siam* himself goes to adore it once a year with a great deal of Pomp and Ceremony. It is covered with a Plate of Gold, and inclosed in a Chappel which is there built. They report that this Rock which is now very flat and like a new mown Field, was formerly a very high Mountain, which shrunk and waxed level on a sudden under the Foot of *Sommona-Codom,* in memory of whom they believe that the Impression of the Foot does there remain. Nevertheless it is certain by the Testimony of ancient men, that the Antiquity of this Tradition exceeds not 90 years. A *Talapoin,* or Religious *Siamese,* of that time, having doubtless made this Impression himself, or procured it to be made, and then feigned to have miraculously discovered it; and without any other appearance of Truth, gave Reputation and Credit to this Fable of the levell'd Mountain. *What it is.*

Now in all this the *Siameses* are only gross Imitators. In the Histories of *India* it is related, with what respect a King of the Island of *Ceylan* kept an Apes Tooth, which the *Indians* averred to be a Relique, and with what Sums he endeavoured to purchase and ransom it from *Constantine* of *Braganza,* then Viceroy of the *Indies,* who had found it amongst the Spoils taken from the *Indians*: But *Constantine* chose rather to burn it, and afterwards threw the Ashes into a River. 'Tis known likewise that in the same Island of *Ceylan,* which the *Indians* do call *Lanca,* and on a real Mountain which is not levelled, there is a pretended print of a Man's foot, which has for a long time been in great Veneration there. It doubtless represents the Left foot: For the *Siameses* report that *Sommona-Codom* set his right foot on their *Prabat,* and his left on *Lanca*; altho the whole Gulph of *Bengala* runs between them. *The Original of this Superstition.*

The *Portugueses* have called the Print at *Ceylan Adam's* Foot, and believe that *Ceylan* was the Terrestrial Paradise, from the Faith of the *Indians* at *Ceylan,* who declare that the Impression which they reverence, is the Print of the first Man: Every one of these Heathenish Nations vigorously affecting that the first Man inhabited their Country. Thus the *Chineses* do call the first man *Pouon-kou,* and believe that he inhabited *China.* I say nothing of some other Impressions of this nature, which are rever'd in several places of the *Indies*; nor of the pretended print of *Hercules* foot, mentioned by *Herodotus.* I return to my subject. *What the Adam's foot of Ceylon is.* *Lib. 4. c. 82.*

CHAP. II.

A Continuation of the Geographical Description of the Kingdom of Siam, *with an Account of its Metropolis.*

Other Cities of the Kingdom of *Siam*.

ON the Frontiers of *Pegu* is seated the City of *Cambory*, and on the borders of *Laos* the Town of *Corazema*, which some do call *Corosema*, both very Famous. And in the Lands which lie between the Rivers above the City of *Locontai*, and on the Channels which have a Communication from one River to the other, there are two other considerable Cities, *Socotai*, almost in the same Latitude with *Pitchit*, and *Sangueloue* more to the North.

A Country intersected with Channels.

The Country being so hot that it is inhabitable only near Rivers, the *Siamese* have cut a great many Channels, and without having better Memoirs or Notes, 'tis impossible to reckon up all the Cities seated thereon.

The City of *Siam* described.

'Tis by the means of these Channels, called by the *Siamese Clom*, that the City of *Siam* is not only become an Island, but is placed in the middle of several Islands, which renders the situation thereof very singular. The Isle wherein it is situated, is at present all inclosed within its walls, which certainly was not in the time of *Ferdinand Mendez Pinto*; if notwithstanding the continual mistakes of this Author, who seems to rely too much on his memory, we may believe what he says, that the Elephants of the King of *Pegu*, who then besieged the City of *Siam*, did so nearly approach the Walls, as with their Trunks to beat down the Palisado's which the *Siamese* had there placed to cover themselves.

Its Latitude, according to Father *Thomas* the Jesuit, is 14 d. 20 m. 40 S. and its Longitude 120 d. 30 m. It has almost the figure of a Purse, the mouth of which is to the East, and the bottom to the West. The River meets it at the North by several Channels, which run into that which environs it, and leaves it on the South, by separating itself again into several streams. The King's Palace stands to the North on the Canal which embraces the City; and by turning to the East, there is a Causey, by which alone, as by an *Isthmus*, People may go out of the City without crossing the water.

The City is spacious, considering the Circuit of its Walls, which, as I have said, incloses the whole Isle; but scarce the sixth part thereof is inhabited, and that to the South-East only. The rest lies desert, where the Temples only stand. 'Tis true that the Suburbs, which are possessed by strangers, do considerably increase the number of the People. The streets thereof are large and strait, and in some places planted with Trees, and paved with Bricks laid edgewise. The Houses are low, and built with Wood; at least those belonging to the Natives, who, for these Reasons are exposed to all the inconveniences of the excessive heat. Most of the streets are watered with strait Canals, which have made *Siam* to be compar'd to *Venice*, and on which are a great many small Bridges of Hurdles, and some of Brick very high and ugly.

Its Name.

The Name of *Siam* is unknown to the *Siamese*. 'Tis one of those words which the *Portugues* of the *Indies* do use, and of which it is very difficult to discover the Original. They use it as the Name of the Nation, and not of the Kingdom: And the Names of *Pegu*, *Lao*, *Mogul*, and most of the Names which we give to the *Indian* Kingdoms, are likewise National Names; so that to speak rightly, we must say, the King of the *Peguins*, *Laos*, *Moguls*, *Siams*, as our Ancestors said, the King of the *Francs*. In a word, those that understand *Portuguese*, do well know that according to their Orthography, *Siao* and *Siam* are the same thing; and that by the Similitude of our Language to theirs, we ought to say the *Siams*, and not the *Siamese*: so when they write in Latin, they call them *Siones*.

The true Name of the *Siamese* signifies *Franks*.

The *Siamese* give to themselves the Name of *Tai*, or *Free*, as the word now signifies in their Language: And thus they flatter themselves with bearing the Name

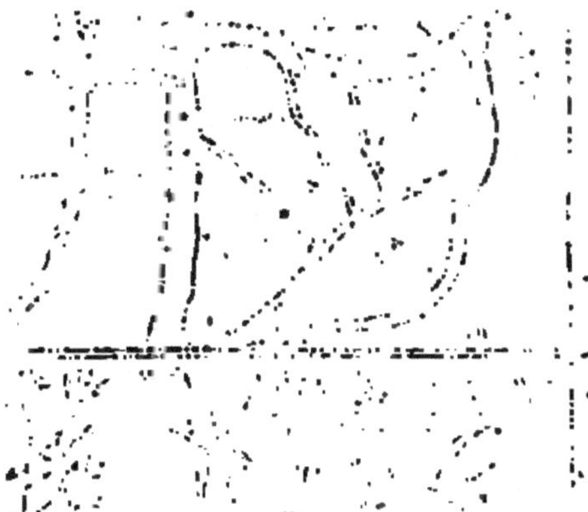

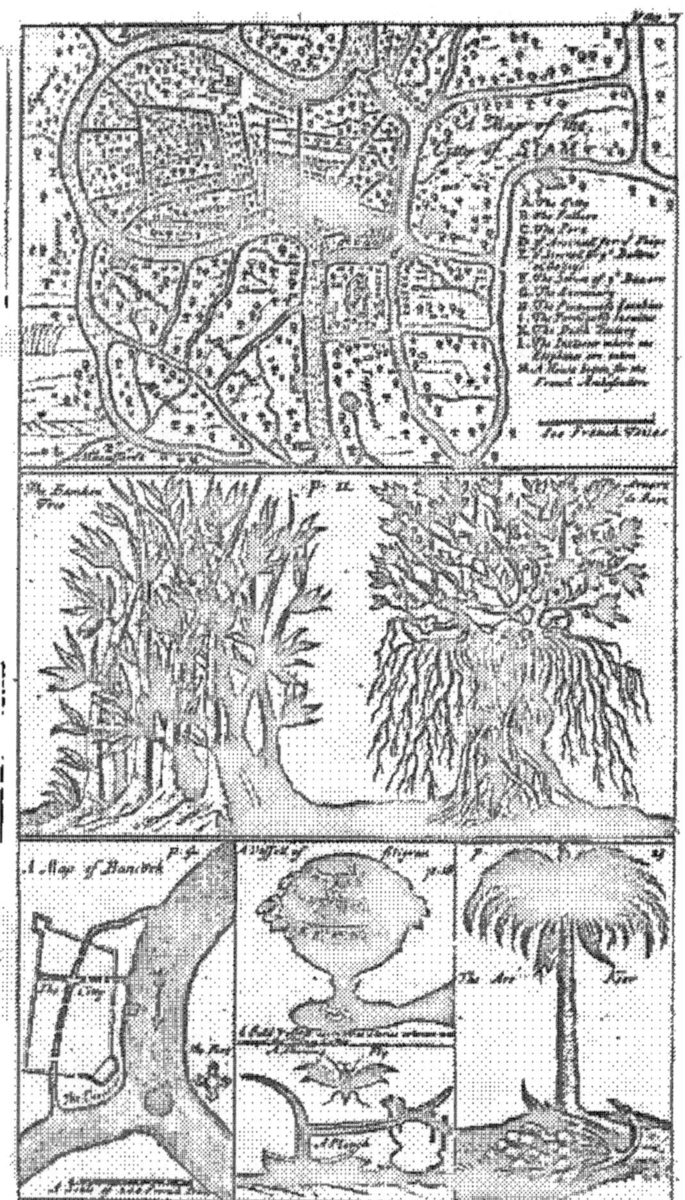
A Map of the City of SIAM
The Bambou Tree
A Map of Bancock
The City
The Fort
A Plough
The Arec Tree

Name of *Franks*, which our Ancestors assum'd when they resolved to deliver the *Gauls* from the *Roman* Power. And those that understand the Language of *Pegu*, affirm that *Siam* in that Tongue signifies *Free*. 'Tis from thence perhaps that the *Portugues* have derived this word, having probably known the *Siameses* by the *Peguins*. Nevertheless *Navarette* in his *Historical Treatises of the Kingdom of* China, *chap.* 1. *art.* 5. relates that the Name of *Siam*, which he writes *Sian*, comes from these two words *Sien lo*, without adding their signification, or of what Language they are; altho' it may be presumed he gives them for *Chinese*. *Meuang Tai* is therefore the *Siamese* Name of the Kingdom of *Siam* (for *Meuang* signifies Kingdom) and this word wrote simply *Muantay*, is found in *Vincent le Blanc*, and in several Geographical Maps, as the Name of a Kingdom adjoining to *Pegu*: But *Vincent le Blanc* apprehended not that this was the Kingdom of *Siam*, not imagining perhaps that *Siam* and *Tai* were two different Names of the same People.

As for the City of *Siam*, the *Siameses* do call it *Si-yo-thi-ya*, the *o* of the Syllable *yo* being closer than our Dipthong *au*. Sometimes also they call it *Crung thep pra mahà nacon*: But most of these words are difficult to understand, because they are taken from the *Balie* Language, which I have already declared to be the learned Language of the *Siameses*, and which they themselves do not always perfectly understand. I have already remark'd what I know concerning the word *Pra*, that of *Mahà* signifies *Great*. Thus in speaking of their King, they stile him *Pra Mahà Crasat*; and the word *Crasat*, according to their report signifies *living*; and because the *Portugues* have thought that *Pra* signifies *God*, they imagin that the *Siameses* called their King, *The great living God*. From *Si-yo-thi-ya*, the *Siamese* Name of the City of *Siam*, Foreigners have made *Judia*, and *Odiaa*, by which it appears that *Vincent le Blanc*, and some other Authors, do very ill distinguish *Odiaa* from *Siam*.

Two different People called Siameses.

In a word, the *Siameses*, of whom I treat, do call themselves *Tai Noe*, *little Siams*. There are others, as I was informed, altogether savage, which are called *Tai yai*, *great Siams*, and which do live in the Northern Mountains. In several Relations of these Countries I find a Kingdom of *Siammon*, or *Siami*: but all do not agree that the People thereof are savage.

Other Mountains, and other Frontiers.

In fine, the Mountains which lie on the common Frontiers of *Ava*, *Pegu* and *Siam*, gradually decreasing as they extend to the South, do form the *Peninsula* of *India extra Gangem*, which terminating at the City of *Sincapura*, separates the Gulphs of *Siam* and *Bengala*, and which with the Island of *Sumatra* forms the famous Strait of *Malaca*, or *Sincapura*. Several Rivers do fall from every part of these Mountains into the Gulphs of *Siam* and *Bengala*, and render these Coasts habitable. The other Mountains which rise between the Kingdom of *Siam* and *Laos*, and extend themselves also towards the South, do run gradually decreasing, till they terminate at the Cape of *Camboya*, the most Eastern of all those in the Continent of *Asia* toward the South. 'Tis about the Latitude of this Cape, that the Gulph of *Siam* begins; and the Kingdom of this Name extends a great way towards the South in form of an Horseshoe on either side of the Gulph, *viz.* along the Eastern Coast to the River *Chantebon*, where the Kingdom of *Camboya* begins; and opposite thereunto, *viz.* in the *Peninsula extra Gangem*, which lies on the West of the Gulph of *Siam*, it extends to *Queda* and *Patana*, the Territories of the *Malayans*, of which *Malaca* was formerly the Metropolis.

The Coasts of Siam.

After this manner it runs about 200 Leagues on the side toward the Gulph of *Siam*, and 180, or thereabouts, on the Gulph of *Bengal*, an advantageous situation which opens unto the Natives of the Countrey the Navigation on all these vast Eastern Seas. Add that as Nature has refus'd all manner of Ports and Roads to the Coast of *Coromandel*, which forms the Gulph of *Bengal* to the West, it has therewith enrich'd that of *Siam* which is opposite to it, and which is on the East of the same Gulph.

Isles of Siam in the Gulph of Bengal.

A great number of Isles do cover it, and render it almost every where a safe Harbor for Ships; besides, that most of these Isles have very excellent Ports, and abundance of fresh water and wood, an invitation for new Colonies. The

King

King of *Siam* affects to be called Lord thereof, altho' his People, who are very thin in the firm Land, have never inhabited them; and he has not strength enough at Sea to prohibit or hinder the entrance thereof to strangers.

The City of *Mergy*. The City of *Mergy* lies on the North-West Point of a great and populous Island, which at the extremity of its course forms a very excellent River, which the *Europeans* have called *Tenasserim*, from the Name of a City seated on its Banks about 15 Leagues from the Sea. This River comes from the North, and after having passed through the Kingdoms of *Ava* and *Pegu*, and enter'd into the Lands under the King of *Siam*'s Jurisdiction, it discharges itself by three Chanels into the Gulph of *Bengal*, and forms the Island I have mention'd. The Ports of *Mergy*, which some report to be the best in all *India*, is between this Isle and another that is inhabited, and lies opposite, and to the West of this, wherein *Mergy* is situated.

CHAP. III.

Concerning the History and Origine of the Siameses.

The *Siamese* little curious of their History.

THE *Siamese* History is full of Fables. The Books thereof are very scarce, by reason the *Siameses* have not the use of Printing: for upon other Accounts I doubt of the report, that they affect to conceal their History, seeing that the *Chineses*, whom in many things they imitate, are not so jealous of theirs. However that matter is, notwithstanding this pretended Jealousy of the *Siameses*, they who have attain'd to read any thing of the History of *Siam*, assert that it ascends not very high with any character of truth.

The Epocha of the *Siamese*.

Behold a very dry and insipid Chronological Arraignment which the *Siameses* have given thereof: But before we proceed, it is necessary to tell you, that the current year 1689, beginning it in the month of *December* 1688, is the 2233 of their *Æra*, from which they date the *Epocha*, or beginning (as they say) from *Sommona-Codom*'s death. But I am perswaded that this *Epocha* has quite another foundation, which I shall afterwards explain.

Their Kings.

Their first King was named *Pra Poat honne sourittep pennaratui sonanne bopitra*; The chief place where he kept his Court was called *Tchai pappe Mahanacon*, the situation of which I ignore; and he began to reign *An.* 1300, computing after their *Epocha*. Ten other Kings succeeded him, the last of which, named *Ipja Louse Thona Thesong Teperat*, remov'd his Royal Seat to the City of *Tasoo Nacora Louang*, which he had built, the situation of which is also unknown to me. The twelfth King after him, whose Name was *Pra Poat Noome Thele seri*, obliged all his People in 1731, to follow him to *Locontai*, a City seated on a River, which descends from the Mountains of *Laos*, and runs into the *Menam* a little above *Porselouc*, from which *Locontai* is between 40 and 50 Leagues distant. But this Prince resided not always at *Locontai*; for he came and built, and inhabited the City of *Pipeli* on a River, the mouth of which is about two Leagues to the West of the most occidental mouth of *Menam*. Four other Kings succeeded him, of which *Rhamatibodi*, the last of the four, began to build the City of *Siam* in 1894, and there established his Court. By which it appears, that they allow to the City of *Siam* the Antiquity of 338 years. The King Regent is the twenty fifth from *Rhamatibodi*, and this year 1689, is the 56th or 57th year of his age. Thus do they reckon 52 Kings in the space of 934 years, but not all of the same Blood.

The Race of the present King.

Mr. *Gervaise* in his *Natural and Political History of the Kingdom of* Siam, gives us the History of the now Regent King's Father; and *Van Vliet* gives it us much more circumstanciated, in his *Historical Relation of the Kingdom of* Siam, printed at the end of Sir *Thomas Herbert's Travels into* Persia. I refer the Reader thither to see an Example of the Revolutions, which are common at *Siam*; for this

King

King who was not of the Royal Race, tho' *Vliet* asserts the contrary, took away the Scepter and Life of his Natural Lords, and put to death all the Princes of their Blood except two, which were alive when *Vliet* writ, but of whom I could not learn any News. Without all doubt this Usurper put them to death like the rest. And in truth, *John Struys*, in the *First Tome of his Voyages*, attests that this was the fate of the last of these two Princes, who was alive in the year 1650, and was then 10 years old; the Tyrant put him to death that very year, with one of his Sisters, upon an Accusation notoriously false. But a remarkable Circumstance of the History of his Usurpation, was, that entering by force of Arms into the Palace, he forced the King to quit it, and flie into a Temple for refuge; and having drag'd this unfortunate Prince out of this Temple, and carry'd him back a Prisoner to the Palace, he caus'd him to be declared unworthy of the Crown and Government, for having deserted the Palace. To this Usurper who died in 1657, after a Reign of 30 years, succeeded his Brother; because his Son could not, or durst not then to dispute the Crown with him. On the contrary, to secure his Life, he sought a Sanctuary in a Cloyster, and cloath'd himself with the inviolable Habit of a *Talapoin*. But he afterwards so politickly took his measures, that he dispossess'd his Uncle, who flying from the Palace on his Elephant, was slain by a *Portuguese* with a Musquet.

Ferdinand Mendez Pinto relates that the King of *Siam*, who reigned in 1547, and to whom he gives great Praises, was poyson'd by the Queen his Wife at his return from a military Expedition. This Princess deliberated thus to prevent the vengeance of her Husband, by reason that during his absence she had maintain'd an amorous Commerce, by which she prov'd with Child. And this Author adds, that she soon after destroy'd the King her own Son in the same manner, and had the Credit to get the Crown set upon her Lover's Head the 11th of *November* 1548. But in *January* 1549, they were both assassinated in a Temple, and a Bastard Prince, the Brother and Uncle of the two last Kings, was taken out of a Cloyster to be advanced to the Throne. The Crowns of *Asia* are always instable, and those of *India*, *China* and *Japan*, much more than the others. Another Example of the Revolutions of *Siam*.

As for what concerns the Origine of the *Siamese*, it would be difficult to judge whether they are only a single People, directly descended from the first Men that inhabited the Country of *Siam*, or whether in process of time some other Nation has not also setled there, notwithstanding the first Inhabitants. A Doubt as to the Origine of the *Siamese*.

The principal Reason of this Doubt proceeds from the *Siamese* understanding two Languages, *viz.* the Vulgar, which is a simple Tongue, consisting almost wholly of Monosyllables, without Conjugation or Declension; and another Language which I have already spoken of, which to them is a dead Tongue, known only by the Learned, which is called the *Balie* Tongue, and which is enricht with the inflexions of words, like the Languages we have in *Europe*. The terms of Religion and Justice, the names of Offices, and all the Ornaments of the Vulgar Tongue are borrow'd from the *Balie*. In this Language they compose their best Songs; so that it seems at least that some Foreign Colony had formerly inhabited the Country of *Siam*, and had carry'd thither a second Language. But this is a Dispute that might be rais'd concerning all the Countries of *India*; for, like *Siam*, they all have two Languages, one of which is still remaining only in their Books. Two Languages at *Siam*.

The *Siamese* assert that their Laws are Foreign, and came to them from the Country of *Laos*, which has, perhaps, no other Foundation than the Conformity of the Laws of *Laos* with those of *Siam*, even as there is a Conformity between the Religions of these two Nations, and with that of the *Peguins*. Now this does not strictly prove that any of these three Kingdoms hath given its Laws and its Religion to the rest, seeing that it may happen that all the three may have deriv'd their Religion and their Laws from another common Source. However it be, as the Tradition is at *Siam*, that their Laws and Kings came from *Laos*, the same Tradition runs at *Laos*, that their Kings and most of their Laws came from *Siam*. What the *Siamese* report concerning the Origine of their Laws and Religion.

Of the Balie Language.

The *Siameses* speak not of any Country where the *Balie* Language, which is that of their Laws and their Religion, is now in use. They suspect indeed, according to the report of some amongst them, which have been at the Coast of *Coromandel*, that the *Balie* Language has some similitude with some one of the Dialects of that Country: but they agree at the same time that the Letters of the *Balie* Language are known only amongst them. The secular Missionaries established at *Siam*, are of opinion that this Language is not entirely extinct: by reason they saw in their Hospital a man come from about the Cape of *Comorin*, who intersperss'd several *Balie* words in his discourse, affirming that they were used in his Country, and that he had never studied, and knew only his Mother Tongue. They moreover aver for truth, that the Religion of the *Siameses* came from those Quarters, because that they have read in a *Balie* Book, that *Sommona-Codom* whom the *Siameses* adore, was the Son of a King of the Island of *Ceylon*.

The Siameses resemble their Neighbours.

But setting aside all these uncertainties, the vulgar Language of the *Siameses*; like in its Simplicity to those of *China*, *Tonquin*, *Cochinchina*, and the other States of the East, sufficiently evinces that those who speak it, are near of the same Genius with their Neighbours. Add hereunto their *Indian* Figure, the colour of their Complexion mixt with red and brown, (which corresponds neither to the North of *Asia*, *Europe*, nor *Africk*.) Add likewise their short Nose rounded at the end, as their Neighbours generally have it; the upper Bone of their Cheeks high and raised, their Eyes slit a little upwards, their Ears larger than ours, in a word all the Lineaments of the *Indian* and *Chinese* Physiognomy; their Countenance naturally squeez'd and bent like that of Apes, and a great many other things which they have in common with these Animals, as well as a marvellous passion for Children. For nothing is equal to the Tenderness which the great Apes expressed to their Cubs, except the Love which the *Siameses* have for all Children, whether for their own, or those of another.

The King of Siam loves Children till 7 or 8 years old.

The King of *Siam* himself is incompass'd with them, and delights to educate them till seven or eight years old: after which as they lose the childish Air, they do also lose his Favour. One alone, say some, was there kept till between twenty and thirty years of Age, and is still his favourite. Some do call him his adopted Son, others suspect him to be his Bastard; He is at least Foster Brother to his Lawful Daughter.

That the Siameses came not from far to inhabit their Country.

But if you consider the extreamly Low Lands of *Siam*, that they seem to escape the Sea as it were by miracle, and that they lye annually under rain water for several Months, the almost infinite number of very incommodious Insects which they engender, and the excessive Heat of the Climate under which they are seated; it is difficult to comprehend that others could resolve to inhabit them, excepting such as came thither by little and little from places adjacent: And it may be thought that they have been inhabited not many Ages, if a Judgment may be made thereof by the few Woods that are stubbed as yet. Moreover it would be necessary to travel more to the North of *Siam*, to find out the warlike People which could yield those innumerable swarms of men, which departed out of their own Country to go and possess others. And how is it possible that they should not be stopp'd on the Road, among some of those soft and effeminate People, which lye between the Country of the *Scythians*, and the Woods and impassible Rivers of the *Siameses*? 'Tis not therefore probable that the *Lesser Siameses*, which we have spoken of, are descended from the Greater, and that the Greater withdrew into the Mountains which they inhabit, to free themselves from the Tyranny of the neighbouring Princes, under which they were born.

Strangers that have come to Siam.

Nevertheless it is certain that the *Siamese* blood is very much mixed with foreign. Not to reckon the *Peguins*, and the Inhabitants of *Lao*, which are at *Siam*, and whom I consider almost as the same Nation with the *Siameses*; 'tis not to be doubted that there formerly fled to *Siam* a great number of Strangers from different Countries, upon the account of a free Liberty of Trade, and by reason of the Wars of the true *India*, *China*, *Japan*, *Tonquin*, *Cochinchina*, and other States in the South part of *Asia*. They report likewise that in the City of

Siam,

Siam, there are forty different Nations: but inasmuch as *Vincent le Blanc* speaks in these very terms concerning the City of *Martaban*, this affected Number of Forty Nations appears unto me an *Indian* Vanity. The entire annihilation of the Commerce of *Siam*, having in these last years forc'd most of the Foreigners, that fled thither, to seek out new Retreats, three or four *Cavaliers* which are of *Bengal*, do now compose a Nation; three *Cochinchinese* Families do make another; the *Moors* alone which ought to be reckon'd only for one, do make more than ten, as well for that they came to *Siam* from different Nations, as for their being of various conditions, as Merchants, Soldiers, and Labourers. (I call *Moors* after the *Spanish* manner, not the *Negroes*, but those *Mahometans* of *Arabian* Extraction, which our Ancestors have called *Sarracens*, and whose race is spread almost through our whole Hemisphere.) And notwithstanding all this, when the Ambassadors of the Foreigners, which at *Siam* are called the Forty Nations, came to salute the King's Envoys, there were reckoned no more than one and twenty Nations, computing as the *Siamese* would have us.

They inhabit different quarters in the City or Suburbs of *Siam*; and yet this City is very little inhabited in respect to its Bigness, and the Country much less in Proportion. It must be imagined that they desire not a greater People, for they count them every year; and do well know, what no person ignores, that the only secret to encrease them, would be to ease them in the Taxes and Impositions. The *Siamese* do therefore keep an exact account of the Men, Women and Children; and in this vast extent of Land, according to their own Confession, they reckon'd up the last time but Nineteen Hundred Thousand Souls. From which I question not that some retrenchment is to be made for Vanity and Lyes, Characters essential to the Eastern people; but on the other hand, thereunto must be added the Fugitives, which do seek a Sanctuary in the Woods against the Government. The people of the Kingdom of *Siam* are very numerous.

CHAP. IV.

Of the Productions of Siam, *and first of the Woods or Trees.*

THE Country of *Siam* lyes almost wholly uncultivated and cover'd with Woods. One of their most eminent Trees is a kind of Reed, called in *Indian*, *Mambou*, in *Portuguese*, *Bambou*, in *Siamese*, *Mai pai*. The *Indians* apply it to an infinite number of uses. *Ælian lib. 5. cap. 34.* mentions it as their most ancient nourishment. At present they use it little; and that only in some of their dishes, when it is tender; and to preserve it, they Pickle it up in Vinegar, as we do *Cucumbers* and *Samphire*. This Tree resembles the Poplar, it is strait and tall, and the Leaves thereof few, pale, and longish. It is hollow, and grows in shoots like our Reeds, and its shoots are separated from one another by knots; but it has Branches and Thorns, which our Reeds have not. It grows very close, and the same Roots do shoot forth several stems, so that nothing is thicker or more difficult to pass than a Forest of *Bambou*; and so much the more because the wood thereof is hard and difficult to cut, although it be easie to cleave. The *Siamese* do set it on fire by Friction, which is a token of its hardness. They have two pieces of *Bambou* cleft, which are like two pieces of Lath, in the edge of the one they do make a notch, and do forcibly rub in this hole with the edge of the other, as with a Saw; and some dry leaves, or other combustible matter, which is put in the notch, fails not to catch fire without firing the *Bambou*. There is no Reed but has naturally somewhat either more or less of a Sugary juice. That of the *Bambou* is famous in some places of *India*, as an excellent Remedy for several Maladies. It escaped my curiosity to ask whether the Sugar of the *Bambou* of *Siam* is as much sought after upon this account, as that of the *Bambou* of *Malaca*, which is not far distant. The Bambou.

The

The Arvore de Raiz.

The *Siameses* report that they likewise have that Tree, which the *Portugues* have called *Arvore de Raiz*, and they *Co pai*, but that they have no plenty: and they add that its wood hath this property (doubtless by its smell) that when any person hath a little of it near him in his Bed it drives away the Gnats. 'Tis from the Branches of this Tree, so frequently described in the Relations of *India*, that several Fibers do hang down to the ground, which there take root, and become as so many new Trunks: so that by little and little this Tree gains a considerable plot of ground, on which it forms a kind of Labyrinth by its stems, which continually multiply, and which adhere to one another by the branches, from which these stems are fall'n. We have seen the *Siameses* seek out other Remedies against the Gnats than that of this wood: and this perswades me either that it is very rare, or that this vertue which is attributed thereunto, is not well attested.

The Cotton Tree and Capoquier.

But the *Siameses* have other Trees more useful, and in great plenty. From the one they do gather Cotton: another yields them *Capoc*, a kind of Cotton-wool extreamly fine, and so short that 'tis impossible to spin it, to them it serves instead of Down.

Trees which produce Oyls or Gums.

From certain Trees they extract several Oyls which they mix in Ciments, to render them more binding. A wall that is plaister'd therewith, is whiter, and bears as good a Polish as Marble; and a Bason made of one of these Ciments preserves water better then glazed Earth. They do likewise make better Mortar than our's: by reason that in the water which they use, they do boyl a certain bark, the skins of Oxen, or Buffalo's, and Sugar. A kind of Trees very common in their Woods yeilds that Gum, which composes the body of that excellent Varnish, which we see on several works of *Japan*, and *China*. The *Portugues* do call this Gum *Cheyram*, a word perhaps derived from *Cheyro*, which signifies a *Perfume*, although this Gum has not any Odor of it self. The *Siameses* do not well know how to put it in use. At *Siam* I saw a *Tonquinese* of this Trade, but he wrought nothing well for want perhaps of a certain Oil which was necessary to mix with the *Cheyram*, and which he supplied, as he could, by a much worse. I would have brought him to *France*, had he not been afraid to pass the Sea, as he had promised me at first. In a word, some say that the best way to render the Varnish more curious, is to lay on the more coverings, but this is to make it much dearer. The Relations of *China* do also declare, that there are two different Materials for the Varnish, and that the one is much better than the other. The *Cheyram* is proved by a drop thereof pour'd into Water; and if this drop sinks to the bottom without separating, the *Cheyram* is good.

Trees whose Bark serves to make Paper.

The *Siameses* make Paper of old Cotton rags, and likewise of the bark of a Tree named *Ton coi*, which they pound as they do the old rags: but these Papers have a great deal less Equality, Body and Whiteness than ours. The *Siameses* cease not to write thereon with *China* Ink. Yet most frequently they black them, which renders them smoother, and gives them a greater body; and then they write thereon with a kind of *Crayon*, which is made only of a clayish Earth dry'd in the Sun. Their Books are not bound, and consist only in a very long Leaf, which they roll not up as our Ancestors did theirs, but which they fold in and out like a Fan: and the way which the Lines are wrote, is according to the length of the folds, and not according to their breadth. Besides this they write with a Styletto and the Leaves of a Tree resembling the Palm: This Tree they call *Tan*, and these Leaves *Bailan*; they cut them in a very long and narrow Square, and on these Tables are writ the Fables and Prayers, which the *Talapoins* do sing in their Temples.

The *Siameses* have also Timber proper for the building of Ships, and furnishing them with Masts: But they having no Hemp, their Cordages are made of the *Bron** of *Coco*, and their Sails are Mats of great Rushes: These Equipments do not countervail ours by much; but their Sails have this advantage, that spontaneously supporting themselves, they do better receive the Wind, when it is near it; that is to say when it blows as much against us as possibly it can, without being contrary to the Course.

* *Bron* is a green Bark or skin which is on the *Coco*, like as on our Nuts; but that at the *Coco* is three fingers thick, and its Fibers may be twisted into a Cord.

In

Wood for other uses.

In fine, the *Siameses* have Timber proper for building of Houſes, for Wainſcotting and Carving; they have both light and very heavy Wood, ſome eaſie to cleave, and others which cleaveth not, what Wedges ſoever it receives. This laſt is called by the *Europeans*, *Wood-Mary*, and is better than any to make the Kils of Ships. That which is heavy and tough is called *Iron-wood*, very well known in our Iſlands of *America*, and it is affirmed in proceſs of time it rots the Iron. They have a Wood which for its Lightneſs and Colour ſome conceive to be Fir, but it takes the Carver's Chiſel in ſo many different ways without ſplitting, that I queſtion whether we have any like it in *Europe*.

Trees for Balons.

But above all, the *Siameſes* have Trees ſo high and ſo ſtrait, that one alone is ſufficient to make a Boat or *Balon*, as the *Portugueſes* ſpeak, between 16 and 20 Fathom long. They hollow the Tree, and then by the heat of the Fire enlarge the Capacity thereof; which done, they raiſe the ſides with an edge, that is to ſay, with a Board of the ſame length: And in fine, at both the ends they faſten a Prow and a Poop very high, and a little bending out, frequently adorn'd with ſculpture and gilding, and with ſome pieces of Mother of Pearl.

They have none of our Wood.

Nevertheleſs amongſt ſo many different ſorts of Wood, they have none of thoſe which we know in *Europe*.

They have not been able to raiſe any Mulberry Trees, and for this reaſon they have no Silk-worms. No Flax alſo grows amongſt them, nor in any other place of *India*, or at leaſt it is not in any eſteem. The Cotton which they have in abundance is, they ſay, more agreeable and more healthful to them; by reaſon that Cotton-cloth grows not cold by being wet with ſweat, and conſequently occaſions not the catching cold, as Linnen does.

The Cinnamon and [illegible] Tree.

They have the Cinnamon Tree, inferior indeed to that of the Iſland of *Ceylon*, but better than any other; they have the *Sapan*, and other Woods proper for Dying.

Wood Aquila.

They have alſo the Wood *Aquila* or Aloes, not ſo good indeed as the *Calamba* of *Cochinchina*, but better than the Wood *Aquila* of any other Country. This Wood is found only in pieces, by reaſon they are only certain rotten places in Trees of a certain kind. And every Tree of this ſame Species has it not, and thoſe which have, have them not all in the ſame place; ſo that it requires a tedious ſearch in the Wood. 'Twas formerly very dear at *Paris*, but is at preſent to be had at a reaſonable rate.

CHAP. V.

Concerning the Mines of Siam.

The Reputation of the Mines of Siam.

NO Country has a greater Reputation of being rich in Mines than the Country of *Siam*, and the great quantity of Idols and other caſt works which are there ſeen, evinces that they have been better cultivated there in former times, than now they are. 'Tis believed likewiſe that they thence extracted that great quantity of Gold, wherewith their Superſtition has adorned not only their almoſt innumerable Idols, but the Wainſcot and Roofs of their Temples. They do likewiſe daily diſcover Pits anciently dug, and the remains of a great many Furnaces, which are thought to have been abandon'd during the ancient Wars of *Pegu*.

The State of the Mines at preſent.

Nevertheleſs the King that now reigns has not been able to find any Vein of Gold or Silver, that is worth the pains that he has therein employed, although he hath applied unto this work ſome *Europeans*, and amongſt the reſt a *Spaniard* that came from *Mexico*, who found, if not a great fortune, at leaſt his Subſiſtence for twenty years, even to his Death, by flattering the Avarice of this Prince, with the imaginary promiſes of infinite Treaſures. After having dug and mined in ſeveral places, they light only on ſome very mean Copper Mines, tho intermixt with a little Gold and Silver: Five hundred weight of Ore scarce yielding an Ounce of Metal; neither understood they how to make the separation of Metals.

Tambac.

But the King of *Siam*, to render his mixture more precious, caus'd some Gold to be added thereunto: and this is what they call *Tambac*. 'Tis said that the Mines of the Isle of *Borneo* do naturally produce it very Rich: and the scarceness augments the price thereof, as it formerly increased that of the famous *Corinthian* Brass; but certainly that which makes the true value thereof amongst the *Siameses*, is the quantity of Gold wherewith it is thought to be mixed. When their Avarice creates desires it is for the Gold, and not for the *Tambac*; and we have seen that when the King of *Siam* has ordered Crucifixes to be made to present to the Christians, the most noble and smallest part, which is the *Christ*, has been of Gold, the Cross alone of *Tambac*. *Vincent le Blanc* relates, that the *Peguins* have a mixture of Lead and Copper, which he calls sometimes *Ganze*, and sometimes *Ganza*, and of which he reports that they make Statues, and a small Money which is not stampt with the Kings Coin, but which every one has a right to make.

Mr. *Vincent* the Physitian retained by the King of *Siam* to work in his Mines.

From *Siam* we brought back Mr. *Vincent* the Physitian. He departed from *France*, to go into *Persia*, with the late Bishop of *Babylon*, and the report of the arrival of the King's first Ships at *Siam*, made him to go thither as well out of a desire to travel, as in hopes of procuring his return into *France*. He understood Mathematicks and Chymistry, and the King of *Siam* retained him some time at the work in his Mines.

What he relates concerning the Mines of *Siam*.

He informed me that he rectified the labours of the *Siameses* in some things, so that they obtain a little more profit than they did. He show'd them a Mine of very good Steel at the top of a Mountain, which had been already discovered, and which they perceived not. He discovered to them one of Crystal, one of Antimony, one of Emeril, and some others, with a Quarry of white Marble. Besides this, he found out a Gold Mine, which to him appear'd very rich, as far as he was able to judge without trying it; but he has not showed it them. Several *Siameses*, most *Talapoins*, came secretly to consult him about the Art of purifying and separating Metals, and brought him divers Specimens of very rich Ore. From some he extracted a very good quantity of fine Silver, and from others, the mixture of several Metals.

Tin and Lead.

As for Tin and Lead, the *Siameses* have long since improved it from very plentiful Mines, and though not very skilful, yet they cease not to get a considerable revenue by it. This Tin, or Calin, as the *Portuguese* report, is sold through all *India*; 'Tis soft and basely purified, and a specimen thereof is seen in the common Tea Boxes or Cannisters, which come from this Country. But to render it harder and whiter, like that of the finest Tea Boxes, they mix it with Cadmia, a sort of Mineral easily reducible to powder, which being melted with the Copper, makes it yellow: but it renders both these Metals more brittle: And 'tis this white Tin which they call *Tintinague*. This is what Mr. *Vincent* relates on the subject of the Mines of *Siam*.

Mines of Loadstone.

In the Neighbourhood of the City of *Louvo* they have a Mountain of Loadstone. They have another also near *Jansalam*, a City seated in an Island of the Gulph of *Bengal*, which is not above the distance of a Mans voice from the Coast of *Siam*: but the Loadstone which is dug at *Jansalam* loses its vertue in three or four Months; I know not whether it is not the same in that of *Louvo*.

Precious Stones.

In their Mountains they find very curious *Agate*, and Mr. *Vincent* inform'd me that he has seen, in the hands of the *Talapoins*, who secretly busie themselves in these researches, some samples or pieces of Saphires and Diamonds that came out of the Mine. He assured me also that some particular Persons having found some Diamonds, and given them to the King's Officers, were retired to *Pegu* by by reason they had not receiv'd any recompence.

Steel.

I have already said that the City of *Campeng-pet* is famous for Mines of excellent Steel. The Inhabitants of the Country do forge Arms thereof after their fashion, as Sabres, Poniards, and Knives. The Knife which they call *Pen* is used by all, and is not look'd upon as Arms, although it may serve upon occasion: The blade

thereof

thereof is three or four Fingers broad, and about a Foot long. The King gives the Sabre and the Poniard. They wear the Poniard on the left side, hanging a little before. The *Portugueses* do call it *Crist*, a word corrupted from *Crid*, which the *Siameses* use. This word is borrow'd from the *Malayan* Language, which is famous throughout the East, and the *Crids* which are made at *Attcen* in the Isle of *Sumatra*, do pass for the best of all. As for the Sabre, a Slave always carries it before his Master on his right shoulder, as we carry the Musquet on the left.

They have Iron Mines which they know how to melt, and some have inform'd me that they have but little thereof; besides, they are bad Forge-men. For their Gallies they have only wooden Anchors, and to the end that these Anchors may sink to the bottom, they fasten stones unto them. They have neither Pins, nor Needles, nor Nails, nor Chisels, nor Saws. They use not a Nail in building their Houses, altho' they be all of Wood. Every one makes Pins of Bambou, even as our Ancestors us'd Thorns for this purpose. To them there comes Padlocks from *Japan*, some of Iron, which are good; and others of Copper, which are very rough. Iron.

They do make very bad Gunpowder. The defect, they say, proceeds from the *Salt-Peter* which they gather from their Rocks, where it is made of the dung of Batts, Animals which are exceeding large and very plentiful throughout *India*. But whether this Salt-Peter be good or bad, the King of *Siam* sells a great deal of it to Strangers. Salt-Peter and Powder.

Having described the natural Riches of the Mountains and Forests of *Siam*, 'twould be proper in this place to speak of the Elephants, Rhinoceros, Tygers, and all other savage Beasts wherewith they are stored: yet seeing this matter has been sufficiently explicated by a great many others, I shall omit it, to pass on to the inhabited and cultivated Lands.

CHAP. VI.

Of the cultivated Lands, and their Fertility.

THey are not Stony, it being very difficult to find a Flint; and this makes me to believe of the Country of *Siam*, what some have reported of *Egypt*, that it has been gradually formed of the clayish Earth which the Rain-waters have carry'd down from the Mountains. Before the mouth of the *Menam*, there is a Bank of Ooze, which, in the Sea-phrase, is call'd the Bar, and which prohibits entrance to great Ships. 'Tis probable that it will increase it self by little and little, and will in time make a new Shore to the firm Land. The Country of Siam is Clayie.

'Tis therefore this Mud descending from the Mountains, that is the real cause of the Fertility of *Siam*, where-ever the Inundation extends it self. In other, and especially on the highest places, all is dry'd and burnt with the Sun, in a little time after the Rains. Under the Torrid Zone, and likewise in *Spain*, whose Climate is more temperate, if the Lands are naturally fertile, (as for Example, between *Murcia* and *Carthagena*, where the Seed yields sometimes an hundred fold) they are nevertheless so subject to Drought, Insects, and other Inconveniences, that it frequently happens that they are deprived of the whole Harvest several years together: And 'tis this which besides all the Countries of *India* which are not subject to be overflowed, and which besides the barrenness of the Soil, do suffer the ravages of contagious and pestilential Distempers which succeed it. But the annual Inundation gives to *Siam* the assurance and plenty of the Rice Harvest, and renders this Kingdom the Nourisher of several others. The annual Inundation fattens the Lands of Siam.

Besides the Inundation fatning the Land, it destroys the Insects; altho' it always leaves a great many, which extremely incommode. Nature instructs all the Animals of *Siam* to avoid the Inundation. The Birds which perch not in It destroys the Insects.

one

our Countries, as Partridges and Pigeons, do all perch in that. The Pismires doubly prudent, do here make their Nests and Magazines on Trees.

White Ants at *Siam*.

There are white Ants, which, amongst other ravages which they make, do pierce Books through and through. The Missionaries are oblig'd to preserve theirs, by varnishing them over the cover and edges with a little *Cheyram*, which hinders them not from opening. After this precaution, the Ants have no more power to bite, and the Books are more agreeable, by reason that this Gum being mixt with nothing that colours it, has the same lustre as the Glasses wherewith we cover Pictures in Miniature. This would be no dear nor difficult Experiment, to try whether the *Cheyram* would not defend the wood of our Beds against Bugs. 'Tis this same *Cheyram*, which being spread upon Canvas, makes it appear like Horn. Therewith they us'd to environ the great Cresset-lights, which some reported to be of Horn, and all of a piece. Sometimes also those little Cups varnish'd with red, which come to us from *Japan*, and whose lightness astonishes us, do consist only of a double Cloth put into the form of a Cup, and cover'd over with this Gum mixt with a colour, which we call *Lacca*, or *China's* Varnish, as I have already declar'd: these Cups last not long, when too hot Liquors are put therein.

The *Maringouins*.

To return to the Insects, which we have began occasionally to speak of, the *Maringouins* are of the same Nature as our Gnats; but the heat of the Climat gives them so much strength, that linnen Stockings defend not our Legs against their Stings. Nevertheless it seems possible to know how to deal with them; for the Natives of the Country, and the *Europeans* that have inhabited there for several years, were not so marked with them as we were.

The *Millepede*.

The *Millepede* or Palmer is known at *Siam*, as in the Isles of *America*. This little Reptile is so called, because it has a great number of feet along its body, all very short in proportion to its length, which is about five or six Inches. What it has most singular (besides the scales in form of rings, which cover its body, and which insert themselves one into the other in its motions) is, that it pinches equally with its head and tail, but its Stings, tho' painful, are not mortal. A *French* Man of that Crew which went to *Siam* with us, and whom we left there in perfect health, suffer'd himself to be stung in his Bed above a quarter of an hour, without daring to lay hold on the Worm to relieve himself. The *Siameses* report, that the *Millepede* has two heads at the extremities of its body, and that it guides it self six months in the year with the one, and six months with the other.

The Ignorance of the *Siameses* in things Natural.

But their History of Animals must not easily be credited, they understand not Bodies better than Souls; and in all matters their inclination is to imagine Wonders, and perswade themselves so much the more easily to believe them, as they are more incredible. What they report of a sort of Lizard named *Toc-quay*, proceeds from an Ignorance and Credulity very singular. They imagine that this Animal feeling his Liver grow too big, makes the Cry which has impos'd on him the name of *Toc-quay*, to call another Insect to its succor; and that this other Insect entering into his Body at his mouth, eats the overplus of the Liver, and after this repast retires out of the *Toc-quay's* body, by the same way that he enter'd therein.

Shining Flyes.

The shining Flyes, like Locusts, have four wings, which do all appear when the Fly takes a flight; but the two thinnest of them are concealed under the strongest when the Fly is at repose. We hardly saw these little Animals, by reason that the rainy time was past when we landed. The North-winds, which begin when the Rains cease, either kill them, or drive them all away. They have some light in their Eyes, but their greatest splendor proceeds from under their wings, and glisters only in the Air, when the wings are display'd. What some report therefore is not true, that they might be us'd in the Night instead of Candles; for tho' they had light enough, what method could be contriv'd to make them always flie, and keep them at a due distance to illuminate? But thus much may suffice to be spoken concerning the Insects of *Siam*; they would afford matter for large Volumes to know them all.

I shall

I shall say only that there are not fewer in the River and Gulph, than on the Land ; and that in the River there are some very dangerous, which is the reason that the rich Men do bathe themselves only in houses of Bambou. *Insects in the waters.*

CHAP. VII.

Of the Grain of Siam.

RICE is the principal Harvest of the *Siamese*, and their best Nourishment ; it refreshes and fattens : And we found our Ship's Crew express some regret, when after a three months allowance thereof, they were return'd to Bisket ; and yet the Bisket was very good, and well kept. *Rice.*

The *Siamese* know by experience how to measure the water, fire and time necessary to the *Rice*, without bursting the Grain, and so it serves them for Bread. Not that they mix it with all their other Food as we do Bread ; when they eat Flesh or Fish for example, they eat the one and the other without *Rice* ; and when they eat *Rice*, they eat it separately. They squeeze it a little between the ends of their Fingers to reduce it into a Paste, and so they put it into their mouth, as our Poor do eat Pottage. The *Chineses* do never touch any meat but with two small Sticks squar'd at the end, which do serve them instead of a Fork. They hold to their lower Lip a small Porcelane or *China* Cup, wherein is their portion of *Rice* ; and holding it steady with their left hand, they strike the *Rice* into their mouth with the two Sticks which they hold in their right hand. *The way of boiling it in pure water.*

The *Levantines*, or Eastern People, do sometimes boil *Rice* with Flesh and Pepper, and then put some Saffron thereunto, and this Dish they call *Pilau*. This is not the practice of the *Siamese* : but generally they boil the *Rice* in clear water, as I have said ; and sometimes they boil it with milk, as we do on fasting days. *Or in milk.*

At *Siam*, in the Lands high enough to avoid the Inundation, there grows Wheat : they water them either with watering Pots like those in our Gardens, or by overflowing it with the Rain-water, which they keep in Cisterns much higher than these Lands. But either by reason of the Care or Expence, or that the *Rice* suffices for common use, the King of *Siam* only has Wheat ; and perhaps more out of Curiosity, than a real Gusto. They call it *Kaou Poslali*, and the word *Kaou* simply signifieth *Rice*. Now these terms being neither *Arabian*, nor *Turkish*, nor *Persian*, I doubt of what was told me, that Wheat was brought to *Siam* by the *Moors*. The *French* which are setled there, do import Meal from *Surrat* ; altho' near *Siam* there is a Windmill to grind Corn, and another near *Louvo*. *Wheat.*

In a word, the Bread which the King of *Siam* gave us, was so dry, that the *Rice* boil'd in pure water, how insipid soever, was more agreeable to me. I less wonder therefore at what the Relations of *China* report, that the Soveraign of this great Kingdom, altho' he has Bread, does rather prefer *Rice* : yet some *Europeans* assur'd me, that the wheaten Bread of *Siam* is good, and that the driness of ours must proceed from a little Rice flower, which is doubtless mixt with the Wheat, for fear perhaps lest the Bread should fail. *Wheaten Bread too dry at Siam.*

At *Siam* I have seen Pease different from ours. The *Siamese*, like us, do make more than one Crop, but they make only one in a year upon the same Land : not that the Soil was not good enough, in my opinion, to yield two Crops in a year, as some have related concerning some other Cantons of *India*, if the Inundation did not last so long. They have Turky-Wheat only in their Gardens. They do boil or parch the whole Ear thereof, without unhusking or breaking off the Grains, and they eat the inside. *Other Grain.*

CHAP. VIII.

Of the Husbandry, and the difference of the Seasons.

Oxen and Buffalo's employ'd in Husbandry.

THey equally employ Oxen and Buffalo's in Husbandry. They guide them with a Rope put through a hole which they make in the Cartilage that separates the Nostrils: And to the end that the Rope may not slip when they draw it, they do tie a knot on each side. This same Cord runs also through a hole, which is at the end of the draught Tree of their Plough.

The *Siamese* Plough.

The Plough of the *Siameses* is plain, and without Wheels. It consists in a long Beam which is the Rudder, in another crooked piece which is the Handle, and in another shorter and stronger piece, fastned almost at Right Angles underneath at the end of the Handle; and 'tis this Third which bears the share. They fasten not these four pieces with Nails, but with leather Thongs.

How they cleanse the Rice from the Chaff.

To unhusk the *Rice*, they employ large Beasts; when it is trodden out, they let it fall by little and little from a very high place, to the end that the wind may carry away the Chaff. And because the *Rice* has an hard Skin like Spelt, a sort of Corn very common in *Flanders*, and other places, they bruise it in a great wooden Mortar, with a Pestle of the same; or in a Hand-mill, all the pieces of which are also of Wood. They knew not how to describe them to me.

Three Seasons only, and two sorts of years.

They know only three Seasons, the *Winter*, which they call *Kanau, the Beginning of Cold*; the *Little Summer*, which they call *Naron, the Beginning of Heat*; and the *Great Summer*, which they call *Naron-yai, the Beginning of Great Heat*, and which strips the Trees of their Leaves, as the Cold does ours. They have two years together consisting of twelve months, and a third of thirteen.

The names of their days from the Planets.

They have no word to express *Week*; but, like us, they call the seven days by the Planets, and their days correspond to ours. I mean, that when it is Monday here, it is Monday there, and so of the rest; but the day begins about six hours sooner there, than here. Amongst the Names they have given to the Planets, that of *Mercury* is *Pout*, a *Persian* word, which signifies an *Idol*; from whence comes *Pout-Ghedà*, a Temple of false Gods; and *Pagode* comes from *Pout-Ghedà*.

From whence they begin their years.

They begin their year on the first day of the Moon in *November* or *December*, according to certain Rules; and they do not always denote the years by their number, but by the names they give them; for they make use of a Cycle of sixty years, like the other Eastern Nations.

The Cycle of 60 years.

A Sexagenary Cycle is a Revolution of sixty years, as a week is a Revolution of seven days; and they have names for the years of the Cycle, as we have for the days of the week. 'Tis true, I have not been able to discover that they have more than twelve different names, which they repeat five times in every Cycle to arrive at the number of sixty, and in my opinion with some additions which do make the differences thereof. They will date therefore, for instance, from the year of the *Pig*, or of the *Great Serpent*, which amongst them are the names of the year; and they will not always denote what year of their *Æra* this shall be, as we sometimes date a Letter upon one of the days of the week to which we set down the name, without noting what number it is in the month. At the end of this Relation, I will give you the twelve names of the years in *Siamese*, with those of the seven days of the week.

Their months.

Their months are vulgarly esteem'd to consist of thirty days. I say vulgarly, because that in Astronomical exactness there may be some month longer or shorter; but the *Siameses* do observe it otherwise than we, in that we give names to the months, and they do not. They call them by their order, the first month, second month, &c.

The distinction of their Seasons.

The two first Months, which answer almost to our Months of *December* and *January*, do make their whole *Winter*; the third, fourth, and fifth, do belong to their *little Summer*, the seven others to their *great Summer*. Thus they have Winter

Winter at the same time as we; by reason they lye to the North line like us. But their greatest Winter is at least as hot as our greatest Summer. After the time of the Inundation they cover the Plants in their Gardens from the heats of the Sun, as we do sometimes cover ours from the cold of the Night or Winter: But as to their Persons, the diminution of the heat appears unto them a very incommodious cold. The little Summer is their Spring, and they utterly ignore the Autumn. They only reckon a great Summer; although it seems that they might reckon two after the manner of the Ancients, who have written of *India*, seeing that they have the Sun perpendicularly over their heads twice a year; once when it comes from the Line to the Tropick of *Cancer*, and another time when it returns from the Tropick of *Cancer* towards the Line.

Their Winter is dry, and their Summer rainy. The Torrid Zone would doubtless be uninhabitable, as the Ancients have held, were it not for that marvellous Providence which makes the Sun continually to draw the Clouds and Rains after it, and the Wind incessantly to blow there from one of the Poles, when the Sun is toward the other. Thus at *Siam* in Winter, the Sun being in the middle of the Line, or towards the Antarctick Pole, the North-winds do constantly prevail, and temper the Air very sensibly to refresh it. In Summer, when the Sun is on the North of the Line, and perpendicularly over the head of the *Siamese*, the South-winds which continually blow there, do cause continual Rains, or at least do make the weather always inclined to Rain; leaving most People in doubt whether this Season of Rain ought not to be called the Winter of *Siam*. 'Tis this constant Rule of the Winds, which the *Portugues* have called *Monçaõ*, and we after them *Monsoon* (*Mutinos ventos*, according to *Ozorius* and *Maffeus*.) And this is the reason that the Ships can hardly arrive at the Bar of *Siam* during the six Months of the North-winds, and that they can hardly depart thence during the six Months of the South-winds. At the end of this work I will give the order of the Winds and Tides in the Gulph of *Siam*, in favour of those that love to reason on Philosophical matters.

Of the Monsons.

The *Siamese* do not give many forms to their Lands. They till them and sowe them, when the Rains have sufficiently softened them; and they gather their harvest when the waters are retired, and sometimes when they are yet remaining on the ground, and they can go only by Boat. All the land that is overflowed is good for Rice, and 'tis said that the Ear always surmounts the waters; and that if they encrease a foot in twenty four hours, the Rice grows a foot also in twenty four hours: but though it be aver'd that this happens sometimes, I cannot without much difficulty believe it in so vast an Inundation: And I rather conceive that when the Inundation surmounts the Rice at any time, it rots it.

The time of ploughing and reaping.

They gather Rice also in divers Cantons of the Kingdom which the Rains do not overflow; and this is more substantial, better relisht, and keeps longer. When it has grown long enough in the Land where it was sown, it is transplanted into another, which is prepared after this manner. They overflow it, as we do the Salt Marshes, until it be throughly soft; and for this purpose it is necessary to have high Cisterns, or rather to keep the Rain-water in the Field it self by little Banks made all round. Then they let the water go to feed the Land, level it, and in fine, transplant the Rice-Roots one after the other, by thrusting them in with the Thumb.

Another sort of Rice.

I am greatly inclin'd to believe, that the Ancient *Siamese* lived only upon Fruits and Fish, as still do several people of the Coasts of *Africk*; and that in process of time Husbandry has been taught them by the *Chinese*. We read in the History of *China* that 'twas anciently the King himself, that annually first set his hand to the Plough in this great Kingdom, and that of the Crop which his Labour yielded him, he made the Bread for the Sacrifices. The Lawful King of *Tonquin* and *Cochinchina* together, who is called the *Bova*, likewise observe this Custom of first breaking up the Lands every year; and of all the Royal Functions, this is almost the only one remaining to him. The most important are exercised by two Hereditary Governors, the one of *Tonquin*, and the other of *Cochinchina*, who wage war, and who are the true Soveraigns; although

The original of Agriculture with the Siamese.

they

they profess to acknowledge the *Bua*, which is at *Tonquin*, for their Sovereign.

The Ceremony of the Siamese touching Agriculture.

The King of *Siam* did formerly also set his hand to the Plough, on a certain day of the year: For about an Age since, and upon some superstitious Observation of a bad Omen, he labours no more; but leaves this Ceremony to an imaginary King, which is purposely created every year: yet they will not permit him to bear the Title of King, but that of *Oc-ya Kaou*, or *Oc-ya* of the *Rice*. He is mounted upon an Ox, and rides to the place where he must plough, attended with a great train of Officers that are obedient to him. This Masquerade for one day gets him wherewithal to live on the whole year. And by the same superstition has deterred the Kings themselves. It is look'd upon as ominous and unlucky to the person. I suspect therefore that this custom of causing the lands to be ploughed by the Prince, came from *China*, to *Tonquin*, and *Siam*, with the Art of Husbandry.

It is Politick and Superstitious both together.

It may perhaps have been invented only to gain credit to Husbandry, by the example of Kings themselves; but it is intermixt with a great many superstitions, to supplicate the good and evil Spirits, whom they think able to help or hurt the goods of the Earth. Amongst other things, the *Oc-ya Kaou* offers them a Sacrifice, in the open field, of an heap of Rice-sheaves, whereunto he sets fire with his own hand.

CHAP. IX.

Of the Gardens of the Siameses, *and occasionally of their Liquors.*

Their Pulse and Roots. The Potatoe.

THE *Siameses* are not less addicted to the manuring of Gardens, than to the ploughing of Arable Lands. They have Pulse and Roots, but for the most part different from ours. Amongst the Roots the *Potatoe* deserves a particular mention. It is of the form and size almost of a Parsnep, and the inside thereof is sometimes white, sometimes red, sometimes purple; but I never saw any but the first sort: Being roasted under the Ashes, it eats like the Chesnut. The Isles of *America* made it known to us; it there frequently supplies, as some report, the place of Bread. At *Siam* I have seen *Chibols*, and no *Onions*, *Garlick*, *Turneps*, *Cucumbers*, *Citruls*, *Water-melons*, *Parsley*, *Ennum*, *Sorrel*. They have no true *Melons*, nor *Strawberries*, nor *Raspberries*, nor *Artichokes*, but a great deal of *Asparagus*, of which they do not eat. They have neither *Sallery*, nor *Beets*, nor *Colewarts*, nor *Coleflore*, nor *Turneps*, nor *Parsneps*, nor *Carrots*, nor *Leeks*, nor *Lettice*, nor *Chervil*, nor most of the Herbs whereof we compose our Sallads. Yet the *Dutch* have most of all these Plants at *Batavia*, which is a sign that the Soil of *Siam* would be proper thereunto. It bears large *Mushrooms*, but few and ill tasted. It yields no *Truffles*, not so much as that insipid and scentless kind, which the *Spaniards* do call *Criadillas de tierra*, and which they put into their pot.

Cucumbers, Chibols, Garlick, Radishes.

The *Siameses* do eat *Cucumbers* raw, as they do throughout the East, and also in *Spain*; and it is not impossible but their *Cucumbers* may be more wholsom than ours, seeing that Vinegar doth not harden them: They look upon them, and call them a kind of Water-Melons. Mr. *Vincent* inform'd me that a *Persian* will eat 36 pound weight of *Melons*, or *Cucumbers*, at the beginning of the season of these Fruits to purge himself. The *Chibols*, *Garlick*, and *Radishes* have a sweeter taste at *Siam*, than in this Country. These sort of Plants do lose their Rankness by the great Heat: And I easily believe what those who have experienc'd it have assured me, that nothing is more pleasant than the *Onions* of *Egypt*, which the *Israelites* so exceedingly regretted.

Flowers.

I have seen a great many *Tuberoses* in the Gardens of *Siam*, and no *Roses*, nor *Gillyflowers*; but it is said there are plenty of *Gillyflowers*, and few *Roses*, and that these

these Flowers have less scent here than in *Europe*; so that the *Roses* have hardly any. The *Jasmine* is likewise so rare, that 'tis said, there are none but at the King's House. We were presented with two or three Flowers as a wonder. They have a great many *Amaranths*, and *Tricolors*. Except these most of the Flowers and Plants which adorn our Gardens, are unknown to them: But in their stead they have others which are peculiar to them, and which are very agreeable for their Beauty and Odor. I have remark'd of some that they smell only in the Night, by reason that the heat of the day dissipates all their Spirits. Our Flowers have most scent about the Evening, and we have some, but few, that smell only at Night.

Whatever has not naturally a great deal of taste and smell, cannot keep them in Countries extreamly hot. Thus though there be Grapes in *Persia*, and at *Surate*, yet there can be no Muscadine Grapes, what care soever is therein employed. The best Plants, which are transported thither from *Europe*, do presently degenerate, and yield the second year ordinary Grapes only.

Why there is no Muscadine Grapes in Persia nor at Surate.

But at *Siam*, where the Climate is much hotter, there are no good Grapes. The few Vines which are planted at *Louvo*, in the King's Garden, produce only some bad Grapes, which are small and of a bitter taste.

Nor Grapes at Siam.

Pure Water is their ordinary Drink; they love only to drink it perfum'd, whereas to our Palate Water which has no smell, is the best. As the *Siameses* go not to draw it at the Springs, which are doubtless too remote, it is wholesom only when it has been setled more or fewer days, according as the Inundation is higher or lower, or wholly run out: For when the Waters retire, and they are filled with Mud, and perhaps with the ill Juices which they take from the Earth, or when the River is re-entred into its Channel sufficiently muddy, they are more corrosive, do cause Dysenteries and Lasks, and cannot be drunk without danger, till they have let them stand in great Jars or Pitchers, the space of three Weeks or a Month.

Pure water the ordinary drink of the Siameses.

At *Louvo* the Waters are much more unwholsome than at *Siam*, by reason that the whole River flows not thither, but only an Arm, which has been turned thither, which runs always decreasing after the Rain, and at last leaves its Channel dry. The King of *Siam* drinks water from a great Cistern made in the Fields, on which is kept a continual Watch. Besides that this Prince has a little house called *Tlee Poussone* or *Rich Sea*, about a League from *Louvo*. It is seated on the brink of certain Low-lands, about two or three Leagues in extent, which receive the Rain-waters and preserve them. This little Sea is of an irregular figure, its Shores are neither handsom nor even; but its Waters are wholesome, by reason they are deep and setled, and I have also heard that the King of *Siam* drinks thereof.

The Waters of Louvo and of Tlee Poussone.

For pleasure and conversation the *Siameses* do take *Tea*, I mean the *Siameses* of the City of *Siam*. For the use of *Tea* is unknown in all the other places of the Kingdom. But at *Siam* the Custom is throughly setled, and 'tis amongst them a necessary Civility to present *Tea* to all that visit them. They call it *Tcha*, as do the *Chineses*, and have not two Terms, the one for what we call *Tea*, and the other for what we call *Cha*, or Flower of *Tea*. 'Tis certain that it is not a Flower: But to assert whether they are the budding Leaves, and consequently the tenderest, or the highest, and consequently the less nourished, or the point of the Leaves, which have been boil'd at *China*, or a kind of particular *Tea*, is what I cannot determine, by reason that various Accounts have been given me thereof.

Tea.

The *Siameses* do reckon three sorts of Tea, the *Tchaboui* or *Boui Tea*, which is reddish, which some say sweetens and is astringent; 'tis look'd upon at *Siam* as a Remedy for the Flux. The *Soumlo Tea*, which on the contrary purges gently. And the third sort of *Tea*, which has no particular Name, that I know, and which neither loosens nor binds.

Three sorts of Tea.

The *Chineses* and all the Orientals, use *Tea* as a Remedy against the Head-ach: But then they make it stronger, and after having drunk five or six Cups, they lye down in their bed, cover themselves up, and sweat. It is not very difficult, in such hot Climates, for Sudorificks to operate, and they are looked upon there almost as general Remedies.

Tea is a sudorifick.

The manner of preparing Tea.

They prepare the *Tea* in this manner. They have Copper Pots tinn'd on the inside, wherein they boil the Water; and it boils in an instant, by reason the Copper thereof is very thin. This Copper comes from *Japan*, if my Memory fails me not; and 'tis so easie to work, that I question whether we have any so pliant in *Europe*. These Pots are called *Boulis*; and on the other hand they have *Boulis* of red Earth, which is without taste, tho without Varnish. They first rince the Earthen *Bouli* with boiling water to heat it, then they put in as much *Tea*, as one can take up with the Finger and Thumb, and afterwards fill it with boiling water; and after having covered it, they still pour boiling water on the outside, they stop not the Spout as we do. When the Tea is sufficiently infused, that is to say when the Leaves are precipitated, they pour the Liquor into *China* dishes; which at first they fill only half, to the end that if it appear too strong or too deep, they may temper it, by pouring in pure water, which they still keep boiling in the Copper *Bouly*. Nevertheless if they will still drink, they do again fill the Earthen *Bouly* with this boiling water, and so they may do several times without adding any more *Tea*, until they see that the water receives no tincture. They put no Sugar into the Dishes, by reason they have none refin'd which is not candy, and the candy melts too slowly. They do therefore take a little in their mouth, which they champ as they drink their *Tea*. When they would have no more *Tea*, they turn the Cup down on the Saucer; because that 'tis the greatest incivility among them to refuse any thing, and that if they leave the Cup standing, they fail not to serve them again with *Tea*, which they are oblig'd to receive. But they forbear to fill the Dish, unless they would testifie to him unto whom they present it full, that 'tis, as some say, for once, and that it is not expected that he ever come again to the House.

Excellent water necessary for Tea.

The most experienced do say that the Water cannot be too clear for Tea, that Cistern-water is the best as being the most pure, and that the finest *Tea* in the world becomes bad in water, which is not excellent.

Whether it is necessary to drink the Tea hot.

In a word, if the *Chineses* drink *Tea* so hot, 'tis not perhaps that they have found it either more wholesom or more pleasant after this manner; for they drink all sorts of Liquor at the same degree of heat, unless the Tartars have now taught them, as it is said, to drink Ice. 'Tis true that the infusion of Tea is perform'd quicker in hot water than cold; but I have drunk with pleasure what I had infused cold for above a day.

The *Siameses* adhere not to Tea: they freely drink Wine, when they have it; altho whatever inebriates is prohibited them by their Morality. The *English* and *Dutch* do sometimes bring it them from *Schiras* in *Persia*, or from *Europe*. Our *Bourdeaux* and *Cahors* Wines came very sound to *Siam*, altho they had twice passed the Line; and at our return the remainder of these Wines, was perhaps much stronger and better kept, than it would have been, had it continued always a shore. I say nothing concerning the Wines of *China* and *Japan*, which are only Beers exceedingly well mixt, but very pleasant. The *China* Wine, of which I have brought a bottle, would not keep to *France*, altho the *Dutch* Beer keeps very well to the *Indies*.

Other Liquors, *Tari* and *Neri*.

The *Siameses* do likewise drink two sorts of Liquors, which are called *Tari* and *Neri*, and which they extract from two sorts of Trees called *Palmiers*, from a name general to every Tree which has great Leaves, like the Palm-tree. The manner of collecting this drink is, in the Evening to make an Incision in the bark of the Tree, near the top of its Trunk, and to apply thereunto a Bottle as close as it is possible, luteing it with Clay, that the Air may not enter therein. The next Morning the Bottle is full, and this Bottle is generally a Pipe of great *Bambou*, to which the knot serves as a bottom. These two Liquors may also be collected in the day time, but it is said that then they are eager, and are used as Vinegar. The *Tari* is drawn from a sort of wild *Cocotier*, or Coco-tree, and *Neri* from the *Arequier*, a sort of Tree which I shall presently speak of.

Aqua vitæ preferred before all, and of what they make it.

But as in hot Countries the continual dissipation of the Spirits, makes them desire what encreases them, they passionately esteem *Aqua Vitæ*, and the strongest more than the others. The *Siameses* do make it of Rice, and do frequently rack it with Lime. Of Rice they do at first make Beer, which they drink not; but

but they convert it into *Aqua Vitæ* which they call *Lau*, and the *Portugueses Arak*, an *Arabian* word, which properly signifies *Sweat*, and metaphorically *Essence*, and by way of excellence *Aqua Vitæ*. Of the Rice Beer they likewise make Vinegar.

Punch, an English Drink.

The *English* inhabiting at *Siam* do use a drink which they call *Pounch*, and which the *Indians* do find very delicious. They put half a pint of Brandy or *Arak*, to a pint of Limonade with Nutmeg and a little Sea Bisket toasted and broke, and beat it all together until the Liquors be well mixed. The *French* call this drink *Bolle Ponche*, and *Bonne Ponche*, from the two *English* words, a Bowl of Punch.

Coffee and Chocolate.

In a word, the Moors of *Siam* drink *Coffee*, which comes to them from *Arabia*, and the *Portugueses* do drink *Chocolate*, when it comes to them from *Manilla*, the chief of the *Philippines*, where it is brought from the *Spanish West-Indies*.

Fruits.

The *Siameses* do esteem fruit better than all things; they eat all the day long if they have it. But excepting *Oranges*, *Citrons* and *Pomegranates*, there is not at *Siam* any of the fruits that we know. The Citrons which they call *Ma-craut*, are small, full of Juice and very sowre, and the skin very smooth. They appeared to me of a singular quality, in that they are rotten on the inside, when their peel is sound and entire. But they have moreover a kind of sowre, and no sweet Lemons, and on the contrary the Oranges and Pomegranates are all sweet; unless for sowre Oranges they would take the *Pampelmouses*, which have the taste and shape thereof, but which are as big as Melons, and have not much Juice. The *Siameses* do with reason range them among the species of Oranges, and call them *Sommo*, and *Som* signifies an *Orange*. Amongst the sweet Oranges the best have the Peel very green and rough; they call them *Som-keou*, or *Crystal Oranges*; not that they have any transparency, but because they appear to them in their kind, of the repute of Crystal, which they highly value. They give of these *Som-keou* to their *sick*, and sell them, as 'tis said, at five *sous* a piece when the season is past; a considerable price in a Country where a man commonly lives for two *Liards* a day.

Certain Fruits at every Season.

Now tho this sort of Oranges lasts not the whole year, yet there is always one sort or other. There is also of that Fruit which the *Europeans* call *Bananas*, or *Indian Figs*, and the *Siameses Clouey*, all the year. All the other Fruits continue only a time. 'Tis at *Achem* only at the North Point of the Isle of *Sumatra*, that Nature produces them all at every season. Those excellent Canes of one single Shoot or Joynt, between nine and ten foot long, do grow only at *Achem*; but Rice, which is their principal nourishment, frequently fails them: and they do then dearly purchase it with the Gold, which they find so plentifully amongst them, that they contemn it without Philosophy.

The difference of the Fruits of Siam from ours.

I designedly omit the Description of several Fruits, and refer it to the end of this work. I will now only speak of the *Areca*, and shall say of the *Indian* Fruits in general, that they have for the most part so strong a taste and smell, that one loves them not, till accustomed thereunto; and I think that then they do no hurt. By a contrary reason, our Fruits are at first insipid and without savor, to him that is accustomed to the *Indian* Fruits.

The Areca and Betel.

The *Areca*, which the *Siameses* do call *Plou*, is a kind of great Acorn, which yet wants that wooden Cup wherein our Acorn grows: When this Fruit is yet tender, it has at the center or heart a greyish substance, which is as soft as Pap. As it drys it waxes yellower and harder, and the soft substance it has at the heart grows hard too: It is always very bitter and savory. After having cut it into four parts with a Knife, they take a piece every time, and chew it with a Leaf resembling Ivy called *Betel* by the *Europeans* which are at the *Indies*, and *Mak* by the *Siameses*. They wrap it up to put it the more easily into the mouth, and do put on each a small quantity of Lime made of Cockle-shells, and redded by I know not what art. For this reason the *Indians* do always carry this sort of Lime in a very little *China* dish, for they put so little on every Leaf, that they consume not much in a day, altho they incessantly make use of the *Areca*, and the *Betel*. The *Areca* whilst tender wholly consumes in the Mouth, but the dry always leaves some remains.

The

Their effect.

The sensible effect of this Acorn and this Leaf is to excite much spitting, if they care not to swallow the Juice; but it is good to spit out the two or three first Mouthfuls at least, to avoid swallowing the Lime. The other less sensible effects, but which are not doubted in the *Indies*, are to carry from the Gums, perhaps by reason of the Lime, whatever may prejudice them, and to fortifie the Stomach, either by reason of the Juice that is swallowed at pleasure, and which may have this quality, or by reason of the superfluous moistures which they discharge by spitting. Thus have I never found any person at *Siam* with a stinking breath, which may be an effect of their natural Sobriety.

Another effect of the *Areca* and *Betel*.

Now as the *Areca* and *Betel* do cause a red spittle independently on the red Lime which is mix'd therewith, so they leave a Vermilion Tincture on the Lips and Teeth. It passes over the Lips, but by little and little it thickens on the Teeth till they become black: So that persons that delight in neatness, do blacken their Teeth, by reason that otherwise the spittle of the *Areca* and *Betel*, mix'd with the natural whiteness of the Teeth, causes an unpleasant effect, which is remarked in the common People. I shall transiently declare, that the Vermilion Lips, which the *Siameses* saw in the Pictures of our Ladies which we had carried to this Country, made them to say that we must needs have in *France*, better *Betel* than theirs.

How they blacken their Teeth, and how they redden the Nails of their little Fingers.

To blacken their Teeth, they do thereon put some pieces of very sowre Lemon, which they hold on their Jaws or Lips for an hour, or more. They report that this softens the Teeth a little. They afterwards rub them with a Juice, which proceeds either from a certain Root, or from the *Coco*, when they are burnt, and so the operation is perform'd. Yet it pleases them sometimes to relate that it continues three days, during which it is necessary, they say, to lye on their Belly and eat no solid Food: But some have assur'd me that this is not true, and that it is sufficient to eat nothing hot for two or three days. I believe rather that their Teeth are too much set on edge, to be able for some time to eat any thing solid. It is necessary continually to renew this operation to make the effect thereof continue; for this blackness sticks not so strong to the Teeth, but that it may be rub'd off with a burnt Crust of Bread reduc'd to Powder. They love also to redden the Nails of their little Fingers, and for this end they scrape them, and then apply a certain Juice, which they extract from a little Rice bruised in Citron Juice with some Leaves of a tree, which in every thing resembles the Pomegranate Tree, but bears no Fruit.

Of the *Palmites* in general.

In brief, the *Arequier* or *Arecier*, and all the Trees which are called *Palmites*, have no Branches, but great, long and broad Leaves, like the Palm-tree; and they have their Leaves only at the top of the stalk, which is hollow. These sorts of Trees do annually produce a new Shoot of Leaves, which spring out of the middle of the Leaves of the preceeding year, which then fall off, and leave a mark round the Trunk; so that by these marks which are so many knots, and which are close together, they can easily compute the Years or Age of the Tree.

This is what I had to say concerning the Extent and Fertility of the Kingdom of *Siam*, I will now discourse of the Manners of the *Siameses* in general; that is to say of their Habit, Houses, Furniture, Table, Equipage, Diversions and Affairs.

PART II.

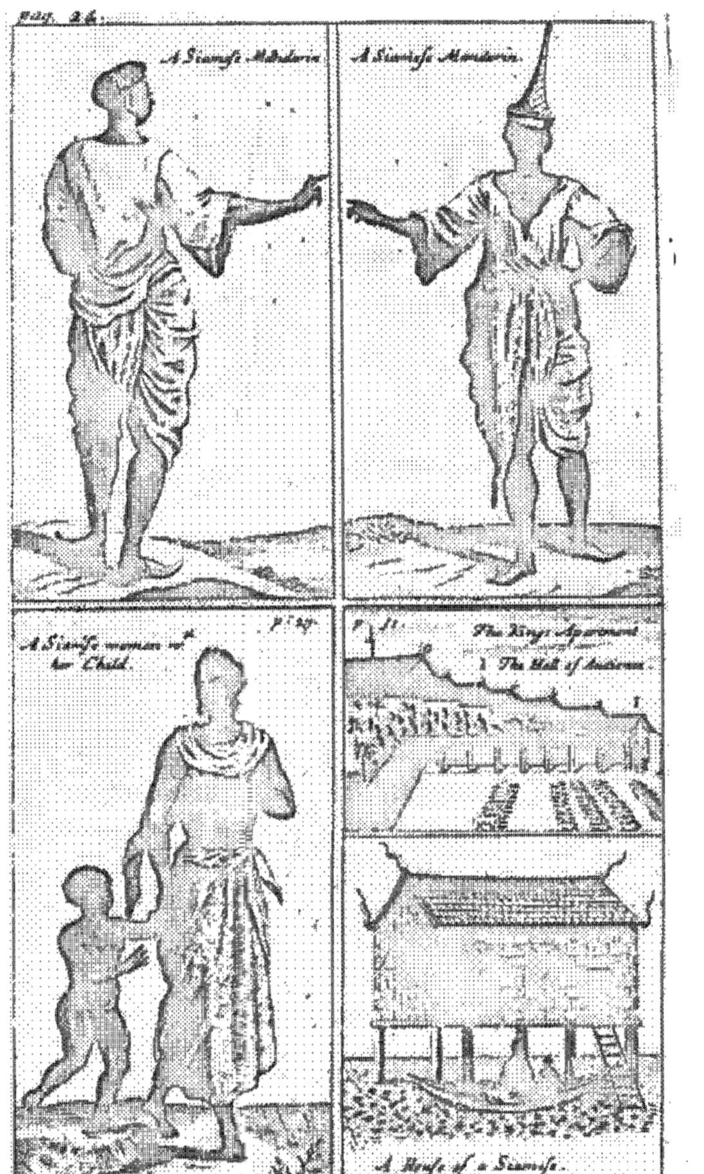

A Siamese Mandarin
A Siamese Mandarin
A Siamese woman wt her Child
The Kings Apartment
The Hall of Audience
A House of a Siamese

PART II.

Of the Manners of the Siameses *in general.*

CHAP. I.

Of the Habit and Meen of the Siameses.

THey hardly cloath themselves. *Tacitus* reports concerning the *German* Infantry in his time, that it was either all naked, or cover'd with light Coats; and even at this present there are some Savages in the Northern *America*, which go almost naked; which proves, in my opinion, that the simplicity of Manners, as well as the Heat, is the cause of the Nakedness of the *Siameses*, as it is of the Nudity of these Savages. 'Tis not but that Cloaths are almost insupportable to the *French* which arrive at *Siam*, and who know not how to forbear acting and stirring; but it is unhealthful for them to uncloath themselves, by reason that the Injuries of the excessively hot Air are not less dreadful, than those of the extreamly cold Air to which one is not accustom'd; yet with this difference, that in very hot Climats 'tis sufficient for health, to cover the Stomach. The *Spaniards* do for this reason cover it with a Buffalo's Skin four double; but the *Siameses*, whose Manners are plain in every thing, have chosen to habituate themselves from their Infancy, to an almost entire Nudity.

They wear few Cloaths, not so much by reason of the heat, as by the simplicity of their Manners.

They go with their Feet naked, and their Head bare; and for Decency only they begirt their Reins and Thighs down to their Knees with a piece of printed Cloth about two Ells and an half long, which the *Portuguese* do call *Pagne*, from the Latin word *Pannus*; sometimes instead of a painted Cloth, the *Pagne* is a silken Stuff, either plain, or embroider'd with a Border of Gold and Silver.

The Pagne, the Habit of the Siameses.

The *Mandarins*, or Officers, do wear besides the *Pagne*, a Muslin Shirt which is as their Vest. They pluck it off, and wrap it about their middle, when they approach a *Mandarin* much higher than them in Dignity, to express unto him their readiness to go where he shall please to send them. And yet the Officers whom we saw at the Audiences of the King of *Siam*, remain'd cloath'd therewith as with their Habit of Ceremony; and by the same reason they always had their Bonnets high, and pointed on the Head. These Shirts have no Neckband, and are open before, they taking no care to fasten them, to cover their Stomach. The Sleeves hang down almost to their Wrists, being about two Foot wide, but without being plaited above or below. Moreover, the Body thereof is so strait, that not slipping nor falling down over the *Pagne*, it sets in several wrinckles.

A Muslin Shirt serves them for a Vest.

In Winter they do sometimes put over their shoulders a breadth of Stuff or painted Linnen, either like a Mantle or a Scarf, the ends of which they wind very neatly about their Arms.

A Scarf against the Cold.

But the King of *Siam* wears a Vest of some excellent Sattin brocaded, the Sleeves of which are very strait, and reach down to the Wrist; and as we apparel our selves against the Cold under our Wastcoats, he puts this Vest under the Shirt which I have described, and which he adorns with Lace, or *European*

How the King wears Vests of Silk.

Point. 'Tis not lawful for any *Siamese* to wear this sort of Vest, unless the King gives it him, and he makes this Present only to the most considerable of his Officers.

A sort of Military Vest.

He sometimes also gives them another Vest or Garment of Scarlet, which is to be worn only in War, or at Hunting. This Garment reaches to the Knees, and has eight or ten Buttons before. The Sleeves thereof are wide, but without Ornament, and so short, that they touch not the Elbows.

The Red Colour for War and Hunting.

'Tis a general Custom at *Siam*, that the Prince, and all his Retinue, in the War or Hunting, be cloath'd in Red. Upon this account the Shirts which are given to the Soldiers, are of Muslin dy'd Red; and on the days of Ceremony, as was that of the Entry of the King's Ambassadors, these Red Shirts were given to the *Siameses*, which they put under their Arms.

The high, and pointed Cap.

The white, high, and pointed Cap, which we saw on the Ambassadors of *Siam*, is a Coif of Ceremony, whereof the King of *Siam* and his Officers do equally make use; but the King of *Siam's* Cap is adorn'd with a Circle, or a Crown of precious Stones, and those of his Officers are embellish'd with divers Circles of Gold, Silver, or Vermilion gilt, to distinguish their Dignities; or, have not any Ornament. The Officers wear them only before the King, or in their Tribunals, or in some Ceremony. They fasten them with a Stay under their Chin, and never pull them off to salute any person.

Babouches.

The *Moors* have introduc'd amongst them the use of *Babouches* or *Slippers*, a kind of pointed Shoes without quarter or heel. They leave them at the Gates of their own and others Houses, to avoid dirtying the places where they enter. But, where-ever their King, or any other person is, to whom they owe Respect, (as is for instance a *Sancrat*, or Superior of their *Talapoins*) they appear not with Slippers.

The Neatness of the Palace of Siam.

Nothing is neater than the King of *Siam's* Palace, as well by reason of the few persons admitted therein, as of the Precautions with which they enter.

Hats for Travelling.

They esteem of Hats for Travelling, and this Prince causes them to be made of all Colours in almost the same shape with his Bonnet; but very few persons amongst the People vouchsafe to cover their Head against the heat of the Sun; and they do it but with a linnen Clout, and only when on the River, where the Reflexion most incommodes.

The Habit of the Women.

The difference of the Womens Habit from the Mens, is, that the Women fastning their *Pagne* length-wise round their Bodies, as likewise the Men do, they let it fall down broad-ways, and imitate a close Coat, which reaches down half-way their Legs; whereas the Men raise up their *Pagne* between their Thighs, by pulling through one of the ends, which they leave longer than the other, and which they tie to the Girdle behind, in which they do in some sort resemble our Breeches. The other end of the *Pagne* hangs before, and as they have no Pockets, they do frequently tye thereunto their Purse for the *Betel*, after the manner that we tye any thing in the corner of our Handkerchief. They do sometimes also wear two *Pagnes* one over the other, to the end that the uppermost may fit more neat.

A Nakedness almost entire.

Excepting the *Pagne*, the Women go all naked, for they have no Muslin Shirts, only the Rich do constantly wear a Scarf. They do sometimes wrap the ends thereof about their Arms; but the best Air for them, is to put it singly over their Bosom at the middle, to make smooth the wrinkles thereof, and to let the two ends hang down behind over their Shoulders.

Modesty in this Nakedness.

Nevertheless so great a Nudity renders them not immodest. On the contrary, the Men and Women of this Country are the most scrupulous in the world of shewing the parts of their Body, which Custom obliges them to conceal. The Women who sat stooping in their *Balons* the day of the King's Ambassador's Entry, turn'd for the most part their Backs to the Show, and the most Curious hardly look'd over their Shoulder. 'Twas necessary to give the *French* Soldiers some *Pagnes* to wash in, to remove the Complaints which these People made, at seeing them go all naked into the River.

The Infants go there without a *Pagne* to four or five years of age, but when once of that age, they are never uncover'd to chastise them; and in the East it is an exceeding Infamy to be beaten naked on the parts of the Body, which are generally conceal'd.

Why they chastise with the Cudgel.

'Tis from hence perhaps, that the use of the Cudgel sprang up amongst them in chastising, by reason that neither the Whip, nor the Rod, would be sufficiently felt through their Cloaths.

Modesty in the Bed, and also in the Bath.

Moreover, they pluck not off their Cloaths to lie down, or at least they only change the *Pagne*, as they do to bathe themselves in the River. The Women bathe themselves like the Men, and do exercise themselves in swimming; and in no part of the world do they swim better.

Other Proofs of their Modesty.

Their Modesty renders the Custom of Bathing almost insupportable unto them, and few amongst them can resolve to do it. They have affixt Infamy to Nakedness. And they are no less careful about the Modesty of the Ears, than of the Eyes; seeing that impure and baudy Songs are prohibited by the Laws of *Siam*, as well as by those of *China*. Yet I cannot affirm that they may not be us'd at all; for the Laws prohibit no other, than the Excess already too much establish'd. And from *China* there comes some Porcelane Figures and Paintings so immodest, that they are no more permitted than the Baudiest Songs.

What Pagnes are permitted.

Those *Pagnes* that are of an extraordinary beauty and gaudiness, as those of Silk with Embroidery, or without Embroidery, and those of painted Linnen very fine, are permitted to those only to whom the Prince presents them. The Women of Quality do greatly esteem the black *Pagnes*, and their Scarf is frequently of plain white Muslin.

Rings, Bracelets, Pendants.

They wear Rings on the three last Fingers of each Hand, and the Fashion permits them to put on as many as possibly can be kept on. They freely give half a Crown for Rings with false Stones, which at *Paris* cost not above two Sols. They have no Necklaces to adorn their Necks, nor their Wives; but the Women and Children of both Sexes wear Pendants. They are generally of Gold, Silver, or Vermilion gilt, in the shape of a Pear. The young Boys and Girls of a good Family have Bracelets, but only to six or seven years of Age; and they equally wear them on their Arms and Legs. They are Rings of Gold, or Silver, or Vermilion gilt.

Their Nakedness surprizeth not.

As these People have their Body of another Colour than ours, it seems that our Eyes do not think them Naked, at least their Nakedness has nothing which surprized me; whereas a Naked White Man, when I met one, always appear'd a new Object unto me.

The Stature of the Siameses.

The *Siameses* are rather Small, than Great; but their Bodies are well proportion'd, which I principally attribute to their not swadling in their Infancy. The care that we take to form the shape of our Children, is not always so successful, as the liberty which they leave to Nature to proceed in forming theirs. 'Tis true, that the Breasts of the *Siamese* Women uphold not themselves from their Childhood, and hang down rather to their Navels, but otherwise, their Body is well proportioned, and their hanging Breasts offend not the Eyes of their Husbands; so true it is that the Phansies, even they which seem to be most natural, do greatly consist in Custom.

Their Mien.

The shape of their Faces, as well of the Men as Women, participate less of the Oval, than the Lozenge; it is broad and high at the Cheek-bones, and on a sudden their Forehead contracts and terminates almost as much in a Point, as their Chin. Moreover, their Eyes slit a little upwards are small, and not overbrisk, and the white thereof is generally yellowish. Their Jaws are hollow, by reason they are too high above; their Mouths are large, their Lips thick and pale, and their Teeth blacken'd. Their Complexion is gross, and of a brown mix'd with red, unto which the continual Sun-burning contributes as much as the Birth.

A blue Colour laid on the Body.

The Women use neither Paint nor Patches; but I have seen a great Lord, whose Legs were blu'd with a dull Blue, like that mark which the Gunpowder leaves. They that shew'd me it, inform'd me that it was a thing affected by the

Great

Great Men, that they had more or less blue according to their dignity; and that the King of *Siam* was blu'd from the sole of his Feet, to the hollow of his Stomach. Others assur'd me that it was not out of Grandeur, but Superstition; and others would make me to doubt whether the King of *Siam* was blue. I know not how it is.

The Nose and Ears of the *Siamese*. The *Siamese*, as I have said, have their Nose short and round at the end, and their Ears bigger than ours; and the larger they have them, the more they esteem them: A Phantasy common to all the East, as it appears by all the Statues of Porcelane and other matter, which come from thence. But in this there is a difference amongst the Orientals; for some do stretch their Ears at the tip to lengthen them, without boring them any more than is necessary to put Pendants therein. Others, after having bor'd them, do by little and little enlarge the hole, to thrust in bigger and bigger Sticks: And it happens, especially in the Country of *Laos*, that they can almost thrust their Fist into the hole, and that the tip of the Ear touches the Shoulders. The *Siamese* have Ears somewhat bigger than ours, but naturally and without Artifice.

Their Hair. Their Hair is black, thick and lank, and both Sexes wear it so short, that all round the Head it reaches only to the top of the Ears. Underneath this they are very closely shaved, and this Fashion pleaseth them. The Women raise it on their Forehead, yet without fastning it again; and some, especially the *Peguins*, do let it grow behind, to wreath it. The young unmarried wear it after a particular manner. They cut with Scissars very close the Crown of the Head, and then all round they pull off a small Circle of Hair about the thickness of two Crown-pieces, and underneath they let the rest of their Hair grow down almost to their Shoulders. The *Spaniards*, by reason of the heat, do thus frequently shave the Crown of their Head, but they pluck off nothing.

The Fancy of the *Siamese* for white Women. Now every one being in love with the things of his own Country, I doubted not but the Pictures of some of the most beautiful persons of the Court, which I had brought into this Country, would ravish the *Siamese* into admiration. The painting thereof was better than that of those little Pictures which are daily sent into Foreign Countries; yet it must be confess'd that the *Siamese* hardly consider'd them, and that after the Pictures of the Royal Family, before which they respectively bowed themselves, not daring stedfastly to behold them, they exceedingly esteemed that of the Duke of *Montmorency*, by reason of his high and warlike Meen. We asked two young *Mandarins* what they thought of a great Puppet or Baby, that we shew'd them. One of them reply'd, that a Woman like this would be worth an hundred *Catis*, or fifteen thousand Livres; and his Companion was of the same mind; but he added, that there was not any person at *Siam* that could purchase it. Whether they put so high a value on a white Woman, either for the singular delight which they take in them, or only by reason that whatever comes from far, ought to be very dear, I leave to be determin'd. 'Tis certain, that whether it be Fancy, or Grandeur, the King of *Siam* has some white *Mingrelian*, or *Georgian* Women, which he purchases in *Persia*: And the *Siamese* that had been in *France* acknowledg'd, that tho' they were not at first very much struck either with the whiteness, or with the features of the *French* Women, yet they presently apprehended that they alone were handsom, and that the *Siamese* were not. As to the habit of the Puppet, the two *Mandarins* absolutely condemn'd it, as too intricate and troublesom for the Husband that would pull it off from his Wife: And I have since consider'd, that they imagin'd perhaps that our Wives lay in their Cloaths, like theirs, which would doubtless be very troublesom.

The *Siamese* are very neat. As the Cloaths imbibe whatever the Body transpires, it is certain that the less one is cloath'd, the more easie it is to be neat, as the *Siamese* are. They perfume themselves in several places of their Body. On their Lips they put a sort of perfum'd Pomatum, which makes them appear much paler than naturally they are. They bathe themselves three or four times a day, or oftner, and it is one of their Neatnesses not to make a Visit of Consequence without bathing; and in this case they make a white spot on the

top

top of their Breast with a piece of Chalk, to shew that they came from the Bath.

They bathe themselves two ways, either by going into the water after our fashion, or by causing water to be pour'd over their Body with Ladles; and they sometimes continue this sort of Bathing for an hour. In a word, they need not to warm the water for their Domestic Baths, notwithstanding it has been kept several days, and in Winter; it always continues naturally hot. Two ways of Bathing.

They take care of their Teeth, altho' they black them: they wash their Hair with Water and sweet Oils, as the *Spaniards* do, and they use no more Powder than they; but they comb themselves, which most of the *Spaniards* do not. They have Combs from *China*, which instead of being all of a piece like ours, are only a great many Points or Teeth tied close together with Wire. They pluck their Beard, and naturally have little; but they cut not their Nails, they are satisfy'd to keep them neat. The Neatness of their Teeth and Hair.

We saw some Dancers by Profession, who, for Beauty, had put on very long Copper Nails, which made them appear like Harpies. At *China*, at least before the Conquest of the *Tartars*, the Custom was neither to cut the Nails, nor the Hair, nor the Beard. The Men wore on their Heads a Net of Hair or Silk, which they fasten'd behind; and which not covering the top of the Head, left a space, through which they pull'd out their Hair, and then wreath'd and fasten'd it with a Bodkin. And it is said that this Dress on which they sometimes also wore Bonnets, or a kind of Hats, did cause Megrims, and other very violent pains in their Head. An Affectation for long Nails.

CHAP. II.

Of the Houses of the Siameses, *and of their Architecture in Publick Buildings.*

If the *Siameses* are plain in their Habits, they are not less in their Houses, in their Furniture, and in their Food: Rich in a general Poverty, because they know how to content themselves with a little. Their Houses are small, but surrounded with pretty large Grounds. Hurdles of cleft Bambou, oftentimes not close compacted, do make the Floors, Walls and Roofs thereof. The Piles, on which they are erected to avoid the Inundation, are Bambou's as thick as one's Leg, and about 13 Foot above the Ground, by reason that the Waters do sometimes rise as much as that. There never is more than four or six, on which they do lay other Bambou's across instead of Beams. The Stairs are a Ladder of Bambou, which hangs on the outside like the Ladder of a Windmill. And by reason that their Stables are also in the Air, they have Climbers made of Hurdles, by which the Cattle enter therein. The *Siameses* keep the same Simplicity in every thing.

If every House stands single, 'tis rather for the privacy of the Family, which would be discover'd through such thin Walls, than for fear of Fire: For besides that, they make their little Fire in the Courts and not in the Houses, it is impossible for them in any case to consume any great matter. Three hundred Houses which were burnt at *Siam* in our time, were rebuilt in two days. On a time when a Boom was shot to please the King of *Siam*, who beheld it at a distance, and from one of the Windows of his Palace, it was necessary for this purpose to remove three Houses, and the Proprietors had taken and carry'd them away with their Furniture in less than an hour. Their Hearth or Chimney is a Basket full of Earth, and supported with three Sticks like a Tripode. And thus they place the Fires wherewith they enclose great spaces in the Forests for the hunting of the Elephants. Houses soon built.

There are no Inns at *Siam*.

'Tis in Houses of this Nature, or rather in these sorts of Tents, but bigger, that they lodged us along the River. They had built them purposely for us, by reason there are not any wherein they could lodge us. There are no Inns at *Siam*, nor in any State of *Asia*. But in *Turkey*, *Persia*, and *Mogul* there are *Caravansera's* for Travellers, that is to say public Buildings without Furniture, in which the *Caravans* may shelter themselves, and where every one eats and lies according to the Provisions and Conveniences which he carries thither. In the Road from *Siam* to *Louvo*, I saw a Hall for this use. 'Tis a space about the bigness of an ordinary Hall, enclosed with a Wall about, as high as one may easily lean over, and covered with a Roof, which is laid upon wooden Pillars set at equal distances in the wall. The King of *Siam* does sometimes dine there in his Travels, but as for particular persons, their Boats serve them for their Inn.

Hospitality why unknown amongst the People of Asia.

Hospitality is a Vertue unknown in *Asia*, which in my opinion proceeds from the care that every one takes to conceal his Wives. The *Siameses* practise it only as to the Beasts, which they freely succour in their Distresses: But the *Talapoins* having no Wives, they are more hospitable than the People. At *Siam* was a *French* man who resolved to keep an Inn there; and some *Europeans* only did sometimes go thither. And although amongst the *Siameses*, as well as amongst the *Chineses*, it be an established practice to entertain one another, yet it is rarely in this Country, and with much Ceremony: and especially no open Table is there kept; so that it would be difficult to lay out much in keeping a Table, if one would.

What Houses were purposely built for the King's Ambassadors.

There being no house proper for us on the banks of the River, they built some after their Country fashion. Hurdles laid on Piles, and covered with Mats of Bambou, did not only make the Floors, but the Area of the Courts. The Hall and Chambers were hung with painted Cloaths, with Cielings of white Muslin, the extremities of which hung sloping. The Floors were cover'd with Rush-mats, finer and more shining than those of the Courts; and in the Chambers where the King's Ambassadors lay, Tapestry-carpets were laid over the Mats. Neatness appeared every where, but no Magnificence. At *Bancok*, *Siam*, and *Louvo*, where the *Europeans*, *Chineses*, and *Moors* have built Houses of Brick, they lodged us in Houses of this sort, and not in Houses purposely built for us.

Brick-Houses for the Ambassadors of France and Portugal, which were not Finished.

Yet we saw two **Brick** Houses which the King of *Siam* had built, one for the Ambassadors of *France*, and the other for those of *Portugal*, but they are not finished; by reason perhaps of the little probability there was, that they would be frequently inhabited. Moreover it is certain that this Prince begins several Brick buildings, and finishes few. The reason of which I know not.

The Houses of the great Officers of Siam.

The great Officers of this Court have Timber Houses, which are said to be great [illegible]; but therein do lodge only the Master of the House, his Principal Wife, and their Children. Every one of the other Wives with her Children, every Slave with his Family, have all their little Apartments separate and alone, but yet inclosed within the same Inclosure of *Bambou* with the Master's House; altho they be so many different Families.

Their Houses have but one Story.

One single story sufficeth them; and I am perswaded that this manner of building is more commodious to them than ours; seeing that they are not straitned for room (for there remains some in the City, and they take it where they please) and seeing they build with those slight materials, which every one takes at pleasure in the Woods, or which he buys at a low rate of him that has been there to take them. Nevertheless it is reported that the reason why their Houses have but one story, is that no Person may be higher in his own House than the King of *Siam*, when he passes thro the Street mounted on his Elephant; and that further to assure themselves that they are all lower than this Prince when he goes either by Water or by Land, they must shut all their Windows, and come into the Street, or into their *Balons* to prostrate themselves. Thus they did on the day of the Entrance of the King's Ambassadors, less out of curiosity for the Show, than out of respect to his Majesties Letters. But it should seem that this custom of coming down out of their Houses, is a sufficient respect to their Prince. For it is not true, that the Houses erected, as they are on

Piles,

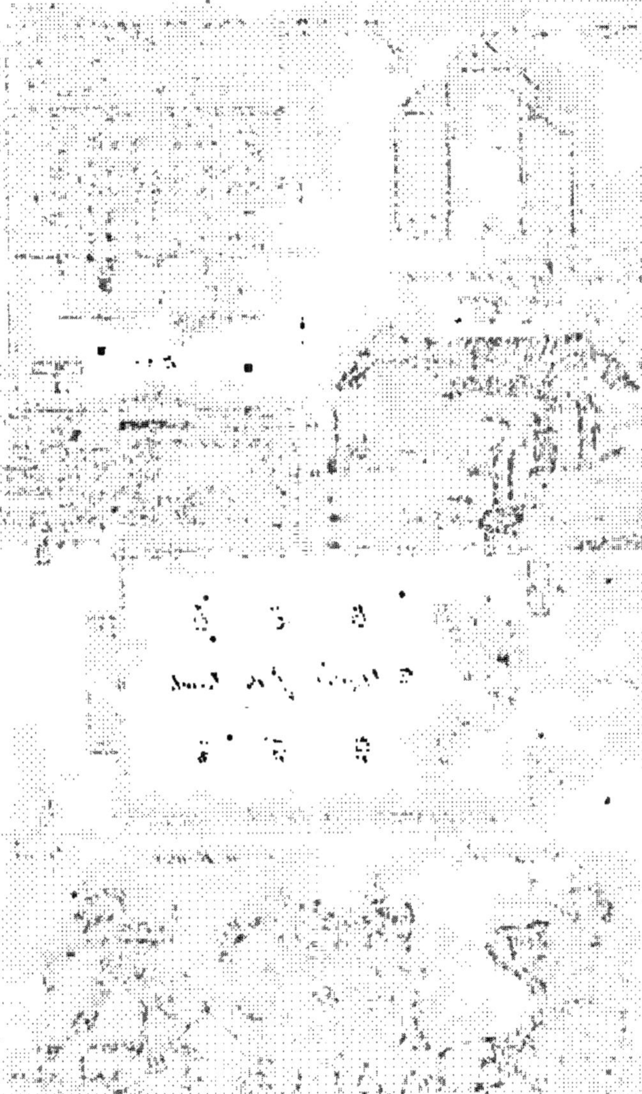

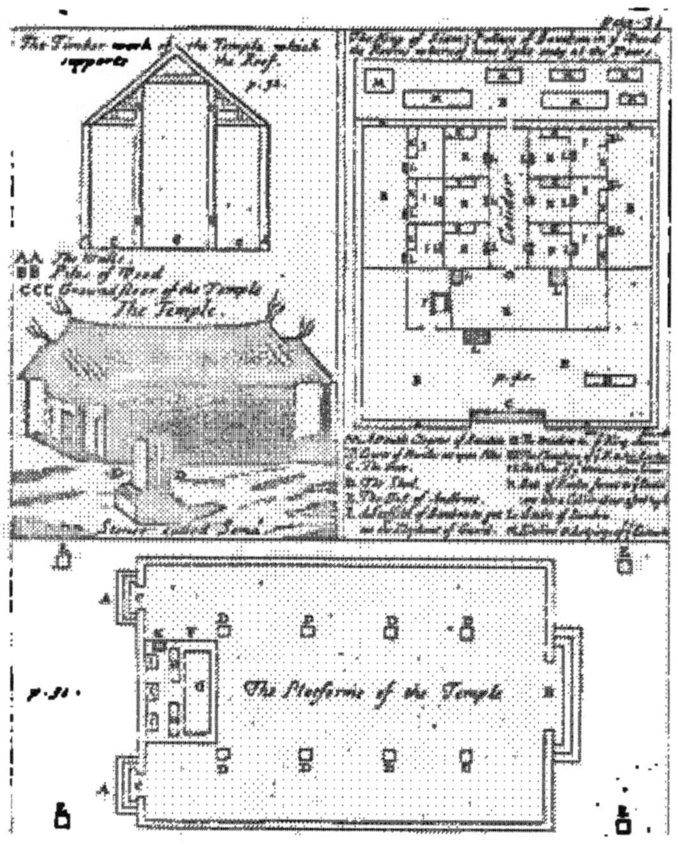
The Timber work of the Temple which supports the Roof.
AA The Walls.
BB Poles of Wood
CCC Ground floor of the Temple
The Temple
Corridor
The Platforme of the Temple
p. 31.

Piles, are lower than the King on his Elephant; and it is less true, that they are not higher than the King in his *Salon*. But what they doubtless observe, is that their Houses are less exalted than the Palaces of this Prince. Moreover his Palaces consisting only of one story, do sufficiently evince, that this is the Phantasie of the Country in their Buildings; the true reason of which I will give you in the sequel.

Brick-Houses for Foreigners.

The *Europeans*, *Chineses*, and *Moors*, do there build with Brick, every one according to his Genius; for that they alone will be at the expence, as I conceive, or that they alone have the Liberty thereof, as it is reported. At the side of their Houses, to keep off the Sun and not hinder the Air, some do add Pent-houses, which are sometimes supported by Pillars. Others do make the bodies of the House double, which do reciprocally receive the light one from the other, to the end that the Air may pass from one to the other. The Chambers are large and full of Windows, to be the more fresh and airy. And those of the first story have lights over the lower Hall, which ought to be so called by reason of its heighth, and which sometimes is almost all enclosed with Buildings, through which it receives the light. And 'tis this they call *Divan*, an *Arabian* word which properly signifies a *Council-Chamber*, or *Judgment-Hall*.

Halls called Divans.

There are other sorts of *Divans*, which being built on three sides do want a fourth Wall, on that side which the Sun shines least on, in the whole Course of the year, for between the Tropicks it illuminates every where according to the several Seasons. On the side which is open they do put a Pent-house as high as the Roof: and the inside of the *Divan* is frequently adorn'd from the top to the bottom with little Niches contrived either in the Wall, or in the Wainscot, in which they put some *China* Dishes. We had a *Divan* of this last sort in our House at *Siam*; and in the Front under the Pent-house there played a little Fountain.

Palaces and Temples of Brick, but low.

The Palaces of *Siam* and *Louvo*, and several Pagodes or Temples are likewise of Brick, but the Palaces are low, by reason they have no more than one story, as I have intimated; and the *Pagodes* are not raised high enough in proportion to their bigness. They are much darker than our Churches; perhaps because the Obscurity imprints more respect, and seems naturally to have something religious. Moreover they are of the shape of our Chappels, but without Vaults, or Cielings; only the Timber-work which supports the Tiles, is varnished with red interspersed with some streaks of Gold.

Brick-Buildings modern at Siam.

The King of *China's* Palace is still of Wood; and this perswades me that Brick Buildings are very modern at *Siam*, and that the *Europeans* have there introduced the practice and use thereof. And because that the first *Europeans*, which have built in this Country, were *Falkes*, and have called their Houses, *Fallories*; the *Siameses*, from the word which in their language signifies *Fallory*, do likewise name their ancientest Brick Pagod, as if they should say *Pagode-Fallory*, or *Pagode* of the *Fallory*.

They know not the five Orders of Architecture.

In a word, they know no exterior Ornament for Palaces, nor for Temples, save in the Roofs, which they cover with that ordinary Tin which they call *Calin*, or with Tiles varnished with yellow, as it is in the King of *China's* Palace. But tho there appears not any Gold in the Palace of *Siam* on the outside, and there is but little gilding on the inside, yet they fail not to call it *Prassat-Tong*, or the Golden Palace, because they give pompous names to every thing which they honour. As for what concerns the five Orders of Architecture, composed of Colomns, Architraves, Frizes, and other Ornaments, the *Siameses* have not any knowledge thereof; and it is not in Ornaments of Architecture, that amongst them consists the real Dignity of the Royal Houses and the Temples.

Stairs and Gates.

Their Stairs are so mean, that a pair of Stairs of ten or twelve steps, by which we went up into the Hall of Audience at *Siam*, exceeded not two foot in breadth. They were of Brick joyning to the Wall on the right side, and without any Rail on the left. But the *Siamese* Lords minded it not; they went up crawling on their Hands and Knees; and so softly, that they might have said that they would surprize the King their Master. The Gate of the Hall being square, but low and strait, was agreeable to the Stairs, and placed on the left

Hand

Hand at the Extremity or Corner of the Wall of the Hall. I know not whether they understand subtilty, and whether they do not believe that a very little Door is too big, seeing it is thought that they ought to prostrate themselves to enter therein. 'Tis true that the entrance into the Hall of *Louvo* is better, according to our Fancy; but besides that, the Palace of *Louvo* is more modern, the Prince does there lay aside his State, which resides principally in the Metropolis, as I shall relate in the sequel.

Wherein the dignity of Palaces consists.

That which amongst them makes the real dignity of the Houses, is that altho there is no more than one story, yet they are not all level. As for example, in the Palace, the King and Lady's Apartment is higher than the rest, and the nearer an Apartment is to it, the higher it is in respect to another, which is further distant: So that there is always some steps to ascend from one to the other: For they all joyn to one another, and the whole is from end to end on a line; and it is that which causes the inequality in the Roofs. The Roofs are all high-ridged, but the one is lower than the other, as it covers a part lower than another. And a lower Roof seems to come out from a higher Roof, and the highest to bear on the lowest, like a Saddle, the fore-bow of which bears on the hind part of another.

The same at China.

In the King of *China*'s Palace it is the same: And this inequality of the Roofs, which seems to proceed one from under another, after the manner that I have explain'd it, denotes grandeur, in that it supposes an inequality of parts, which is not found in these Countries, at least in considerable number, but at the King's Houses; to the end that the further one is permitted to go into this set of Buildings, the more indeed he ascends, and the greater distinction he perceives. The great Officers will have three parts, one higher than another, which are divided by three Roofs of different elevation. But at the Palace of the City of *Siam* I have seen seven Roofs proceeding one from under another before the Building: I know not whether there were not others behind. Some square Towers, which are in the Palace, do seem also to have several Roofs, one three, another five, another seven, as if they were square Goblets laid one upon another; and in one of these Towers is a very great Drum headed with an Elephants Skin, to beat the *Tocsin* or Alarum in case of need.

The same in the Temples or Pagodes.

As to the *Pagodes*, in those that I have seen, I observed only one single Penthouse before, and another behind. The highest Roof is that under which the Idol stands, the other two which are lower, are thought to be only for the People; although the People forbear not to enter every where on the days when the Temple is open.

Pyramids.

But the Principal Ornament of the Pagodes, is to be accompanied, as generally they are, with several Pyramids of Lime and Brick, the Ornaments of which are very grosly performed. The highest are as high as our ordinary Steeples, and the lowest not exceeding two Fathom. They are all round, and do little diminish in bigness as they rise; so that they terminate like a Dome: It is true that when they are very low, there proceeds from this Dome-like extremity a Tin Spire very small and sharp pointed, and high enough in relation to the rest of the Pyramid. Some there are which diminish and grow thick again four or five times in their heighth, so that the Profile of them goes waving: But these Bellyings out are smaller as they are in a higher part of the Pyramid. They are adorn'd in three or four places of their Contour, with several Furrows or Flutings at Right Angles, as well as in that they have some hollow, as in that they have some railed, which diminishing gradually in proportion to the Diminution of the Pyramid, do run terminating in a point at the beginning of the next bellying out, from whence do again arise new Flutings.

A Description of certain Halls of the Palace.

I cannot tell what the King of *Siam*'s Apartments are; I have only seen the first piece thereof, which is the Hall of Audience at *Siam* and *Louvo*. 'Tis said that no person enters further, not the King's Domesticks themselves, excepting his Wives and Eunuchs; in which, if it is true, this Prince maintains a greater heighth than the King of *China*. I likewise saw the Council-chamber in the Palace of *Louvo*; but it was also a first Room of another Pile of Building, I mean that it was not preceeded by any Anti Chamber. At the Front and two

sides

sides of this Hall lyes a Terras, which commands as well over the Garden which environs it, as it is commanded by the Hall; and it is on this Terras, and under a Canopy, purposely erected on the North-side, that the King's Ambassadors were at a private Audience, which the King of *Siam* gave them; and this Prince was in a Chair of State at one of the Hall Windows. In the middle of the Garden and in the Courts there are some single open Rooms, which are called Halls; I mean those square places, that I have already described, which inclosed with a Wall, no higher than one may lean over, and cover'd with a Roof, which bears only upon Pillars placed at equal distances in the Wall. These Halls are for the chief *Mandarins*, who do there sit cross-legg'd, either for the Functions of their Offices, or to make their Court, or to expect the Prince's Orders, *&c.* in the Morning very late, and in the Evening until the approach of the Night, and they stir not thence without Order. The less considerable *Mandarins* sit in the open Air, in the Courts or Gardens; and when they know by certain signals that the King of *Siam* sees them, altho he be invisible, they do all prostrate themselves on their Hands and Knees.

When we din'd in the Palace of *Siam*, 'twas in a very pleasant place under great Trees, and at the side of a stone-pond, wherein it was said that amongst several sorts of Fish there are some which resemble a Man and Woman, but I saw none of any sort. In the Palace of *Louvo* we dined in the Garden, in a single Hall, the Walls of which supported the Roof. They are plaistered with a Ciment extremely white, smooth, and shining, upon occasion of which it was told us there was much better made at *Surat*. The Hall has a Door at each end, and is encompast with a Ditch between two or three Fathoms in breadth, and perhaps one in depth, in which there are twenty little *Jet-d'eaus*, at equal distances. They play like a watering pot, pierced with several very little holes, and they spurt no higher than the edge of the Ditch, or thereabouts, because that instead of raising the Water, they have dug away the Earth to make the Basons low.

The places of the Palace where we dined.

The Garden is not very spacious; the Compartments and Borders thereof are very little and formed by Bricks laid edgeways. The Paths between the Borders cannot contain two a breft, nor the Walks more: But the whole being planted with Flowers, and several sorts of Palmites and other Trees, the Garden, Hall, and Fountains, had I know not what Air of Simplicity and Coolness, which caused Delight. 'Tis a remarkable thing that these Princes should never be inclined to use Magnificence in their Gardens, altho from all Antiquity the Orientals have admired them.

The Garden of Louvo.

The King of *Siam* exercising the Chace sometimes for several days, there are in the Woods some Palaces of Bambou, or if you please, some fixed Tents, which only need furnishing to receive him. They are red on the outside, like those of the great *Mogul*, when he goes into the Country, and like the Walls which serve as an Inclosure for the King of *China*'s Palace. I have given the Model thereof, not only that the Simplicity of it may be seen, but principally because some assur'd me that the King of *Siam*'s Apartments, in his Palaces of *Siam* and *Louvo* is according to the same Model. 'Tis only a little Dormitory, where the King and his Wives have each a little Cell: Nevertheless the truth of what few persons do see, is always hard to know. However some also assur'd me concerning this Prince, what I have heard reported of *Cromwel*, which is that for fear of being surprized by any Conspiracy, this Prince hath several Apartments wherein he locks himself at night, it being impossible to divine exactly in which he lyes. *Strabo* reports of the *Indian* Kings in his time, that this very reason obliged them to change their Bed and Apartment several times in the same Night. And this is almost all that can be spoken concerning the manner of Building amongst the *Siamese*. Their Furniture is as follows.

Palaces of Bambou in the Woods.

CHAP. III.

Of the Furniture of the Siameses.

Their gross Houshold-stuff.

THeir Bedstead is a wooden Frame very strait and matted, but without Head or Posts. It has sometimes six Feet, which are not joined by cross pieces; sometimes it has none at all; but the generality have no other Bed than a Matt of Bulrush. Their Table is like a Drum-head with the Edges raised, and without Feet. They have at Table neither Cloth nor Napkin, nor Spoon, nor Fork, nor Knife, they are serv'd with Morsels ready cut. No Seats, but Bulrush Matts, finer or courser: No Carpets, when the Prince gives them not to them: And those of fine Cloth are very honourable, by reason of the dearness thereof. The Rich have Cushions to lean on, but they use them not to sit on, nor the King himself. That which amongst us is of Stuff or Wooll, or Silk, is generally amongst them of white or painted Cotton.

Their Vessels.

Their Vessels are either of Porcelane, or Potters Clay, with some Vessels of Copper. Wood plain, or varnish'd, *Coco* and *Bambou* afford them all the rest. If they have any Vessel of Gold or Silver, 'tis very little, and almost only by the Liberality of the Prince, and as a Chattel belonging to their Offices. Their Buckets to draw up Water are of *Bambou*, very neatly woven. In the Markets the People are seen to boil their *Rice* in a *Coco*, and the *Rice* to be sufficiently drest, before the *Coco* begins to burn; but the *Coco* serves no more than once.

Their Tools.

In short, every one builds his House, if he causeth it not to be built by his Slaves; and for this Reason the Saw and the Plane are every ones Tools. At the end of this Volume the most Curious will find a List, which two *Mandarins* gave me of the ordinary Moveables in their Families. 'Tis not that every particular person has so many, but perhaps none has more. They do there add the names of the principal parts of a House, of their Habits, and of their Arms. There may be seen the plain, but neat manner after which they built, and furnish themselves with Moveables; and several particulars of their Manners, which I there relate upon the occasion of certain Moveables.

The King's Furniture.

Their King's Furniture is almost the same, but richer and more precious than those of particular persons. The Halls, which I saw at the Palaces of *Siam* and *Louvo*, are all Wainscoted, and the Wainscot is varnish'd Red, with some streaks and foliages of Gold. The Floors were cover'd with Carpets. The Hall of Audience at *Louvo* was all over embellish'd with Looking-glasses, which the King's Squadron had brought to *Siam*. The Council-Chamber was furnish'd after this manner. In the Room there was a Sopha made exactly like a great Bedstead with its Posts, its Bottom and its Curtain-Rods all cover'd with a Plate of Gold, and the bottom with a Carpet, but without Tester or Curtains, or any sort of Garniture; instead of the Bolster there were Cushions pil'd, on which the King lean'd, but sat not thereon, as I have already remark'd, he had only a Carpet under him. In this Hall, at the Wall of the right side in relation to the Sopha, there was an excellent Glass which the King had sent to the King of *Siam* by *M. de Chaumont*. There was likewise a wooden Chair of State gilded, in which this Prince shew'd himself to the King's Ambassadors at a private Audience, which I have mention'd; and a *Tsiab* or Cup to put *Betel* in, about two Foot high, or thereabouts, and cas'd with Silver curiously wrought, and gilded in some places.

The Table-Plate which we saw at the King's Palace.

In all the Entertainments which we receiv'd at the Palace, we saw great store of Silver Plate, especially great Basons round and deep, with a Brim about a Finger's breadth, in which were serv'd up great round Boxes about a Foot and an half in Diameter. They were cover'd, and had a Foot proportion'd to their bigness, and 'twas in these Boxes that the *Rice* was serv'd up. For the Fruit they gave us some gold Plates, which were reported to have been made purposely for the

the Entertainments which the King of *Siam* made for *M. de Chaumont*; and it is true that this Prince eats not in the Plate. They esteem for his Dignity, that the Messes which are serv'd up to him are only in high Vessels, and Porcelane is more common at his Table, than Gold or Silver: A general Custom in all the Courts of *Asia*, and even in that of *Constantinople*.

CHAP. IV.

Concerning the Table of the Siamese.

That the *Siamese* eat little, and what their Food is.

THE Table of the *Siamese* is not sumptuous: As we eat less in Summer than in Winter, they eat less than we, by reason of the continual Summer in which they live; their common Food is Rice and Fish. The Sea affords them very delicate small Oysters, very excellent small Turtles, Lobsters of all sizes, and admirable Fish, the sorts of which are unknown to us. Their River is also very plentiful of Fish, and principally very good and curious Eels: But they make little esteem of fresh Fish.

A Wonder reported of two sorts of Fish.

Amongst the Fresh-water Fish, they have some little ones of two sorts, which do here deserve to be mention'd. They call them *Pla out*, and *Pla tode*, that is to say the Fish *out*, and the Fish *tode*. To free me from all doubts, some have assur'd me, that after they have salted them together, as the *Siamese* used to do, if they leave them in an earthen Pot in their Pickle, where they soon corrupt, by reason they salt ill at *Siam*, then, that is to say when they are corrupted, and as it were in a very liquid Paste, they do exactly follow the flux and reflux of the Sea, growing higher and lower in the Pitcher as the Sea ebbs or flows. Mr. *Vincent* gave me a Pot thereof at his arrival in *France*, and assur'd me that this Experiment was true, and that he had seen it; but I cannot add my Testimony thereunto, by reason I was too late advertised thereof at *Siam*, to have an occasion of ascertaining it by my own Eyes; and that the Pot which Mr. *Vincent* gave me, and which I brought to *Paris*, perform'd this Effect no more: perhaps because the Fish were too much corrupted, or that their virtue of imitating the flux and reflux of the Sea continues only a certain time.

Bad Salt at *Siam*: The desire of the *Siamese* for corrupt meats.

The *Siamese* find much difficulty to make good Salt, by reason that Meats do hardly take Salt in excessive hot Countries; but they love Fish ill season'd and dry better than fresh, even stinking Fish displeaseth them not no more than rotten Eggs, Locusts, Rats, Lizards, and most Insects: Nature doubtless framing their Appetite to things, the Digestion whereof is more easie to them. And it may be that all these things have not such an ill taste as we imagine. *Navarette* in Pag. 45. Tom. I. *of his Historical Discourses of* China, relates that he at first exceedingly detested the Brooded Eggs of a Bird which he calls *Tahon*, but that when he eat thereof, he found them excellent. 'Tis certain that at *Siam* new-laid Eggs are very unwholsom; we do here eat Vipers, we draw not certain Birds to eat them; and sometimes Venison a little over-hunted is best relishe.

Whatever smells ill, is not always ill tasted.

What a *Siamese* expends a day in Food.

A *Siamese* makes a very good Meal with a pound of *Rice* a day, which amounts not to more than a Farthing; and with a little dry or salt Fish, which costs no more. The *Arak* or *Rice Brandy* is not worth above two Sols for that quantity, which amounts to a *Parisian* Pint; after which it is no wonder if the *Siamese* are not in any great care about their Subsistence, and if in the Evening there is heard nothing but Singing in their Houses.

Their Sauces.

Their Sauces are plain, a little Water with some Spices, Garlic, Chibols, or some sweet Herb, as Baulm. They do very much esteem a liquid Sauce, like Mustard, which is only Cray Fish corrupted, because they are ill salted; they call it *Capi*. They gave Mr. *Ceberet* some Pots thereof, which had no bad Smell.

That

They yellow their Children.

That which serves them instead of Saffron is a root, which has the Taste and Colour thereof when it is dry and reduc'd to Powder; the Plant thereof is known under the Name of *Croco Indiano*. They account it very wholesom for their Children, to yellow the Body and Face therewith. So that in the streets there are only seen Children with a tawny Complexion.

What Oil they eat.

They have neither Nuts, nor Olives, nor any eating Oil, save that which they extract from the Fruit of *Coco*; which, tho always a little bitter, yet is good, when it is fresh drawn: but it presently becomes very strong, insomuch that it is not eatable by such as are not accustomed to eat bad Oil. The Taste is always made, and it happened at my return from a very long Voyage, where I met with no extraordinary Oil, that I found the excellent Oil of *Paris* insipid and tasteless.

How Relations must be understood with reference to him that writes them.

Wherefore I cannot forbear making a remark very necessary, truly to understand the Relations of Foreign Countries. 'Tis that the words, *good, excellent, magnificent, great, bad, ugly, simple,* and *small*; equivocal in themselves, must always be understood with reference to the Phantasie of the Author of the Relation, if otherwise he does not particularly explain what he writes. As for example, if a *Dutch* Factor, or a *Portuguese* Monk do exaggerate the Magnificence, and good Entertainment of the East; if the least House of the King of *China's* Palace appear unto them worthy of an *European* King, it must be supposed that this is true, in reference to the Court of *Portugal*. And yet some may doubt hereof, seeing that in truth the Apartments of the Palace of *China* are no other than Wood varnished on the inside and outside, which is rather agreeable and neat than magnificent. Thus (because it would not be just to contemn every thing, that resembles not what we do now see in the Court of *France*, and which was never seen before this great and glorious Reign) I have endeavour'd to express nothing in ambiguous Terms, but to describe exactly what I have seen, thereby to prevent the surprising any person by my particular Fancy, and to the end that every one make as true a Judgment of what I write, as if he had performed the Voyage that I have done.

Another Reflection on the same Subject.

Another defect in Relations is the Translation of the Foreign Words. As for instance, amongst the King of *China's* Wives, there is only one that hath the Honours and Title of Queen: the rest are under her, although they be all legitimate, that is to say permitted by the Laws of the Country. They are called *verbatim* the *Ladies of the Palace,* and at *Siam* they have the same Name. The Children of these Ladies honour not their natural Mothers, as the *Chinese* are obliged theirs, but they render this Respect, and give the Name of Mother to the Queen; as if the second Wives bore Children only for the principal Wife. And this is also the Custom at *China*, in the Houses of private Persons, who have several Wives; to the end that there may be an entire subordination, which maintains Peace there as much as possible. And that the Children be not permitted to dispute amongst them the merit of their Mothers. We read almost the same thing of *Sarah*, who gave *Hagar* her Bond-maid unto *Abraham*, to have, as she said, some Children by her Slave, being past Child-bearing her self. Some other Wives of the Patriarchs practised the same, and it is evident that being the principal Wives, every one was thought the Mother of all her Husband's Children. But to return to what I have spoken concerning the danger of being deceived by the Translations of the Foreign words in Relations, who sees not the Equivocation of these words, *the Ladies of the Palace*, put into the mouth of a *Chinese*, or *Portuguese*, or in the mouth of a *French-man*, who translates a *Portuguese* Relation of *China*? The same Equivocations are found in the names of Offices? Because that all Courts and all Governments do not resemble. All Functions are not found every where, and the same are not every where attributed to the same Offices, that is to say to Offices of the same name; besides that such a Function will be great and considerable in one Country, which may be inconsiderable in another. As for example, the *Spaniards* have Marshals, which they at first design'd in imitation of the Marshals of *France*, and yet an Ambassador would find himself exceedingly mistaken, if being accompanied to the Audience of the King of *Spain*, by a Marshal of *Spain*, he should think him-

self

self as highly honoured, as if he were accompany'd to the King's Audience by a Marshal of *France*. Now the more remote the Courts are, the greater is the defect, when the same Words and the same *Idea's* are transferred from the one to the other. As *Siam* it is a very honourable Employment to empty the King's Close-stool, which is always emptied in a place appointed, and carefully kept for this purpose; it may be out of some superstitious Fear of the Sorceries which they imagine may be perform'd on the Excrements. At *China* all the Splendor and Authority is in the Offices which we call the Long Robe: And their Military Officers, at least before the Domination of the *Tartars*, consisted only of unfortunate Wretches, who were not thought endow'd with Merit sufficient to raise themselves by Learning.

A third defect of Relations is to describe things only in one Particular, if I may so say. The Reader conceives that in every thing else the Nation whereof he is inform'd resembles his, and that in this only it is either extravagant or admirable. Thus if it be simply said, that the King of *Siam* puts his Shirt over his Vest, this would appear ridiculous to us; but when the whole is understood, it is found, that, tho' all Nations act almost on different Principles, the whole amounts almost to the same; and that there is not in any place any thing marvellous or extravagant. But enough is spoken on this Subject, I return to the good Cheer of the *Siamese*.

Another Reflection on the same Subject.

They have Milk from the Female *Buffalo*, which has more Cream than the Milk of our Cows; but they make not any sort of Cheese, and scarce any Butter. Butter does hardly take any Consistence there by reason of the Heat; and that which is brought from *Surat* and *Bengale*, through Climates so extreamly hot, is very bad, and almost melted in arriving there.

The Milk at Siam.

They disguise dry Fish after several manners, without varying the Preparation. For Example, they will cut it into thin Slices, twisted like the *Vermicelli* of the *Italians*, or the *neufs filez* of the *Spaniards*. The *Chinese* are so addicted to this way of disguising their Meats, that of a Drake, for Example, they will make a Soldier, of an *Ananas* a Dragon, and this Dragon shall be painted in several Colours. Heretofore in *Europe* several Sugar Figures were serv'd up amongst the Fruit, but they eat them not; and the *Germans* call'd them *Schaw essen*, or *Food to look upon*.

How the Siamese disguise their Meats.

Of more than thirty Dishes, wherewith we were served at *Siam* after the Fashion of the *Chinese*, it was not possible for me to eat of one: Altho' it be naturally as easie to me as to any other, to accommodate my self to strange Tastes. At the sight therefore of so strange a Repast, I rested more satisfy'd with what some report of the *Chinese*, that they taste, without loathing, the Excrements of Men and other Animals, to chuse out the most proper to manure and improve their Lands; and that they commonly eat of all the Viands, which we abhor, as Cats, Dogs, Horses, Asses, Mules, *&c.*

A Chinese Repast.

In which they are very opposite to the *Siamese*, who do rarely eat of any Flesh, tho' it be given them. But when they vouchsafe so far as to eat thereof, they rather chuse the Guts, and whatever is most loathsom to us in the Intestines. In their Bazars or Markets they do sell Insects broil'd or roasted, and they have not any other Roast-meat. The King of *Siam* gave us some Poultry, and other live Animals, for our Servants to kill and dress for our Table. But in general all Food there is tough, Juiceless and Crude; and by degrees the *Europeans* themselves, which inhabit at *Siam*, do refrain eating thereof. The ancient Inhabitants of the Isle of *Rhodes*, according to *Ælian*, esteemed not those who preferred Flesh before Fish. The *Spaniards* and *Italians* do eat little, and do eat it dry roasted; and we find that the *English* eat too much, and that they eat it too raw: 'Tis that as the Countries are hotter, Sobriety is more natural.

The Siamese do love Flesh little, and have no Butchers Meat.

The *Siamese* take no care of Poultry. They have two sorts of Hens, some are like to ours, others have the Skin and Comb black, but the Flesh and the

The Poultry.

Bones white; and when these black Hens are boil'd, it is impossible to distinguish them from the white ones either by the taste or colour; altho' there are some persons who generally esteem the black best. Ducks are very plentiful and very good, but 'tis a Food, which, as it is said, does easily cloy. The *Indian Cocks* are brought to us from the *West-Indies*, and there are none at *Siam*.

Game. Peacocks and Pigeons are wild there; all Partridges are gray: Hares are very scarce, and no Rabbets to be seen. It may be that the Race could not preserve itself in the Woods, amongst all the carnivorous Animals, wherewith they are stored. There is great plenty of *Francolins*, and excellent Snipes; here they do eat Turtle-doves, whose Plumage is variegated, Parrots, and divers small Birds, which are good.

Wild-Fowl. But Wild-Fowl is secure amongst the *Siameses*, they love neither to kill them, nor hinder their liberty. They have the Dogs that will take them; and moreover, the heighth of their Herbage and the thickness of the Woods do render the Chace difficult; yet the *Moors* do exceedingly divert themselves in the flight of Faulcons, and these Birds do come to them from *Persia*.

The Peculiarity of the Birds of *Siam*. A thing which will appear singular, (altho' it be common at *Brasil*, and it may be in other hot Countries) is, that almost all the Birds at *Siam* are beautiful to behold, and are all very unpleasant to hear. There are several sorts, which imitate the Voice; all have some Cry, but no warbling Note. And tho' in this Country there are some of the Birds which we have here, they are, for Example, neither Nightingales nor Canary-Birds, but Sparrows, Peacocks, Crows, and Vultures. The Sparrows do enter boldly into the Chambers, there to pick up the little Insects, wherewith they swarm. The Crows and Vultures are very plentiful, and very familiar; because no person frights them, and the people feed them out of Charity. They do generally give them the Children, which die before three or four years old.

What we call Butcher's Meat, is worth nothing at *Siam*. Goats and Sheep are here very scarce, small, and not over-good; they are to be bought only of the *Moors*: the King of *Siam* caused a quantity of them to be nourished for himself. They generally keep the Ox and *Buffalo* for Tillage, and sell the Cows, and the whole is very bad to eat.

The goodness of the Pig. The Pig is there very small, and so fat, that it is distasteful; yet the flesh thereof is the wholsomest that can be eaten in most of the Countries of the Torrid Zone, and is given to sick persons. The Pigs are excellent also on the Sea, when they eat Bisket; whereas the Sheep do frequently taste of the wooll, by reason they eat it one from another, as Poultry eats their feathers.

The price of Meats. As to the price of Meats in the Kingdom of *Siam*, a Cow is not worth above ten Sols in the Provinces; and a Crown, or thereabouts, in the Metropolis: A Sheep four Crowns: A Goat two or three Crowns, (tho' the *Moors* do sell them very unwillingly, because this is their principal Food:) A Pig is not worth above seven Sols, by reason the *Moors* eat not thereof; Hens are worth about twenty pence a dozen, and a dozen of Ducks is worth a Crown.

Volatiles do multiply exceedingly at *Siam*. All Volatiles do multiply extreamly at *Siam*; the heat of the Climate almost hatches the Eggs. Venison also is not wanting, notwithstanding the spoil which the wild Beasts make thereof, if the *Siameses* were greedy of Dainties: But when they kill Bucks, and other Beasts, it is only to sell the Skins thereof to the *Dutch*, who make a great Trade thereof to *Japan*.

The Distempers of the *Siameses*. Yet to the discredit, in my opinion, of Sobriety, or because that in proportion to the heat of their Stomach, the *Siameses* are not more sober than us, they live not longer, and their Life is not less attack'd with Diseases than ours. Amongst the most dangerous, the most frequent are Fluxes and Dissenteries, from which the *Europeans* that arrive at this Country, have more trouble to defend themselves, than the Natives of the Country, by reason they cannot live sober enough. The *Siameses* are sometimes attackt with burning Fevers, in which the transport to the Brain is easily formed, with defluxions on the Stomach. Moreover, Inflamations are rare, and the ordinary continual Fever kills none, no more than in the other places of the Torrid Zone: Intermitting Fevers are also rare, but violent, tho' the cold Fit be very short. The External does so exceedingly

ceedingly weaken the Natural Heat, that here are not seen almost any of these Distempers, which our Physitians do call Agues and this is so throughout *India*, and also in *Persia*, where of an hundred sick persons, Mr. *Vincent* the provincial Physician, whom I have already mention'd, declar'd that he scarce found one which had the Fever, or any other hot distemper. Coughs, Coque-luches or Quinancies, and all sorts of Defluxions and Rheumatisms are not less frequent at *Siam*, than in these Countries; and I wonder not thereat, seeing that the weather is inclined to Rain so great a part of the year: but the Gout, Epilepsy, Appoplexy, Pthysick, and all sorts of Cholick, especially the Stone, are very rare.

There are a great many *Cankers, Abcesses*, and *Fistula's*. *Erysipela* are here so frequent, that among twenty men, nineteen are infected therewith: and some have two thirds of their body cover'd therewith. There is no Scurvy, nor Dropsie, but a great many of those extraordinary distempers, which the people conceive to be caused by Witchcraft. The ill consequences of a debauch are here very frequent, but they know not whether they are ancient or modern in their Country.

In a word, there are some contagious diseases, but the real Plague of this Country is the Small Pox: It oftentimes makes dreadful ravage, and then they Interr the bodies without burning them: but because their Piety always makes them desire to render them this last respect, they do afterwards dig them up again: and that which exceedingly surprizes me, is, that they dare not do it till three years after, or longer, by reason, as they say, that they have experimented, that this Contagion breaks out afresh, if they dig them up sooner. What is the Plague at Siam.

CHAP. V.

Concerning the Carriages and Equipage of the Siameses, *in general.*

BEsides the *Ox* and *Buffalo*, which they commonly ride, the Elephant is their sole Domestick Animal. The Hunting of Elephants is free for all, but they pursue this Chase only to catch them, and never to kill them. They never cut them, but for ordinary service they use only the Female Elephants: the Males they design for the War. Their Country is not proper for the breeding of Horses, or they know not how to breed them: but I believe also that their Pastures are too course and moorish, to give Courage and Mettle to their Horses; and this is the reason that they need not to cut them to render them more tractable. They have neither Asses nor Mules; but the *Moors* which are settled at *Siam*, have some Camels, which come to them from abroad. Their domestick Animals.

The King of *Siam* only keeps about two thousand Horses: He has a dozen of *Persian*, which are now nothing worth. The *Persian* Ambassador presented them to him about four or five years since, from the King his Master. Ordinarily he sends to buy some Horses at *Batavia*, where they are all small and very brisk, but as resty as the *Javan* people are mutinous; either for that the Country makes them so, or that the *Hollanders* know not to manage them. The King of Siam's Horses.

I have more than once seen in the streets of *Batavia* the Burgesses of the City on Horseback; but in an instant their Ranks were broken, by reason that most of their Horses would stop on a sudden, and would refuse to march: and mine Host hereupon inform'd me, that the common fault of the *Javan* Horses was to prove very resty. The *Dutch* Company maintain Infantry at *Batavia*, amongst which there is a good number of *French*. As for what concerns the Cavalry, there is no other than the Burgesses, who notwithstanding the heat of the Climate, do cloath themselves with good Buff, with rich trappings embroider'd with Gold and Silver. No Burgher serves in the Infantry: but if a Souldier demonstrates The Cavalry and Infantry of Batavia.

ſtrates that he has wherewith to ſettle and maintain himſelf at *Batavia*, either by a Marriage or a Trade, they never refuſe him neither his liberty, nor his right of Burghership.

The King of *Siam* rides little or not at all on Horſeback.

When we arriv'd there were two *Siameſes* to buy two hundred Horſes for the King their Maſter, about an hundred and fifty of which they had already ſent away for *Siam*. 'Tis not that this Prince loves to ride on Horſeback; this way ſeems to him both too mean and of too little defence: for the Elephant appears to them much more proper for Battel, though when all comes to all, it may reaſonably be doubted whether he be more proper for War, as I ſhall ſhew in the ſequel. They report that this Animal knows how to defend his Maſter, and to ſet him upon his back again with his Trunk, if he is faln, and to throw his Enemy on the ground. When the King of *Siam* ſeiz'd on the Crown, the King his Uncle fled from the Palace on an Elephant, and not on Horſeback, altho a Horſe ſeems much properer to fly.

A Guard Elephant in the Palace.

In the Palace there is always an Elephant on the Guard, that is to ſay Harneſſed and ready to mount, and no Guard-Horſe. Yet ſome have aſſur'd me, that the King of *Siam* diſdains not abſolutely to ride on Horſeback, but that he does it very rarely.

The King of *Siam* never ſeen on Foot.

In this place of the Palace where the Guard-Elephant ſtands, there is a little Scaffold, to which the King walks from his Apartment, and from this Scaffold he eaſily gets upon his Elephant. But if he would be carry'd in a Chair by men, which he ſometimes is, he comes to this ſort of carriage, at the due heighth of placing himſelf therein, either by a Window or a Terrace, and by this means neither his Subjects nor Strangers do ever ſee him on Foot. This Honour is only reſerved for his Wives and Eunuchs, when he is lock'd up within his Palace.

Their Sedans.

Their Chairs or Sedans are not like ours, they are ſquare and flat Seats, more or leſs elevated, which they place and fix on Biers. Four or eight men (for the Dignity herein conſiſts in the Number) do carry them on their naked Shoulders, one or two to each Staff, and other men relieve theſe. Sometimes theſe Seats have a Back and Arms like our Chairs of State, and ſometimes they are ſimply compaſt, except before, with a ſmall Balliſter about half a Foot high; but the *Siameſes* do always place themſelves croſs-legged. Sometimes theſe Seats are open, ſometimes they have an Imperial; and theſe Imperials are of ſeveral ſorts, which I will deſcribe in ſpeaking of the Balons, in the middle of which they do likewiſe place theſe Seats, as well as on the backs of Elephants.

The Imperial not very honourable at *Siam*, but the Parasol is.

As often as I have ſeen the King of *Siam* on an Elephant, his Seat was without an Imperial, and all open before. At the ſides and behind do riſe up to the top of his Shoulders three great Foliages, or Feathers gilt, and bent outwards at the Point: but when this Prince ſtops, a Footman, who ſtands ten or twelve paces from him, ſhelters him from the Sun with a very high Umbrella like a Pike, with the Head three or four Foot in Diameter: and this is not a ſmall fatigue, when the Wind blows thereon. This ſort of Umbrella, which is only for the King, is called *Pat-bouk*.

How they get upon an Elephant.

To return to the riding of the Elephant, thoſe that would guide him themſelves do ſeat themſelves on his Neck, as on a Horſe, but without any kind of Saddle; and with a punch of Iron or Silver they prick him on the head, ſometimes on the right ſide, ſometimes on the left, or exactly in the middle of the Forehead, telling him at the ſame time whether he muſt go, and when he muſt ſtop; and on the Road in the *deſcents* of the ways they adviſe him to go deſcending, *Pat, Pat*, that is to ſay, deſcend, deſcend. But if one will not take the pains to guide him, he places himſelf on his back in a Chair, inſtead of a Saddle, or without a Chair and on his Hair, if we may ſo ſpeak of an Animal that has none: And then a Servant, or commonly he that takes care of feeding the Elephant, gets up on his Neck and guides him; and ſometimes there is alſo another man ſeated on the Crupper. The *Siameſes* do call him that is placed on the Crupper *Hona ſip*, or the *Chief* of *Ten*, becauſe that they ſuppoſe out of Pride, that an Elephant has a great number of men to ſerve him, and that there are ten under the command of the *Hona-ſip*. Him that ſits upon the Elephants

Neck

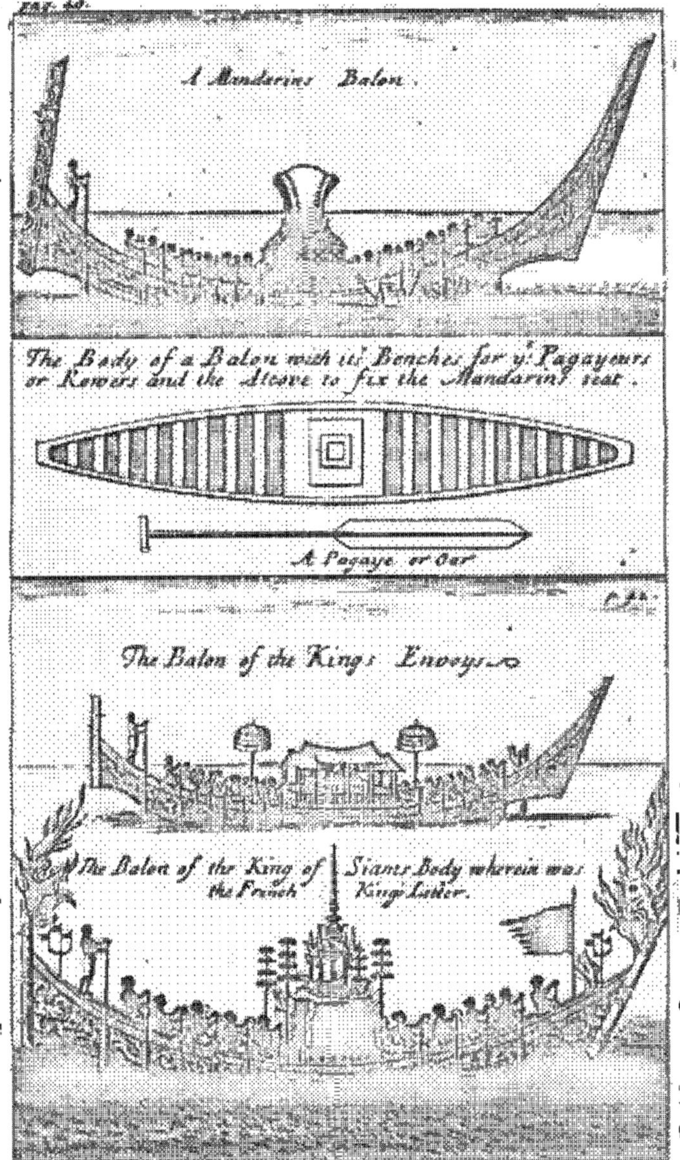
A Mandarins Balon
The Body of a Balon with its Benches for ye Pagayeurs
or Rowers and the Alcove to fix the Mandarins seat.
A Pagaye or Oar
The Balon of the Kings Envoys
The Balon of the King of Siams Body wherein was
the French Kings Letter.

Neck they do call *Nai-Tchang*, or *Captain* of the *Elephant*, and he commands over all thoſe that are appointed for the ſervice of the Elephant.

The Carriage of the Balons.

But becauſe that in this Country they go more by Water than by Land, the King of *Siam* has very fine *Balons*. I have already ſaid that the Body of a *Balon* is compoſed only of one ſingle Tree, ſometimes from ſixteen to twenty Fathom in length. Two men ſitting croſs-leg'd by the ſide one of another, on a Plank laid acroſs, are ſufficient to take up the whole breadth thereof. The one *Pagayes* at the right, and the other on the left ſide. *Pagayer* is to row with the *Pagaye*, and the *Pagaye* is a ſhort Oar, which one holds with both hands, by the middle, and at the end. It ſeems that he can only ſweep the water though with force. It is not fixed to the edge of the *Balon*, and he that manages it, looks where he goes; whereas he that rows, turns his back to his Road.

An exact Deſcription of a Balon.

In a ſingle *Balon* there are ſometimes an hundred, or an hundred and twenty *Pagayeurs*, thus ranged two and two with their Legs croſſed on Plancks; but the inferior Officers have *Balons* a great deal ſhorter, where few *Pagayes* or *Oars*, as ſixteen, or twenty do ſuffice. The *Pagayeurs* or Rowers, do ſtrike the *Pagaye* in Conſort, do ſing, or make ſome meaſured Noiſes; and they plunge the *Pagaye* in a juſt cadence with a motion of the Arms and Shoulders, which is vigorous, but eaſy, and graceful. The weight of this Bank of Oars ſerves as Ballaſt to the *Balon*, and keeps it almoſt even with the water, which is the reaſon that the *Pagayes* are very ſhort. And the Impreſſion which the *Balon* receives from ſo many men which vigorouſly plunge the *Pagaye* at the ſame time, makes it always totter with a motion which pleaſes the Eye, and which is obſerv'd much more at the Poop and Prow; becauſe they are higher, and like to the Neck and Tail of ſome Dragon, or ſome monſtrous Fiſh, of which the *Pagayes* on either ſide ſhew like the Wings or the Fins. At the Prow one ſingle *Pagayeur* takes up the firſt Rank, without having any Comrade at his ſide. He has not room enough to croſs his left Leg with his right, and he is forced to ſtretch it out over an end of a ſtick, which proceeds from the ſide of the Prow. 'Tis this firſt *Pagayeur* that gives the motion to all the reſt. His *Pagaye* is ſomewhat longer, by reaſon that he is poſted in that place where the Prow begins to riſe, and that he is ſo much the further from the Water. He plunges the *Pagaye* once to every meaſure, and when it is neceſſary to go ſwifter he plunges it twice; and lifting up the *Pagaye* continually, and only for decency with a ſhout, he throws the water a great way, and the next ſtroak all the Equipage imitates him. The Pilot ſtands always at the Poop, where it riſes exceedingly. The Rudder is a very long *Pagaye*, which is not fixed to the *Balon*, and to which the Steerſman ſeems to give no other Motion, than to keep it truly perpendicular in the water, and againſt the edge of the *Balon* ſometimes on the right ſide, and ſometimes on the left. The Women Slaves do row the Ladies *Balons*.

Several ſorts of Balons.

In the *Balons* of ordinary ſervice, wherein there are fewer *Pagayeurs*, there is in the middle a Cabin of *Bambou*, or other Wood, without Painting or Varniſh, in which a whole Family may be held, and ſometimes this Cabin has a lower Pent-houſe before, under which the Slaves are; and many of the *Siameſes* have no other Habitation. But in the *Balons* of Ceremony, or in thoſe of the King of *Siam*'s body, which the *Portugueſe* have called *Balons of State*, there is in the middle but one Seat, which takes up almoſt the whole breadth of the *Balon*, and wherein there is only one Perſon and his Arms, the Sabre and Lance. If it is an ordinary *Mandarin*, he has only a ſingle Umbrella like ours to ſhelter himſelf; if it is a more conſiderable *Mandarin*, beſides that his Seat is higher, he is covered with what the *Portugueſes* call *Chirole*, and the *Siameſes Coup*. 'Tis an Arbor all open before and behind, made of *Bambous* cleft and interlac'd, and cover'd within and without with a black or red Varniſh. The red Varniſh is for the *Mandarins* at the right hand, the black for thoſe of the left, a diſtinction which I ſhall explain in its due place. Beſides this the extremities of the *Chirole* are gilded on the outſide the breadth of three or four Inches, and ſome pretend that 'tis in the faſhion of theſe Guildings, which are not plain, but like Embroidery, that the Marks of the *Mandarins* Dignity are. There are alſo ſome *Chiroles* cover'd with Stuff, but they ſerve not for rainy weather. He that commands the Equipage sometimes cudgels, but very rarely, those which row softly and out of measure, places himself cross-leg'd before the *Mandarins* Seat, on the extremity of the Table, on which the Seat is fixed. But if the King chances to pass by, the *Mandarin* himself descends upon this Table, and there prostrates himself; his whole Equipage does likewise follow his example, and his *Balon* stirs not till the King's be out of sight.

The Balons of the Body which are called Balons of State.

The Imperials of the *Balons* of State are all over gilded, as well as the *Pagoda's*. They are supported by Columns, and loaded with several pieces of Sculpture in *Pyramids*, and some have sheds against the Sun. In the *Balon* where the King's Person is, there are four Captains or Officers to command the Equipage, two before and two behind they sit cross-leg'd, and this is the Ornament of the *Balons*.

The Swiftness of the Balons.

Now as these Vessels are very narrow, and very proper to cut the water, and the Equipage thereof numerous, it cannot be imagin'd with what swiftness it carries them, even against the Stream, and how pleasant a sight it is to behold a great number of *Balons* to row together in good order.

The Entrance of the Kings Ambassadors into the River.

I confess that when the King's Ambassadors entred in the River, the Beauty of the Show surpriz'd me. The River is of an agreeable breadth, and notwithstanding its *Meanders*, there is always discover'd a very great extent of its Channel, the Banks whereof are two Hedge-rows continually green. This would be the best Theater in the World for the most sumptuous and magnificent Feasts; but no Magnificence appears like a great number of men devoted to serve you. There were near three Thousand embarkt in seventy or eighty *Balons*, which made the Train of the Ambassador. They rowed in two ranks, and left the *Balon* with the King's Ambassadors in the middle. Every one was animated and in motion; All eyes were taken up with the diversity and number of the *Balons*, and with the pleasantness of the River's Channel; and yet the ears were diverted by a barbarous, but agreeable noise of Songs, Acclamations and Instruments; in the intervals of which the Imagination ceased not to have a sensible taste of the natural silence of the River. In the night there was another sort of Beauty, by reason that every *Balon* had its Lanthorn; and that a noise which pleases, is much more pleasant in the night.

The ancient Magnificence of the Court of Siam.

'Tis asserted at *Siam* that the Court was formerly very magnificent, that is to say, there was a great number of Lords adorn'd with rich Stuffs, and a great many precious Stones, and always attended with an hundred or two hundred Slaves, and with a considerable number of Elephants: but this is gone ever since the Father of the present King cut off almost all the most considerable, and consequently the most formidable *Siameses*, as well those who had served him in his Revolt, as those which had opposed him. At present three or four Lords only have permission to use those Chairs or Sedans, which I have spoken of. The *Palankin* (which is a kind of Bed, that hangs almost to the ground, from a great Bar, which men carry on their Shoulders) is permitted to sick persons, and some diseased old men, for 'tis a Carriage wherein they can only lie along. But though the *Siameses* may not freely use these sorts of Conveniences, the *Europeans* which are at *Siam*, have more permission herein.

Umbrella's.

The use of *Umbrella's*, in *Siamese Ruom*, is also a Favour which the King of *Siam* grants not to all his Subjects, although the *Umbrella* be permitted to all the *Europeans*. Those which are like to ours, that is to say, which have but one round, is the least honorable, and most of the *Mandarins* have thereof. Those that have more rounds about the same handle, as if they were several *Umbrella's* fixd one upon another, are for the King alone. Those which the *Siameses* do call *Clot*, which only have one round, but from which do hang two or three painted Cloaths like so many Hangings, one lower than the other, are those which the King of *Siam* gives to the *Sancrats* or Superiors of the *Talapoins*. Those which he gave to the King's Ambassadors were of this last sort, and with three Cloaths. You may see the figure thereof in that of the *Balon* of the King's Ambassadors.

The Umbrella of the Talapoins, and the Origine of the word Talapoin.

The *Talapoins* have *Umbrella's* in the form of a Screen, which they carry in their hand. They are of a kind of Palmito leaf cut round and folded, and the folds thereof are tyed with a thread near the stem, and the stem which they

make

made crooked like an S is the handle thereof. In *Siamese* they call them *Talapat*, and 'tis probable that from hence comes the name of *Talapoi* or *Talapoin*, which is in use amongst Foreigners only, and which is unknown to the *Talapoins* themselves, whose *Siamese* name is *Tchaou-cou*.

The Elephant is the carriage of every one that can take one by hunting, or purchase one; but the Boat is the more universal carriage; no person can travel without one, by reason of the annual Inundation of the Country. *The Elephant and Boat permitted to all.*

Whilst the King of *Siam* is in his Metropolis, the ancient custom of his Court requires that he show himself to the people five or six days of the year only, and that he does it with Pomp. Heretofore the Kings his Predecessors did first break up the ground every year, till they left this Function to the *Oc-ya-kaoo*; and it was attended with great Splendor. They also went out another day to perform on the water another Ceremony, which was not less superstitious, nor less splendid. 'Twas to conjure the River to return into its Channel, when the Agriculture requir'd it, and when the Wind inclining to the North assured the return of fair weather. The present King was the first that dispenc'd with this troublesom work, and it is several years since it seem'd abolished; because, say they, that the last time he perform'd it, he had the disgrace of being surpriz'd with rain, altho his Astrologers had promised him a fair day. *When and how the King of Siam shews himself.*

Ferdinand Mendez Pinto relates that in his time the King of *Siam* used to shew himself one day in a year upon his white Elephant, to ride through nine streets of the City, and to extend great Liberalities to the People. This Ceremony, if it has been in use, is now abolished. The King of *Siam* never mounts the white Elephant, and the reason which they give is, that the white Elephant is as great a Lord as himself, because he has a King's soul like him. Thus this Prince shews himself in his Metropolis no more than twice a year, at the beginning of the sixth and twelfth month, to go and present Alms of Silver, yellow *Pagnes*, and fruits to the *Talapoins* of the Principal Pagods. On these days, which the *Siamese* do call *Van pra, a holy, or excellent day*, he goes upon an Elephant to the Pagodes which are in the same City, and by water to another, which is about two leagues from the City down the River. On the days following he sends the like Alms to the less considerable Pagods: but this extends not above two leagues from the Metropolis, or thereabouts. And in the last month of the year 1687, this Prince went no where in person, he contented himself with sending every where.

If therefore the King of *Siam* shews himself in his Metropolis, 'tis upon some Ceremonies of Religion. At *Louvo*, where it is permitted him to lay aside his Kingship, he frequently goes abroad, either for the hunting of the Tyger and Elephant, or to stir himself; he goes with so little Pomp, that when he marches from *Louvo* to his little house of *Thlée-poussone* with his Ladies, he gives not any carriage to the women which are of the Company: which is doubtless a respect from these women Slaves to their Mistresses. *The King of Siam less with his pomp at Louvo than at Siam.*

Nevertheless he has always in his retinue two or three hundred men as well on foot as on horseback; but what is this in comparison of those Trains of fifteen and twenty thousand men which the Relations do give him on days of Ceremony? Before him do march some Footmen with Staves, or with long Truncks to shoot Peas with, to drive all the People out of his way, and especially when the Ladies follow him; and likewise before he goes out the *Europeans* are therewith acquainted, if there are any lately arrived, to avoid meeting him: As for all the *Asiaticks*, they very well know this custom, which is the same in all the Courts of *Asia*. *Barros* reports, that in the true *India*, when a Nobleman walks in the Streets he is always preceded by one of his Domesticks, who crys *po, po*, that is to say, close, close, to the end that all the Ploughmen may disperse themselves. *Osorius* reports, that 'tis the Ploughman that is obliged to cry out, and he subjoyns, that it is for fear lest any Nobleman should touch him unawares, and revenge this Affront by killing him. The *Nairos* I call Nobles, who alone make profession of Arms, and who think themselves defiled, when they touch a Ploughman. At *Siam* and *China* the principal Magistrates have Officers that go before them, who make the People to stand in Ranks, and who would cudgel those that would not retire, or which would *The King of Siam's Retinue.*

not

not render to their Master all the other respects which are due unto him, and which in these Countries we found very insupportable. 'Tis no wonder therefore if the King of *China*, the Great *Mogol*, the King of *Persia*, and the other *Asiatick* Potentates have thought it consistent with their Dignity, thus to advertize the People of their March. Those that do for this purpose precede the King of *Siam*, are called *Contabar* and *Cong*. The *Contabars* do keep the right hand, and the *Cong*'s the left: and we shall see in the List of certain Officers, that *Cong* is the Title of the Provost. 'Tis upon the same account, that is to say, to disperse the People from the person of the King of *Siam* when he travels, that two Officers of his Horse Guard, of *Mén* and *Lous*, do march on both sides, but about 50 or 60 paces from him. His Courtiers appear first at the Rendevouz, or they do sometimes follow on Foot with their hands joyn'd on their Breast. Sometimes they follow on Horseback, sometimes on Elephants, but in this case their Elephants have no Chairs. The Foot and Horse-Guards do likewise follow, but confusedly and without any order; and if this Prince stops, all that follow him on Foot, prostrate themselves on their Knees and Elbows, and those that follow on Horseback, or on Elephants, do entirely bow down themselves on these Animals. Those which are named *Schaou mia*, do also follow a Foot: They are the King's Domesticks, which are not Slaves. Some do carry his Arms, and others his Boxes with *Betel* and *Areca*.

The singular Respect of the *Siamese* for their King.

When this Prince gave to the King's Ambassadors the diversion of taking an Elephant, twelve Lords cloath'd in Scarlet, and with their red Caps, arrived before the King at the place of the Show, and seated themselves cross-leg'd on the ground before the place, where the King their Master was to stand. They were turn'd toward the place of the Show; but so soon as they heard the Noise of this Prince's March, they prostrated themselves on their Knees and Elbows towards the place from whence the sound came, and as the Noise approached they turned themselves by little and little towards the Noise, and still remained prostrate: So that when the King their Master was come they were prostrate before him, and their back was turned to the Show; and whilst the Show continued they made not any motion, and exprest not any sign of Curiosity. But my Discourse insensibly leads me to speak of the Shows and other Diversions of the *Siamese*.

CHAP. VI.

Concerning the Shows, and other Diversions of the Siamese.

The way of catching a wild Elephant.

THE place, where the Elephant is that they would take, is as it were a very broad and very long Trench: I say, as it were a Trench, because it is not made by digging, but by raising the Earth almost perpendicular on each side, and it is upon these Terrasses that the Spectators stand. In the bottom, which is between these Terrasses, is a double row of Trunks of Trees above ten Foot high, planted in the Earth, big enough to resist the Attacks of the Elephant, and far enough from one another to let a Man pass between, but too close to let an Elephant pass through. 'Tis between these two rows of Trunks, that the tame Female Elephants, which they had led into the Woods, had enticed a wild Male Elephant. Those which guide them thither, do cover themselves with Leaves, to avoid frighting the Elephants of the Woods, and the Female Elephants have understanding enough, to make the Cries proper to call the Males. He was already intrap'd in the double row of Trunks, by following the Females, and could no more return into the Woods; but the design was to take him and tie him, to shut him up and tame him. The Exess from the space wherein he was, is a strait *Cortina*, composed also of great Trunks of Trees.

Trees. So soon as the Elephant is enter'd into this Cortine, the Gate through which he enters, and which he opens by thrusting it before him with his *Proboscis*, shuts again with its own weight: the other Gate through which he must pass is shut; and besides the space is so narrow, that he cannot turn himself therein. The difficulty was to engage the wild Elephant in this Cortine, and to engage him single; for the Females were still with him in the Trench, and he did not separate from them. Several *Siamese* who stood behind the Pallisado's of the Trunks, and the Foot of the Terrasses, where the Elephant could not come at them, enter'd every where between the Trunks into the space, where the Elephant was, to vex him; and when the Elephant pursued one of them, he fled very swiftly behind the Pallisado's, between which the enraged Elephant vainly thrust his *Proboscis*, and against which he broke the end of one of his Teeth. Whilst he thus pursued after those which provoked him, others laid long Nooses for him. One of the ends of which they kept; and they threw them at him with so much dexterity, that the Elephant in running never fail'd to put one of his hind-feet therein: so that by diligently putting the end of the Noose, they clos'd and fasten'd it a little above the Elephant's foot. These Nooses were of great Ropes, one of the ends of which was put into the other like a Slip-knot, and the Elephant dragged three or four of them at each hind-foot. For as soon as the Noose is once knit, he lets go the end thereof, to avoid being drag'd himself by the Elephant. The more he is exasperated, the less he associates with the Females; and yet to make them quit this space, a Man mounted on another Female enter'd therein, and went back again several times through the Cortine, and this Female which he mounted, called the others, by a dry blow, which she struck against the ground with her *Proboscis*. She darted it perpendicularly downwards, yet avoiding to strike altogether with the end, which she kept bended upwards. And when she had repeated this Call twice or thrice, he that rid her, made her to return back again through the Cortine. In fine, after he had perform'd this Trick five or six times with this Female, the other Female follow'd her, and soon after the Elephant return'd to himself, because they forbore to vex him, resolv'd to go after them. He push'd open the first door of the Cortine with his *Proboscis*, and so soon as he was enter'd, they threw several Buckets of water on his Body to refresh him, and with an incredible swiftness and dexterity they ty'd him to the Trunks of the Cortine with the Nooses, which were already at his feet. Then they made a tame Elephant to enter backwards into the Cortine, to whose Neck they also ty'd the savage Elephant by the Neck, and at the same time unloos'd him from the Trunks; and two other tame Elephants being likewise led to the Succor, all the three, the one on one side, the other on the other, and the third behind, do conduct the wild Elephant under a Pent-house near adjoining, where they fasten and tie him close by the Neck to a Pivot planted upright, which he made to turn as he turn'd round. They said that he need remain at this Pivot but 24 hours, and that in this space of time they would lead some tame Elephants to him to keep him company, and comfort him: that after 24 hours they would carry him into the Stable appointed for him; and that in eight days he would bethink himself, and submit to Slavery.

They speak of an Elephant as of a Man; they believe him perfectly rational, and they relate such rational things of him, that he only wants Speech. This is one, for Example, to which you may give what Credit you please. Some have related to us for a known Truth, that a Man having crack'd a *Cocoa* on the head of an Elephant which he rode, and using for this purpose the back of that kind of Punch, with which I have said that they guide the Elephants, this Elephant took up a resolution of revenging himself as soon as he could. He gather'd up with his *Proboscis* as they say, one of the Shells of the *Cocoa*, and kept it several days, never letting it go but to eat, during which he kept it carefully between his two fore-feet. In fine, he that had affronted him, approaching him to give him food, the Elephant seiz'd him, trampled him under his feet, and slew him, and for his Justification laid the *Cocoa*-Shell on the dead Body. 'Tis in these terms that the Relation was made to us: for the *Siamese* do think that

What the *Siamese* do think of the Elephants.

Elephants are capable of Justice, and of profiting by the punishments one of another; and they alledge that in War, for Instance, when these Animals mutiny, it is needful only to kill one on the spot, to render all the others wise. But these Relations, and several others, which I have forgot, do seem very fabulous; and not to digress from the Example, which I have mentioned, it is, in my opinion, very evident, that if the offended Elephant had consulted reason, he would not have waited another opportunity of revenge, but would have wreak'd his vengeance on the spot; seeing that every Elephant can with his *Proboscis* throw off the Rider, and having thrown him on the ground, trample him under foot, and kill him.

How the *Siamese* took leave of the three Elephants, which the King of *Siam* sent into *France*.

As for my self, during the time I was at *Siam*, I saw no marvellous Act perform'd by any of these Animals, tho' I am perswaded that they are more docible than others. They embarked three young ones, which the King of *Siam* sent to the three Princes the Grandsons of *France*. The *Siamese* which brought them on Board our Ships to embark them, took leave of them, as they would have done of three of their Companions, and whisper'd them in their Ears, saying; *Go, depart chearfully, you will be Slaves indeed, but you will be so to three the greatest Princes of the World, whose Service is as moderate as it is glorious.* They afterwards hoisted them into the Ships, and because they bow'd down themselves to go under the Decks, they cry'd out with admiration, as if all Animals did not as much to pass under low places.

The Elephant is very dangerous when he is enraged.

One day at *Louvo* an Elephant tore in pieces in the Street the Brother of a young *Mandarin*, who was with the King's Ambassadors, as Mr. *Torpf* had been with the Ambassadors of *Siam*. They said indeed that the Elephant was enraged, but this Rage was not of a Beast more reasonable, but only more cruel than the rest. Thus to render the Elephants of War more tame, they are accompany'd with Females, when they are led out to water and wash themselves, and I know not whether without this Train it could ever be accomplished. The *Siamese* report, that the Elephants are sensible of Grandeur; that they love to have a great House, that is to say, several Grooms for their service, and some Females for their Mistresses, (with whom nevertheless it is said that the Elephants desire familiarity only in the Woods, so long as they are savage, and at full liberty;) that without this state, they afflict themselves at the little regard had for them; and that when they commit any great Fault, the severest punishment that can be inflicted on them, is to retrench their House, to take away their Females, to remove them from the Palace, and to send them into Stables abroad. They say that an Elephant having been punish'd after this manner and being set at liberty, returns to his Lodge at the Palace, and kills the Elephant which was put in his place; which seems neither incredible nor strange, provided the way be free and open; for every Animal loves his usual Lodging, and according as he is more or less Couragious, he will use more or less Violence to drive out another Animal.

A Fight of Elephants.

To return to the Diversions of the Court of *Siam*, we saw a Fight of two Elephants of War. They were retained by the hind-feet with Cables, which several *Siamese* held, and which besides this were fasten'd to Capstains. The Elephants could hardly cross their Trunks in the Fight, two Men were mounted on each of them to animate them; but after five or six Attacks the Combat ended, and they brought in the Females, who parted them. At the great *Mogul's* Palace, the Elephants are permitted to approach nearer, and these Animals endeavour to beat off each other's Rider, and frequently they knock him down and kill him. At *Siam* they neither expose the Life of Men nor Beasts, by way of Sport or Exercise.

Cock-fighting.

They love Cock-Fighting. The most Couragious are not always the biggest, but those which are naturally the best armed, that is to say, those which have the best Spurs. If a Cock falls, they give him drink; by reason that they experimentally know that it is oftentimes only an effect of Thirst, and indeed he generally renews the Fight after quenching his Thirst. But as it almost always cost the life of one of the Cocks, the King of *Siam* prohibited these sort of Duels; because the *Talapoins* cry'd, and said, *That the Owners of the Cocks would for their punishment be bastinado'd in the other World with Bars of Iron.* I forbore going to a Fight of an Elephant and a Tyger, because the King of *Siam* would not be there, and that I knew they would not permit to these Animals the liberty of using all their Courage. Some inform'd me that the Tyger had been very Cowardly, and that the Show had succeeded ill. The hunting of Elephants perform'd by an enclosure of Fires in the Woods, has been described by others: the King of *Siam* went not to that which was perform'd whilst the King's Ambassadors were at his Court, neither were they invited; but the other Diversions which were exhibited to them all at once, and in a vast Court, were these.

The one was a *Chinese* Comedy, which I would willingly have seen to the end, but it was adjourned, after some Scenes, to go to Dinner. The *Chinese* Comedians, whom the *Siameses* do love without understanding them, do speak in the Throat. All their words are Monosyllables, and I heard them not pronounce one single one, but with a new breath: some would say that it throttles them. Their Habit was such as the Relations of *China* describe it, almost like that of the *Carthusians*, being clasp'd on the side by three or four Buckles, which reach from the Arm pit to the Hip, with great square Placards before and behind, wherein were painted Dragons, and with a Girdle three Fingers broad, on which, at equal distances, were little squares, and small rounds either of Tortoise-Shell or Horn, or of some sort of Wood: And these Girdles being loose, they were run into a Buckle on each side to sustain them. One of the Actors who represented a Magistrate, walk'd so gravely, that he first trod upon his Heel, and then successively and slowly upon the Sole and Toes; and as he rested on the Sole, he rais'd the Heel; and when he rested on his Toes, the Sole touch'd the ground no more. On the contrary, another Actor, walking like a Madman, threw his Feet and Arms in several extravagant Postures, and after a threatning manner, but much more excessive, than the whole Action of our Captains or Matamores. He was the General of an Army; and if the Relations of *China* are true, this Actor naturally represented the Affectations common to the Soldiers of his Country. The Theater had a Cloth on the bottom, and nothing on the sides, like the Stages of our Rope-dancers and Jack-puddings.

A Chinese Comedy.

The Puppets are mute at *Siam*, and those which come from the Country of *Lao* are much more esteemed than the *Siamese*. Neither the one nor the other have any thing, which is not very common in this Country.

Puppets.

But the *Siamese* Tumblers are excellent, and the Court of *Siam* gives the diversion thereof to the King, when he arrives at *Louvo*. *Ælian* reports, that *Alexander* had some *Indian* Rope-dancers at his Wedding, and that they were esteem'd more nimble than those of other Nations. These are their Actions, which it is necessary to confess I did not closely and carefully consider, because I was more attentive to the *Chinese* Comedy, than to all the other Shows, which were at the same time exhibited to us. They plant a *Bambou* in the ground, and to the end of this they join another, and to the end of this second a third, and to the end of the third a Hoop: so that this makes as it were the wood of a round Racket, the Handle of which would be very long. A Man holding the two sides of the Hoop with his two Hands, puts his Head upon the inferior and inward part of the Hoop, raises his Body and his Feet on high, and continues in this posture an hour, and sometimes an hour and half: then he will put a Foot where he had plac'd his Head, and without standing otherwise, and without fixing the other Foot, he will dance after their manner, that is to say, without raising himself, but only by making Contorsions. And what renders all this more perilous and difficult, is the continual wavering of the *Bambou*. A *Bambou* dancer of this sort, they call *Lo Bouang*; *Lo* signifies *to pass*, and *Bouang* a *Hoop*.

Rope-dancers, and other sorts of excellent Tumblers.

There dyed one, some Years since, who leap'd from the Hoop, supporting himself only by two *Umbrello's*, the hands of which were firmly fix'd to his Girdle: the Wind carry'd him accidentally sometimes to the Ground, sometimes on Trees or Houses, and sometimes into the River. He so exceedingly diverted the

A Tumbler exceedingly honour'd by the King of Siam.

the King of *Siam*, that this Prince had made him a great Lord: he had lodged him in the Palace, and had given him a great Title; or, as they say, a great Name. Others do walk and dance, after the mode of the Country, without raising themselves; but with Contorsions on a Copper-wire as big as the little Finger, and stretch'd after the same manner as our Rope-dancers do stretch their Rope: And they say, that the more the Wire is stretched, the more difficult it is to stand, by reason it gives a greater spring, and is so much the more uncertain. But what they account most difficult, is to get upon this Wire by the part of that same Wire which is fasten'd to the ground, and to descend thence by one of the *Bambou's*, which are plac'd like a *St. Andrew's Cross* to support it; as also to sit on the Wire cross-legg'd, to hold there one of those Bands, which serves them as a Table to eat on it, and to raise themselves on their Feet. They cease not likewise to ascend and dance upon an extended Rope, but without a Counterpoise, and with *Babouches* or Slippers on their Feet, and with *Sabres*, and Buckets of water fasten'd to their Legs. There are such who plant a very high Ladder in the ground, the two sides of which are of *Bambou's*, and the steps of *Sabres*, the edges of which are turned upwards. He goes to the top of this Ladder, and stands, and dances without any support on the edge of the *Sabre*, which makes the last step thereof; whilst the Ladder has more motion than a Tree shaken by the wind: then he descends Head foremost, and passes nimbly, winding between all the *Sabres*. I saw him descend, but observed not when he was on the highest *Sabre*; and I went not to examine whether the Steps were *Sabres*: not reckoning that the *Sabres* could be seen, except perhaps the lowest, because they are most expos'd to view. I omit the rest of this matter, as little important, and because I have not sufficiently observ'd it to support it with my Testimony.

Tame Serpents.

The Emperor *Galba* being in his Praetorship, exhibited to the *Roman* People the sight of some Elephants dancing upon Ropes. The Elephants of *Siam* are not so experienc'd, and the only Animals that I know the *Siamese* instruct, are great Serpents, which, they say, are very dangerous. These Animals do move themselves at the sound of the Instruments, as if they would dance. But this passes for Magic, because that always in that Country, as oftentimes in this, those who have some extraordinary Artifice, do pretend that it consists in some mysterious words.

Religious Shows: An Illumination on the Waters, and another on the Land, and in the Palace.

The *Siamese* have also some Religious Shows. When the Waters begin to retreat, the People returns them Thanks for several Nights together with a great Illumination; not only for that they are retired, but for the Fertility which they render to the Lands. The whole River is then seen cover'd with floating Lanthorns, which pass with it. There are of different Sizes, according to the Devotion of every particular Person; the variously painted Paper, whereof they are made, augments the agreeable effect of so many Lights. Moreover, to thank the Earth for the Harvest, they do on the first days of their Year make another magnificent Illumination. The first time we arriv'd at *Louvo* was in the Night, and at the time of this Illumination; and we saw the Walls of the City adorned with lighted Lanthorns at equal distances; but the inside of the Palace was much more pleasant to behold. In the Walls which do make the Inclosures of the Courts, there were contrived three rows of small Niches all round, in every of which burnt a Lamp. The Windows and Doors were likewise all adorn'd with several Fires, and several great and small Lanthorns, of different Figures, garnished with Paper, or Canvas, and differently painted, were hung up with an agreeable Symmetry on the Branches of Trees, or on Posts.

Excellent Artificial Fire-works.

I saw no Fire-works, in which nevertheless the *Chinese* of *Siam* do excel, and they made some very curious during our residence at *Siam* and *Louvo*. At *China* there is also made a solemn Illumination at the beginning of their Year, and at another time another great Festival on the Water without any Illumination. The *Chinese* agree not in the Reasons they give thereof, but they give none upon the account of Religion, and those which they give are puerile and fabulous.

We

A Paper-Kite.

We must not omit the Paper-Kite, in *Siamese Vao*, the Amusement of all the Courts of the *Indies* in Winter. I know not whether it be a piece of Religion, or not; but the great *Mogul*, who is a Mahometan, and not an Idolater, delights himself also therein. Sometimes they fasten Fire thereunto, which in the Air appears like a Planet. And sometimes they do there put a piece of Gold, which is for him that finds the Kite, in case the String breaks, or that the Kite falls so far distant, that it cannot be drawn back again. That of the King of *Siam* is in the Air every Night for the two Winter months, and some *Mandarins* are nominated to ease one another in holding the String.

Three sorts of Stage-Plays amongst the Siamese.

The *Siamese* have three sorts of Stage-Plays. That which they call *Cone* is a Figure-dance, to the Sound of the Violin, and some other Instruments. The Dancers are masqued and armed, and represent rather a Combat than a Dance: And tho every one runs into high Motions, and extravagant Postures, they cease not continually to intermix some word. Most of their Masks are hideous, and represent either monstrous Beasts, or kinds of Devils. The Show which they call *Lacone*, is a Poem intermixt with Epic and Dramatic, which lasts three days, from eight in the Morning till seven at Night. They are Histories in Verse, serious, and sung by several Actors always present, and which do only sing reciprocally. One of them sings the Historian's part, and the rest those of the Personages which the History makes to speak; but they are all Men that sing, and no Women. The *Rabam* is a double Dance of Men and Women, which is not Martial, but Gallant; and they presented unto us the Diversion thereof with the others which I have before mentioned. These Dancers, both Men and Women, have all false Nails, and very long ones, of Copper: They sing some words in their dancing, and they can perform it without much tyring themselves, because their way of dancing is a simple march round, very slow, and without any high motion; but with a great many slow Contorsions of the Body and Arms, so they hold not one another. Mean while two Men entertain the Spectators with several Fooleries, which the one utters in the name of all the Men-dancers, and the other in the name of all the Women-dancers. All these Actors have nothing singular in their Habits: only those that dance in the *Rabam*, and *Cone*, have gilded Paper-Bonnets, high and pointed, like the *Mandarins* Caps of Ceremony, but which hang down at the sides below their Ears, and which are adorned with counterfeit Stones, and with two Pendants of gilded wood. The *Cone* and the *Rabam* are always call'd at Funerals, and sometimes on other occasions; and 'tis probable that these Shows contain nothing Religious, since the *Talapoins* are prohibited to be present thereat. The *Lacone* serves principally to solemnize the Feast of the Dedication of a new Temple, when a new Statue of their *Sommona-Codom* is plac'd therein.

Wrestling and Boxing.

This Festival is likewise accompanied with races of Oxen, and several other Diversions, as of Wrestlers, and Men that fight with their Elbow and Fist. In Boxing, they guard their Hand with three or four rounds of Cord instead of the Copper Rings, which those of *Laos* do use in such Combats.

A Race of Oxen.

The Running of Oxen is perform'd in this manner. They mark out a Plat of 500 Fathom in length, and two in breadth, with four Trunks, which are planted at the four Corners, to serve as Boundaries; and it is round these Limits that the Course is run. In the middle of this place they erect a Scaffold for the Judges: and the more precisely to mark out the middle, which is the place from whence the Oxen were to start, they do plant a very high Post against the Scaffold. Sometimes 'tis only a single Ox which runs against another, the one and the other being guided by two Men running afoot, which do hold the Reins, or rather the String put into their Noses, the one on the one side, and the other on the other side; and other Men are posted at certain distances, to ease those which run. But most frequently it is a Yoke of Oxen fasten'd to a Plough, which runs against another Yoke of Oxen joined to another Plough, some Men guide them on the right side and on the left, as when it is only a single Ox which runs against another: But besides this, it is necessary that each Plough be so well sustained in the Air by a Man running, that it never touch the ground, for fear it retard the Animals that draw it; and these Men which thus support the Ploughs, are more frequently reliev'd than the others.

Now tho' the Ploughs run both after the same manner, turning always to the right round the space which I have described, they set not out from the same place. The one starts at one side of the Scaffold, and the other at the other, to run reciprocally one after the other. Thus at the beginning of their Course they look from opposite places, and they are distant one from the other half a Circle, or half the space over which they were to run. Yet they run after the same manner, as I have said, turning several times round the four Boundaries, which I have mentioned, till the one overtakes the other. The Spectators are nevertheless all round, yet is it not necessary to have Bars to hinder from approaching too near. These Courses are sometimes the subjects of Bettings, and the Lords do breed and train up small, but well-proportion'd Oxen for this Exercise; and instead of Oxen, they do likewise make use of *Buffalo's*.

A Race of *Balons*.

I know not whether I ought to rank amongst the Shows, the Diversion which was given us of a Race of *Balons*; for in respect of the *Siameses* it is rather a Sport, than a Show. They chose two *Balons* the most equal in all things as is possible, and they divide themselves into two Parties to bett. Then the Captains do beat a precipitate measure, not only by knocking with the end of a long Bambou which they have in their hands, but by their Cryes, and the Agitation of their whole Body. The Crew of Rowers excites itself also by several redoubled Acclamations, and the Spectator which betts, hollows also, and is in no less motion than if he really rowed. Oftentimes they commit not to the Captains the care of animating the Rowers, but two of the Bettors do execute this Office themselves.

The excessive love of Gaming.

The *Siameses* love Gaming to such an Excess as to ruine themselves, and lose their Liberty, or that of their Children: for in this Country, whoever has not wherewith to satisfy his Creditor, sells his Children to discharge the Debt; and if this satisfies not, he himself becomes a Slave. The Play which they love best, is *Tick-Tack*, which they call *Saca*, and which they have learnt perhaps from the *Portugueses*; for they play it like them and us. They play not at Cards, and their other hazardous Sports I know not; but they play at Chesse after our and the *Chinese* way. At the end of this Work I will insert the Game of Chesse of the *Chineses*.

The *Siameses* love to smoke *Tobacco*.

Tobacco-Smoke (for they take none in Snuff) is also one of their greatest pleasures, and the Women, even the most considerable, are entirely addicted thereunto. They have *Tobacco* from *Manilla*, *China*, and *Siam*; and tho' these sorts of *Tobacco* are very strong, the *Siameses* do smoke it without any weakning it; but the *Chineses* and *Moors* do draw the Smoke through water, to diminish the strength thereof. The method of the *Chineses* is, to take a little water into their mouth, and then proceed to fill their mouth with *Tobacco*-Smoke, and afterwards they spit out the water and the Smoke at the same time. The *Moors* make use of a singular Instrument, the Description and Figure of which you will find at the end of this Work.

The common life of a *Siamese*.

Such are the Diversions of the *Siameses*, to which may be added the Domestic. They love their Wives and Children exceedingly, and it appears that they are greatly beloved by them. Whilst the Men acquit themselves of the six months work, which they every one yearly owe to the Prince, it belongs to their Wife, their Mother, or their Children to maintain them. And when they have satisfy'd the Service of their King, and they are return'd home, the generality know not unto what business to apply themselves, being little accustomed to any particular Profession; by reason the Prince employs them indifferently to all, as it pleaseth him. Hence it may be judged how lazy the ordinary life of a *Siamese* is. He works not at all, when he works not for his King: he walks not abroad; he hunts not: he does nothing almost but continue sitting or lying, eating, playing, smoking and sleeping. His Wife will wake him at 7 a clock in the morning, and will serve him with Rice and Fish: He will fall asleep again hereupon; and at Noon he will eat again, and will sup at the end of the day. Between these two last Meals will be his day; Conversation or Play will spend all the rest. The Women plough the Land, they sell and buy in the Cities. But it is time to speak of the Affairs and serious Occupations of the *Siameses*, that is to say of their Marriages, of the Education they give to their Children, of the Studies and Professions to which they apply themselves.

CHAP.

CHAP. VII.

Concerning the Marriage and Divorce of the Siameses.

The care they have of keeping their Daughters.

'TIs not the Custom in this Country to permit unto Maids the Conversation of young men. The Mothers chastise them, when they surprize them so; but the Girls forbear not to get out, when they can; and this is not impossible towards the Evening.

At what Age they marry them.

They are capable of having children at twelve years of Age, and sometimes sooner; and the greatest part have none past forty. The Custom is therefore to marry them very young, and the Boys in proportion. Yet there is found some *Siameses*, who disdain Marriage all their life, but there is not any that can turn *Talapoinesse*, that is to say, consecrate her self to a Religious life, who is not advanc'd in years.

How a Siamese seeks a Maid in Marriage and how their Marriage is concluded.

When a Marriage is design'd, the Parents of the young man demand the Maid of her Parents, by women advanced in years and of good Reputation. If the Parents of the Maid have any inclination thereunto, they return a favourable Answer. Nevertheless they reserve unto themselves the liberty of consulting first the mind of their Daughter; and at the same time they take the hour of the young mans Nativity, and give that of the Birth of the Maid: and both sides go to the Southsayers to know principally whether the Party proposed is rich, and whether the Marriage will continue till death without a divorce. As every one carefully conceals his riches, to secure them from the oppression of the Magistrate, and the Covetousness of the Prince, it is necessity that they go to the Southsayer, to know whether a Family is rich, and it is upon the advice of the Southsayers that they take their Resolution. If the Marriage must be concluded, the young man goes to visit the Lady three times, and carries her some presents of *Betel* and Fruit, and nothing more precious. At the third Visit the Relations on both sides appear there likewise, and they count the Portion of the *Bride*, and what is given to the Bridegroom to whom the whole is delivered upon the spot, and in presence of the Relations, but without any writing. The new married couple do also commonly receive on this occasion some presents from their Uncles: and from that time, and without any Religious Ceremony, the Bridegroom has a right to consummate the Marriage. The *Talapoins* are prohibited to be present thereat. Only some days after they go to the house of the New Married folks to sprinkle some Holy-water, and to repeat some Prayers in the *Baly* Tongue.

The Nuptial Feast.

The Wedding as in all other places, is attended with Feasts and shows. They do hire and invite profest Dancers thereunto; but neither the Bridegroom, nor the Bride, nor any of the Guests do dance. The Feast is made at the house of the Brides Relations, where the Bridegroom takes care to build an Hall on purpose, which stands alone: And from thence the new married persons are conducted into another single Building, built also on purpose, at the expence and care of the Bridegroom, in the Inclosure of *Bambou*, which makes the Inclosure of the House of the Brides Relations. The new married persons continue there some Months, and then go to settle where it pleases them best to build an House for themselves. A singular Ornament for the Daughters of the *Mandarins* which are married, is to put on their head that Circle of Gold, which the *Mandarins* put on their Bonnet of Ceremony. Next to this the decking consists in having finer Pagnes then ordinary, more excellent Pendants, and more curious Rings on their Fingers, and in greater quantity. Some there are who report that the pretended father-in-Law, before the conclusion of the Marriage of his Daughter with his Son-in-Law, keeps him six Months in his house, to know him better. Some absolutely deny that this is true. And all that, in my opinion, may have given occasion to the report, is that it belongs to the Bridegroom to build the Wedding Room, and House, which he is to have at his Fa-

ther's

ther-in-Law's, during which, that is to say for two or three days at most, his future Spouse brings him Food, without dreading the Consequences thereof, because the Marriage is already concluded, tho' the Feast be deferred.

The Riches of the Marriages at *Siam*.

The greatest Portion at *Siam* is an hundred *Catis*, which do make 15000 Livres; and because it is common that the Bridegroom's Estate equals the Portion of the Bride, it follows that at *Siam* the greatest Fortune of two new married Persons exceeds not 10000 Crowns.

Of Plurality of Wives.

The *Siameses* may have several Wives, tho' they think it would be best to have but one; and it is only the Rich that affect to have more, and that more out of Pomp and Grandeur, than out of Debauchery.

A considerable distinction between them.

When they have several Wives, there is always one that is the chief: they call her the great Wife. The others, which they call the lesser Wives, are indeed legitimate, I mean permitted by the Laws, but they are subject to the Principal. They are only purchas'd Wives, and consequently Slaves; so that the Children of the little Wives do call their Father *Po Tchaou*, that is to say *Father Lord*, whereas the Children of the principal Wife do call him simply *Po*, or *Father*.

The degrees of Alliance prohibited, and how the Kings of *Siam* dispense with this Article.

Marriage in the first degrees of Kindred is prohibited them, yet they may marry their Cousin-German. And as to the degrees of Alliance, a Man may marry two Sisters one after the other, and not at the same time. Nevertheless the Kings of *Siam* do dispense with these Rules, and do think it hardly possible to find a Wife worthy of them, but in persons that are nearly related to them. The present King married his Sister, and by this Marriage was born the Princess his only Daughter, whom it is said he has married. I could not find out the truth, but this is the common Report: And I think it probable, in that her House is erected as unto a Queen; and the *Europeans* who have call'd her the Princess Queen, have made the same judgment thereof with me. The Relations inform us, that in other places as well as at *Siam*, there are some Examples of these Marriages of the Brother with the Sister; and it is certain that they have been anciently frequent amongst a great many *Pagan* Nations, at least in the Royal Families: either to the end that the Daughter might succeed to the Crown with the Son, or out of the fear I have mention'd, that these Kings have had of misplacing their Alliances, if they married not their own Sisters. For as to what others add, that it is to the end that the People may not doubt of having a Soveraign of the Royal Blood, at least by his Mother, I find no probability therein as to the East, where the People are so little wedded to the Blood of their Kings, and where the Kings do think to assure themselves of the Fidelity of their Wives, by keeping them very closely.

Thus *Jupiter* had married his Sister.

The Laws of Succession for Widows and Children.

The Succession in particular Families is all for the great Wife, and then for her Children, who inherit from their Parents by equal Portions. The little Wives and their Children may be sold by the Heir; and they have only what the Heir gives them, or what the Father before his death has given them from hand to hand, for the *Siameses* know not the use of Wills. The Daughters born of the little Wives, are sold to be themselves little Wives; and the most powerful purchasing the handsomest, without having any regard to the Parents from whom they descend, do after this manner make very unequal Alliances: and those with whom they make them, do not thereby acquire any more Honour or Protection.

Wherein consists the Fortune of a *Siamese*.

The Estate of the *Siameses* consist chiefly in Moveables. If they have Lands, they have not much, by reason they cannot obtain the full Property thereof: It belongs always to their King, who at his pleasure takes away the Lands which he has sold to particular persons, and who frequently takes them again without returning the value. Nevertheless the Law of the Country is, that Lands should be hereditary in Families, and that particular persons may sell them one to another: But this Prince has regard only to this Law, as far as it suits him, because it cannot prejudice his Domains, which generally extend over all that his Subjects possess. This is the Reason that they get as few Immoveables as they can, and that they always endeavor to conceal their Moveables from the knowledge of their Kings: and because that Diamonds are Moveables the most easie to hide and transport, they are mightily sought after at *Siam*, and in all *India*, and they sell them very dear. Sometimes the *Indian* Lords do at their death give part of their Estate to the King their Master, to secure the rest to their Family, and this generally succeeds.

A Divorce.

The Families are almost all happy at *Siam*, as may be judged by the Fidelity of the Wives in nourishing their Husband, whilst he serves the King: A Service which by a kind of Oppression lasts not only six Months in a Year, but sometimes one, two, and three Years together. But when the Husband and Wife cannot support one another, they have the remedy of Divorce. 'Tis true that it is in practice only amongst the Populace; the Rich who have several Wives, do equally keep those they love not, and those they love.

What are the Laws thereof.

The Husband is naturally the Master of the Divorce, but he never refuseth it to his Wife, when she absolutely desires it. He restores her Portion to her, and their Children are divided amongst them in this manner. The Mother has the first, the third, the fifth, and so all the odd ones. The Father has the second, fourth, sixth, and all the even ones. Hence it happens, that if there is no more than one Child, it is for the Mother; and that if the number of Children is unequal, the Mother has one more; whether that they judge the Mother would take more care thereof, than the Father; or that having born them in her womb, or nourished them with her milk, she seems to have a greater Right therein, than the Father; or that being weaker, she has more need of the succor of her Children than he.

And the Consequences.

After the Divorce, it is lawful for the Husband and Wife to marry again with whom they please; and it is free for the Woman to do it in the very day of the Divorce, they not troubling themselves with the Doubt that may thence arise touching the Father of the first Child, that may be born after the second Marriage. They rely on what the Wife says thereof; a great sign of the little Jealousie of this People. But tho' the Divorce be permitted them, yet they consider it as a very great Evil, and as the almost certain Ruine of the Children, which are ordinarily very ill treated in the second Marriages of their Parents. So that this is one of the Causes assigned why the Country is not populous, altho' the *Siameses* are fruitful, and do very frequently bring Twins.

Of the Paternal Power.

The power of the Husband is despotical in his Family, even to the selling his Children and Wives, his principal Wife excepted, whom he can only repudiate. The Widows inherit the power of their Husbands, with this restriction, that they cannot sell the Children which they have of the even number, if the Father's Relations oppose it; for the Children date not. After the Divorce, the Father and Mother may each sell the Children which fell to them by lot, according to the Division I have mentioned. But the Parents cannot kill their Children, nor the Husband his Wives, by reason that in general all Murder is prohibited at *Siam*.

Amorous Conversations.

The Love of free persons is not ignominious, at least amongst the Populace: It is there look'd upon as a Marriage, and Incontinency as a Divorce. Nevertheless the Parents do carefully watch their Daughters, as I have said; and Children are no where permitted to dispose of themselves to the prejudice of the paternal Power, which is the most natural of all Laws. Moreover, the *Siameses* are naturally too proud easily to give themselves to Foreigners, or at least to invite them. The *Peguins* which are at *Siam*, as being Strangers themselves, do more highly esteem of Foreigners; and do pass for debauched persons in the minds of those who understand not that they seek a Husband. Thus they continue faithful until they are abandon'd; and if they prove big with Child, they are not less esteem'd amongst those of their Nation, and they do even glory in having had a white Man for a Husband. It may be also that they are of a more amorous Complexion than the *Siameses*; they have at least more spirit and briskness. 'Tis an established opinion in the *Indies*, that the people have more or less vigor and spirit, according as they are nearer, or remoter from *Pegu*.

CHAP. VIII.

Of the Education of the Siamese *Children, and first of their Civility.*

The love of the *Siamese* Children for their Parents.

THE *Siamese* Children have docility and sweetness, provided they be not discountenanc'd. Their Parents know how to make themselves extreamly beloved and respected, and to inspire an extream Civility in them. Their Instructions are marvellously assisted by the Despotic Power, which I have said they have in their Family; but the Parents do also answer unto the Prince for the Faults of their Children. They share in their Chastisements, and more especially are obliged to deliver them up when they have offended. And tho' the Son be fled, he never fails to return and surrender himself, when the Prince apprehends his Father, or his Mother, or his other collateral Relations, but older than himself, and to whom he owes Respect: And this is a great proof of the love of the *Siamese* Children to their Parents.

Civility necessary to the *Siamese*.

As to Civility, it is so great throughout the East, even amongst Strangers, that an *European* who has liv'd there a long time, finds much difficulty to re-accustom himself to the Familiarities of these Countries. The *Indian* Princes being very much given to Traffic, they love to invite Strangers amongst them, and they protect them even against their own Subjects. And hence it is that the *Siamese* do for Example appear savage, and that they eschew the Conversation of Strangers. They know that they are thought always to be in the wrong, and that they are always punish'd in the Quarrels they have with them. The *Siamese* do therefore educate their Children in an extream Modesty, by reason that it is necessary in Trade, and much more in the Service, which for six Months in the Year they render unto the King, or to the *Mandarins* by order of their King.

Their Inclination to Silence.

Silence is not greater amongst the *Carthusians*, than it is in the Palace of this Prince; the Lords dispense not therewith more than others. The sole desire of speaking, never excites the *Siamese* to say any thing that may displease. 'Tis necessary that they be thoroughly convinced that you would know the truth of any thing, to embolden them to declare it against your opinion. They do in nothing affect to appear better instructed than you, not in the things of their own Country, altho' you be a Stranger.

The Raillery amongst them.

They appear'd to me very far from all sort of Raillery, by reason they understand not any, perhaps thro' the fault of the Interpreters. 'Tis principally in matter of Raillery, that this ancient Proverb of the *Indians* is verified, *That things best weighed, when deliver'd by an Interpreter, are as a pure Spring which runs thro' mud.* Most false it is to droll little with Strangers, even with those that understand our Language; because that Railleries are the last thing that they understand, and that it is easie to offend them with a Raillery which they understand not. I doubt not therefore that the *Siamese* know how to jest wittily one with another. Some have assur'd me, that they do it frequently amongst Equals, and even in Verse; and that as well the Women as the Men are all very readily verst therein; the most ordinary method of which is amongst them a continued Raillery, wherein emulously appears the briskness of the Answers and Repartees. I have observ'd the same thing amongst the people of *Spain*.

The Politeness of the *Siamese* Language.

But when they enter into earnest, their Language is much more capable than our's, of whatever denotes Respect and Distinction. They give, for instance, certain Titles to certain Officers, as amongst us are the Titles of *Excellence* and *Greatness*. Moreover, these words *I* and *Me*, indifferent in our Language, do express themselves by several terms in the *Siamese* Tongue; the one of which is from the Master to the Slave, and the other from the Slave to the Master. Another is from the Man of the people to a Lord; and a fourth is us'd

amongst

amongst Equals; and some there are which are only in the mouth of *Talapoins*. The word *You* and *He* are not expressed in fewer manners. And when they speak of Women, (because that in their Tongue there is no distinction of Genders into Masculine and Feminine) they add to the Masculine the word *Nang*, which in the *Balie* Language signifies *Young*, to imply the Feminine, as if we should say for Example, *Young Prince*, instead of *Princess*. It seems that their Civility hinders them from thinking that Women can ever grow old.

By the same Complaisance they call them by the most precious or most agreeable things of Nature, as *young Diamond, young Gold, young Crystal, young Flower*. The Princess, the King's Daughter, is called *Nang fa, young Heaven*; if he had a Son, he would be called, in some respect, *Tchaou fa, Lord of Heaven*. 'Tis certain that the white Elephant which *Mr. de Chaumont* saw at *Siam*, and which was dead when we arriv'd there, had attain'd to an extream old Age; yet because it was a Female, and that they believe moreover that in the Body of white Elephants there is always a Royal Soul, they called her *verbatim, Nang Paya Tchang peuak, young Prince white Elephant*. The Names of the Siamese.

The words which the *Siamese* use by way of Salute, are *Caxai Tchaou, I salute Lord*. And, if 'tis really a Lord that salutes an Inferior, he will bluntly answer, *Kaou vai, I salute*, or *ca vai*, which signifies the same thing; altho' the word *ca*, which signifies *me*, ought to be naturally only in the mouth of a Slave speaking to his Master; and that the word *Kaou*, which also signifies *me*, denotes some dignity in him that speaks. To ask, *How do you?* they say, *Tgiau di? Kin di?* That is to say, *Do you continue well? Do you eat well?* The words which the Siamese use in saluting.

But it is a singular Observation, that it is not permitted a *Siamese* to ask his Inferior any News concerning their King's health; as if it was a Crime in him, that approaches near the person of the Prince, to be less informed thereof, than another that is obliged to keep at a greater distance. How they are permitted to ask News of their King's health.

Their civil posture of Sitting is as the *Spaniards* sit, crossing their Legs; and they are so well accustom'd thereunto, that, even on a Seat when given them, they place themselves no otherwise. How they sit.

When they bow, they do not stand; but if they sit not cross legg'd, they bow themselves out of respect to one another. The Slaves and the Servants before their Masters, and the common People before the Lords keep on their knees, with their Body seated on their heels, their head a little inclin'd, and their hands joined at the top of their forehead. A *Siamese* which passeth by another, to whom he would render Respect, will pass by stooping with joined hands more or less elevated, and will salute him no otherwise. Their Postures.

In their Visits, if it is a very inferior person that makes it, he enters stooping into the Chamber, he prostrates himself, and remains upon his knees, and sitting upon his heels after the manner that I have described; but he dares not to speak first. He must wait till he to whom he pays the Visit, speaks to him: and thus the *Mandarins* that came to visit us on the behalf of the King of *Siam*, waited always till I spake to them first. If it is a Visit amongst Equals, or if the Superior goes to see the Inferior, the Master of the House receives him at the Hall-door, and at the end of the Visit he accompanies him thither, and never any further. Moreover, he walks either upright, or stooping, according to the degree of Respect which he owes to the Visitor. He likewise observes to speak first, or last, according as he can, or as he ought; but he always offers his place to him whom he receives at his House, and invites him to accept it. He afterwards serves him with Fruit and Preserves, and sometimes with Rice and Fish; and more especially he with his own hand presents him with *Arek* and *Betel*, and *Tea*. The common People forget not *Arek*, and Persons of Quality do sometimes accommodate themselves therewith. At the end of the Visit, the Stranger first testifies that he will go, as amongst us, and the Master of the House consents thereto with very obliging Expressions, and he must be greatly superior to him that renders him the Visit, to bid him depart. Their Ceremonies in Visits.

The highest place is so far the most honourable according to them, that they dared not to go into the first Story, even for the service of the House, when the To what degree the highest place is the most honourable.

King's

Kings Ambassadors were in the lower Hall. In the Houses, which strangers do build of Brick above one story, they observe that the undermost part of the Stairs never serves for a passage, for fear lest any one should go under the feet of another that ascends; but the *Siameses* build no more than one story, by reason that the bottom would be useless to them, no person amongst them being willing either to go or lodge under the feet of another. For this reason, though the *Siamese* Houses be erected on Piles, they never make use of the under part, not so much as in the Kings House, whose Palace being uneven, has some pieces higher than others, the under part of which might be inhabited. I remember that when the Ambassadors of *Siam* came to an Inn near *Vincennes*, the first Ambassador being lodged in the first story, and the others in the second, the second Ambassador perceiving that he was above the King his Masters Letter, which the first Ambassador had with him, ran hastily out of his Chamber bewailing his offence, and tearing his hair in despair.

The right hand more honourable than the left at Siam.

At *Siam* the right hand is more honourable than the left; the floor of the Chamber opposite to the door is more honourable than the sides, and the sides more than the wall where the door is, and the wall which is on the right hand of him that sits on the floor, is more honourable than that which is on his left hand. Thus in the Tribunals, no person sits on the Bench fixed to the wall which is directly opposite to the door, save the President, who alone has a determinative Vote. The Councellors, who only have a Consultative Vote, are seated on other lower Benches along the side-walls, and the other Officers along the wall of the door. After the same manner, if any one receives an important visit, he places the Visitor alone on the floor of the Chamber, and seats himself with his back towards the door, or towards one of the sides of the Chamber.

Why the Cities at China are all after one Model.

These Ceremonies and a great many others are so precise at *China*, that it is necessary that the Forms of the Houses, and the Rooms where particular persons receive their Visits, and those where they entertain their Friends, be all after one model, to be able to observe the same Civilities. But this Uniformity of building, and of turning the buildings to the South, so that they front the North in their entering in, has been much more indispensible in the Tribunals, and in all the other publick houses; insomuch that whoever sees one City in this great Kingdom sees them all.

The exactness of the Siameses in their Ceremonies.

New Ceremonies are as essential, and almost as numerous at *Siam* as at *China*. A *Mandarin* carries himself one way before his Inferiors, and another way before his Superiors. If there are several *Siameses* together, and there unexpectedly comes in another, it frequently happens that the posture of all changes. They know before whom, and to what degree, they must keep themselves inclined or strait, or sitting; whether they must joyn their hands or not, and keep them high, or low; whether being seated they may advance one Foot, or both, or whether they must keep them both conceal'd by sitting on their heels. And the miscarriages in these sorts of duties may be punished with the cudgel by him to whom they are committed, or by his orders, and on the spot. So that there is not introduced amongst them those Airs of familiarity, which in diversions do attract rudeness, injuries, blows and quarrels, and sometimes intemperance and impudence; they are always restrained by reciprocal respects. What some report concerning the *Chinese* Hat, is a thing very pleasant. It has no brim before nor behind, but only at the sides; and this brim, which terminates in an oval, is so little fastened to the body of the Hat, that it flaps, and renders a man ridiculous, at the least irregular motion which he makes of his head. Thus these people have imagined, that the less men are at ease, the fewer faults they commit.

They are accustomed thereunto from their infancy.

But all these forms, which seem to us very troublesom, appear not so to them, by reason they are early accustomed thereunto. Custom renders the distinctions less severe to them, than they would be to us; and much more the thoughts that they may enjoy it in their turn: He that is Superior or Inferior to day, changing his condition to morrow, according to the Prudence, or the Capricious Humor of the Prince. The hereditary distinctions which the Birth does

here

here give to so many persons who are sometimes without merit, will not appear less hard to undergo, to him who should not be thereto accustomed, or who should not comprehend that the most precious recompence of Vertue is that, which one hopes to transmit to his posterity.

How the great ones dispense with their Inferiors.

The Custom is therefore at *Siam* and *China*, that when the Superior would discreetly manage the Inferior, and testify a great deal of consideration for him (as it sometimes happens in the intrigues of Court) the Superior affects publickly to avoid the meeting the Inferior, to spare him the publick submission, with which he could not dispense if they should meet him. Moreover, affability towards Inferiors, Easiness of access, or going before them, do pass for weakness in the *Indies*.

Certain things indecent enough as are not so amongst them, and on the contrary.

The *Siamese* constrain not themselves to belching in conversation, neither turn they aside their face, or put any thing before their mouth, no more than the *Spaniards*. 'Tis no incivility amongst them to wipe off the Sweat of their forehead with their Fingers, and then to shake them against the ground. For this purpose we use a Handkerchief, and few of the *Siamese* have any; which is the reason why they very slovenly perform every thing whereunto the Handkerchief is necessary. They dare to spit neither on the Mats, nor the Carpets; and because they are in all houses a little furnished, they make use of spitting-pots which they carry in their hand. In the Kings Palace they neither cough, nor spit, nor wipe their Nose. The *Betel* which they continually chew, and the juice of which they swallow at pleasure, hinders them: Nevertheless they cannot take *Betel* in the Prince's presence, but only continue to chew that which they have already in their Mouth. They refuse nothing that is offered them, and dare not to say, I have enough.

What is the greatest Affront among the Siamese.

As the most eminent place is always amongst them the most honourable, the head, as the highest part of the body, is also the most respected. To touch any person on the head or the hair, or to stroke ones hand over the head, is to offer him the greatest of all affronts. To touch his Bonnet, if he leaves it any where, is a great incivility. The mode of this Country amongst the *Europeans* which dwell there, is never to leave their Hat in a low place, but to give it to a Servant, who carries it higher than his Head, at the end of a Stick, and without touching it; and this Stick has a foot, to the end that it may stand up if he that carries it, be obliged to leave it.

What postures are more or less respectful.

The most respectful, or to say better, the most humble posture, is that in which they do all keep themselves continually before their King: in which they express to him more respect than the *Chineses* do to theirs. They keep themselves prostrate on their knees and elbows, with their hands joyned at the top of their forehead, and their body seated on their heels, to the end that they may lean less on their elbows, and that it may be possible (without assisting themselves with their hands, but keeping them still joyned to the top of their forehead) to raise themselves on their knees, and fall again upon their elbows, as they do thrice together, as often as they would speak to their King. I have remark'd, that when they are thus prostrate, they lean their back-part on one side or other, as much as possibly they can, without displacing their knees, as it were to lessen and undervalue themselves the more.

By the same principle, it is not only more honourable, according to them, to be seated on a high seat, than on a low seat; but it is much more honourable to be standing than sitting. When *Mr. de Chaumont* had his first audience, it was necessary that the *French* Gentlemen which accompany'd him, should enter first into the Hall, and seat themselves on their heels, before the King of *Siam* appeared; to the end that this Prince might not see them a moment standing. They were prohibited to rise up to salute him, when he appeared. This Prince never suffered the Bishops nor the Jesuits to appear standing before him in the Audience. It is not permitted to stand in any place of the Palace, unless while walking: and if in this last Voyage of 1687, at the first audience of the Kings Ambassadors, the *French* Gentlemen had the honour of entring, when the King of *Siam* was already visible, it was only because the *Mandarins*, which had accompanied the Ambassadors of *Siam* into *France*, were admitted into the

Q Gallery

Gallery of *Versailles*, when the King was seated on the Throne which he had erected there.

How the King of Siam accommodates the Ceremonies of his Court, to those of the Court of France.

The King of *Siam* had that respect for the King of *France*, as to acquaint him by M^r^. *de Chaumont*, that if there was any Custom in his Court which was not in the Court of *France*, he would alter it; and when the King's Ambassadors arrived in this Country, the King of *Siam* affected indeed to make them a Reception different in several things from that which he had made to M^r^. *de Chaumont*, to conform it the more to that which he understood the King had made to his Ambassadors. He did one thing, when M^r^. *des Farges* saluted him, which never had any Precedent at *Siam*: for he commanded that all the Officers of his Court should stand in his presence, as did M^r^. *des Farges*, and the other *French* Officers which accompany'd him.

Why I chose to speak to the King of Siam rather standing, than sitting.

Remembring therefore that M^r^. *de Chaumont* had demanded to compliment him sitting, and knowing that his Ambassadors had spoken standing to the King, (an Honour which he highly esteem'd) he informed me, that he would grant me the liberty to speak to him sitting or standing; and I chose to deliver all my Compliments standing. And if I could have raised my self higher, I should have received more Honour. 'Twas in the King of *Siam*, as they informed me, a mark of respect for the King's Letters, not to receive them standing, but sitting.

Another Siamese Civility.

To lay a thing upon one's head, which is given, or received, is at *Siam*, and in a great many other Countries, a very great mark of respect. The *Spaniards*, for Example, are obliged by an express Law to render this respect to the *Cedulas*, or written Orders, which they receive from their King. The King of *Siam* was pleas'd to see me put the King's Letter on my head, in delivering it to him: he cry'd out, and demanded, *Where I had learnt that Civility us'd in his Country?* He had lifted up to his Forehead the King's Letter, which M^r^. *de Chaumont* deliver'd him; but understanding, by the report of his Ambassadors, that this Civility was not known in the Court of *France*, he omitted it, in regard of the King's Letter, which I had the Honour to deliver him.

The manner of saluting among the Siameses.

When a *Siamese* salutes, he lifts up either both his hands join'd, or at least his right hand to the top of his forehead, as it were to put him whom he salutes on his head. As often as they take the liberty to answer to their King, they always begin again with these words, *Pra pouti Tchaou-ca, ca rap pra ouncan sai clao sai cramom*: That is to say, *High and Mighty Lord of me thy Slave, I desire to take thy Royal Word, and put it on my Brain, and on the top of my Head.* And it is from these words *Tchaou-ca*, which signifie *Lord of me thy Slave*, that amongst the *French* is sprung up this way of speaking *faire chaca*, to signifie *To make homage, or to prostrate himself after the* Siamese *manner*. *Faire le Zombaye* to the King of *Siam*, signifies *to present him a Petition*, which cannot be done without performing the *[illegible]*. I know not from whence the *Portugueses* have borrow'd this way of speaking. If you stretch out your hand to a *Siamese* to take hold on his, he puts both his hands underneath yours, as to put himself entirely into your power. 'Tis an Incivility, in their opinion, to give only one hand, as also not to hold what they present you, with both their hands, and not to take with both hands what they receive from you. But let this suffice as concerning the Civility with which the *Siameses* inspire their Children, altho' I have not exhausted this Subject.

CHAP. IX.

Of the Studies of the Siameses.

They put their Children to the Talapoins.

WHen they have educated their Children to seven or eight years old, they put them into a Convent of *Talapoins*, and make them assume the habit of a *Talapoin*: for it is a Profession which obliges not, and which is quitted at pleasure without disgrace. These little *Talapoins* are called *Nens*: they are not Pensioners, but their Friends do daily send them Food. Some of these *Nens* are of a good Family, and have one or more Slaves to wait upon them.

What they learn.

They are taught principally to Read, to Write, and to cast Accompts, by reason that nothing is more necessary to Merchants, and that all the *Siameses* do exercise Traffic. They are taught the Principles of their Morality, and the Fables of their *Sommona-Codom*, but no History, nor Law, nor any Science. They likewise teach them the *Balie* Tongue, which, as I have more than once declared, is the language of their Religion, and their Laws; and few amongst them do make any progress therein, if they do not a long time adhere to the profession of the *Talapoin*, or if they enter not into some offices: for it is in these two Cases only that this language is useful to them.

The *Balie* and *Siamese* Languages compared with the *Chinese*.

They write the *Siamese* and *Balie* from the left hand to the right, after the same manner as we write our Languages of *Europe*: in which they differ from most of the other *Asiatics*, who have ever wrote from the right to the left; and from the *Chineses* also, who draw the line from the top to the bottom; and who in the ranging of the lines in one Page, do put the first on the right hand, and the others successively towards the left. They are different also from the *Chineses*, in that they have not like them a Character for every word, or even for every signification of a single word; to the end that the writing may have no Equivocations like the Language. The *Siamese* and *Balie* Tongues have, like ours, an Alphabet of few letters, of which are compos'd syllables and words. Moreover, the *Siamese* Language participates greatly of the *Chinese*, in that it has a great deal of Accent, (for their Voice frequently rises above one fourth) and in that it consists almost all of Monosyllables: so that it may be presumed, that if one perfectly understood it, one should find that the few words which it has of several syllables, are either foreign, or composed of Monosyllables, some of which are used only in these Compositions.

The *Siamese* and *Chinese* Languages have no Declensions of words, the *Balie* has.

But the most remarkable Similitude that is between these two Languages, and which is not found in the *Balie*, is that neither the one nor the other have any Declension or Conjugation, nor perhaps Derivations, which the *Balie* has. As for Example, the word which signifies *Content*, may likewise signifie *Contentment*; and that which signifies *Good*, will signifie *Well*, and *Bounty*, according to the various ways of using them. The placing alone denotes the Cases in Nouns, and herein their disposition is hardly different from ours. And as to the Conjugations, the *Siameses* have only four or five small Particles, which they put sometimes before the Verb, and sometimes after, to signifie the Numbers, Tenses, and Moods thereof. I will insert them at the end of this Volume, with the *Siamese* and *Balie* Alphabets; and it is in this that their whole Grammar almost consists.

The *Siamese* Language not copious, but very figurative.

Their Dictionary is not less simple: I mean, that their Language is not copious; but the turn of their Phrase is only more various, and more difficult. In cold Countries, where the Imagination is cold, every thing is called by its Name; and they do there abound as much or more in words, than in things: And when one has fixed all these words in his memory, he may promise himself to speak well. It is not the same in hot Countries, few words do there suffice to express much, by reason that the quickness of the Imagination employs them in an hundred different ways, all figurative. Take two or three Examples of the methods of speaking *Siamese*. *Good Heart* signifies *Content*, thus to say, *If I was at* Siam, *I should be content*; they said, *If I were City* Siam, *me heart good much*. *Sii* signifies *Light*, and by a Metaphor *Beauty*; and by a second Metaphor, this word *Sii* being joined with *Pak*, which signifies *Mouth*; *Sii-pak*, signifies the *Lips*; as if one should say, *The Light, or Beauty of the Mouth*. Thus, *The Glory of the Wood*, signifies *a Flower*; the *Son of the Water* implies in general, whatever *is engender'd in the Water without it be Fish*, as Crocodiles, and all sorts of aquatic Insects. And on other occasions, the word *Son* will only denote *Smallness*, as *the Sons of the Weights*, to signifie *small Weights*, contrary to the word *Mother*, which in certain things they make use of to signifie *Greatness*. In short, I have not seen any words in this Language that have resemblance to ours.

ours, excepting those of *pa* and *ma*, which signifie *Father* and *Mother*, in *Chinese* *fu, mu*.

Arithmetic.

I proceed to Arithmetic, which after Reading and Writing, is the principal Study of the *Siameses*. Their Arithmetic, like ours, hath ten Characters, with which they figure the Nought like us, and to which they give the same Powers as we, in the same disposition, placing, like us, from the Right to the Left, Unites, Tens, Hundreds, Thousands, and all the other Powers of the Number Ten. The *Indian* Merchants are so well vers'd in casting Accompt, and their Imagination is so clear thereupon, that it is said they can presently resolve very difficult Questions of Arithmetic; but I suppose likewise that they do never resolve what they cannot resolve immediately. They love not to trouble their heads, and they have no use of *Algebra*.

An Instrument which serves the *Chinese* for an *Abacus*, or Counting Table.

The *Siameses* do always calculate with a Pen; but the *Chineses* make use of an Instrument which resembles the *Abacus*, and which *F. Martinius*, in his History of *China*, intimates, that they invented about 2600 or 2700 years before Jesus Christ. However it be, *Pignorius*, in his Book *de Servis*, informs us, that this Instrument was familiar to the ancient *Roman* Slaves that were appointed to cast Accompt. I give the Description and Figure thereof at the end of this Work.

The *Siameses* not proper for Studies of Application.

The Studies to which we apply our selves in our Colledges, are almost absolutely unknown to the *Siameses*; and it may be doubted whether they are fit for such. The essential Character of the People of Countries extreamly hot, or extreamly cold, is sluggishness of Mind and Body; with this difference, that it degenerates into Stupidity in Countries too cold, and that in Countries too hot, there is always Spirit and Imagination; but of that sort of Imagination and Spirit, which soon flaggs with the least Application.

They have Imagination and Laziness.

The *Siameses* do conceive easily and clearly, their Repartees are witty and quick, their Objections are rational. They imitate immediately, and from the first day they are tolerable good Workmen: so that one would think a little Study would render them very accomplish'd, either in the highest Sciences, or in the most difficult Arts; but their invincible Laziness suddenly destroys these hopes. It is no wonder therefore if they invent nothing in the Sciences which they love best, as Chymistry and Astronomy.

They are naturally Poets, and their Poetry is Rhyme.

I have already said that they are naturally Poets. Their Poetry, like ours; and that which is now used throughout the known World, consists in the number of Syllables, and in Rhyme. Some do attribute the Invention thereof to the *Arabians*, by reason it seems to have been they that have carried it every where. The Relations of *China* report, that the *Chinese* Poetry at present is in Rhyme; but tho' they speak of their ancient Poetry, of which they still have several Works, they declare not of what nature it was, because, in my opinion, it is difficult to judge thereof: for tho' the *Chineses* have preserved the sense of their ancient Writing, they have not preserved their ancient Language. However, I can hardly comprehend from a Language wholly consisting of Monosyllables, and full of accented Vowels, and compounded Dipthongs, that if the Poetry consists not in Rhyme, it can consist in Quantity, as did the *Greek* and *Latin* Poems.

They read the ancient Characters in the present Language.

Their *Genius* in Poetry.

I could not get a *Siamese* Song well translated, so different is their way of thinking from ours; yet I have seen some Pictures, as for Example, of a pleasant Garden, where a Lover invites his Mistress to come. I have also seen some Expressions, which to me appear'd full of Smuttiness, and gross Immodesty; altho' this had not the same Effect in their Language. But besides Love Songs, they have likewise some Historical and Moral Songs altogether: I have heard the *Pagayeurs* sing some, of which they made me to understand the sense. The *Lacone* which I have mentioned, is no other than a Moral and Historical Song; and some have told me, that one of the Brothers of the King of *Siam* compos'd some Moral Poems very highly esteem'd, to which he himself set the Tune.

They are no Orators.

But if the *Siameses* are born Poets, they neither are born, nor do become Orators. Their Books are either Narrations of a plain Style, or some Sentences

of

were t
of *Lond*
of *Bin*
them
of goin
which
h sum
o thar

Laws be there in the hands of all persons, and that there are publick Schools, to teach them. As for example, in the Provisions of a *Corregidor* they will insert the whole Title of the *Corregidors*, which is in the compiling of their Ordinances and Decrees. I have likewise seen some example of this in *France*.

CHAP. X.

What the Siameses *do know in Medicine and Chymistry.*

The King of Siam has his Physicians from divers Countries.

MEdicine cannot merit the name of a Science amongst the *Siameses*. The King of *Siam*'s principal Physicians are *Chineses*; and he has also some *Siameses* and *Peguins*: and within two or three years he has admitted into this quality *Mr. Paumart*, one of the *French* Secular Missionaries, on whom he relies more than on all his other Physicians. The others are obliged to report daily unto him the state of this Prince's health, and to receive from his hand the Remedies which he prepares for him.

They understand not Chyrurgery nor Anatomy.

Their chief Ignorance is to know nothing in Chyrurgery, and to stand in need of the *Europeans*, not only for Trapans, and for all the other difficult Operations of Chyrurgery, but for simple Blood-lettings. They are utterly ignorant of Anatomy: and so far from having excited their Curiosity to discover either the Circulation of the Blood, or all the new things, that we know touching the structure of the body of Animals, that they open not the dead bodies, till after having rosted them in their Funeral solemnities, under pretence of burning them; and they open them only to seek wherewith to abuse the superstitious credulity of the people. For example, they alledge that they sometimes find in the Stomach of the dead, great pieces of fresh Pig's flesh, or of some other Animal, about eight or ten pound in weight: and they suppose that it has been put therein by some Divination, and that it is good to perform others.

They have not any principle, but Receipts.

They trouble not themselves to have any principle of Medicine, but only a number of Receipts, which they have learnt from their Ancestors, and in which they never alter any thing. They have no regard to the particular symptoms of diseases: and yet they fail not to cure a great many; because that the natural Temperance of the *Siameses* preserves them from a great many evils difficult to cure. But when at last it happens that the Distemper is stronger than the Remedies, they fail not to attribute the cause thereof to Inchantment.

The Chinese Physicians are great Mountebanks.

The King of *Siam* understanding one day that I was somewhat indisposed, tho it was so little, that I kept not my Chamber, he had the goodness to send all his Physicians to me. The *Chineses* offer'd some Civility to the *Siameses* and *Peguins*; and then they made me sit, and sat down themselves: and after having demanded silence, for the company was numerous, they felt my pulse one after the other a long time, to make me suspect that it was not only a grimace. I had read that at *China* there is no School for Physicians, and that one is there admitted to exercise the profession thereof, at most by a slight examination made by a Magistrate of Justice, and not by Doctors in Physick. And I knew moreover, that the *Indians* are great Cheats, and the *Chineses* much greater: so that I had throughly resolved to get rid of these Doctors without making any experience of their Remedies. After having felt my pulse, they said that I was a little feverish, but I discerned it not at all: they added that my Stomach was out of order, and I perceived it not, save that my voice was a little weak. The next morning the *Chineses* return'd alone to present me a small Potion warm, in a China Cup cover'd and very neat. The smell of the remedy pleas'd me, and made me to drink it, and I found my self neither better nor worse.

The difference of the Chinese Mountebanks from ours.

'Tis well known that there are Mountebanks every where, and that every Man who will boldly promise Health, Pleasures, Riches, Honors, and the knowledge of Futurities, will always find Fools. But the difference that there

is

is between the Mountebanks of *China* and the Quacks of *Europe* on the account of Medicine, is that the *Chineses* do abuse the sick by pleasant and enticing Remedies, and that the *Europeans* do give us Drugs, which the humane Body seeks to get rid off by all manner of means: so that we are inclined to believe that they would not thus torment a sick person, if it was not certainly very necessary.

What Remedies are used at *Siam*.

When any person is sick at *Siam*, he begins with causing his whole body to be moulded by one that is skilful herein, who gets upon the Body of the sick person, and tramples him under his feet. 'Tis likewise reported that great belly'd women do thus cause themselves to be trodden under foot by a Child, to procure themselves to be delivered with less pain: for in hot Countries, though their Deliveries seem to be more easie by the natural Conformation of the women, yet they are very painful, by reason perhaps that they are preceded with less Evacuation.

Anciently the *Indians* apply'd no other Remedy to plenitude, than an Excessive diet; and this is still the principal subtilty of the *Chineses* in Medicine. The *Chineses* do now make use of Blood-letting, provided they may have an *European* Chyrurgion: and sometimes instead of Blood-letting they do use Cupping-glasses, Scarifications and Leeches.

They have some Purgatives which we make use of, and others which are peculiar to them; but they know not the *Hellebore*, so familiar to the Antient Greek Physicians. Moreover they observe not any time in purging, and know not what the Crisis is: though they understand the benefit of Sweats in distempers, and do highly applaud the use of Sudorificks.

In their Remedies they do use Minerals and Simples, and the *Europeans* have made known the *Quinquina* unto them. In general all their Remedies are very hot; and they use not any inward Refreshment: but they bath themselves in Fevers, and in all sorts of diseases. It seems that whatever concenters or augments the natural heat, is beneficial to them.

The Diet of the sick Siameses.

Their sick do nourish themselves only with boiled Rice, which they do make extreamly liquid: the *Portugueses* of the *Indies* do call it *cange*. Meat-Broths are mortal at *Siam*, because they too much relax the Stomach: and when their Patients are in a condition to eat any thing solid, they give them Pigs flesh preferable to any other.

Their Ignorance in Chymistry, and their Fables about this matter.

They do not understand Chymistry, although they passionately affect it; and that several amongst them do boast of possessing the most profound secrets thereof. *Siam*, like all the rest of the East, is full of two sorts of persons upon this account, Impostors and Fools. The late King of *Siam*, the Father of the present Prince, spent two Millions, a great summ for his Country, in the vain research of the Philosophers Stone: and the *Chineses*, reputed so wise, have for three or four thousand years had the folly of seeking out an Universal Remedy, by which they hope to exempt themselves from the necessity of dying. And as amongst us there are some foolish Traditions concerning some rare persons that are reported to have made Gold, or to have lived some Ages; there are some very strongly established amongst the *Chineses*, the *Siameses*, and the other Orientals, concerning those that know how to render themselves immortal, either absolutely, or in such a manner, that they can die no otherwise than of a violent death. Wherefore it is supposed, that some have withdrawn themselves from the sight of men, either to enjoy a free and peaceable Immortality, or to secure themselves from all foreign force, which might deprive them of their life, which no distemper could do. They relate wonders concerning the knowledge of these pretended Immortals, and it is no matter of astonishment that they think themselves capable of forcing Nature in several things, since they imagine that they have had the Art of freeing themselves from Death.

CHAP.

CHAP. XI.

What the Siameses *do know of the Mathematicks.*

The great Heat of *Siam*, is repugnant to all application of Mind.

THE quick and clear Imagination of the *Siameses* should seem more proper for the Mathematicks, than the other Studies, if it did not soon weary them; but they cannot follow a long thread of Ratiocinations, of which they do foresee neither the end nor the profit. And it must be confessed for their Excuse, that all application of Mind is so laborious in a Climate so hot as theirs, that the very *Europeans* could hardly study there, what desire soever they might have thereunto.

The Ignorance of the *Siameses* touching the principal parts of Mathematicks.

The *Siameses* do therefore know nothing in Geometry or Mechanicks, because they can be absolutely without them: And Astronomy concerns them only as far as they conceive it may be assistant to Divination. They know only some Practical part thereof, the Reasons of which they disdain to penetrate; but of which they make use in the Horoscopes of particular Persons, and in the Composition of their Almanac, which, as it were, is a general Horoscope.

Of the *Siamese* Calendar, and why they have two *Epocha's*.

It appears that they have twice caused their Calendar to be reformed by able Astronomers, who, to supply the Astronomical Tables, have taken two arbitrary *Epocha's*, but yet remarkable for some rare Conjunction of the Planets. Having once established certain Numbers upon these Observations, they by the means of several Additions, Substractions, Multiplications and Divisions, have given for the following Years the secret of finding the place of the Planets, almost as we find the Epact of every Year, by adding eleven to the Epact of the Year foregoing.

The most Modern is evidently Arbitrary.

The most Modern of the two *Siamese Epocha's*, is referred to the Year of Grace 638. I gave to Mr. *Cassini*, Director of the Observatory at *Paris*, the *Siamese* Method of finding the place of the Sun and Moon by a Calculation, the ground of which is taken from this *Epocha*. And the singular Merit which Mr. *Cassini* has had of unfolding a thing so difficult, and penetrating the Reasons thereof, will doubtless be admired by all the Learned. Now as this *Epocha* is visibly the ground only of an Astronomical Calculation, and has been chosen rather than another, only because it appear'd more commodious to Calculation than another, it is evident that we must thence conclude nothing which respects the *Siamese* History; nor imagine that the Year 638, has been more Famous amongst them than another for any Event, from which they have thought fit to begin to compute their Years, as we compute ours, from the Birth of the Saviour of the World.

The most Ancient also appears Arbitrary.

By the same Reason I am persuaded, that their most Ancient *Epocha*, from which in this Year 1689, they compute 2233 Years, has not been remarkable at *Siam* for any thing worthy of Memory, and that it proves not that the Kingdom of *Siam* is of that Antiquity. It is purely Astronomical, and serves as a Foundation to another way of calculating the places of the Planets, which they have relinquished for that new Method which I have given to Mr. *Cassini*. Some person may discover to them the Mistakes, whereby in process of time this ancient Method must fall; as in time we have found out the Errors of the Reformation of the Calendar made by the Order of *Julius Cesar*.

And is not taken from the death of *Sommona Codom*.

The Historical Memoirs of the *Siameses* re-ascending, as I have remark'd in the beginning, to 900 Years, or thereabouts, it is not necessary to seek the Foundation of their Kingdom in the 545th Year before the Birth of Jesus Christ; nor to suppose that from this time they have enjoyed a Succession of Kings, which they themselves are absolutely ignorant of. And tho' the *Siameses* do vulgarly report, that this first *Epocha*, from which they compute, as I have said, 2233 Years, is that of the death of their *Sommona-Codom*; and altho' it refers almost to the time in which *Pythagoras* liv'd, who has spread in the West the Doctrine of the *Metempsychosis*, which he had learnt from the *Egyptians*, yet it is

certain

certain that the *Siamese* have not any Memoirs of the time in which their *Sommona-Codom* might have lived: And I cannot persuade my self that their *Sommona-Codom* could be *Pythagoras*, who was not in the *East*, nor that their ancient *Epocha* is other than *Astronomical* and *Arbitrary*, no more than their Modern *Epocha*.

But if the *Siamese* do still make use thereof in their Dates, after having relinquish'd it in their Astronomical Calculations, it is because that in things of Style they do not easily alter the Usages unto which they are accustomed; and yet they cease not to date sometimes with respect to that modern *Epocha* which they have taken, as I have said, from the Year of our Lord 638. But their first Month is always the Moon of *November* or *December*, in which they depart not from the ancient Style, even then when they date the Year according to their new Stile; tho' the first Month of the Year, according to this new Style, be the fifth or sixth of the old Style.

The Variety of Style in their Dates.

This, in few words, is the whole Skill of the *Siamese* in Astronomy. Moreover, they understand nothing of the true System of the World, because they know nothing by Reason. They believe therefore, like all the East, that the Eclipses are caused by some Dragon, which devours the Sun and Moon (perhaps by reason of the Astronomer's metaphorical way of speaking, that the Eclipses are made in the Head and Tail of the Dragon;) And they make a great noise, with Fire-shovels and Kettles, to scare and drive away this pernicious Animal, and to deliver those beauteous Planets. They believe the Earth Four square, and of vast Extent, on which the Arch of Heaven rests at its extremities, as if it was one of our Glass-Bells with which we cover some of our Plants in our Gardens. They assert, that the Earth is divided into four habitable parts of the World, so separated one from the other by Seas, that they are, as it were, *four* different *Worlds*. In the middle of these *four Worlds*, they suppose an exceeding high Pyramidal Mountain with four equal sides, called, *Caou pra Soumene* (*Caou* signifies, a *Mountain*, and to *Mount*:) and from the Surface of the Earth, or the Sea, to the top of this Mountain, which, as they say, touches the Stars, they compute 84000 *Iods*, and every *Iod* contains about 8000 Fathoms. They reckon as many *Iods* from the Surface of the Sea to the Foundations of the Mountain; and they likewise reckon 84000 *Iods* extent of Sea from each of the four sides of this Mountain to every of the four Worlds which I have mentioned. Now our World, which they call *Tchiampou*, lies, as they report, to the South of this Mountain, and the Sun, Moon and Stars do incessantly turn round it; and it is that, which according to them, makes the *Day* and *Night*. At the top of this Mountain is a Heaven, which they call *Intratiraka*, which is surmounted by the Heaven of Angels. This Sample, which is all I know thereof, will suffice to demonstrate their Grosness; and if it does not exactly accord to what others have writ before me concerning this matter, we must not more admire the variety of the *Siamese* Opinions in a thing they understand not, than the contrariety of our Systems in Astronomy, which we pretend to understand.

What the *Siamese* do think of the System of the World.

The extream Superstition of the *Indians* is therefore a very natural Consequence of their profound Ignorance; but for their Excuse, some People, more illuminated than them, have not been less Superstitious. Have not the *Greeks*, and after them the *Romans*, believed in Judiciary Astrology, Augurs, Presages, and all sorts of Arts invented under pretence of Divining and Predicting? They thought that it was the goodness of the Gods, to bestow on Men some Succors to penetrate Futurities; and the words *Divination* and *Divine* are the same word in their Origine, because that according to the ancient *Pagans*, the Art of Divining was only an Art to consult the Deities. The *Siamese* are also of opinion, that there is an Art of Prophecying, as there is one of restoring Health to the Sick: And when the King of *Siam*'s Soothsayers are mistaken, he causes them to be bastinado'd, not as Impostors, but as negligent persons; as he commands his Physicians to be cudgell'd, when the Remedies they give him, perform not the Effect which is thereby promised.

The *Indians* are Superstitious proportionably to their extream Ignorance.

The Authority of Soothsayers over the Siamese.

This Prince, no more than his Subjects, undertakes no Affair, nor Expedition, till his Diviners, which are all *Brames* or *Peguins*, have fix'd him an hour prosperously to set upon it. He stirs not out of his House, or if he be gone, he enters not again, so long as his Diviners prohibit him. *Sunday* seems to him more lucky than the other days, because that in his Tongue he has preserv'd the name of the *Sun-day*. He believes the Increase of the Moon more lucky than the Decrease; and besides this, the Almanac which he causes Annually to be made by a *Brame* Astrologer, denotes to him and his Subjects, the lucky or unlucky days for most of the things they used to do: A Folly which is perhaps too much tolerated amongst the Christians, witness the Almanac of *Milan*, to which so many persons do now give such a blind Belief.

And Presages.

The *Siamese* do take the Howlings of wild Beasts, and the Cryes of Stags and Apes, for an ill *Omen*; as several persons amongst us are frighted with the Barking of the Dogs in the Night. A Serpent which crosses the way, the Thunderbolt which falls on a House, any thing that falls as it were of it self, and without any apparent Cause, are Subjects of dread to the *Siamese*, and the reasons of laying aside or setting upon an Affair, how important and pressing soever it be. One of the ways they make use of to foretel things to come, and which is common to all the Orientals, is to perform some superstitious Ceremonies, then to go into the City, and to take for an Oracle about what they desire to know, the first words which they hear accidentally spoken in the Streets, or in the Houses. I could learn no more thereof, by reason that the Christian Interpreters, which I made use of, look'd upon these things with Horror, as Witchcraft and Compacts with the *Dæmon*; altho' it be very possible that they are only Fooleries full of Credulity and Ignorance. The ancient *French*, by a like Superstition, consulted in their Wars the first words which they heard sung in the Church, at their entring thereinto. At this very day several persons have a Superstitious Belief in certain Herbs which they gather the Evening of *St. John*, from whence is risen this Proverb, To use or employ all the Herbs of *St. John*, that is, the utmost skill in an Affair: And amongst the *Italians*, there are some, who, after having wash'd their Feet in Wine on *St. John's* Eve, do throw the Wine out at Window, and so stand afterwards to hear those that pass along the Street, taking for a certain Augury on what they desire to know, the first word they hear spoken.

The Indians accused of Sorcery, and why.

But that which has rais'd the Reputation of great Sorcerers amongst the *Indians*, is principally the continual Conjurations which they use to drive away the evil Spirits with, and attract the good. They pretend to have some *Talismans*, or Characters which they call *Cata*, to accomplish whatever they please; as to kill, or to render invulnerable; and to impose Silence on Persons and Dogs, when they would commit a wicked Action, and not be discovered. If they prepare a Medicine, they will fasten to the brim of the Vessel several Papers, wherein they will write some mysterious words, to hinder the *Prayetons* from carrying away the vertue of the Remedy with the Steam. These *Prayetons* are in their Opinion some Spirits diffused in the Air, of whom they believe, amongst other things, that they do first enjoy all the Maidens; and that they do them that pretended hurt, which is renewed every Month. In a Storm at Sea, they will fasten to all the Tackle such like written Papers, which they believe proper to asswage the Winds.

Superstitions for Women in Child-bed.

The superstitions which they use towards Women in Child-bed, appear not less ridiculous, although they be founded perhaps on some benefit for health. They believe that Women in Child-bed have need of being purified: whether that the *Jews*, spread throughout the Earth, have sowed this Tradition amongst several Nations, or that the people of hot Countries are more easily prejudiced than those of cold Countries with the natural impurities of Women. The *Siamese* keep the Women in Child-bed before a continual and great fire for a month, where they turn them sometimes on one side, sometimes on the other. The smoak does greatly incommode them, and passes slowly through an Aperture, which they make in the roof of their houses. The *Peguins* do put their Wives on a kind of Bambou grate, very nigh, with fire underneath; but they

they keep them thus no more than four or five days. At the up-rising, the one and the other return thanks to the Fire for having purified their Wives; and in the Entertainment which they give on this occasion to their Friends, they eat nothing which they have not first offered to the Fire, leaving it some time near it. During the whole time of lying in Child-bed, the Women neither eat nor drink any thing that is not hot; and I understand that our *Abyssines*, forbid their Women also to drink any thing cold.

Philtres look'd upon as the effect of Magick.

But the most speedy and most sensible effects of the pretended Divinations of the *Indians* are in the use of certain Philtres, which are only natural drinks. The *Indies* do produce some Simples, the kinds, force, or use of which we understand not. The Amorous *Philtres*, or Love-potions, are those which debilitate the Imagination, and make a Man to become a Child; so that after this it is easie to govern him. My domesticks assur'd me that they had seen a man at *Batavia*, of whom it was reported that his wife had render'd him senseless after this manner. Other drinks do cause other effects. The Relations are full of those which the women of *Goa* frequently give their Husbands; and which render them so stupid for 24 hours, that they can then be unfaithful to them in their presence. *Opium*, or the quintessence of Poppies, causes such different effects, that it procures sleep, or watchfulness, as it is variously prepared. The *Indians* going to Battel, do take thereof to inspire them with courage, or rather with fury. They then run headlong upon the Enemy like wild Boars. It is dangerous to attend them, but one may avoid them by turning out of the way, for they go forwards. Moreover, the effect of *Opium* lasts only some hours, after which they relapse not only into their natural cowardice, but into a faintness, which leaves them but little action for their defence. And such were those *Macassers*, which had conspired against the King of *Siam*, some months before the Kings Ambassadors arrived there.

Distempers considered as the Effects of Magick.

The *Siamese* have likewise some Distempers, the symptoms of which are sometimes so strange, that they think the cause thereof can be attributed only to Witchcraft. But besides these extraordinary cases, their Physicians do almost continually accuse the greater Energy of the Spirits, with the inefficaciousness of their Remedies; and they do herein play such subtile jugling tricks, or rather they deal with persons so credulous, that whilst we were at *Siam*, they made a sick man believe, that he had voided a Deers skin with a Medicine, and that he must have swallowed this Deers skin by a Magical effect, and without perceiving it. This is what I judged necessary to relate concerning the *Siamese* Superstitions, of which every one may judge as he pleases: for if on the one hand I have seen nothing which obliges me to accuse them of Sorcery, on the other hand I am not concern'd to justifie them entirely.

Superstition or Vanity touching the walls of Cities.

But before we quit this subject I will here add one thing, which may be attributed at your pleasure, to Superstition or Vanity. One day when the Kings Ambassadors were saluted by the real or supposed Ambassadors from *Patana*, *Camboya*, and some other neighbouring Courts, the Ambassadors of some of the several Nations which are at *Siam*, were also at this Visit; and among the rest there were two, who said that the City of their Origine, the name of which I have forgot, remained no more: but that it had been so considerable, that it was impossible to go round it in three Months. I smil'd thereat as at a groundless folly; and in a few days after Mr. *de la Mare* the Ingineer, whom Mr. *de Chaumont* had left at *Siam*, informed me, that when by the King of *Siam*'s order he had been at *Ligor* to take the draught thereof, the Governour would not permit him to go round it under two days, though he could have done it in less than an hour. Let us proceed to the study of the last part of the Mathematicks.

CHAP.

CHAP. XII.

Concerning Musick, and the Exercises of the Body.

The *Siameses* have no Art in singing.

MUsick is not better understood at *Siam*, than Geometry and Astronomy. They make Airs by Fancy, and know not how to prick them by Notes. They have neither Cadence, nor Quaver no more than the *Castilians*: but they sometimes sing like us without words, which the *Castilians* think very strange; and in the stead of words, they only say *noi, noi*, as we do say *lan-la-lari*. I have not remark'd one single Air, whose measure was triple, whereas those are without comparison the most familiar to the *Spaniards*. The King of *Siam*, without shewing himself, heard several Airs of our *Opera* on the Violin, and it was told us that he did not think them of a movement grave enough: Nevertheless the *Siameses* have nothing very grave in their Songs; and whatever they play on their Instruments, even in their Kings march, is very brisk.

They have not several parts in their Consorts.

They understand not more than the *Chineses* the diversity of Parts in composition; they understand not the Variety of the Parts, they do all sing Unisons. Their Instruments are not well chose, and it must be thought that those, wherein there appears any knowledge of Musick, have them brought from other parts.

Their Instruments the Rebeck, Hoboy, Basons.

They have very ugly little *Rebecks* or Violins with three strings, which they call *Tro*, and some very shrill Hoboys which they call *Pi*, and the *Spaniards Chirimias*. They play not ill, and accompany them with the noise of certain copper Basons, on each of which a man strikes a blow with a short stick, at certain times * in each measure. These Basons are hung up by a string, each has a Pole laid across upon two upright Forks: the one is called *Schoungschang*, and it is thinner, broader, and of a graver sound than the other, which they call *Cong*.

* The Europeans mark them, no person beating the Time.

The Tlounpounpan.

To this they add two sorts of Drum, the *Tlounpounpan*, and the *Tapon*. The wood of the *Tlounpounpan* is about the size of our Timbrels, but it is cover'd with skin on both sides like a true Drum, and on each side of the wood hangs a leaden ball to a string. Besides this the wood of the *Tlounpounpan* is run through with a stick which serves as a handle, by which it is held. They rowl it between their hands like a Chocolate stick, only that the Chocolate stick is held inverted, and the *Tlounpounpan* strait: and by this motion which I have described, the Leaden Balls which hang down from each side of the *Tlounpounpan*, do strike on each side upon the two Skins.

The *Tapon*.

The *Tapon* resembles a Barrel; they carry it before them, hung to the Neck by a Rope; and they beat it on the two Skins with each fist.

They have another Instrument composed of . . . . , which they call *Pat-cong*. The . . . . . . are all placed successively every one on a short stick, and planted perpendicular on a demi-circumference of Wood, like to the felleys of a little Wheel of a Coach. He that plays on this Instrument is seated at the center cross-legg'd; and he strikes the . . . . with two sticks, one of which he holds in his right hand, and the other in his left. To me it seems that this Instrument had only a fifth redoubled in extent, but certainly there was not any half notes, nor any thing to stop the sound of one . . . . , when another was struck.

The Consort which follows the King in his Marches.

The March which they sounded at the entrance of the Kings Ambassadors, was a confused noise with all these Instruments together: The like is sounded in attending on the King of *Siam*; and this noise, as fantastical and odd as it is, has nothing unpleasant, especially on the River.

Instruments accompanying the Voice.

They sometimes accompany the Voice with two short sticks, which they call *Crab*, and which they strike one against the other; and he that sings thus, is stiled *Tchang cap*. They hire him at Weddings with several of these Instruments I have mentioned. The people do also accompany the Voice in the Evening

into

into the Courts of the Houses, with a kind of Drum called *Tong*. They hold it with the Left hand, and strike it continually with the Right hand. 'Tis an earthen Bottle without a bottom, and which instead thereof is covered with a Skin tyed to the Neck with Ropes.

The *Siamese* do extreamly love our Trumpets, theirs are small and harsh, they call them *Tre*, and besides this they have true Drums, which they call *Clong*. But tho' their Drums be lesser than ours, they carry them not hanging upon their Shoulder: They set them upon one of the Skins, and they beat them on the other, themselves sitting cross-leg'd before their Drums. They do also make use of this sort of Drum to accompany the Voice, but they seldom sing with these Drums but to dance. — Trumpets and Drums.

On the day of the first Audience of the King's Ambassadors, there were in the Innermost Court of the Palace an hundred Men lying prostrate, some holding for show those ugly little Trumpets which they sounded not, and which I suspect to be of wood, and the others having before them every one a little Drum without beating it. — They have little ones to make a show.

By all that I have said, it appears that in some cases the Mathematicks are as much neglected at *Siam*, as the other Sciences. They have Exercises of the Body in no more Esteem than those of the Mind. They know not what the Art of Riding the Great Horse is: Arms they have none, except the King gives them some; and they cannot purchase any, till he has given them some. They exercise them only by the Order of this Prince. They never fire the Musquet standing, no not in War: To discharge it, they place one Knee on the ground, and frequently proceed to sit on their Heel, stretching forward the other Leg, which they have not bent. They hardly know to march, or keep themselves on their Feet with a good grace. They never stretch out their Hams well, because they are accustomed to keep them bended. The *French* taught them how to stand to their Arms, and till the arrival of the King's Ships at *Siam*, their Sentinels themselves sat upon the ground. So far are they from running Races, purely for Recreation sake, that they never walk abroad. The heat of the Climate causes a great Consumption in them. Wrestling, and Fisty-cuffs, are the Jugler's Trade. The running of *Balons* is therefore their sole Exercise. The Oar and *Pagaye* are in this Country the Trade of all the People from four or five years old. They can Row three days and three nights almost without resting, altho' they cannot undergo any other Work. — The Exercises of the Body.

CHAP. XIII.

Of the Arts exercised by the Siamese.

THey have no Companies of Trades, and the Arts flourish not amongst them, not only by reason of their natural sluggishness, but much more by reason of the Government under which they live. There being no security for the wealth of particular persons, but to conceal it well every one there continues in so great a simplicity, that most of the Arts are not necessary to them, and that the Workmen cannot meet with the just value of the Works on which they would bestow a great deal of Expence and Labour. Moreover, as every particular Person does Annually owe six Months service to the King, and that frequently he is not discharged for six Months, there is no Person in this Country that dares to distinguish himself in any Art, for fear of being forced to work gratis all his life for the service of this Prince. And because that they are indifferently employ'd in these Works, every one applies himself to know how to do a little of all, to avoid the Bastinados; but none would do too well, because that Servitude is the reward of Ingenuity. They neither know, nor desire to know how to do otherwise, than what they have always done. 'Tis no matter to them to have 500 Workmen, for several Months, upon what a few — They are bad Artificers, and why.

Europeans, well paid, would finish in a few days. If any Stranger gives them any direction, or any Machine, they forget it so soon as their Prince forgets it. Wherefore no *European* offers his service to an *Indian* Prince, who is not receiv'd, as I may say, with open Arms. How little Merit soever he may have, he always has more than the natural *Indians*; and not only for the Mechanic Arts, but for the Sea, and for Commerce, to which they are much more affected. The Inconveniencе is, that the *Indian* Kings do well know the Secret, either of enriching a Stranger only with hopes, or of detaining him amongst them if they have really enrich'd him. Nothing is so magnificent as the Grants which the great *Mogul* gives: But is there found one *European* that has carry'd away much wealth out of his Service?

What Arts they exercise.

To return to the Industry of the *Siamese*, the Arts which they understand are these. They are reasonable good Joyners, and because they have no Nails, they very well understand how to fasten pieces together. They pretend to Sculpture, but grosly perform it. The Statues of their Temples are very ill made. They know how to burn Brick, and make excellent Ciments, and are not unskill'd in Masonry. Nevertheless their Brick Buildings do not last, for want of Foundations: they do not make any, even in their Fortifications. They have no melted Crystal, nor Glass; and it is one of the things they most esteem. The King of *Siam* was extreamly pleased with those Facet-cut Glasses, which multiply an Object; and he demanded entire Windows with the same property.

The Windows of the Chinese.

The Windows of the *Chinese* are compos'd with Threads of Glass as big as Straws, laid one by another, and glued at the ends to Paper, as we solder the Quarries of Glass into our Window-frames. They do frequently put some Paintings on these sorts of Glasses, and with these Glasses thus painted, they sometimes make Pannels of Screens, behind which they love to set some lights, because they extreamly admire the Fancy of Illuminations.

How the Siamese do use Metals.

The *Siamese* do know to melt Metals, and cast some Works in Molds. They do cover their Idols, which are sometimes enormous masses of Brick and Lime, with a very thin Plate either of Gold or Silver, or Copper. I have in my possession a little *Sommona Codom*, which is thus cover'd over with a Copper Plate gilded, and which is yet full of the Ciment, which served as the Model. With such a Plate of Gold or Silver they cover certain of their King's Moveables, and the Iron hilt of the Sabres and Daggers, which he presents to some of his Officers, and sometimes to Strangers. They are not wholly ignorant of the Goldsmith's Trade; but they neither know how to polish, nor to set precious Stones.

How they write on a Leaf of Gold.

They are excellent Gilders, and know very well how to beat the Gold. As often as the King of *Siam* writes to another King, he does it upon a Leaf of that Metal as thin as a Leaf of Paper. The Letters are imprinted thereon with a blunt Poinson or Bodkin, like those with which we write in our Table-Books.

They are bad Smiths, and no Tanners.

They make use of Iron only as it is Cast, by reason they are bad Forge-men; their Horses are not shod, and have commonly Stirrups of Rope, and very paltry Snaffles. They have no better Saddles, the Art of Tanning and preparing Skins, being absolutely unknown at *Siam*.

They make little Linnen, and no Stuffs.

They make little Cotton-Cloth, and that very course, with a very nasty Painting, and only in the Metropolis. They make no Stuffs, neither of Silk, nor Wooll, nor any Tapestry-work: Wooll is here very scarce. They understand Embroidery, and their Designs please.

The painting of the Siamese and Chinese.

In one of their Temples I saw a very pleasant Picture in *Fresco*, the Colours of which were lively. There was no Ordonance, and it made us to remember our ancient Tapestries: 'Twas not certainly the work of a *Siamese* hand.

The *Siamese* and *Chinese* know not how to paint in Oil; and, moreover, they are bad Painters. Their Fancy is to slight and disesteem whatever is after Nature only. To them it seems that an exact Imitation is too easie, wherefore they

they overdo every thing. They will therefore have Extravagancies in Painting, as we will have Wonders in Poetry. They represent Trees, Flowers, Birds, and other Animals, which never were. They sometimes give unto Men impossible Proportions, and the Secret is, to give to all these things a Facility, which may make them to appear Natural. This is what concerns the Arts.

CHAP. XIV.

Of the Traffic amongst the Siameses.

Fishing and Commerce are the two Professions which do almost employ all the Siameses.

THE most general Professions at *Siam* are Fishing for the common People, and Merchandize for all those that have wherewith to follow it. I say all, not excepting their King himself. But the Foreign Trade being reserved almost entire to the King, the Home Trade is so inconsiderable, that it is impossible to raise any competent Fortune thereby. That simplicity of Manners, which makes the *Siameses* to let go most of the Arts, makes them also to slight most of the Commodities which are necessary to the *Europeans*; yet see how the *Siameses* carry on their Commerce.

What their private Writings are.

In their Loans, a third person, whosoever he be, writes down the Promise; and this sufficeth them in Justice, because it is determined against the word of the Debtor who denies, upon the double Testimony of him that produces the Promise, and of him that writ. It is necessary only that it appear by the viewing of the Writing, that it is not the Creditor that writ the Promise.

What their Signature is.

Moreover, they sign no Writings, neither do they apply any Seal to private Writings. 'Tis only the Magistrates that have a Seal, that is properly a Seal which the King gives them as an Instrument of their Offices. Particular Persons, instead of a Signature, do put a single Cross; and tho' this kind of Signature be practised by all, yet every one knows the Cross which is under his own hand; and it is very rare, they say, that any one is of a Reputation so bad as to disown it in Justice. In a word, I shall ingenuously declare, that we must not search out any Mystery in that they sign with a Cross: 'Tis amongst them only a kind of Flourish which they have preferr'd before any other, probably because it is more plain.

They have no publick Writing nor Notaries.

I have said, that they endow the Virgins at their marrying; and that the Portion is paid to the Husband in presence of the Parents, but without any Writing. I have said also, that they make no Will, and that before their death they dispose of their Estate with their own hand, and to whom they please, and that after this manner Custom disposes of their Inheritance. They Trade little with Immoveables, no person amongst them thinking it safe to purchase Land of another; the Prince gives, or sells thereof, to whoever would have it. But the real Property remaining always in him, is the reason that none in this Country does care to purchase much Land, nor to meliorate it, for fear of exciting a desire of it in one more powerful than himself. And thus needing no Writings of long continuance, they have not thought fit to have any Notaries.

The small Trades.

As to the small Trades, they are almost all of so little Consequence, and Fidelity is there so great, that in the Bazars or Markets the Seller counts not the Money which he receives, nor the Buyer the Commodity, which he purchases by Tale. They were scandaliz'd to see the *French* buy the least things with more Caution.

They use no Ell.

The Hour of the Market is from Five in the Evening to Eight or Nine. They use no Ell, by reason they buy Muslins, and other Linnens, all in whole Pieces. They are very poor and miserable in this Country, when they buy

Cloth

Cloth by *Ken*, a term which signifies the *Elbow* and *Cubit* both, and for these they measure with their Arm, and not with any sort of Ell.

They have the Fathom, which they use in several things, and especially in measuring the Roads.

Nevertheless they have their Fathom, which equals the *French* Toise within an Inch. They use it in Buildings, in surveying of Land, and perhaps in other things; and especially in measuring the Roads, or Channels, through which the King generally passes. Thus from *Siam* to *Louvo*, every Mile is marked with a Post, on which they have writ the number of the Mile. The same thing is observ'd in the Country of the great *Mogul*, where *Bernier* reports, that they mark the *Kosses*, or Half-miles, with Tourrettes, or little Pyramids; and every one knows that the *Romans* denoted their Miles with Stones.

The *Coco* serves the *Siamese* as Measure for Grains and Liquors.

The *Coco* serves as a Measure for Grain and Liquors in this manner. As all the *Cocos* are naturally unequal, they measure the Capacity thereof by those little Shells called *Cori*, which serve for small Money at *Siam*, and which are not sensibly greater one than the other. There is therefore such a *Coco* which contains a thousand *Cori*, as some have informed me, such an one which contains five hundred, and such another more or less. To measure Corn they have a kind of *Basket*, called *Sat* in the *Siamese*, which is made only with interlaced Bambou's; and to measure Liquors, they have a Pitcher called *Canan* in *Siamese*, *Choup* in *Portuguese*; and it is according to these sorts of Measures, that they make their Markets. But for want of Policy, and a *Standard*, according to which the Measures should legally be regulated, the Buyer accepts them only after having measured them with his *Coco*, the Capacity of which he knows by the *Cori*; and he uses either Water, or Rice, according as he would measure either the *Canan* or the *Sat* with his *Coco*. In a word, the quarter of the *Canan* is called *Leeng*, and forty *Sats* do make the *Seste*, and forty *Sestes* the *Cohi*. It is impossible to declare the resemblance which Measures so little exact have with ours. I have said moreover, that a Pound of Rice a day sufficeth a Man, and that it is worth no more than a Farthing. Mr. *Gervaise* says, that the *Seste* of Rice is reckon'd to weigh an hundred *Catis*, that is to say, two hundred twenty and five of our Pounds.

Money serves them for Weights.

They are not more exact as to their Weights, in general they call them *Ding*; and the pieces of their Money are more nice and true, and almost the only ones which they use, altho' their Money be frequently false or light. Some inform'd me, as a thing very remarkable, that the *Siamese* sold course Silver by weight, because they had seen in the Market that Commodity in one of the Scales, and the silver Money which serv'd as a Weight in the other. The same Names do therefore signifie the Weights and Money both.

Their Monies.

Their silver Coins are all of the same Figure, and struck with the same Stamps, only some are smaller than others. They are of the Figure of a little Cylinder or Roll very short, and bowed quite at the middle, so that both ends of the Cylinder touch'd one another. Their Stamps (for they have two on each piece, struck one at the side of the other in the middle of the Cylinder, and not at the ends) do represent nothing that we knew, and they have not explain'd them to me. The proportion of their Money to ours is, that their *Tical*, which weighs no more than half a Crown, is yet worth three shillings and three half-pence. I give the Figure and Size thereof, and at the end of this Work you will find their Measures for the Lengths, as well as their Coins and their Weights. They have no Gold, nor Copper-Money. Gold is a Merchandise amongst them, and is twelve times the value of Silver, the purity being supposed equal in both the Metals.

The *China's* Money.

Neither Gold nor Silver are Monies at *China*. They cut these Metals into ill shaped pieces, with which they pay for other Commodities; and for this purpose it is necessary, that they always have a pair of Gold Scales, and a Touchstone in their hand. Their pair of Gold Scales is a little *Roman* Balance; but amongst them there is such cheap living, that for ordinary Provisions their own Money, which is only Copper, sufficeth them. They thread it in a certain number on a Cord, for it is perforated in the middle, and they count by strings, and not by pieces.

The

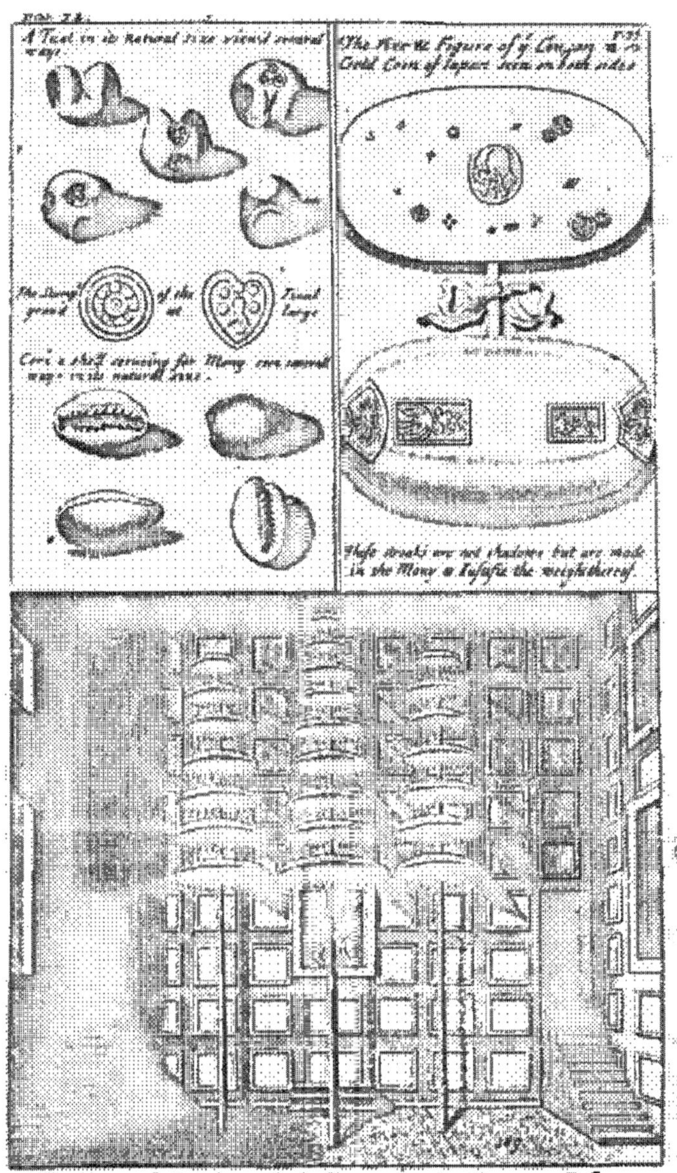

A Prospect of the Hall of Audience in the Pallace of Siam.

The Copan, the Gold Money of Japan.

The *Japanese* have a flat Gold Coin somewhat longer than broad, and rounded like an oval. I give exactly the size and figure thereof. It is struck at several stamps with hatchings. Its weight is four Drams and a half, and twelve grains, and is at least Twenty three Carats, as far as we can judge thereof without melting it. It is called *Coupan*, and its value is vulgarly esteemed Ten Crowns a piece.

Shells, the base Money of Siam.

The base Coin at *Siam* is no other than those little Shells I have already mentioned, and of which I have likewise given the size and figure. The *Europeans* which are at *Siam* do call them *Coris*, and the *Siameses Bia*. They fish them up abundantly at the *Maldives* Islands, and sometimes at the *Philippine* Isles, but in very little quantity, as some have informed me. Nevertheless *Navarette* in his *Discourse of* China, *pag.* 64. speaks thus concerning the *Coris*, which he calls *Sigueyes*, *'Tis imported*, saith he, *from the coast of* India *and* Manille: *They are innumerable at the Isle of* Luban, *which is one of the* Philippines. And a little after he subjoyns, *the Sigueyes are brought from the Isles of* Baldivia, which are the *Maldives*.

How much the use of this Money is extended.

'Tis not easie to say how far the use of this Money extends it self. It is current throughout *India*, and almost over all the coasts of *Africk*; and some have informed me that it is received in some places of *Hungary*: but I can hardly believe it, by reason I see it not worth the trouble to carry it thither. It breaks much in the use; and as there is less of it, it is more worth in respect to the Silver Money; as likewise it lowers its price when there arrives any considerable cargo by any Ship; for it is a kind of Merchandise. The ordinary price at *Siam* is that a *Fouan*, or the eighth part of a *Tical*, is worth eight hundred *Coris*, or that 7 or 800 *Coris* are hardly worth a Penny: The lowness of Money being a certain sign of a good Market, or rather of the cheapness of Commodities.

CHAP. XV.

A Character of the Siameses *in general.*

The Siameses are good People.

As easiness of living consists in the reasonable price of things necessary for life, and as good manners are more easily preserved in a moderate easiness, than in a Poverty attended with too much labour, or in an over-abundant Idleness, it may be affirm'd that the *Siameses* are good men. Vices are detestable amongst them, and they excuse them not as witty conceits, nor as sublimity of mind. A *Siamese* never so little above the refuse of the people, is so far from making himself drunk, that he accounts it a shame to drink *Arak*.

Adultery is rare at Siam.

Adultery is rare at *Siam*, not so much because the Husband has the power of doing himself Justice over his Wife, (that is to say, to kill her if he finds her in a palpable offence, or to sell her, if he can convict her of Infidelity) as because the Women are not corrupted by Idleness (for it is they that maintain the men by their Labour) nor by the Luxury of the Table or of Cloaths, nor by Gameing, nor by Shows. The *Siamese* Women do not play; they receive no Visits from men; and Plays are very rare at *Siam*, and have no appointed days, nor certain price, nor publick Theater. It must not however be thought that all Marriages are chaste, but at least any other Love more immoderate, than that of the Wives is, they say, without example.

The Jealousie of the Siameses to their Wives.

Jealousie is amongst them only a meer opinion of Glory, which is greater in those, that are most highly advanced in Dignity. The Wives of the People managing all the Trade do enjoy a perfect Liberty. Those of the Nobles are very reserved, and stir not abroad but seldom, either upon some Family visit, or to go to the *Pagodes*. But when they go out, they go with their face uncovered, even when they go on foot; and sometimes it is hard to distinguish them from the Women-slaves which accompany them. In a word, they not only find nothing austere in the constraint under which they live, but they place their glory therein. They look upon a greater liberty as a shame; and would think themselves slighted and contemned by a Husband that would permit it them. They are jealous for them as much as they are themselves.

The Glory of the *Asiatick* Women.

There is not a vertuous Woman in *Asia*, who in time of War chuses not rather that her Husband should kill her, than that he should suffer her to fall under the power of the Enemies. *Tacitus* in the Twelfth Book of his *Annals*, gives an example thereof in *Zenobia*, the wife of *Rhadamistus*. The Husbands themselves do think it the most shameful thing in the world to them, that their Wives should fall into the Enemies hands; and when this happens, the greatest affront that can be done them, is not to restore them their Wives. But tho the Women of *Asia* be capable of sacrificing their life to their glory, there ceases not to be some amongst them, who take secret pleasures when they can, and who hazard their glory and their life upon this account. 'Tis reported that there have been some examples hereof amongst the King of *Siam's* Wives. How closely soever they be shut up, they do sometimes find out a way to have Lovers. Some have assur'd me, that the ordinary method by which this Prince punishes them, is first to submit them to a Horse, accustomed I know not how, to the love of Women, and then to put them to death. 'Tis some years since he gave one to the Tygers, and because these Animals spared her at the first, he offered her a Pardon; but this Woman was so unworthy as to refuse it, and with so many affronts, that the King looking upon her as distracted, ordered again that she should dye. They irritated the Tygers, and they tore her in pieces in his presence. It is not so certain that he puts the Lovers to death, but at the least he causes them to be severely chastized. The common opinion at *Siam* is, that 'twas a fault of this nature, which caused the last disgrace of the late *Barcalon*, elder Brother to the King of *Siam's* first Ambassadour to the King. The King his Master caused him to be very severely battinado'd, and forbore to see him, yet without taking away his Offices. On the contrary, he continued to make use of him during the six months, that he survived the blows which he had received; and he with his own hand prepared all the Remedies which the *Barcalon* took in his last sickness, because no person dared to give him any, for fear of being accused of the death of a man, who appeared so dear to his Master. *Bernier* relates some examples, by which it appears that the Great *Mogul* does not always punish the Women of his *Seraglio* that offended in their duty, nor the Men that are their Accomplices, with death. These Princes consider these sorts of Crimes, like the others, which may be committed against their Majesty, unless any sentiment of Love renders them more sensible of Jealousie.

The Jealousie of the *Siamese* towards their Daughters.

The *Siamese* Lords are not less jealous of their Daughters than of their Wives; and if any one commits a fault, they sell her to a certain man, who has a priviledge of prostituting them for Money, in consideration of a Tribute which he pays the King. 'Tis said that he has six hundred, all Daughters of Officers in esteem. He likewise purchases Wives, when the Husbands sell them, being convicted of Infidelity.

Their respect towards Old Men.

Disrespect towards Old Men is not less rare at *Siam* than at *China*. Of the two *Mandarins* which came on board the Kings Ambassadours Ship, to bring them the first Compliment from the King of *Siam*, the younger tho the highest in dignity, yielded the first place and speech to the elder, who was not above three or four years older.

The *Siamese* great Lyars.

Lying towards Superiours is punished by the Superiour himself; and the King of *Siam* punishes it more severely than any other; and notwithstanding all this, they lye as much or more at *Siam*, than in *Europe*.

Great Union in their Families.

The Union of Families there is such, that a Son who would plead against his Parents, would pass for a Monster: Wherefore no person in this Country dreads Marriage, nor a number of Children: Interest divides not Families; Poverty renders not Marriage burdensome.

Begging is rare and Shameful at *Siam*.

Our Domesticks observed only three sorts of Beggars, Aged, Impotent and Friendless persons. Relations permit not their Kindred to beg Alms: They charitably maintain those that cannot maintain themselves out of their Estate

or

or Labour. Begging is shameful there, not only to the Beggar, but to all his Family.

The Siamese are Robbers.

But Robbing is much more ignominious than Begging, I say not to the Robber himself, but to his Relations. The nearest Friend dare not concern themselves about a Man accused of Theft; and it is not strange that Thievery should be reputed so infamous, where they may live so cheap: Thus are their Houses much less secure, than our worst Chests. Nevertheless as it is not possible to have true Vertue, but in the eternal prospects of Christianity, the *Siamese* do seldome as I may say refuse to steal whatever they meet with. 'Tis properly amongst them that opportunity makes the Thief. They place the Idea of perfect Justice in not gathering up lost things, that is to say in not laying hold on so easie an occasion of getting. After the same manner the *Chineses* to exaggerate the good Government of some of their Princes, do say that under their Reign Justice was in so high an esteem among the People, that no person medled with what he found scattered in the high Road; and this Idea has not been unknown to the *Greeks*. Anciently in *Greece* the *Stagyrites* made a Law in these words: What you have not laid down take not up; and it is perhaps from them that *Plato* learned it, when he inserted it amongst his Laws. But the *Siamese* are very remote from so exquisite a probity.

Some examples of Thefts committed by the Siamese.

Father *d'Espagnac*, one of those pious and learned Jesuits which we carried to *Siam*, being one day alone in the Divan of their House, a *Siamese* came boldly to take away an excellent *Persian* Carpet from off a Table that was before him; and Father *d'Espagnac* let him do it, because he imagined not that he was a Robber. In the Journey which the King caused the Ambassadors from *Siam* to make into *Flanders*, one of the *Mandarins* which accompanied them, took twenty Scions in a house, where the Ambassadors were invited to dine, as they sojourned in one of the principal Cities of *Picardy*. The next day this *Mandarin* conceiving that these Scions were Money; gave one to a Footman to drink; and his Theft was hereby discovered, but no Notice taken thereof.

Behold likewise an ingenious prank, which proves that the opportunity of stealing has so much power over them, that it sometimes sways them, even when it is perilous. One of the Officers of the King of *Siam*'s Magazines having stolen some Silver, this Prince ordered him to be put to death, by forcing him to swallow three or four Ounces of melted Silver, and it happened, that he who had order to take those three or four Ounces of Silver out of that Wretch's throat, could not forbear filching part of it. The King therefore caused him to die of the same punishment, and a third exposed himself to the same hazard by committing the like Offence: I mean by stealing part of the Silver, which he took out of the last dead Man's throat. So that the King of *Siam*, pardoning him his Life, said, there is enough punish'd, I should destroy all my Subjects, if I should not resolve to pardon them at last.

Robbers in the Woods of Siam and China, which do very rarely kill.

It must not be doubted after this, of what is reported of the *Siamese* who live in the Woods, to withdraw themselves from the Government, that they frequently rob the Passengers, yet without killing any. The Woods of *China* have been continually pestered with such Robbers; and there are some who after having enticed a great many Companions with them, have formed whole Armies, and at last rendered themselves Masters of that great Kingdom.

The fidelity of the Siamese in Commerce, their boundless Usury, and their Avarice.

On the other hand, Fidelity is exceeding great at *Siam*, in all sorts of Traffick, as I have elsewhere remarked: but Usury is there practised without bounds. Their Laws have not provided against it, though their Morality prohibits it. Avarice is their essential Vice; and what is more wonderful herein, is that they heap not up riches to use them, but to bury them.

They are very revengeful, and how.

As they traffick not almost with immoveables, make no Wills, nor publick Contracts, and as in a word they have no Notaries, it seems that they cannot almost have any Suits, and they have indeed few Civil, but a great many Criminal causes. 'Tis principally out of spight that they exercise their secret Hatreds and Revenges; and they find facility therein with the Judges, who in this Country, as in *Europe*, do live on their profession. The *Siamese* have naturally an aversion to blood: but when they hate, even unto death, which is very rare,

they

they assassinate, or they poyson, and understand not the uncertain Revenge of Duels, yet most of their quarrels do terminate only in blows, or reciprocal defamations.

Other qualities of the Siamese.

The Ancients have remark'd that it is the Humidity of the Elements, which defends the *Indians* against that action of the Sun, which burns the Complexion of the *Negro's*, and makes their Hair to grow like Cotton. The Nourishment of the *Siamese* is likewise more aqueous, than that of any other People of the *Indies*, and unto them may be fairly attributed all the good, and all the bad qualities, which proceed from Phlegm and Spittle; because that Phlegm and Spittle are the necessary effects of their Nourishment. They are courteous, polite, fearful, and careless. They contain themselves a long time, but when once their Rage is kindled, they have perhaps less discretion than we have. Their Timidity, their Avarice, their Dissimulation, their Silence, their Inclination to lying do increase with them. They are stiff in their Customs, as much out of Idleness, as out of respect to their Ancestors, who have transmitted them to them. They have no curiosity, and do admire nothing. They are proud with those that deal gently with them, and humble to those that treat them with rigour. They are subtile and variable, like all those that perceive their own weakness.

Their Friendship is perfidious.

Their manner of promising themselves an eternal amity, is by drinking of the same *Aqua Vitæ* in the same Cup, and when they would swear themselves more solemnly, they taste the blood one of another; which *Lucian* gives us for a Custom of the ancient *Scythians*, and which is practised also by the *Chinese*, and by other Nations: but the *Siamese* cease not sometimes to betray after all these Ceremonies.

They are naturally more moderate than we are, because they are more dull.

In general they have more Moderation than us: their Humors are as calm as their Heaven, which changes only twice a year and insensibly, when it turns by little and little from Rain to Fair-weather, and from Fair-weather to Rain. They act only by necessity, and do not like us place merit in Action. It seems not rational to them that Labour and Pains should be the Fruit and Reward of Vertue. They have the good Fortune to be born Philosophers, and it may be that if they were not born such, they would not become so more than we. I therefore willingly believe what the Ancients have reported, that Philosophy came from the *Indies* into *Europe*, and that we have been more concerned at the insensibility of the *Indians*, than the *Indians* have been at the wonders, which our Inquietude has produced in the discovery of so many different Arts, whereof we flatter our selves, perhaps to no purpose, that necessity was the Mother. But enough is spoken of the *Siamese* in general, let us enter into the particulars of their manners, according to their various conditions.

PART III.

PART III.

Of the Manners of the Siameses, *according to their several Conditions.*

CHAP. I.

Of the several Conditions among the Siameses.

AT *Siam* all Persons are either Freemen or Slaves. The Master has all power over the Slave, except that of killing him: And tho' some may report, that Slaves are severely beaten there, (which is very probable in a Country where free persons are so rigidly bastinado'd) yet the Slavery there is so gentle, or, if you will, the Liberty is so abject, that it is become a Proverb, that the *Siameses* sell it to eat of a Fruit, which they call *Durions*. I have already said, that they chuse rather to enjoy it, than to enjoy none at all: 'Tis certain also, that they dread Beggary more than Slavery; and this makes me to think, that Beggary is there as painful as ignominious, and that the *Siameses*, who express a great deal of Charity for Beasts, even to the relieving them, if they find any sick in the Fields, have very little for the Men. *Of the Slavery according to the Manners of Siam.*

They employ their Slaves in cultivating their Lands and Gardens, and in some domestic Services; or rather, they permit them to work to gain their livelihood, under a Tribute which they receive, from four to eight *Ticals* a Year, that is to say, from seven Livres ten Sols, to fifteen Livres. *In what the Slaves are employed.*

One may be born, or become a Slave. One becomes so either for Debt, as I have said, or for having been taken Captive in War, or for having been confiscated by Justice. When one is made a Slave for Debt, his Liberty returns again by making satisfaction; but the Children born during this Slavery, tho' it be but for a time, continue Slaves. *A Siamese may be born, or become a Slave.*

One is born a Slave, when born of a Mother-slave; and in the Slavery, the Children are divided as in the Divorce. The first, third, fifth, and all the rest in the odd number belong to the Master of the Mother: the second, fourth, and all the others in the even rank belong to the Father, if he is free; or to his Master, if he is a Slave. 'Tis true, that it is necessary upon this account, that the Father and Mother should have had Commerce together, with the consent of the Master of the Mother: for otherwise all the Children would belong to the Master of the Mother. *How he is born a Slave, and to whom he belongs.*

The difference of the King of *Siam's* Slaves from his Subjects of free condition, is, that he continually employs his Slaves in personal labours, and maintains them; whereas his free Subjects only owe him six months service every Year, but at their own expence. *The difference between the King of Siam's Slaves, and his other Subjects.*

In a word, the Slaves of particular men owe not any service to that Prince; and tho' for this Reason he loses a Freeman, when this man falls into slavery, either for Debt, or to avoid Beggary, yet this Prince opposes it not, neither pretends any Indemnity upon this account. *The Slaves of private men owe not any service to the King.*

Properly speaking, there is not two sorts of Conditions among free persons. Nobility is no other thing than the actual possession of Offices, the Families *Of the Siamese Nobility.*

X which

which do long maintain themselves therein, do become doubtless more illustrious and more powerful; but they are rare: and so soon as they have lost their Offices, they have nothing, which distinguishes them from the common People. There is frequently seen at the *Pagod*, the Grandson of a Man who died a great Lord, and sometimes his own Son.

Of the Priests or Talapoins.

The distinction between the People and the Priests is only an uncertain distinction, seeing that one may continually pass from one of these States to the other. The Priests are the *Talapoins*, of whom we shall speak in the sequel. Under the Name of People I comprehend whatever is not a Priest, *viz.* the King, Officers, and People, of whom we now proceed to speak.

CHAP. II.

Of the Siamese *People.*

The Siamese people is a Militia.

THE *Siamese* People is a Militia, where every particular person is registred: They are all Souldiers, in *Siamese Tahan*, and do all owe six Months service annually to their Prince. It belongs to the Prince to arm them, and give them Elephants or Horses, if he would have them serve either on Elephants, or on Horseback: but it belongs to them to cloath and to maintain themselves. And as the Prince never employs all his Subjects in his Armies, and that oftentimes he sends no Army into the Field, though he be at War with some of his Neighbours, yet for six months in the year he employs in such a work, or in such a service as pleases him, those Subjects which he employs not in the War.

It is counted and divided into men on the right hand, and on the left.

Wherefore, to the end that no person may escape the personal service of the Prince, there is kept an exact account of the People. 'Tis divided into men on the right hand, and men on the left, to the end that every one may know on what side he ought to range himself in his Functions.

And by Bands.

And besides this it is divided into Bands, each of which has its Chief, which they call *Nai*: so that this word *Nai* is become a term of Civility, which the *Siamese* do reciprocally give one to the other, as the *Chineses* do interchange the Title of Master or Governor.

What difference there is between a Band and a Company.

I have said that the *Siamese* People is divided by Bands, rather than by Companies; because that the number of Soldiers of the same Band is not fix'd, and because that all those of the same Band, are not of the same Company in the Army: and I have said, that *Nai* signifies Chief, though some translate it by the word *Captain*; because that the *Nai* does not always lead his Band to the War, no more than to the six months Service: His care is to furnish as many men out of his Band, as are required, either for the War, or for the six months Service.

The Children are of the same Band with their Parents.

The Children are of the same Band with their Parents; and if the Parents are of different Bands, the Children in the odd rank are of the Mother's Band, and the Children in the even rank of the Father's; provided nevertheless that the Mother's *Nai* hath been acquainted with the Marriage, and that he hath given his consent thereunto: otherwise the Children would be all of the Mother's Band.

The Talapoins and Women are exempt from Service, and yet are register'd, and why.

Thus, though the *Talapoins* and Women do enjoy an exemption from Service, as not being esteemed Soldiers, yet they cease not to be set down in the Rolls of the People: the *Talapoins*, because they may return when they please to a secular condition, and that then they fall again under the power of their natural *Nai*: the Women because their Children are of their Band, or all, or the greatest part, as I have said.

The Advantages of the Nai.

'Tis one of the *Nai's* Priviledges to be able to lend to his Soldier sooner than any other, and to be able to satisfie his Soldiers Creditor; thereby to make his Soldier his Slave, when he is insolvable. As the King gives a *Balon* to each

Officer

Officer with a certain number of *Pagayors*, and as these are the Officers, which are also the *Nai*, every Officer has his *Pagayors* in his Band. They brand them on the outside of the Wrist with an hot Iron and an Anchor over it; and these sort of Domesticks are called *Bao*. But none of the *Bao's* or *Pagayors* owes to his *Nai* only this service, and that only six months in the year, wherefore they are released from six months to six months, or by month, as it pleases the *Nai*: the *Nai* has also some Offices in the Law as we shall see.

What at *Siam* are the dignities of *Pa-ya*, *Oc-ya* and the rest.

Now the more numerous his Band is, the more powerful he is esteemed: The Offices and Employments of *Siam* being important only in this. The Dignities of *Pa-ya*, *Oc-ya*, *Oc-Pra*, *Oc-Louang*, *Oc-Counne*, *Oc-Meuing*, and *Oc-Pan*, are seven degrees of these *Nai*. 'Tis true that the Title of *Oc-Pan* is now disused. *Pan* signifies a *Thousand*, and it was thought that an *Oc-Pan* was Chief of a Thousand Men. *Meuing* signifies *Ten Thousand*, and it is thought that an *Oc-Meuing* is the Chief of Ten Thousand Men: not that in truth it was so, but that in the *Indies* they magnifie the Titles. No person could give me the true signification of these words, *Pa-ya*, *Oc-ya*, *Oc-Pra*, *Oc-Louang*, *Oc-Counne*, nor how many men are assigned to each of the five Dignities; but it is probable that as the words *Pan* and *Meuing* are Terms of Number, the rest are so too.

Of the word *Oc*.

The word *Oc* seems to signifie Chief; for they have another Title without Function, viz. *Oc-Meuang*, which seems to signifie *Chief of a City*, in that *Meuang* signifies a *City*, and in that it is necessary to have been made *Oc-Meuang* before he be effectually made Governor, whom they call *Tchaou-Meuang*, Lord of a City.

This word is not *Siamese*, and how they use it.

But this word *Oc* is not *Siamese*; *Chief* in *Siamese* is called *Houa*, and this word *Houa* properly signifies the *Head*. From hence comes *Houa Sip*, *Chief of Ten*, which is, as I have elsewhere said, the Title of him that mounts the Elephant at the Crupper. After the same manner they call him, that bears the Royal Standard in the *Balon* where the King is, *Houapan*, or *Chief of a Thousand*. To return to the word *Oc*, a Superior never useth it to an Inferior. Thus the King of *Siam* speaking to *Oc-Pra Pipitcharatcha*, will not, for example, say *Oc Pra Pipitcharatcha*, but only *Pra Pipitcharatcha*; A man relating his own Titles himself, will also modestly suppress the term *Oc*; and in fine, the inferiour People in speaking of the highest Officers will omit the word *Oc*, and will say for example, *ya-yommat*, for *Oc-ya-yommat*; *Meuing Vai*, for *Oc Meuing Vai*.

Of the word *Pa-ya*.

The *Portugues* have translated the word *Pa-ya*, by that of Prince; not in my opinion, from their right understanding it, but because they have seen this Title given to Princes, and that the King of *Siam* gives it himself; but he sometimes gives it also to the Officers of his Court, which are not Princes, and he gives it not always to the Princes of the Blood. The Lords of the Great *Moguls* Court are called, according to *Bernier*, *Hazary*, *Dou hazary*, *Pengy*, *hecht*, and *Deh hazary*, that is to say, *One Thousand*, *Two Thousand*, *Five*, *Eight*, and *Ten Thousand*, as if one should say, Lords over so many Thousands of Horse though in reality they could neither maintain, nor command so great a number. The great *Moguls* eldest Son, he says, is called *Twelve Thousand*, as if he had the effective command of Twelve Thousand Horse. 'Tis no strange thing therefore that the King of *Siam's* Subjects being esteemed Soldiers, as those of the Great *Mogul* are esteemed Horsemen, have equally assumed in both Courts the term of number, to express the highest Dignities, and to name the Princes themselves; yet I cannot affirm this is so at *Siam*, by reason that I know only that the words *Pan* and *Meuing* are *Siamese* and numeral Terms; but as to the other names of Dignity, which I have mentioned, some have informed me that they are *Balie*, and that they understood them not. I know that in the Country of *Laos* the Dignities of *Pa-ya* and *Meuang*, and the honourable Epithets of *Pra* are in use; it may be also that the other Terms of Dignity are common to both Nations, as well as the Laws.

Six orders of Cities of *Siam*.

In reference to the six Dignities (for that of *Oc-pan* is obsolete, as I have said) there are now at *Siam* six Orders of Cities, which have been anciently determined according to the Rolls of the Inhabitants. So that such a City, which was then found very populous had a *Pa-ya* for Governor, and such which was less popu-

populous had an *Oc-ya*, and the rest had also other Dignities in proportion to the Inhabitants which they contained. But it is not necessary to believe that these Cities have ever been so populous as the Titles of their Governors import; by reason, as I have often alledged, that these People are very proud in Titles. Only the greatest Titles were given to the Governors of the biggest Cities, and the least Titles to the Governors of the Cities less inhabited. Thus the City of *Me-Tac*, of which I have spoken at the beginning, had a Governor called *Pa-ya-Tac*, and the word *Me* which signifies *Mother*, and which is joyned to *Tac*, seems to intimate that the City of *Me-Tac* was very great. The City of *Porselouc* had also a *Pa-ya*; *Tenasserim*, *Ligor*, *Corazema* and others, have still some *Oc-ya*. Lesser Cities, as *Pipili* and *Bancock*, have the *Oc-pra*, others have the *Oc-Louang*, or the *Oc-Counne*, and the least of all have the *Oc-Meuing*. The *Portuguese* have translated these Titles according to their fancy by those of *King*, *Vice-Roy*, *Duke*, *Marquis*, *Earl*, &c. They have given the Title of Kingdom to *Merguy*, *Tenasserim*, *Porselouc*, *Ligor*, and *Pipeli*; either by reason of their hereditary Governours, or for having been like *Pipeli* the residence of the Kings of *Siam*; and to the Kings of *Siam* they have given the Title of Emperor, because the *Spaniards* have ever thought the Title of Emperor ought to be given to Kings, that have other Kings for Feudataries: So that upon this single reason some Kings of *Castille* have born the Title of Emperor, giving to their Children the Title of Kings of the several Kingdoms which were united to their Crown.

The dignities of the *Siamese* are not annext to the single Government of City or Province.

To return to the Titles of the *Siamese*, they are given not only to the Governors, but to all the Officers of the Kingdom; because that they are all *Nai*: and the same Title is not always joyned to the same Office. The *Barcalon*, for example, has sometimes had that of *Pa-ya*, as some have informed me, and now he has only that of *Oc-ya*. But if a Man has two Offices, he may have two different Titles in respect to his two Offices: and it is not rare that one Man has two Offices, one in the City and the other in the Province, or rather one in Title and the other by Commission. Thus *Oc-ya Pra-Sedet* who is Governor of the City of *Siam* in Title, is now *Oc-ya Barcalon* by Commission: the King of *Siam* finding it his interest, because that upon this account he gives not to one Officer a double Sallery.

The Equivocations which this causes in Relations.

But this Multiplication of Offices on the same Head causes a great deal of Obscurity and Equivocation in the ancient Relations of *Siam*; because that when a man has two Offices, he has two Titles, and two Names, and when the Relation imports that such an *Oc-ya* for example, is concerned in such a thing, one is inclined to believe that the Relation has stil'd this *Oc-ya* by the title of the function which it attributes to him, and frequently it has named him by the title of another Office. Thus if a Relation of the Kingdom of *France* made by a *Siamese* should intimate, that the Duke of *Maine* is General of the *Swiss*, the *Siamese* might groundlesly perswade themselves, that every General of the *Swiss* bears the Title of Duke of *Maine*. And this is what I had to say touching the People of *Siam*.

CHAP. III.

Of the Officers of the Kingdom of Siam *in general.*

The proper signification of the word *Mandarin*.

THE *Portuguese* have generally called all the Officers throughout the whole extent of the East *Mandarins*; and it is probable that they have formed this word from that of *Mandar*, which in their Language signifies to *command*. *Navarrete*, whom I have already cited, is of this opinion; and we may confirm it, because that the *Arabian* word *Emir*, which is used at the Court of the Great *Mogul* and in several other Mahometan Courts of the *Indies*, to signifie the Officers, is derived from the *Arabian* Verb *amara*, which signifies to *command*. The word *Manda-*

rin

Nai extends also to the Children of the Principal Officers, which are considered as Children of Quality, called *Mom* in *Siamese*. But I shall make use of the word *Mandarin*, only to signify the Officers.

The King of *Siam* gives Names to the considerable *Mandarins*.

The King of *Siam* therefore makes no considerable *Mandarin*, but he gives him a new Name; a Custom established also at *China*, and in other States of the East. This Name is always an *Elogium*; sometimes it is purposely invented, like that which he gave to the Bishop of *Metellopolis*, and like those which he gives to the Foreigners that are at his Court; but oftentimes these Names are ancient, and known for having been formerly given to others; and those are the most honourable, which have been heretofore born by persons very highly advanced in Dignity, or by the Princes of the Royal Blood. And although such Names be not always accompanied with Offices and Authority, they cease not to be a great Mark of Favour. It likewise happens that the same Name is given to several persons of different Dignities; so that at the same time the one, for example, will call himself, *Oc Pra Pipitcharacha*, and the other *Oc-Counne Pipitcharacha*. These Names, of which the first words are only spoken, and which do every one make a Period, are taken almost all entire out of the *Baly* Tongue, and are not always well understood: But this, and the Stile of the Laws, which participate very much of the *Baly*, and the Books of Religion, which are *Baly*, are the cause why the Kings of *Siam* ought not to ignore this Tongue. Forasmuch as, I have elsewhere said, it lends all its Ornaments to the *Siamese*, and that oftentimes they do elegantly intermix them, either in speaking or in writing.

All Offices are hereditary.

The Law of the State is, that all Offices should be hereditary; and the same Law is in the Kingdom of *Laos*, and was anciently at *China*. But the selling of Offices is not there permitted: and moreover the least fault of the Parent, or the capricious Humor of the Prince, or the Dotage of the Inheritor may take away the Offices from the Families, and when this happens it is always without Recompence. Very few Families do long maintain themselves therein, especially in the Offices of the Court, which are more than the rest under the Master's power.

The Profits of the Offices.

Moreover, no Officer at *Siam* has any Sallary. The Prince lodges them, which is no great matter; and gives them some moveables, as Boxes of Gold or Silver for *Betel*; some Arms, and a *Balon*; some Beasts, as Elephants, Horses, and Buffalo's; some Services, Slaves, and in fine some Arable Lands. All which return to the King with the Office, and which do principally make the King to be the Heir of his Officers. But the principal gain of the Offices consists in Extortions, because that in the them is no Justice for the weak. All the Officers do hold a correspondence in pillaging; and the Corruption is greatest in those from whence the Remedy ought to come. The Trade of Presents is publick; the least Officers do give unto the greatest, under a Title of Respect; and a Judge is not there punished for having received Presents, if otherwise he be not convicted of Injustice, which is not very easie to do.

The Oath of Fidelity.

The Form of the Oath of Fidelity consists in swallowing the water over which the *Talapoins* do pronounce some Imprecations against him, who is to drink it, in case he fails in the Fidelity which he owes to his King. This Prince dispenses not with this Oath to any persons that engage themselves in his Service, of what Religion or Nation soever.

The Publick Law of *Siam* is written.

The Publick Law of *Siam* is written in three Volumes. The first is called *Pra Tam Ra*, and contains the Names, Functions, and Prerogatives of all the Offices. The second is intituled, *Pra Tam Nun*, and is a Collection of the Constitutions of the Ancient Kings; and the third is the *Pra Raja Cammanot*, wherein are the Constitutions of the now Regent King's Father.

The difficulty of procuring the Books thereof.

Nothing would have been more necessary than a faithful extract of these three Volumes, rightly to make known the Constitution of the Kingdom of *Siam*: but so far was I from being able to get a Translation, that I could not procure a Copy thereof in *Siamese*. It would have been necessary upon this account to continue longer at *Siam*, and with less business. This is therefore what I could learn certainly about this matter, without the assistance of those Books, and in a Country where every one is afraid to speak. The greatest token of Servitude of the *Siameses* is, that they dare not to open their mouth about any thing that relates to their Country.

CHAP. IV.

Concerning the Offices of Judicatory.

The Division of the Kingdom of Siam by Provinces.

THE Kingdom of *Siam* is divided into the upper and lower. The upper lies towards the North, (seeing that the River descends from thence) and contains seven Provinces, which are named by their Chief Cities, *Porselouc*, *Sanquelouc*, *Lacontai*, *Campeng-pet*, *Coconrepina*, *Pechebonne*, and *Pitchai*. At *Porselouc* do immediately arise ten Jurisdictions, at *Sanquelouc* eight, at *Lacontai* seven, at *Campeng pet* ten, at *Coconrepina* five, at *Pechebonne* two, and at *Pitchai* seven. And besides this there are in the upper *Siam* one and twenty other Jurisdictions, to which no other Jurisdiction resorts; but which do resort to the Court, and are as so many little Provinces.

In the lower *Siam*, that is to say in the South part of the Kingdom, they reckon the Provinces of *Jor*, *Patana*, *Ligor*, *Tenasserim*, *Chantebonne*, *Petelong* or *Bardelong*, and *Tchiai*. On *Jor* do immediately depend seven Jurisdictions, on *Patana* eight, on *Ligor* twenty, on *Tenasserim* twelve, on *Chantebonne* seven, on *Petelong* eight, and on *Tchiai* two. And besides this, there are likewise in the lower *Siam* thirteen small Jurisdictions, which are as so many particular Provinces, which resort only to the Court, and to which no other Jurisdiction resorts. The City of *Siam* has its Province apart, in the heart of the State, between the upper and lower *Siam*.

The Governour is the Judge.

The whole Tribunal of Judicature consists properly only in a single Officer, seeing that it is the Chief or President only that has the deliberate voice, and that all the other Officers have only a consultative voice, according to the Custom received also at *China*, and in the other Neighbouring States. But the most important prerogative of the President is to be the Governour of his whole Jurisdiction, and to command even the Garrisons, if there be any; unless the Prince hath otherwise disposed thereof by an express order. So that as in other places these Offices are hereditary, it is no difficult matter for some of these Governours, and especially the most powerful, and for the most remote from Court, to withdraw themselves wholly or in part from the Royal Authority.

Jor belongs no more to the Kingdom of of Siam.

Thus the Governor of *Jor* renders Obedience no longer, and the *Portuguese* give him the Title of King. And it may be he never intends to obey, unless the Kingdom of *Siam* should extend it self, as Relations declare, to the whole *Peninsula extra Gangem*. *Jor* is the most Southern City thereof, seated on a River, which has its Mouth at the Cape of *Sincapura*, and which forms a very excellent Port.

Nor Patana.

The People of *Patana* live, like those of *Achem* in the Isle of *Sumatra*, under the Dominion of a Woman, whom they always elect in the same Family, and always old, to the end that she may have no occasion to marry, and in the name of whom the most trusty persons do rule. The *Portuguese* have likewise given her the Title of Queen, and for Tribute she sends to the King of *Siam* every three Years two small Trees, the one of Gold, the other of Silver, and both loaded with Flowers and Fruits; but she owes not any assistance to this Prince in his Wars. Whether these Gold and Silver Trees are a real Homage, or only a Respect to maintain the liberty of Commerce, as the King of *Siam* sends Presents every three Years to the King of *China*, in consideration of Trade only, is what I cannot alledge; but as the King of *China* honours himself with these sorts of Presents, and takes them for a kind of Homage, it may well be, that

that the King of *Siam* does not less value himself on the Presents he receives from the Queen of *Patana*, altho' she be not perhaps his Vassal.

The Governor is Lord.

The *Siameses* do call an Hereditary Governor *Tchaou-Meuang*; *Tchaou* signifies *Lord*, and *Meuang* a *City* or *Province*, and sometimes a *Kingdom*. The Kings of *Siam* have ruin'd and destroy'd the most potent *Tchaou-Meuang*, as much as they could, and have substituted in their place some Triennial Governors by Commission. These Commission-Governors are called *Pouran*, and *Pou* signifies a Person.

The Profits or Rights of the Tchaou-Meuang.

Besides the Presents which the *Tchaou-Meuang* may receive, as I have declar'd, his other legal Rights are,

First, Equally to share with the King the Rents that the arable Lands do yield, which they call *Na*, that is to say *Fields*; and according to the ancient Law, these Rents are a *Mayon*, or quarter part of a *Tical* for forty Fathom, or two hundred Foot square.

2dly, The *Tchaou-Meuang* has the profit of all Confiscations, of all the Penalties to the Exchequer, and ten *per Cent.* of all the Fines to the Party. The Confiscations are fixed by Law according to the Cases, and are not always the whole Estate, not even in case of sentence of Death; but sometimes also they extend to the Body, not only of the Person condemn'd, but of his Children too.

3dly, The King of *Siam* gives the *Tchaou-Meuang* some men to execute his Orders; they accompany him everywhere, and they row in his *Balon*. The *Siameses* do call them *Kenlai*, or *Painted Arms*; by reason that they pink and mangle their Arms, and lay Gunpowder on the Wounds, which paints their Arms with a faded Blew. The *Portugueses* do call them *Painted Arms*, and *Officers*; and these Painted Arms, are still used in the Country of *Laos*.

4thly, In the Maritime Governments, the *Tchaou-Meuang* sometimes takes Customs of the Merchant Ships, but it is generally inconsiderable. At *Tenasserim* it is eight *per Cent.* in the kind, according to the Relation of the Foreign Missions.

The Humanity of the Siameses towards those that have suffer'd Shipwrack.

Some have assur'd me, that the *Siameses* have the Humanity not to appropriate any thing to themselves of what the Tempest casts on their Coasts by Shipwrack; yet *Ferdinand Mendez Pinto* relates, that *Lewis de Montarroyo*, a *Portuguese*, having suffer'd Shipwrack on the Coast of *Siam* near *Patana*, the *Chabandar*, or Custom-house Officer, which he names *Chaim*, confiscated not only the Ship and its Cargo, but *Montarroyo* himself, and some Children; alledging, that by the ancient Custom of the Kingdom, whatever the Sea cast upon the Coasts, was the profit of his Office. 'Tis true, that this Author adds, with great Praises on the King of *Siam* who then reigned, that this Prince, at the Request of the *Portugueses* which were at his Court, set *Montarroyo* at liberty, and restor'd him all the Prize, and the Children; but he subjoins also that it was out of Charity, and on the day that this Prince went through the City mounted on a white Elephant, to distribute Alms to the People.

A continuance of the Rights or Profits of the Tchaou-Meuang.

5thly, The *Tchaou-Meuang* arrogating to themselves all the Rights of Soveraignty over the Frontiers, do levy, when they can, extraordinary Taxes on the People.

6thly, The *Tchaou-Meuang* do exercise Commerce every where, but under the name of their Secretary, or some other of their Domesticks. And this last Circumstance demonstrates that they have some shame, and that the Law perhaps prohibits them; but that in this they are not more scrupulous than their King.

7thly, In some places where there are Fish-ponds, the *Tchaou-Meuang* take the best of the Fish when the Pond is emptied; but he takes for his own use only, and not to sell, and the rest he leaves to the People.

8thly, Venison and Salt are free throughout the Kingdom, and the King himself has laid no Prohibition nor Impost thereon. Salt is there of little value. I have heard that they have Rock-salt, and they make it of Sea-water; some have told me with the Sun, others with Fire; and, perhaps, both is true. At the places where the Shoars are too high to receive the Sea, and in those, where Wood is not near at hand, the Salt may fail, or cost too much to make, as in the

the Island of *Jonsalam*, the Inhabitants whereof do rather chuse to import their Salt from *Tenasserim*.

The Rights or Profits of the *Pou-ran*.

The *Pou-ran*, or Governor by Commission, has the same Honours, and the same Authority as the *Tchaou-Meuang*, but not the same Profits. The King of *Siam* names the *Pou-ran* upon two Accounts, either when he would have no *Tchaou-Meuang*, or when the *Tchaou-Meuang* is obliged to absent himself from his Government; for the *Tchaou-Meuang* has no ordinary Lieutenant who can supply his place in his absence, as in *France* the Chancellor has none. In the first Case the *Pou-ran* has only the Profits which the King assigns him at naming him; in the second Case he takes the Moyety of the Profits from the *Tchaou-Meuang*, and leaves him the other Moyety.

The Names and Functions of the Officers which compose a Tribunal.

Now follows the ordinary Officers of a Tribunal of Judicature, not that there are so many in every one, but that in any one perhaps there is not more.

Oc-ya Tchaou-Meuang. The *Tchaou-Meuang* is not always *Oc-ya*, he has sometimes another Title, and the other Officers of his Tribunal have always some Titles proportion'd to his.

Oc-Pra Palat. His Name signifies *Second*, but he presides not in the absence of the *Tchaou-Meuang*, because he has no determinative Voice.

Oc-Pra Jockebat, a kind of Attorney-General, and his Office is to be a strict Spy upon the Governor. His Office is not Hereditary, the King nominates some person of Trust; but Experience evinces, that there is no Fidelity in these Men, and that all the Officers hold a private Correspondence to pillage the People.

Oc-Pra Peng commands the Garrison, if there is any, but under the Orders of the *Tchaou-Meuang*; and he has no Authority over his Soldiers, but when they are in the Field.

Oc-Pra Mahat-Thai, is, as it were, the Chief of the People. His Name seems to signifie the *Great Siamese*; for *Mahat* signifies *Great*, and *Tai* signifies *Siamese*. 'Tis he that levies the Soldiers, or rather that demands them of the *Nai*; who sends Provisions to the Army, who watches that the Rolls of the People be well made; and who, in general, executes all the Governor's Orders which concern the People.

Oc-Pra Sassedi makes and keeps the Rolls of the People. 'Tis an Office very subject to Corruption, by reason that every particular person endeavours to get himself omitted out of the Rolls for mony. The *Nai* do likewise seek to favor those of their Band, who make Presents to them, and to oppress those with labour who have nothing to give them. The *Mahat Tai*, and the *Sassedi*, would prevent this disorder, if they were not the first corrupted. The *Sassedi* begins to enter down Children upon the Rolls when they are three or four Years old.

Oc-Louang Meuang is, as it were, the Mayor of the City; for, as I have already said, *Meuang* signifies City; but as for what concerns the Title of *Oc-Louang*, it does not signifie *Mayor*, and is no more applied to that Office than another Title. This Mayor takes care of the Policy and Watch. They kept a Watch every Night round the Ambassador's Lodgings, as round the King of *Siam*'s Palace, and this was a very great Token of Honour.

Oc-Louang Vang is the Master of the Governor's Palace, for *Vang* signifies *Palace*. He causes it to be repair'd, he commands the Governor's Guards, and even their Captain; and, in a word, he orders in the Governor's Palace, whatever has relation to the Governor's charge.

Oc-Louang Peng keeps the Book of the Law and the Custom, according to which they judge; and when Judgment is passed, he reads the Article thereof, which serves for the Judgment of the Process: and, in a word, it is he that pronounces the Sentence.

Oc-Louang Clang has the Charge of the King's Magazine, *Clang* signifies *Magazine*. He receives certain of the King's Revenues, and sells to the People the King's Commodities, that is to say those, the Trade of which the King appropriates to himself, as in *Europe* the Princes do generally appropriate the Trade of Salt to themselves.

Oc-Lou-

Oc-Louang Cetta has the Inspection over Foreigners; he protects them, or accuses them to the Governor.

Moreover there are some Officers in every superior Tribunal to send to the inferior Justices, when the *Tchaou-Meuang* or *Pouran* are dead, whilst that the King fills the place: and the number of these Officers are as great as that of the inferior Justices.

Oc-Louang or *Oc-Counne Cong* is the Provost: he is always armed with a Sabre, and has *Painted Arms* like Archers.

Oc-Counne Pa-ya Bat is the Keeper of the Goal or Prisons: and the word *Pa-ya*, which the *Portugueses* have translated by that of *Prince*, seems exceedingly vilified in the Title of this Office. *Nai-Cuc* is the true Goaler, *Cuc* signifies a *Prison*, and nothing is more cruel than the Prisons of *Siam*. They are Cages of *Bambou* exposed to all the injuries of the Air.

Oc-Counne Narin commands those that have the care of the Elephants, which the King has in the Province: for there are some in several places, because it would be difficult to lodge and feed a very great number of Elephants together.

Oc-Counne Nai rang is the Purveyor of the Elephants. In a word, there is an Officer in every Tribunal to read the *Tara* or Orders from the King to the Governor, and an House in an eminent place for to keep them: As within the inclosure of the King of *Siam's* Palace there is a single House, on an eminent place, to keep all the Letters which the King of *Siam* receives from other Kings.

These are the Officers which are called from within. Besides these, there are others which are called from without, for the Service of the Province. All have an entire dependance upon the Governor; and altho those without have the like Titles, yet they are very inferior to the Officers within. Thus an *Oc-Meuang* within the Palace, is superior to an *Oc-ya* without; and in a word it is not necessary to believe that all those who bear great Titles, must always be great Lords: That infamous fellow who buys Women and Maids to prostitute them bears the Title of *Oc-ya*; he is called *Oc-ya Meen*, and is a very contemptible person. There are none but debauch'd persons that have any Correspondence with him. Every one of the Officers within has his Lieutenant, in *Siamese Balat*, and his Register in *Siamese Smien*, and in his House, which the King gives him, he has generally an Hall to give his Audiences.

An Important distinction as to Officers within and Officers without.

CHAP. V.

Of the Judiciary Stile and Form of Pleading.

They have only one Stile for all matters in Law, and they have not thought fit to divide them into Civil and Criminal; either because there is always some punishment due to him that is cast, even in a matter purely Civil, or because that suits in matters purely Civil are very rare there.

They have not a double Stile.

'Tis a general Rule amongst them, that all Process should be in writing, and that they plead not without giving Caution.

They plead only in writing and by giving Bail.

But as the whole People of the Jurisdiction is divided by Bands, and that their principal *Nai* are the Officers of the Tribunal, whom I shall call by the general name of Councellors; in case of process the Plaintiff goes first to the Councellor who is his *Nai*, or to his Country-*Nai*, who goes to the Councellor *Nai*. He presents him his Petition, and the Councellor presents it to the Governor. The Duty of the Governour is nicely to examin it; and to admit or reject it, according as to him it seems just or unjust; and in this last case to Chastise the Party, who presented it, to the end that no person might begin any process rashly, and this is likewise the Stile or form of *China*, but it is little observed at *Siam*.

The Function of the *Nai* in Law Suits.

How a Process is prepared at Siam.

The Governor then admits the Petition, and refers it to one of the Councellors; and ordinarily he remains it to him that presented it, if he is the common *Nai* of both parties: but then he puts his Seal thereunto, and he counts the lines and the cancelling thereof, to the end that no alteration may be made. The Councellor gives it to his Deputy and to his Clerk, who make their report to him at his House in his Hall of Audience: And this report, and all those which I shall treat of in the sequel, are only a Lecture. After this the Councellor's Clerk presented by his Master, reports or reads this very Petition, in the Governour's Hall, at an Assembly of all the Councellors; but in the absence of the Governor, who vouchsafes not to appear at whatever serves only to prepare the Cause. The Parties are there called in under pretence of endeavouring to reconcile them: and they are summon'd three times, more for fashions sake, than with a sincere intention of procuring the accommodation. This Reconciliation not succeeding, the Court orders, if there are witnesses, that they should be heard before the same Clerk, unless he be declared suspected. And in such another Session, that is to say, where the Governor is not present, the Clerk reads the Process and the depositions of the Witnesses, and they proceed to the Opinions, which are only consultative, and which are all writ down, beginning with the Opinion of the last Officer.

The Form of the Judgment.

The Process being thus prepar'd, and the Council standing in presence of the Governor, his Clerk reads unto him the Process and the Opinions; and the Governor, after having resumed them all, interrogates those whose Opinions seem to him not just, to know of them upon what reasons they grounded them. After this Examination he pronounces in general terms, that such of the Parties shall be condemned according to the Law.

The Law or Custom is read.

Then it belongs to *Ok-Louang-Peng* to read with a loud voice the Article of the Law, which respects the fact: but in that Country, as in this, they dispute the sense of the Laws. They do there seek out some accommodations under the title of Equity; and under pretence that all the circumstances of the fact are never in the Law, they never follow the Law. The Governour alone decides these disputes, and the Sentence is pronounced upon the parties, and set down in Writing. But if it be contrary to all appearance of Justice, it belongs to the *Jokebat*, or the Kings Attorney General, to advertise the Court thereof, but not to oppose it.

Suits are a long time depending.

Every suit ought to end in three days, and some there are which last three years.

They have no Advocate nor Attorney.

The parties do speak before the Clerk, who writes down what they tell him; and they speak either by themselves, or by another: but it is necessary that this other, who herein performs the office of an Attorney or Advocate, should be at least Cousin German to him for whom he speaks; otherwise he would be punished, and not heard.

Before whom they produce.

The Clerk receives likewise all the Titles and Deeds, but in presence of the Court, who counts all the lines thereof.

Proofs subsidiary to the Torture.

When ordinary proofs do not suffice, they have recourse to Torture in Accusations, which are very grievous upon this account; and they apply it rigorously, and in several ways: or rather they use the proofs of Water and of Fire, or of some others as superstitious, but not of Duelling.

The Proof of the Fire.

In the Proof of Fire they erect a Pile of Faggots in a Ditch, in such a manner that the surface of the Pile be level with the edge of the Ditch. This Pile is five fathoms long, and one broad. Both the parties do walk with their naked Feet from one end to the other, and he that has not the sole of his Feet hurt gains his Suit. But as they are accustomed to go with naked Feet, and that they have the sole of the Foot hard like Horn, they say that it is very common that the Fire spares them, provided they rest the Foot upon the Coals: for the way to burn themselves is to go quick and lightly. Two men do generally walk by the side of him that passes over the Fire, and they lean with force upon his Shoulders, to hinder him from getting too quick over this proof and it is said that this weight is so far from exposing him more to be burnt, that on the contrary he stifles the Action of the Fire under his Feet.

Some-

Another sort of Proof by Fire.

Sometimes the proof of the Fire is performed with Oil, or other boiling matter, into which the parties do thrust their hand. A *Frenchman*, from whom a *Siamese* had stole some Tin, was perswaded, for want of proof, to put his hand into the melted Tin; and he drew it out almost consumed. The *Siamese* being more cunning extricated himself, I know not how, without burning; and was sent away absolved: and yet six Months after, in another Suit, wherein he was engaged, he was convicted of the Robbery, wherewith the *Frenchman* had accused him. But a Thousand such like events perswade not the *Siameses* to change their form.

The Proof of the Water.

The Proof of the Water is performed after this manner. The two parties do plunge themselves into the Water at the same time, each holding by a Pole, along which they descend; and he that remains longest under Water is thought to have a good Cause. Every one therefore practises from their Youth, in this Country, to familiarize himself with Fire, and to continue a long time under Water.

A Proof by Vomits.

They have another sort of Proof, which is performed by certain Pills prepared by the *Talapoins*, and accompanied with Imprecations: Both the parties do swallow them, and the token of the right Cause is to be able to keep them in the Stomach without casting them up, for they are vomitive.

The various successes of their Proofs.

All these Proofs are not only before the Judges, but before the People, and if the two parties do escape equally well, or equally ill with one, they have recourse to another Tryal. The King of *Siam* uses them also in his Judgments, but besides this he sometimes delivers up the parties to Tygers, and he whom the Tygers spare for a certain time is adjudged innocent. But if the Tygers devour them both, they are both esteemed guilty. If on the contrary the Tygers do meddle neither with the one nor the other, they have recourse to some other Proof, or rather they wait till the Tygers determine to devour one or both of the Parties. The Constancy with which it is reported that the *Siameses* do undergo this kind of death, is incredible in persons, who express so little Courage in War.

The Degrees of Appeal.

There are sometimes several Provinces which appeal one to the other; which multiplies the degrees of Appeal to three or four. An Appeal is permitted in all cases, but the charges thereof are always greater, as it is necessary to travel further to plead, and in a Tribunal superior.

Judgment of Death reserved to the Prince, or to some extraordinary Commissioners.

But when there ought to pass the sentence of Death, the decision thereof is reserved to the King alone. No other Judge than himself can order a capital punishment, if this Prince does not expresly grant him the power thereof; and there is hardly any precedent, that he grants it otherwise than to some extraordinary Judges, whom this Prince sends sometimes into the Provinces, either upon a particular case, or to execute Justice at the places of all the crimes worthy of death. All the Criminals are kept in the Prisons till the arrival of the Commissioners: and they have sometimes, as at *China*, the power of deposing and punishing the ordinary Officers with death, if they deserve it. But if the King of *Siam* grants other Commissions for his Service, or for the Service of the State, it is rare that he exempts the Commissioner from taking the assistance of the Governor of the places where he sends him.

The Punishment of Robbery extended to Estates.

The usual Punishment of Robbery is the Condemnation to the double, and sometimes to the triple; by equal portions to the Judge and Party: But it is most singular in this, that the *Siameses* extend the Punishment of Robbery to every unjust Possessor in a Real Estate: So that whoever is evicted out of an Inheritance by Law, not only restores the Inheritance to the Party, but likewise pays the value thereof, half to the Party, and half to the Judge. But if by the King's special permission the Judge can put the Robber to death, then he can at his own discretion order either Death, or the pecuniary Mulct, but not Death and the pecuniary Mulct together.

But to shew how dear Justice is in a Country, where Provisions are so cheap, I will add at the end of this work, a Note that was given me of the charges of Justice, where you will likewise see a particular of the form: but the charges are not the same in all the Tribunals, as I have already declared. He for whom

this

this Roll is, has four inferior Jurisdictions, and he appeals to another, which appeals to the Court.

CHAP. VI.

The Functions of the Governor and Judge in the Metropolis.

The King is the Tchaou-Meuang of the Metropolis.

IN the *Metropolis*, where there is no other *Tchaou-Meuang* than the King, the Functions of Governor and Judge are divided into two Offices; and the other Functions of the lesser Offices, which compose a Tribunal of *Tchaou-Meuang*, are distributed to the principal Officers of the State; but with greater Extent and Authority, and with higher and more pompous Titles.

The Office of Ommarat, which they pronounce Ommarat.

The President of the Tribunal of the City of *Siam*, to whom all the Appeals of the Kingdom do go, they call *Ommarat*. He generally bears the Title of *Oc-ya*, and his Tribunal is in the King's Palace; but he follows not the King, when that Prince removes from his *Metropolis*; and then he renders Justice in a Tower, which is in the City of *Siam*, and without the inclosure of the Palace. To him alone belongs the determinative Voice; and from him there also lyes an Appeal to the King, if any one will bear the expence.

The Judiciary form before the King.

In this case the Process is referred and examined by the King's Council; but in his absence to a Sentence inclusively consultative, as is practised in the Council of the *Tchaou-Meuang*. The King is present only when it is necessary that he pronounce a definitive Judgment; and according to the general form of the Kingdom, this Prince, before passing the Sentence, reforms all the opinions and debates with his Counsellors, those which to him seem unjust; and some have assured me, that the present King acquits himself herein with a great deal of Ingenuity and Judgment.

The Office of Pra-sedet, which is pronounced Pra-sedet.

The Governor of the City of *Siam* is called *Pra-sedet*, and generally also bears the Title of *Oc-ya*. His Name, which is *Bali*, is composed of the word *Pra*, which I have several times explained, and of the word *Sedet* which signifies, to go out, *the King is gone*; and indeed they speak not otherwise, to say that the King is gone. But this does not sufficiently explain what the Office of *Pra-sedet* is; and in several things it appears, that they have very much lost the exact understanding of the *Bali*. Mr. *Gervaise* calls this Office *Pesedet*; I always heard it called *Pra-sedet*, and by able men, altho they write it *Pra-sadet*.

The Reception which the Government gave to the King's Ambassadors, each in its own Government.

The course of the River from its Mouth to the *Metropolis*, is divided into several small Governments. The first is *Pipeli*, the second *Prapadam*, the third *Bancok*, the fourth *Talacoan*, and the fifth *Siam*. The Officers of every one of these Governments received the King's Ambassadors at the entrance into their Jurisdiction, and they left them not till the Officers of the next Jurisdiction had joyned and saluted them; and they were the particular Officers of each Government that made the Head of the Train. Besides this there were some Officers more considerable, that came to offer the King their Master's *Balon* to the Ambassadors, at the Mouth of the River; and every day there joyned new Officers, that came to bring new Compliments to the Ambassadors; and who quitted not the Ambassadors after they had joined them.

The place where the King's Ambassadors expected the day of their entrance.

The King's Ambassadors arrived thus within two Leagues of *Siam*, at a place which the *French* called the *Tabanque*; and they waited there eight or ten days for the time of their entrance into the *Metropolis*. *Tabanque* in *Siamese* signifies the *Custom House*; and because the Officer's House, which stands at the Mouth of the River, is of *Bambou* like all the rest, the *French* gave the name of *Tabanque* to all the Bambou-houses where they lodged, from the name of the Officers House, which they had seen first of all.

The

The day therefore that the King's Ambassadors made their enterance, *Oc-ya Prasedet* as Governour of the Metropolis came to visit, and compliment them at this pretended *Tabanque*. The Governor of Siam came to visit them.

CHAP. VII.

Of the State Officers, and particularly of the Tchacry, Calla-hom, *and of the* General *of the* Elephants.

AMongst the Court Officers are principally those, to whom are annexed the Functions of our Secretaries of State: but before an enterance be made into this matter, I must declare that all the chief Officers in any kind of Affairs whatever, have under them as many of those Subaltern Officers which compose the Tribunal of the *Tchaou-Meuang*. Of the chief Officers in general.

The *Tchacry* has the distribution of all the Interior polity of the Kingdom; to him revert all the Affairs of the Provinces: All the Governours do immediately render him an Account, and do immediately receive Orders from him: he is President of the Council of State. Of the *Tchacry*.

The *Calla-hom* has the appointment of the War: he has the care of the Fortifications, Arms, and Ammunitions: He issues out all the Orders, that concern the Armies, and he is naturally the General thereof, altho the King may name whom he pleases for General. By *Van Vliet's* Relation it appears that the Command of the Elephants belonged also to the *Calla-hom*, even without the Army. But now this is a separate Employment, as some have assured me: either for that the present King's Father, after having made use of the Office of the *Calla-hom* to gain the Throne, resolved to divide the Power thereof, or that naturally they are two distinct Offices, which may be given to a single Person. Of the *Calla-hom*.

However it be, 'tis *Oc-Pra Pipitcharatcha* corruptly called *Petratcha*, who commands all the Elephants, and all the Horses: and it is one of the greatest Employments of the Kingdom, because that the Elephants are esteemed the King of *Siam*'s Principal Forces. Some there are who report that this Prince maintains Ten Thousand, but is impossible to be known, by reason that Vanity always inclines these People to Lying: and they are more vain in the matter of Elephants, than in any thing else. The Metropolis of the Kingdom of *Laos* is called *Lan Tchang*, and its name in the Language of the Country, which is almost the same as the *Siamese*, signifies *The Millions of Elephants*. The King of *Siam* keeps therefore a very great number: and it is said that three men at least are required for the service of every Elephant: and these men, with all the Officers that command them, are under the orders of *Oc-Pra Pipitcharatcha*: who though he has only the Title of *Oc-Pra*, is yet a very great Lord. The people love him because he appears moderate; and think him invulnerable, because he express'd a great deal of Courage in some Fight against the *Peguins*: his Courage has likewise procur'd him the Favour of the King his Master. His Family has continued a long time in the highest Offices: is frequently allied to the Crown; and it is publickly reported that he or his Son *Oc-Louang Sorasac* may pretend to it, if either of them survive the King that now Reigns. The Mother of *Oc-Pra Pipitcharatcha* was the King's Nurse, and the Mother of the first Ambassador whom we saw here; and when the King commanded the great *Barcalon*, the Brother of this Ambassador, to be bastinado'd the last time, 'twas *Oc-Louang Sorasac* the Son of *Oc-Pra Pipitcharatcha* that bastinado'd him by the King's order, and in his presence, the Prince's Nurse, the Mother of the *Barcalon*, lying prostrate at his Feet, to obtain pardon for her Son. Of the General of the Elephants.

CHAP. VIII.

Concerning the Art of War amongst the Siameses, *and of their Forces by Sea and Land.*

The Siameses not proper for War.

THE Art of War is exceedingly ignor'd at *Siam*: the *Siameses* are little inclined to this Trade. The over-quick imagination of the excessive hot Countries, is not more proper for Courage, than the slow imagination of Countries extreamly cold. The sight of a naked Sword is sufficient to put an hundred *Siameses* to flight; there needs only the assured Tone of an *European*, that wears a Sword at his side, or a Cane in his hand, to make them forget the most express Orders of their Superiors.

How contemptible the men in the Indies are as to their Courage.

I say moreover, that every one born in the *Indies* is without Courage; although he be born of *European* Parents. And the *Portugueses* born in the *Indies* have been a real proof thereof. A society of *Dutch* Merchants found in them only the Name and the Language, and not the Bravery of the *Portugueses*: and if other *Europeans* went to seek out the *Dutch*, they would not be found more Valorous. The best constituted men are those of the Temperate Zones: and amongst these the difference of their common aliments, and of the places which they inhabit, more or less hot, dry or moist, exposed to the Winds or to the Seas, Plains or Mountains, Woods or Champains, and much more the several Governments do cause very great differences. For who doubts, for example, that the Antient *Greeks*, brought up in liberty, where incomparably more Valorous then the present *Greeks*, depressed by so long a Servitude? All these reasons do concur to effeminate the Courage of the *Siameses*, I mean the heat of the Climate, the flegmatick Aliments, and the Despotick Government.

The Siameses abhor blood.

The Opinion of the *Metempsychosis* inspiring them with an horror of blood, deprives them likewise of the Spirit of War. They busie themselves only in making Slaves. If the *Peguins*, for example, do on one side invade the lands of *Siam*, the *Siameses* will at another place enter on the Lands of *Pegu*, and both Parties will carry away whole Villages into Captivity.

How in fighting they disguise the design of killing their Enemies.

But if the Armies meet, they will not shoot directly one against the other, but higher: and yet as they endeavour to make these random Shots to fall back upon the Enemies, to the end that they may be overtaken therewith, if they do not retreat, one of the two Parties does not long defer from taking flight, upon perceiving it never so little to rain Darts or Bullets. But if the design be to stop the Troops that come upon them, they will shoot lower than it is necessary; to the end that if the Enemies approach, the fault may be their own in coming within the reach of being wounded or slain. *Kill not* is the order, which the King of *Siam* gives his Troops, when he sends them into the Field: which cannot signifie that they should not kill absolutely, but that they shoot not directly upon the Enemy.

How the King of Singor was taken by a Frenchman.

Some have upon this account informed me a thing, which in my opinion, will appear most incredible. 'Tis of a provincial named *Cyprien*, who is still at *Surat* in the *French* Company's Service, if he has not quitted it, or if he is not lately dead: the name of his Family I know not. Before his entrance into the Companies service, he had served some time in the King of *Siam's* Army in quality of Cannoneer; and because he was prohibited from shooting strait, he doubted not that the *Siamese* General would betray the King his Master. This Prince sending afterwards some Troops against the *Tchiam-Meuang*, or if you will, against the King of *Singor*, on the western Coast of the Gulph of *Siam*, *Cyprien* wearied with seeing the Armies in view, which attempted no persons life, determin'd one night to go alone to the Camp of the Rebels, and to fetch the King of *Singor* into his Tent. He took him indeed, and brought him to the *Siamese* General, and so terminated a War of above twenty years. The King of of *Siam* intended to recompence this service of *Cyprian* with a quantity of *Sapan-wood*; but by some intrigue of Court he got nothing, and retir'd to *Surat*.

The Siameses have little to fear from their Neighbours.

Now though the *Siameses* appear to us so little proper for War, yet they cease not to make it frequently and advantageously, by reason that their Neighbours are neither more potent nor more valiant than them.

The King of Siam has no other Troops maintain'd than his foreign Guard.

The King of *Siam* has no other Troops maintained than his foreign Guard, of which I will speak in the sequel. 'Tis true that the Chevalier *de Fourbin* had showed the Exercise of Arms to four hundred *Siameses*, which we found at *Bancock*; and that after he had quitted this Kingdom, an Englishman, who had been a Sergeant in the Garrison of *Madras-patan*, on the Coast of *Coromandel*, showed this same exercise, which he had learnt under the Chevalier *de Fourbin*, to about eight hundred other *Siameses*, to show the King of *Siam* that the Chevalier *de Fourbin* was not necessary to him. But all these Soldiers have no other pay, than the Exemption from the six Months Service for some of their Family. And as they cannot easily maintain themselves from their own Houses, by reason they receive no money, they remain at their own Habitations; the four hundred about *Bancock*, and the other eight hundred at *Louvo*, or thereabouts. Only for the security of *Bancock* some Detachments went thither by turns to keep a continual Guard, and the rest being thereabouts might render themselves in case of an Alarm. But according to the common practice of the Kingdom of *Siam*, the Garrisons which it may have, are composed of persons, who serve in this by six Months, as they should serve in another thing; and who are relieved by others when they have served their full time.

The Country of Siam is very strong without Forts.

The Kingdom of *Siam* being very strong by its impenetrable Woods, and by the great number of Channels, wherewith it is interspersed, and in fine by the annual Inundation of six Months, the *Siameses* would not hitherto have places well fortified for fear of losing them, and not being able to retake them; and this is the reason they gave me thereof. The Castles they have would hardly sustain the first shock of our Soldiers; and though they be small and ugly, because they would have them such, yet is it necessary to employ the skill of the *Europeans* to delineate them.

The Siameses know not how to make a wooden Fort.

'Tis some years since the King of *Siam* designing to make a wooden Fort on the Frontier of *Pegu*, had no abler a person to whom he could entrust the care thereof, than to one named Brother *René Charbonneau*, who after having been a Servant of the Mission of S^t^. *Lazarus* at *Paris*, had passed to the Service of the Foreign Missions, and was gone to *Siam*. Brother *René*, who by his Industry knew how to let blood, and give a Remedy to a sick Person (for it is by such like charitable Employments, and by some presents, that the Missionaries are permitted and loved in this Country) defended himself as much as he could from making this Fort, protesting that he was not capable: but in short he could not prevent rendering obedience, when it was signified to him that the King of *Siam* absolutely requir'd it. He was afterwards three or four years Governor of *Jonsalam* by Commission, and with great approbation: and because he desired to return to the City of *Siam* to his Wife's Relations, which are *Portugueses*, Mr. *Billi*, the Master of Mr. *de Chaumont*'s Palace, succeeded him in the Employment of *Jonsalam*.

Of their Artillery.

The *Siameses* have not much Artillery. A *Portuguese* of *Macao*, who died in their service, cast them some pieces of Cannon; but as for them, I question whether they know how to make any moderately good: though some have informed me that they have hammered some out of cold Iron.

In what their Armies consist.

As they have no Horses (for what is two thousand Horse at most, which 'tis reported that the King of *Siam* keeps?) their Armies consist only in Elephants, and in Infantry, naked and ill armed, after the mode of the Country. Their order of Battel and Encampment is thus.

What is their order of battle and of their Encampment.

They range themselves in three lines, each of which is composed of three great square Battalions; and the King, or the General whom he names in his absence, stands in the middle Battalion, which he composes of the best Troops, for the security of his Person. Every particular Captain of a Battalion keeps himself also in the midst of the Battalion which he commands: and if the nine

Battali-

Battalions are too big, they are each divided into nine less, with the same Symmetry as the whole body of the Army.

Elephants of War.

The Army being thus ranged, every one of the nine Battalions has sixteen male Elephants in the rear. They call them Elephants of War; and each of these Elephants carries his particular standard, and is accompanied with two female Elephants; but as well females as males are mounted each with three armed Men; and besides this the Army has some Elephants with Baggage. The *Siamoses* report that the female Elephants are only for the dignity of the males; but as I have already declared in the other part, it would be very difficult always to govern the males without the Company of the females.

The Artillery begins the Fight.

The Artillery, at the places where the River grows shallow, is carried on Waggons drawn by Buffalo's, or Oxen, for it has no carriage. It begins the Fight, and if it ends it not, then they place themselves within reach to make use of the small shot, and Arrows, after the manner as I have explained, but they never fall on with vigour enough, nor defend themselves with constancy enough, to come to a close Fight.

The *Siamoses* easie to break, and to rally.

They break themselves and fly into Woods, but ordinarily they rally with the same facility as they are broken; and if on some occasion, as in the last Conspiracy of the *Macassars*, it is absolutely necessary to stand firm, they can promise themselves to retain the Soldiers, only by placing some Officers behind, to kill those that shall fly. I have elsewhere related how these *Macassars* made use of Opium to endow themselves with Courage; 'tis a custom practised principally by the *Rajipouts*, and the *Moors*, but not by the *Siamoses*: the *Siamoses* would be afraid to become too Couragious.

Elephants not proper for War.

They very much rely upon the Elephants in Combats, though this Animal for want of Bit or Bridle, cannot be securely governed, and he frequently returns upon his own Masters when he is wounded. Moreover he so exceedingly dreads the fire, that he is never almost accustomed thereunto. Yet they exercise them to carry, and to see fired from their back little pieces about three foot long, and about a pound of Balls and *Bernier* reports that this very practice is observed in the *Mogul*'s Country.

The *Siamoses* incapable of Sieges.

As for Sieges they are wholly incapable thereof, for men that dare not set upon the Enemies when in view, will not vigorously attack a place never so little Fortified, but only by Treachery, in which they are very cunning, or by Famine, if the Besieged cannot have provision.

Their weakness by Sea.

They are yet more feeble by Sea than by Land. Not without much ado the King of *Siam* hath five or six very small Ships, which he principally makes use of for Merchandises, and sometimes he arms them as Privateers against those of his Neighbours, with whom he is at War. But the Officers and Seamen, on whom he confides, are Foreigners; and till these latter times he had chosen *English* and *Portuguese*: but within these few years he hath employed some *French*. The King of *Siam*'s Intention is, that his Corsairs should kill no person, no more than his Land Forces, but that they use all the Tricks imaginable to take some Prizes. In his War at Sea, he proposes to himself only some Reprizals from some of his Neighbours, from whom he believes himself to have received some injury in Trade. And the contrivances succeed whilst his Enemies are not in any distrust. Besides this he has fifty or sixty Galleys, whose Anchors, I have said, are of Wood. They are only moderate Boats for a Bridge, which do every one carry fifty or sixty men to Row and to Fight. These men do fight by turns, as in every thing else: There is only one to each Oar; and he is obliged to Row standing, because the Oar is so short, for lightness sake, that it would not touch the water, if not held almost perpendicular. These Gallies only coast it along the Gulph of *Siam*.

I

CHAP.

CHAP. IX.

Of the Barcalon, *and of the Revenues.*

Of the Barcalon.

THe *Pra-Clang*, or by a corruption of the *Portugueses*, the *Barcalon*, is the Officer which has the appointment of the Commerce, as well within as without the Kingdom. He is the Superintendent of the King of *Siam's* Magazines, or if you will, his chief Factor. His name is composed of the *Balie* word *Pra*, which I have so often discoursed of, and of the word *Clang*, which signifies Magazine. He is the Minister of the foreign affairs, because they almost all relate to Commerce; and 'tis to him that the fugitive Nations at *Siam* address themselves in their affairs, because 'tis only the liberty of Trade that formerly invited them thither. In a word, it is the *Barcalon* that receives the Revenues of the Cities.

The King of Siam's Revenues arise from two Sources.

The King of *Siam's* Revenues are of two sorts, Revenues of the Cities, and Revenues of the Country. The Country Revenues are received by *Oc-ya Pollatep*, according to some, or *Forthep*, according to Mr. *Gervaise*.

They are all reduced to the Heads following.

His Duties on cultivated Lands.

1. On Forty Fathom Square of cultivated Lands, a *Mayon* or quarter of a *Tical* by year: but this Rent is divided with the *Tchaou-Meuang* where there is one; and it is never well paid to the King on the Frontiers. Besides this, the Law of the Kingdom is, that whoever ploughs not his ground pays nothing, though it be by his own negligence that he reaps nothing. But the present King of *Siam* to force his Subjects to work, has exacted this duty from those that have possessed Lands for a certain time, although they omit to cultivate them. Yet this is executed only in the places where his Authority is absolute. He loved nothing so much, as to see Strangers come to settle in his States, there to manure those great uncultivated Spaces, which without comparison do make the most considerable part thereof: in this case he would be liberal of untilled grounds, and of Beasts to cultivate them, though they had been cleared and prepared for Tillage.

On Boats.

2. On Boats or *Balons*, the Natives of the Country pay a *Tical* for every Fathom in length. Under this Reign they have added that every *Balon* or Boat above six Cubits broad should pay six *Ticals*, and that Foreigners should be obliged to this duty, as well as the Natives of the Country. This duty is levied like a kind of Custom at certain places of the River, and amongst others at *Tchainat*, four Leagues above *Siam*, where all the Streams unite.

Customs.

3. Customs on whatever is imported or exported by Sea. Besides which, the body of the Ship pays something in proportion to its Capacities, like the *Balons*.

On Arek.

4. On *Arek* or Rice-Brandy, or rather on every Furnace where it is made, which they call *Tau-Lau*, the People of the Country do pay a *Tical per Annum*. This Duty has been doubled under this Reign, and is exacted on the Natives of the Country, and on Strangers alike. 'Tis likewise added, that every Seller of *Arek* by retail, should pay a *Tical* a year, and every Seller by whole sale, a *Tical per Annum* for every great Pot, the size of which I find no otherwise described in the Note which was given me.

On Durions.

5. On the Fruit called *Durion*, for every Tree already bearing, or not bearing Fruit, two *Mayons* or half a *Tical per annum*.

On Betel.

6. On every Tree of *Betel*, a *Tical per Annum*.

On the Arek.

7. On every *Arekier* they formerly paid three Nuts of *Arek* in kind: under this Reign, they pay six.

New Imposts.

8. Revenues entirely new, or established under this Reign, are in the first place, a certain Duty on a School of Recreation permitted at *Siam*. The Tribute which the *Oc-ya Meen* pays, is almost of the same Nature, but I know not whether it is not ancienter than the former. In the second place, on every Coco-

Tree, half a *Tical per Annum*; and in the third place on Orange-Trees, Mango-Trees, Mangoustaniers and Pimentiers, for each, a *Tical per Annum*. There is no duty on Pepper, by reason that the King would have his Subjects addict themselves more to plant it.

A Demesn reserved to the King.

9. This Prince has in several places of his States some Gardens and Lands, which he causes to be cultivated, as his particular demesn, as well by his Slaves, as by the six Months Service. He causes the Fruits to be gathered and kept on the places, for the maintenance of his House, and for the nourishment of his Slaves, his Elephants, his Horses, and other Cattle; and the rest he sells.

10. A Casual Revenue is the Presents which this Prince receives, as well as all the Officers of his Kingdom, the Legacies which the Officers bequeath him at their death, or which he takes from their Succession; and in fine, the extraordinary Duties, which he takes from his Subjects on several occasions: as for the Maintenance of Foreign Ambassadors, to which the Governors, into whose Jurisdiction the Ambassadors do pass, or sojourn, are obliged to contribute; and for the building of Forts, and other publick works, an expence which he levies on the People, amongst whom these works are made.

Confiscations and Fines. Six Months Service.

11. The Revenues of Justice do consist in Confiscations and Fines.

12. Six Months service of every one of his Subjects *per Annum*: a Service which he or his Officers frequently extend much further, who alone discharges it from every thing, and from which there remains to him a good Increase. For in certain places this Service is converted into a payment made in Rice, or in Sapan-wood, or Lignum-aloes, or Salpetre, or in Elephants, or in Beasts Skins, or in Ivory, or in other Commodities: and in fine, this Service is sometimes esteemed and paid in ready Money: and it is for the ready Money that the Rich are exempted. Anciently this Service was esteemed at a *Tical* a Month, because that one *Tical* is sufficient to maintain one Man: and this composition serves likewise as an assessment on the days Labour of the Workmen, which a particular Person employs. They amount to two *Ticals* a Month at least, by reason that it is reckon'd that a Workman must in 6 Months gain his Maintenance for the whole year, seeing that he can get nothing the other six Months' that he serves the Prince. The Prince now exacts two *Ticals* a Month for the exemption from the six Months Service.

Commerce, a Revenue extraordinary or casual.

13. His other Revenues do arise from the Commerce, which he exercises with his Subjects and Foreigners. He has carried it to such a degree, that Merchandise is now no more the Trade of particular persons at *Siam*. He is not contented with selling by Whole-sale, he has some Shops in the Bazars or Markets, to sell by Retail.

Cotton-cloath.

The principal thing that he sells to his Subjects is Cotton-cloaths; he sends them into his Magazines of the Provinces. Heretofore his Predecessors and he sent them thither only every Ten Years, and a moderate quantity, which being sold, particular persons had liberty to make Commerce thereof: now he continually furnishes them, he has in his Magazines more than he can possibly sell, and it sometimes happens that to vend more, that he has forced his Subjects to cloath their Children before the accustomed Age. Before the *Hollanders* came into the Kingdom of *Laos*, and into others adjacent, the King of *Siam* did there make the whole Commerce of Linnen with a considerable profit.

The Calin or Tin.

All the *Calin* is his, and he sells it as well to Strangers as to his own Subjects, excepting that which is dug out of the Mines of *Jonsalam* on the Gulph of *Bengal*: for this being a remote Frontier, he leaves the Inhabitants in their ancient Rights, so that they enjoy the Mines which they dig, paying a small profit to this Prince.

Ivory, Saltpeter, Lead, Sapan.

All the Ivory comes to the King, his Subjects are obliged to vend him all that they sell, and Strangers can buy only at his Magazine. The Trade of Saltpetre, Lead and Sapan, belongs also to the King: they can buy and sell them only at his Magazine, whether one be a *Siamese* or Stranger.

Arek.

Arek, a great deal of which is exported out of the Kingdom, can be sold to Foreigners only by the King: and for this end he buys some of his Subjects, besides that which he has from his particular Revenues.

Pro-

Prohibited Goods.

Prohibited Goods, as Powder, Sulphur and Arms, can be bought or sold at *Siam*, only at the King's Magazine.

Skins of Beasts.

As to the Skins of Beasts, this Prince is obliged, by a Treaty made with the *Hollanders*, to sell them all to them; and for this purpose he buys them of his Subjects: but his Subjects do convey away a great many, which the *Hollanders* buy of them in secret.

The Commerce free to all persons.

The rest of the Commerce at *Siam* is permitted to all, as that of Rice, Fish, Salt, Brown Sugar, Sugar-Candy, Ambergreese, Wax, the Gum with which Varnish is made, Mother of Pearl, those edable Birds Nests which come from *Tunquin* and *Cochinchina*, which *Navarette* reports to be made of the Sea-froth in some Rocks, by a kind of small Sea-Birds, which resemble Swallows, Gumme Gutte, Incense, Oyl, Coco, Cotton, Cinnamon, Nenuphar, which is not exactly like ours; Cassia, Dates, and several other things, as well the growth of the Kingdom, as brought from abroad.

Salt, Fishing, Hunting.

Every one may make and sell Salt; fish and hunt, as I have declared, and without paying any thing to the King. It is true, that the necessary Policy is used in Fishing; and *Oc-Pra Tainam*, who receives the particular Revenues of the River, hinders those ways of Fishing, which destroy too much Fish at once.

To what Sum the King of Siam's Revenues amount.

The King of *Siam* has never been well paid his Revenues in lands remote from his Court. 'Tis said that the ready Money that he formerly received, amounted to Twelve hundred thousand Livres, and that what he now gets amounts to Six hundred thousand Crowns, or to Two Millions. 'Tis a difficult thing to know exactly: all that I can assert is, that in this Country it is reported (as a thing very considerable, and which seems Hyperbolical) that the present King of *Siam* has augmented his Revenues a Million.

CHAP. X.

Of the Royal Seal, and of the Maha Obarat.

There is no Chancellor at Siam. The King gives not his Seal to any person.

There is no Chancellor at *Siam*. Every Officer that has the Power of giving the Sentences, or Orders in Writing, which they call *Tra* in general, has a Seal which the King gives him: and the King himself has his Royal Seal, which he commits to no person whatever, and of which he makes use for the Letters he writes, and for whatever proceeds immediately from him. The Figure which is in the Seals, is not hollow, but in Relievo. The Seal is rub'd over with a kind of Red Ink, and is printed on the Paper with the Hand. An inferior Officer takes this Pains; but 'tis the duty of the Officer to whom the Seal belongs, to pluck it with his own Hand from the Print.

Of the Maha-Obarat.

After several remarks, which I have made, it seems to me, that whatever is done in the King of *Siam's* Name has no Power, if it is not done at the place where this King actually resides. Certain reasons have hindered, why they have not certainly inform'd me thereof. However, it is certain, that for the reason which I have alledged, or for some other, there is at *Siam* as it were a Vice-Roy, who represents the King, and performs the Regal Functions in the King's Absence; as when this Prince is at War. This Officer is called *Maha Obarat*, as it was given me in writing, or *Oumarat*, according to the Abbot *de Choisy*, and Mr. *Gervaise*. And the Abbot *de Choisy* adds, that the *Maha Oumarat* has a right of sitting down in the King's Presence, a Circumstance which some have informed me to be peculiar to another Officer, of whom I shall speak in the sequel. At present they give him the Title of *Pa-ya*, and they do thereunto add the word *Tchaou*, which signifies *Lord*; *Tchaou Pa-ya Maha Oumarat*: Sometimes he has only the Title of *Oc-ya*, as in *Vliet's* Relation, where he is called *Oc-ya Oumarat*. He is thereunto qualified as Chief of the Nobility, which signifies nothing, but the first Officer of the Kingdom.

CHAP.

CHAP. XI.

Of the Palace, and of the King of Siam's Guards.

Officers within and without.

IT now remains for me to speak of the King, and of his House. This Prince's Palace has its Officers within, and its Officers without; but so different in dignity, that an *Oc-Mening* within commands all the *Oc-ya* without. They call Officers within, not only those which lodge always in the Palace, but those whose functions are exercised in the Palace: And they call Officers without the Palace, not all the Officers of the Kingdom, which have no Function in the Palace, but those which having no Function in the Palace, yet have not any without which respects not the Service of the Palace. Thus the *Spaniards* have Servants, which they call *de Escalera arriba*, and others which they call *de Escalera abaxo*, that is to say Servants at the top of the Stairs, or which may go up the Stairs to their Master, and to those to whom their Master sends them, and others who wait always at the bottom of the Stairs.

Three Inclosures in the King of Siam's Palace.

The King of *Siam*'s Palaces have three Inclosures; and that of the City of *Siam* has them so distant one from the other, that the space thereof appears like vast Courts. All that the inward Close includes, *viz.* the King's Apartment, some Court, and some Garden, is called *Vang* in *Siamese*. The whole Palace with all its Inclosures is called *Prasat*, though *Vliet* in the Title of his Relation translates the word *Prasat* by that of Throne. The *Siameses* neither enter into the *Vang*, nor depart thence without prostrating themselves, and they pass not before the *Prasat*. And if sometimes the stream of the Water carries them, and forces them to pass thereby, they are pelted with showers of Pease, which the King's Servants shoot over them with Trunks. Mr. *de Chaumont* and the King's Ambassadors landed, and left their Umbrella's at the first entrance of the *Prasat*.

Of the Oc-ya Vang.

The *Oc-ya Vang* commands in the *Vang*; and in him centres all the Functions which respect the Reparations of the Palace, the Order which must be observed in the Palace, and the Expence which is made for the Maintenance of the King, of his Wives and of his Eunuchs, and of all those whom this Prince maintains in the *Vang*. 'Twas the *Oc-ya Vang* who, after the Example of all the other Governours, which had received the King's Ambassadors at the entrance of their Government, came to receive them at the Gate of the *Vang*; and who introduced them to the Audience of the King his Master.

The Gates of the Palace, and of the precautions with which persons are admitted.

The Gates of the Palace are always shut; and behind each stands a Porter, who has some Arms, but who instead of bearing them, keeps them in his Lodge near the Gate. If any one knocks, the Porter advertises the Officer, who commands in the first Inclosure, and without whose permission no person enters in, nor goes out: but no person enters armed, nor after having drunk *Arak*, to assure himself that no drunken man enters therein. Wherefore the Officer views, and smells the breath of all those that must enter therein.

The Mening Tchion.

This Office is double, and those that are in it do serve alternately and by day. The days of Service they continue twenty four whole hours in the Palace, and the other days they may be at home. Their Title is *Oc-Mening Tchion*, or rather *Pra Mening Tchion*: for at the Palace before the word *Mening* there are some who put the word *Pra* instead of *Oc*, though some have told me that it is *Oc-Mening*, and not *Pra-Mening* that he must be always called. 'Twas one of these *Mening Tchion* who brought the first Compliment from the King of *Siam* to the Ambassadors, when they were in the Road; and who stayed constantly with them after they were landed, as Mr. *Torff*, continued always with the Ambassador of *Siam*.

Painted Arms.

Between the two first Inclosures, and under a Pent-house, is a small number of Soldiers unarmed and squatting. They are those *Kenlai* or *Painted Arms*, of whom I have spoken. The Officer who commands them immediately, and who is a Painted-Arm himself, is called *Ongarac*, and he and they are the Prince's Execu-

Executioners; as the Officers and Soldiers of the *Pretorian* Cohorts, were the Executioners of the *Roman* Emperors. But at the same time they omit not to watch the Prince's person; for in the Palace there is wherewith to arm them in case of need. They row the *Balon* of State, and the King of *Siam* has no other Foot-guard. Their Employment is hereditary, like all the rest of the Kingdom; and the ancient Law imports that they ought not to exceed six hundred: But this must doubtless be understood that there ought to be no more than six hundred for the Palace; for there must needs be many more in the whole extent of the State; because that the King, as I have said elsewhere, gives thereof to a very great number of Officers.

A Guard of Slaves for a Show.

But this Prince is not contented with this Guard on days of Ceremony, as was that of the first Audience of the King's Ambassadors. On such occasions he causes his Slaves to be armed; and if their number is not sufficient, the Slaves of the principal Officers are armed. He gives to them all some Muslin Shirts dyed red, Muskets, or Bows, or Lances, and Pots of gilded wood on their Heads, which for this purpose are taken out of the Magazine: and the quantity of which, in my opinion, determines the number of these Soldiers of show. They formed a double Rank at the reception of Mr. *de Chaumont*; and so soon as he was past, those which he had left behind, made haste to get before by the by-ways, to go to fill up the vacant places which were left for them. In our time they marched by the sides of the Ambassadors, till they stopt up the space through which they were to pass. We also found part of these Slaves prostrate before the little Stairs, which go up to the Hall of Audience. Some held those little useless Trumpets, which I have spoken of; and others had before them those little Drums, which they never beat. The *Mendin Tchion* are the *Nai* of all these Slaves; and these Slaves row the *Balons* of the King's retinue, and are moreover employed on several works.

The King of *Siam* has no standing *Japonese* Guard.

Anciently the Kings of *Siam* had a *Japonese* Guard, composed of six hundred men: but because these six hundred men alone, could make the whole Kingdom to tremble when they pleased, the present King's Father, after having made use of them to invade the Throne, found out a way to rid himself of them, more by policy than force.

The Horse-Guard from *Meen*, and *Laos*.

The King of *Siam*'s Horse-guard is composed of Men from *Lao*, and another neighbouring Country, the chief City whereof is called *Meen*: and as the *Meens* and *Laos* do serve him by six Months, he makes this Guard as numerous as he pleases, and as many Horse as he would employ therein.

Oc-Coune Ran Patchi commands this Guard on the right hand: His Son is in *France*, and has for some years learnt the Trade of a Fountain-maker at *Trianon*. *Oc-Coune Pipitcharatcha*, or as the People say, *Oc Coune Petratcha*, commands the half of this Guard, which serves on the left hand: but over these two Officers *Oc-ya Lao* commands the Guard of the *Laos*, and *Oc-ya Meen* the Guard of the *Meens*: and this *Oc-ya Meen* is a different person from him that prostitutes lewd Women.

A Foreign Horse-Guard.

Besides this the King of *Siam* has a foreign standing Horse-guard, which consists in an Hundred and Thirty Gentlemen: but neither they, nor the *Meens*, nor the *Laos*, do ever keep Guard in the Palace. Notice is given them to accompany the King when he goes out, and thereat this is esteemed the exterior Service, and not the interior Service of the Palace.

Of what it is composed.

This foreign Guard consists, first in two Companies of thirty *Moors* each, Natives, or originally descended from the States of the *Mogul*, of an excellent Meen, but accounted Cowards. Secondly, in a Company of twenty *Chinese Tartars* armed with Bows and Arrows, and formidable for their Courage; and lastly in two Companies of Twenty five Men each, Pagans of the true *India*, habited like the *Moors*, which are called *Rasbouts*, or *Ragipouts*, who boast themselves to be of the Royal blood, and whose Courage is very famous, though it be only the effect of Opium, as I have before remarked.

What it costs.

The King of *Siam* supplies this whole Guard with Arms, and with Horses: and besides this every *Moor* costs him three *Catis* and twelve *Tials* a year, that is to say 540 *Livres*, or thereabouts, and a red Stuff Vest; and every of the their *Moorish* Captains five *Catis* and twelve *Tails*, or 840 *Livres*, and a Scarlet Vest. The *Ragipoutes* are maintained according to the same rate; but every *Chinese Tartar* costs him only six *Tails*, or 45 *Livres* a year, and their Captain fifteen *Tails*, or 112 *Livres*, ten *Sols*.

The Elephants and Horses of the Palace.

In the first Inclosures are likewise the Stables of the Elephants and Horses, which the King of *Siam* esteems the best, and which are called Elephants and Horses by *Name*; because that this King gives them a Name, as he gives to all the Officers within his Palace, and to the important Officers of the State, which in this are very much distinguished from the Officers on whom he imposes none. He that hath the care of the Horses, either for their maintenance, or to train them up, and who is as it were the chief Querry, is called *Oc Louang Tchioumpou*; his *Balat*, or Lieutenant is *Oc-Meuang Si Sing Tong Pa-tchai*; but he alone has the Priviledge of speaking to the King: Neither his *Balat* nor his other inferior Officers do speak unto him.

The Elephants of Name.

The Elephants of *Name* are treated with more or less Dignity, according to the more or less honourable Name they bear; but every one of them has several Men at his Service. They stir not out, as I have elsewhere declared, without trappings; and because that all the Elephants of Name cannot be kept within the Compass of the Palace, there are some which have their Stables close by.

Of the White Elephant.

These People have naturally so great an esteem of Elephants, that they are perswaded that an Animal so noble, so strong, and so docile, can be animated only with an illustrious Soul, which has formerly been in the body of some Prince, or of some great Person: but they have yet a much higher Idea of the White Elephants. These Animals are rare, and are found, say they, only in the Woods of *Siam*. They are not altogether White, but of a flesh colour, and for this reason it is that *Vliet* in the Title of his Relation has said, the White and Red Elephant. The *Siameses* do call this colour *Peuak*, and I do not not that it is this colour inclining to White, and moreover so rare in this Animal, which has procured it the Veneration of those People to such a degree, as to perswade them what they report thereof, that a Soul of some Prince is always lodged in the body of a White Elephant, whether Male or Female it matters not.

The Esteem which the *Siameses* do make of the White colour in Animals.

By the same reason of the colour, White Horses are those which the *Siameses* most esteem. I proceed to give a proof thereof. The King of *Siam* having one of his Horses sick, intreated M^r. *Vincent*, that Physician which I have frequently mentioned, to prescribe him some Remedy. And to perswade him to it (for he well knew that the *European* Physicians debased not themselves to meddle with Beasts) he acquainted him that the Horse was *Mogol* (that is to say White) of four races by Sire and Dam, without any mixture of *Indian* blood; and that had it not been for this consideration he would not have made him this request. The *Indians* call the White, *Mogols*, which they distinguish into *Mogols* of *Asia*, and *Mogols* of *Europe*. Therefore whence soever this respect is for the White colour, as well in Men as in Beasts, I could discover no other reason at *Siam*, than that of the veneration which the *Siameses* have for the White Elephants. Next to the White they most esteem those which are quite Black, because they are likewise very rare; and they Dye some of this colour, when they are not naturally Black enough. The King of *Siam* always keeps a White Elephant in his Palace, which is treated like the King of all those Elephants, which this Prince maintains. That which Mr. *de Chaumont* saw in this Country, was dead, as I have said, when we arrived there. There was born another as they reported on the 9th of *December* 1687, a few days before our departure: but this Elephant was still in the Woods, and received no Visit, and so we saw no White Elephant. Other Relations have informed us how this Animal is served with Vessels of Gold.

The King of *Siam's Balons*.

The Care of the King's *Balons*, and of his Gallies, belongs to the *Calla-hom*. Their Arsenal is over against the Palace, the River running between. There every one of these Barges is lock'd up in a Trench, whereinto runs the Water of the River; and each Trench is shut up in an Inclosure made of Wood, and covered. These Inclosures are locked up, and besides this a person watches there at Night. The *Balons* of ordinary Service are not so secured as those for

Cere-

Ceremony; and amongst those for Ceremony there are some which the King gives to his Officers for these occasions only; for those which he allows them for ordinary Ceremonies, are less curious and fine.

CHAP. XII.

Of the Officers which nearest approach the King of Siam's *Person.*

IN the *Vang* are some of those single Halls which I have described; in which the Officers do meet, either for their Functions, or to make their Court, or to wait the Orders of the Prince.

In what place of the Palace the Courtiers wait.

The usual place were he shows himself unto them, is the Hall, where he gave Audience to the King's Ambassadors; and he shows himself only through a Window, as did antiently the King of *China*. This Window is from a higher Chamber, which has this prospect over the Hall, and which may be said to be of the first Story. It is nine Foot high or thereabouts; and it was necessary to place three steps underneath, to raise me high enough to present the King's Letter to the King of *Siam*. This Prince chose rather to cause these three steps to be put, than to see himself again obliged to stoop, to take the King's Letter from my hand, as he had been obliged to do, to take that which Mr. *de Chaumont* deliver'd him. 'Tis evident by the Relation of Mr. *de Chaumont*, that he had in his hands a kind of Gold Cup, which had a very long handle of the same matter; to the end that he might use it to give the King's Letter to the King of *Siam*. He did it, but he would not take this Cup by the handle to raise the Letter; so that it was necessary that the King of *Siam* should stoop out of the Window to receive it. 'Tis with the same Cup, that the Officers of this Prince deliver him every thing that he receives from their hands. At the two Corners of the Hall which are at the sides of this Window, are two doors about the heighth of the Windows, and two pair of very narrow Stairs to ascend. For the Furniture there is only three *Umbrellas*, one before the Window with nine rounds, and two with seven rounds on both sides of the Window. The *Umbrella* is in this Country as the *Dais* or Canopy is in *France*.

How the King of Siam shows himself to them.

'Tis in this Hall that the King of *Siam's* Officers, which if you please, may be named from his Chamber, or rather his Antichamber, do expect his Orders. He has Forty four young men, the oldest of which hardly exceeds twenty five years of Age: the *Siamese* do call them *Mahatlek*, the *Europeans* have called them *Pages*. These Forty four Pages therefore are divided into four Bands, each consisting of eleven: the two first are on the right hand, and do prostrate themselves in the Hall at the King's right hand; the two others are on the left hand, and do prostrate themselves on the left hand. This Prince gives them every one a Name and a Sabre; and they carry his Orders to the Pages without, which are numerous, and which have no Name, that is imposed on them by the King. The *Siameses* do call them *Cabang*, and 'tis these *Cabangs* that the King ordinarily sends into the Provinces upon Commissions, whether ordinary, or extraordinary.

The King of Siam's Pages.

Besides this the Forty four Pages within have their Functions regulated. Some, for example, do serve Betel to the King, others take care of his Arms, others do keep his Books, and when he pleases they read in his presence.

Their Functions.

This Prince is curious to the highest degree. He caused *Q. Curtius* to be translated into *Siamese*, whilst we were there, and has since order'd several of our Histories to be translated. He understands the States of *Europe*; and I doubt not thereof, because that once, as he gave me occasion to inform him that the Empire of *Germany* is Elective, he asked me whether besides the Empire and

How the King of Siam loves Reading.

Poland,

Poland, there was any other Elective State in *Europe*? And I heard him pronounce the word *Polonia*, of which I had not spoken to him. Some have assur'd me that he has frequently affirmed, that the Art of Ruling is not inspired, and that with great Experience and Reading he perceived that he was not yet perfect in understanding it. But he design'd principally to study it from the History of the King: he is desirous of all the News from *France*; and so soon as his Ambassadors were arrived, he retained the third with him, until he had read their Relation to him from one end to the other.

The Officers which command the Pages within.

To return to the Forty-four Pages, Four Officers command them; who, because they so nearly approach the Prince, are in great esteem, but yet not in an equal degree: for there is a great difference from the first to the second, from the second to the third, and from the third to the fourth. They bear only the Title of *Oc-Meuing*, or of *Pra-Meuing*: *Meuing Vai*, *Meuing Sarapet*, *Meuing Semmengrabat*, *Meuinghi*. The Sabres and Poniards which the King gives them are adorned with some precious Stones. All four are very considerable *Nai*, having a great many subaltern Officers under them; and though they have only the Title of *Meuing*, they cease not to be Officers in chief. The *Paya*, the *Oc-ya*, the *Oc-pra*, and the other Titles are not always subordinate to them, only the one must command more persons than the other. In a word, 'twas *Meuinghi* which accompany'd *Meuing Tchion* on Board our Ships, to bring to the King's Ambassadors the first Compliment from the King of *Siam*, and it was to him that *Meuing Tchion*, tho' higher in dignity, gave the precedency and the word; because that *Meuinghi* was three or four years older, but the eldest of both was not thirty.

Of the single Officer which prostrates not himself before the King of Siam.

Whilst the Ambassadors were at Audience, there was in one place an Officer, whom we perceived not, who alone, as they informed me, has the Priviledge of not prostrating himself before the King his Master; and this renders his Office very honourable. I forgot to write down his Title in my Memoirs. He always has his Eyes fixed upon this Prince, to receive his Orders, which he understands by certain Signs, and which he signifies by Signs to the other Officers which are without the Hall. Thus when the Audience was ended, I wou'd say when the King had done speaking to us, this Prince, in that silence which is profound, gave some Signal, to which we gave no heed; and immediately at the bottom of the Hall, and in an high place, which is not visible, was heard a tinkling Noise, like that of a Timbrel. This Noise was accompany'd with a Blow, which was ever and anon struck on a Drum, which is hung up under a Penthouse without the Hall, and which for being very great, renders its sound grave and Majestic; it is cover'd with an Elephant's Skin: yet no person made any motion, till that the King, whose Chair an invisible hand did by little and little draw back, removed himself from the window, and closed the Shutters thereof; and then the Noise of the tinkling and of the great Drum ceased.

CHAP. XIII.

Of the Women of the Palace, and of the Officers of the Wardrobe.

The King of Siam's Chamber.

As to the King of *Siam*'s Chamber, the true Officers thereof are Women, 'tis they only that have a Priviledge of entering therein. They make his Bed, and dress his Meat; they cloath him and wait on him at Table: but none but himself touches his Head when he is attir'd, nor puts any thing over his Head. The Pourveyors carry the Provisions to the Eunuchs, and they give them to the Women; and she which plays the Cook, uses Salt and Spices only by weight, thereby never to put in more nor less: A practice, which, in my opinion, is only a Rule of the Physicians, by reason of the King's unhealthy disposition, and not an ancient custom of the Palace.

The

Of the late Queen his Wife and his Sister.

The Women do never stir out but with the King, nor the Eunuchs without express Order. 'Tis reported that he has eight or ten Eunuchs only, as well white as black. The late Queen, who was both his Wife and his Sister, was called *Nang Achamalisi*. It is not easie to know the King's Name, they carefully and superstitiously conceal it, for fear lest any Enchantment should be made on his Name. And others report, that their Kings have no Name till after their death, and that it is their Successor which names them, and this would be more certain against the pretended Sorceries.

Of the Princess his only Daughter.

Of Queen *Achamalisi* is born, as I have related in the other Part, the Princess, the King of *Siam's* only Daughter, who now has the Rank and House of a Queen. The King's other Wives (which in general are called *Tchaou Vang*, because that the word *Tchaou*, which signifies *Lord*, signifies likewise *Lady* and *Mistress*) do render Obedience to her, and respect her as their Soveraign. They are subject to her Justice, as well as the Women and Eunuchs which serve them; because that not being able to stir out, to go plead elsewhere, it necessarily follows that the Queen should judge them, and cause them to be chastised, to keep them in peace. This is thus practised in all the Courts of *Asia*; but it is not true neither at *Siam*, nor perhaps in any part of the East, that the Queen has any Province to govern. 'Tis easie also to comprehend, that if the King loves any of his Ladies more than the rest, he causes her to remove from the Jealousie and harsh Usage of the Queen.

The King of *Siam* takes the Daughters of his Subjects for his Palace, when he pleases.

At *Siam* they continually take Ladies for the service of the *King*, or to be Concubines to the King, if this Prince makes use thereof. But the *Siamese* deliver up their Daughters only by force, because it is never to see them again; and they redeem them so long as they can for Money. So that this becomes a kind of Extortion; for they designedly take a great many Virgins merely to restore them to their Parents, who redeem them.

He has few Mistresses.

The King of *Siam* has few Mistresses, that is to say eight or ten in all, not out of Continency, but Parsimony. I have already declared, that to have a great many Wives, is in this Country rather Magnificence, than Debauchery. Wherefore they are very much surprized to hear that so great a King as ours has no more than one Wife, that he had no Elephants, and that his Lands bear no Rice; as we might be, when it was told us that the King of *Siam* has no Horses, nor standing Forces, and that his Country bears no Corn nor Grapes, altho' all the Relations do so highly extol the Riches and Power of the Kingdom of *Siam*.

The Queen's House.

The Queen hath her Elephants and her Balons, and some Officers to take care of her, and accompany her when she goes abroad; but none but her Women and Eunuchs do see her. She is conceal'd from all the rest of the People; and when she goes out either on an Elephant, or in a Balon, it is in a Chair made up with Curtains, which permit her to see what she pleases, and do prevent her being seen: And Respect commands, that if they cannot avoid her, they should turn their back to her, by prostrating themselves when she passes along.

Her Magazine and her Ships.

Besides this she has her Magazine, her Ships, and her Treasures. She exercises Commerce; and when we arrived in this Country, the Princess, whom I have reported to be treated like a Queen, was exceedingly embroiled with the King her Father, because that he reserved to himself alone almost all the Foreign Trade, and that thereby she found herself deprived thereof, contrary to the ancient Custom of the Kingdom.

Of the Succession to the Crown, and the Causes which render it uncertain.

Daughters succeed not to the Crown, they are hardly look'd upon as free. 'Tis the eldest Son of the Queen that ought always to succeed by the Laws. Nevertheless because that the *Siamese* can hardly conceive that amongst Princes of near the same Rank, the most aged should prostrate himself before the younger; it frequently happens that amongst Brethren, tho' they be not all Sons of the Queen, and that amongst Uncles and Nephews, the most advanced in Age is preferred, or rather it is Force which always decides it. The Kings themselves contribute to render the Royal Succession uncertain, because that instead of chusing for their Successor the eldest Son of the Queen, they most frequently follow the Inclination which they have for the Son of some one of their Concubines with whom they were enamour'd.

The occasion which rendred the Hollanders Masters of Bantam.

'Tis upon this account that the King of *Bantam*, for example, has lost his Crown and his Liberty. He endeavoured to get one of his Sons, whom he had by one of his Concubines, to be acknowledged for his Successor before his Death: and the eldest Son which he had by the Queen put himself into the hands of the *Hollanders*. They set him upon the Throne after having vanquished his Father, whom they still keep in Prison, if he is not dead: but for the reward of this Service they remain Masters of the Port, and of the whole Commerce of *Bantam*.

Of the Succession to the Kingdom of China.

The Succession is not better regulated at *China*, though there be an express and very ancient Law in favour of the eldest Son of the Queen. But what Rule can there be in a thing, how important soever it be, when the Passions of the Kings do always seek to imbroil it? All the Orientals, in the choice of a Governor, adhere most to the Royal Family, and not to a certain Prince of the Royal Family: uncertain in the sole thing wherein all the *Europeans* are not. In all the rest we vary every day, and they never do. Always the same Manners amongst them, always the same Laws, the same Religion, the same Worship; as may be judged by comparing what the Ancients have writ concerning the *Indians*, with what we do now see.

Of the King of Siam's Wardrobe.

I have said that 'tis the Women of the Palace which dress the King of *Siam*; but they have no charge of his Wardrobe; he has Officers on purpose. The most considerable of all is he that touches his Bonnet, altho he be not permitted to put it upon the Head of the King his Master. 'Tis a Prince of the Royal blood of *Camboya*; by reason that the King of *Siam* boasts in being thence descended, not being able to vaunt in being of the race of the Kings his Predecessors. The Title of this Master of the Wardrobe is *Oc-ya Out haya tamé*, which sufficiently evinces that the Title of *Pa-ya* does not signifie *Prince*, seeing that this Prince wears it not. Under him *Oc-Pra Raja Vanefa* has the charge of the cloaths. *Raja* or *Raja* or *Ragi* or *Raicha*, are only an *Indian* term variously pronounced, which signifies King, or *Royal*, and which enters into the composition of several Names amongst the *Indians*.

CHAP. XIV.

Of the Customs of the Court of Siam, *and of the Policy of its Kings.*

The Hours of Council.

THe common usage of the Court of *Siam* is to hold a Council twice a day; about Ten a clock in the Morning, and about Ten in the Evening, reckoning the hours after our fashion.

The division of the day and night according to the Siameses.

As for them they divide the day into Twelve hours from the Morning to the Night: The Hours they call *Mong*: they reckon them like us, and give them not a particular name to each, as the *Chineses* do. As for the Night, they divide it into four Watches, which they call *Tgiam*, and it is always broad Day at the end of the Fourth. The *Latins*, *Greeks*, *Jews*, and other people have divided the Day and Night, after the same manner.

Their Clock.

The People of *Siam* have no Clocks but as the Days are almost equal there all the Year, it is easie for them to know what Hour it is, by the sight of the Sun. In the King's Palace they are a kind of Water-Clock: 'Tis a thin Copper Cup, at the bottom of which they do make an almost imperceptible hole. They put it quite empty upon the water: which by little and little enters therein through the hole; and when the Cup is full enough to sink down, this is one of the hours, or a twelfth part of the day. They measure the Watches of the Night by such a like method, and they make a Noise on Copper Basons when the Watch is ended.

I have

I have related how Causes are determined in the King of *Siam*'s Council: Affairs of State are there examined, and decided almost after the same manner. That Councellor to whom this Prince has committed a business, makes the report thereof, which consists in reading it, and then proceeds to the consultative Opinions; and hitherto the King's Presence is not necessary. When he is come he hears the report, which is read to him concerning the former Consult, he resumes all the advices, confutes those which he approves not, and thus decides. But if the Affair seems to him to merit a more mature deliberation, he makes no decision: but after having proposed his difficulties, he commits the examination thereof to some of his Council, whom he purposely appoints; and principally to those who were of a different Opinion from his. They, after having again consulted together, do cause the report of their new Consultation to be made by one of them, in a full Council, and before the King; and hereupon this Prince consummates his Determination. Yet sometimes, but very rarely, and in affairs of a certain Nature, he will consult the principal *Sancrats*, which are the Superiors of the *Talapoins*; whose credit in other matters he depresses as much as he can, though in appearance he honors them exceedingly. In a word, there is such a sort of affairs, wherein he will call the Officers of the Provinces: but on all occasions, and in all affairs, he decides when he pleases; and he is never constrained to either ask advice of any person, or to follow any other advice than his own.

How the King of *Siam* examines Affairs in his Council, and how he terminates them.

He oftentimes punishes ill Advice, or recompences good. I say good or bad according to his sense, for he alone is the Judge thereof. Thus his Ministers do much more apply themselves to divine his sentiments, than to declare him theirs, and they misunderstand him, by reason he also endeavours to conceal his Opinion from them.

He punishes bad Counsels, and recompences good.

In a word, the affair on which he consults them, is not always a real concern; 'tis sometimes a question, which he propounds to them by way of exercise.

Sometimes he consults about Affairs invented by way of Exercise.

He likewise has a custom of examining his Officers about the *Pra-Tam-Ra*, which is that Book, which I have said contains all their Duties; and causes such to be chastized with the Bastinado, who answer not very exactly; even as a Father chastizes his Children in instructing them.

He examines his Officers about their Obligations.

'Tis an ancient Law of the State established for the security of the King, whose Authority is naturally almost unarmed, that the Courtiers should not render him any visit without his express leave, and only at Weddings and Funerals, and that when they meet, they should speak with a loud voice, and in the presence of a third person: but if the Kings of *Siam* be unactive, or negligent, not any Law secures them. At present the Courtiers may appear again at the Academy of Sports, where the great number seems to take away all opportunity of Caballings.

A Law against the Ambition of the Great Men.

The Trade of an Informer, so detested in all places where men are born free, is commanded to every person at *Siam*, under pain of death for the least things; and so whatever is known by two Witnesses, is almost infallibly related to the King: because that every one hastens to give information thereof, for fear of being herein prevented by his Companion, and remain guilty of Silence.

The Trade of an Informer commanded at *Siam* by the Law.

The present King of *Siam* relies not in an important affair upon the single report of him to whom he has committed it; but neither does he rely also on the report of a single Informer. He has a number of secret Spies, whom he separately interrogates; and he sometimes sends more than one to interrogate those who have acted in the affair, whereof he would be informed.

The King of *Siam*'s Precaution to prevent being deceived.

And yet it is easie for him to be deceived; for throughout the Country every Informer is a dishonest man, and every dishonest man is an Infidel. Moreover Flattery is so great in *India*, that it has persuaded the *Indian* Kings, that if it is their interest to be informed, it is their dignity to hear nothing that may displease them. As for example, they will not tell the King of *Siam*, that he wants Slaves or Vassals, for any enterprize he would go about. They will not tell him that they cannot perform his Commands: but they execute them ill, and when the mischief appears, they will excuse it by some defect. They will tell him

Why they are frequently ineffectual.

him all news quite otherwise than it is; to the end that the truth reaching his Ears only by degrees, may vex him less, and that it might be easier to pacifie him at several times. They will not counsel him a bad thing; but will so insinuate it, that he may think himself the Author, and only take to himself the bad success. And then they will not tell him that he must alter a thing that he has done amiss; but they will persuade him to do it better some other way, which will only be a pretence: and in the new project they will suppress, without acquainting him, what they designed to reform, and will put in the place what they designed to establish. I my self have seen part of what I relate, and and they have assured me the rest.

The King of Siam's rigorous Justice.

Now such like Artifices are always very perilous; they offend the present King in nothing without being punished. Being severe to extream rigour, he puts to death whom he pleases without any formality of Justice, and by the hand of whom he pleases, and in his own Presence: And sometimes the Accuser with the Criminal, the Innocent with the Calumniator: for when the proofs remain doubtful, he, as I have said, exposes both parties to the Tygers.

How he insults over the dead body.

After the Execution he insults over the dead body with some words, which are a lesson to the living; as for example, after having made him who had robbed his Magazine, to swallow some melted Silver, he says to the dead body, Miserable wretch, thou hast robb'd me of Ten Pieces of Silver, and Three Ounces only are sufficient to take away thy life. Then he complains that they with-held him not in his Anger; either that he indeed repents sometimes of his precipitate Cruelties, or that he would make believe that he is cruel only in the first Transport.

The Various Punishments of the Court of Siam.

Sometimes he exposes a Criminal to an enraged Bull, and the Criminal is armed with a hollow stick, consequently proper to cause fear, but not to wound, with which he defends himself some time. At other times he will give the Criminal to Elephants, sometimes to be trampled under foot and slain, sometimes to be tossed without killing: for they affirm that the Elephants are docible to that degree, and that if a Man is only to be tossed, they throw him one to the other, and receive him on their Trunck, and on their Teeth, without letting him fall on the ground. I have not seen it, but I cannot doubt of the manner which they have assured me.

The Punishments have respect to the Crimes.

But the Ordinary Chastisements are those, which have some relation to the Nature of the Crimes. As for example, Extortion exercised on the People, and a Robbery committed on the Prince's Money, will be punished by the swallowing of Gold or Silver melted: Lying, or a Secret revealed, will be punished by Sowing up the Mouth. They will slit it to punish Silence, where it is not to be kept. Any Fault in the execution of Orders, will be Chastised by pricking the Head, as to punish the Memory. To prick the Head, is to cut it with the edge of a Sabre: but to manage it securely, and not to make too great wounds, they hold it with one hand by the Back, and not by the Handle.

The punishment of the Sword and the Cudgel.

The punishment of the Glave or Sword is not executed only by cutting the Head off, but by cutting a man through the middle of the Body: And the Cudgel is sometimes also a punishment of death. But when the Chastisement of the Cudgel ought not to extend to death, it ceaseth not to be very rigorous, and frequently to cause the loss of all knowledge.

The Punishment with which Princes are punished.

If the matter is to put a Prince to death in form, as it may happen, or when a King would rid himself of some of his Relations, or when an Usurper would extinguish the race, from which he has ravish'd the Crown, they make it a piece of Religion not to shed the Royal blood: but they will make him to die with hunger, and sometimes with a lingring hunger, by daily substracting from him something of his food: or they will stifle him with Rich Stuffs, or rather they will stretch him on Scarlet, which they mightily esteem, because the Wool is rare, and dear; and there they will thrust into his Stomach a billet of Sanders Wood. This Wood is odoriferous, and highly esteem'd. There are three sorts; the white is better than the yellow, and both do grow only in the Isles of *Solor* and *Timor*, to the East of *Java*. The red is esteemed the least of all, and it grows in several places.

The

The extreme distrust of the Kings of Siam.

The Kings of *Asia* do place their whole security in rendering themselves formidable, and from time out of mind they have had no other Policy: whether that a long Experience has evinced that their People are uncapable of Love for their Sovereign; or that these Kings would not be advised that the more they are fear'd, the more they have to fear. However it be, the extream distrust in which the Kings of *Siam* do always live, appears sufficiently in the cares which they take to prevent all secret Correspondence amongst the great Men, to keep the Gates of their Palace shut, and to permit no armed person to enter, and to disarm their own Guards. A Gun fired, by accident or otherwise, so near the Palace that the King hears it, is a capital Crime; and the noise of a Pistol being heard in the Palace, a little after the Conspiracy of the *Macassers*, 'twas doubted whether the King had not with this shot killed one of his Brothers; because that the King alone has power to shoot, and that moreover one of his Brethren had been suspected of having mix'd in this Conspiracy: and this doubt was not cleared when we left *Siam*.

Infamous Punishments.

Besides these Punishments which I have mentioned, they have some less dolorous, but more infamous, as to expose a Man in a public place loaded with Irons, or with his Neck put into a kind of Ladder or Pillory, which is called *Cangue*, in *Siamese Ka*. The two sides of this Ladder are about six foot long, and are fastned to a Wall, or to Posts, each at one end, with a Cord; insomuch that the Ladder may be rais'd up, and let down, as if it was fasten'd to Pullies. In the middle of the Ladder are two Steps or Rounds, between which is the Neck of the Offender, and there are no more Rounds than these two. The Offender may sit on the ground, or stand, when the weight of the Ladder, which bears upon his Shoulders, is not too big, as it is sometimes; or when the Ladder is not fastned at the four ends: for in this last Case it is planted in the Air, bearing at the ends upon Props, and then the Criminal is as it were hung by the Neck; he hardly touches the ground with the Tips of his Toes. Besides this, they have the use of Stocks and Manacles.

The Criminal is sometimes in a Ditch to be lower than the ground; and this Ditch is not always broad, but oftentimes it is extremely narrow, and the Criminal, properly speaking, is buried up to the Shoulders. There, for the greater Ignominy, they give him Cuffs or Blows on the Head; or they only stroke the hand over his Head, Affronts esteemed very great, especially if received from the hand of a Woman.

The shame of the Punishments lasts no longer than the Punishments.

But what is herein very particular, is, that the most infamous Punishment is reproachful only as long as it lasts. He that suffers it to day, will re-enter to morrow, if the Prince think fit, into the most important Offices.

It is attended with Honour.

Moreover, they boast of the Punishments which they receive by Order of their King, as of his paternal care for him whom he has the goodness to chastise. He receives Compliments and Presents after the Bastinado, and it is principally in the East that Chastisements do pass for testimonies of Affection. We saw a young *Mandarin* shut up to be punished, and a *Frenchman* offering him to go and ask his Pardon of his Superior: *No*, replied the *Mandarin* in *Portuguese*, *I would see how far his Love would reach*; or as an *European* would have said, *I would see how far he will extend his Rigor*. To be reduced from an eminent place to a lower is no Reproach, and this befel the second Ambassador whom we saw here. Yet it happens also, that in this Country they hang themselves in despair, when they see themselves reduced from an high Employment to an extreme Poverty, and to the six Months Service due to the Prince, tho' this Fall be not shameful.

Others are included in the Punishments with the Criminals.

I have said in another place, that a Father shares sometimes in the punishment of the Son, as being bound to answer for the Education which he has given him. At *China* an Officer answers for the Faults of all the persons of his Family, because they pretend that he who knows not how to govern his own Family is not capable of any public Function. The Fear therefore, which particular persons have of seeing their Families turned out of the Employments, which do make the Splendor and Support thereof, renders them all wise, as if they were all Magistrates. In like manner at *Siam*, and at *China*, an Officer is punished for

 the

the Offences of another Officer that is subject to his Orders, by reason that he is to watch over him that depends on him; and that having power to correct him, he ought to answer for his conduct. Thus about three years since we saw at *Siam* for three days, *Oc-Pra Sheula-fai*, by Nation a *Peguan*, who is now in the King of *Siam's* Council of State, exposed to the *Cangue* with the head of a Malefactor, which they had put to Death, hung about his Neck; without being accused of having had any other hand in the crime of him, whose head was hung to his Neck, than too great Negligence in watching over a Man that was subject to him. After this 'tis no wonder in my opinion, that the Bastinado should be so frequent at *Siam*. Sometimes there may be seen several Officers at the *Cangue*, disposed in a Circle; and in the midst of them will be the head of a Man, which they have put to death; and this head will hang by several strings from the Neck of every one of these Officers.

The least pretence for a Crime is punished.

The worst is, that the least appearance of guilt renders an action criminal: To be accused is almost sufficient to be culpable. An action in it self innocent becomes bad, so soon as any one thinks to make a Crime thereof. And from thence proceed the so frequent disgraces of the principal Officers. They know not how, for instance, to reckon up all the *Barcalons* that the King of *Siam* has had since he reigned.

The Policy of the Kings of *Siam*, cruel against all, and against their own Brethren.

The Greatness of the Kings, whose Authority is despotical, is to exercise Power over all, and over their own Brethren. The Kings of *Siam* do maim them, in several ways, when they can: they take away or debilitate their sight by fire; they render them Impotent by dislocation of Members, or fourthly by Drinks, securing themselves and their Children against the Enterprizes of their Brethren, only by rendring them incapable of reigning: he that now reigns has not treated his better. This Prince will not therefore envy our King, the sweetness of being beloved by his Subjects, and the Glory of being dreaded by his Enemies. The Idea of a great King is not at *Siam*, that he should render himself terrible to his Neighbours, provided he be so to his Subjects.

The Government of *Siam* more burdensome to the Nobles than to the Populace.

Yet there is this Reflection to be made on this sort of Government, that the Yoke thereof is less heavy, if I may so say, on the Populace than on the Nobles. Ambition in this Country leads to Slavery: Liberty, and the other Enjoyments of Life are for the vulgar Conditions. The more one is unknown to the Prince, and the further from him, the greater Ease he enjoys; and for this reason the Employments of the Provinces are there considered, as a Recompence of the Services done in the Palace.

How tempestuous the Ministry is at *Siam*.

The Ministry there is tempestuous: not only thro the natural Inconstancy, which may appear in the Prince's Mind; but because that the ways are open for all persons to carry complaints to the Prince against his Ministers. And though the Ministers and all the other Officers, do employ all their artifices to render these ways of complaint ineffectual, whereby one may attack them all, yet all complaints are dangerous, and sometimes it is the slightest which hurts, and which subverts the best established favour. These examples, which very frequently happen, do edifie the People; and if the present King had not too far extended his exactions without any real necessity, his Government would as much please the Populace, as it is terrible to the Nobles.

The King of *Siam's* regards for his people.

Nevertheless he has had that regard for his People, as not to augment his Duties on cultivated Lands, and to lay no imposition on Corn and Fish; to the end that what is necessary to Life might not be dear: A moderation so much the more admirable, as it seems that they ought not to expect any from a Prince educated in this Maxim, that his Glory consists in not setting limits to his power, and always in augmenting his Treasure.

The inconveniences of this Government. It renders the Prince wavering on his Throne.

But these Kings which are so absolutely the Masters of the Fortune and Life of their Subjects, are so much the more wavering in the Throne. They find not in any person, or at most in a small number of Domesticks, that Fidelity or Love which we have for our Kings. The People which possess nothing in property, and which do reckon only upon what they have buried in the ground, as they have no solid establishment in their Country, so they have no obligation thereto. Being resolved to bear the same Yoke under any Prince whatever, and

having

having the assurance of not being able to bear a heavier, they concern not themselves in the Fortune of their Prince; and experience evinces that upon the least trouble they let the Crown go, to whom Force or Policy will give it. A *Siamese*, a *Chinese*, an *Indian*, will easily die to exert a particular Hatred, or to avoid a miserable Life, or a too cruel Death: but to die for their Prince and their Country, is not a Vertue in their practice. Amongst them are not found the powerful motives by which our People animate themselves to a vigorous Defence. They have no Inheritance to lose, and Liberty is oftentimes more burdensom to them than Servitude. The *Siameses* which the King of *Pegu* has taken in war, will live peaceable in *Pegu*, at Twenty miles distant from the Frontiers of *Siam*, and they will there cultivate the Lands which the King of *Pegu* has given them, no remembrance of their Country making them to hate their new Servitude. And it is the same of the *Peguins*, which are in the Kingdom of *Siam*.

How uncertain the external Respect of the Orientals is for their Kings.

The Eastern Kings are looked upon as the adoptive Sons of Heaven. 'Tis believed that they have Souls celestial, and as high above other Souls by their Merit, as the Royal Condition appears more happy than that of other men. Nevertheless, if any one of their Subjects revolts, the People doubt presently which of the two Souls is most valuable, whether that of the Lawful Prince, or that of the Rebellious Subject; and whether the Adoption of Heaven has not passed from the King to the Subject. Their Histories are all full of these examples; and that of *China*, which Father *Martinius* has given us, is curious in the ratiocinations by which the *Chineses*, I mean the *Chinese* Philosophers, are often perswaded that they followed the Inclination of Heaven in changing their Sovereign, and sometimes in preferring a High-way-man before their Lawful Prince.

These Princes do oftentimes lose their Authority by being too jealous.

But besides that the despotick Authority is almost destitute of defence, it is moreover rather usurped by him that possesses it, in that the exercise thereof is less communicated. Whoever takes upon him the Spirit or Person of a Prince, has almost nothing more to do to dispossess the Prince; because that the exercise of the Authority being too much reunited in the Prince, there is none besides him that prohibits it in case of need. Thus is it not lawful for a King to be a Minor, or too easie to let himself be governed. The Scepter of this Country soon falls from hands that need a support to sustain it. On the contrary, in Kingdoms where several permanent bodies of Magistracy divide the Splendor and the Exercise of the Royal Authority, these same bodies do preserve it entire for the King, who imparts it to them; because they deliver not to the Usurper that part which is in their hands, and which alone suffices to save that which the King himself knows not how to keep.

The peril in re-uniting all the Royal Authority in the Seal.

In the ancient Rebellions of *China* it appears, that he who seized on the Royal Seal, presently rendered himself Master of all; because that the people obeyed the Orders where the Seal appear'd, without informing themselves in whose hands the Seal was. And the Jealousie which the King of *Siam* has of his, that I have said he intrusts with no person, perswades me that it is the same in his Country. The danger therefore to these Princes is in that wherein they place their security. Their Policy requires that their whole Authority should be in their Seal, to exercise it more entire themselves alone: And this Policy as much exposes their Authority, as their Seal is easie to lose.

A publick Treasure necessary to despotick Governments, and what are the Inconveniences thereof.

The same danger is found in a great Treasure, the only saving of all the Despotick Governments, where the ruin'd people cannot supply extraordinary Subsidies in publick necessities. In a great Treasure all the Forces of the State reunite themselves, and he that seizes on the Treasure, seizes on the State. So that besides Treasures ruining the People, on whom it is levied, it frequently serves against those that accumulate it; and this likewise draws the dissipation thereof.

The Conclusion of this Chapter.

The *Indian* Government has therefore all the defects of the Despotick Government. It renders the Prince and his Subjects equally uncertain: It betrays the Royal Authority, and delivers it up entire, under pretence of putting the more entire Management thereof into the hands of a single person; and moreover it deprives it of its natural defence, by separating the whole Interest of the

Subjects

Subjects from that of the Prince and State. Having therefore related how the Kings of *Siam* do treat their Subjects, it remains to show how they treat, as well with foreign Princes by Embassies, as with the foreign Nations which are fled to *Siam*.

CHAP. XV.

Concerning the Form of Embassies at Siam.

The Eastern Ambassadors represent not their Masters, and are less honoured than in Europe.

AN Ambassador throughout the East is no other than a Kings Messenger: he represents not his Master. They honour him little, in comparison of the respects which are tender'd to the Letters of Credence whereof he is Bearer. Mr. *de Chaumont*, tho an Ambassador extraordinary, never had a *Balon* of the Body, nor on the very day of his entrance; and it was in a *Balon* of the Body that the Kings Letter was put, which he had to deliver to the King of *Siam*. This *Balon* had four *Umbrello's*, one at each corner of the Seat; and it was attended with four other *Balons* of the Body, adorn'd with their *Umbrello's*, but empty; as the King of *Spain*, when he goes abroad in his Coach, and that he would be seen and known, has always one which follows him empty, which is called *de respeto*, a word and custom come from *Italy*. The Kings Presents were likewise carry'd in *Balons* of the Body; and the same things were observed at the entrance of the King's Envoys. Thus the Orientals make no difference between an Ambassador and an Envoy: And they understand not Ambassadors, nor ordinary Envoys, nor Residents; because they send no person to reside at a foreign Court, but there to dispatch a business, and return.

The Siamese Embassies consist in three persons.

The *Siamese* do never send more nor less than three Ambassadors together. The first is called *Rajja Tout*, that is to say, Royal Messenger, the second *Oubba Tout*, and the third *Tri Tout* (terms which I understand not) but the two last Ambassadors are obliged in every thing to follow the Advice of the first.

They are looked upon as Messengers which carry a Letter.

Every one therefore who is the carrier of a Letter from the King, is reputed an Ambassador throughout the East. Wherefore, after the Ambassador of *Persia*, which Mr. *de Chaumont* left in the Country of *Siam*, was dead at *Tenasserim*, his Domesticks having elected one amongst them, to deliver the King of *Persia's* Letter to the King of *Siam*; he that was elected was received without any other Character, as the real Ambassador would have been, and with the same honours which the King of *Persia* had formerly granted to the Ambassador of *Siam*.

He returns them no Answer, but a Recepisse.

But that wherein they treat an Ambassador like a meer Messenger, is, that the King of *Siam*, in the Audience of Leave, gives him a *Recepisse* of the Letter he has received from him; and if this Prince returns an Answer, he gives it not to him, but he sends his own Ambassadors with him to carry it.

How the King of Siam is advertised of the Arrival of an Ambassador.

A foreign Ambassador which arrives at *Siam*, is stopped at the Entrance of the Kingdom, until the King of *Siam* has received intelligence thereof; and if he is accompanied with *Siamese* Ambassadors, as we were; it belongs to the *Siamese* Ambassadors to go before, to carry unto the King their Master, the news of their Arrival, and of the Arrival of the foreign Ambassador, whom they brought with them.

An Ambassador has his Charges born at Siam. He must Communicate his Instructions.

Every foreign Ambassador is lodged and maintained by the King of *Siam*, and during the time of his Embassy he may exercise Merchandize; but he cannot treat of any affair till he has delivered his Letter of Credence, and communicated his Original Instructions. They dispenced with this last Article to Mr. *de Chaumont*, and the King's Envoys; but the Ambassadors of *Siam* dispenc'd not therewith in *France*: They communicated their Instructions.

The

He enters not into the Metropolis till he goes to Audience, and departs thence in going from the Audience of Leave.

The Ambassador cannot enter into the Metropolis, till he goes directly to Audience, nor continue therein till after the Audience of Leave: in going from the Audience of Leave he departs out of the City, and negotiates nothing more. Wherefore on the Evening before the Audience of Leave, the King of *Siam* demands of him, *Whether he has any thing to propose?* And in the Audience of Leave, he asks him, *If he is contented?*

The Solemn Audiences.

The Majesty of the Prince resides principally in the Metropolis, 'tis there that the Solemn Audiences are given; out of this City every Audience is accounted private, and without Ceremony. The whole Guard, as well the Ordinary, as that of Ostentation, was put in Arms for the Audience at *Siam*: the Elephants and the Horses appear'd with their best Harness, and in great number, on the Entry of the King's Envoys, and there was almost nothing of all this for the Audiences at *Louvo*. At *Siam* the *Umbrella*, which was before the Kings window, had nine Rounds, and the two which were at the side had seven each. At *Louvo* the King had no *Umbrella* before him, but two on each side, which had each four Rounds apiece, and which mounted up much lower than those of *Siam*. The King was not at *Louvo* at a single window, as at *Siam*; he was in a wooden Tower joined to the Floor of the Hall into which he enter'd behind, and immediately, by a Step higher than the Hall. So that tho' this Prince was as high at *Louvo* as at *Siam*, yet he was at *Louvo* in the Hall of Audience; whereas at *Siam* he was in another Room, which had a Prospect into the Hall. Moreover, the Gate of the Hall at *Louvo* was large, and in the middle of the Tower, that is to say opposite to the King; whereas at *Siam* the door was low and strait, and almost at the corner of the Hall: differences, which have all their reasons in this Country, where the least things are measured and performed with diligence. At the Audience at *Siam* there were 50 Mandarins prostrate in the Hall, 25 on each side, in five Ranks, each consisting of five. At the Audiences at *Louvo* there were no more than 32, 16 on each side, in four Ranks, of four in a Rank. The Audience of Reception, where the Letter of Credence is delivered, is always given in the chief City, and with all the magnificence imaginable, in respect to the Letter of Credence: the other Audiences are given without the City, and with less Pomp, because there appears no Letter from the King.

What is observed in Audiences.

The Custom in all Audiences is, that the King speaks first, and not the Ambassador. What he speaks in Audiences of Ceremony, is reduced to some Questions almost always the same; after which, he orders the Ambassador to address himself to the *Barcalon* upon all the Propositions which he has to make. Harangues please him not at all; tho' he had the goodness to acquaint me, upon the Compliments I had the Honour to make to him, that I was a great Contriver of Words. We were fain to embellish them with Figures, and therein to use the Sun, Moon and Stars, Ornaments of Discourse, which may please them in other things: This Prince thinks that the longer an Ambassador speaks the first time, the less he honours him. And indeed when the Ambassador is only a Messenger, which delivers a Letter, it is natural that he has nothing to say which is not asked him. After the King has spoken to the Ambassador, he gives him *Arek* and *Betel*, and a Vest, with which the Ambassador cloaths himself immediately, and sometimes a Sabre, and a Chain of Gold.

To Foreigners which are not Ambassadors, he gives Audience only by accident.

This Prince gave Sabres, Chains of Gold and Vests, or sometimes only Vests to the principal *French* Officers, but gave them Audience only as it were by accident in his Gardens, or out of his Palace at some Show.

The Indians are cunning and deceitful in their Negotiations.

In all sorts of Business, the *Indians* are slow in concluding, by reason of the length of their Councils, for they never depart from their Customs. They are very phlegmatic and hypocritical. They are insinuating in their Speeches, captious in their Writings, deceitful, to such a degree as to Cheat. The praise which the King of *Siam*'s Wives and Concubines give him, when they would flatter him to the highest degree, was to tell him, not that he was an Hero, or the greatest General in the World, but that he had always been more politic and witty, than all the Princes with whom he had to do. They engage themselves in writing as little as they can. They will rather receive you into a Port,

 or

or into a Castle, than they will agree with you to surrender them up to you by a Treaty in ample Form, and sealed by their *Barcolon*.

That the *Europeans* have ever found it necessary to treat the *Indians* with arrogance.

The *Portugueses* being naturally bold and distrustful, have always treated the *Indians* with a great deal of Loftiness, and with very little Confidence: And the *Dutch* have thought they could not do better, than herein to imitate the *Portugueses*; because that indeed the *Indians* being educated in a Spirit of Servitude, are crafty; and, as I have said in another place, subservient to those who treat them haughtily, and insolent to those that use them gently. The King of *Siam* says of his Subjects, that they are of the temper of Apes, who tremble so long as one holds the end of their Band, and who disown their Master, when the Band is loosed. Examples are not rare in *India* of simple *European* Factors, who have bastinado'd the Officers of the *Indian* Kings without being punished. And it is evident, that the certain vigorous Repartees which are sometimes made in our Countries, appear to us more daring, than the Bastinado is in theirs; provided it be given them in cold Blood, and not in Anger: A Man that suffers himself to be transported with Passion, is what the *Indians* most contemn.

Presents are essential to Embassies in the East.

But as Trade is their most sensible Interest, Presents are essential for them in Embassies. 'Tis a trafficking under an honourable Title, and from King to King. Their Politeness excites them to testify by several Demonstrations, how they esteem the Presents which they have received. If it is any thing of use, tho' it be not for their use, they publickly prepare whatever shall be necessary to use it, as if they had a real desire thereof. If it is any thing to wear, they will adorn themselves therewith in your presence. If they are Horses, they will build a Stable on purpose to lodge them. Was it only a Telescope, they would build a Tower to see with this Glass. And so they will seem to make an high account of all sorts of Presents, to honour the Prince which sends them, unless he has received Presents from their part with less demonstrations of Esteem. Nevertheless they are really concern'd only for the Profit. Before that the King's Presents went out of our hands, some of the King of *Siam*'s Officers came to take an exact description thereof in writing, even to the counting all the Stones of every sort which were intersper'd in the Embroideries; and to the end that it might not seem that the King their Master took this care to prevent being robbed by his Officers, through whose hands the Presents were to pass, they pretended that this Prince was curious and impatient, and that it was necessary to go render him an account of what this was, and to be ready to answer him exactly upon the least things.

The Orientals do esteem it a great Honour to receive Embassies.

All the Oriental Princes do esteem it a great Honour to receive Embassies, and to send the fewest they can: Because that, in their Opinion, it is a Badge which cannot be alien'd from them and their Riches, and that they can content themselves without the Riches of Foreigners. They look upon Embassies as a kind of Homage; and in their Courts they retain the Foreign Ministers as long as it is possible, to prolong, as much as in them lies, the Honour which they receive. Thus the great *Mogul*, and the Kings of *China* and *Japan*, do never send Ambassadors. The King of *Persia* likewise sends only to *Siam*, because that the King of *Siam*'s Ambassador had demanded it, as I proceed to relate.

The *Siamese* Ambassadors are accountable.

The *Siamese* Ambassadors are accountable, because that they are loaded with Goods; and it rarely happens, that they render an Account good enough entirely to avoid the Bastinado. Thus *Agi Selim* ('tis the name of a *Moor*, whom the King of *Siam* sent eight or nine years since into *Persia*, as his Ambassador) was severely chastised at his return, tho' in appearance he had served very faithfully. He had established Commerce with *Persia*, and had brought with him that *Persian* Ambassador, who, as I have several times related, dyed at *Tenasserim*. He was a *Moula*, or Doctor of the Law of *Mahomet*, whom *Agi Selim* had demanded of the King of *Persia*, to instruct, as he pretended, the King of *Siam* in Mahumetanism. *Bernier* Tome II. pag. 54. reports that during his abode in the *Indies*, some Ambassadors from *Prester John*, who, as every one knows, professes to be a Christian, demanded of the great *Mogul* an *Alcoran*, and eight of the most renowned Books that were in the *Mahometan* Religion; a base Flattery, which exceedingly scandalized *Bernier*. But generally speaking, these trading Kings do exceedingly make use of the pretence of Religion, for the increase of their Commerce.

Expli-

Explication of the Platform of the Hall of Audience of *Siam.*

A *Three Steps which are placed under the Window, where the King of* Siam *was, to raise me high enough to deliver him the King's Letter from hand to hand.*
B *Three Parasols or Umbrella's.*
C *Two pair of Stairs to go up into the place where the King of* Siam *was.*
D *Two Tables covered with Tapestry, on which were laid the King's Present, which could be held there.*
E *The Son of Mr.* Cebéret *standing, holding the King's Letter in a Gold Bason of Filigreen with a triple Story, the Figure of which is seen at Page*
F *Two little square and low Stools, each covered with a little Carpet, for the King's Envoys to sit on. Monsieur* de Chaumont *had such another.*
G *The Bishop of* Metellopolis, *Apostolick Vicar, sitting cross-legg'd.*
H *Monsieur* Constance *prostrate at my right hand, and behind me to serve as my Interpreter.*
I *Father* Tachart *sitting cross-legg'd.*
K *Fifty* Mandarin, *prostrate.*
L *The* French *Gentlemen sitting with their Legs across.*
M *A little pair of Brick Stairs to go up to the Hall of Audience.*
N *The Wall whereunto this pair of Stairs is fixed.*

The Explication of the Platform of the Temple, which should have been inserted in *Chap.* 2. *Part* 2.

A *The Steps before the Gates of the Temple.*
B *The principal Gate.*
C *The two Gates behind.*
D *The Piles of Wood which bear the Roof.*
E *The Piles of Wood which bear before and behind the Temple.*
FF *The Altar.*
G *The Figure of* Sommona-Codam *taking up the all the forepart of the Altar.*
HH *The Statues of* Pra Mogla, *and of* Pra Sarabout, *less and lower than the first.*
III *Other Statues lesser than the former.*
K *Steps to ascend on the Altar, which is a Mass built with Bricks about 4 Feet high.*

CHAP.

CHAP. XVI.

Of the Foreigners of different Nations fled to, and setled at Siam.

The Policy observed in respect of the Strangers fled to Siam.

TWas, as I have said, the Liberty of Commerce, which had formerly invited to *Siam* a great multitude of Strangers of different Nations; who setled there with the Liberty of living according to their Customs, and of publickly exercising their several ways of Worship. Every Nation possesses a different Quarter. The Quarters which are without the City, and which do compose the Suburbs thereof, the *Portugueses* do call *Camp*, and the *Siamese Ban*. Moreover every Nation chooses its Chief, or its *Nai*, as the *Siamese* do speak, and this Chief manages the Affairs of his Nation with the *Mandarin*, whom the King of *Siam* nominates for this purpose, and whom they call the *Mandarin* of this Nation. But Affairs of the least importance are not determined by this *Mandarin*, they are carried to the *Barcalon*.

The Fortune of the Moors very different at Siam, at several times.

Amongst the several Nations, that of the *Moors* has been the best established under this Reign. It once hapned that the *Barcalon* was a *Moor*, probably because the King of *Siam* thought by this means better to establish his Commerce, amongst the most powerful of his Neighbouring Princes, who do all make profession of Mahumetanism: The principal Offices of the Court, and of the Provinces were then in the hands of the *Moors*: The King of *Siam* caused several Mosques to be erected for them at his expence, and he still bears the charges of their principal Festival, which they celebrate for several days together, in memory of the Death of *Haly*, or of his Children. The *Siamese*, which embraced the Religion of the *Moors*, had the Priviledge of being exempted from the personal Service: But the *Barcalon Moor* soon experienced the Inconstancy of the Fortunes of *Siam*, he fell into Disgrace, and the Credit of those of his Nation fell afterwards into Decay. The considerable Offices and Employments were taken away from them, and the *Siamese* which were turned Mahumetans, were forc'd to pay in ready Money for the six Months Service, from which they had been exempted. Nevertheless their Mosques are remaining to them, as well as the publick Protection which the King of *Siam* gives to their Religion, as to all foreign Religions. There are therefore three or four Thousand *Moors* at *Siam*, as many *Portugueses* born in *India*, and as many *Chinese*, and perhaps as many *Malays*, besides what there is of other Nations.

The Foreign Commerce ceased at Siam has caused the Richest Strangers, and especially the Moors to depart thence.

But the richest Foreigners, and especially the *Moors*, are retired elsewhere, since the King of *Siam* has reserved to himself alone almost all the foreign Commerce. The King his Father had heretofore done the same thing, and perhaps it is the Policy of *Siam* to do it thus from time to time; otherwise it is certain that they have almost always left the Trade free, and that it has frequently flourished at *Siam*. *Ferdinand Mendez Pinto* reports, that in his time there were annually above a thousand foreign Ships; whereas at present there goes no more than two or three *Dutch* Barks.

Why the Foreign Trade ceased at Siam.

Commerce requires a certain liberty: no person can resolve to go to *Siam*, necessarily to sell unto the King what is carry'd thither, and to buy of him alone what one would carry thence, when this was not the product of the Kingdom. For though there were several foreign Ships together at *Siam*, the Trade was not permitted from one Ship to the other, nor with the Inhabitants of the Country, Natives or Foreigners, till that the King, under the pretence of a preference due to his Royal dignity, had purchased what was best in the Ships, and at his own rate, to sell it afterwards as he pleased: because that when the season for the departure of the Ships presses on, the Merchants choose rather to sell to great loss, and dearly to buy a new Cargo, than to wait at *Siam* a new season to depart, without hopes of making a better Trade.

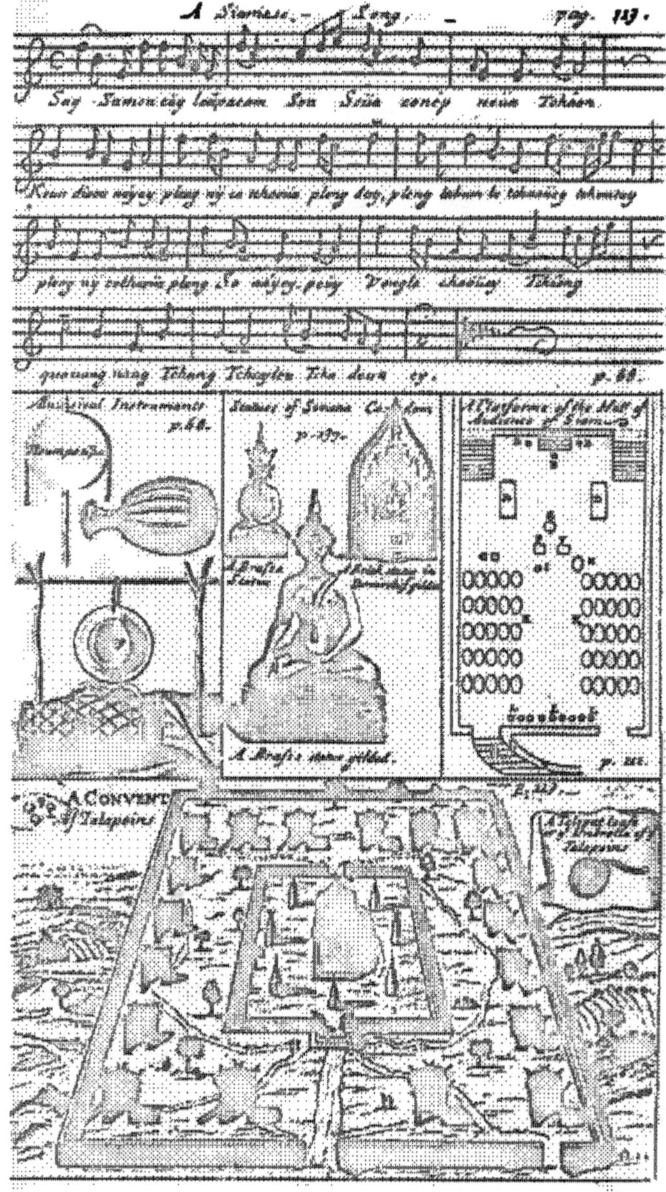
A Siamese Song
pag. 113.
Say Sumon cáy loüpacam Son Sсüa conéy neüa Tchäon
plong ny colthamu plang So náyey peny Vongle choüay Tchang
quouang nang Tchang Tchaylen Tcha doun cy.
p. 68.
Musical Instruments
p. 68.
Statues of Siamese Cardons
A Brass statue gilded.
A Convent of Talapoins
p. 111.

The Natural *Siameses* cannot afford a great Trade.

In a word, 'tis neither the natural Riches, nor the Manufactures of the Kingdom of *Siam*, that should tempt one to go thither. The natural *Siameses*, ruin'd as they are by Impositions and Services, cannot carry on a great Trade, though they should have all the liberty imaginable. The Trade is manag'd only with the superfluous Money, and in the places where the Impositions are very great, there is scarcely found Money necessary for life. The vast summs levied on the people return slowly to the people, and especially in the remote Provinces; and the whole does not return, because that a great part thereof remains in the hands of those, that tend upon the receipts and expences of the Prince. And as to that part which returns to the people, it remains not in their hands for their uses; it soon goes thence to return to the Princes Coffers: so that it must needs be, that all the small Trades do cease for want of Money; which cannot be, but the general Commerce of a State does greatly suffer. But this is yet much truer at *Siam*, where the Prince annually accumulates his Revenues, instead of expending them. Having thus explained what respects the King, the Officers, and the People of *Siam*, it remains to speak of their *Talapoins*, or Priests.

CHAP. XVII.

Of the Talapoins, *and their Convents.*

The origine of the word *Pagod*.

THey live in Convents, which the *Siameses* do call *Vat*; and they make use of the Temples, which the *Siameses* do call *Pihan*, and the *Portugueses* *Pagode*, from the *Persian* word *Pouthgheda*, which signifies a Temple of Idols; but the *Portugueses* do use the word *Pagode*, to signify equally the Idol and the Temple.

A Description of the Convents of the *Talapoins*.

The Temple and the Convent do take up a very great square piece of ground, encompast with an Inclosure of Bambou. In the middle of the ground stands the Temple, as in the place esteemed the most honourable in their Encampments; and at the corners of this ground, and along the Bambou Inclosure, are ranged the Cells of the *Talapoins*, like the Tents of an Army; and sometimes the Rows thereof are double, or triple: These Cells are little single Houses, erected on Piles, and that of the Superior is after the same manner, but a little bigger and higher than the rest. The Pyramids stand near and quite round the Temple: and the ground which the Temple and the Pyramids take up, besides its being higher, is inclosed between four Walls: but from these Walls to the Cells there likewise remains a great void piece of Ground, which is as it were the Court of the Convent. Sometimes these Walls are all bare, and serve only as an Inclosure to the ground, which the Temple and the Pyramids take up: Sometimes along these Walls there are covered Galleries of the Figure of those, which in our Religious Houses we call the Cloyster: and on a counterwall breast high, which runs along these Galleries, they place in a Train, and close together, a great number of Idols sometimes gilded.

They have Cells for the *Talapoinesses*.

Though at *Siam* there are some *Talapoinesses*, or Women, who in most things do observe the Rule of the *Talapoins*, yet they have no other Convents than those of the *Talapoins* themselves: The *Siameses* do think that the advanced Age of all these Women, for there are none young, is a sufficient caution of their Chastity. There are not *Talapoinesses* in all the Convents; but in those where any are, their Cells run along one of the sides of the Bambou Inclosure, which I have mentioned, without being otherwise separated from those of the *Talapoins*.

How the *Talapoin* Children are lodg'd.

The *Nens*, or *Talapoin Children*, are dispersed one, two, or three into every *Talapoin* Cell, and they serve the *Talapoin* with whom they lodge, that is to say with whom they have been placed by their Parents: So that when a *Talapoin* has two or three *Nens*, he receives no more. In a word, these *Nens* are not all young; some there are which do grow old in this Condition, which is not thought entirely religious, and the eldest of all they call *Taten*. It belongs to him

him to pluck up the Weeds which grow in the ground of the Convent, which the *Talapoins* themselves cannot do, in their opinion, without sin.

The Halls of the Convent. The School of the *Nens* is a Hall of Bambou standing alone; and besides this Hall, there is always such another, where the People carry their Alms on the days when the Temple is shut, and where the *Talapoins* assemble for their ordinary Conferences.

The Steeple. The Steeple is a Wooden Tower standing also alone, they call it *Horacang*, or the Belfry; but the Bell has no Clapper. They strike it with a Mallet or Wooden Hammer to sound it: and it is only in War, or for things of War, that they strike their Basons, and other Instruments of Brass or Copper, with Iron Hammers.

Of the Superiors. Every Convent is under the Conduct of a Superior called *Tchaou Vat*, that is to say, Lord or Master of the Convent; but all the Superiors are not of equal dignity. The most honorable are those which they call *Sancrat*, and the *Sancrat* of the Convent of the Palace is the most reverend of all. Yet no Superior, nor no *Sancrat*, has Authority or Jurisdiction over another. This body would be too formidable if it had but one head, and if it acted always unanimously, and according to the same Maxims.

Of the Sancrats. The Missionaries have compared the *Sancrats* to our Bishops, and the simple Superiors to our Curates; and they have some inclination to believe that this Country has formerly had some Christian Bishops, to whom the *Sancrats* have succeeded. None but the *Sancrats* indeed can make *Talapoins*, as none but Bishops can make Priests. But otherwise the *Sancrats* have not any Jurisdiction nor any Authority, neither over the People, nor over the *Talapoins*, which are not of their Convent; and they could not inform me whether they have any particular Character which makes them *Sancrats*, save that they are Superiors of certain Convents designed for *Sancrats*. Every Convent therefore design'd for a *Sancrat* is distinguished from the other Convents, wherein there are only simple Superiors, by some Stones planted round the Temple, and near its Walls, each of which is double, and bears some resemblance, but at a very great distance, with a Mitre set upon a Pedestal. I have inserted the Figure thereof in the Print of a Temple. Their Name in *Siamese* is *Sema*. Now 'tis this resemblance of these Stones with the Mitres, that is the principal Foundation of the Suspicion, which the Missionaries have, that the *Sancrats* have succeeded some Bishops. The more of these Stones there is round a Temple, the more the *Sancrat* is thought advanced in Dignity; but there never is fewer than two, nor more than eight. The Ignorance under which the *Siameses* are, as to what these Stones do signifie, has put the Missionaries upon seeking the Origine thereof in Christianity.

The honors of the Sancrats. The King of *Siam* gives to the principal *Sancrats* a Name, an Umbrella, a Sedan, and some men to carry it; but the *Sancrats* do make use of this Equipage only to wait upon the King, and they never see *Talapoins* that carry the Sedan. The *Sancrat* of the Palace is now called *Pra Vikat*.

The Spirit of the Institution. The Spirit of the Institution of the *Talapoins*, is, to keep themselves from the Sins of the People, to lead a penitent Life for the Sins of those that bestow Alms upon them, and to live on Alms. They eat not in common, and tho they be very hospitable to the Seculars, which have recourse to them, and even to Christians, yet it is prohibited them to share the Alms which they receive, or at least to do it presently; because that every one of them being thought to repent sufficiently, has no need to redeem his Sins by bestowing Alms on his Companion, and perhaps they would also oblige them all to the fatigue of begging. Nevertheless a *Talapoin* is not prohibited from ever giving any thing to his Brother, or from assisting him in a real Necessity. They have two Lodgings, one on each side of their door to receive the Passengers, who desire a bed amongst them.

There are two sorts of Talapoins. There are two sorts of *Talapoins* at *Siam*, as in all the rest of the *Indies*. Some do live in the Woods, and others in the Cities. And those of the Woods do lead, as they say, a Life which would appear intolerable, and which would doubtless be so in Countries less hot than *Siam*, or than the *Thebais* of *Egypt*.

All

All, that is to say those of the Cities, and those of the Woods, are obliged under pain of Fire strictly to keep Celibacy, so long as they continue in their Profession; and the King of *Siam*, from whose Jurisdiction they cannot withdraw themselves, pardons them not in this point: for as they have great Priviledges, and amongst other things are exempted from the six Months Service, It imports him that the Profession of *Talapoin* become not altogether convenient, for fear lest all his Subjects embrace it.

They are obliged to Celibacy under the penalty of the Fire.

To diminish the number of these priviledged Persons, he causes them to be from time to time examined as to their Knowledge, which respects the *Balie* Language and its Books: and when we arrived in this Country, he had just reduc'd several Thousands to the Secular condition, because they had not been found learned enough. Their Examiner was *Oc Louang Souracac*, a young man of about Twenty eight or Thirty years old, the Son of that *Oc Pra Pipitcharatcha*, who, as I have said, commands the Elephants; but the *Talapoins* of the Woods had refused to submit to the Examination of a Secular, and consented to be examined only by one of their Superiors.

And to a certain degree of Literature under pain of being expelled out of the Convent.

They educate the Youth, as I have related; and they explain their Doctrine to the People, according as it is written in their *Balie* Books. They preach the next day after every new and every full Moon, and the People are ever very constant in the Temples. When the Channel of the River is full of Rain-water, until the Inundation begins to sink, they preach every day, from six in the Morning till Dinner-time, and from one in the Afternoon till five in the Evening. The Preacher is seated cross-leg'd in a high Chair of State, and several *Talapoins* releave one another in this Office.

They Educate the Youth and instruct the People.

The People approves the Doctrine which is preach'd to them in these *Balie* words, *Sa tou sa*, which signifies, *it is so Sir*, or in other *Siamese* words which amount to the same sense; and then they give Alms to the Preacher: and those that do preach frequently, not only at this time, but during the whole course of the year, do easily become rich.

This Trade is gainful.

Now it is this time which the *Europeans* have called the Lent of the *Talapoins*. Their Fasting is to eat nothing from Noon, unless they may chew *Betel*: but when they do not fast, they only eat Fruit in the Afternoon. The *Indians* are naturally so sober, that a Fast of Forty, nay of an Hundred days, appears not incredible to them. *Twist*, a *Dutch* Author, in his *Description* of the *Indies* reports, that *Experience has certainly evinced that there are some* Indians *that can fast Twenty, Thirty*, and *Forty* days, without taking any thing but a little Liquor mixed with some bitter Wood reduced to Powder. The *Siameses* have cited the example of a *Talapoin*, whom they pretend to have fasted an hundred and seven days, without eating any thing But when I sounded their opinion thereon, I found that they attributed this Fast to Magick, and to prove it to me, they added, that it was easie to live on the Grass of the Fields, provided they breathed thereon, and utter'd certain words, which they understood not, or which they would not inform me, or which they said that others understood.

Of the Lent of the Talapoins and of their facility in fasting.

After the Rice-Harvest the *Talapoins* do go for three Weeks to watch in the Nights in the middle of the Fields, under small Huts of branches of Leaves ranged square; and in the day they return to visit the Temple, and to sleep in their Cells. The Hut of the Superior stands in the middle of the others, and higher. They make no Fire in the Night to scare away the wild Beasts, as all those that travel in the Woods of this Country us'd to do, and as was done round the *Tabarques* wherein we lodged: So that the People look upon it as a Miracle, that the *Talapoins* are not devoured; and I know not what precaution they use, except that of enclosing themselves in a Park of *Bambou*. But doubtless they chose places little exposed, remote from the Woods, and where the savage Beasts cannot come with Hunger, but after having found a great deal of Food, for it is the season wherein there is plenty of Forage on the ground. The People admire also the security, in which the *Talapoins* of the Woods do live: For they have neither Convent nor Temple to retire into. They think that the Tygers, Elephants, and Rhinoceros do respect them, and lick their hands and feet, when they find any one asleep: but these may make a Fire of *Bambou*,

The Watch of the Talapoins in the Fields, and the Esteem which the People make thereof.

to

to defend themselves from these Animals, they may lie in the closest Thickets; and moreover, though the people should find the remains of some man devoured, it would never be presumed he was a *Talapoin*; and when they could not doubt thereof, they would presume that this *Talapoin* had been wicked, and would not cease to believe that the Beasts respect the good. And it must needs be that the Woods are not so dangerous as they report, seeing that so many Families do seek Sanctuary there against the Government.

The Talapoins have a Chaplet.

I know not what the *Talapoins* do pretend, either by this Watch, or by their Lent: I ignore also what the Chaplets of one Hundred and eight Grains, on which they recite certain *Bali* words, do mean.

Their Habit.

They go with naked feet and bare-headed, like the rest of the People: round their Reins and Thighs they wear the *Pagne* of the Seculars, but of yellow Linnen, which is the colour of their Kings, and of the Kings of *China*: and they have no Muslin Shirt, nor any Vest. Their Habit consists of four pieces. The first which they call *Angsa*, is a kind of Shoulder Belt of yellow Linnen, five or six Inches broad; they wear it on their left Shoulder, and button it with a single button on the right Hip; and it descends not lower than the Hip. Over this Belt they put another great yellow Cloath, which is called the *Pagne* of the *Talapoin*, and which they call *Pa Schivon*, or the Cloth of several pieces, because it ought to be patched in several places. 'Tis a kind of Scapulary, which reaches down to the ground behind and before; and which covering only the left Shoulder returns to the right Hip, and leaves the two Arms and all the right Shoulder free. Over the *Pa Schivon* is the *Pa Pat*. 'Tis another cloth four or five Inches broad which they do likewise put over the left Shoulder, but like a Hood; it descends to the Navel before, and as much behind as before. Its colour is sometimes red: the *Sancrats* and the most ancient *Talapoins* do wear it thus, but the *Angsa* and the *Pa Schivon* can never be other than yellow. To keep the *Pa Pat* and the *Pa Schivon* in a posture, they girt the middle of their body with a Scarf of yellow Cloth which they call *Rappacod* and which is the fourth and last piece of their Habit.

They have a little Iron-Bason for begging.

When they go a begging they carry an Iron Bason, to receive what is given them; and they carry it in a Linnen Bag, which hangs on the left side, by two ends of a Rope hung like a Belt over the right Shoulder.

They shave all the Head, and have a Screen in their hand.

They shave all their Beard, Head, and Eyebrows; and to defend themselves from the Sun they have the *Talapat*, which is their little *Umbrella*, in form of a Screen, as I have already said in the other part. The Superior is forced to shave himself, because no person can touch his head, without showing him disrespect. By the same reason a young *Talapoin* dares not to shave an old one; but it is lawful for the old to shave the young, I mean those Children whose Education is committed to them, and who know not how to shave themselves. Nevertheless when the Superior is very old, it is necessary that he permit another to shave him; and this other does it after having desired an express Permission. In a word, the Razors of *Siam* are of Copper.

The days on which they shave themselves, are days of Devotion to the People.

The days on which they shave themselves, are those of the new and full Moon; and on these days the *Talapoins* and the People do fast, that is to say, they eat nothing from Noon. The People abstain also on these days from going a Fishing, not that Fishing is a work, for they abstain not from any other Labor, but because that, in my opinion, they esteem not Fishing wholly Innocent, as we shall see in the sequel. And in fine, the People on these days do carry unto the Convents some Alms, which consist in Money, Fruits, Pagnes, or Cattle. If the Cattle are dead, the *Talapoins* do eat them: if they are alive, they let them live and die about the Temple; and they eat them only when they die of themselves. Near certain Temples there is also a Pond for the living Fish, which is offer'd to the Temple: and besides these Festival days, common to all the Temples, every Temple has a particular one appointed to receive the Alms, as if it was the Feast of its Dedication: for I could not learn what it is.

The People love to adorn themselves to go to the Temples: and their Charity to Animals.

The People voluntarily assist at these Festivals, and make a show with their new Cloaths. One of their greatest Charities is to give Liberty to some Animals, which they buy of those that have taken them in the Fields. What they

give

give to the Idol, they offer not immediately to the Idol, but to the *Talapoins*; and they present it to the Idol, either by holding it in their hand before the Idol, or by laying it upon the Altar; and in a little time after they take it away, and convert it to their own uses. Sometimes the People offer up lighted Tapers, which the *Talapoins* do fasten to the knees of the Statue, and this is the reason why one of the knees of a great many Idols is ungilt. As for bloody Sacrifices, they never offer up any, on the contrary they are prohibited from killing any thing.

The Siamese do wash their Idols, their Talapoins, and their Parents.

At the Full Moon of the fifth Month, the *Talapoins* do wash the Idol with perfumed waters, but respect permits them not to wash its head. They afterwards wash the *Sancrat*. And the People go also to wash the *Sancrat*, and the other *Talapoins*. And then in particular Families the Children do wash their Parents, without having regard to the Sex; for the Son and the Daughter do equally wash the Father and the Mother, the Grandfather and the Grandmother. This Custom is observed also in the Country of *Laos*, with this Singularity, that the King himself is washed in the River.

The hour on which the Talapoins do wash themselves.

The *Talapoins* have no Clock; and they wash themselves only when it is light enough to be able to discern the veins of their hands, for fear lest if they should wash themselves earlier in the morning, they should in walking kill any Insect without perceiving it. This is the reason why they wash later in the shortest days, tho' their Bell fails not to wake them before day.

They go to the Temples in the morning.

Being raised, they go with their Superior to the Temple for two hours. There they sing or repeat out of the *Balie*, and what they sing is written on the Leafs of a Tree somewhat longish, and fasten'd at one of the ends, as I have said in discoursing of the Tree which bears them. The People have not any Prayer-Book. The posture of the *Talapoins*, whilst they sing, is to sit cross-leg'd, and continually to toss their *Talipat* or Fan, as if they would continually fan themselves; so that their Fan goes or comes at each Syllable which they pronounce, and they pronounce them all at equal times, and after the same tone. In entering in and going out of the Temple, they prostrate themselves three times before the Statue, and the Seculars do observe the same; but the one and the other do remain in the Temple sitting cross-leg'd, and not always prostrate.

Then to begging on which alone they do not always live.

In going from Prayer, the *Talapoins* go into the City to beg Alms for an hour; but they never go out of the Convent, and never re-enter, without going to salute their Superior, before whom they prostrate themselves to touch the ground with their Forehead; and because that the Superior sits generally cross-leg'd, they take one of his Feet with both their hands, and put it on their head. To crave Alms they stand at the Gates, without saying any thing; and they pass on after a little time, if nothing is given them. It is rare that the People sends them away without giving them, and besides this their Parents never fail them. The Convents have likewise some Gardens, and cultivated Lands, and Slaves to plough them. All their Lands are free from Taxes, and the Prince touches them not; altho' he has the real property thereof, if he divests not himself by writing, which he almost never does.

How they fill up the day.

At their return from begging, the *Talapoins* do breakfast if they will, and are not always regular in presenting to the Idol what they eat, tho' they do it sometimes after the manner that I have related. Till Dinner-time they study, or employ themselves as to them seems meet, and at Noon they dine. After Dinner they read a Lecture to the little *Talapoins*, and sleep; and at the declining of the day they sweep the Temple, and do there sing as in the morning for two hours, after which they lie down. If they eat in the evening, it is only Fruits; and tho' their day's work seems full by what I have said, they cease not to walk in the City after Dinner for their pleasure.

The Secular Servants of the Talapoins.

Besides the Slaves which the Convents may have, they have each one or two Servants which they call *Tapacaou*, and which are really Seculars, tho' they be habited like the *Talapoins*, excepting that their Habit is white, and not yellow. They receive the money which is given to the *Talapoins*, because the *Talapoins*

 can-

cannot touch it without sinning: they have the care of the Gardens and Lands, which the Convent may have, and in a word they act in the Convents for the *Talapoins*, whatever the *Talapoins* conceive cannot be done by themselves, as we shall see in the Sequel.

CHAP. XVIII.

Of the Election of the Superior, and of the Reception of the Talapoins *and* Talapoinesses.

The Election of the Superior.

WHen the Superior is dead, be he *Sancrat* or not, the Convent elects another, and ordinarily it chuses the oldest *Talapoin* of the House, or at least the most learned.

How a Secular does, who builds a Temple, and begins a Convent.

If a particular person builds a Temple, he agrees with some old *Talapoin* at his own choice to be the Superior of the Convent, which is built round this Temple, as other *Talapoins* come thither to inhabit; for he builds no *Talapoins* Lodging before-hand.

How a Talapoin is admitted.

If any one would make himself a *Talapoin*, he begins with agreeing with some Superior that would receive him into his Convent; and because there is none but a *Sancrat*, as I have said, can give him the Habit, he goes to demand it of some *Sancrat*, if the Superior with whom he would remain, is not himself a *Sancrat*; and the *Sancrat* appoints him an hour some few days after, and for the Afternoon. Whoever should oppose him would sin; and as this Profession is painful, and it lasts not necessarily the whole life, the Parents are always very glad to see their Children embrace it. I have not heard what Mr. *Gervaise* reports, that it is needful to have a permission in writing from *Oc-ya Pra Sedet*, to be receiv'd a *Talapoin*. I see not likewise how this could be practicable in the whole extent of the Kingdom; and they have always assured me, that it is free for every one to make himself a *Talapoin*, and that if any one did oppose the reception of another into this Profession, he would sin. When any one therefore is to be admitted, his Parents and his Friends accompany him to this Ceremony with Instruments and Dancers, and they stop frequently by the way to see dancing. During the Ceremony, the Demandant, and the Men that are of his Retinue, do enter into the Temple where the *Sancrat* is; but the Women, the Instruments, and the Dancers enter not therein. I know not who shaves the Head, the Eye-brows and the Beard of the Demandant, or whether he shaves it not himself. The *Sancrat* gives the Habit with his own hand, and he cloaths himself therewith, letting the secular Habit fall underneath when he has put on the other. Mean while the *Sancrat* pronounces several *Balie* words; and when the Ceremony is ended, the new *Talapoin* goes to the Convent, where he must remain, and his Parents and Friends accompany him thither: But from this time he must no more hear any Instruments, nor behold any Dance. Some days after the Parents do give an Entertainment to the Convent, and they exhibit a great many Shows before the Temple, which the *Talapoins* are prohibited to see.

Whether there are several degrees of Talapoins.

Mr. *Gervaise* distinguishes the *Talapoins* into *Balouang*, *Tchaou-cou* and *Picou*. As for me, I have always heard say that *Balouang*, which the *Siameses* do write *Pat-louang*, is only a Title of Respect. The *Siameses* gave it to the Jesuits, as we do give them the Title of Reverence. In this Country I never heard speak of the word *Picou*, but only of *Tchaou-cou*, which I shall explain in the Sequel, and which some have informed me to be the *Siamese* word which signifies *Talapoin*. So that they say, *He is a Tchaou-cou*, and *I would be Tchaou-cou*, to signifie *he is a Talapoin, and I would be a Talapoin*. Nevertheless as there may be some difference between the *Sancrats* and *Talapoins*, which the persons whom I consulted, knew not, tho' otherwise expert, it may well be that there is some like-

wise

wise between the *Talapoins* themselves, some of which might be *Pat-bouang*, and others *Pirin*, and that the general name of all might be *Tchaou-cou*; I refer my self to Mr. *Gervaise*.

Of the *Talapoinesses*.

The *Talapoinesses* do call themselves *Nang Tchii*: They are clad in white, like the *Tapacaou*, and are not esteemed altogether Religious. A simple Superior sufficeth to give them the Habit, as well as to the *Nens*: And altho' they cannot have any carnal Commerce with Men, yet are they not burnt upon this account, as the *Talapoins* are, which are surprized in a Fault with the Women. They deliver them up to their Parents to bastinado them, because that neither the *Talapoins* nor the *Talapoinesses* can strike any person.

CHAP. XIX.

Concerning the Doctrine of the Talapoins.

Divers kinds of *Talapoins* in the *Indies*.

ALL the *Indies* are full of *Talapoins*, tho' they have not everywhere this Name, and live not everywhere after the same manner. Some marry, and others strictly observe Celibacy. Some eat Meat, provided it is given them slain, others never eat any. Some do kill Animals, others kill none at all; and others do kill very rarely, and for some Sacrifice. Their Doctrine appears not more exactly the same in all places, tho' the Foundation thereof be always the opinion of the *Metempsychosis*; and their Worship is also various, tho' it always refers to the dead.

How they believe the whole universal Nature, and what Idea they have of the Animation.

It seems that they believe all Nature animated, not only Men, Beasts and Plants, but the Heaven, the Planets, the Earth, and the other Elements, the Rivers, the Mountains, the Cities, the Houses themselves. And moreover, as all Souls appear to them of the same Nature, and indifferent to enter into all Bodies, of what kind soever they be, it seems that they have not the *Idea* of the Animation as we have. They believe that the Soul is in the Body, and that it rules the Body, but it appears not that they believe like us, that the Soul is physically united to the Body, to make one with it. So far are they from thinking that the natural Inclination of Souls is to be in Bodies, that they believe it is a Penance for them, to extirpate their Sins by their Sufferings, because that indeed there is no kind of Life which has not its Troubles. The supreme Felicity of the Soul, in their opinion, is not to be obliged to animate any Body, but to remain eternally in repose. And the true Hell of the Soul is on the contrary, according to them, the perpetual necessity of animating Bodies, and of passing from one to another by continual Transmigrations. 'Tis said, that amongst the *Talapoins*, there are some which boldly affirm, that they remember their past Transmigrations; and these Testimonies do doubtless suffice to confirm the People in the Opinion of the *Metempsychosis*. The *Europeans* have sometimes translated by the word *Tutelar Genius*, the Souls which the *Indians* give to the Bodies, which we esteem inanimate: But these *Genii* are certainly in the Opinion of the *Indians* only real Souls, which they suppose equally to animate all the Bodies wherein they are present, but after a manner which corresponds not to the *Physical Union* of our Schools.

What they think of the Eternity of the World.

The Matter of the World, according to their Doctrine, is eternal; but the World which we see is not, for whatever we see therein, lives in their Opinion, and must die; and at the same time there will spring up other Beings of the same kind, another Heaven, another Earth, and other Stars; and this is the ground of what they say, that they have seen Nature decay and revive again several times.

Of the nature of the Soul according to them.

No Opinion has been so generally receiv'd amongst Men, as that of the Immortality of the Soul; but that the Soul is immaterial, is a Truth the knowledge of which is not so much propagated. Thus is it a very great difficulty to give

unto

unto a *Siamese* the *Idea* of a pure Spirit; and this is the Testimony which the Missionaries give thereof, that have been longest amongst them. All the *Pagans* of the East do believe indeed that there remains something of Man after his death, which subsists separately and independantly from its body; but they give extent and figure to what remains, and in a word they attribute unto it all the same Members, and all the same solid and liquid Substances whereof our Bodies are composed. They suppose only that the Souls are of a matter subtile enough, to be free from touch and sight; tho' they believe that if any one be wounded, the blood which flows from its wound, may appear. Such were the *Manes* and *Shades* of the *Greeks* and *Romans*, and it is by this figure of the Souls like unto that of the Bodies, that *Virgil* supposes that *Æneas* knew *Palinurus, Dido,* and *Anchises* in Hell.

The Absurdity of their Opinion.

Now what is altogether impertinent in this Opinion, is, that the Orientals cannot tell why they attribute the humane Figure, rather than any other, to the Soul, which they suppose able to animate all sorts of Bodies, besides the humane Body. When the *Tartar* which now reigns at *China*, would force the *Chineses* to shave their hair after the *Tartarian* fashion, several of them chose rather to suffer death, than to go, they said, into the other World, to appear before their Ancestors without hair; imagining, that they shaved the head of the Soul, by shaving that of the Body.

Of the Punishments and Recompences to the Soul after death.

The Souls therefore, tho' material, are yet imperishable in their Opinion; and at their departure out of this life, they are punished or recompenced, with Punishments or Pleasures proportioned in greatness and duration to their good or evil works, until they re-enter into the humane Body, wherein they must enjoy a Life more or less happy, according to the Good or Evil they have committed in a former Life.

How they explain the Prosperity of the Wicked, and the Misfortunes of the Good.

If a Man is unfortunate before he has done amiss, as if he is dead-born, the *Indians* believe that he has merited it in a former Life, and that then perhaps he caused some Great-belly'd Woman to miscarry. If, on the contrary, they observe a wicked Man to prosper, they believe that he enjoys the Recompence which he has merited in another Life by good Actions. If the Life of the Man is mixt with Prosperity and Adversity, 'tis because every Man, they say, has done Good and Evil when he formerly lived. In a word, no Person suffers any Misfortune, according to their Opinion, if he has always been innocent; nor is he always happy, if he has at any time been culpable; nor does he enjoy any Prosperity, which he has not merited by some good Action.

Of the several places where the Soul passes after death.

Besides the divers manners of being of this World, as of Plant, or of Animal, to which the Souls are successively linked after death, they reckon several places out of this World, where the Souls are punished or rewarded. Some are more happy, and others more miserable than the World wherein we are. They make all these places as Stages in the whole extent of Nature, and their Books do vary in the number; tho' the most common Opinion is, that there are nine happy, and as many unhappy. The nine happy places are over our heads, the nine unhappy are under our feet; and the higher a place is, the happier it is; as also the lower it is, the more unhappy it is: so that the happy extend far above the Stars, as the unhappy do sink a great way beneath the earth. The *Siameses* do call the Inhabitants of the superior Worlds *Thevada*, those of the inferior Worlds *Pii*, and those of this World *Manusse*. The *Portugueses* have translated the word *Thevada* by that of *Angels*, and the word *Pii* by that of *Devils*, and they have given the Name of *Paradise* to the superior Worlds, and that of *Hell* to the inferior.

It there revives again.

But the *Siameses* do not believe that the Souls in departing out of the Body do pass into these places, as the *Greeks* and *Romans* thought that they went into Hell: they are born, according to them, at the places where they go; and there they do live a life, which from us is conceal'd, but which is subject to the infirmities of this, and unto death. Death and a new Birth are always the road from one of these places to another, and it is not till after having lived in a certain number of places, and during a certain time, which ordinarily extends to some thousands of years, that the Souls there punished or recompenced, do happen to spring up again in the World wherein we are.

Now

To live a life full of Cares like this.

Now as they suppose that the Souls have a new habitation in the places where they arrive, they think they stand in need of the things of this Life; and all the ancient Paganism believed the same. With the body of a dead man, they burnt the things which he had most esteemed, during his Life, Moveables, Animals, Slaves, and even free Persons, if he had any singularly devoted to his Service.

Why the Indian women burn themselves with the body of their Husband.

They still practice worse than this, if it is possible, among the Pagans of the true *India*, where the Wife glories in burning herself alive with the body of her Husband, to meet his Soul in the other world. I well know that some presume that this Custom was formerly introduced in the *Indies*, to secure the Husbands from the Treason of their Wives, by forcing them to die with them. *Mandesto* reports this opinion, and *Strabo* had reported it before him, and had disapproved it, thinking it improbable either that such a Law was established, or that such a reason for establishing it was true: Indeed, besides that this Custom is extended to the Moveables and Animals, things all innocent, it is free in regard of the Women, none of which dies after this manner, if she desires it not; and it has been received in too great a part of the Country, to imagine that the Crimes of the Women have given occasion thereunto. Wives to be Slaves, or as Slaves to their Husbands, are not either more dissatisfied with their Condition, nor greater Enemies to their Husbands, and they change no part of the Condition as to this regard, by a second Marriage. Thus it is observed that the *Indian* Women have always look'd upon the Liberty they have of dying with their Husbands, not as a Punishment, but as a Felicity which is offered them. The Women slaves do sometimes follow their Mistress to the Funeral Pile, but voluntarily and without compulsion. And moreover it is not a thing without precedent in the *Indies*, that an Husband enamour'd with his Wife, will burn himself with her, in hopes of going to enjoy another Life with her.

This Custom is received among the Tartars, and is not without example among the Chinese.

Navarette reports it is a Custom of the *Tartars*, that when there dies one amongst them, one of his Wives hangs herself, to follow him into the other World; but that the *Tartar* which reigned at *China* in 1668, abolished this Custom: and he adds, that though it be not common to the *Chinese*, nor approved by *Confucius*, yet it is not without example. He relates one in his time, of the Vice-Roy of *Canton*, who being poysoned himself, and feeling the approach of Death, called her, whom he loved the best of his Wives, and desired her to follow him: which she did by hanging herself so soon as he was dead.

The Oeconomy of the Chinese and of their Neighbours in Burials.

But certainly neither the *Chinese*, nor the *Tonquinese*, nor the *Siamese*, nor the other *Indians* beyond the *Ganges*, have ever, as it is known, received the Custom of permitting the Women to burn: and moreover they have by a wise Oeconomy established, that instead of real Furniture and Money, it should suffice to burn with the dead bodies, those very things delineated in paper cut, and oftentimes painted or gilded: under pretence, in my opinion, that in matter of Types, those of the things in Paper were as good as those of the things themselves, which the Paper represents. Wherefore the People report, that this Paper which is burnt, is converted in the other Life to the things which it represents. The richest *Chinese* cease not to burn at least some real Stuffs, and they burn moreover so much Paper, that this expence alone is considerable.

The power of the Dead over the Living the Source of the worship of the Dead.

But all these Oriental People do not only believe that they may be helpful to the dead, as I have already explained; they think also that the dead have the power of tormenting and succouring the living: and from hence comes their Care and Magnificence in Funerals; for it is only in this that they are magnificent. Hence it comes also that they pray to the dead, and especially the *Manes* of their Ancestors to the Great-Grand-Father, or to the Great-Great-Grand-Father; presuming that the rest are so dispersed by divers Transmigrations, that they can hear them no more. The *Romans* likewise prayed to their dead Ancestors, tho they believed them not to be Gods. Thus *Germanicus* in *Tacitus*, at the beginning of a military expedition besought the *Manes* of his Father *Drusus* to render it happy, because that *Drusus* himself had made war in that Country.

They fear only their dead Acquaintance.

But by a prevention, which I see diffused likewise among the Christians, that are afraid of Spirits, the Orientals neither expect nor fear any thing from the dead of foreign Countries, but from the dead of their City, or of their Quarter, or of their Profession, or of their Family.

CHAP. XX.

Of the Burials of the Chineses *and* Siameses.

The Reason of speaking of the Burials of the *Chineses*.

THE Burials of the *Chineses* are described in several Relations, but I shall not forbear speaking a word thereof, to render those of the *Siameses* more intelligible; because that the Customs of a Country do always better illustrate themselves, by the comparison of the Customs of the neighbouring Countries.

What are the Principal Circumstances thereof.

The first care of the *Chineses* in Burials is to have a Coffin of precious Wood; in which they do sometimes make an expence above their Fortune: and though they bury their bodies without burning them, they forbear not, at their Interment, to burn Goods, Houses, Animals, Money, and whatever is necessary to the Conveniences of Life; but all in Paper, except some real Stuffs which are burnt at the Funerals of the rich. Father *Semedo* reports, that at the Burial of a Queen of *China* her goods were really burnt. The second care of the *Chin.* is in Burials is, to chuse out a place proper for the Tomb. They chuse it according to the advice of the Soothsayers, imagining that the repose of the deceased depends on this choice, and that of the felicity and repose of the living depends on the repose of the dead. If therefore they are not the Proprietors of the place declared by the Soothsayers, they fail not to buy it, and sometimes dearly. And in the third place, besides the Funeral Train, which is great, they give magnificent entertainments to the dead person, not only when they bury him, but annually on the same day, and several times in the year.

The worship of the Dead.

In their House they have a Chamber designed for the *Manes* of their Ancestors, where from time to time they go to render the same Devotions to their Figure, as they render'd to their Body in interring it. They do again burn Perfumes, Stuffs, and cut Papers; and they do make them new repasts. The *Tonquineses*, according to Father *de Rhodes*, do intermix these sorts of repasts with Paper-meats, which they burn. The same Author very largely relates the Prayers which the *Tonquineses* make to the dead, how they demand of them a long and happy Life; with what zeal they redouble their Worship and Prayers in their Misfortunes, when the Soothsayers assure them that they ought to attribute the cause thereof to the Anger of their Parents.

The *Chineses* at present are entirely impious.

Several Relations of *China* assert, that the learned men, which in this Country are the most important Citizens, do consider the Ceremonies of Funerals, only as civil Duties, to which they add no Prayers: That at present they have not any sense of Religion, and do not believe the existence of any God, nor the Immortality of the Soul; and that tho they render unto *Confucius* an exterior Worship in the Temples which are consecrated to him, yet they demand not of him the Knowledge, which the learned Men of *Tonquin* demand of him.

The Doctrine of the Ancient *Chineses* on the worship of the Dead, and that it is very probable that they never prayed to the dead in Funerals.

But, whether the Funerals which the learned *Chineses* do make for their Parents be without Prayers, or not; it is certain that the ancient Spirit of the Doctrine of the *Chineses*, was to believe the Immortality of the Soul, to expect good and evil from the dead, and to address some Prayers unto them, if not in Burials, at least in the disgraces of Life to attract their protection. Moreover, what opinion soever they have had of the Power of the dead to succor the living, it is very probable that they thought, that the dead were in need at the moment of the Burial, that is to say in the Entrance and Establishment of another Life, and that it then belonged to the living to succor the dead, and not to demand succor of them.

But

The Burials of the *Siameses*.

But it is time to relate what the Funerals of the *Siameses* are. So soon as a man is dead his body is shut up in a wooden Coffin, which is varnished and gilded on the outside: and as the Varnish of *Siam* is not so good as that of *China*, and hinders not the stench of the dead body from passing through the cracks of the Coffin, they endeavour at least to consume the Intestines of the dead with Mercury, which they pour into his Mouth, and which, they say, comes out at the Fundament. They sometimes make use also of Leaden Coffins, and sometimes also they gild them: but the Wood of their Coffins is not so precious as at *China*, because they are not so rich as the *Chineses*. Out of a respect they place the Coffin on some high thing, and generally on a Bedsted which hath feet, and so long as the body is kept at the house, whether to expect the Head of the Family, if he is absent, or to prepare the Funeral Solemnities, they burn Perfumes and Tapers by the Coffin; and every night the *Talapoins* come to sing in the *Balie* Language, in the Chamber where it is exposed: they do range themselves along the Walls. They entertain them, and give them some Money: and what they sing are some moral Subjects upon Death, with the Road to Heaven, which they pretend to show to the Soul of the deceased.

How they burn the bodies.

Mean while the Family chuses a place in the Field, there to carry and burn the body. This place is generally a Spot near the Temple, which the Deceased, or some of his Ancestors had built; or near some other Temple, if there is none peculiar to the Family of the deceased. This space is inclosed with a square inclosure made of *Bambou*, with some kind of Architecture, almost of the same work as the Arbours and Bowers of our Gardens, and adorned with those Papers Painted or Gilded, which they cut to represent the Houses, Moveables, and Domestic and Savage Animals. In the middle of this Inclosure the Pile composed entirely or partly of Odoriferous wood, as are the white or yellow Saunders, and Lignum Aloes, and this according to the Wealth and Dignity of the deceased. But the greatest honour of the Funeral consists in erecting the Pile, not in eagerly heaping up Wood, but in great Scaffolds, on which they do put Earth, and then Wood. At the Burial of the late Queen, who died seven or eight years ago, the Scaffold was higher than ever was yet seen in this Country, and a Machine was desired of the *Europeans*, to raise the Coffin decently to that heighth.

The Train.

When it is resolved to carry the Corps to the Pile (which is always done in the Morning) the Parents and Friends do carry it with the sound of a great many Instruments. The Body marches first, then the Family of the deceased, Men and Women all cloathed in White, their Head covered with a White Vail, and lamenting exceedingly; and in fine, the rest of the Friends and Relations. If the Train can go all the way by water, it is so done. In very magnificent Funerals they carry great Machines of Bamboo covered with painted and gilded Paper, which represents not only Palaces, Moveables, Elephants, and other common Animals, but some hideous Monsters, some of which resemble the humane Figure, and which the Christians take for the Figures of Devils. They burn not the Coffin, but they take out the body which they leave on the Pile: and the *Talapoins* of the Convent, near which the body is burnt, do sing for a quarter of an hour, and then retire to appear no more. Then begin the shows of the *Cone* and of the *Rabam*, which are at the same time, and all the day long, but on different Theaters. The *Talapoins* think not that they can be present thereat without Sin: and these Shows are not exhibited at Funerals upon any religious Account, but only to render them more magnificent. To the Ceremony they add a festival Air, and yet the Relations of the deceased forbear not to make great Lamentations, and to shed many Tears, but they hire no Mourners, as some have assured me.

The Servant of the *Talapoins* lights the Funeral Pile.

About Noon the *Tapacaou*, or Servant of the *Talapoins*, sets fire to the Pile, which generally burns for two hours. The Fire never consumes the body, it only roasts it, and oftentimes very ill: but it is always reputed for the Honour of the deceased, that he has been wholly consumed in an eminent place, and that there remains only his Ashes. If it is the Body of a Prince of the Blood, or of a Lord whom the King has loved, the King himself sets fire to the Pile,

with-

without stirring out of his Palace. He lets go a lighted Torch along a Rope, which is extended from one of the Windows of the Palace to the Pile. As to the cut Papers, which are naturally designed for the Flames, the *Talapoins* do frequently secure them, and seize them to lend them to other Funerals; and the Family of the deceased permits them to do it. In which it appears that they have forgot the reason, why the neighbouring Nations dispence not from burning such Papers effectually: and in general it may be asserted, that there are no Persons in the world, which do ignore their own Religion so much as the *Talapoins*. It is very difficult, say some, to find any one amongst them that knows any thing. It is necessary to seek their Opinions in the *Balie* Books, which they keep, and which they study very little.

Alms at Funerals.

The Family of the deceased entertains the Train, and for three days it bestows Alms, *viz.* On the day that the body is burnt, to the *Talapoins* which have sung over the body, the next day to their whole Convent, and the third day to their Temple.

Funerals redoubled.

This is what is practised at the Funerals of the *Siameses*; to which it is requisite only to add, that they imbellish the Show with a great many Fire-works, and that if the Funerals are for a man of great consequence, they last with the same Shows for three days.

Bodies dug up to receive greater Funeral Honors.

It sometimes also happens that a Person of great Quality causes the body of his Father to be digged up again, though a long time dead, to make him a pompous Funeral; if when he died, they made him not such a one, as was worthy of the present Elevation of the Son. This participates of the Customs of the *Chineses*, who communicate as much as they can to their dead Relations, the Honors to which they arrive. Thus when a man not born a Kings Son arrives at the Crown of *China*, he will with certain Ceremonies cause the Title of King to be given to his deceased Father.

What the fire consumes not, is buried under Pyramids: and how the *Siameses* do call these Pyramids.

After the body of a *Siamese* has been burnt, as I have said, the whole Show is ended; they shut up the remains of his Body in the Coffin, without any Order; and this depositum is laid under one of these Pyramids, wherewith they encompass their Temples. Sometimes also they bury precious Stones, and other Riches with the body, because that it is to put them in a place which Religion renders inviolable. Some there are who say, that they cast the Ashes of their Kings into the River, and I have read of the *Peguins*, that they make a Paste of the Ashes of their Kings with Milk, and that they bury it at the mouth of their River when the Sea is retired: but as the Fire never consumes all, and as it principally spares the Bones, the *Siameses* and *Peguins* do put these remains of their Kings under Pyramids. These Pyramids are called *Pra Tchiai di*, *Pra* is that *Baly* Term, which I have frequently mentioned. *Tchiai-di* signifies *Good Heart*, that is to say *Contentment*, as I have explained it in the other part: So that *Pra Tchiai-di* amounts to these words *sacred repose*, as much as those of Repose and Contentment do resemble.

From whence came the fancy of Pyramids for Tombs.

A Tomb quite flat like ours would not in their opinion be honourable enough, they must have something of Eminence: and this is the fancy of the Pyramids of *Ægypt*, and the *Mausolæa*. Some People yet more vain have joyned Epitaphs thereto: and because that time effaces the Inscriptions, which are exposed to view, others have secretly put their names on the principal Stones of certain stately edifices: So that when they are discovered, their work is already demolished to the Foundation. The *Siameses* still keep to the first degree of Vanity, which is single Pyramids without any Epitaph, and so slightly erected, that those which last longest, do never last an Age.

Why the *Siameses* love to build Temples.

Those that have neither Temple nor Pyramid, do sometimes keep at their house the ill burnt remains of their Parents: But there hardly is a *Siamese* rich enough to build a Temple, who does it not, and who buries not the Riches he has remaining. The Temples are inviolable Sanctuaries, as I have said, and the Kings of *Siam*, as well as particular persons, commit their Treasures to them. I know that the *Siameses* have demanded some smooth Files of the *Europeans*, to cut the great Iron Bars which linked the Stones in the Temples, under which there was Gold concealed. The *Siameses* which have not wherewith to build a

Temple,

Temple, ex ſteem it at leaſt to make ſome Idol, which they give to ſome of the Temples already built: Which in theſe People is a ſentiment of Vanity or Religion, whereas the building of Temples may be as much the Intereſt of preſerving their Riches to their Family, as any other thing.

The Funerals of the Poor.

The Poor inter their Parents without burning them; but if it is poſſible for them, they invite the *Talapoins*, who ſtir not without a Gratuity. Thoſe that have not wherewithal to pay the *Talapoins*, do think they do honor enough to their dead Parents, to expoſe them in the Field on an eminent place; that is to ſay on a Scaffold, where the Vulturs and the Crows devour them.

Funeral honors retarded.

I have already ſaid, that in Epidemical Diſtempers they bury the Bodies without burning them; and that they dig them up and burn them ſome years after, when they think all the danger of the Infection is paſt.

Thoſe that are deprived of Funeral Honors.

But they never burn thoſe that Juſtice cuts off, nor Infants dead-born, nor Women that die in Child-bed, nor theſe which drown themſelves, or which periſh by any other extraordinary diſaſter, as by a Thunderbolt. They rank theſe unfortunate perſons amongſt the guilty, because they believe that ſuch Misfortunes never happen to innocent Perſons.

Mourning.

Mourning at *China* is preſcribed by the Laws, and that for the Father and Mother laſts three years, and deprives or bereaves the Son during this time, of all ſorts of publick Employment, if it is not Military: though to me it ſeems that this exception as to Military Employments, is a late eſtabliſhment. On the contrary, the *Siameſes* have no forced Mourning: they give marks of Sorrow only as much as they are Afflicted; ſo that it is more common at *Siam*, that the Father and the Mother put on Mourning for their Children, than that the Children wear it for their Father and Mother. Sometimes the Father turns *Talapoin* and the Mother *Talapoineſſe*, or at leaſt they ſhave the head one of the other: but there is only the true *Talapoins*, that can likewiſe ſhave the Eye-brows.

Whether the *Siameſes* pray to the Dead.

To me it appeared not that the *Siameſes* invoke their dead Parents, what enquiry ſoever I have made upon it; but they ceaſe not to believe themſelves frequently tormented with their Apparitions: and then they carry Viands to their Tombs, which the Beaſts do eat; and they give Alms for them to the *Talapoins*, becauſe they think that Charity is a Ranſom for the Sins of the dead, as well as of the living. Beſides this the *Siameſes* almoſt on all occaſions, do offer up Prayers to the good *Genij*, and imprecations againſt the bad, of which I have already given ſome examples; And theſe *Genij* are certainly in their opinion only Souls, all as I have ſaid, of the ſame Nature.

How it muſt be underſtood that the Souls of the Good are changed into Angels, and the Souls of the wicked into Devils.

The wicked *Genij* are the Souls of thoſe, which dye, either by the hand of Juſtice, or by ſome of thoſe extraordinary misfortunes, which make them to be judged unworthy of Funeral Honors. The good *Genij* are all the other Souls, eſteemed more or leſs good, according as they have been more or leſs Virtuous in this life. And this wholly reſembles the Opinion of *Plato*, who requires that one ſhould adhere to Vertue during life, to the end that the cuſtom thereof may continue after death. This amounts likewiſe to that Antient Opinion, which was ſpread alſo amongſt ſome of the Antient Chriſtians, that the Souls of the good are changed into Angels, and the Souls of the wicked into Devils. But amongſt the *Indians*, this doctrine is no other, than that the Souls of the good, ſpring up again after Death, in one of thoſe places, which the *Portugueſes* have called *Paradice*, and the Souls of the wicked, in one of thoſe other places, which they do call *Hell*. Some continuing to be good after Death, do good to men, others continuing to be wicked, do hurt to men, and every thing elſe, as much as they can. And who knows whether theſe ſeveral *Paradices* which they believe, are not a confuſed remembrance of the ſeveral Orders of the Celeſtial Spirits.

The *Indians* have no God which is the Judge of Humane Actions.

Now through an incredible blindneſs, the *Indians* admit not any Intelligent Being, which judges of the goodneſs or badneſs of Humane actions, and which orders the Puniſhment or Recompence thereof. Upon this account they admit only a blind fatality, which, ſay they, is the reaſon that Proſperity accompanies Vertue, and Misfortune Vice; as it determines heavy things to deſcend, and light things to ascend. And because that nothing more repugns reason, than to suppose an exact Justice in chance, or in the Necessity of Fate, the *Indian* People incline themselves to believe something Corporeal in good or bad works, which, they say, has the power of doing unto men, the Good or Evil which they deserve. But since we have often said, that the *Indians* do own the distinction of good or bad Works, it is necessary to set down the Principles of of their Morality.

CHAP. XXI.

Of the Principles of the Indian *Morals.*

Five Negative Precepts.

THey are reduced to five Negative Precepts, very near the same in all the Cantons of the *Indies*. Those of the *Siamese* are such as follow.

1. Kill nothing.
2. Steal nothing.
3. Commit not any impurity.
4. Lye not.
5. Drink no intoxicating Liquor, which in general they call *Laou*.

The first Precept extends to Plants and Seeds.

The first Precept is not limited to the Killing either Men or Animals: but it extends to Plants, and to Seeds; because that by a very probable Opinion, they believe that the Seed is only the Plant it self in a Cover. The Man therefore observing this Precept, as they understand it, can live only on Fruits; forasmuch as they consider the Fruit not as a thing which has Life, but as a part of a thing which has Life, and which suffers not, though its Fruit be pluck'd. In eating the Fruit it is necessary only not to eat the Kernel nor Stone, because they are Seeds: and it is necessary not to eat Fruit out of season, that is to say, in my opinion, before the Season; because that it is to make the Seed, which the Fruit contains, abortive, by hindering it from ripening.

And to the not destroying any thing in Nature.

Besides this, the Precept of not killing, extends to the not destroying any thing in Nature: by reason they think that every thing is animated, or if you will, that there are Souls every where, and that to destroy any thing whatever, is forceably to dispossess a Soul. They will not, for instance, break a Branch of a Tree, as they will not break the Arm of an innocent Person. They believe that it is to offend the Soul of the Tree. But when once the Soul has been expelled out of a body, they look upon this as a Destruction already wrought, and think nothing to be destroyed in nourishing themselves with this Body. The *Talapoins* make not any scruple of eating what is dead, but of killing what they think alive.

In several things they do more abhor Blood than Murder.

In several things they testify a greater Abhorrence of Blood, than of Murder: It is prohibited them to make any Incision, from whence there gushes out Blood; as if the Soul was principally in the Blood, or that it was only the Blood. And this perhaps is a confused remembrance of the ancient Command of God, who permitting unto man the use of Meat, prohibited him from eating the Blood of the Animals, *because that the Blood supplys in them the place of the Soul.* There are some *Indians* which dare not to cut a certain Plant, because there comes out a red Juice, which they take for the Blood of this Plant. The *Siamese* do scruple to go a fishing, only on the days when the *Talapoins* shave their Head. This done, it seems to them that when they fish, they commit no Crime; by reason they think not themselves guilty of the Death of the Fishes. They say they only pull them out of the Water, and shed not their Blood. The least evasion sufficeth them to elude the Precept. Thus they think not to sin by killing in War, because they shoot not direct at the Enemy: though at the bottom they endeavour to kill, as I have already explained it, discoursing of their manner of fighting.

But

But if any one tells them, that according to the opinion of the *Metempsychosists*, Murder oftentimes appears laudable, seeing that it may deliver a Soul from a miserable Life: They answer that forcibly to dispossess Souls is always to offend them; and that moreover they are not relieved, because they re-enter into the like Bodies, there to fill up the rest of the time, during which they are destined for this sort of Life. But they consider not that this reason would also prove that they did no real Injury in killing: and the *Chinese* who in this do think otherwise than the *Siamese*, do kill their Children when they have too many, and they alledge that it is to make them spring up more happy.

The Opinion of the *Metempsychosis* favourable to the Murder of the unhappy, it renders not all Murder indifferent.

Moreover all the *Indians* do think, that to kill themselves is not only a thing permitted, because they believe themselves Masters of their selves; but that it is a Sacrifice advantageous to the Soul, and which acquires it a great degree of Vertue and Felicity. Thus the *Siamese* do sometimes hang themselves out of Devotion, on a Tree which in *Balie* they call *Pra si maha Pout*, and in *Siamese Ton po*. These *Balie* words do seem to signifie the *excellent*, or the *holy Tree* of the *great Mercury*; for *Pout* signifies *Mercury*, in the *Balie* Name of *Wednesday*. The *Europeans* do call this Tree, *the Tree of the Pagods*, because the *Siamese* do plant it before the Pagods. It grows in the Woods like the other Trees of the Country, but no particular Person can have thereof in his Garden; and it is of this Wood, that they make all the Statues of *Sommona Codom*, which they would make of Wood. But in that Zeal which sometimes determines the *Siamese* to hang themselves, there is always some evident subject of a great distaste of Life, or of a great Fear; as is that of the Anger of the Prince.

To kill themselves appears to them a very laudable thing.

'Tis about six or seven years since a *Peguin* burnt himself, in one of the Temples, which the *Peguins* at *Siam* have called *Sam Pihan*. He seated himself cross-leg'd, and besmear'd his whole body, with a very thick Oil, or rather with a sort of Gum, and set fire thereunto. 'Twas reported that he was very much discontented with his Family, which nevertheless lamented exceedingly about him. After the Fire had smother'd and roasted him well, his body was covered with a kind of Plaister; and thereof they made a Statue which was gilded and put upon the Altar, behind that of the *Sommona Codom*. They call these sorts of Saints *Pra than tee*; *than* signifies *true*, *tee* signifies *certainly*. Behold then how the *Siamese* understand the first Precept of their Moral Law.

The Story of a *Peguin* which burnt himself.

I have nothing particular to say upon the second: but as to the third which prohibits all manner of Uncleanness, it extends not only to Adultery, but to all carnal Commerce of a Man with a Woman, and to Marriage itself. Not only Celibacy is amongst them a state of Perfection, but Marriage is a state of Sin: either through that Spirit of Modesty, which amongst all Nations is annext to the use of Marriage, and which seems therein to suppose an evil whereat they blush: or through a general Aversion to all natural indecencies, some of which were legal Impurities among the *Jews*. They wash themselves amongst certain People after having seen their Wives, as after some other sort of Pollution. *Mahomet* thought Women unworthy of Paradise, and without declaring what they shall become, he promises some fairer and more beautiful to his Elect.

The Prohibition of Impurity extends to the Prohibition of Marriage.

The *Chinese* Philosophers do say, that a Wife is a thing evil in itself, and that one must neither keep his own, nor take another, when he has Children, that may render unto their Parents from whom they are born, and to their Ancestors, the Duties which the Christian Religion thinks necessary to the repose of the dead. Without this pretended necessity they would believe Marriage unlawful, and so soon as they have Children, they think it a Vertue to make a Divorce. They cite the example of *Confucius*, who quitted his Wife when he had a Son; they alledge the example of this Son, who likewise quitted his; and the example and opinion of several other *Chinese* Philosophers, who have made a Divorce with their Wives, and who have esteemed the Divorce amongst the virtuous Actions. They condemn as a Corruption of the ancient manners of *China*, the Opinion of the modern *Chinese* People, who as well as the *Siamese*, guided by the sentiments of Nature, look upon Divorce, if not as an Evil, at least as a Misfortune. I know nothing concerning the fourth Precept, which deserves to be explained.

The *Chinese* Philosophers esteem Divorce a Vertuous Action.

The

Every Liquor which intoxicates, is prohibited.

The fifth not only prohibits intoxicating, but the drinking of any Liquor, which may intoxicate, though one makes not himself drunk therewith. They esteem a thing evil in it self, which may hurt by the quantity.

'Tis thus that they understand their Precepts, neither do they believe that real Vertue is made for every one, but only for the *Talapoins*. They think that what is Sin in it self, is Sin for all; and the *Talapoins* make neither Vow, nor any thing whatever, which is a Sin in them, which is not a Sin to all the World: but according to them, the Trade of Seculars is to sin, and that of the *Talapoins* not to sin, and to exercise Repentance for those that sin. They comprehend like us, that those who are designed to expiate the Sins of others by Repentance, ought to be more pure than others; and that the Punishment due and necessarily annext to Sin, may yet pass from the guilty to the innocent, if the innocent will willingly submit himself to deliver the guilty. Moreover they conceive the Nature of Sin very grosly, and very materially; for the *Talapoins* content themselves with abstaining from Actions which they think wicked, but they scruple not to make the Seculars commit them, to get Advantage thereby. Thus when they would eat Rice, Rice being a Seed they cannot boil it without Sin, because it is to kill it: But they make their *Tapacons*, which are their Domestic Seculars, or rather they cause the *Talapoin-Children*, which they educate, to commit this pretended Sin; and when the Rice is boiled, then they eat it. They are also prohibited to piss on the Fire, or in the Water, or on the Earth, because that this would be to extinguish the Fire, or to corrupt those two other Elements: they piss in some Vessel, and a Secular Servant pours it where he pleases, and it matters not whether he sins. The Seculars do therefore observe, or elude the Precepts only through the fear of the publick Chastisements, or through the natural strangeness which they might have to what they shall think Sin; but they ransom their Sins by their good Works, which principally consist in bestowing Alms on the Temples and *Talapoins*, according to the ancient Tradition known perhaps throughout the Earth, and so frequently repeated in the Holy Scripture, that Alms doth ransom Sins. It is easie also to observe in them a very natural and very just sentiment, which is that they much more condemn the Sins which may be easily avoided, than those which are inevitable, though they think that all are Sins. But to the end that the Morality of the *Talapoins* may be better understood, I will insert at the end of this Work, most of their Maxims verbatim, as they were given me. I will add only some Remarks to make them better understood.

The Spirit of the Maxims of the Talapoins.

There will be seen the respect which they have for the Elements, and for all Nature. They are prohibited to speak injuriously of any thing natural; to dig any hole in the Earth, and not to fill it up again after they have done it; to boil the Earth, as to boil Rice; to kindle the Fire, because it is to destroy that with which it is kindled; and to extinguish it when it is once kindled. There we shall see that they take care of Purity and Decency, as much as of real Virtue: that they have some Idea's of almost all the Virtues, and that they have hardly any that is exact; because they carry some to superstitious scruples, and that they live short of others.

Vertue according to them is impossible.

Moreover these Maxims are only for the *Talapoins*; not that they think that any person can violate them without Sin: but it is that they see it is impossible for any one not to infringe them: as for example, it is very necessary that some person make the Fire. They are surprized at the Beauty of our Morality, when it is told them that it equally invites all men to Vertue, because they comprehend not that this can be a thing practicable: but when they are made to understand it, and are informed that Vertue consists not in those impossible things, wherein they place it, they contemn what is told them, and do believe themselves more pure and virtuous than the Christians: or rather they return again to believe that they alone are *Creng*, that is to say pure, and that the Christians are *Cahin* or designed to sin, like the rest of Mankind: A prevention which must quite confound us, and which proves the extreme necessity which humane reason has of a superior Light, not to err in the knowledge of good and evil, the Idea's of which do nevertheless appear unto us so easie, and so natural.

It

The Vanity of the Talapoins.

If therefore the *Talapoins* do think themselves only vertuous, it is no wonder if they likewise allow themselves all the Pride imaginable in regard of the Seculars. This Pride appears in all things, as in that they affect to seat themselves higher than the Seculars, never to salute any Secular, and never to bewail the death of any person, not even that of their Parents. They have a Practice which resembles Confession, for from time to time they seem secretly to render an account of their Deportments to their Superior; but are so far from confessing themselves Sinners, that they only run over the Precepts, to say they have not violated them. I have not stolen, say they, I have not lied, and so of the rest. And in a word they are not humble, and they have rather the Idea's of Humiliations and Mortifications than of Humility.

Some Appearances of certain Monastick Vertues in the Talapoins.

They seem to understand Entertaining and Retirement. A Talapoin *sins, if in walking along the Streets, he has not his Sense's composed.* A Talapoin *sins, if he meddles with State Affairs.* They concern not themselves therein, without a great deal of Distraction, and without attracting the Envy and Hatred of several; which suits not to a *Talapoin*, who ought only to mind his Convent, and to edifie every one by his Modesty. But moreover I believe that a wise Policy has greatly contributed to interdict State-Affairs to persons, who have so great a Power upon the Minds of the People. They understand Religious Obedience. Obedience is the Vertue of every one in this Country, and it is no wonder that it is found in their Cloisters. They likewise understand Chastity. A *Talapoin sins*, if he coughs to attract on him the Eyes of the Women, if he beholds a Woman with Complacency, or if he desires one; if he uses Perfumes about his Person, if he puts Flowers to his Ears: and in a word, if he adorns himself with too much Care. And some would likewise say, they understand Poverty, because it is prohibited them to have more than one Vestment, and to have it precious: To keep any thing to eat from the Evening, till the next day; to touch either Gold or Silver, or to desire it. But at the bottom, as they may abandon their Profession, they act so well, that if they live poorly whilst they are *Talapoins*, they fail not to heap wherewith to live at their Ease, when they cease to be so. And these are the Idea's which the *Siameses* have of Vertue.

CHAP. XXII.

Of the Supream Felicity, and Extream Infelicity amongst the Siameses.

Perfect Felicity.

IT remains for me to explain wherein they place perfect Felicity, that is to say, the supream Recompence of good Works, and the utmost Degree of Unhappiness, that is to say the greatest Punishment of the Guilty. They believe therefore that if by several Transmigrations, and by a great number of good Works in all the Lives, a Soul acquires so much Merit, that there is not in any World any mortal Condition, that is worthy of it; they believe, I say, that this Soul is then exempt from every Transmigration, and every Animation, that it has nothing more to do; that it neither revives, nor dies any more; but that it enjoys an eternal Unactivity, and a real Impassibility. *Nireupan*, say they, that is to say this Soul has disappeared: it will return no more in any World: and 'tis this word which the *Portugueses* have translated *it is annihilated*; and likewise thus, *It is become a God*, though in the Opinion of the *Siameses*, this is not a real Annihilation, nor an Acquisition of any divine Nature.

What the Portugueses have called Paradise and Hell, are neither the Perfect Felicity, nor the extream Infelicity according to the Siameses.

Such is therefore the true Paradice of the *Indians*; for tho' they suppose a great Felicity in the highest of the nine Paradices, of which we have already discoursed; yet they say that this Felicity is not eternal, nor exempt from all Inquietude; seeing that it is a kind of life, where one is born, and where one dies.

dies. By the like reason, their true Hell is not any of these nine places which we have called Hell, and in some of which they suppose Torments and eternal Flames: for tho' there may eternally be some Souls in these Hells, these will not always be the same: No Soul will be eternally punished; they will revive again to live there a certain time, and to depart thence by death.

The utmost degree of Infelicity.

But the true Hell of the *Indians* is only, as I have already said, the eternal Transmigrations of these Souls, which will never arrive at the *Nireupan*, that is to say, will never *disappear* in the whole duration of the World, which they do think must be eternal. They believe, that it is for the Sins of these Souls, and for their want of ever acquiring a sufficient merit, that they shall continually pass from one Body to another. The Body, whatever it be, is always according to them, a Prison for the Soul, wherein it is punished for its Faults.

The Wonders which they relate of a Man that deserves the Nireupan, and how they consecrate their Temples to him.

But before that a Man enters into the supreme Felicity, before that he *disappears*, to speak like them, they believe that after the Action, by which he concludes to merit the *Nireupan*, he enjoys great Priviledges from this life. They believe that it is then that such a Man preaches up Vertue to others with much more efficacy; that he acquires a prodigious Science, an invincible strength of Body, the power of doing Miracles, and the knowledge of whatever has befallen him in all the Transmigrations of his Soul, and of whatever should happen to him till his death. His death must likewise be of a singular sort, which they think more noble than the common way of dying. *He disappears*, they say, *like a Spark, which is lost in the Air*. And it is to the memory of these sorts of Men, that the *Siameses* do consecrate their Temples.

Tho' they believe it several, they honour only one named Sommona-Codom.

Now tho' they say that several have attain'd to this Felicity, (to the end, in my opinion, that several may hope to arrive thereat) yet they honour only one alone, whom they esteem to have surpassed all the rest in Vertue. They call him *Sommona-Codom*; and they say that *Codom* was his Name, and that *Sommona* signifies in the *Balie* Tongue, *a Talapoin of the Woods*. According to them, there is no true Vertue out of the *Talapoin* Profession, and they believe the *Talapoins* of the Woods much more vertuous than those of the Cities.

No Idea of a Divinity amongst the Siameses.

And this is certainly the whole Doctrine of the *Siameses*, in which I find no *Idea* of a Divinity. The Gods of the ancient *Paganism* which we know, govern'd Nature, punished the wicked, and recompenc'd the good; and tho' they were born like Men, they came of an immortal Race, and knew not death. The Gods of *Epicurus* took care of nothing, no more than *Sommona-Codom*; but it appears not that they were Men arrived thro' the r Vertue at that state of an happy Inactivity, they were not born, neither did they dye. *Aristotle* has acknowledged a first Mover, that is to say a powerful Being, who had ranged Nature, and who had given it, as I may say, the swing, which preserv'd the harmony therein. But the *Siameses* have not any such *Idea*, being far from acknowledging a God Creator; and so I believe it may be asserted, that the *Siameses* have no *Idea* of any God, and that their Religion is reduced all intire to the worship of the dead. And it is necessary that the *Chineses* understand it thus, and that they think not that *Pagode* signifies *God*: for Father *Magaillans* informs us, that they are offended when *Confucius* is treated as a *Pagode*; because this is to treat him not as God, which would not be an injury to *Confucius*: but as a Man arrived at the supreme Vertue of the *Indians*, which the *Chineses* do think very much inferior to the Vertue of *Confucius*.

CHAP. XXIII.

Concerning the Origine of the Talapoins, *and of their Opinions.*

It seems that it may be found in the Chinese Antiquity.

WHen I would seek by what degrees Humane Reason could precipitate it self into such strange Digressions, I think to find the Footsteps thereof in the *Chinese* Antiquity.

The

If the ancient Chinese acknowledge the Deity, they have corrupted the Idea thereof.

The *Chinese* are fo ancient, that it muft be prefumed that at the beginning they knew the true God, and by him good and bad Works, and the Recompences or Punifhments which the one and the other were to expect from this Omnipotent Judge; but that by little and little they have obfcur'd and corrupted thefe *Idea's*. God, that Being fo pure and fo perfect, is almoft become the material Soul of the entire World, or of its moft beautiful part, which is the Heaven. His Providence and his Power have been no more than a limited Providence and Power, tho' neverthelefs a great deal more extenfive than the ftrength and prudence of Men. *It feems*, fays Father *Trigaut*, *in the firft Book of his Chriftian Expedition to* China, chap. 10. *That the ancient* Chinefes *have believed the Heaven and the Earth animated, and that they have ador'd the Soul as a Supreme God, calling him the King of Heaven, or fimply the Heaven and the Earth.* Father *Trigaut* might raife the fame doubt upon all things; for the Doctrine of the *Chinefes* has continually attributed Spirits to the four parts of the World, to the Planets, to the Mountains, to the Rivers, to the Plants, to the Cities and their Ditches, to Houfes and their Chimnies, and, in a word, to all things. And all the Spirits appear not good to them; they acknowledge fome wicked ones, to be the immediate caufe of the mifchiefs and difafters to which the humane life is fubject. Moreover, as they thought the Earth and the Sea fixt to the Heaven by the Horizon, they have attributed but one Spirit or one Soul to the Heaven and the Earth; tho' neverthelefs, and perhaps by fome thought contrary to their firft opinion, they have built two different Temples, the one confecrated to the Heaven, and the other to the Earth.

They have taken from God the infinite Providence and Omnipotence.

As therefore the Soul of Man was, in their opinion, the fource of all the vital Actions of Man; fo they gave a Soul unto the Sun, to be the fource of its qualities and of its motions: and on this Principle the Souls diffufed every where, caufing in all Bodies the Actions which appear natural to thefe Bodies, there needs no more to explain in this opinion the whole œconomie of Nature, and to fupply the Omnipotence, and infinite Providence, which they admit not in any Spirit, not even in that of the Heaven.

They have made God as a King of all Nature, but not a King always obeyed.

In truth, as it feems that Man, ufing things natural for his nourifhment, or for his conveniency, has fome power over things Natural, the ancient opinion of the *Chinefes*, allowing fuch a like power proportionably to all the Souls, fuppofed that that of the Heaven might act over Nature, with a prudence and ftrength incomparably greater than Humane Prudence and Power. But at the fame time it acknowledg'd in the Soul of every thing, an interior force, independent by its nature from the Power of Heaven, and which acted fometimes againft the Defigns of Heaven. The Heaven governed Nature as a powerful King; the other Souls paid Obedience to him; He almoft continually forced them, but fome there were which fometimes diffented with obeying him.

Confucius believes extream Vertue impoffible, and confequently he thinks the Idea we have of God impoffible.

Confucius difcourfing of boundlefs Vertue, which is the true Idea that we have of the Divinity, thinks it impoffible. *How vertuous foever*, faith he, *a man is, there will yet be a degree of Vertue, to which he cannot attain. The Heaven and the Earth*, adds he, *tho' fo great, fo perfect, and fo curioufly wrought, cannot yet fatisfy the Defires of all; by reafon of the Inconftancy of the Seafons, and of the Elements: fo that Man finds in them wherewith to reprehend, and even juft Subjects of Indignation. Wherefore if we throughly comprehend the greatnefs of extream Vertue, we fhall neceffarily confefs that the whole Univerfe can neither contain nor fuftain the weight thereof. If, on the contrary, we think upon that fubtil and conceal'd point of Perfection in which it confifts, we fhall confefs that the whole World can neither divide nor penetrate it.* Thefe are the words of *Confucius*, as Father *Couplet* has given them us, by which this Philofopher feems to have had no other Intention, than to defcribe the real Divinity, which he believes impoffible, fceing that he finds it no where, not even in the Spirit of the Heaven and the Earth, which is what he conceived moft perfect.

The Worfhip due to the Creator divided amongft the Creatures by the Ancient Chinefes.

The Devine Power and Providence being thus diftributed as by Piece meals, to an infinite number of Souls, the ancient *Chinefes* thought themfelves obliged to addrefs to this infinite multitude of Souls and Spirits, the Vows and Worfhip which they ow'd only to one alone.

Of

Of Nature they make a State like to theirs.

Of Nature they make an invisible Monarchy, which they mould theirs upon, and of which they believe that the invisible members had a continual correspondence with the members of the *Chinese* Monarchy, which they thought to possess near the whole Earth. To the Spirit of Heaven they allot six principal Ministers, as the King of *China* has six, which are the Presidents of the six chief Tribunals, wherein they only have a determinative Voice. They believe that the King of Heaven (for they give this Title to the Spirit of Heaven) intermeddled only with the person and manners of the King of *China*: That all men ought to honour this supream Spirit, but that the King of *China* only was worthy to offer Sacrifices unto him; and for these Sacrifices they had no other Priest. The Ministers of *China* offer'd Sacrifices to the Ministers of Heaven: and every *Chinese* Officer thus honoured an Officer like to him near Heaven. The People sacrificed to a multitude of Spirits diffused every where, and every one was Priest in this sort of worship: there being not any Order, or Religious body, for the service of the Temples, and for the Sacrifices.

What the Indians have added to these Errors.

The *Indians* do now believe, like the ancient *Chineses*, some Souls, as well good as bad, diffused every where, to which they have distributed the Divine Omnipotence. And there is yet found some remains of this very Opinion amongst the *Indians*, which have embraced Mahometanism. But by a new Error the Pagans of the *Indies* have thought all these Souls of the same nature, and they have made them all to rowl from one body to another: The Spirit of the Heaven of the ancient *Chineses* had some Air of Divinity: It was, I think, immortal, and not subject to wax old, and to die, and to leave its place to a Successor: but in the *Indian* Doctrine of the *Metempsychosis*, the Souls are fixed no where, and succeeding one another every where, they are not one better than another by their nature: they are only designed to higher or lower functions in Nature, according to the merit of their work.

Why the Indians have consecrated no Temple to the Spirits, not even to that of Heaven.

Thus the *Indians* have consecrated no Temples to the Spirits, not so much as to that of Heaven: because they believe them all Souls, like all the rest, which are still in the course of Transmigration, that is to say in Sin, and in the Torments of different sorts of life, and consequently unworthy of having Altars.

The Antient Chineses have divided the Justice of God.

But if the ancient *Chineses* have, as I may say, reduc'd the Providence and Omnipotence of God into piece-meals, they have not less divided his Justice. They assert that the Spirits, like concealed Ministers, were principally busied in punishing the hidden faults of men; that the Spirit of Heaven punished the faults of the King, the Ministring Spirits of Heaven the faults of the King's Ministers, and so of other Spirits in regard of other men.

The Justice of Heaven was principally busied in punishing the faults of the Kings of China.

On this Foundation they said to their King, that though he was the adoptive Son of Heaven, yet the Heaven would not have any regard to him by any sort of Afflictions, but by the sole consideration of the good or evil, that he should do in the Government of his Kingdom. They called the *Chinese* Empire, the *Celestial Command*; because, said they, a King of *China* ought to govern his State, as Heaven governed Nature, and that it was to Heaven, that he ought to seek the Science of Governing. They acknowledged that not only the Art of Ruling was a Present from Heaven; but that Regality it self was given by Heaven, and that it was a present difficult to keep; because that they supposed that Kings could not maintain themselves on the Throne without the favour of Heaven, nor please Heaven but by Vertue.

How they believe their Kings responsible to Heaven for the manners of their Subjects.

They carried this Doctrine so far, that they pretended that the sole Vertue of Kings, might render their Subjects Vertuous; and that thereby the Kings were held responsible to Heaven for the wicked manners of their Kingdom. The Vertue of Kings, that is to say, the Art of Ruling according to the Laws of *China*, was, in their Opinion a Donative from Heaven, which they called *Celestial Reason*, or Reason given by Heaven, and like to that of Heaven: The Vertue of Subjects, according to them, *the regards of the Citizens, as well from one to another, as from all towards their Prince, according to the Laws of China*, was the work of good Kings. 'Tis a small matter, said they, to punish Crimes, it is necessary, that a King prevents them by his Vertue. They extoll one of their Kings for having reigned Twenty two years, the People not perceiving, that is to say, not feeling the weight of the Royal Authority, no more than the force which moves Nature, and which they attribute to Heaven. They report then that for these Twenty two years there was not one single Process in all *China*, not one single Execution of Justice; a Wonder which they call *to govern imperceptibly like the Heaven*, and which alone may cause a doubt of the Fidelity of their History. Another of their Kings meeting, as they say, a Criminal, which was lead to Punishment, took it upon himself, for that under his Reign he committed Crimes worthy of Death. And another seeing *China* afflicted with Sterility for seven years, condemned himself, if their History may be credited, to bear the Crimes of his People, as thinking himself only culpable; and resolved to devote himself to death, and to sacrifice himself to the Spirit of Heaven, the Revenger of the Crimes of Kings. But their History adds, that Heaven, satisfied with the Piety of that Prince, exempted him from that Sacrifice, and restored Fertility to the Lands by a sudden and plentiful Rain. As the Heaven therefore executes Justice only upon the King, and that it inflicts it only upon the King for what it sees punishable in the People, the Ministers of Heaven do execute Justice on the secret Faults which the King's Ministers commit, and all the Officers which depend upon them: and after the same manner the other Spirits do watch over the Actions of the Men, that in the Kingdom of *China* have a rank equal to that, which these Spirits do possess in the invincible Monarchy of Nature, whereof the Spirit of Heaven is King.

The Chinese fear their dead Parents.

Besides this the natural Honor which most men have of the dead, whom they knew very well in their Life-time; and the Opinion which several have of having seen them appear to them, whether by an effect of this natural Honor, which represents them to them, or by Dreams so lively, that they resemble the Truth; do induce the ancient *Chinese* to believe that the Souls of their Ancestors, which they judged to be of very subtile matter, pleased themselves in continuing about their Posterity; and that they might, though after their death, chastise the Faults of their Children. The *Chinese* People still continue in these opinions of the temporal Punishments, and Rewards which come from the Soul of Heaven, and from all the other Souls; though moreover for the greatest part they have embraced the Opinion of the *Metempsychosis*, unknown to their Ancestors.

The Impiety of the present Chinese, which are men of Learning.

But by little and little the Men of Letters, that is to say, those that have some degrees of Literature, and who alone have a Hand in the Government, being become altogether impious, and yet having altered nothing in the Language of their Predecessors, have made of the Soul of Heaven, and of all the other Souls, I know not what aerial substances, unprovided of Intelligence; and for the Judge of our Works, they have established a blind Fatality; which, in their opinion, makes that which might exercise an Omnipotent and Illuminated Justice. How ancient this Impiety is at *China*, belongs not to me to determin. Father *de Rhodes* in his History of *Tonquin*, accuses *Confucius* himself therewith: Father *Couplet*, to whom we owe the Translation of several of this Philosophers Works, pretends to justifie him; and he at the same time recites several Arguments of the modern *Chinese*, by which they endeavour to demonstrate, that it is a thing wholly conformable to the Principles of Nature, that by the secret, but certain Sympathies, between Vertue and Felicity, and between Vice and Infelicity, Vertue must always be prosperous, and Vice always unhappy: but in truth their Arguments are so elevated, and so forced, and correspond so ill to the Language of their Ancestors, that it is very apparent that they are only the effect of a great extravagancy of Imagination, which was not in their Ancestors.

The Siamese have no other Judge of Humane Actions than Fatality.

The *Siamese* do not less dread Spirits, than the *Chinese*; though they imagine not perhaps the Conformity between the Kingdom of the dead and theirs; and moreover they have not lost the Idea of the Divinity less than the *Chinese*, and that they have yet preserved this ancient Maxim, which promises Rewards to Vertue, and which threatens Sin with Punishments; they have found out no other way, than to attribute this distributive Justice to a blind Fatality. So that according to them, 'tis the Fatality which makes the Soul to pass from one state to a better or a worse, and which retains them more or less proportionably to their good or bad works. And it is by these degrees that men are wholly fallen from the Truth, when they would guide themselves by that weak reason, in which they so mightily glory.

The *Indians* believe the *Talapoins* and their Doctrine as Antient as Mankind.

As to the Origin of the *Talapoins* and their Compeers, which are spread throughout the East, under several Names, as *Bramins*, *Jogues*, and *Bonzes*; it is so obscure in Antiquity, that it is difficult, in my opinion, ever to discover it. It appears that the *Indians* do believe this kind of men, and their Doctrine, as ancient as the World. They name not their Founder; and they think that it is of this Profession, that all the men have been, whose Statues are honoured in their Temples, and all those others which they suppose to have been adored before those, which they now adore.

The *Chinese* do name *Che-Kia* for the Author of this Doctrine.

The *Chinese* report, that the *Bonzes* and their Doctrine came to them from the *Indies*, in the eighth year of the Reign of *Mim-ti*, which answers to the 65th of our Salvation: and as they love to give the Origin of all things, they say that it was a *Siamese* named *Che Kia*, who was the Author thereof, about One Thousand years before the Nativity of Jesus Christ, though the *Siameses* themselves do pretend no such thing, and who boasting Antiquity in all things, like all the other *Indians*, they imagine that the Doctrine of the *Metempsychosis*, is as ancient as the Souls themselves. The *Japponeses* do call the *Che-Kia* of the *Chineses*, *Chaka*, and the *Tonquineses* have corrupted this same word after another manner: for according to Father *de Rhodes*, they call it *Thika*.

That this *Che-Kia* is certainly the *Siamese* name of the *Talapoins*.

Now these words *Che-Kia*, and *Chaka*, do nearly enough approach these *Siamese* words *Tchaou-ca*, and *Tchaou cou*, to make suspect that they are only a light corruption thereof. *Tchaou-ca* and *Tchaou-cou* signifies *Lord*, or literally *Lord of me*, with this difference, that the word *ca* which signifies *me*, is us'd only by Slaves in speaking to their Masters, or by those who would render such a respect to him, to whom they speak: whereas the word *cou* which likewise signifies *me*, is not so respectful, and is joyned to the word *Tchaou*, to speak in the third Person to him that discourses of his Lord. In speaking therefore to a *Talapoin*, they will say unto him *Tchaou-ca*, and in speaking of him to another they will call him *Tchaou-cou*. But what is remarkable is, that the *Talapoins* have no other name in *Siamese*; so that they say literally, *crai-pen Tchaou-cou*, *I would be Lord*, to signifie *I would be* Talapoin. Their *Sommona-Codom* they call *Pra-poute Tchaou*, which verbatim signifies *the Great and Excellent Lord*, and it is in this sense that they speak it of their King: but these words may also signifie, *the Great and Excellent* Talapoin. After the same manner amongst the *Arabians*, the word *Moula*, which signifies a Doctor of Law, properly signifies *Lord*, and the word Master is equivocal in our Language: it is spoken of a Doctor, and likewise of the King. I find therefore some reason to believe, that the *Chineses* having received the Doctrine of the *Metempsychosis* from some *Siamese Talapoin*, they have taken the general Name of the Profession, for the proper Name of the Author of the Doctrine: and this is so much the more plausible, as it is certain that the *Chineses* do also call their *Bonzes* by the Name of *Che-Kia*, as the *Siameses* do call their *Talapoins Tchaou-cou*. 'Tis therefore impossible to assert, from the Testimony of the *Chineses*, that there was an *Indian* named *Che-Kia*, Author of the Opinion of the *Metempsychosis*, a Thousand years before Jesus Christ: seeing that the *Chineses*, who have received this Opinion since the Death of Christ, and perhaps much later than they alledge, are forced to confess, that they have nothing related concerning this *Che-Kia*, but upon the Faith of the *Indians*; who speak not one word thereof, not thinking that there ever was any first Author of their Opinions.

The Antient way of Instructing the People, was by Poetry and by Musick.

Before the *Bonzes* came from the *Indies* to *China*, the *Chineses* had not any Priests nor Religious; and they have none as yet for their Antient Religion, which is that of the State. Amongst them, as amongst the *Greeks*, the most Antient way of instructing the People, was by Poetry and Musick. They had three hundred Odes, whereof *Confucius* made great Esteem, like to the Works of *Solomon*: for they contained not only the knowledge of the Plants, but all the

Duties

Duties of a good *Chinese* Citizen, and doubtless all their Philosophy: and it may be that these Odes are still preserved. The Magistrates took care to have them sung Publickly, and *Confucius* complains for that in his time he saw this Practice almost extinguished, and all the Antient Musick lost. According to him, the most sure mark of the loss of a State was the loss of the Musick; and *Plato*, like him, thinks Musick essential to good Policy. These two great Philosophers had learnt that Manners cannot be preserved, without the continual instruction of the People, and that the Laws, that is to say, the only Foundation of the Publick Authority and Repose, cannot long continue, where the Manners are corrupted: for where the Manners are corrupted, they only Study to Violate or Elude the Laws. The Learned remark in the Pentateuch, the Tracts of such a like Poetry, which contain'd the History of Illustrious Men, even of those that were more Antient than the Deluge: *Moses* cites certain places thereof, wherein is remarked the Poetick Stile.

How the *Talapoins* and their Brethren might have succeeded the Antient Poetry and Musick.

I conceive therefore that Men being wearied with singing always the same things, and losing by little and little the sense of the old Songs, have ceased to sing them, and have sought some commentaries on the Verses, which they they sung no more, for lack of understanding them: That then the Magistrates left the care of these Commentaries to other Men, and that they by little and little imposing on the belief of the People, have inserted in their Lectures, many things to their particular advantage, which are the Source of the Superstitious Veneration, which the *Indians* do still retain for the *Talapoins* and their Fellow-Brethren.

However it be, their Habit, their Convents, and their Temples are Inviolable, though the Revolutions of this Country, may have showed some examples of the contrary. *Vliet* whom I have often quoted, relates that when the present King's Father seized on the Crown, he thought it impossible securely to make an attempt upon the Person of one of the Princes of the Royal Family, till he had cunningly made him first to quit the *Talapoins Pagne* which he wore. After the same manner when this Usurper was dead, his Son who now Reigns, seeing his Uncle by the Father's side seize on the Throne, turned *Talapoin* to secure his Life, as I have reported at the beginning of this Relation.

CHAP. XXIV.

Of the Fabulous Stories which the Talapoins *and their Brethren have framed on their Doctrine.*

Fables common to all the *Indians*.

THE *Talapoins* are therefore obliged to supply the ancient Musick, and to explain their *Balie* Books unto the People with an audible Voice. These Books are filled with extravagant stories, grafted on the Doctrine which I have explained: and these Fables are almost the same throughout *India*, as the ground of the Doctrine is every where the same, or very near. They every where believe the *Metempsychosis*, and that it is only a way to punish the Souls for their faults, and to carry them gradually unto Perfection. They believe Spirits every where diffused, good and bad, capable of aiding and of hurting, but which are no other than the Souls of the dead; and they admit the Worship of these Spirits, though they raise no Altars to them; but only to the *Manes* of the men, whom they conceive to be arrived at the highest degree of Vertue, as far as they think Vertue possible. They all have some Quadruped, which they prefer before all others; some favourite Bird, and some Tree, which they principally adore. They all believe the same thing of the pretended Dragon which causes the Eclipses, and of the pretended Mountain, round which the whole Heaven turns, to make the Days and the Nights. They have almost the same five Precepts of Morality, they reckon near the same number of Hells and Para-

dises;

dice. They all expect other men, who ought to merit Altars, like those to whom they have already consecrated some; to the end that every one may have the Field free to pretend to the soveraign Vertue. They all suppose that the Planets, the Mountains, the Rivers, and particularly the *Ganges*, may think, speak, marry and have Children. They all relate the ridiculous *Metempsychoses* of the men whom they adore, in Pigs, Apes and other Beasts. *Abraham Roger* in his Book of the Religion of the *Bramins* relates, that the Pagans of *Paliacate*, on the Coast of *Coromandel*, do believe that their *Brama* whom they adore, was born almost, as some *Balie* Books do say *Sommona-Codom* was born, viz. of a Flower, which was sprung from the Navel of an Infant, which, they say, was a leaf a Tree in the form of an Infant biting its Toe, and swimming on the Water, which alone subsisted with God. They take no notice that the *Leaf-Infant*, subsisted too: and according to *Abraham Roger*, they in this Country believe in God, but in a God which is not adored: and without doubt he has with as little ground advanced, that others have writ that the *Siameses* believe a God.

The Fables which the Siameses relate of their Sommona-Codom.

'Tis no fault of mine that they gave me not the life of *Sommona Codom* translated from their Books, but not being able to obtain it, I will here relate what was told me thereof. How marvellous soever they pretend his Birth has been, they cease not to give him a Father and a Mother. His Mother, whose Name is found in some of their *Balie* Books, was called, as they say, *Maha Maria*, which seems to signifie the *great Mary*, for *Maha* signifies *great*. But it is found written *Mania*, as often as *Maria*: which proves almost that these are two words *Mania*, because that the *Siameses* do confound the *n* with the *r* only at the end of the words, or at the end of the Syllables, which are followed with a Consonant. However it be, this ceases not to give attention to the Missionaries, and has perhaps given occasion to the *Siameses* to believe, that *Jesus* being the Son of *Mary*, was Brother to *Sommona Codom*, and that having been crucified, he was that wicked Brother whom they give to *Sommona-Codom*, under the Name of *Thevetat*, and whom they report to be punished in Hell, with a Punishment which participates something of the Cross. The Father of *Sommona Codom* was, according to this same *Balie* Book, a King of *Teve Lanca*, that is to say, a King of the famous *Ceylon*. But the *Balie* Books being without Date, and without the Author's Name, have no more Authority than all the Traditions, whose Origin is unkown. This now is what they relate of *Sommona-Codom*.

'Tis said, that he bestowed all his Estate in Alms, and that his Charity not being yet satisfied, he pluck'd out his Eyes, and slew his Wife and Children, to give them to the *Talapoins* of his Age to eat. A strange contrariety of Idea's in this People, who prohibit nothing so much as to kill, and who relate the most execrable Parricides, as the most meritorious works of *Sommona Codom*. Perhaps they think that under the Title of Property a Man has as much Power over the Lives of his Wife and Children, as to them it seems he has over his own: For it matters not if otherwise the Royal Authority prohibits particular *Siameses* from making use of this pretended Right of Life and Death over their Wives, Children and Slaves; whereas it alone exerts it equally over all its Subjects, it may upon this Maxim of the despotic Government, that the Life of the Subjects properly belong to the King.

The *Siameses* expect another *Sommona Codom*, I mean another miraculous man like him, whom they already name *Pra Narotte*, and whom they suppose to have been foretold by *Sommona-Codom*. And they before-hand report of him, that he shall kill two Children which he shall have, that he will give them to the *Talapoins* to eat, and that it will be by this pious Charity that he will consummate his Vertue. This expectation of a new God, to make use of this Term, renders them careful and credulous, as often as any one is proposed to them, as an extraordinary Person; especially if he that is proposed to them, is entirely stupid, because that the entire Stupidity resembles what they represent by the Inactivity and Impassibility of the *Nireupan*. As for example, there appeared some years since at *Siam*, a young Boy born dumb, and so stupid, that he seemed to have nothing humane but the Shape: yet the Report spread it self

through

through the whole Kingdom, that he was of the first men, which inhabited this Country, and that he would one day become a God, that is to say arrive at the *Nireupan*. The People flocked to him from all parts, to adore him and make him Presents, till that the King fearing the consequences of this Folly, caused it to cease by the Chastisement of some of those, that suffered themselves to be seduced. I have read some such thing in *Tosi's India Orientale*, Tom. I. pag. 203. He reports that the *Bonzes* of *Cochinchina*, having taken away from their a stupid Infant, shew'd him to the People as a God, and that after having enrich'd themselves with the Presents which the People made him, they published that this pretended God would burn himself; and he adds that they indeed burnt him publickly, after having stupified his Senses by some Drink, and calling the insensible state, wherein they had put him, Extasie. This last History is given as a crafty Trick of the *Bonzes*, but it demonstrates, as well as the first, the Belief which these People have, that there may daily spring up some new God, and the Inclination which they have to take extream Stupidity, for a beginning of the *Nireupan*.

Sommona-Codom being disingaged, by the Almsdeeds which I have mentioned, from all the Bands of Life, devoted himself to Fasting, to Prayer, and to the other Exercises of the perfect Life: But as these Practises are possible only to the *Talapoins*, he embraced the Profession of a *Talapoin*; and when he had heaped up his good works, he immediately acquired all the Priviledges thereof.

He found himself endowed with so great a Strength, that in a Duel he vanquished another man of a consummated Vertue, whom they call *Pra Souane*, and who doubting of the Perfection whereunto *Sommona-Codom* was arrived, challenged him to try his Strength, and was vanquisht. This *Pra Souane* is not the sole God, or rather the sole perfect Man, which they pretend to have been contemporary with *Sommona-Codom*. They name several others, as *Pra Ariaseria*, of whom they report that he was Forty Fadoms high, that his Eyes were three and a half broad, and two and a half round, that is to say, less in Circumference than Diameter, if there is no fault in the Writing from whence I have taken this Remark. The *Siamese* have a time of Wonders, as had the *Egyptians* and the *Greeks*, and as the *Chinese* have. For Instance, their principal Book, which they believe to be the work of *Sommona-Codom*, relates, that a certain Elephant had Three and thirty Heads, that each of its Heads had seven Teeth, every Tooth seven Pools, every Pool seven Flowers, every Flower seven Leafs, every Leaf seven Towers, and every Tower seven other things, which had each seven others, and these likewise others, and always by seven; for the numbers have always been a great Subject of Superstition. Thus in the Alcoran, if my Memory deceives me not, there is an Angel with a very great number of Heads, each of which hath as many Mouths, and every Mouth as many Tongues, which do praise God as many times every day.

Besides corporal strength, *Sommona-Codom* had the power of doing all sorts of Miracles. For example, he could make himself as big and as great as he pleas'd; and on the contrary, he could render himself so little, that he could steal out of sight, and stand on the head of another man, without being felt either by his weight, or perceived by the Eyes of another. Then he could annihilate himself, and place some other man in his stead; that is to say, that then he could enjoy the repose of the *Nireupan*. He suddenly and perfectly understood all the things of the World: He equally penetrated things past and to come, and having given to his body an entire Agility, he easily transported himself from one place to another, to preach Vertue to all Nations.

He had two principal Disciples, the one on the right Hand, and the other on the left: they were both plac'd behind him, and by each other's side on the Altars, but their Statues are less than his. He that is plac'd on his right Hand is called *Pra Mogla*, and he that is on his left Hand is called *Pra Scaribout*. Behind these three Statues, and on the same Altar, they only represent the Officers within the Palace of *Sommona-Codom*. I know not whether they have Names. Along the Galleries or Cloysters, which are sometimes round the Temples, are the Statues of the other Officers without the Palace of *Sommona-Codom*. Of

Pra Mogla they report, that at the request of the damned he overturned the Earth, and took the whole Fire of Hell into the hollow of his Hand; but that designing to extinguish it, he could not effect it, because that this Fire dried up the Rivers, instead of extinguishing, and that it consumed all that whereon *Pra Mogla* placed it: *Pra Mogla* therefore went to beseech *Pra Pouti Tchaou*, or *Sommona-Codom*, to extinguish Hell Fire: but though *Pra Pouti Tchaou* could do it, he thought it not convenient, because, he said, that men would grow too wicked, if he should destroy the Fear of this Punishment.

But after that *Pra Pouti Tchaou* was arrived at this high Vertue, he ceased not to kill a *Mar*, or a *Man* (for they write *Mar* and *Man*, though they pronounce always Man) and as a Punishment for this great fault, his Life exceeded not Eighty years, after which he died, by disappearing on a sudden, like a Spark which is lost in the Air.

The *Man* were a People Enemies to *Sommona-Codom*, whom they called *Pays Mans*, and because they suppose that this People was an Enemy to so holy a Man, they do represent them as a monstrous People, with a very large Visage, with Teeth horrible for their Size, and with Serpents on their Head instead of Hair.

One day then as *Pra Pouti Tchaou* eat Pig's flesh, he had a Chollick fit which killed him: An admirable end for a man so abstemious: but it was necessary that he died by a Pig, because they suppose that the Soul of the *Man* whom he slew, was not then in the Body of a *Man*, but in the Body of a *Pig*: as if a Soul could be esteemed, even according to their Opinion, the Soul of a *Man*, when it is in the Body of a Pig. But all these inventers of Stories are not so attentive to the Principles of their Doctrine.

Sommona-Codom before his Death ordered that some Statues and Temples should be Consecrated to him, and since his Death he is in that State of repose, which they express by they word *Nireupan*. This is not a place but a kind of Being: for to speak truly, they say *Sommona-Codom* is no where, and he enjoys not any Felicity: he is without power, and out of a condition to do either Good or Evil unto Men: expressions which the *Portugueses* have rendered by the word Annihilation. Nevertheless on the other hand the *Siameses* do esteem *Sommona-Codom* happy, they offer up Prayers unto him, and demand of him whatever they want: whether that their Doctrine agrees not with it self, or that they extend their worship beyond their Doctrine: but in what Sense soever they attribute Power to *Sommona-Codom*, they agree that he has it only over the *Siameses*, and that he concerns not himself with other People, who adore other Men besides him.

That it is probable that *Sommona Codom* never has been.

As therefore they report nothing but Fables of their *Sommona-Codom*, that they respect him not as the Author of their Laws and their Doctrine, but at most as him who has re-established them amongst Men, and that in fine they have no reasonable Memory of him, it may be doubted, in my Opinion, that there ever was such a man. He seems to have been invented to be the Idea of a Man, whom Vertue, as they apprehend it, has rendered happy, in the times of their Fables, that is to say beyond what their Histories contain certain. And because that they have thought necessary to give at the same time an opposite Idea of a Man, whom his wickedness has subjected to great Torments, they have certainly invented that *Thevetat*, whom they suppose to have been Brother to *Sommona-Codom*, and his Enemy. They make them both to be *Talapoins*, and when they alledge that *Sommona-Codom* has been King, they report it, as they declare he has been an Ape and a Pig. They suppose that in the several Transmigrations of his Soul he has been all things, and always excellent in every kind, that is to say he has been the most commendable of all Pigs, as the most commendable of all Kings. I know not from whence Mr. *Gervaise* judges that the *Chineses* pretend that *Sommona-Codom* was of their Country: I have seen nothing thereof in the Relations of *China*, but only what I have spoken concerning *Chekia* or *Chaka*.

The Life of *Thevetat* was given me translated from the *Balie*, but not to interrupt my discourse, I will put it at the end of this Relation. 'Tis also a Tex-

ture

ture of Fables, and a curious specimen of the thoughts of these men, touching the Vertues and Vices, the Punishments and Rewards, the Nature and the Transmigration of Souls.

I must not omit what I borrow from Mr. *Herbelot*. I have thought it necessary to consult him about what I know of the *Siamese*; to the end that he might observe what the words which I know thereof, have in common with the *Arabian*, *Turkish* and *Persian*: and he informed that *Sommona*, which must be pronounced *Soman*, signifies *Heaven* in *Persian*: and that *Codom*, or *Codam*, signifies *Ancient* in the same Tongue; so that *Sommona Codom* seems to signifie the *eternal*, or *uncreated Heaven*, because that in *Persian* and in *Hebrew*, the word which signifies Ancient implys likewise *uncreated* or *eternal*. And as touching the *Baly* Tongue, he informed me, that the ancient *Persian* is called *Pahalevi*, or *Pahali*, and that between *Pahali* and *Bahali* the *Persians* make no Difference. Add that the word *Pout*, which in *Persian* signifies an *Idol*, or *false God*, and which doubtless signified *Mercury*, when the *Persians* were Idolaters, signifies *Mercury* amongst the *Siamese*, as I have already remark'd. *Mercury*, who was the God of the Sciences, seems to have been adored through the whole Earth; by reason doubtless that Knowledge is one of the most essential Attributes of the true God. Remarks which may hereafter excite the curiosity of the learned men, that shall be designed to travel into the East.

A conjecture upon the Etymology of *Sommona Codom*, and what Language the *Baly* may be.

But I know not whether to this hour it is not lawful to believe that this is a proof of what I have said, that the Ancestors of the *Siamese* must have adored the Heaven, like the ancient *Chineses*, and as perhaps the ancient *Persians* did, and that having afterwards embraced the Doctrine of the *Metempsychosis*, and forgot the true meaning of the name of *Sommona Codom*, they have made a man of the Spirit of Heaven, and have attributed unto him all the fables that I have related. 'Tis a great Art to change the belief of the People, to leave unto them their ancient words, by cloathing them with new Idea's. Thus, it may be, that the Ancestors of the *Siamese* have thought that the Spirit of Heaven ruled the whole Nature, though the modern *Siamese* do not believe it of *Sommona-Codom*: they believe on the contrary, as I have said, that such a care is opposite to the supream felicity. They believe also that *Sommona-Codom* has sinned, and that he has been punished, at the time that he was worthy of the *Nireupan*, because they believe the extream virtue impossible. They believe that the worship of *Sommona-Codom* is only for them, and that amongst the other Nations there are other men, who have render'd themselves worthy of Altars, and which those other Nations must adore.

It seems to prove that the worship of the *Chinese* is more ancient at *Siam* than the Opinion of the *Metempsychosis*.

All the *Indians* in general are therefore perswaded, that different people must have different Worships, but by approving that other People have each their worship, they comprehend not that some would exterminate theirs. They think not like us that Faith is a Vertue: they believe because they know not how to doubt; but they perswade not themselves that there is a Faith and Worship which ought to be the Faith and the Worship of all Nations. Their Priests preach not that a Soul shall be punished in the other world, for not having believed the Traditions of his Country in this, because they understand not that any of them denies the Fables of their Books. They are ready to believe whatever is told them of a foreign Religion, how incomprehensible soever it be; but they cannot believe that their own is false: and much less can they resolve to change their Laws, their Manners, and their Worship. One had better to show them the contrarieties and gross Ignorance in their Books: they do sometimes agree herein, but for all this they reject not their Books; as for some falsity we reject not every Historian, nor every Physical Book. They believe not that their Doctrine has been dictated by an eternal and infallible Truth, of which they have not only the Idea; they believe their Doctrine born with the man, and written by some men, which to them appear to have had an extraordinary knowledge, and to have led a very innocent life: but they believe not that these men have ever sinned; nor that they could be ever deceived. As they acknowledge no Author of the Universe, so they acknowledge no first Legislator. They erect Temples to the Memory of cer-

What is the Spirit of the Faith of the *Indians*, or the Submission which they have to their Traditions.

tain

tain men, of whom they believe a thousand Fables, which the superstition of their Ancestors have invented in the course of several Ages: and this is what the *Portugueses* have called the Gods of the *Indies*. The *Portugueses* have thought that what was honoured with a Publick Worship, could be only a God: and when the *Indians* accepted this word God for those men, to the Memory of whom they consecrate their Temples, its that they understand not the force thereof.

That the worship of the *Siameses* proves not that they believe a Divinity.

There is nothing that may be taken in more various Senses, nor which may receive more different Interpretations than exterior Worship. Statues have not always been the Marks of a Divine Honor. The *Greeks* and the *Romans* have erected them, like us, to Persons yet living, without any design to make them Gods. The *Chineses* do proceed further, and they not only consecrate Statues to some Magistrates yet living, but they erect unto them some sorts of Temples, and sacred Edifices: They establish to them a Worship accompanied with Prostrations, Perfumes and Lights; and they preserve certain things of their Apparel as Relicks: though it cannot be thought that they respect these Magistrates, yet living as Gods, but as men very much inferior to the King of *China* their Master, of whom they make no Divinity. There are several Christian Princes which are served upon the Knee, and the Deputies of the third State speak to the King only in this Posture. We give Incense to particular Persons in our Churches; and the Christians do honor their Princes with many and great Marks of exterior Worship. Thus the exterior Worship of the *Indians* is not a proof that they acknowledge, at least at present, any Divinity; and hitherto we ought rather to call them Atheists than Idolaters. But when they offer Sacrifices to others than to God, and they joyn Vows to render themselves propitious, we cannot excuse them of Idolatry: for in having entirely forgotten the Divinity, they only are greater Idolaters, when they terminate their Worship to what is not God, and that they make it the sole Object of their Religion.

CHAP. XXV.

Diverse Observations to be made in preaching the Gospel to the Orientals.

That our Belief scandalizes the Orientals in several things that one must not preach to them without caution, if one has not the gift of Miracles.

FRom what I have said concerning the Opinions of the Orientals, it is easie to comprehend how difficult an enterprize it is to bring them over to the Christian Religion; and of what consequence it is, that the Missionaries, which preach the Gospel in the East, do perfectly understand the Manners and Belief of these People. For as the Apostles and first Christians, when God supported their Preaching by so many wonders, did not on a sudden discover to the Heathens all the Mysteries which we adore, but a long time conceal'd from them, and the Catechumens themselves, the knowledge of those which might scandalize them; it seems very rational to me, that the Missionaries, who have not the gift of Miracles, ought not presently to discover to the Orientals all the Mysteries nor all the Practices of Christianity. 'Twould be convenient, for example, if I am not mistaken, not to preach unto them, without great caution, the worshipping of Saints: and as to the knowledge of Jesus Christ, I think it would be necessary to manage it with them, if I may so say, and not to speak to them of the Mysterie of the Incarnation, till after having convinced them of the Existence of a God Creator. For what probability is there to begin with perswading the *Siameses* to remove *Sommona-Codom*, *Pra Mogla*, and *Pra Saribout* from the Altars, to set up Jesus Christ, St. *Peter* and St. *Paul*, in their stead? 'Twould not perhaps be more proper to preach unto them Jesus Christ crucified, till they have first comprehended that one may be unfortunate and innocent; and that by the rule received, even amongst them, which is, that the

the Innocent might load himself with the Crimes of the Guilty, it was necessary that a God should become Man, to the end that this Man-God should by a laborious life, and a shameful, but voluntary Death satisfie for all the Sins of men: but before all things it would be necessary to give them the true Idea of a God Creator, and justly provoked against men. The Eucharist after this will not scandalize the *Siameses*, as it formerly scandalized the Pagans of *Europe*: forasmuch as the *Siameses* do believe that *Sommona-Codom* could give his Wife and Children to the *Talapoins* to eat.

On the contrary, as the *Chineses* are respectful towards their Parents even to a scruple, I doubt not that if the Gospel should be presently put into their Hands, they would be scandalized at that place, where when some told J. Christ that his Mother and his Brethren asked after him, he answered in such a manner, that he seems so little to regard them, that he affected not to know them. They would not be less offended at those other mysterious words, which our divine Saviour spake to the young Man, who desired time to go and bury his Parents. Let the dead, saith he, bury the dead. Every one knows the trouble which the *Jappanneses* expressed to St. *Francis Xavier* upon the Eternity of Damnation, not being able to believe that their dead Parents should fall into so horrible a Misfortune, for want of having embraced Christianity, which they had never heard of. It seems necessary therefore to prevent and mollifie this thought, by the means which that great Apostle of the *Indies* used, in first establishing the Idea of an omnipotent, all-wise, and most just God, the Author of all good, to whom only every thing is due, and by whose will we owe unto Kings, Bishops, Magistrates, and to our Parents, the Respects which we owe them. These Examples are sufficient to show with what precautions it is necessary to prepare the minds of the Orientals, to think like us, and not to be offended with most of the Articles of the Christian Faith.

That the reading of the Holy Scripture ought to be permitted to them only with Caution.

The *Chineses* do not less respect their Teachers than their Parents; and this sentiment is so well established amongst them, that they chastise the Tutor to the Prince, the presumptive Heir of the Crown, for the Faults which that Prince commits; and that there are some Princes, who being made Kings, have revenged their Tutors. The *Indians* do likewise greatly honour the Memory of those, whom they believe to have preach'd up Virtue efficaciously: they are those, whom they have judged worthy of their whole Worship; and they take Offence that we are scandalized thereat. Could we, say they, do less for those, who have preached unto us so holy a Doctrine? Father *Hierom Xavier*, a *Portuguese* Jesuit, having published at *Agra* a kind of Catechism, under the Title of the *Mirrour of Truth*: A *Persian* of *Ispahan* named *Zinel Abedin* wrote an answer thereunto, under the Title of the *Mirrour repolish'd*, which the Congregation *de Propaganda fide* thought necessary to have confuted: and it committed the care thereof to Father *Philip Guadagnol*, of the Order of the Regular Minimes. But he spake so unworthily of *Mahomet*, that his confutation proved ineffectualy; because that the Mission of *Ispahan* dar'd never to publish it: and this Mission desiring Father *Guadagnol* somewhat to moderate his Stile, this good Father running into the other extream, made a Panegyrick upon *Mahomet*, which drew upon him a Reprimand from the Congregation *de propaganda*. 'Tis therefore necessary in these sorts of matters to observe a wise Moderation, and to speak respectfully, at least to the *Indians*, of *Brama*, *Sommona-Codom*, and all the rest, whose Statues are seen on their Altars. 'Tis necessary to agree with them, that these men have had great natural lights, and intentions worthy of Praise; and at the same time to insinuate to them, that being men, they are deceived in several things important to the eternal Salvation of Mankind, and principally in that they have not known the Creator.

'Tis necessary to speak to the Orientals with an esteem of their Legislators.

But next to this Blindness, which is is necessity to demonstrate inexcusable, why should we not praise the Legislators of the East, as well as the *Greek* Legislators, for that they have applied themselves to inspire into the People, what to them has appeared most virtuous, and most proper to keep them in Peace and Innocence? Why should we blame them for the Fables, which a long succession of Ages full of Ignorance has invented upon their account, and of which

That these Law-givers may be praised in some things.

 proba-

probably they have not been the Authors: considering that when they had spoken magnificently of their persons, they had only done what is pardonable in almost all other Legislators? They have the merit of having known before the *Greeks* some intelligent Beings superior to man, and the Immortality of the Soul.

That the Doctrine of Metempsychosis may be excused by Physical Reasons.

But if they have believed the *Metempsychosis*, they have been thereto induced by apparent Reasons. Ignoring all Creation, and establishing moreover that a Soul cannot proceed from a Soul, and that there could not be an infinite number of Souls; they were forced to conclude that the infinite number of the living, which had succeeded one another in the World, during all this past Eternity, which they supposed that the World had already lasted; could not be animated by this finite number of Spirits, unless they had passed an infinite number of times from one body to another. The Opinion of the *Metempsychosis* is therefore founded on several Principles which we receive; and certainly contains only one Falsity, which is the pretended Impossibility of the Creation.

And by Politick Reasons.

As to the natural consequences of this Doctrine, the Prohibition of Meats is very wholsom in the *Indies*, and the Horror of Blood would be every where useful. The great *Barcalon*, elder Brother to the first Ambassador of *Siam*, ceased not to reproach the Christians for the bloody Madness of our Wars. On the other hand, the Opinion of the *Metempsychosis* comforts men in the Misfortunes of Life, and fortifies them against the Horrors of Death, by the Hopes which it gives of reviving another time more happily: and because that men are credulous in proportion to their desires, 'tis observed that those, who esteem themselves the most unhappy People in this Life, as Eunuchs, do strongly adhere to this hope of another better Life, which the Doctrine of the *Metempsychosis* has given to good men.

The fear of the dead Parents excused by Politick Reasons.

But if Error can be advantageous, what other can be so much as that Fear of Children for their dead Parents. *Confucius* makes it the only Foundation of all good Policy. And indeed it establishes the Peace of Families, and of Kingdoms: it bends men to Obedience, and renders them more submissive to their Parents and to their Magistrates; it preserves good Manners and the Laws. These People comprehend not that they can ever abandon the Opinions and Customs, which they have received from their Fathers, nor avoid, if they did, the Resentment which, in their Opinion, their Ancestors would express thereat. The *Chinese* Doctrine has no other Paradice, nor Hell, than this Republic of the dead, where they believe that the Soul is received at the departure out of this Life, and where it is well or ill entertained with the Souls of its Ancestors, according to its Vertues or its Vices.

This fear causes the stability of the Laws of China.

'Tis upon this consideration, that the Lawful Kings of *China* have abstained from making any Innovations on the Government. None but Usurpers dare to do this, not only by the Right which force gives them, but because that not being descended from the Kings their Predecessors, they have not thought any respect due to their Establishments.

Yet it has its Inconveniences.

Nevertheless as all errors have bad sides, *Confucius* being ask'd by one of his Disciples, whether the dead had any sense of the Respects which their Children paid them, answer'd, That it was not fitting to make these over-curious sorts of Questions; that by answering negatively, he fear'd to abolish the respect of Children for their dead Parents; and by answering affirmatively, he dreaded the exciting the best Persons to kill themselves, to go and joyn their Ancestors.

The Talapoins must not be thought knowing and interested Impostors.

'Twould also be, I know not what Injustice to treat the *Talapoins* as Impostors, and interessed Persons. They deceive only because they are first deceived: they are not more cunning, nor more interested than the Seculars. When they preach to the Seculars to bestow Alms upon them, they think their Preaching their Duty; and in every Country the Ministers of the Altar do live on the Altar.

That it is necessary with the Orientals to use all the insinuations which our Religion and the example of the first Christians can permit us.

I am therefore convinced, that the true secret of Insinuating into the mind of these People, supposing one has not the Gift of Miracles, is not directly to contradict them in any thing, but to show them, as at unawares, their Errors in the Sciences, and especially in the Mathematicks and Anatomy, wherein they are most

most palpable: 'Tis to change the Terms of their Worship the least Imaginable, by giving to the true God, either the Name of Sovereign Lord, or that of King of Heaven and Earth, or some other Name which signifies in the Language of the Country, what is most worthy of Veneration, as the word *Pra* in *Siamese*; But at the same time it be necessary to instruct them to annex unto these Names the intire Idea of the Deity, an Idea so much the more easie to receive, as it only heightens and embellishes the mean Idea's of the false Gods. *Got* which now signifies *God* in *German*, was anciently, according to *Vossius*, the Name of *Mercury*, who seems to have been every where adored. Certainly the words *Theos* and *Deus* have not always signified in *Greece* and *Italy* the God, which we adore. What then have the Christians done? They have accepted these Names in the stead of the ineffable Name of God, and they have explained them after their manner. From the Knowledge of an eternal, spiritual God and Creator, it would be easie to descend to the Faith of Jesus Christ: and these People would make no Opposition, if first they saw themselves cured of some sensible Ignorance. The Spirit of man is such, that he almost implicitly receives the Opinions of him, who has visibly convinc'd him of his first Errors. Thoroughly convince a sick person that the Remedy which he uses is not good, and he will immediately take yours.

But in my opinion it is one of the most important Articles of the conduct of the Missionaries, to accommodate themselves entirely to the simplicity of the Manners of the Orientals, in their Food, Furniture, Lodging, and whatever the Rules of the *Talapoins* prescribe, wherein they have nothing contrary to Christianity. The example of Father *de Nobilibus* the Jesuit is famous. Being in Mission to the Kingdom of *Madura* in the *Indies*, he resolved to live like a *Jogue*, that is to say, like a *Bramin* of the Woods; to go with his Feet naked, and his Head bare, and his Body almost naked in the scorching Sands of this Country, and to nourish himself with that excess of frugality, which appear'd intollerable: and it is reported that by this means he converted near forty thousand persons. Now as this exact imitation of the *Indian* severity is the true way to make some Conversions, so the further one should remove therefrom, the more one should attract the hatred and contempt of the *Indians*. It is necessary to learn in these Countries, to make a shift with whatever they do, and not to sustain the necessities, or rather the superfluities of these Countries, if one would not cause Jealousie and Envy to some Nations, the particular persons of which conceal their fortune, because they can preserve it only by hiding. The less the Missionaries appear settled, the more the Mission is established, and the better it promotes Religion. As the East is not a Country of settlement for private persons, it would be an injury to think to accomplish it: the Natives of the Country do not themselves enjoy any solid fortune; and they would not fail to pick quarrels with those that should appear richer than them, to deprive them of their Riches. Moreover, the Orientals seem to have no prejudice for any Religion; and it must be confessed, that if the beauty of Christianity has not convinc'd them, it is principally by reason of the bad opinion, which the Avarice, Treachery, Invasions, and Tyranny of the *Portuguese*, and some Christians in the *Indies*, have implanted and rivetted in them. But it is time to conclude this Relation with the Life of *Thevetat*, the Brother of *Sommona Codom*, and with all the other things that I have promised.

How the Missionaries ought to accommodate themselves to the simple customs of the Orientals, in what concerns not Religion.

The End of the First Tome.

A NEW

Historical Relation

OF THE

KINGDOM

OF

SIAM.

BY

Monsieur *DE LA LOUBERE*,

Envoy Extraordinary from the *FRENCH* KING, to the KING of *SIAM*, in the years 1687 and 1688.

Wherein a full and curious Account is given of the *Chinese* Way of Arithmetick, and Mathematick Learning.

TOME II.

Illustrated with SCULPTURES.

Done out of *French*, by *A. P.* Gen. R. S.S.

LONDON,

Printed by *F. L.* for *Tho. Horne* at the *Royal Exchange*, *Francis Saunders* at the *New Exchange*, and *Tho. Bennet* at the *Half-Moon* in St. *Pauls* Church-yard. M DC XCIII.

TO THE

READER.

I Have almost no other hand in this Volume, than the collecting the Pieces thereof. Some are Translations, which are not mine, in some others I only have held the Pen, whilst the substance thereof was dictated unto me. If there are any which appear too foreign to a Relation of *Siam*, they are not so to my Voyage; the History of which would perhaps have pardon'd me, if I had undertaken to do it: and much less to the general Knowledge, which I have endeavoured to give of all the East, thereby to make known the Genius of the *Siameses*. However, I crave Pardon for two or three Pieces at most, which will not perhaps displease in themselves, and which I have given to satisfie the Curiosity of some Persons, whom I honor.

A

A

TABLE

OF THE

PIECES contained in this VOLUME.

THE

THE LIFE OF THEVETAT,

Translated from the Balic.

AFter the birth of *Pouti Sat* *, who by his good works in process of time arrived at the *Nireupan*, his Father, King *Tanssontau*, consulted the Soothsayers to know what would betide him, and the fortune that a Son would have, at whose Nativity there had appeared so many Wonders. They all assur'd him that he had great reason to rejoyce, seeing that if his Son did continue in the World, he would be Emperor of the whole Earth; or that if he turned *Talapoin*, by abandoning the Pleasures of the Age, he would arrive at the *Nireupan*. It is necessary to know that this Emperor had seven sorts of things, which were so peculiar to him, that there was none besides him that had them. The first was a Glass-bowl, which he made use of to rid himself of his Enemies, by throwing it against those whom he would kill; which being let go, went to cut off the Enemies head, and then return'd of it self. The second were Elephants and Horses of an extraordinary goodness and beauty, which did fly with the same facility as they walked. The third was a piece of Glass, by the means of which he could have as much Gold and Silver as he pleased: for to this end he needed only to throw it into the Air, and of the heighth that it went, there would grow a Pillar of Gold or Silver. The fourth was a Lady, come from the North, of a marvellous Beauty, who had a great glass Pot sustained by three Columns of the same: then when she would boil any Rice, she needed only to put never so little Rice therein, and the Fire would kindle of it self, and extinguished also of it self when the Rice was boiled: the Rice multiplied so exceedingly in the boiling, that it would feed five hundred men and more. The fifth was a man, who took care of the House, and who had Eyes so penetrating, that he did see Gold, Silver, and Precious Stones in the Bowels of the Earth. The sixth was a great *Mandarin* of an extraordinary Strength and Valour. The last was, that he had a Thousand Children by one Queen, which indeed did not all come out of her Womb. One alone came out thence, and the rest were engendered of the Water, Blood, and whatever comes out at the Delivery. Every one of these Children in particular being grown up, was capable of subduing and vanquishing all the Enemies, which their Father could have. Now there was one of the Soothsayers, who taking the Father aside, told him, that assuredly his Son would abandon the World, would quit the Kingdom, and would consecrate himself to Repentance by turning *Talapoin*, to be able by his good works to arrive at the *Nireupan*.

* This is one of the names of *Sommona-Codom*: *Sat*, in my Opinion signifies Lord in *Baly*, as *Tchaou* in *Siamese*, and so he is called *Pouti Sat*, and *Pouti Tchaou*: the word *Pouti* is *Baly*.

His Relations, to the Number of Ten Thousand, understanding by the Answer of the Soothsayer, that the Universal Demeine of this whole World, or the *Nireupan* were ascertained to this young Prince, resolv'd amongst themselves every one to give him, when he should be a little advanced in years, one of their Sons to make up his Train; and so they did. When therefore this Prince, after the Repentance of some seven years, which he performed in the Woods, was become worthy of the *Nireupan*, a great many of these young men, whom we mentioned, which were of his Retinue, turn'd *Talapoins* with him, but amongst this great Company there were six, who though they were his Relations, and in his Train, would not yet follow him. We will recite the Names thereof, by reason that in the sequel we shall speak only of them. The first is called *Pattia*, the second *Anourout*, the third *Anant*, the fourth *Patiea*, the fifth *Quemila*, the sixth *Thevetat*: and it is of this last that we write the History. One day the Fathers of these six young Princes being accidentally met together, after having discoursed a long time about several indifferent things, one of them observed to the rest that not any of their Sons had followed the Prince to turn *Talapoin*; and they said amongst themselves, is it because that not any of our Children will turn *Talapoins*, that we shall upon this account cease to be his Relations? Hereupon therefore the Father of *Anourout*, one of these six young Princes, who was the Successor of *Tamsoutout*, said to his Son, that though he was of Royal Blood, yet if *Sommona-Codom* would receive him into his Company as a *Talapoin*, he would not hinder him, though some Persons of his Quality would not follow this Example.

* The *Siameses* report that *Thevetat* was the Brother of *Sommona-Codom*, by this History he only is his Relation.

Prince *Anourout* being accustomed to his Pleasures, and to have whatever he desired, understood not what this word of refusal, *No*, did mean. One day as these six young Princes diverted themselves at Bowls, and played for Confects for a Collation, *Anourout* having lost, sent a Man to his Mother, to intreat her to send him some Confects, which she did: having eaten them, they played for a second Collation, then a third and a fourth; and his Mother sent him some Confects, till all were gone. But as *Anourout* still sent to have more, his Mother then told the Servant: *No, there are no more*. Which being related to the Son, and the Son not understanding what these words, *No there are no more*, did signify, having never heard them spoken, thought that his Mother meant that she had yet others more excellent, the name of which must be these words, *No there are no more*. He therefore sent back his Servant to his Mother, desiring her to send him some of the Confects *No there are no more*; his Mother perceiving hereby that her Son understood not these words, *No there are no more*, resolved to explain them to him. She took a great empty Dish, covered it with another, and gave it to the Servant to carry to her Son. But then the *Genij* of the City *Kaubilpat* reflecting on all that had passed between Prince *Anourout* and his Mother, and knowing that the Prince understood not these words, *No there are no more*, (because that formerly in another Generation he had Charitably given to the *Talapoins* his Portion of Rice, and had demanded and desired, that in process of time, when he should come to revive again in this World, he might not understand what these words, *No there are no more*, did mean; neither did he understand or know the place where the Rice did grow.) they said that it was necessary speedily to assemble themselves with the other *Genij*, to consult what was proper to be done, because that if *Anourout* found the Plate empty, their head as a Punishment would be broke in seven pieces. It was therefore resolved that they would fill it with Confects brought from Heaven, which they did. The Servant who carried the Plate, having laid it at the place, where these young Princes were diverting themselves, *Anourout*, who only expected this to pay his Debt to his Companions, ran to the Plate and uncovered it, and found it as before, full of Confects, but so excellent that the whole City was perfumed with their Odor: The excellent taste which they found in these Confects, diffused it self through their whole Body. The Plate was soon empty, and hereupon *Anourout* reflecting on the goodness of these Confects said unto himself: It must needs be that my Mother has scarcely loved me till now, seeing that she never gave me the Confects, *No there are no more*.

These *Genij* are not invisible, and their care is to recompence and punish.

more. Returning home, he went to ask his Mother, whether she loved her Son. His Mother, who passionately loved him, was exceedingly surprized at this question, and answered him that she loved him as her own Heart, and Eyes. And why, if what you say is true, have you never given me the Confects, *Mother there are no more,* For the future I beseech you to give me no other: I am resolved to eat only of these. His Mother, astonished to hear her Son speak thus, addressed her self to the Servant, who had carried the Plate, and asked him secretly, whether he saw any thing therein, to whom he answered yes, that he saw the Dish filled with a kind of Confects, which he had never seen before: and then the Mother of *Anurout* comprehended the Mystery, and judged rightly that the Antient Merit of her Son had procured him these Confects, and that the Superior *Genii* had rendered him this good Office. Afterwards therefore when the Prince demanded these Confects of his Mother, she only took an empty Dish, covered it with another, and sent it him, and the Plate was always found full as I have said.

Anourout understood not likewise the meaning of these words, to assume the *Pagne* or *Talapoin* Habit, and having one day desired his elder Brother *Pattia* to explain them to him, *Pattia* informed him what he knew, that to assume the *Talapoins* Habit, was intirely to shave his Hair and Beard, to sleep on a Hurdle, and to cloath himself with a yellow *Pagne.* Which *Anourout* understanding, he told his Brother that being accustomed to live at his ease, and to have all things at pleasure, he should find much difficulty to lead this Life: And *Pattia* replyed, seeing then my Brother that you will not resolve to turn *Talapoin*, consider which is best: but also not to live Idly, learn to work and continue at my Father's House as long as you please. *Anourout* asked him what he meant by this word to *Work*, which he understood not: *Pattia* then said unto him, how can you know what it is to work, seeing that you neither know where nor how the Rice grows? One day indeed *Quimila*, *Pattia*, and *Anourout* discoursing together upon the Place where the Rice might grow, *Quimila* replyed that it growed in the Barn: *Pattia*, said no, and asserted that it grew in the Pot: And *Anourout* told them both that they understood nothing, and that it grew in the Dish. The first having one day observed that the Rice was taken out of the Barn, thought it was there that it grew. The second had seen it taken out of the Pot, and 'tis that which gave him occasion to think that it grew in the Pot: But the third who had never seen it otherwise than in the Dish, really believed that the Rice grew in the Dish, when one had a desire to eat: and thus all three knew nothing of the matter.

Anourout declared afterwards to the other two that he was not inclined to work, and that he chose rather to turn *Talapoin*: and he went to ask leave of his Mother. She refused him two or three times: but as he would not be denied, and as he continually pressed her more and more, she told him that if *Pattia* would turn *Talapoin*, she would permit him to follow him. *Anourout* went therefore to sollicit his five other Companions to make themselves *Talapoins*, and they resolved to do it seven days after. These seven days being elapsed they went out of the City, with a great Equipage, seeming to go to divert themselves in the Country. In their retinue they had a great many *Mandarins* mounted on Elephants, with a good number of Footmen. But principally they had in their Train a Barber by Profession, named *Oubbali*. Being arrived at the Confines of the Kingdom, they sent back all their retinue except *Oubbali*: then they stript themselves of their Cloaths, folded them up very neatly, and put them into the hands of *Oubbali*, to make him a present thereof, telling him that he should return into the City, and that he had wherewithal to live at his ease the remainder of his days. *Oubbali*, very much afflicted to separate himself from these six Princes, and yet not daring to contradict what they order'd him, after having taken his leave of them departed weeping, and took his road towards the City, from whence they had set out together. But it presently came into his mind, that if he returned, and that the Parents of these young Princes should see the cloaths of their Children, they would have reason to suspect him of their death, and likewise to put him to death, not believing that these young

Princes

Princes would have quitted such precious Habits to give them to him. Hereupon he hung up these Habits on a Tree, and returned to seek out these young Lords. So soon as they saw him, they demanded the reason of his return, and having declared it to them, he testified that he would continue with them, and assume the Habit of a *Talapoin*. These young Princes presented him then to *Sommona-Codom*, beseeching him to give the Habit to him, rather than to them: for finding themselves yet full of the Spirit of the World, and proud of heart, and willing to humble themselves, they desired that *Oubbali*, who was very inferior to them in the World, might be their Elder in Religion, to the end they might be obliged to respect him, and to yield to him in all things: the * Rule, requiring that between two *Talapoins* the Eldest have all the Honours, though the youngest be much the more Learned. *Sommona Codom* granted them their Request, and they assumed the Habit a little while after *Oubbali*. Being therefore entred into the time of Repentance, *Patiia* by his merit had a Cœlestial Heart, Eyes, and Ears; that is to say he understood every thing, he knew the Hearts of others, he saw all things, and heard every thing, notwithstanding the distance and all obstacles. One day after *Sommona-Codom* had preached, *Anantont* was advanced to the degree of an Angel. At the same time *Ananr* a *Talapoin*, dear to *Sommona-Codom*, went to *Soda* the first degree of Perfection. *Pakon* and *Quimila* after having a long time exercised themselves in Prayer and Meditation, were advanced to be Angels. There was *Thevetat* alone that could obtain no other thing than a great strength, and the power of doing Miracles *.

* I suppose that this is a remark which the Translator has inserted into the Text, and we may therein remark some other.

* The Miracles of Jesus Christ perswade them that he is *Thevetat*; but it is necessary to convince to them that the Miracles which they attribute to *Thevetat* are to do Evil, and that those of Jesus Christ are for Good.

Sommona Codom being gone with his *Talapoins* to the City of *Kausampi*, the Inhabitants came daily to make them presents, sometimes to *Sommona-Codom*, sometimes to *Mogla* and to *Saributr*, his two principal Favourites, one of which sat on his Right hand, and the other on his Left: some to *Kasip* and *Patiia*, others to *Quimila* and *Pakon*, or to *Anantont*; but what is remarkable, no body presented to *Thevetat*: and they spake no more of him than if he had never been in the world, whereat he was extreamly inraged. Is it, said he, that I am not a *Talapoin* as well as the others? Is it that I am not of the Royal Blood like them? Why has no one made any Present to me? He therefore resolved instantly to seek out some body that should present him, and to allure some Disciples. The King of the City *Pimpisan*, was arrived to the first degree of Perfection, with One Hundred and Ten Thousand men, all Disciples of *Sommona-Codom*: and he had a Son as yet young, and who knew not what Evil was, *Thevetat* contriving to seduce this Son, to make use of him in his wicked designs, went from the City of *Pimmesan*, to go to *Rhacaren*, and assumed by the power he had, the shape of a little Infant, with a Serpent round each Leg, another round his Neck, and another round his Head. Besides this he had one, who embracing him on the left Shoulder, descended underneath the right Shoulder before and behind. In this equipage he took wing, and went through the Air to the City of *Rachaten*. He lights at the Feet of *Achatasatan*, who was that young Prince the Son of the King of the City of * *Pimmepisan*, and who seeing *Thevetat* after this manner, with his whole body twisted about with Serpents, conceived a great Terror thereat. Being affrighted at a thing so strange, he asked *Thevetat* who he was, and *Thevetat* having told him his Name, and entirely confirmed him, reassumed his first shape, that is to say his *Talapoins* Habit, and his Serpents disappeared. *Achatasatan* hereupon conceived a great esteem of *Thevetat*, and made him great Presents, an Honour which effected the ruine of *Thevetat* by the Pride he conceived thereat; for from that time he contrived the design of making himself Master and Chief of his Brethren. He went therefore to *Sommona-Codom*, he found him out who preached to the King, saluted him, approached him, and after some discourse told him, that being already in a very advanced Age, it was not fit that for the future he should take so much Pains, but that he ought to think of spending the rest of his days pleasantly and at his own Ease. I am, added he, ready to assist you to the utmost of my power, and as the care of so many Religious overwhelms you, you may for the future discharge it upon me. This is the Language, which the extream

* Just before he said *Pimpisan*.

desire

desire of seeing himself above all, did put into his Mouth. *Sommona-Codom* who knew him, refus'd and condemn'd his demand, whereat *Thevetat* was so enraged, that he only plotted ways to revenge himself. He returned to the City of *Rachaureu* to find out *Achatasatrou* his Disciple, and perswaded him to get rid of his Father, the sooner to get upon the Throne, and afterwards to afford him the means of putting *Sommona-Codom* to Death, and of setting up himself in his stead. *Achatasatrou* then caused his Father to be put into a Dungeon loaded with Irons, and seized on the Throne: *Thevetat* expressed unto him his Joy, and desired him to remember the Promise he had made him. The new King presently granted him 500 men armed with Arrows, to go and kill *Sommona-Codom*. They found him walking at the Foot of a Mountain; and his sight alone impressed in them so much Fear and Respect, that there was not any one who dared to let fly an Arrow; they all remained immoveable, every one with their Bow bent. *Sommona-Codom* intreated them to tell him the Author of their Enterprize; and when they had informed him, he preached a Sermon unto them, at the end of which they arrived at the first degree of Perfection, and returned home. So soon as *Thevetat* saw that they had missed their blow, he went himself on the Mountain, and applied himself to roul down Stones to the bottom, designedly to kill *Sommona-Codom*; and when he thought he had thrown down enough to kill him, he descended thence, and called him two or three times by his Name; *Sommona-Codom* who had ascended the Mountain at one side, when *Thevetat* descended at the other, answered that he was at top; *Thevetat* presently re-mounted, and at the same time *Sommona-Codom*, who knew him without seeing him, descended without being seen. *Thevetat* re-ascended again in vain, and he died with rage. Mean while *Sommona-Codom* seeing himself thus persecuted, said unto himself, what Crime, what Sin have I committed? Now that I am at the height of perfection, that I have performed so great a Penitence that I have preached so much and taught so holy a doctrine, yet they cease not to persecute me to kill me. And by thus examining himself he remember'd, that one day being drunk, he had hit a *Talapoin* with a little stone which he had flung, and which had drawn out a little blood, and he knew that he was to be punished in five hundred Generations successively; that he had already been punished in 499, and that this was the five hundredth: besides which, he had been a long time in Hell. Wherefore knowing moreover that if he permitted not *Thevetat* to do him some mischief, he should kill him with rage, and go into Hell after his death, he rather chose that a small shiver of a Flint which *Thevetat* threw at him, and which dash'd in pieces against another, should wound him in the foot to draw out a little blood. 'Twas he that stretch'd out his foot to receive the blow, and thereby he appeased the anger of *Thevetat*, who for some time forgot the Resolution of killing him.

Sommona-Codom sins and is punished in Hell.

One day as *Sommona-Codom* went to beg Alms in the City of *Rachaureu*, *Thevetat* being advertised thereof, procur'd the King to send his most mischievous Elephants to do him a mischief, if he did not retreat. *Sommona-Codom* ceased not to continue his road with his *Talapoins*: and as they came near the Elephants, *Anam* went before his Master, to secure him from the fury of the Elephants, by exposing himself, but they hurt no body.

At his departure out of the City, *Sommona-Codom* retir'd into a *Pagod*, where the people brought him to eat. He eat, and preached afterwards to all this multitude, which was come out to the number of Ten Millions of persons, to hear him: and he converted fourscore and four Thousand, some of which went to the first degree, others to the second, others to the third, others to the fourth degree of Perfection. Several enlarged themselves on the Praises of *Anam*, who loved his master so dearly, as to expose his life for him. Whereupon *Sommona-Codom* informed them, that this was not the first time *Anam* had done it. Another time he said unto them, when I was King of the *Org* ('tis a kind of Bird) *Anam* being also an *Org*, and my younger Brother, he saved my life by exposing his in my place. When the King *Achatasatrou* had heard *Anam* thus commended, for having exposed his life for his Master, he recalled the 500 men, which he had given to *Thevetat*: and thus *Thevetat* saw himself abandon'd

 by

by every one. He had leave to beg, but no body gave him wherewith to live: being reduced to the extremity of seeking a livelihood himself, he returned to *Sommona-Codom*, and offered him five Propositions, which he intreated him to grant. The first was, that if there were some *Talapoins* who would oblige themselves to live in the Woods, and sequester'd from the World, he would permit them. The second, that those who would engage themselves to live only on Alms, might submit themselves thereto. The third, that he would grant the liberty of cloathing themselves poorly to such who would desire always to do it, and who would oblige themselves to be always contented with old *Pagnes*, patched and nasty. The fourth, that he would permit those which should desire it, to refuse all their life to have any other Convent or Lodging, than under a Tree; and in fine, that they who would never eat Meat or Fish, might deprive themselves thereof. *Sommona-Codom* answer'd him, that it was necessary to leave to every one his own will, and to oblige no person to more than he would, or even than he could. *Thevetat* rose up after *Sommona-Codom*'s Answer, and cried aloud to all the *Talapoins* that were present, let all those that would be happy follow me; and immediately a Troop of ignorant persons, to the number of five hundred, deceived by the specious appearance of his false intentions, resolved to follow him, and exactly to keep the five things which he proposed. They had some devoto's which nourish'd them, and which supply'd all their wants: although they knew that *Thevetat* had kindled the War amongst the *Talapoins*, by separating himself from his Master. When *Sommona-Codom* saw that he took so wicked a Conduct, he endeavoured to reclaim him, by divers Sermons which he made to him, to convince him that there was not a greater Crime than this. *Thevetat* heard him very patiently, but without making any benefit thereby; for he briskly quitted *Sommona-Codom*. On the Road he met *Anon*, who demanded Charity from door to door in the City of *Rathagren*, and told him that he had just quitted his Master, to live for the future after his own humor. *Anon* told it to *Sommona-Codom*, who replied, that he knew it very well, that he saw that *Thevetat* was an unhappy wretch, that he would go into Hell. This, adds he, is exactly as Sinners do; they commit great Crimes, and this they call doing Good, and what is Good they call Evil. Virtuous Men do good without trouble, whereas it is a punishment to the wicked; and on the contrary, Evil displeaseth the Good, and the wicked make a pleasure thereof. Knowing therefore the place and quarter where *Thevetat* was retir'd with his 500 Disciples, he sent *Mogla* and *Saribout* thither to bring them away. They found *Thevetat* preaching, and when he saw them, he thought that like him they had quitted their Master. Wherefore after his Sermon, he said unto them: I know that when you were with *Sommona-Codom* you were his two Favourites, and that he made you to sit one at his right hand, and the other at his left. I desire you to accept the same thing from me. Not to know him, and the better to cover their design, they told him that they kindly accepted it, and seated themselves indeed at his sides. Then he intreated them to preach in his stead whilst he went to repose. *Saribout* preached, and after his Sermon all those 500 *Talapoins* arrived at the perfection of an Angel, rose up into the Air and disappear'd. *Conkali* the Disciple of *Thevetat* ran to wake him and tell him, what had past. I had well advised you not to trust them, said he unto him: then he began to be vexed, and to such a degree, that he beat *Conkali* so as to make his Mouth to bleed. On the other hand, when the *Talapoins*, which were with *Sommona-Codom*, saw *Mogla* and *Saribout* return with their Company, they went immediately to acquaint their Master, and to express unto him the astonishment wherein they were to see *Mogla* and *Saribout* return so well accompanied, after having seen them depart alone. *Mogla* and *Saribout* came also to salute their Master, and the new come *Talapoins* told *Sommona-Codom* that *Thevetat* imitated him in all things. You very much deceive your selves, said he unto them, to think that he does what I do: formerly indeed he Counterfeited me, but now he practises the same. Then his Disciples said unto him, we know our dear Master that *Thevetat* Counterfeits you at present, but that he has Counterfeited you in times past we know nothing thereof, wherefore we desire you to explain it to us. He then open'd his mouth and said,

said, you know that heretofore being a Bird, but a Bird which sought his living sometimes in the Water, sometimes on the Land, *Thevetat* at the same time was a Land-Fowl and had great Feet. After my example he would catch Fish, but he entangled his Neck in the Weeds, not being able to pluck it out, and died there. I remember also that I once was one of these little red Birds, which do eat the Worms of the Trees. *Thevetat* was a Bird of another sort, and he affected to nourish himself like me. I sought the Worms in the Trees, which have the heart included in the middle of the Trunck, and I sought out these Trees in a great and spacious Forest, he sought the Worms in Trees without heart, but which have an appearance thereof; and his head was bruised as a punishment. Another time I was born a *Rachasi*, and he was born a wild Dog. Now the *Rachasi* do live only on the Elephants which they kill in the Woods, and the Dog of the Woods would act like me, but he reapt the evil thereof; for the Elephants trampled him under their Feet and crushed him in pieces.

Another day *Sommona Codom* preaching to his Disciples, spake to them of *Thevetat*, and said unto them: Once I was one of the Land-fowl with great Feet, and he was *Rachasi*. In eating of meat he would swallow a bone, which sticking in his Throat would strangle him. I had compassion on him, I drew the bone out of his Throat at the request he made me, confessing that what force soever he had used, yet he could not relieve himself. I entered therefore into his great Throat, which he open'd, and pluck'd out this bone with my Beak: and as he had promised me a recompence, I only demanded of him something to eat, but he answered me, that having permitted me to enter into his Throat, and to come out safe and sound, was the greatest Favour he could show me. Another time I was a Stag, and *Thevetat* a Hunter. Going one day a Hunting, he climb'd upon a Tree, which bore the little Fruits which Stags do eat, and there made himself as it were a little Hutt, to keep himself close and conceal'd in, expecting his Prey: and as the Stag * *Pontisat* was come very near the Tree, *Thevetat* threw him some Fruits to entice him to approach nearer; but the Stag *Pontisat* seeing these Fruits fall on either side, doubted of the business, and observed the Hunter upon the Tree, to whom he said 'twas in vain to wait longer, that he would not approach him nearer. 'Tis thus that *Thevetat* desires much. Another time *Thevetat* was a Fisherman. Having one day thrown his Line, the Hook catch'd on a Tree fallen into the water, he thought that the hook held a great Fish, and considering already that he must share it among his Friends, he was troubled thereat, because that these presents would deprive him of the greatest part. To prevent this inconvenience he sent his Son whom he had with him, to carry unto his Wife the news of the prize he thought to catch, and orders to go immediately to quarrel with all her Neighbours. She then took her little dog, and repaired presently to the nearest, went into the house, and began to scold at him and his Wife: from thence she went to another, and at last to them all. In the mean time *Thevetat* was looking after his Line which he could not get out, so that to have it he strips himself, laid his Cloaths on the bank of the River, threw himself into the water, and gave such an unhappy blow against the Tree, that he beat out both his Eyes. The Passengers stole away his Cloaths: and the quarrel of his Wife with his Neighbours, cost him all the little Money he had, by a Suit which they brought against him for this injury. After this *Sommona-Codom* departed out of the City of *Rachaxow* to go to *Sevati*: he was there sick in a Convent where he lodged: and at the same time *Thevetat* was likewise sick of a distemper, which held him nine Months. He had an extream desire to see his Master *Sommona-Codom*, and he signified it to his disciples, desiring them to do him the kindness to carry him to him. They asked him how he dared to think thereof, and what Good and Succour he could expect from him, after having persecuted him so much. 'Tis true, said he unto them, that for the Good he has done me, I have only return'd him Evil; but that's no matter carry me to him, that sufficeth me. They obeyed him, and having laid him on an Hurdle, they set out on the road, to seek out *Sommona Codom*. As they approach'd, the Disciples of *Sommona-Codom* ran to acquaint their Master, that *Thevetat* being sick came to visit him. I know

* 'Tis one of the names of *Sommona-Codom*.

know it, answered he, I know that he comes, but he shall not see me. Since that you refused him, reply'd the Disciples, the favour he demanded of you, touching the five Articles which he desired to observe, we have not hitherto seen him. Upon these words *Sommona-Codom* said unto them; *Thevetat* is a miserable wretch, who has always followed his own capricious humour, and never took care to keep the Rule, which I have taken so much pains to teach him; wherefore, though he comes purposely to visit me, and how good a mind soever he has thereunto, yet he shall not see me; because he has endeavoured to oppose me, and raise a division among my Disciples. As *Thevetat* was within a Mile of the Place, where *Sommona-Codom* was, his Disciples went again to advertise him thereof; and he still told them, I know it very well, but yet *Thevetat* shall not see me. When *Thevetat* was within a half a mile of the City, the Disciples returned to acquaint *Sommona-Codom*; 'Tis true, said he, yet he shall not see me. When *Thevetat* was arrived at the Pool, which they call *Pokeral*, near the place where *Sommona-Codom* was, the *Talapoins* went again to *Sommona-Codom* to tell him that he was near at hand; to which he reply'd, how near soever he be yet he shall not see me. *Thevetat* being therefore come to this Pool, his Disciples set him on the ground on the bank of the water: and as he endeavoured to walk, his Feet sunk, and entred into the Earth, and by little and little he sunk up to the Neck, and then to the Chin. Seeing himself in this condition he began to recommend himself to *Sommona-Codom*, and offer himself to him, confessing that he was very perfect, very great: that he brought back Persons strayed out of the good way, as does a Groom, who takes care to beat his Horses, to correct them when they are mischievous: that he knew and understood every thing: that he was full of merit. He humbled himself, acknowledged the fault he had committed, and desired pardon. Mean while *Sommona-Codom* considering on this wretch, said unto himself, Why hast thou received him into thine house? Why hast thou given him the habit? Would it not be better to let him continue in the world? But no, reply'd he, for if he was lefted there, he would have continued only to transgress the five † Commandments, and to sin. He would destroy the life of an infinite number of Animals: He would seize on anothers estate, where ever he could entrap it: He would be permitted to run into all sort of Impurity: He would have been a Lyar and Impostor; he would always be seen drunk, like a Beast: and in fine, he would never have done any good, and would never have meditated for the Future. This is the reason why I have received him. After this *Sommona-Codom* prophesied that after an hundred Thousand * *Kes*, *Thevetat* should be a God and be named *Ariffaripathiepeponi*. Mean while *Thevetat* was buried in the Earth, and even to Hell where he is without possibility of removing, for want of having loved *Sommona-Codom*. His Body is the heighth of a *Jod*, that is to say, Eight Thousand Fadom: he is in the Hell *Avethi*, 640 Leagues in greatness: on his head he has a great Iron pot all red with fire, and which came to his Shoulders: he has his Feet sunk into the Earth up to the Ankles, and all inflamed. Moreover a great Iron Spit which reaches from the West to the East, pierces through his Shoulders and comes out at his Breast. Another pierces him through the sides, which comes from the South, and goes to the North, and crosses all Hell. And another enters through his Head, and pierces him to the Feet. Now all these Spits do stick at both ends, and are thrust a great way into the Earth. He is standing, without being able to stir, or lye down. The disciples of *Sommona-Codom* discoursed amongst themselves of the poor *Thevetat*, saying, that he was able to come only to the lake *Pokeral*, and not to the Convent, which is near it: And *Sommona-Codom* taking up the discourse, told them, that this was not the first time that such a punishment had happen'd to *Thevetat*, to be swallow'd up and buried in Hell. I remember, pursued he, that *Thevetat* in one of his Generations was an Hunter, and that then I was an Elephant of the Woods. One day then as he was hunting, and as he wandered and was lost, not knowing where he was, I seeing him in so great an affliction had Compassion upon him, I took him upon my back, drew him out of the Woods, set him down near his House, and then returned. Going another

† By this place it appears what the five Commandments of the *Siamese* are.

* Perhaps it must be *Lan*, that is to say Ten Millions, to say Ten Millions of years; as in other places of the *Indies* *Lac* is taken for an Hundred Thousand Years, though *Lac* signifies simple an Hundred Thousand. It is seen by this place how they pretend that the Souls of the wicked may purifie themselves by the means of Transmigration. It appears also that the word *Pout* which signifies Mercury, enters into this name of God, and I doubt not that the *Bali* Adjective *Prasi* comes from *Pout*, though I have seen the *Siamese* write these two words with different Letters; but they are not exact in their Orthography.

another time a hunting, as he saw me with very excellent Teeth, it came into his mind, that if he had such, he could sell them very well, and hereupon he cut off the two ends of mine. Having swallow'd the Silver that he had made thereof, he return'd to cut off as much more, and a third time he made an end of cutting what remain'd. I was extreamly afflicted thereat, and expressed all the resentments whereof I was capable: but he carry'd not his crime very far, for as he left me, the earth open'd and swallow'd him up, without giving him time to ask pardon. Upon these words of *Sommona-Codom*, every one rejoiced at *Thevetat's* death: And *Sommona-Codom* said likewise, I remember that anciently *Thevetat* was born King of the City of *Pavanasi*. His name was *Pingpandara-tha*. He so tormented his Subjects that not one of them loved him: on the contrary every one desired to see him dead: and his death happen'd when he least expected it. Every one made publick rejoycings, except the Porter of the City, who wept heartily: and being demanded the reason thereof: Ah! said he, I weep because that this wretch, wicked as he is, will torment the Devils, as he has tormented us, and the Devils not being able to bear him, will restore him to us, and we shall be as miserable as before. This is the cause of my Tears.

Sommona Codom ceasing to speak, the *Talapoins* desired him to inform them where *Thevetat* was then, and in what place he was gone to revive: and he told them that he was gone to revive in the great Hell *Avehi*: but, said they to him, is it that after having suffered so much in this Life, he is gone likewise to suffer in Hell? yes, replyed *Sommona-Codom*, for you must know that all Sinners, whatever they are, and of what condition soever they may be, whether *Talapoins*, or *Laicks*, after all the sufferings of this World, will have others incomparably greater and more grevious.

The End of Thevetat's *Life.*

This Life was given me at the Moment that I departed for my Return; and I received it without having time to peruse it. At the end I found the beginning of another Work, on which I could interrogate no Person. I give you what I have thereof.

An Explication of the Patimouc, *or Text of the* Vinac.

THere are four things, that we ought to do before we enter into the Explication of the *Patimouc*, according to what *Sommona-Codom* has taught. 1. It is necessary to sweep the Hall where they assemble. 2. It is necessary to light the Lamps or Wax candles. 3. They ought to prepare water in the Spout-pots, or in other Vessels designed to this purpose, for those that shall desire to drink. 4. They ought to spread Matts or Carpets to sit upon. After the disciples have swept it, they go to tell it to the Master, who answers them that they have done well: then they acquaint him that they have lighted the Lamps, and the Master replys that it was not necessary seeing that the Sun shines, and it is broad day. Afterwards the disciples inform him that they have brought the Water, and spread the Matts: Good, said the Master unto them, this is good. Behold then, said the disciples to the Master, these four things which *Sommona-Codom* has taught and ordain'd before they begin the reading of the *Vinac*. Yes, reply'd the Master. *The Disciple.* What are the four things which it is necessary to do after those which we have mentioned, and which *Sommona-Codom* has likewise prescribed: are they not these? 1. When there comes in any new *Talapoins*, after the explication begun, if they are fewer in number than the Auditors, they are obliged to declare that they believe and heartily receive what they have already explained: that if, on the contrary, those that come are more in number than the first, it is necessary to begin again what they have already read. 2. It is necessary to know and to tell in what Season of the Year it is. 3. To count the number of the Auditors. 4. To instruct. Begin then, if you please with the first of these four things.

The End of the Fragment.

The *Principal Maxims of the* Talapoins *of* Siam, *translated from the* Siamese.

Kill no Man. *The Talapoins do not only not kill, but they never strike any Person.*

Steal not.

Commit not the Sin of the Flesh.

Glorify not your self, saying, that you are arrived at Sanctity. *Every Man, who is not a Talapoin, cannot become holy, that is to say he cannot arrive at a certain degree of Merit.*

Dig not the Earth. *'Tis out of respect to this Element.*

Cause not any Tree to die. *They are prohibited to cut any branch thereof.*

Kill not any Animal.

Drink not any intoxicating Liquor.

Eat not Rice after dinner. *They may eat Fruit in the Evening, and chew Betel all the day long.*

Regard not Songs, Dances, nor Players on Instruments.

Use no perfumes about you.

Neither Sit nor Sleep in a place so high as that of your Superior.

Keep neither Gold nor Silver. *They are prohibited to touch it; but they ill observe this Rule, the Trade of a* Talapoin *is a Trade to grow Rich, and when they are Wealthy enough, they quit the Cloister and Marry.*

Entertain not your self with things, which concern not Religion.

Do no work, which is not the work of Religion.

Give not Flowers unto Women.

Draw not water in a place, where Worms are engender'd.

A *Talapoin* that goes to do his Needs, and who has not first drawn water, to wash himself, Sins. *Natural Impurities seem faults unto them.*

Contract not Friendship with Seculars, in hopes of receiving Alms from them.

Borrow nothing of Seculars.

Lend not unto Usury, though it be only a single Cory.

Keep neither Lance, nor Sword, nor any Arms of War.

Eat not excessively.

Sleep not too much.

Sing not worldly Songs.

Play not on any Instrument, and eschew all sorts of Sports and Diversions.

Judge not your Neighbor; say not, He is good, this is wicked.

Shake not your Arms in walking. *They little observe this Precept.*

Climb not upon Trees. *'Tis for fear of breaking any Branch thereof.*

Bake no Tile, nor burn any Wood. *'Tis out of Respect to the Earth and Wood. It is as bad to bake a Tile as Kill, and it is a wicked act to destroy the Wood.*

Twinkle not with your Eyes in speaking, and look not with Contempt.

Labour not for Money. *They ought to live on Charity, and not on the Work of their hands.*

Give not strong Medicines to Women with Child. *For fear of killing the Infant.*

Look not upon Women to please your Eyes.

Make not any Incisions that may cause the blood to come out.

Neither sell nor buy any thing.

In eating make not the noise *tchibe tchibe, tchiabe tchiabe*, as do Dogs. *'Tis the ungraceful noise which certain Persons do make in chewing slowly and gently. The* Siameses *do take a great care of Decency.*

Sleep not in a place exposed to view.

Give no Medicine wherein Poyson is put. *By reason of the danger of killing. The Art of Physick is not prohibited them: they practise it very much. Wherefore the* Siameses *are so far from being scandalized, to see the Missionaries practise Physic, that it is principally upon this account that they suffer them, and love them. It is necessary that the*

the *Missionaries do freely cure the sick, either by the Art of Medicine, or by Miracle.*

A *Talapoin* sins, if in walking along the Streets he has not his Senses composed.

A *Talapoin* who shaves not his Beard, his Hair, and his Eye-brows, and who puts not on his Nails, sins. *I know not whether this has any other Foundation than an excess of Neatness.*

A *Talapoin* who being seated, has his Feet extended or suspended, sins. *Modesty, in their Opinion, requires that the Legs be crossed, and the Feet placed near the Knees.*

After that you have eaten, gather not the remains for the next day. *They give them to the Beasts.*

Have not several Garments. *The People frequently gives them some out of Charity, and they distribute them to their Family.*

A *Talapoin* who loves the lesser *Talapoins*, and caresses them as if they were Women, sins.

A *Talapoin* who seems to be as austere as a *Talapoin* of the Woods, and to keep the Rule more exactly than another, who performs Meditation to be seen, and who being alone, observes nothing of all this, he sins.

A *Talapoin* who has received an Alms, and who goes presently to bestow it on another, sins.

A *Talapoin* who speaks to a Woman in a secret place, sins.

A *Talapoin* who concerns himself in the King's Affairs, which respect not Religion, sins.

A *Talapoin* who cultivates the Earth, or who breeds Ducks, Poultry, Cows, Buffalo's, Elephants, Horses, Pigs, Dogs, after the manner of Seculars, sins. *Not to cultivate the Earth is a respect for this Element; the rest purely represents the Monastic Poverty.*

A *Talapoin* who in Preaching speaks not *Balie*, sins. *This Maxim is not well render'd by the Translator. Their way of preaching is to read out of the* Balie, *where they ought to change nothing, but they must begin in* Siamese, *and say nothing which is not in the* Balie.

A *Talapoin* who speaks one thing, and thinks another, sins.

A *Talapoin* who speaks evil of another, sins.

A *Talapoin* who being waked rises not immediately, and turns himself on one side, and on the other, sins. *It is necessary that it be the hour of rising, that is to say, that they may discern the Veins of their Hands.*

A *Talapoin* who seats himself on the same Mat with a Woman, sins.

A *Talapoin* who embraces a Woman, sins.

A *Talapoin* who bakes Rice, sins, because it is to kill the Seed.

A *Talapoin* who eats any thing which has not been offer'd to him with joyned hands, sins. *'Tis a Vanity, for the respect in this Country, requires that every thing be given with both hands.* The Talapoins *believing themselves holy, are very vain in respect of the Seculars, whom they think loaded with Sin. They salute no Person, not the King himself, and when the* Sancrat *preaches, or speaks to the King, the King is behind a Vail to conceal his Majesty: but when this Prince cannot avoid a* Talapoin, *he salutes him, and the* Talapoin *salutes not the Prince.*

A *Talapoin* who dreams in his sleep that he sees a Woman, so that the effect of the Dream wakes him, sins. *Though all this be involuntary.*

A *Talapoin* who covets another's Estate, sins.

A *Talapoin* who pisses on the Fire, on the Earth, or in the Water, sins. *This would be to extinguish the Fire, and corrupt the two other Elements.* Mandeslo *reports, that the* Banians *are prohibited to piss upon the ground. He knew not the whole Precept; and he has been deceived, when he thought it grounded on the fear of killing some Insect. If this were so, the* Banians *would be prohibited to spill any Liquor, and moreover, they do not believe any Insect in the Fire.* Pythagoras *forbad pissing against the Sun.*

A *Talapoin* who reviles the Earth, the Wind, the Fire, the Water, or any other thing whatever, sins.

A *Talapoin* who excites Persons to fall out, sins.

A *Talapoin* who goes upon an Horse, or an Elephant, or in a Palenquin, sins. *He ought not to burden man, nor beast, nor tree.*

A Tala-

A *Talapoin* who cloaths himself with rich Garments, sins.

A *Talapoin* who rubs his body against any thing, sins.

A *Talapoin* who puts Flowers in his Ears, sins.

A *Talapoin* who uses Shoes, which conceal his Heels, sins.

A *Talapoin* who plants Flowers, or Trees, sins. *They think it not lawful to dig holes in the ground.*

A *Talapoin* who receives any thing from the Hand of a Woman, sins. *The Woman lays the Alms which she bestows on the* Talapoin *in some place, and the* Talapoin *takes it where the Woman puts it.*

A *Talapoin* who loves not every one equally, sins. *That is not to say, that he must love another as well as himself.*

A *Talapoin* who eats any thing that has Life, as for example, the Grains which may yet bear Fruit, sins. *They forbid not to eat any thing that has had Life.*

A *Talapoin* who cuts, or plucks up any thing, which has yet Life, sins.

A *Talapoin* who makes an Idol, sins. *'Tis, say they, because that the Idol is above the man, and that it is incongruous that the Idol should be the work of the man, forasmuch as in Justice the Work is inferior to the Workman. The Secular therefore who makes the Idol, sins also, but according to them the Sin is inevitable to the Seculars. In a word, particular Persons have no Idol amongst them, and the* Siameses *do make and sell them only to set up in the Temples.*

A *Talapoin* who fills not up a Ditch, which he has made, sins. *He sins in making the Ditch, and he sins in not repairing the Evil which he has done.*

A *Talapoin* who having no work to do, tucks up the Tail of his *Pagne*, sins.

A *Talapoin* who eats in Gold or Silver, sins.

A *Talapoin* who sleeps after having eaten, instead of performing the Service of Religion, sins.

A *Talapoin* who after having eaten what has been given him in Charity, pleases to say, this was good, or this was not good, sins. *These Discourses do savor of Sensuality, and not of Mortification.*

A *Talapoin* who glorifies himself, saying, I am the Son of a *Mandarin*, my Mother is rich, sins.

A *Talapoin* who wears red, black, green, or white *Pagnes*, sins. *Under these four Colors, and under the yellow, they comprehend all the other Colors, except the Colors of Animals, which have frequently some particular Names. The yellow and feuillemorte, for example, have one Name, blue and green the same; the blue they call little green.*

A *Talapoin* who in Laughing raises his Voice, sins.

A *Talapoin* who in Preaching changes something in the *Baly* Text to please, sins.

A *Talapoin* who gives Charms to render invulnerable, sins. *They believe it possible to render themselves invulnerable against the blows of the Executioners, in the Execution of Justice.*

A *Talapoin* who boasts himself to be more learned than the rest, sins.

A *Talapoin* who covets Gold or Silver, saying: when I shall go out of the Convent I will Marry, and be at expence, sins.

A *Talapoin* who grieves to lose his Relations by death, sins. *It is not Lawful for the* Crenz, *that is to say, the Saints, to lament the* Cahat, *or the Seculars.*

A *Talapoin* who goes out in the Evening to visit other than his Father, or his Mother, or his Sisters, or his Brethren, and who unawares contrives to quarrel in the way, sins.

A *Talapoin* who gives *Pagnes* of Gold or Silver, to other than his Father and Mother, Brethren and Sisters, sins.

A *Talapoin* who runs out of the Convent, to seize *Pagnes*, or Gold or Silver, which he supposes that some has stoln, sins.

A *Talapoin* who sits upon a Carpet interwoven with Gold or Silver, which has not been given him, but which himself shall have caused to be made, sins.

A *Talapoin* who sits down, without taking a *Pagne* to sit upon, sins. *This* Pagne *is called* Santat, *and serves to raise the* Talapoin, *when he is seated. Sometimes they make use of a Buffalo's skin folded in several doubles for this purpose.*

A *Tala-*

A *Talapoin* who walking in the streets, has not buttoned a Button which they have in their habit, sins: and if going into a *Balon*, he has not unbuttoned this very Button, he sins also. *'Tis the Button of the Angsa. I know not the reason of the Precept.*

A *Talapoin* who seeing a company of Maidens sitting, coughs, or makes a noise, to cause them to turn their head, sins.

A *Talapoin* who has not the under *Pagne* edged, sins: and if that which he has on the shoulder consists not of several pieces, he sins likewise.

A *Talapoin* who puts not his Cloaths on very early in the morning, sins.

A *Talapoin* who runs in the streets, as pursued, sins.

A *Talapoin* who after having washed his Feet, makes a noise with his Feet, either on Wood or on Stone, then goes to the house of a Secular, sins. *This noise is to make the cleanness of his Feet observed.*

A *Talapoin* who has not learnt certain numbers, or calculations, sins. They are superstitious numbers. Father *Martinius* in his History of *China*, p. 16. informs us, that the *Chineses* are likewise extreamly superstitious on numbers; and that amongst other things, they think the number 9 the most perfect and most lucky of all, and that of 10 the most imperfect and most unlucky. For this reason, the King of *China* has for the service of his Palace 9999 Barks, and not 10000, and in one of his Provinces he has 999 Stues, or Fish-ponds, and not 1000. He prefers the lucky and odd number, before the even and unlucky. When the *Chineses* salute him, it is with nine Prostrations.

A *Talapoin* who going into any one's House makes a Noise with his Feet, and walks heavily, sins. *In several of these Rules are discovered several things, wherein the* Siameses *do partly place politeness, for they require it extreamly in the* Talapoins.

A *Talapoin* who raises his *Pagne* to pass the Water, sins.

A *Talapoin* who raises his *Pagne* in walking the streets, sins.

A *Talapoin* who judges of the persons that he sees, saying, This is handsome, that unhandsome, sins.

A *Talapoin* who boldly looks upon men, sins.

A *Talapoin* who derides any one, or who rails at him, sins.

A *Talapoin* who sleeps on something high, sins. *They have no other Bedsted than a Hurdle.*

A *Talapoin* cleansing his Teeth with a certain Wood common to this purpose, if the Wood is long, or if he cleanses them in discoursing with others, he sins.

A *Talapoin* who eats, and who at the same time wrangles with any one, sins.

A *Talapoin* who in eating, lets Rice fall on one side and on the other, sins.

A *Talapoin* who after having eaten, and washed his Feet, picks his Teeth, and then whistles with his Lips, in presence of the Seculars, sins.

A *Talapoin* who girds his *Pagne* under his Navel, sins.

A *Talapoin* who takes the Cloaths of a dead person, which are not yet pierced, sins. *They willingly accept from a man that is a dying.*

A *Talapoin* who threatens any one to bind him, or to have him put to the *Cangue*, or to be buffeted, or who threatens him with any other punishment, or to inform the King, or some great man against him; that *Talapoin* who does thus to make himself feared, sins.

A *Talapoin* who going any where, resolves not to keep the Commandments, sins.

A *Talapoin* who washes his body, and takes the current of the water above another *Talapoin* more ancient than him, sins.

A *Talapoin* who forges Iron, sins. *This is not performed without extinguishing the Fire, with which the Iron is red.*

A *Talapoin* who meditating upon the things of Religion, doubts of any thing, which he does not clearly understand; and who out of Vanity will not ask another, that might illustrate it, sins.

A *Talapoin* who knows not the three Seasons of the Year, and how he ought to make Conferences at every Season, sins. *I have said in discoursing of the Seasons, that the* Siameses *have only three, the Winter, the Little Summer, and the Great Summer.*

A *Talapoin* who knows that another *Talapoin* owes Money to any one, and who nevertheless enters into the Temple with this *Talapoin*, sins. *We have before seen a Rule which prohibits them to borrow of Seculars.*

A *Talapoin* who is at Enmity, or in a rage with another *Talapoin*, and who nevertheless comes with that *Talapoin* to the Conferences, which are made about the things of Religion, sins.

A *Talapoin* who terrifies any one, sins.

A *Talapoin* who causes any one to be seized, by whom he loses Money, if it is less than a Tical, sins; if more than a Tical, this *Talapoin* must be cashier'd.

A *Talapoin* who gives Medicines to a man, who is not sick, sins. *They allow no presenting Medicines.*

A *Talapoin* who whistles with his mouth to divert himself, sins. This Precept is general. *The* Talapoins *are prohibited to whistle upon any account whatever, and to play on any Instrument*: So that these words, with his Mouth to divert himself, *which are in this Precept, are not to extenuate the signification, but only because the* Siamese *tongue loves to express the manner of the things which it expresses. The* Hebrew *tongue is of the same Nature;* mulier si suscepto semine pepererit filium, &c. *And this Remark may be applied to some other of these Maxims of the* Talapoins.

A *Talapoin* who crys like Robbers, sins.

A *Talapoin* who uses to envy any one, sins. *Some would say that, according to them, an Act of Envy is no Sin; but it may be that in this the Translation corresponds not exactly to the natural sense of the Precept.*

A *Talapoin* who makes a Fire himself, or who covers it, sins. *It is not lawful to kindle the Fire, because it is to destroy what is burnt; nor to cover the Fire for fear of extinguishing it.* Pythagoras *prohibited the striking a Sword into the Flame.*

A *Talapoin* who eats Fruit out of the Season of this Fruit, sins. *I am persuaded that these words*, out of Season, *must be understood* before the Season, *because that it is to kill the seed, which is in the Fruit, by not permitting it to ripen.*

A *Talapoin* who eats one of these eight sorts of Flesh, *viz.* of a Man, of an Elephant, of an Horse, of a Serpent, of a Tyger, of a Crocodile, of a Dog, or of a Cat, sins.

A *Talapoin* who goes daily to beg Alms at the same place, sins.

A *Talapoin* who causes a Bason to be made of Gold or Silver, to receive Alms, sins. *They receive Alms in an Iron Plate.*

A *Talapoin* who sleeps in the same Bed with his Disciples, or any other Persons whatever, sins.

A *Talapoin* who puts his hand into the pot, sins. *'Tis for this reason that the affront of* the Spoon in the Pot, *is the greatest that can be given to a* Siamese.

A *Talapoin* who pounds Rice himself, winnows it, and cleanses it, or who takes Water to boil it, sins. To be a Servant to Sin, is Sin.

A *Talapoin* who in eating besmears himself round the mouth, like a little Child, sins.

A *Talapoin* who begs Alms, and takes more then he can eat in one day, sins.

A *Talapoin* who goes to do his Needs in an open place, sins.

A *Talapoin* who takes Wood, or any thing else to make a Fire, in a place where some Animal uses to take his repose, sins. *In the expression of this Precept there is something of the Genius of the* Siamese *tongue, for this Precept does not insinuate* **that** *the* Talapoin *may for any reason whatever, take Wood in a place, where any Animal has used to take his repose, nor that he may kindle a Fire with any Wood whatever; but the meaning of the Precept is, that it is a double Fault to make the Fire, and take the Wood* **in** *a place, where some Animal has chosen his Lodging.*

A *Talapoin* who going to beg Alms coughs, to the end that he may be seen, sins. *He sins likewise as often as he coughs to attract the Eyes of others, though it be not in going to crave Alms.*

A *Talapoin* who walking in the Streets covers his Head with his *Pagne*, or puts on a Hat, as do sometimes the Seculars, sins. *The* Talapoins *shelter themselves from the Sun with their Fan, in form of a Screen, which they call* Talapat.

A *Talapoin* who takes off his *Pagne*, that his body may be seen, sins.

A *Talapoin* who goes to sing, or rather to rehearse, at a dead man's House, sins, if he reflects not upon Death, upon the Certainty of all Persons dying, upon the Instability of humane things, upon the Frailty of Man's Life. *This is partly the matter of their Song over dead bodies.*

A *Talapoin* who in eating has not his Legs crossed, sins. *In general they cannot sit otherwise on any occasion.*

A *Talapoin* who sleeps in a place where others have lain together, sins.

A *Talapoin* who being with other Seculars, and wrangling with them extends his Feet, sins. *Modesty requires that they cross their Legs.*

An Account of the Charges of Justice, translated out of the Siamese.

WHen the Judge receives the first Petition, for this 1 Livr.

The Judge, or *Tckom Meuang* counts the Lines and the Cancellings; and affixes his Seal to the Petition, for this 3 Livres.

The *Tckom-Meuang* sends the Petition to one of the Councellors, such as he pleases, but generally to the *Nai* of the Parties, to examine, and to show the habitation of both the securities of the Parties, 1 Livre.

For him that goes to summon the two Parties to come to the Hall of Justice, 3 Livres.

When he must lye a Night on the Road, 4 Livres.

To have the Liberty of giving each a Security, for the Judge 16 Livres, for the Clerk that writes 3 Livres, this is the receiving of the Bail.

For copying the reasons of the two Parties to present to the Judge, to the Clerk 3 Livres, to the Judge 3 Livres.

For the Clerk who goes to hear the Witnesses, 3 Livres. And if there be a day and a Night on the road, 4 Livres. *In this Country they go to find the Witnesses at their Houses, to receive their Depositions, and for this purpose there is deputed only one Clerk. The Law prescribes neither a Re-examination nor confronting of Witnesses, though the Judges cease not sometimes to confront the Accuser with the Accused. Reproaches against the Witnesses are not here in use, and oftentimes the Accused knows not who are the Witnesses that depose against him.*

If the Parties do examin several Witnesses, he takes one Livre for every Witness.

To copy the Evidences or Testimonies of the two Parties, and to make them fit to be presented to the Judge, to judge thereof, Four Livres, as well to the Councellor as to the Clerk.

For the Governour or Judge to sit in the Hall of Justice, five Livres. When there are *Oc-Pra* for *Second* or *Belat*, and for Councellors, to each five *Livres.* To the *Oc-Louang* three Livres.

When the Case is judged, for him that keeps it, three Livres.

A Collation or Entertainment for the Councellors, three Livres.

When it is order'd and judg'd to consult the Law of the Country, which they call, *Pra Raja cit di caa ajat cany*, for the Councellor who reads it, whom they call *Prag*, three Livres. More a white Cloath of about four Ells, more about five pound weight of Rice, more a Taper of yellow Wax, more five mouthfuls of *Arek* and *Betel*, more a Hen, more two Pots of *Arak*, more some Flowers and a Mat to put under the Books. Of which the two Parties do pay as much one as the other.

Concerning the Measures, Weights and Moneys of Siam.

The Measures. THe *Siamese* Measures are formed or composed after this manner.

Pent met vate pleuan, that is to say, *eight Grains of whole Rice*, the first cover of which has not been bruised in the Mill, amount to a Fingers breadth, in *Siamese niou*.

Twelve Fingers breadth do make a *Keub*, that is to say, a *Palm*, or the opening of the Thumb and the middle Finger.

Two *Keub* do make a *Sok*, that is to say, from the Elbow to the ends of the Fingers.

Two *Soks* do make a *Ken*, that is to say a Cubit, from the ends of the Fingers to the middle of the Breast.

Two *Kens* make a Fadom, which they call *Vona*, and which is near an Inch less than our Toises: so that within a very little their eight Grains of Rice, which do make their *Fingers breath*, do amount to 9 of our Lines, which we esteem equal to 9 Barly Corns.

Twenty *Vona* do make a Cord, which they call *Sen*.

And an hundred *Sens*, that is to say an hundred Cords, do make one of their Leagues, which amounts to two Thousand Fadom. They call their League *roe neng*, that is to say, a *Hundred*, *roe* signifies a *Hundred*, and *neng* signifies *One*: Thus the *Italians* do say a Thousand.

In a word, four of their Leagues, or 8000 *Vona* or *Fadom*, do make a *Jod*. And these are all their Measures of Length.

The Weights and Moneys. The Names and Values of the Weights and Moneys together are these. 'Tis true that some of these names do not signifie the Moneys, but the Values or the Sums: as in *France*, the word *Livre* signifies not a Money, but the value of a pound weight of Copper, which is a Sum of Twenty *Sols*.

The *Pic* is worth Fifty *Catis*.

The *Cati* is worth Twenty *Teils*.

The *Teil* four *Ticals*.

The *Tical* is a Silver Coin, and is worth four *Mayons*, and it is the weight of half an Ounce, by reason of which the *Cati* weighs two pounds and a half.

The *Mayon* is a Silver Coin, and is worth two *Fouangs*.

The *Fouang* is also a Silver Money, and is worth four *Payes*.

The *Paye* is not a Coin, and it is worth two *Clams*. But the *Song-Paye*, that is to say the two *Payes*, are a Silver Coin, which is worth half a *Fouang*.

The *Clam* likewise is not a Coin, but it is thought to weigh twelve Grains of Rice. This is what was told me, and upon this ground the *Tical* should weigh 768 grains of whole Rice, which I have not tryed.

All these names are not *Siamese*, but common amongst the *Europeans* which are at *Siam*. I know not of what Tongue the word *Pic* is. In the *Levant* it signifies a sort of Ell, nine of which do make five of *Paris*: At *Siam* it is the weight of One Hundred twenty five Pounds, of sixteen Ounces to the Pound.

The word *Cati* is *Chinese*, and is called *Schang* in *Siamese*, but the *Chinese Cati* is worth two *Siamese Cati's*.

Teil, or as others do write *Tael*, is also a *Chinese* word, which is called *Tamling* in *Siamese*, but the *Siamese Cati* is worth but eight *Chinese Taels*, whereas it is worth twenty *Siamese*, as I have said.

Tical and *Mayon* are words the Origine of which I am Ignorant of and which the *Siamese* do call *Baat* and *Seling*. *Fouang*, *Paye* and *Clam* are of the *Siamese* Language.

As to the Agreement of this Money with ours, to take it vulgarly, and without this exactness, which is not necessary to Commerce, a *Baat* or *Tical*, although it weighs only half a Crown, yet it is worth Thirty seven Sols and a half of our Money, by reason of which a *Cati* is worth Fifty Crowns.

A List

A List of the Moveables, Arms, and Habits of the Siameses, *and of the Parts of their Houses.*

Pra, a great Cleaver which serves them instead of a Hatchet. Instruments common to all.

Siou, a Joyner's Chisel.

Lenai, a Saw.

Kob, a Joyner's Plane.

Kiliez, a Wimble.

Kaiok, a Spade.

Rewang, a House.

Saou the *Bambou*-Pillars which bear the House, being four or six in number, planted at equal distances in two rows; They are twelve or thirteen foot above the ground. The parts of a House.

Rore, the two Transomes or *Bambous* laid a-cross, like Beams on Piles, along the front, and along the back part of the House.

Rawang, the other Transomes or *Bambous* laid on the Piles, two or three in number, along both the sides of the House, and on the two middle Piles, when the House is set upon six Pillars.

Preuang, Hurdles serving to plank the lower, or first Floor.

Fak, Sticks flatted and joyned together at equal distances, to lay over the Floor, instead of a Carpet: They lay them also on the Hurdles, which serve the wall instead of Wainscot.

Ake-a, the Mother wall, they are the Hurdles or Wainscoting, which serves as the outward wall.

Fa, the Hurdles which do make the principal Inclosures.

Look fa, the Son of the Inclosure, that is to say, the lesser Inclosures.

Pakpan, the fore mouth or door of the House. *Pak* signifies a mouth.

Na tang, a Visage keeper or Window, they are kind of Penthouses which are raised, and supported with a stick, and which are let down again when they would shut the Window. There is no Glass. *Na* signifies a Visage, *tang*, to keep.

Ken, the Hurdle which serves for the upper Floor, or Cieling.

Dang, the two *Bambou* Pillars to bear the roof.

Okkai, the Transome or *Bambou* laid on these two Pillars, to make the Ridge of the Roof.

Cloon, the Hurdles of the Roof laid sloping on both sides the *Okkai*.

Kiak, Foliages which serve instead of Straw.

Krabuang, the Tiles: but the Houses of particular persons have none if they are not of Brick; on which account they belong to the *Europeans*, the *Chineses* or the *Moors*.

Pe, the Roof.

Hong, a Chamber.

Gadai, the Ladder of the House.

Tong, the two Bambou's which make the two sides of the Ladder.

Kan gadai, the Rounds.

Sena, a Matt of Bulrush.

Ti-non, the place where the Bed is laid to lye upon, when they have no Bedsted: *Non* signifies to *Sleep*. *Ti* signifies a *Place*. Their Moveables.

Tangcon, a Bedsted without Posts or Head, but with four or six feet, which are not joyned by overthwart Beams. The bottom of this Bedsted is a Lettice of Bulrush, like as have the Chairs which come to us from *England*, and the Wood of which the English do send to the *Indies*, to be there garnished with Bulrush.

Cre, such a sort of Bedsted, but without feet. All these Bedsteds are very narrow, because they only serve a single person. 'Tis only some of the meaner people, who lye in the same Bed with their Wives; and they have no Bedsted. Amongst the Rich every one has his Bed and his Chamber apart, but in little.

Foukroung-non, the Mattress, or rather the Bed of *Capoc*, a kind of Cotton-wool, instead of Feathers. They are not quilted; *roung* signifies *nest*, *non* to *sleep*.

Pa-pou-non, the under Sheet to sleep on. They have no upper Sheet, which is other than the Coverlet.

Pa houm-non, the upper Sheet, that is to say the Coverlet. They are only single Cotton-sheets.

Mon, a longish Pillow, but when they lye together, every one has his own, as in *Spain*. *Mon* signifies also a Cushion to lean on, for they never sit thereon.

Man-can ti-non, a Curtain before the Sleeping-place. *Man* signifies a Curtain or Tapistry. *Can* signifies before. They put a Curtain before their Bed, to prevent being seen, because that from one Chamber to the other there is no Door which shuts.

Man-can-fak-reuan, a Linnen Curtain. *Man* a Curtain, *can* before, *fak* the flat sticks fasten'd at equal distances, to serve as Wainscot, *reuan* signifies a House.

Prom, a Carpet for the Feet.

Kiam, 'tis the same thing.

Thaum, Tables with a Border and without Feet, called otherwise *Lardiers*, and by our Merchants *flat and thin* Tables. When they eat together, every one has his Table at *Siam*, as at *China*. They have neither Table-cloaths nor Napkins, but the varnish'd Wood of their Tables is very easily cleansed with hot water: and so they easily make a shift without a Table-cloath.

Hip, a Chest.

Hip chipoun, a *Japan* Chest.

Hip-lin, a Cabinet with Drawers.

Tad, a Copper Dish, they generally serve up their Dish therein.

Me-can, a Pot to put Water in; *Can* signifies a *Pot*, *Me* signifies *Mother*.

Can nam, a *bowl* of Copper to boil Water for Tea; *nam* signifies Water.

Can-nam-nol, a little *Glass*. 'Tis a Cup round at the bottom, and without Feet.

Kon thoo, a Drinking-pot.

Kon thil, an earthen *bowl* for Tea.

Tiae my, a little Tea-Cup.

Tiae yai, a larger Cup.

Tabei-tong kin-nam, a Copper Ladle to drink Water. They also have some of *Coco* for this use: They bore a Cup of *Coco* on both sides, and thrust a Stick into the two holes, which crosses the *Coco*, and serves as a handle. *Tong* equally signifies Gold and Brass, *Tong di*, good Gold; *Tong Leuang*, false Gold or Latten. *Kin* signifies equally to eat and drink, according as it is spoken of a thing solid or liquid. Thus the words, to take and to swallow are common in our language, to solid Aliments and to Liquors.

Touan, the Ladle in the Pot. 'Tis the greatest affront that can be spoken to any one, as if one should tax him to be such a Glutton, as with his own hand to take out of the Pot, and not to stay till the Pot be emptied into the Dish. None but Slaves take the Ladles out of the Pot, or use them.

Touan, a Porcelane Plate, or Dish.

Tcham, a Porcelane Bowl to put Rice in. They use a great deal of Porcelane, because they have some very course, and very cheap.

Tiaa, a little Saucer to put under the Tea-dish.

Ma cam, a Skellet to boil the Rice; *Mo* a kind of Pot or Skellet, *cam*, Rice.

Quim, a Spoon. They use it only to take the Sweet-meats, which are always served in little Porcelane Saucers with the Tea. They have neither Fork nor Salt-seller. They use no Salt at Table.

Mid, a Knife. They have every one a little one to cut the *Arek*; they use it not like us, by holding what they would cut between the Thumb and the edge of the Knife, but they always place the Thumb on the back of the Knife, and they guide the edge with the fore-finger of the Right hand, which they keep extended.

Mid-tonne, a Razor or Knife to shave. Their Razors are of Copper; *tonne* signifies to shave.

Tiar

Tim-quian, a Candlestick; *quian* is a Candle of yellow Wax. They know not how to whiten the Wax, which they have in abundance; and as they have no Butchers meat, they have no Tallow; and Tallow in this Country would be of a nasty use, it would melt too much by reason of the heat.

Pra, another sort of larger Knife, which they carry about them for their use, and which might serve them for Arms in case of need.

Mid-rak, a sort of Knife to cut the Wood, with which they fasten the foliage which serves them for Straw.

Krob, a Gold or Silver Box for the *Arek* and the *Betel*. The King gives them, but it is only to certain considerable Officers. They are large, and cover'd, and very light: They have them before them at the Kings Palace, and in all Ceremonies.

Tiab, another Box for the same use, but without a lid, and which lyes at the house. 'Tis like a great Cup, sometimes of Wood varnished; and the higher the family is, the more honourable he is. For ordinary use they wear a Purse about them, wherein they put their *Arek* and their *Betel*, their little Cup of Red Calx, and their little Knife. The *Portugueses* do call a Purse *Bosseta*, and they have given this name to *Krob*, which I have discoursed of, and after them we have call'd them *Bossettes*.

Ca-ton, a Spitting-pot, which they all use by reason of the *Betel*, which makes them to spit very much.

Rena, a Balon, or strait and long Boat for a single Officer.

Cean, a Balon for a whole Family.

Mung, a Fly-net. 'Tis a Tester and close Curtain of Tiffany, which the *Talapoins* alone do use, not to be incommoded with the Gnats, and to prevent being forced to kill them. The Seculars have none of these Fly-nets, but they kill the Gnats without scruple.

Kamai, a Chair of State. None but the King and *Talapoins* have thereof, to seat themselves higher than others. The *Talapoins* do think themselves very much above other men.

Mouamon, a Chamber-pot. The *Talapoins* alone do use them, because they are prohibited to piss upon the ground, or in the water, or in the fire.

Lom-pok, a Bonnet of Ceremony. *Lom* signifies a Bonnet, *pok* high. It is commonly White, but in Hunting and in War it is Red. Their Habits.

Pa-nung, a Linnen Sash. 'Tis the *Pagne* which they wear round their Reins and Thighs. The King gives the finest, which are called *Pasompac*, and no person can wear them of this fineness, to whom he does not give them.

Sena-bana, the Muslin Shirt, which is their true habit. The word *Sena* signifies also a Mat, but then it has another Accent, and the *Siamese* do write it with other Characters.

Tiber-na, a Handkerchief. The Lords have it carry'd by their Slaves, and do take it themselves only in entering into the Palace; but they dare not to wipe themselves before the King: the generality are without Handkerchiefs.

Pahom, the upper Linnen. 'Tis that Linnen, which they wear like a Mantle against the cold, or like a Scarf on their Shoulders and round their Arms.

Rat-sa-you, a Belt into which they put their Dagger. They wear it also like a Scarf over the Coat of Mail.

Pasabai, a Woman Scarf.

Sena crenang, a Vest to put under the Muslin Shirt.

Sena-horm, a close Coat of Mail, or Red Shirt for the War, and for Hunting.

Muak, a Hat. They love them of all colours, high, pointed, and the edge about a fingers breadth.

Peun nok-sap, a Musket or Fusil. *Peun* signifies a Cannon. Their Arms.

Peun pai, a great Cannon.

Touan, a Lance after the *Siamese* fashion.

Stok, a *Zagaye* or Lance, after the *Moors* fashion; 'tis like the blade of a Sabre at the end of a Stick.

Dab, a Sabre. They have it carry'd by a Slave, who holds it respectfully on his Right Shoulder, as we carry the Musket on the Left.

Krid, a Dagger which the King gives to the *Mandarins*. They wear it thrust into a Girdle on the Left side, but very much before. The *Europeans* do corruptly call it *Cris*.

Kantat, a Bow.

Ke, a round Target.

Na-mai, a Cross-bow; *mai* signifies a Stick.

Lao, a Dart. 'Tis a Bambou arm'd with Iron.

Laou, a Dart of Bambou, harden'd in the fire, without Iron. *Lau* writ after another manner signifies all intoxicating Liquors.

Mai-tabong, a Battle-axe.

Mai-souan, a Truncheon.

The Names of the Days of the Months and of the Years of the Siameses.

The Days.

V*an* in *Siamese* signifies a Day. The names of the Days are,

Van Athit, Sunday.

Van Tchan, Monday.

Van Angkaan, the days of *Mars*, or Tuesday.

Van Pout, the day of *Mercury*, or Wednesday.

Van Prahaat, the day of *Jupiter*, or Thursday.

Van Souc, the day of *Venus*, or Friday.

Van Saou, the day of *Saturn*, or Saturday.

The names of the Planets are therefore *Athit*, *Tchan*, *Angkaan* &c. It is true they name not the Planets without the names of the Days, without giving them the Title of *Pra*, which, as I have several times declared, denotes a very great excellency. Thus *Pra Athit* signifies the Sun, *Pra Tchan* the Moon, *Pra Pra Prahaat* Jupiter: but the word *Pra* is written with a P. stronger than that which is in the first syllable of the word *Prahaat*. In short all these names are of the *Baly* Tongue, the Sun is called *Tavan*, and the Moon *Doüen*, in *Siamese*. *Abraham Roger* in his *History* of the *Manners* of the *Bramines* has given us the names of the Days in *Samscortam*, which, saith he, is the learned Language of the *Bramines* of *Palicatta* on the Coast of *Coromandel*. They are taken also from the Planets. *Souriawaram* Sunday, *Jendrawaram* Monday, *Angarawarawaram* Tuesday, *Boutawaram* Wednesday, *Brahaspitawaram* Thursday, *Soucrawaram* Friday, *Senniwaram* Saturday. It is evident that *Waram* signifies Day, that *Souria* is the name of the Sun, perhaps with some inflection to denote the Genitive; and that *Jendra* is the name of the *Moon*, perhaps also with some inflection, which being taken away, would leave some resemblance between this word, and the *Baly Tchan*. As to the other names, *Angaraua* participates enough of *Angkaan*: *Bouta*, which it is necessary to pronounce *Bouda*, is no other than *Pout*: *Prahat* agrees with the beginning of *Brahaspita*, and *Soucra* and *Souc* are the same word, *Senni* and *Saou* appear more remote, and *Souria* and *Athit* have nothing common: but what the same Author adds, is remarkable, that Sunday is called *Adittawaram* in the vulgar Language of *Palicatta*: for it is there that we do again find the *Baly* word *Athit*.

The *Chinese*, according to Father *Martinius* in his *Historia Sinica*, p. 31. do not name the Days by the Planets, but by the sixty names, which they give to the sixty Years of every Cycle: so that their Week, so to explain my self, is a Revolution of sixty Days.

The Months.

The *Siameses* do call the Months in their Order.

Deuen signifies a Month.

Deuen ai, the first Month.

Deuen Yi, the second Month.

Deuen Sam, the third Month.

Duan Sii, the Fourth Month.
Duan Haa, the Fifth Month.
Duan Hok, the Sixth Month.
Duan Ket, the Seventh Month.
Duan Pet, the Eighth Month.
Duan Cau, the Ninth Month.
Duan Sib, the Tenth Month.
Duan Sib et, the Eleventh Month.
Duan Sib Song, the Twelfth Month.

The *Siamese* People understand not the Words *Ai* and *Tgii*, which are the names of the two first Months; but it is probable that these are two old numerical Words, which signifie *One* and *Two*; and this is evident from the Word *Tgii*, because that the *Siamese* do say *Tgii-Sib*, to signifie Twenty, which *verbatim* is two Tens. All the other names of Months are still in use to signifie Numbers, with this difference, that when they are put before the Substantive, they signifie pure Numbers; and that when they are plac'd after, they become Names, which denote Order. Thus *Sam Duan* signifies Three Months, and *Duan Sam*, the Third Month.

Pii signifies a Year. The Twelve Names of the Year are: The Years.
Pii ma mia, the Year of the Little Mare.
Pii ma me, the Year of the Great Mare.
Pii Vok, the Year of the Ape.
Pii Rakaa, the Year of the Crow.
Pii Tebio, the Year of the Sheep.
Pii Counou, the Year of the Pig.
Pii Chouat, the Year of the Rabbet.
Pii Tohlou, the Year of the Lizard.
Pii Kan, the Year of the Hens.
Pii Tho, the Year of the Goat.
Pii ma Rong, the Year of the Sea-Gull.
Pii ma Seng, the Year of the Great Serpent.

Most of these Names are also of the *Balie* Tongue. Now as the *Siamese* do make use of the Cycle of Sixty Years, they ought to have Sixty Names to name the Sixty Years of every Cycle; and yet the Persons, whom I have consulted, could give me no more than Twelve, which are repeated five times in every Cycle, to arrive at the Number of Sixty: But I doubt not that it is with some additions, which do make the differences thereof; and I think to find the proof thereof in two dates of *Siamese* Letters, which I have carefully taken from the Originals. The first is thus: *In the First Month, the Ninth Day after the Full Moon in the Æra* 2229, *the Year* Tchlou Sapsoc. And the second is thus: *The Eighth Month, and the First Day of the Moon's Decrease in the Year* Pii Tho Sapsoc *of the Æra* 2231. The Word *Æra* in these two dates simply signifies *Year*, according to the *Spanish* language; so that it is all one to say the *Æra* 2229, and to say the Year *Tchlou Sapsoc*: to say the *Æra* 2231, and to say the Year *Pii Tho Sapsoc*. Besides, as the Word *Pii* signifies Year, they might put *Tho Sapsoc* instead of *Pii Tho Sapsoc*, as they have put *Tchlou Sapsoc*, and not *Pii Tchlou Sapsoc*. Now these two Years which are the Years 1685, and 1687 of Jesus Christ, are not called simply either by *Tchlou* and *Tho*, that is to say of the *Lizard* and *Goat*; but to the Words *Tchlou* and *Tho*, is added the Word *Sapsoc*, which I understand not, and which was added to the Names of the Twelfth of the Years, which run then to distinguish it from the four other Twelfths of the Years of the same Cycle.

Of the Monsons and Tides of the Gulph of Siam.

WE find upon our Seas, that tho' the Winds be very variable, yet they change with this almost infallible Rule, of passing from the North to the South only by the East; or from the South to the North, only by the West; or from the East to the West, only by the South; or from the West to the East, only by the North. So that the Wind continually veers about the Heaven, passing from the North to the East, and from the East to the South; and from the South to the West, and from the West to the North; and almost never in the contrary manner: Yet in the temperate Zone, which is on the South of the Line, when we navigated those Seas which are on the East of *Africk*, we experimented in our return from *Siam*, that the Winds went always contrary to this Rule; but to assert whether this may be always so, requires more than one Proof. However it be, the Wind goes not so in the Gulph of *Siam*, but it only encompasses the Heaven in a year; whereas on our Seas it does it in a small number of days, and sometimes in one day. When in the *Indies* the Wind blows round the Compass in a day, it is stormy: This is what they properly call a Hurricane.

In the Months of *March*, *April* and *May*, the South-wind prevails at *Siam*, the Heaven is disorder'd, the Rains begin, and are very frequent in *April*. In *June* they are almost continual, and the Winds do turn to the West, that is to say, do blow from the West and the South. In *July*, *August*, and *September*, the Winds are in the West, or almost West, and always accompany'd with Rains, the Waters overflowing the Earth to the breadth of nine or ten Miles, and above One hundred and fifty to the North of the Gulph.

During this time, and especially towards the middle of *July*, the Tides are so strong, that they ascend up to *Siam*, and sometimes to *Louvo*; and they decrease in twenty four hours with that measure, that the Water becomes sweet again before *Bancock* in an hour; tho' *Bancock* be seven Miles from the mouth of the River, yet the Water is always somewhat brackish.

In *October* the Winds do blow from the West and the North, and the Rains do cease. In *November* and *December* the Winds are North, do clear the Heavens, and seem so exceedingly to lower the Sea, that in few days it receives all the Waters of the Inundation. Then the Tides are so insensible, that the Water is always sweet two or three Leagues in the River, and that at certain hours of the day, it is the same for a League in the Road. But at *Siam* there never is more than an Ebb and Floud in twenty four hours. In *January* the Winds have already turn'd to the East, and in *February* they blow from the East and the South.

'Tis a considerable Circumstance, that at the time when the Winds are in the West, or that they blow from the West, the Currents of the Gulph do rapidly carry the Ships on the Eastern Coast, which is that of *Camboya*, and do hinder them from coming back again; and that at the time when the Winds are to the East, or that they blow from the East, the Currents do run on the Western Coast, so that then in Sailing it is necessary to fear being bore away. Now this proves, in my opinion, that the Winds have a great share in the motions of the Sea, forasmuch as some have proved, that these Currents are only in the upper parts of the Waters, and that underneath they have a quite contrary Current, because that the upper Waters being continually rowled on the Shore, returns underneath towards the Coast from whence it came. After the same manner it seems that they are the South-winds, which drive on the Flux, and maintain it for six Months further up in the River, and that they are the North-winds which do hinder it the entrance of the River for the six other Months.

A Di-

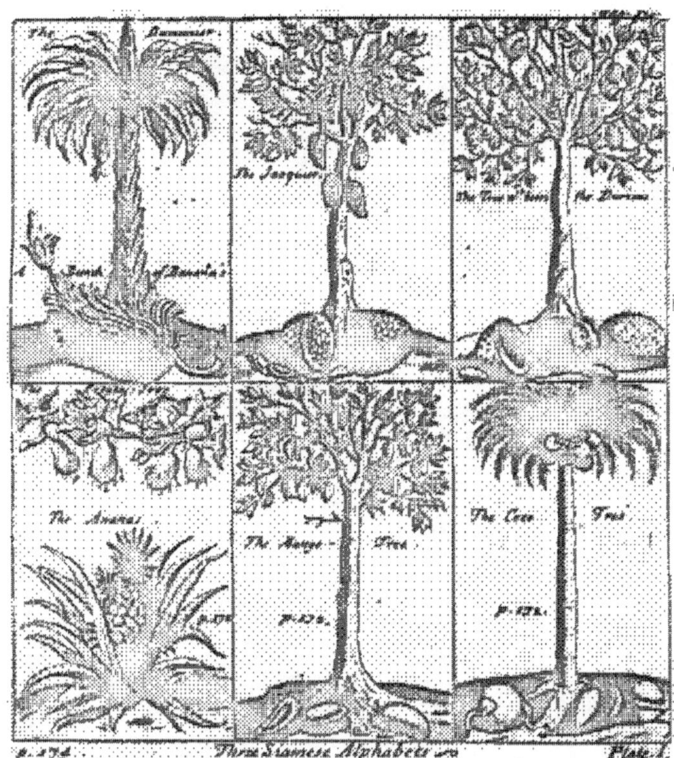

p. 274. Three Siamese Alphabets Plate I.

1 Ka Khi Khe Khò Khoa Khoa-ngo cho che che Sò chou yo do to the thi

thoo no ho po ppé fo ffpi fo ppo mo ro lo vo Sa Sò

Sò hò lo

2 Ka Ki Ki Kru Kru Kou Ku Ké Ké Kaï Kaïk

Kaon Kam Ka

Keüy Kaaï Kâou Kiou Kiom Kaüy Keüi Koüy Kouï

3

Keoü Kéou Koüy Köi Kouaï Kiaôu Kiâ

The Sequel of this Alphabet is in the following Plate.

A Description of the principal Fruits of Siam.

THE Figs of *India*, which the *Siameses* do call *Cluey-ngoan-tchang*, Elephant's Trunks, have not the taste of our Figs, and, in my mind, they are not so good. Thus the Melons of *Siam* are not true Melons, but the Fruit of a Tree known in the Isles of *America* under the name of *Papayer*. I have not eaten of this Fruit. But to return to the Fig, it is of the size and shape of a Sausage. Its green Skin, which waxes yellow and speckled with black in its maturity, is easily separated from its soft and clammy pulp, and 'tis that which has given it the name of Fig; but in the midst of its pulp there is no vacuity, nor any of those kernels which do make as it were a little gravel in our Figs, when they are a little dry'd. Its taste is strong, and it has something of sharpness and sweetness both together.

The *Bananas*, which the *Siameses* do call *Cluey-ngaa-tchang*, or Elephant's Tooth, is almost the same thing as the Fig, save that it is greener and longer, and that it has Angles, and Faces or flat Sides, which are re-united point-wise at both ends. These Fruits do hang like Nosegays, or rather like great Bunches of Grapes, from the top of the Trunk of the Trees which bear them. The Figs grow hard in the Fire, the *Bananas* which are not altogether so delicate raw, do wax soft again, do there lose their sweetness, and do acquire the taste of our Pippins ripen'd on the Apple Tree.

The *Goyave* (In *Siamese Louc-Kiae*, *Louc* signifies *Son*, *Kiae* is the name of the *Goyavier*) is about the size of a middling Apple. Its Skin is of a grayish green, like that of certain Pears: under this Skin is a pulp of the consistence of that of the Citron, but not so white. When it is put into the mouth, it favors the Strawberry; but this Strawberry taste soon loses itself, because it becomes too strong. This pulp, which exceeds not the thickness of a Crown-piece, contains a liquid substance like Broth, but grayish, and which would not be less pleasant to eat than the pulp, if it was not mix'd with an innumerable number of small kernels so hard, that it would be difficult to chew them.

The *Jacques*, *in Siamese Canoun*, are of the shape of a great Melon ill rounded. Under a grayish Skin fashioned like Chagrin, they have a very great number of kernels, or stones; stones, if we consider their magnitude, which is almost like a Pigeon's Egg; kernels, by the thin and smooth wood which incloses them. These stones therefore or kernels being broil'd or boil'd, differ not from our Chestnuts either in taste or consistence, excepting that they are, in my opinion, more delicate. At one end they stick to a pulp which invelops them all, and separates them one from the other. It is easily torn off, according to the course of its fibres; it is yellow, juicy, clammy, and glutinous, of a sweet taste, and strong smell. It is not possible to chew it, they only suck it.

They gave us a Fruit like to Plums, and we at the first appearance were deceived. It had the pulp and taste of a Medler, and sometimes two, sometimes three stones, but bigger, flatter, and smoother, than the Medler has them. This Fruit is called *Akouffida* in *Siamese*.

The *Ox-heart* was so named by reason of its size and shape. The Skin thereof is thin, and this Fruit is soft, because that on the inside it is only a kind of white Cream, and of a very agreeable taste. The *Siameses* do call it *Manoon*.

The *Durion*, in *Siamese Thourrien*, which is a Fruit very much esteem'd in the *Indies*, appear'd insupportable to me for its ill smell. This Fruit is of the size of our Melons cover'd with a prickly Coat like our Chestnuts. It has also, like the *Jacques*, several stones, but as big as Eggs, in which is contained what they eat, in the inside of which there is also another stone. The fewer there is of these stones in a *Durion*, the more pleasant the Fruit is. There never is less than three.

The *Mango*, in *Siamese Ma-mouan*, participates at first of the taste of the Peach and

and the Apricot; toward the end this taste waxes stronger, and less agreeable. The *Mango's* are highly esteem'd, I have seen some as big as a Child's hand, they are flat and oval, but pointed at the two ends almost like our Almonds. Their Skin is of the consistence of that of our Peaches, of colour inclining to yellow; but their meat is only a pulp which must be suck'd, and which quits not a great flat stone which it envelops.

I have not seen the *Mangoustan*, which is said to be much better than the *Mango's*.

The *Siamese* have some sharp Fruits which quench the thirst, and which upon this account appear'd unto me the most agreeable of all. They are small as Plums, and have a stone encompast with a white pulp, which easily melts in the mouth.

The *Tamarinds* is also sharp. 'Tis a Fruit enclosed in a shell like an Almond, and then several of these Fruits are likewise included in a Cod. I preserved some, and found the Syrup thereof very pleasant during my return; but by little and little it lost its sharpness, and there remain'd only the taste of the Pimpernel. The Tree which bears it, and which is very large, has a Leaf resembling Pimpernel.

From this Country I brought several sorts of liquid Sweet-meats, which were come from *China* to *Siam* about two years, and they ceased not to keep very well to *Paris*. The Syrup especially was very good, and had nothing of Candy, notwithstanding the heat of the Climats through which it had passed. These Sweet-meats had perhaps been made with Sugar-candy, which is the sole Purifier that the Orientals have. I refer my self to the Confectioners.

I speak not of the Sugar-canes wherewith *Siam* abounds, nor of the Pepper, because I saw none thereof. The King of *Siam*, they say, has caused an hundred thousand thereof to be planted. 'Tis a Plant which needs Props like the Vine, and the Pepper hangs thereon also by little Bunches, like to those of Currents.

The *Ananas*, in *Siamese Sapparot*, has the meat white, and the taste of our Peaches. Its meat is mixed with a little wood, not a wood which separates, as there is in our Nuts, but with a wood that adheres thereto, and which is only the meat over-hardned; and it is at the Center that it begins to grow hard. The *Ananas* is believed unwholsom, because that its juice, they say, corrodes Iron. It is yellow when it is ripe, and then to smell it without opening it, it has the scent of a roasted Apple. Its Figure is like a great Pine Apple, it has little rinds curiously ranged, under which, to behold them, one would think that the kernels are. The Plant which produces it bears it at the top of its stalk, which is not three foot high. The *Ananas* keeps directly upon the little end; and at the great end there is a tuft of Leaves, like little Corn-flags, short, bent outwards, and toothed. Sometimes from the body of this Fruit, and at the sides, there grows like Wens, one or two other little *Ananas*, which have also their Tufts. Now every Tuft cut and put in the ground, may produce another *Ananas*, but every Plant bears only one, and bears no more than once.

The *Coco*, in *Siamese Ma-praou*, is a kind of Filbert, but much bigger indeed than a Filbert, as may be seen by those Cups of *Coco* which they sell us. 'Tis the wood thereof which is naturally cover'd like that of our Nuts, with a *brou* or green bark an inch thick, and full of fibres, whereof Cordages may be made. In the wood of the *Coco* is a very pleasant liquor, and the wood thereof is so full, that it spurts a great way when it is pierced. As this Fruit ripens, this liquor congeals at the extremities, that is to say near the wood, and there forms a Nut very white, and of a very good taste; the water which is not yet congealed remains still at the Center of the Fruit, and at length it all congeals.

Of

Of the Siamese *and* Balie *Languages.*

THE *Siamese* Tongue has Thirty seven Letters, and the *Baly* Thirty three, but they are all Consonants. As to the Vowels and Dipthongs, of which there is a great number in the one and the other Language, they have indeed some particular Characters, whereof are made other Alphabets: but of these Characters some are placed always before the Consonant, some others always after, others above, others underneath: and yet all these Vowels, and all these Dipthongs thus variously disposed in respect of the Consonant, must only be pronounced after it.

But if in the Pronunciation the Syllable begins with a Vowel, or with a Dipthong, or if it is only a pure Vowel, or a pure Dipthong, then they have a mute Character, which supplys the place of a Consonant, and which must not be pronounced.

This mute Character is the last in the two Alphabets, the *Siamese* and *Balie*. In the *Siamese* it has the figure of our *o*, and indeed it countervails an *o*, when it must be pronounced, and not be a mute Consonant, that is to say, when it is preceeded with a Consonant or by it self. In the *Balie* Alphabet this last Character countervails *ang*, when it is not a mute Consonant; but its figure has no resemblance to any one of our Letters. Thus the first Letter of the *Hebrew* Alphabet, which is *Aleph*, serves as a mute Consonant, in relation to which they place the Points which are the Vowels; and it is probable that the *Aleph* was anciently pronounced like the *Alpha* of the *Greeks*, which has taken its name from the *Aleph*.

The *Siamese* Pronunciations are very difficult for us to imitate, and they correspond so ill to most of ours, that of ten *Siamese* words written in *French* Characters, and read by a *Frenchman*, there will not perhaps be one, that is known and understood by a natural *Siamese*, what care soever is taken to accommodate our Orthography to their Pronunciation.

They have the *r*, which the *Chineses* have not. They have our *v* Consonant, but they pronounce it frequently like the *w* of the *High-Germans*, and sometime like the *w* of the *English*. They have likewise the *ng* of the *Germans*, which we have not: For the *Germans* pronounce *Engel*, for example, after a manner that we hardly apprehend, and which is only a *g* pronounc'd before the *e*, and the *i* as before the *a*, but very softly and much through the Nose.

They have a middle Pronunciation between our two Pronunciations of *ye* and *ja*, and from hence it is that the *Europeans* do say sometimes *Cambaja*, and sometimes *Camboya*, because they know not how to pronounce these sorts of words exactly after the *Siamese*.

'Tis the same as to the word *Kiai*, which signifies, *Heart*. It is not known whether they rather say *Kiai* than *Ciai*, pronounced after the *Italian* manner, because that indeed they do not exactly speak either the one or the other, but something which partakes of the one and the other.

They have our Aspiration, which yet they pronounce very softly, and when they put the Character thereof before a Consonant (which the *French* tongue never permits) they do it only to weaken the pronunciation of the Consonant: and in general they speak so softly, that it is not known often whether they pronounce an *m* or a *h*, *cia* or *tchia*.

They have not our *u* Vowel which the *Chineses* have, but they have our *e*, such as we pronounce it in our Monosyllables, *ce*, *le*, *me*, *que*, *se*, *te*: but this *e* suffers no elision in their Tongue as in ours. I dare even affirm that they have no other *e* than this, not in the Cries of the Pagayeurs, *he*, *he*, *he*, which they pronounce as we would pronounce *heu*, *heu*, *heu*; nor in the Syllables which end with a Consonant, like this, *Pet*, which signifies a rough Diamond, and which they rather pronounce *peut*, than *pet*.

They have an *a* extreamly short, which they write with two points, thus :, and which they pronounce clearly at the end of the words, as in this *Balie* word

word *Pra*, which they give to whatever they honour most; but when this *a* is found in the middle of a word, it passes so quick that it is not discerned, and that it answers to our *e* mute. Hence it is that the word *Pa-ya*, which we have translated by that of Prince, and of which the first *a* written with the two points, is pronounced *Peya*, or *Pia*, though in the Relations we find it written *Pya* and *Pi*a, by the confusion of the *e* mute with the *a*, and of the *y* with the *j* consonant. This *a* marked with two points suffers no other Letter after it in the same Syllable.

'Tis a thing very singular that in the Syllables which end with a Consonant, they pronounce it not after our manner; but their tongue remains fix'd either to the palate of the Mouth, or to the Teeth, according to the nature of the Consonant; or rather their Lips remain shut: and it is thus that they terminate these sorts of pronunciations, I mean without unloosing the Tongue, and opening the Lips again. They cannot pronounce an Aspirate at the end of a Syllable, was it in the middle of a word. They pronounce *Porpayang*, though they write *Prochpayang*. The Convent of the Palace they call *wat Si-Sanpet*, though they write *Sarapech*. Thus when they would say *an ouf* they said *an ouk*, but they open'd not their Lips again to finish after our manner the pronunciation of the *k*. By the same reason they will pronounce an *n* for an *r* and for an *l*, at the end of a word, because that at the end of the words they unloose not the Tongue from the Palate, and it is necessary to unloose it in the pronunciation of the *r* or of the *l*: for in that of the *l* the Tongue cleaves not to the Palate at sides. They will write *Tahar* and *Akar*, and they will say *Tahan* and *Akan*.

They have a great deal of Accent, like the *Chineses*: they do almost sing in speaking: and the *Siamese* Alphabet begins with six different Characters, which do all countervail only a *K*, more or less strong, and variously accented. For though in the pronunciation the Accents be naturally upon Vowels, yet they do mark some by varying the Consonants, which otherwise are of the same weight. From whence it is perhaps permitted to conjecture that they writ at first without Vowels, like the *Hebrews*, and that at last they have marked them by some strokes foreign to their Alphabet: and which for the most part are placed out of the rank of the Letters, like the Points, which the modern *Hebrews* have added to their ancient manner of writing. Whoever therefore has learn'd to give the true Accent to the six first Characters of the *Siamese* Alphabet, easily pronounces the rest; because that they are all ranged with that art, that in their pronunciation it is necessary to repeat almost the same Accents. They read the *Balie* Alphabet after the same manner, save that they give it only five Accents, which they repeat five times in the twenty five first letters, the eight last having no accent. And as far as I can judge of the Hanscrit by the Alphabet, which Father *Kirker* has given us thereof in his *China Illustrata*, this Tongue, which is the learned Tongue of the *Mogul's* States, has five Accents like the *Balie* Tongue: for the Characters of its Alphabet are divided by fives.

Of the first Siamese *Alphabet.*

THe first Alphabet is of Consonants, which are thirty seven in number, and which I have plac'd in their natural order, with their value at the top, as far as to me has been possible. This double stroke (||) which is found six times, is to denote the places where they stop in saying their Alphabet by heart; for it is a kind of Song. They say seven Letters at first, and then the others six and six.

The little stroke which is between the names of two Letters, denotes that they pronounce the Letter which precedes the stroke very quick, and that it makes a shrink with the following Letter, when they say their Alphabet by heart.

I have

I have put an *h* after the *K*. 'tis to show that the *K* must be pronounced with an Aspiration after the *German* way, and not so simply as our *c* hard; and where I have put two *pp*, it is to denote a *p* harder than ours.

The *Ngo* is pronounced before all the Vowels, like our *g* before the *a*, the *o* and the *u*; with this difference, that it is pronounced a great deal more carelessly, and altogether from the Nose, which gives it something of *n* at the beginning of its pronunciation. At the end of the words, it is pronounced without loosing the Tongue from the roof of the Mouth: they will say *Tong*, and not *Tongue*.

The three first Letters of the second division are pronounced between the *tcia* and *cia* of the *Italians*.

The *yo* is pronounced after the *Castilian* manner by hissing.

The *do* which is in the third division, is pronounced like a *to* at the end of words, and they have no other *to* final.

They have a double *yo*, the one at the second division and the other at the fifth: they pronounce them between our *y* and our *jo*, and there is no other difference between these two Letters, save that the last *yo* which is that of the fifth division, is the true *yo* final: they place it after the Vowels to make Dipthongs, though they cease not sometimes to place the other there, but through ignorance: for this Orthography is not in their Alphabet, where all their Dipthongs are. Now these *yo* are however thought Consonants, as the *i* is thought a Consonant in *German* and *Spanish* in these Dipthongs *ja*, *je*, *jo*, *ju*, with which a Vowel which precedes them in Verses, is not confounded, but makes its Syllable apart. And yet though the *Siameses* put the *yo* among the Consonants, they so clearly perceive that they sound like Vowels, that in writing the words, which begin with a *yo* in the Pronunciation, they place an *o* mute at the head, as they do at the head of the words, which begin with the Vowel: this is not regular, but they are all incapable of all these little attentions.

The *No* which is the last Letter of the third division is not pronounced at the end of words like our *n*, but like the *n* of the *Gascons* and *Spaniards*. I have writ it with an *n* simple, in writing the *Siamese* words with our Characters; and sometimes to avoid ill agreement, which these words caused with those of our Language, I have thereunto added an *e* feminine, although this be ill, in that the *Siameses* pronounce it not, seeing that they unloose not not the Tongue from the roof of the Mouth, in pronouncing their *n* at the end of words.

The *Vo* is pronounced indifferently like our *v* Consonant, or like the *w* of the *High Germans*, which is a *b* pronounced softly, or without closing the Lips, or in fine like the *w* of the *English*, that is to say like our *ou* in the word *oui*. The *Vo* is likewise put after Vowels to form certain Dipthongs, in which case it is pronounced like our *ou*.

The three *So* of the last division, have the accent somewhat more sharp one than the other, the Voice ascending gradually to the last.

The *ho* is put sometimes before the Consonants, to mollifie the pronunciation thereof.

The *o* is a mute Consonant, as I have said, which serves to place the Vowels, as the *Aleph* serves to place the Points of the *Hebrew*, when the Syllable begins with a Vowel, or when it is only a Vowel; but the *o* becomes a Vowel, and is pronounced like our *o* when it is preceded by another Consonant, or by itself.

Of the second Siamese *Alphabet.*

THE second *Siamese* Alphabet is that of the Vowels placed in respect of the first *Ko*, as they are placed in respect of every other Consonant, and in respect of the *o* mute.

Ea,

Eu, *ou* and *ai* are simple Pronunciations, though we write them each with two Letters.

Ai is a Dipthong and not a single Vowel, and is pronounced as in our exclamation of complaint, *ai*.

Aou is also a Dipthong, which must be pronounced as *au* in *Italian* and in *Spanish*, but the *Siamese* Orthography is altogether fantastical: for it answers to *ea*.

Am is a Syllable and not a Vowel. The *a* is there clearly marked after the *Ks*, and that little *o* which is at top, denotes the *m* final. They have put the *m* final amongst the Vowels, because they have marked it above the Consonants, after the manner of the Vowels. They do sometimes also place at the end of the Syllables and Words, the *m* which is in their Alphabet of Consonants.

The last *a* which is marked with two points is an *a* very short, which suffers no other Letter after it in the same Syllable, and which is pronounced only at the end of words: for in the middle it is frequently lost, and becomes our *e* mute, such as the first *e* of *pereat*: wherefore in several *Siamese* words I have omitted this *a*, and sometimes I have written it with an *e*. Thus I have put *Jochar* for *Jocabar*, *Bla* or *Bela* for *Bala*, by reason that this Orthography more nearly approaches their Pronunciation.

The Character of the first *a* is always joyned to the Consonant, and is always placed after it, 'tis an *a* long, which is as two, as we anciently write *aage* for age.

The four following Vowels are placed always over the Consonant, and the long are marked with a stroke also. The two Vowels after, *viz.* the sixth and the seventh are placed underneath, and the seventh is only the double stroke of the sixth. The five following are placed before the Consonant, and the *e* long is only the *e* short redoubled.

The *eu* consists in two Characters, which answers *ea* as I have said, and the *e* is always put before the Consonant, and the *a* after, according to their Nature.

The *m* final marked with a little *o* is placed always on the Consonant, and is pronounced without opening the Lips.

The *a* short and sharp, marked with two points, is always put after the Consonant, and suffers no Letter after it in the same Syllable.

All these Vowels thus disposed, sometimes above, sometimes below, sometimes before, sometimes after the Consonant, are always pronounced after it, as I have already declared. This would be a trouble to us, when the Syllable begins with a Mute and a Liquid, like *pra*, the Letters of which they would range thus *apr*, so that we could not know if it were necessary to say *pra* or *par*: but they always pronounce the Liquid before the Vowel, saying *pra*, and not *par*. They cannot pronounce *pre* but *pere*: they will also say *peur* for *pri*, and they will range the Letters in this manner, *lape*, or *riept*, or *urpt*. The *e* pronouncing itself always after the Consonant, which follows it in the writing, leaves not any doubt to them in this Orthography. For *paut*, or *peai*, *pnue* or *pewe*, they will always pronounce *pret* and *preme*.

Of the third Siamese *Alphabet*.

THis Alphabet is of Dipthongs, most of which are truly orthographied and easie to read; but some of which are pronounc'd after a manner very different from their Orthography. We shall observe in these that the Vowels are pronounced according to their disposition; those which precede the Consonant pronounced first, altho they nevertheless are pronounced after the Consonant. Whence it appears, that designing to place certain Vowels before the Consonant, they have chosen those, which in the pronunciation of the Dipthongs

are

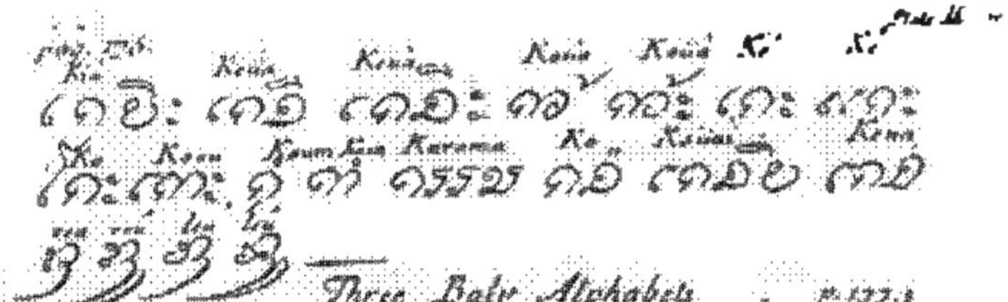

Three Bali Alphabets p. 177.

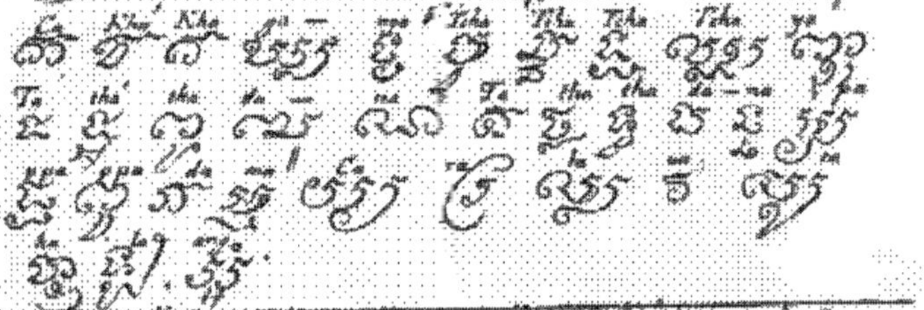

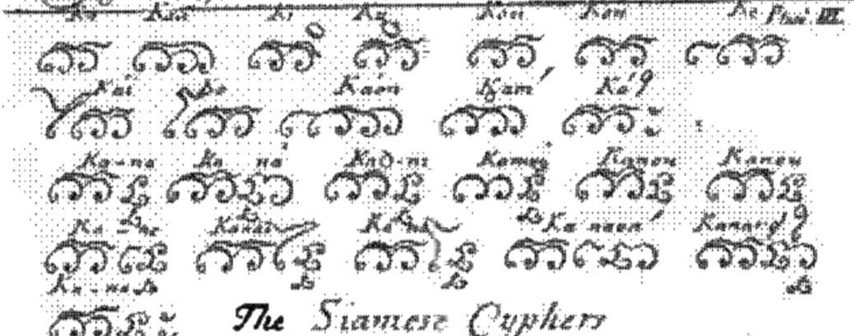

Plate III.

The Siamese Cyphers

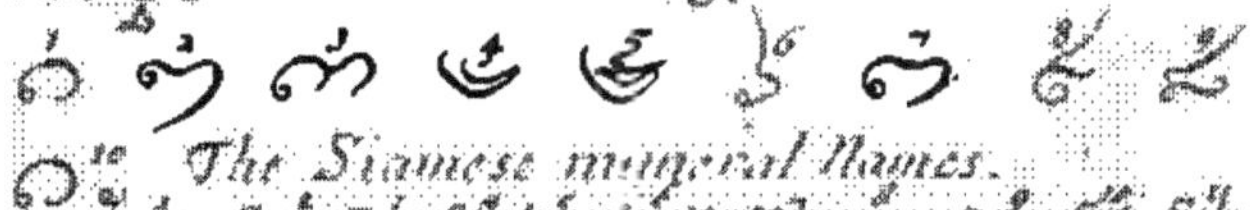

The Siamese numeral names.

Nong. Song. Sam. Sii. hâ. hauk. Ket. peet. Cau. Sib. Sibet. Sib Song. Tgii Sib. Sam Sib &c.

A Smoaking Instrument in Siam de use. p. 180.

A. A Pipe of Bambou or Smoaking

The Chinese Chess Board

1 The King
2 The Guards
3 The Elephant
4 The Knights
5 The Waggons
6 The Cannon
7 The Pawns
8 The River

p. 182.

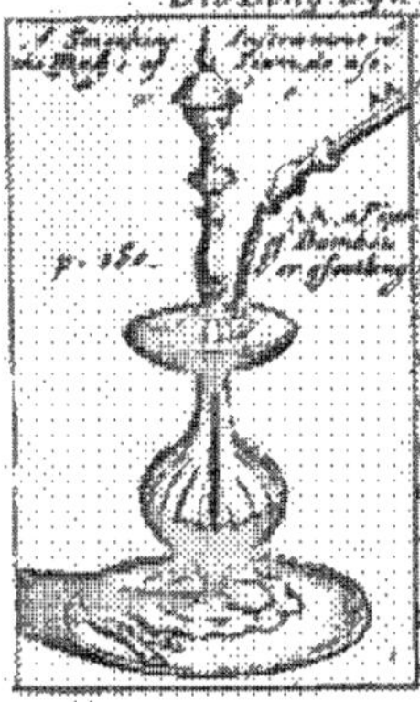

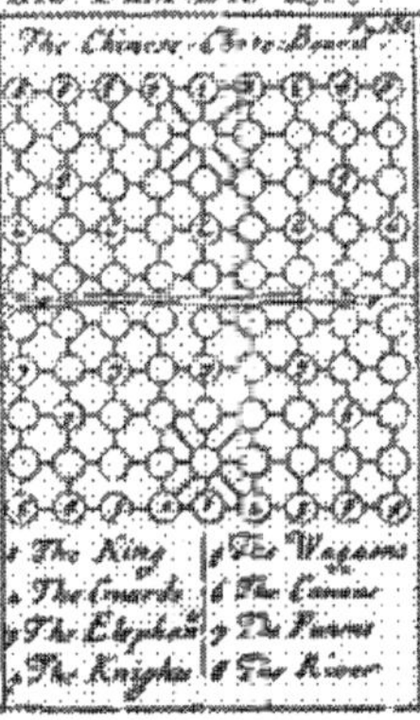

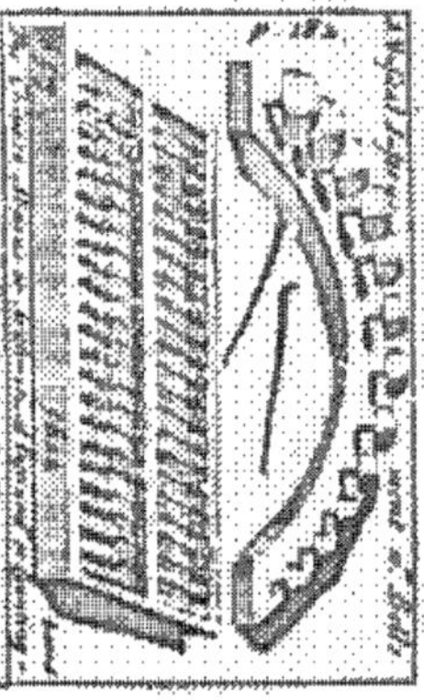

are first pronounced. In this Alphabet there is also some Syllables, which are not Dipthongs.

Of a fourth Siamese *Alphabet, which I have not graved.*

THis Alphabet is of the Syllables which begin, and which end with Consonants, and it teaches two things. First, there are two Vowels, an *a* and an *o*, which must never begin the Syllable nor end it, but be always between two Consonants. They have a particular Accent. The *a* is marked with a sharp accent ', oftentimes very much lengthned, and always placed over the first Consonant of the Syllable; and the *o* is marked with a double Accent sharp '', which they put likewise over the first Consonant of the Syllable. When in the pronunciation the Syllable ends not with a Consonant, they put the *o* mute in the place of the second Consonant, as may be seen in the Syllable *Ko* in the Alphabet of the *Siamese* Dipthongs: yet they sometimes dispense therewith after the accent ', which marks the *a*, but never after the two accents '', which mark the *o*. Sometimes also instead of the double accent, which marks the *o*, they put a little *o* over the first Consonant, and sometimes they put nothing; and as often as two Consonants make a Syllable, it is the *o* that must be understood. The second thing which this Alphabet teaches, are the final Consonants, *viz.* the first *ko*, the *ngo*, the *do*, the *no*, the *mo*, and the *bo*. As often as they end a Syllable, with any other Consonant, it is a fault against their Orthography. They pronounce these only at the end of the Syllables, and they never show their Children any Syllable to read, which ends with any other Consonant, than with those I have mentioned. It is true that they pronounce the *do* like a *to*, and the *bo* like a *po* at the end of some Syllables and Words.

Of the Balie *Alphabets.*

THey are not difficult to understand, after what I have related of the *Siamese*: The stroke shows that the two Letters between which it is found, do make a halt in the pronunciation. The five which follow the twentieth are not now of different value from the five, which immediately precede them: but perhaps this was otherwise, when this Tongue flourished.

Of the Siamese *Cyphers.*

I Have nothing to say of the *Siamese* Characters, save that an experienc'd man inform'd me that they resembled those, which he had found on some *Arabian* Medals between four and five hundred years old. The *Siamese* names of the Powers of the number Ten are these.

Nore, which they pronounce *Nuei*, signifies *Number*.

Sib, which they pronounce *Sip*, signifies *Ten*, and *Tenth*.

Roi, which they pronounce *Roe*, signifies a *Hundred*, and *Hundredth*.

Pan, a *Thousand*.

Meuing, *Ten Thousand*.

Seen, or *Sen*, an *Hundred Thousand*, or *Hundredth of Thousand*. *Abraham Roger*, p. 104. *Of the Manners of the Bramines*, says that at *Paliacata*, *Lac* signifies an *Hundred Thousand*; and *Bernier* says *Lacque*, in his Relation of the *Gentiles of Indostan*, pag. 221.

Cot, a *Million*. *Abraham Roger* in the before-quoted place, saith that at *Paliacata*, *Coti* signifies *Ten Millions*.

Lan, Ten Millions.

The numbers are plac'd before the Substantive, as in our Tongue: but these numbers are put after the Substantive, to signifie the names of Orders. Thus *Sam Deuan* signifies *Three Months*, and *Deuan Sam* the *Third Month*.

Of the Pronouns of the First Person.

Cou, ca, raou, atamapap, ca Tchaou, Ca-ppa, tchaou, atama, are eight ways of expressing *I* or *we*: for there is no difference between Singular and Plural.

Cou, is of the Master speaking to his Slave.

Ca, is a respectful term from the Inferior to the Superior, and in civility amongst equals: the *Talapoins* never use it, by reason that they believe themselves above other men.

Raou, denotes some superiority or dignity, as when we say *We* in Proclamations.

Rauk, properly signifies body, 'tis as if one should say my body: to say *we*, 'tis only the *Talapoins* that use it sometimes.

Atamapap, is a *Balie* term, more affected by the *Talapoins* than any other.

Ca Tchaou, is compos'd of *ca*, which signifies *me*, and *Tchaou*, which signifies *Lord*; as who should say me of the Lord, or me who belong to you my Lord; that is to say, who am your Slave. The Slaves do use it to their Masters, the common people to the Nobles, and every one in speaking to the *Talapoins*.

Ca ppa Tchaou, has likewise something more submissive.

Atama is a *Balie* word, introduced within three or four years into the *Siamese* Tongue, to be able to speak of himself with an intire indifference, that is to say without Pride and without Submission.

Of the Pronouns of the Second and Third Persons.

TEU, *Tan, Eng, Man, Orchaou*, do serve equally to the Second and Third Persons for the Singular and Plural Numbers: but oftentimes they make use of the Name or Quality of the person to whom they speak.

Teu, is a very honourable term, but is used only for the third person, or for the *Talapoins* in the second, that is to say in speaking to them.

Tan, is a term of Civility amongst equals. The *French* have translated it by the word Monsieur, Sir.

Eng, to an inferior person.

Man, with contempt.

Orchaou, to a mean person unknown.

Of the Particles which supply the place of Conjugations.

THe Present Tense is without Particle: As for example, *pen* signifies *to be*, and *raou pen*, signifies *I am*; *eng pen*, *thou art*, and *he is*. And again, *raou pen*, signifies *we are*. *Tan tang-lai pen*, *ye be*. *Kon tang-lai pen*, *they are*. *Tang lai* signifies *all*, or *a great many*; and it is the mark of the Plural. *Kon* signifies *People*, as who should say *the People are*, to say in general, they are, or he is.

The Imperfect is verbatim *at this time, I being*, or *time this*, or *when I being*, to say *I was*, *mona nan rau pen*. *Mona* signifies *time*, or when, *nan* signifies *this*. The Perfect is denoted by *dai*, or by *laou*, and sometimes by both. But *dai* is plac'd always before the Verb, and *laou* after: Thus *dai pen*, or *rau dai pen*, I have

have been, or rather *raou pen leou*, or rather yet *Raou dai pen leou*. *Dai* signifies *to find*, *leou* signifies *end*.

The Pluperfect is composed of the Particles of the Imperfect, and the Perfect. Thus to say, when you came I had already eaten, they will say, *mewa tan ma, raou dai kin sam red leou*; that is to say word for word, *time*, or *when you come*, I already to eat end. *Ma* signifies *to come*, and with other Accents and another Orthography, it signifies *Horse* and *Dog*. *Kin* signifies to *eat*, *samred* signifies to *end*: and this term is added to the Perfect to form the Pluperfect.

Tcha is the sign of the Future: *raou tchapen*, I shall or will be; this Particle always precedes the Verb.

Hai denotes the Imperative, and is put before the Verb. *Tent* also denotes it, and is placed always at the end of the Phrase: *hai kin* eat, or rather *kin tent*, or rather *hai kin tent*. *Hai* properly signifies to give, and is used likewise to signifie to the end.

Ren is the Note of Interrogation. *Kin leou ren?* Hath he eaten? or have you eaten? *Leou*, as we have said, is the sign of the Perfect, *ren* is plac'd always at the end of the Phrase.

To say *I did eat*, they say I would eat, *tcha crai kin*. *Tcha* is the sign of the future, *crai* signifies to will, and so *tcha crai* signifies *I would*, and *kin* signifies to eat.

To say *if I was at Siam, I should be satisfied*, they would say word for word, *if me to be City Siam, my heart good much*. *Heart good* signifies *content*, and the Verb *I should be* is there understood.

Of the Construction.

THey have Pronouns demonstrative, and not relative. They have Prepositions and Adverbs, or at least Nouns taken in this sense.

The Nominative always precedes the Verb, and the Verb precedes the governed.

The Preposition precedes also what it governs.

When two Substantives come together, the latter is taken in the Genitive. *Van athit*, day of the Sun, *athit* which signifies Sun is in the Genitive.

The Adjective is always after the Substantive, and the Adverb after the Adjective, or after the Verb to which it refers.

Their Construction is always shorter than ours, because it wants Articles, and a great many Particles which we have, and oftentimes a Verb; but the turn of their expressions seems long to us, if we translate them word for word. To say, *How is this thing named?* they say, *an seben rai*, that is to say verbatim, *this thing name how?* where they suppress the Verb. But to say, *bring me that*, they will say, *go, take that, and come*. To say, *give some Rice to thy Child*, they say, *take Rice, give Child to eat*: The Construction is always short, but the turn of the expression is long, because they express all the circumstances of the Action.

In naming particular things, they do almost always make use of the general word, to which they add another word for the difference. They say, *Head of Diamond*, to signifie a Diamond; and they have two words, the one for the Rough Diamond, *pet*, and the other for the Diamond set in work, *Ven*: *houa pet*, *houa ven*. *Houa* signifies *Head*.

To say a *Man*, they say *pou tchay*, to say a *Woman*, *pou ying*, which they pronounce almost *pou-ging*, and *pou* signifies *person*: to name the Beasts, they put the word *body*: *body of an Ox*, *body of a Cow*. *Louk* signifies *Son*, *Louk Schaome*, *young Son*, that is to say *Dongivon*; *Schaome* in *Siamese*, signifies *young*, as *vang* in *Italian*. To denote the Female amongst the Animals, they use the word *mia*. They join the word *ban*, which signifies *Village*, to almost all their Names of their Villages. *Ban-pac tret yai*, *Village* of the *Mouth* of the *great Strait*, *Ban-pac-tret-noe Village* of the *Mouth* of the *little Strait*. *Ban-vat Village* of the *Convent*. *Ban-pac-nam*, *Village* of the *Mouth* of the *Water*.

The

The Pater Noster, *and* Ave Maria *in* Siamese, *with an Interlineary Translation.*

PO raou yu Savang. Scheu Pra hai prakat touk heng kon tang-lai rouai Pra pen. Meuang Pra to hai dai ke raou. Hai loue ning tchai pra Menang Pendin some savang. Ahan raou touk Van co hai dai ke raou Van ni, to prat bap raou, some raou prat pua tam bap ke raou. Ta hai raou tok nai kuuan bap: hai poun kiat anrai tang paang. Amen.

The Ave Maria.

*AVE Maria Tem anisong, Pra you heng † Nang. Nang somm-bouï yinghena Nang Tang-lai, Tam bouk outong, heng nang Pra, Ogkha Jesu somm-bouï yinghena Tanglai. Sancta Maria Me Pra thoui ning tone Pra pre raou kon bap tois bou ni le moun raou * teha tai. Amen.*

† Nang is that Italic word, which signifies young, and which added to Nouns Masculine renders them Feminine.

* 'Tis the Latin Word.

A Smoaking Instrument made use of by the Moors, *which are at* Siam.

THey have a glass bottle of the figure of our Caraffas, excepting that it has a foot to be more firm, they fill it up half with water, and into the neck, which is all of a bigness and very long, they put a Silver Pipe wound about with a Fillet, to the end that it close the better: but this Pipe enters only the length of two Fingers breadth, though it be more than half a Foot long. At the upper end is a little Cup, either of Silver or Porcelane, which has the bottom perforated to communicate with the Pipe; and in this Cup is the Tobacco, on which they put a live coal. From the side of the Pipe there proceeds another much less in form of a Spout, or rather it is the little one which enters into the great one at the side, and it descends within the great one, and as far as the great one it self, yet without filling the whole capacity thereof, but leaving a space through which the smoak of the Tobacco, which is consumed in the Porcelane Cup, may descend into the Bottle. In fine, to the inferior Orifice of the little Pipe, they put another little Pipe of Bambou, bound about also with a little Ribbon or black Silk, which descends into the water. Now he that would smoak, setting this glass bottle, or rather all this Machine which I have described upon the ground, puts into the superior orifice of the little silver pipe, the end of a Bambou-slip, which though of one single shoot is sometimes between seven and eight foot long. The two ends thereof are garnished with Gold or Silver, and besides this one of the two is garnished with a little Chrystal Pipe, which he that smoaks puts between his Lips. From this manner it seems that in smoaking, he would attract to his Mouth the Water of the Bottle, by reason of the Communication that there is from the Mouth of the Smoaker to the Water of the Bottle, *viz.* through the great Bambou slip, thro the little Silver Pipe to which it joyns, and thro the little Bambou Pipe which enters into the Water, and which unites at the lower end of the small silver Pipe: but instead of this, the exterior air not being able to enter into the Bottle, the Smoak of the Tobacco descends along the great silver Tube, not only into the Bottle, but even into the Water, to insinuate it self into the little tube of Bambou, from whence it ascends to the Mouth of the Smoaker. So that he who invented this Instrument, has very ingeniously apprehended that it would be more natural that the smoak should be drawn into the water, and from the water to the Mouth of the Smoaker, then that the water, which is heavier than the smoak, should yield to the force of this Attraction. Sometimes

Sometimes there are several small Tubes round the great one, to the end that several persons may smoak in company with the same Instrument, and the better to settle it, it is placed on a copper Bason, covered in that place with a little piece of cloth, which hinders the foot of the Boule from slipping over the Bason.

The Chess-Play of the Chineses.

A Description of their Chess-board, and the number of their Men.

THeir Chess-board is composed like ours of 64 squares, but which are not distinguished by white and black. Neither do they place their pieces in the Squares, but at the corners of the Squares, that is to say at the points where the lines of the Chess-board do intersect. Moreover the Chess-board is divided into two halves, thirty two Squares for each of the two Players, and these two halves are separated by a space, which they call the River. It is about the bigness of a row of Squares, and runs not from one Player to the other: but after the same manner wherewith the pieces are ranged on the Chess-board. 'Tis not therefore the Squares which are the Points of their game, but the corners of the Squares. And so they have nine Points on each line, and there are five times nine or forty five on each half of the Chess-board; I have marked them with circles.

They have thirty two Men like us, sixteen for each Gamester, the one white, the other black; but these Men are not all the same as ours, and they dispose them not altogether after the same manner. Every Gamester has a King and no Queen, two Guards, two Elephants, two Horsemen, two Waggons, two Cannons, and five Pawns. Each Gamester places nine Men on the first Line of the Chess-board, which is on his side, at the Points where this first Line is divided, and on those where it is terminated. These nine Men are, the King, whom they place in the middle; the two Guards which are next him, the one on the right and the other on the left; the two Elephants which are next the Guards, the one on the right and the other on the left; then the two Horsemen, the one on the right and the other on the left; and in fine the two Waggons which take up the two corners of the Chess-board. The two Cannons are placed in the second Point before the two Horsemen, and the Pawns in the first, third, fifth, seventh, and ninth Points of the fourth Line, that is to say on that which is our Chess-board, separates the first Points before the Men, from the second.

The motion of their Men.

The King makes only one step as in our Game, but he cannot do it every way: he goes forward, or backward, or side ways, as do our Rooks, but he marches not bias-wise like our Bishops. Moreover he cannot stir out of a Square, which is his field of Battle or his Palace, and which contains four Squares, which on our Chess-board are those, where we place the King and Queen, and the Pawns of the King and Queen.

The two Guards do not move also out of the Square, and they never make more than one step, but bias-wise like our Bishops, and not otherwise.

The two Elephants do move after the manner of our Bishops, but they do always make two steps, and never more nor less, and they pass not the River: they enter not into the Enemy's Camp. I understood that the Elephant is called *fil* in *Arabia*, and that it is from this word *fil* that we have taken that of *fol* or Bishop for that of our Chess-men which answers to the Elephant.

The Horseman skips two points like our Knight, the one of which is according to the march of our Rocks, and the other is according to the walk of our Bishop But their Horseman leaps not over the other Men: it is necessary that he have the way open, at least on one side. I explain my self. The walk of the Horseman is composed of two steps, as I have said, the one of which is according to the march of our Rook, and the other according to that of our Bishop. It is therefore necessary that the first step of the Horseman, be free in one sense, that is to say, either according to the march of the Rook, or according to that of the Bishop. Besides the Horseman may pass the River, and the breadth of the River is esteem'd one of the two steps that he must take, as if it was a Rank of Squares.

The Waggons march like our Rooks, and may pass the River. The Cannons have also the walk of our Rooks, and may pass the River.

The Pawns do only make one step as amongst us, and they never have the liberty of making two, not even the first time that they are used. They may pass the River which is always reckoned for one step, and when they have passed it, they may move not only forwards, but also sideways like the Rook, and never bias-ways like the Bishop, and like our Pawns when they take, nor also backward, not even when they have been at the end of the Game, which we call making a Queen.

The design of the Game. The design of the Game is to give Check-mate, as amongst us; and the King is obliged amongst them, as amongst us, to free himself from Check, either by removing place, or by covering himself from Check.

How their men do take. Every Man takes, by putting it self in the place of the Man which it takes, provided that the walk from the one to the other be free. There is only the Cannon which requires that there be a Man between it, and that which it takes, and it matters not whether this Man be Friend or Enemy. 'Tis said that it serves as a carriage. Thus it is necessary that there be a Man between the Cannon and the King, for that the Cannon gives Check to the King; and if the Man which is between both, is on the King's side, he whose King is in Check, may free him from Check by taking away this Man, and by exposing the King before the Cannon. In a word one Cannon may serve as a carriage to another Cannon.

Their Pawns take not bias-ways like ours, but in the natural sense of their walk, which is forward, when they have not passed the River; and forward or sideways according to the march of our Rook, when they have passed the River.

One cannot put nor leave his King opposite to the other King, when there is not a Man between both, he that should do it, or would take the Man that is between both, would himself put his own King in Check, which cannot be done, yet the King can take nothing but what is at a point near him, and according to the march of our Rook, and not according to the march of our Bishop.

The Abacus, *or Counting-Table of the* Chineses.

THe Counting-Table which the *Chineses* use, is a wooden frame of a square figure, but much longer than broad. It is divided into two long squares, with a flat stick of Lath parallel to the two great sides, and terminated at the two little ones. These three parallel sticks, (I mean the two great sides of the frame and the middle stick) are threaded at right Angles, by several small sticks of wood, or copper wires, which are all parallel to one another, and parallel to the two little sides of the Frame, and placed at equal distances for Decency. And in fine, on each of these sticks are put seven Beads or Balls, two on one side of the middle piece, and five on the other, which will slide, or come along the Sticks; that is to say, to approach to, and remove from the middle Lath, or Partition.

This Instrument, which is composed at most of Twenty, or Twenty five sticks, for the number thereof is uncertain, is laid flat, and not on the side, and one turns to him the ends of those sticks, which do each bear five Beads, or Balls. The way of using it is grounded, 1st. On this, that the Beads do signifie only when slid near the middle Lath or Partition. 2d. On this, that each of the five Beads stands for a point, and each of the two Beads five points, as

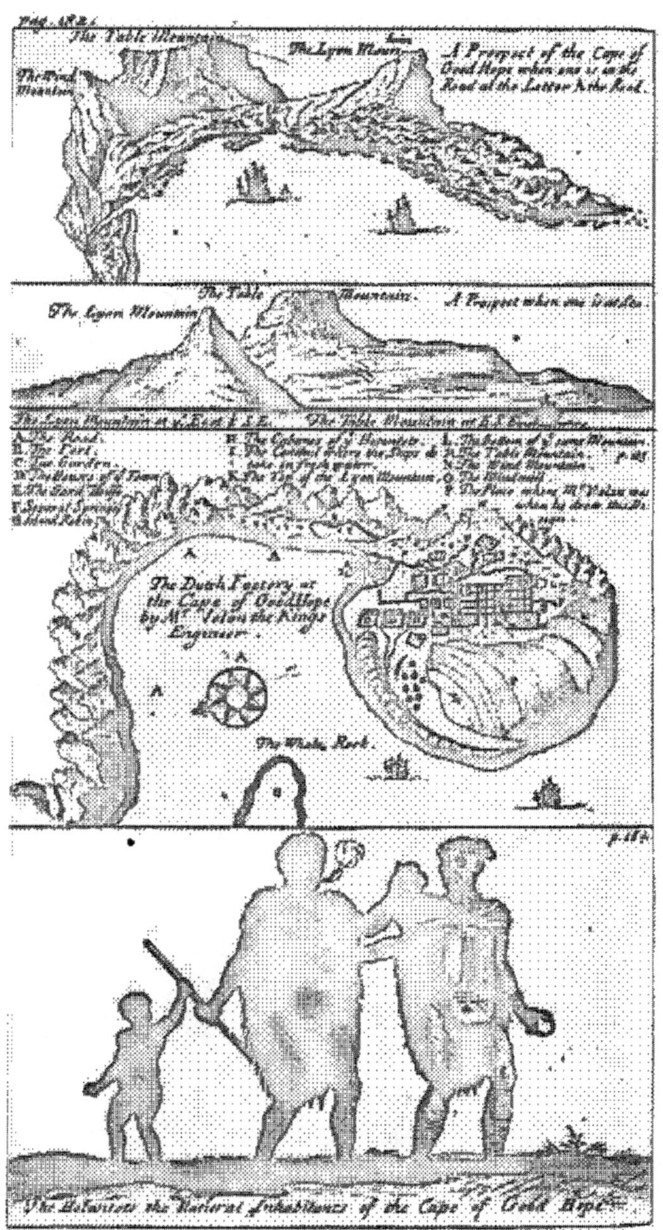

The Hottentots the Natural Inhabitants of the Cape of Good Hope.

often as these Beads do stand for any thing, that is to say, as often as they approach them near the middle Partition. 3d. On this, that the sticks are reckoned, from the right to the left, and do stand for *Number*, or *Unites*, *Tens*, *Hundreds*, and *Thousands*, and all the other powers of the number *ten* in their natural Order. In a word, one may at the same time denote several sums in divers places of this Instrument, by taking such sticks, as one will to denote Unites, and the next on the left to denote Tens and Hundreds, and so successively. And this is sufficient to illustrate the use of this Instrument to those, that know how to reckon with Counters. The Swiftness with which I have seen the *Chineses*, which are at *Siam*, make use thereof, is inconceivable; but they say that it is an effect of two years Apprenticeship. The Instrument may be more simple if one will, by putting only four Beads on one side, and one on the other, because that this is sufficient to mark to nine on each stick, which is all that is requir'd; and in this simplicity was the *Roman* Instrument, which in my Relation I have mentioned, that *Pignorius* has given us. From whence the Learned may, at their pleasure, draw their Conjectures, to decide which of these two Instruments is probably the Original, either the most compound, or the most simple. The Simple seems a Correction of the Compound, the Compound seems to have added to the Simple, for the more facility and exactness in practice.

Of the Cape of Good-Hope.

I Have given three different Prospects thereof, two of which are entirely new, and the third, which is that whose place of view is in the Road, is copied after a very good *Dutch* Map.

Every one knows that the *Dutch* have an important Establishment there, which secures their Navigation from the *East-Indies*. The Fort which defends it, would perhaps be no considerable thing in *Europe*; but it is sufficient in a Country, where there is no Neighbour to fear, and where there can go no considerable Enemy, but from a great distance, and consequently with a great deal of difficulty.

The Company's Garden, the Platform whereof is in one of these Prints, is very spacious, as may be judged by comparing it to the Fort: And tho' the Soil be not over-good, it plentifully produces Coleworts, Citruls, Oranges, Pomegranates, and, in a word, Pulse and Fruits, which keep at Sea, and of which the Mariners are desirous in long Voyages. In a corner, and under a shelter, I saw a Camphire-Tree, an *European* Fig-Tree, and a Shrub about two Foot high, which was said to be that which bears the Tea, and which I had taken for a young Pear-Tree. It had neither Flowers nor Fruit, and very few Leaves. Close by, and under another shelter, were two or three Foot of *Ananas*, and this was all the Rarity they shew'd me for the Country. The Grape is not more rare, but there is only that which the *Hollanders* have planted there. The Wine thereof is white, and very good. Some of our Crew went to the top of the Table Mountain, to seek some extraordinary Plants, but they found none. Nevertheless, upon a strict Scrutiny, there is not any that has not something particular, which the Plants of these Countries have not. The Shells there found are not the Remains of the Deluge, as some have conjectur'd. The Birds, the Apes, and the *Hotantots*, do bring them, and leave them there.

The Walks of the Garden do almost spontaneously maintain themselves, because that the Soil produces only Moss if it is not cultivated: Besides the neatness of the Garden has nothing, which savours not a wise oeconomy, nor any thing which favours a too great negligence, like a Kitchen Garden of Merchants, more wedded to the profit, which they reap thence, than to the Pleasures, which they could not enjoy.

The water which waters it through several little Channels, enters therein at the going out from a Mill which it turns, and underneath the Garden, it serves for blanching. They only divert a part thereof, which is conducted to a Cistern, which is on the bank of the Road, and where the Ships do go to take in their fresh water.

The Garden is divided into several great Squares, almost like the Plot of the place Royal. They are encompassed with Pales, to shelter them from the Winds, which are sometimes furious enough to wreck the Ships in the Road, if they have not good Anchors and good Cables. These Winds are formed of the thick Clouds, which do sometimes assemble between the Table-Mountain, and that which is called the Mountain of the Wind, by reason of these Storms. A walk of Citron-trees and Orange-trees planted in Earth, which go from one end of the Garden to the other, do altogether resent their fury. Next to this the situation of the Garden, and that of the Village which is a little nearer to the Road, are very good; for they are wholly exposed to the Sun, and sheltered from the South Winds, which are the cold Winds of this Country. The *Hollanders* which are setled there, do say, that if the South-west Wind blows not during their Summer, which is our Winter, the Distempers of the Lungs are frequent and dangerous.

The short stay that I made, permitted me not throughly to instruct my self concerning the Manners of the *Hotantots*, the natural Inhabitants of the Cape, though in the extream Simplicity in which they live, this can be no long study. They are called *Hotantots*, because that when they dance, they always in singing say this word *Hotantot*. The Love of the Tobacco and Brandy, which the Strangers offer them, and which has made them to receive the *Hollanders* into their Country, makes them to dance so long as one will, that is to say, to stamp sometimes with one Foot, and sometimes with the other, as he that treads the Grapes, and incessantly, and vigorously to say, *Hotantot*, *Hotantot*, but with a very low voice, as if they were out of breath, or that they fear'd to awaken any one. This mute Song has no diversity of Tones, but of Measure: the two first Syllables of *Hotantot* are always two Blacks, or Crochets, and the last always a White or Minime.

They go all naked, as may be seen in the figure, which I have given. They have but one skin over their Shoulders, like a Cloak; yet do they quit it at every place: and then they have only a little Leather Purse, hung to their Neck by a string, and a piece of a Skin a little bigger than one's Hand, hung before, and fastned with another string round their body: but this little piece covers them not, either when they show themselves side-ways, or when they do make a brisk motion.

Their stature is acceptable, and their gate more easy, than can be expressed. They are born as white as the *Spaniards*, but they have their Hair very much frized, and Features participating somewhat of those of the *Negro's*: and besides they are always very black; because that they grease their Body and Face. They do also grease their Head, and we smell them twenty Paces, when they have the Wind. Our men gave them Pots, and Cauldrons to bath in; and before all things, they took the Fat by hands-full, and herewith anointed their whole Body, from the Head to the Feet. The Grease defends them from the Air and the Sun, renders them sound and well disposed, and they prefer these natural Advantages before Sweet Scents and Pleasure. They are so active, that several among them do out-run Horses. There is no Brook which they swim not over. They are expert in drawing the Bow, and throwing the Dart; and they have Courage even to Undauntedness. They do sometimes worst a Lion, provided they have Skins enough, and Furniture enough to garnish their left Arm. They do thrust it thus into the Throat of this Animal, and they pierce it with a Dart or Knife, which they will have in their right hand. If they are two, the one kills the Lion, whilst the other amuses him. If they are several, and they have nothing to secure themselves from the Claws of the Lion, they fail not to expose themselves all at once: The one of them generally perishes, but the Lion perishes likewise by the Blows which

the

the others give him. Sometimes they are all fixed, and they kill the Lion.

Their Wives do likewise grease themselves, though they affect some Ornaments; as to fasten little Bones and Shells to their short Cottony, and greasie Hair. They also have Necklaces with divers colors of Glass, Bone, or such other matter, according as the Foreigners do give them, or sell them to them. On each Leg they have fifty Rings of Leather, which do beat one upon the other, and make some Noise when they dance, and which defend them from the Briers, when they go to get Wood: for this care concerns them, and not their Husbands.

The Men and the Women did eat Guts, almost without cleansing them, when our men presented them therewith, and they did hardly put them a moment on the Coals. If we offer'd them Brandy, they would gather up the first Shell, they found on the ground to receive it, and after having blow'd therein, they used to drink in it. They eat their Lice, as well as the *Cochinchinese*: and when we thought it strange, they answer'd pleasantly, that 'tis because their Lice eat them.

They lodge under little Huts made of Branches, or great Bulrush Mats, the top of which hardly reach'd to my middle; and to me it seem'd that I could not lye therein, my whole length. Under these Mats they make a hole in the ground, and in this Hole, about two Foot deep, they make their Fire, not caring for the Smoak, wherewith their Huts do not empty themselves. They live on Hunting, Fishing, Milk and the Flesh of their Flocks.

In this Poverty they are always merry, singing and dancing continually, living without Pains and Business; and caring for Gold and Silver, only as far as it is necessary for them to buy a little Tobacco and Brandy; a Corruption which the Foreign Commerce has introduced into their Customs.

As some amongst them were exercising themselves, in throwing the Dart before us, I offer'd them five or six Papers of Necklaces with Beads of coloured Glass; and they all so exactly seized my Hand, that I could not open it to let go the Necklaces, and I could not besides explain my self unto them. I was sometime in this perplexity, till they perceived that they must set me at Liberty to obtain what they desired. They love these Necklaces for their Wives, and when we had set sail again, I understood that a Laquais of ours had sold one for a Crown to one of them. The little Money they have, and of which they have little esteem, is the Wages for the Service which they render sometimes to the *Hollanders*, and to the other Foreigners, which land at the *Cape*: but they care but little to work.

Every one has but one Wife, their Chief only has three, and Adultery amongst them is punished with Death. They kill their Children, when they have too many; and as they marry those which they keep exceeding young, there is seen amongst them a great many Grand-Daughters, already Widows; who want a Joynt in their little Finger: For when a Woman loses her Husband, she cuts off a Joynt of the little Finger, or of the fourth Finger, if she has so often been a Widow, as to have her whole little Finger cut off. Nevertheless she may dispence therewith, if she please; and there are some Husbands who dispence not therewith, when they have lost their Wife. Most of them do make themselves Ridgils, to be more fit for the Women; and when the Age of renouncing comes, they make themselves entirely Eunuchs, to deprive themselves wholly of their Commerce, and to enjoy a more vigorous old Age. The *Hollander* had educated an *Hottentot* Infant after the *European* manner, and had sent him into *Holland*. Sometime after they caused him to return to the Cape, where he might be useful to them amongst those of his own Nation. But so soon as he found himself again amongst them, he continued there, and renounced the *Dutch* Habit, and Manner of living.

They commit no Robbery amongst themselves, nor in the Houses of the *Hollanders*, where they are received without Care: and if the thing happens, they punish it with Death. Nevertheless in the Country, when they can do it securely, and that they think not to be discovered, they do sometimes assassinate to rob; and do shew that the Contempt of Riches is, amongst them, only the Hatred of work.

The *Dutch* do nominate their Chief, and this Chief is their Judge: but those who could not bear this Foreign Dependance, are gone further into the Country, to live with the other *Caffrees*.

Some informed me at first, that they had no sence of Religion; but at last I understood, that tho they have neither Priests nor Temples, yet they make public rejoycing, which favor of Worship, at the New and Full Moons. I suspect that they have some Tincture of *Manicheism*, because that they acknowledge a Principle of Good, and another of Evil, which they call the *Captain above*, and the *Captain below*. The *Captain above*, they say, is good, it is not necessary to pray to him, 'tis only needful to let him act freely, he always does good: But the *Captain below* is wicked, he must be prayed to, and intreated to divert him from mischief. 'Tis thus that they speak, but it appears not in their exterior Conduct, that they pray much. A *Dutchman* of Wit and Knowledge informed me, that amongst the *Hotantots*, he had found the Names of *Afoukal* and of *Borthac*.

Rules of the Siamese *Astronomy, for calculating the Motions of the Sun and Moon, translated from the* Siamese, *and since examined and explained by* M. Cassini, *a Member of the Royal Academy of Sciences.*

MOnsieur *de la Loubere*, the King's Ambassador extraordinary at *Siam* brought back a *Siamese* Manuscript, which comprehends the Rules for calculating the motions of the Sun and Moon, according to the method of that Country, the Translation thereof he likewise brought from *Siam*, and communicated unto me.

This method is extraordinary. They make no use of Tables; but only of the Addition, Substraction, Multiplication, and Division of certain numbers, of which we do not presently discern the Ground, nor to what these numbers refer.

Under these numbers are conceal'd divers Periods of Solar Years, of Lunar Months, and other Revolutions, and the Relation of the one with the other. Under these numbers are likewise conceal'd several sorts of *Epoches* which are not distinguished, as the Civil Epoche, the Epoche of the Lunar Month, that of the Equinoxes, Apogæa, and Solar Cycle. The numbers in which the difference between these Epoches consists, are not ordinarily at the head of the Operations to which they serve, as they ought to be according to the Natural Order: they are often mixed with certain numbers, and the Sums or differences are multiplied or divided by others, for they are not always simple numbers, but frequently they are Fractions, sometimes Simple, sometimes Compound, without being ranged after the manner of Fractions, the Numerator being sometimes in one Article, and the Denominator in another; as if they had had a contrived design to conceal the Nature and Use of these numbers. In the Calculation of the Sun, they intermix some things which appertain only to the Moon, and others which are not necessary, either to the one or to the other, without making any distinction. They confound together the Solar and the Lunisolar Years, the Months of the Moon, and the Months of the Sun, the Civil and the Astronomical Months, the Days Natural and the Days Artificial. The Zodiack is divided sometimes into twelve Signs, according to the number of the Month of the Year, sometimes into 27 parts, according to the number of the Days that the Moon runs through the Zodiack, and sometimes in 30 parts, according to the number of the Days, that the Moon returns to the Sun. In the Division of the Day there is no discourse of Hours, but therein is found the 11th the 703d and the 800th parts of the Day, which result from the Arithmetical Operations which are prescribed.

This Method is ingenious; and being illustrated, rectified, and purged from Supe-

Superfluities, it will be of some use, being practicable without books, by the means of divers Cycles, and of the difference of their Epoches. Wherefore it is that I have endeavoured to decypher it, what difficulty soever I found at first, not only by reason of the confusion which every where appeared, and of the Names which are wanting in the supposed numbers; but likewise by reason of the extraordinary names, which are given to what results from the Operations, of which there are more than Twenty which have not been interpreted by the Translator, and of which I could never have found the Signification, if I had not first discover'd the method; which has likewise evinced to me, that the Interpretation, which the Translator has made of three or four other names, is not very exact.

In this research I have first distinguished, and separated from the other numbers, those which belong to the Epoches, having observed that these numbers, are those which were given to add or to substract, either simply, or by dividing or multiplying them by certain other numbers.

Secondly, I have considered the Analogies which result from the Multiplications and Divisions of the other numbers, separated from the Epoches; and it is in the Terms of these Analogies, that I have found the Periods of the Years, of the Months, and of the Days, and the differences of the one from the other, which the experience of things Astronomical, and the occasion of divers operations which I have made, has given me to understand.

I thought that the Missionaries, to whom Astronomy gives admittance amongst the great and learned throughout the East, might reap some advantage from this work, for the Understanding, and for the Explication of the Oriental Astronomy, which might easily be rectified and adapted to ours, with a little altering the Method, by correcting the numbers which it uses.

I thought also that it would not be useless to reduce the Astronomy of *Europe* to this form, to be able to supply the want of the Tables which greatly abridge the work. This method would be much more easie to practise in the form of the *Julian* and *Gregorian* year of which we make use, than in the form of the Lunisolar year, which the Orientals observe: for their principal difficulty consists in reducing the Lunisolar years and the Civil Lunary months to the years and months of the Sun, which the form of our Kalender immediately gives us; and what has given me the most trouble, has been to find out the method which they use to reduce them, in which the several sorts of Years, Months and Days, which are supposed and sought, are not distinguished. Wherefore the reason of the Explication which I give, and of the Determination of the Genus to the Species which I make in the beginning, will not presently be understood; but in the sequel it will be comprehended by the Connexion of things, and by what necessarily results therefrom.

Concerning the Astronomical Epocha of this Method.

I Have endeavoured to discover what is the *Epocha*, from whence they here begin to compute the Motions of the Sun and Moon; and to what year, what month, and what day of our Kalender it refers: for it is not treated of in this extract, which supposes it either known, or explained perhaps in the preceding Chapters from whence this extract has been taken, seeing that without the knowledge of the *Epocha*, it is absolutely impossible to practice this Method.

I have found that this *Epocha* is Astronomical, and that it is different from the Civil, which I have understood, because it is here prescribed to begin to compute the Months of the Year, current with the fifth Month in the Leap Year, which consists of 13 Months, and with the sixth Month in the common Year, which consists of 12 Months. For this would not be intelligible, if they supposed not two different *Epoches* of Years, the one whereof, which must be the Astrono-

Astronomical, begins sometimes in the fifth, and sometimes in the sixth Month of the other, which is the Civil. That which likewise evinc'd to me that the Astronomical *Epocha*, is different from the Civil *Epocha*, not only in the Months, but also in the Years, is the Operation which is here made to find the Year of ones Nativity, by substracting his Age from the number of the Years elaps'd since the *Epocha*; for this Operation would be useless, if they demand only the Year of the Birth after the Civil *Epocha*, which is immediately known, and which is compared to the Year current, to know the Age of a Person.

This being supposed, I have first searched out the Age to which this Astronomical *Epocha* may refer; and having found in the Calculation of the Sun, performed by this method, that two Signs and twenty Degrees which are therein employed, can only denote the place of the *Zodiack*, where was found the *Apogeum* of the Sun in the *Epocha*, which *Apogeum* must be in the twentieth Degree of *Gemini*; I judged that this *Epocha* must be about the seventh Age, where the *Apogeum* of the Sun is found in the twentieth Degree of *Gemini* according to most Astronomical Tables.

Secondly, having found that the number 621, which is intermixed in the Calculation of the Sun, can only be the number of the days comprized, between the Astronomical *Epocha*, and the return of the Moon's *Apogeum*, to the beginning of the *Zodiack*; and that the number 3232, which is afterwards employed therein, can be only the number of the Days, during which, this *Apogeum* makes a Revolution; I have confirmed that the *Apogeum* of the Moon, which in 621 Days makes two Signs and nine Degrees, was in this *Epocha*, in the 21 Degrees of *Capricorn*: And because that the Moon's *Apogeum* by the Revolution it makes in eight Years three quarters, returns to the same degree of the *Zodiack* twelve times in one Age; I have distinguished the Years of the Age, in which the Moon's *Apogeum* is found in this Degree, and I have excluded the other Year.

Thirdly, having found by the method here used for Calculating the place of the Sun, that this Astronomical *Epocha* is very near the vernal *Æquinox*, which in the seventh Age fell on the 20th or 21st of *March*; Amongst these select Years I have found one in which the Moon's *Apogeum* arrived at this Degree of *Capricorn*, about the 21st of *March*, which is found but once in 62 Years, wanting some Degrees; and I have found that in the 638th Year of Jesus Christ, the *Apogeum* of the Moon was at the 21st Degree of *Capricorn* the 21st of *March*.

Fourthly, I have remarked that this Astronomical *Epocha* must have begun at a new Moon; because the Lunar Months are reduced into Days, to find the number of the Days from the *Epocha*, and the value of the whole Months being deducted from the Sum of the Days, the rest serves to find the Moon's distance from the Sun.

In the 638th Year of Jesus Christ, the *Æquinoxial* new Moon happened the 21st of *March* at three a Clock in the Morning at *Siam*, when the Sun by its middle Motion ran through the first degree of *Aries*, the Sun's *Apogeum* being in the 20th Degree of *Gemini*, and the Moon's in the 21st Degree of *Capricorn*. This Day was likewise remarkable for a great Eclipse of the Sun, which happened the same day, but 14 Hours after the mean Conjunction.

Fifthly, By the manner of finding the day of the week, which is here observed, it appears that the day of the *Epocha*, was a *Saturday*; and the 21st of *March*, in the Year 638 was also a *Saturday*. This likewise confirms the certainty of this Epocha, and demonstrates the Knowledge and Judgment of those that have established it, who contented not themselves with a Civil Epocha, as other Astronomers have done; but who have chosen an Astronomical one, which was the Natural Principle of several Revolutions, which could not begin again, till after several Ages. This *Epocha* is 5 Years and 278 Days distant from the *Persian Epocha* of *Jesdegerdes*, the first year of which began on the 16th of *June*, in the Year of Jesus Christ, 632. Yet these *Indian* Rules are not taken from the *Persian* Tables related by *Crisococa*; for these Tables do make the

the Sun's *Apogeum* two degrees more backward, and the Moon's *Apogeum* above six degrees forwarder; which agrees not so exactly with our modern Tables. The *Persian* Tables do also make the Sun's Æquation 12 Minutes less, and that of the Moon 4 Minutes greater, which agrees better with the Moderns.

These *Indian* Rules are not drawn neither from the Tables of *Ptolemy*, where the Sun's *Apogeum* is fixed to the 5th degree and a half of *Gemini*, nor from the other Tables since made, which have all this moveable *Apogeum*. It seems therefore that they have been invented by the *Indians*; or that perhaps they have been taken from the *Chinese* Astronomy, as may be conjectured from this, that in this extract the Numbers are written from the top downwards, after the manner of the *Chineses*: but it may be that this way of writing the numbers might be common to these two Nations.

Having found the Astronomical *Epocha* of this method, and the Relation it has with the *Julian* years, we may rectifie the *Epocha*'s of the motions of the Sun and Moon by the modern Tables, by adding about a Minute a Year to the Sun's *Apogeum*, and by correcting the other Periods. Thus there will be no difficulty, to reduce the Years and Months since the *Epocha* into days, and if the Equations are likewise corrected conformably to the modern Tables, we shall by the same Method, find the place of the Sun and Moon with a great deal more exactness. We will give this Correction, with the Supplement of what is wanting in these Rules, after that we have explained them.

Rules to find the place of the Sun and Moon at the time of any Person's Birth.	*Explication.*

I.

1st. SET *down the Æra.*

1st. THE *Æra* in this place is the number of the years since the Astronomical *Epocha* from whence is taken the motion of the Planets to the current years, which will appear in the sequel.

2d. *Subtract the Age of the Person from the Æra, you will have the Age of the Birth.*

2d. *The Age of the Person*, is the number of the Years from his Birth to the Year current, which being deducted from the *Æra*, there remains the Age or Time of the Birth, that is to say, the Year from the Astronomical *Epocha* in which the Nativity happened.

3d. *Multiply it by 12.*

3d. By multiplying the years by 12 they are reduced into Months. These Months will be solar, each consisting of 30 days, 10 hours and a half, a little more or less, according to the several hypotheses, if the years are solar; or near upon if they are lunisolar, and in so great number, that the excess of the one recompences the defect of the others.

4th. *Add hereunto the number of the Months of the year current: and for this purpose if the year current is* Attikamaat, *that is to say, if it has 13 Lunar months, you shall begin to compute with the 5th month; but if it is not* Attikamaat, *you shall begin to compute with the 6th month.*

4th. The form of the Year here mentioned, is lunisolar, seeing there are some common of 12 lunar months, and abundant or Embolismal, called *Attikamaat*, of 13 lunar months. For that they begin to compute the months, not with the first month of the year, but with the fifth, if it is Leap-year, and with the sixth if it is not: I have inferred that there are two Epocha's, and two forms of different

 Years,

Years, the one Astronomical and the other Civil: that the first Month of the Astronomical Year begins in the fifth Month of the Civil Leap-year, which would be the sixth Month without the intercalation of the Leap-month, which is not reckoned amongst the 12 Months, and which is supposed to be inserted before; and that in the other Years, all the Months of which are successively computed without Intercalation, the first Month of the Astronomical Year, is computed only from the sixth Month of the Civil Year.

But as it is not expresly determined here, whether one ought to begin to compute an entire month at the beginning or end of the 5th or 6th month, it may be that for the first month of the Astronomical Year they take, that which ends at the beginning of the months whereof it is discoursed in this Article. In this case, the Interval between the beginning of the Civil Year, and the beginning of the Astronomical Year, would be only of 3 or 4 entire months: whereas if an entire month is reckoned only at the end of the 5th or of the 6th month, and that the first month which is reckoned, according to this Rule, be the first of the Astronomical Year; the interval between the beginnings of these two sorts of years, will be 4 or 5 whole months. We shall see in the sequel, that the *Indians* have diverse sorts of Astronomical Years, the beginnings of which are different, and are not much distant from the Vernal Æquinox; whereas the Civil Year must begin before the Winter Solstice, sometimes in the month of *November*, sometimes in the month of *December* of the *Gregorian* Year.

They add the number of the months of the current year, which are lunar months, to those that they have found by the third Article, which are solar months; and they suppose that the sum, as heterogeneous as it is, should be equal to the number of the solar months elapsed from the Astronomical *Epocha*. They neglect the difference that there may be, which in a year cannot amount to an entire month: but they might be deceived a month in the succession of the years, if they took not good heed to the Intercalations of the months, after which the number of the months which are computed in the Civil Year, is lesser than that which they would reckon without the precedent Intercalations.

5th. *Multiply by 7 the number found Art. 4.*

6th. *Divide the sum by 228.*

7th. *Join the quotient of the division to the number found Art. 4. This will give you the* Masaken *(that is to say, the number of the months) which you shall keep.*

5th, 6th, 7th. They here seek the number of the lunar months from the Astronomical *Epocha*, discoursed of in the 1st. Article, to the beginning of the current month: which is performed by reducing the solar months, which are supposed to have been found above, into lunar months, by the means of the difference, which is between the one and the other. In the operations which are made, it is supposed that as 228 is to 7, so the number of the solar months given, is to the difference which the number of the lunary months surpasses the number given of the solar months elapsed, during the same space of time; that thus in 228 solar months, which do make 19 years, there are 228 lunary months, and 7 months more, that is to say 235 lunary months. This therefore is a Period like to that of *Numa* and *Meto*, and to our Cycle of the golden number of 19 years, during which the Moon rejoyn'd it self 235 times to the Sun.

Yet in the sequel we shall see, that these Periods which accord together in the number of the lunar months and solar years, agree not in the number of the hours, by reason of the greatness of the solar year and of the lunar month, which is supposed various in these several Periods: and that the *Indian* is not subject to a fault so great, as the ancient Cycle of the Golden Number, which they have been obliged to expunge out of the *Roman* Kalender, in the *Gregorian* correction, because it gave the new Moons later than they are, almost a day in 312 years; whereas the New Moons determined by this *Indian* Period, agree with the true in this interval of time to near an hour, as will be found by comparing these Rules with the following.

II.

1. *Set down the* Maasaken.
2. *Multiply it by 30.*
3. *Joyn thereunto the days of the current Month.*

II.

The months of the Moon are here reduced into days: but because they make all the months to consist of 30 days, there only will be some artificial months about 11 hours 16 minutes longer than the Astronomical, or some artificial days which begin at the New Moon, and are 22 minutes, 32 seconds shorter than the natural days of 24 hours, which begin always at the return of the Sun to the same Meridian.

4. *Multiply the whole by 11.*
5. *Add thereunto also the number of* 650.

They reduce the days into 11 parts, by multiplying them by 11; and they add thereto 650 elevenths, which do make 59 days and $\frac{1}{11}$. I find that these 59 days and $\frac{1}{11}$ are the artificial days, which were elapsed to the day of the *Epocha*, since that an eleventh part of the natural day, and an eleventh of the artificial had began together under the meridian of the *Indies*, to which these Rules are accommodated.

6. *Divide the whole by 703.*
7. *Keep the Numerator which you shall call* Anamaan.
8. *Take the quotient of the Fraction found Art. 6. and substract it from the number found Art. 3. The remainder will be the* Horocoune *(that is to say, the number of the days of the Æra) which you shall keep.*

Having laid apart what is always added by the 5th. Article, it appears by the 2d. 3d. 4th. 6th and 8th. operation, that as 703 is to 11, so the number of the artificial days, which results from the Operations of the 2d. and 3d. Art. is to the number of the days deducted to have the number of the natural days, which answers to this number of the artificial days: whence it appears, that by making the lunar month to consist of 30 artificial days, 703 of these days do surpass the number of the natural days, which equal them above eleven days.

One may find the greatness of the Lunar Month, which results from this *Hypothesis*: for if 703 Artificial Days do give an excess of 11 Days; 30 of these Days which do make a Lunar Month, do give an excess of $\frac{330}{703}$ in the Day; and as 703 is to 330, so 24 Hours are to 11 Hours, 15 Minutes, 57 Seconds; and deducting this *Overplus* from 30 Days, there remains 29 Days, 12 Hours, 44 Minutes, 3 Seconds for the Lunar Month, which agrees within a Second to the Lunar Month determined by our Astronomers.

As to the value of 59 Days and $\frac{1}{11}$ which is added before the Division, it appears that if 703 Days do give 11 to substract, 59 Days and $\frac{1}{11}$ do give $\frac{650}{703}$ in the Day, which do make 22 Hours, 11 Minutes and a half, by which the end of the Artificial Day, must arrive before the end of the Natural Day, which is taken for the *Epocha*.

The *Anamaan* is the number of the 703 parts of the Day, which remain from the end of the Artificial Day, to the end of the current Natural Day. Use is made hereof in the sequel to calculate the motion of the Moon, as shall be afterwards explained.

The Quotient which is taken from the number of the Days found by the third Art. is the difference of the entire Days, which is found between the number of the Artificial Days, and the number of the Natural Days from the *Epocha*.

The *Horocoune* is the number of the Natural Days elapsed from the Astronomical *Epocha* to the current Day. It should seem that in rigour the Addition of the Days of the current Month, prescribed by the third Article, should not be made till after the Multiplication and Division, which serves to find the difference of the Artificial Days from the Natural, because that the Days of the Current Month are Natural, and not Artificial of 30 *per mensem*; but by by the sequel it appears that this is done more exactly to have the *Anomaly* which serves for the calculation of the motion of the Moon.

III.

1. *Set down the* Horoconne.
2. *Divide it by* 7.
3. *The Numerator of the Fraction is the day of the Week.*

Note, *That the first day of the Week is* Sunday.

III.

It follows from this Operation and Advertisement, that if after the Division there remains 1, the current day will be a *Sunday*; and if nothing remains, it will be a *Saturday*: the Astronomical *Epocha* of the *Horoconne* is therefore a *Saturday*.

If it be known likewise what day of the Week is the day current, it will be seen whether the Precedent Operations have been well made.

IV.

1. *Set down the* Horoconne.
2. *Multiply it by* 800.
3. *Substract it by* 373.
4. *Divide it by* 292207.
5. *The Quotient will be the Æra, and the Numerator of the Fraction will be the* Kronmethiapponne, *which you shall keep.*

IV.

The days are here reduced into 800 parts. The number 373 of the third Article makes $\frac{373}{800}$ of the day, which do make 11 hours and 11 minutes. They can proceed only from the difference of the *Epocha's*, or from some correction, seeing that it is always the same number that is substracted. The *Epocha* of this fourth Section may therefore be 11 hours and 11 minutes after the former.

The *Æra* will be a number of Periods of Days from this new *Epocha*, 800 of which will make 292207. The Question is to know what these Periods will be? 800 *Gregorian* Years, which very nearly approach as many Tropical Solar Years, do make 292194 Days. If then we suppose that the *Æra* be the number of the Tropical Solar Years from the *Epocha*, 800 of these Years will be 13 Days too long, according to the *Gregorian* correction.

But if we suppose that they are Anomalous Years, during which the Sun returns to his *Apogeum*, or Astral Years during which the Sun returns to the same fixt Stars; there will be almost no error: for in 13 Days, which is the overplus of 800 of these Periods above 800 *Gregorian* Years, the Sun by its middle motion makes 12d. 48'. 48", which the *Apogeum* of the Sun does in 800 Years by reason of 57". 39"'. *per annum*. *Albategnius* makes the Annual motion of the Sun's *Apogeum* 59". 4"'. and that of the fix'd Stars 54". 34"'. and there are some modern Astronomers which do make this annual motion of the Sun's *Apogeum* 57", and that of the fix'd Stars 51"; Therefore if what is here called *Æra*, is the number of the Anomalous or Astral Years: these Years will be almost conformable to those which are established by the ancient and modern Astronomers. Nevertheless it appears by the following Rules, that they use this form of Year as if it were Tropical, during which the Sun returns to the same place of the Zodiack, and that it is not distinguished from the other two sorts of Years.

The *Kronmethiapponne* which remains after the preceeding Division, that is to say, after having taken all the entire Years from the *Epocha*, will therefore be the 800 parts of the Day, which remain after the Sun's return to the same place of the *Zodiack*: and it appears by the following Operations that this place was the beginning of *Aries*. Thus according to this *Hypothesis* the Vernal middle Æquinox will happen 11 Hours 11' after the *Epocha* of the preceeding Section.

V. 1. *Sit*

V.

1. *Set down the* Krommethiapponne.
2. *Subtract from it the* Æra.
3. *Divide the remainder by* 2.
4. *Neglecting the Fraction, subtract* 1 *from the Quotient.*
5. *Divide the remainder by* 7, *the Fraction will give you the day of the Week,*

Seeing that in the third Art. the day of the Week is found by the *Horoconne*, after a very easie manner, it is needless to stay on this which is longer and more compounded.

Note, *That when I shall say the Fraction, I mean only of the Numerator.*

VI.

1. Horoconne.
2. *Subtract from it* 621.
3. *Divide the remainder by* 3232. *The Fraction is called* Outhiapponne, *which you shall keep.*

This Substraction of 621, which is always deducted from the *Horoconne*, what number soever the *Horoconne* contains, denotes an *Epocha*, which is 621 days after the *Epocha* of the *Horoconne*.

The number 3232 must be the number of the Days, which the Moon's *Apogæum* employs in running through the Circle of the *Zodiack*: 3232 Days do make 8 *Julian* Years and 310 Days. During that time this *Apogæum* finishes a Revolution after the rate of 6'. 41" which it performs in a Day, even according to the Astronomers of *Europe*. The *Apogæum* of the Moon does consequently finish its Revolution 621 days after the *Epocha* of the *Horoconne*. 'Tis here performed then; as 3232 days are to a Revolution of the *Apogæum*, so the number of the days is to the number of the Revolutions of the *Apogæum*. They keep the remainder which is the number of the days called *Outhiapponne*. The *Outhiapponne* will therefore be the number of the days elapsed from the return of the Moon's *Apogæum* to the beginning of the Zodiac; which will more evidently appear in the sequel.

If you would have the day of the Week by the Outhiapponne, *take the Quotient of the aforesaid Division; multiply it by* 5, *then joyn it to the* Outhiapponne, *then subtract thence two days, divide it by* 7, *the Fraction will shew the day.*

Whatever is before is called Poutiasourit, *as if one should say the Force of the Sun.*

Having already explained the true method of finding the day of the Week, it is needless to stay here. Leaving the care of examining it, and searching the ground thereof, to those that shall have the curiosity.

Notwithstanding the name of the Sun's Force which is here given to the precedent Operations, it is certain that what has hitherto been explained, belongs not only to the Sun, but likewise to the Moon.

VII.

1. *Set down the* Krommethiapponne.
2. *Divide it by* 24350.
3. *Keep the quotient, which will be the* Raasi, *that is to say, the Sign where the Sun will be.*

To find what the number 24350 is; it is necessary to consider, that the *Krommethiapponne* are the 800 parts of the day which remains after the Sun's return to the same place of the *Zodiac*, and that the solar year contains 292207 of these parts, as has been declared in the explication of the fourth Section. The twelfth part of a year will therefore contain 24350 and 7/12 of these 800 parts: wherefore the number 24350 denotes the twelfth part of a solar year, during which the Sun by its middle motion makes a Sign.

Seeing then that 24350 7/12 of a day do give a Sign, the *Krommethiapponne* divided by 24350 will give to the Quotient the Signs which the Sun has run since his return by his middle motion to the same place; The *Raasi* then is the number of the Signs, run through by the middle motion of the Sun. They here neglect the Fraction 7/10, so that the solar year remains here of 292207/800, that is to say, of 365 days 1/4, like the *Julian* year.

4. *Lay down the Fraction of the aforesaid Division, and divide it by 811.*

5. *The Quotient of the Division will be the* Ongsaa, *that is to say, the degree wherein the Sun will be.*

Seeing that by the preceding Article 24350/800 of a day do give a Sign of the Sun's middle Motion, the 30th part of 24350/800 will give a degree which is the 30th part of a Sign. The 30th part of 24350 is 811 2/3; which do make a degree: dividing then the remainder by 811 2/3, they will have the degree of the Sun's middle motion. Here they neglect the 2/3 which can make no considerable difference.

6. *Set down the Fraction of this last Division, and divide it by 14.*

7. *The Quotient will be the* Libedaa, *that is to say the Minute.*

8. *Substract 3 from the* Libedaa.

9. *Place what belongs to the* Libedaa, *underneath the* Ongsaa, *and the* Ongsaa *underneath the* Raasi: *This will make a Figure which shall be called the* Matte-jomme *of the Sun, which you shall keep. I suppose it is* locus medius Solis.

Seeing that in a degree there are 811/800 parts; in a minute, which is the 60th part of a degree, there will be 13 31/60 of these parts. Neglecting the Fraction, they take the number 14, which dividing the remainder, will give the minutes. The Substraction which is here made of three minutes is a reduction whereof we shall speak in the sequel.

It is here prescribed to put the Degrees under the Signs, and the Minutes under the Degrees in this manner,

Raasi, Signs.
Ongsaa, Degrees.
Libedaa, Minutes.

This Disposition of the Signs, Degrees, and Minutes one under the other is called a *Figure*, and it here denotes the middle place of the Sun.

VIII.

To find the true place of the Sun.

1. *Set down the* Mattejomme *of the Sun, that is to say, the figure which comprehends what is in the* Raasi, Ongsaa, *and* Libedaa.

2. *Substract 2 from the* Raasi. *But if this cannot be, add 12 to the* Raasi, *to be able to do it, then do it.*

3. *Substract 20 from the* Ongsaa. *But if this cannot be, deduct 1 from the* Raasi, *which will amount to 30 in the* Ongsaa, *then you shall deduct the aforesaid 20.*

VIII.

The number 2, which is substracted from the *Raasi* in the second Article, and the number 20 in the third Article, are 2 Signs and 20 degrees, which doubtless denotes the place of the Suns *Apogeum* according to this *Hypothesis*; in which there is not seen any number which answers to the motion of the *Apogeum*. It appears then that this *Apogeum* is supposed fix'd to the 20th degree of *Gemini*, which precedes the true place of the *Apogeum*, as it is at present 17 degrees, which this *Apogeum* performs not in less than 1000 Years, or thereabouts: From whence it may be judged that the *Epocha* of this method is about a thousand years before the present age. But as the greatness of the year agrees better here with the Suns return to the *Apogeum* and the fixed Stars, than with the Suns return to the Equinoxes; it may be that the beginning of the Signs here used, is not at present in the Equinoctial point, but that it is advanced 17 or 18 degrees, and so it will be necessary to be corrected by the Anticipation of the Equinoxes. Here then they substract the Suns *Apogeum* from its middle place called *Mattejomme*, to have the Suns *Anomalia*: and the number of the Signs of this *Anomalia* is that which they call *Kenne*.

4. *What will afterwards remain, shall be called* Kenne.

5. *If the* Kenne *is 0, 1, or 2, multiply it by 2, you will have the* Kenne.

6. *If the* Kenne *is 3, 4, or 5; you shall*

It appeareth by these Rules that the *Kenne* is the number of the half-signs of the distance of the *Apogeum* or *Perigeum*, taken according to the succession of the Signs, according as the Sun

shall substract the figure from this figure

5
29
60

which is called Attachim, *and amounts to 6 Signs.*

7. *If the* Kenne *is* 6, 7, 8, *substract 6 from the* Raasi, *the remainder will be the* Kanne.

8. *If the* Kenne *is* 9, 10, 11, *substract the figure from this figure*

11
29
60

which is called Toutaasamonnetonne, *and amounts to 12 Signs: the remainder in the* Raasi *will be the* Kanne.

9. *If you can deduct* 15 *from the* Ongsa, *add* 1 *to the* Kanne, *if you cannot, add nothing.*

10. *Multiply the* Ongsaa *by* 60.

11. *Add thereunto the* Libedaa, *this will be the* Pouchalit, *which you shall keep.*

12. *Consider the* Kanne. *If the* Kanne *is* 0, *take the first number of the* Chaiaa *of the Sun, which is* 35, *and multiply it by the* Pouchalit.

13. *If the* Kanne *is some other number, take according to the number, the number of the* Chaiaa *aareit, and substract it from the number underneath. Then what shall remain in the lower number, multiply by it the* Pouchalit. *As for example, if the* Kanne *is* 1, *substract* 35 *from* 67, *and by the rest multiply. If the* Kanne *is* 2, *substract* 67 *from* 94, *and by the rest multiply the* Pouchalit.

14. *Divide the Sum of the* Pouchalit *multiplied by* 900.

15. *Add the Quotient to the superior number of the* Chaiaa, *which you have made use of.*

16. *Divide the Sum by* 60.

17. *The Quotient will be* Ongsaa, *the Fraction will be the* Libedaa. *Put an* 0 *in the place of the* Raasi.

18. *Set the figure found by the preceding Article over against the* Mattejomme *of the Sun.*

19. *Consider the* Ken *aforesaid. If the* Ken *is* 0, 1, 2, 3, 4, 5, *it is called* Ken *substracting: Then you shall substract the figure found in the* 17 *Article from the* Mattejomme *of the Sun.*

20. *If the* Ken *is* 6, 7, 8, 9, 10, 11, *it is called* Ken *additional: So you shall join the said figure to the* Mattejomme *of the Sun: which will give out at last the* Sommepont

Sun is nearer one term than the other: So that in the 5th Article is taken the distance of the *Apogeon* according to the succession of the Signs: in Article 6th the distance of the *Perigeon* against the succession of the Signs: in Article 7th the distance of the *Perigeon* according to the succession of the Signs, and in Article 8th the distance of the *Apogeon*, contrary to the succession of the Signs. In the 6th, 7th, and 8th Articles it seems, that it must always be understood. Multiply the *Raasi* by 2, as it appears in the sequel.

In the 5th Article when the degrees of the *Anomalia* exceed 15, they add 1 to the *Kanne*; because that the *Kanne*, which is a half Sign, amounts to 15 degrees.

The degrees and minutes of the *Kanne* are here reduced into minutes, the number of which is called the *Pouchalit*.

It appears by these Operations, that the *Chaiaa* is the Æquation of the Sun calculated from 15 to 15 degrees, the first number of which is 35, the second 67, the third 94, and that they are minutes, which are to one another as the *Sines* of 15, 30, and 45 degrees from whence

It follows that the Equation of 60, 75, and 90 degrees are, 116, 129, 134.	35 67 94 116 129 134

which are set apart in this form, and do answer in order to the number of the *Kanne*, 1, 2, 3, 4, 5, 6.

As for the other degrees they take the proportional part of the difference of one number to the other, which answers to 15 degrees, which do make 900 minutes, making 1 as 900, to the difference of two Equations; so the minutes which are in the *overplus* of the *Kanne*, to the proportional part of the Equation, which it is necessary to add to the minutes which answer to the *Kanne* to make the total Equation. They reduce these minutes of the Equation into degrees and minutes, dividing them by 60. The greatest Equation of the Sun is here of 2 degrees, 12 min. The *Alphonsine* Tables do make it 2 degrees, 10 minutes: We find it of 1 degree, 57 minutes. They apply the Equation to the middle place mepont *of the Sun, which you shall preciseley keep.*

place of the Sun, to have its true place which is called *Sommepont.*"

19. This Equation, conformably to the rule of our Astronomers in the first demi-circle of the *Ammalia*, is substractive; and in the second demi-circle, additional. Here they perform the Arithmetical operations placing one under the other, what we place side-ways; and on the contrary, placing side-ways, what we place one under the other. As for Example:

	The *Mattejomme*, Middle Place.	The *Chayaa*, Equation.	The *Sommepont*, True Place.	
Raasi,	8	0	8	Signs.
Ongsaa,	25	2	27	Degrees.
Libedaa,	40	4	44	Minutes.

IX.

1. *Set down the* Sommepont *of the Sun.*
2. ***Multiply by 30 what is in the* Raasi.**
3. ***Add thereto what is in the* Ongsaa.**
4. ***Multiply the whole by 60.***
5. ***Add thereunto what is in the* Libedaa.**
6. ***Divide the whole by 800, the Quotient will be the* Reuc *of the Sun.***
7. ***Divide the remaining Fraction by 13, the Quotient will be the* Nasil reuc, *which you shall keep underneath the* Reuc.**

IX.

It appears by these Operations that the *Indians* divide the *Zodiac* into 27 equal parts, which are each of 13 degrees, 40 minutes. For by the six first Operations the signs are reduced into degrees, and the minutes of the true place of the Sun into minutes; and in dividing them afterwards by 800, they are reduced into 27 parts of a Circle; for 800 minutes are the 27th part of 21600 minutes which are in the Circle, the number of the 27 parts of the *Zodiack* are therefore called *Reuc*, each of which consists of 800 minutes, that is to say, of 13 degrees, 40 minutes. This division is grounded upon the diurnal motion of the Moon, which is about 13 Degrees, 40 Minutes; as the division of the *Zodiack* unto 360 Degrees has for foundation the diurnal motion of the Sun in the *Zodiack*, which is near a Degree.

The 60 of these parts is $13\frac{1}{3}$, as it appears in dividing 800 by 60, wherefore they divide the Remainder by 13, neglecting the fraction, to have what is here called *Nasi-reuc*, which are the Minutes or 60 parts of a *Reuc*.

X.

For the Moon. ***To find the* Mattejomme *of the Moon.***

1. *Set down the* Anaman.
2. *Divide it by 15.*
3. *Neglect the Fraction, and join the Quotient with the* Anaman.

Divide

X.

According to the 7th Article of the III Section, the *Anaman* is the number of the 903 parts of the day, which remain from the end of the Artificial day to the end of the Natural day. Also according to this rule, the *Anaman*

4. *Divide the whole by* 60, *the Quotient will be* Ongsa, *the Fraction will be* Libedaa, *and you shall put an* 0 *to the* Raasi.

5. *Set down as many days as you have before put to the month current.* Sect. II. n. 3.

6. *Multiply this number by* 12.

7. *Divide the whole by* 30 *the Quotient, put it to the* Raasi *of the preceding figure which has an* 0 *at the* Raasi, *and join the fraction to the* Ongsaa *of the figure.*

8. *Join this whole figure to the* Mattejomme *of the Sun.*

9. *Subtract* 40 *from the* Libedaa. *But if this cannot be, you may abate* 1 *from the* Ongsaa, *which will be* 60 Libedaa.

10. *What shall remain in the figure is the* Mattejomme *of the Moon sought.*

maan can never amount to 703: yet if 703 be set down for the *Anamaan*, and it be divided by 25, according to the 2d Article, they have 28, for the Quotient. Adding 28 to 703, according to the third Article, the sum 731 will be a number of minutes of a degree. Dividing 731 by 60, according to the fourth Article, the Quotient which is 12^d. $11'$ is the middle diurnal motion, by which the Moon removes from the Sun.

From what hasbeen said in the II Section, it results that in 30 days the *Anamaan* augments 330. Dividing 330 by 25, there is in the Quotient 13. Adding this Quotient to the *Anamaan*, the summ is 343, that is to say, 5^d, $43'$, which the Moon removes from the Sun in 30 days, besides the entire Circle.

The *European* Tables do make the diurnal motion of 12^d. $11'$. and middle motion in 30 days, of 5^d, $43'$, $21''$, besides the entire Circle.

After having found out the degrees and the minutes which agree to the *Anamaan*, they seek the signs and degrees which agree to the Artificial days of the current month. For to multiply them by 12, and to divide them by 30, is the same thing as to say, If thirty Artificial days do give 12 Signs, what will the Artificial days of the current month give? they will have the Signs in the Quotient. The Fractions are the 30ths of a Sign, that is to say, of the degrees. They join them therefore to the degrees found by the *Anamaan*, which is the surplusage of the Natural days above the Artificial.

The Figure here treated of is the Moons distance from the Sun, after they have deducted 40 minutes, which is either a Correction made to the *Epocha*, or the reduction of one Meridian to another: as shall be explain'd in the sequel. This distance of the Moon from the Sun being added to the middle place of the Sun, gives the middle-place of the Moon.

XI.

1. *Set down the* Outhiapponne.
2. *Multiply by* 3.
3. *Divide by* 808.
4. *Put the Quotient to the* Raasi.
5. *Multiply the fraction by* 30.
6. *Divide it by* 808. *the Quotient will be* Ongsaa.
7. *Take the remaining fraction, and multiply it by* 60.
8. *Divide the summ by* 808, *the Quotient will be* Libedaa.
9. *Add* 2 *to the* Libedaa; *the* Raasi, *the* Ongsaa, *and the* Libedaa *will be the* Mattejomme *of* Louthia, *which you shall keep.*

XI.

Upon the VI Section it is remarked that the *Outhiapponne* is the number of the Days after the return of the Moon's *Apogeum*, which is performed in 3232 Days: 808 Days are therefore the fourth part of the time of the Revolution of the Moon's *Apogeum*, during which it makes 3 Signs, which are the fourth part of the Circle.

By these Operations therefore they find the motion of the Moon's *Apogeum*, making as 808 Days are to 3 Signs; so the time passed from the return of the Moon's *Apogeum* is to the motion of the same *Apogeum* during this time. It appears by the following Operation that this motion is taken from the same Principle of the *Zodiack*, from whence the motion of the Sun is taken.

- The *Mattejomme* of *Louthia*, is the Place of the Moon's *Apogeum*.

XII.

For the Sommepont *of the Moon.*

1. *Set down the* Mattejomme *of the Moon.*

2. *Over against it set the* Mattejomme *of* Louthia.

3. *Substract the* Mattejomme *of* Louthia *from the* Mattejomme *of the Moon.*

4. *What remains in the* Raasi *will be the* Kenne.

5. *If the* Kenne *is* 0, 1, 2, *multiply it by* 2, *and it will be the* Kanne.

6. *If the* Ken *is* 3, 4, 5, *substract it from this figure,*

   5
   29
   60

7. *If the* Ken *is* 6, 7, 8, *substract from it* 6.

8. *If the* Ken *is* 9, 10, 11, *substract it from this figure*

   11
   29
   60

9. *If the* Kenne *is* 1 *or* 2, *multiply it by* 2; *this will be the* Kanne.

10. *Deduct* 15 *from the* Ongsia, *if possible*; *you shall add* 1 *to the* Raasi; *if not, you shall not do it.*

11. *Multiply the* Ongsia *by* 60, *and add thereunto the* Libedas, *and it will be the* Pouchalic, *that you shall keep.*

12. *Take into the Moons* Chajaa *the number conformable to the* Kanne, *as it has been said of the Sun; substract the upper number from the lower.*

13. *Take the remainder, and therewith multiply the* Pouchalic.

14. *Divide this by* 900.

15. *Add this Quotient to the upper number of the Moon* Chajaa.

16. *Divide this by* 60, *the Quotient will be* Ongsia, *the Residue* Libedas, *and so is for the* Raasi.

17. *Opposite to this figure set the* Mattejomme *of the Moon.*

18. *Consider the* Ken. *If the* Ken *is* 0, 1, 2, 3, 4, 5, *substract the figure of the Moons* Mattejomme; *if the* Ken *is* 6, 7, 8, 9, 10, 11, *join the two figures together, and you will have the* Sommepont *of the Moon, which you shall keep.*

XII.

All these Rules are conformable to those of the VIII. Section, to find the place of the Sun, and are sufficiently illustrated, by the explication made of that Section.

The difference in the *Chajaa* of the Moon, discoursed of in the 14th and 15th Article. This *Chajaa* consists in these numbers.

77
148
209
256
286
296

The greatest Equation of the Moon is therefore of 4 degrees 56 minutes, as some Modern Astronomers do make it, though the generality do make it of 5 degrees in the Conjunctions and Oppositions.

XIII.

Set down the Sommepont *of the Moon, and operating as you have done in the* Sommepont *of the Sun, you will find the* Reoc *and* Nassatoc *of the Moon.*

XIII.

This Operation has been made for the Sun in the IX Section. It is to find the position of the Moon in her Stations, which are the 27 parts of the *Zodiac*.

XIV.

1. *Set down the* Sommepont *of the Moon.*

2. *Over against it set the* Sommepont *of the Sun.*

3. *Substract the* Sommepont *of the Sun from the* Sommepont *of the Moon, and the* Pianne *will remain, which you shall keep.*

XIV.

The *Pianne* is therefore the Moon's distance from the Sun.

XV. 1. *Take*

XV.

1. *Take the* Plaone *and set it down.*

2. *Multiply the* Raasi *by* 30, *add the* Ongsa *thereunto.*

3. *Multiply the whole by* 60, *and thereunto add the* Libedra.

4. *Divide the whole by* 720, *the Quotient is called* Irti, *which you shall keep.*

5. *Divide the Fraction by* 12, *the Quotient will be* Natti Irti.

The end of the Souriat.

XV.

These three first Operations do serve to reduce the Moon's distance from the Sun into minutes; dividing it by 720, it is reduced to the 30 part of a Circle, for 720 minutes are the 30th part of 21600 minutes, which do make the whole circumference. The ground of this division is the Moons diurnal motion from the Sun, which is near the 30th part of the whole Circle. They consider then the Position of the Moon, not only in the Signs and in her stations, but also in the 30th parts of the *Zodiack*, which do each consist of 12 degrees, and are called *irti*; dividing the remainder by 12, they have the minutes, or sixtieth parts of an *irti*, which do each consist of 12 minutes of degrees, which the Moon removes from the Sun in the sixtieth part of a day; these sixtieth parts are called *natti irti*.

Reflexions upon the *Indian* Rules.

I. *Of the particular* Epocha's *of the* Indian *Method.*

HAving explained the Rules comprised in the preceding Sections, and found out several Periods of Years, Months, and Days, which they suppose: It remains to us particularly to explain divers particular *Epocha's*, which we have found in the numbers employed in this Method, which being compared together may serve to determine the Year, the Month, the Day, the Hour, and the Meridian of the Astronomical *Epocha*, which is not spoken of in the *Indian* Rules, which suppose it known.

By the Rules of the I. Section, is sought the number of the Lunary Months elapsed from the Astronomical *Epocha*. The *Epocha* which they suppose in this Section is therefore that of the Lunar Months, and consequently it must be at the Hour of the middle Conjunction from whence begins the Month wherein the *Epocha* is.

By the Rules of the II. Section, they first reduce the Lunar Months elapsed from the *Epocha* into Artificial Days of 30 *per mensem*, which are shorter than the Natural Days, from one Noon to the other, by $\frac{11}{703}$ a Day, that is to say by 22 Minutes 32 Seconds of an Hour. These Artificial Days have therefore their beginning at the new Moons, and at every thirtieth part of the Lunar Month; but the Natural Days do always begin mutually at Midnight under the same Meridian. The Term of the Artificial Days agrees not then with the Term of the Natural Days, in the same Hour and same Minute, unless when the Month, or one of the 30 parts of the Month, begins at Midnight under the Meridian given at the choice of the Astronomer. After this common beginning the end of the Artificial Day, prevents the end of the Natural Day under the same Meridian $\frac{11}{703}$ a Day, in which does then consist the *Avaman*, which always augments one 703^{d} of a Day to every eleventh part of the Day, until that the number of the 703 parts, amounts to 703, or surpasses this number; for then they take 703 of these parts for a Day, whereby the number of the Artificial Days surpasses the number of the Natural Days, elaps'd since the *Epocha*; and the remainder, if there is any, is the *Avaman*. The day of this meeting or concourse of the term of the Artificial days with the term of the Natural Days under the Meridian which is chosen, is always a new *Epocha* of the *Avaman*, *men*, which is reduced to nothing, or to less than 11, after having attained this number 703; which arrives only at every Period of 64 Days, as it appears in dividing 703 by 11, and more exactly eleven times in 703 Days. At every time given for the *Epocha* of the *Avamen* they then take the Day of the preceeding rencounter of the beginning of the Artificial Days with the beginning of the Natural Days, which under the same Meridian happens only five or six times in a Year.

Seeing then that in the fifth Article of the II. Section, they add 650 elevenths of a Day to those which are elapsed from the *Epocha* of the I. Section, they suppose that this *Epocha* was preceded from another *Epocha* which could only be that of the *Avamen*, of 650 elevenths of a Day; that is to say, of 59 Days 1/11, which do give 1/11 of a Day for the *Avamen*, under the Meridian of the *East Indies*, to which the Rules of this II. Section are accommodated; which shows that under this Meridian the middle Conjunction which gave beginning to the Artificial Day since the Astronomical *Epocha*, was 1/11 of a Day before the end of the Natural Day in which this conjunction happen'd; And consequently that it happen'd at one a Clock 49 Minutes in the morning, under the Meridian which is supposed in the same Section: but in the 9th Article of the 10th Section, they deduct 40 Minutes from the motion of the Moon, and in the 8th Article of the 7th Section, they deduct 3 minutes from the motion of the Sun: which removes the Moon 37 minutes from the Sun, at the hour that they suppose the middle Conjunction of the Moon with the Sun, in the II. Section.

Wherefore I have judged that the 40 minutes taken from the motion of the Moon, and the 3 minutes taken from the motion of the Sun, do result from some difference between the meridian to which these Rules were accommodated at the beginning, and of another meridian to which they have since reduced them: so that under the meridian supposed in the II. Section, the new Moon in the *Epocha* arrived at one a Clock 49 minutes in the morning; but under the meridian which is supposed in the 9th Article of the X. Section, at the same hour of 1. and 49 minutes after midnight, the Moon was distant from the Sun 37 minutes, which it makes in an hour 13 minutes; therefore under the Meridian supposed in the 9th Article of the X. Section, the new Moon could not arrive till 3 a Clock 2 minutes after midnight. The meridian to which these Rules have been reduced, would therefore be more oriental than the meridian chosen at the beginning by 1 hour 13 minutes, that is to say, 18 degrees and a quarter; and having supposed that they have reduced them to the meridian of *Siam*, they would be accommodated from the beginning, almost, to the meridian of *Narsinga*.

What more convinces that this substraction of 40 minutes from the motion of the Moon, and of three minutes from the motion of the Sun, is caused from the difference of the meridians of 1 hour 13 minutes, is that in 1 hour 13 minutes the Moon makes 40 minutes, and the Sun 3. 'Tis therefore by the same difference of 1 hour 13 minutes, that they have deducted 3 minutes from the motion of the Sun, and 40 minutes from the motion of the Moon.

Without this correspondence of what they have deducted from the motion of the Sun, with what they have taken from the motion of the Moon, which appears to have for foundation the same difference of time, and consequently the same difference of meridians, one might have reason to believe that the substraction of these 40 minutes has been made a long time after these first rules; because that it is perceived in process of time, that the motion of the Moon was not exactly so quick, as it results from the preceding Rules, which do make the lunar month about three quarters of a second shorter than the modern Tables; and this difference amounts to 1 hour and 13 minutes in 450 years, or thereabouts. Thus, if 450 years after the *Epocha* they had compared the first rules to the observations, one might have judged that the Moon retarded, in respect of these first rules, 1 hour and 13 minutes, or 40 minutes of a degree. But this difference, which is always the same, when attributed to the difference of the meridians, would not be always the same if it depended on the motion of the

the Moon, for it would augment one minute to 22 years, to which 'twould be necessary to have regard in the Correction of these Rules.

II. *The Determination of the Astronomical Epocha of the Indian Method.*

SEeing that these *Indian* Rules have been brought from *Siam*, and that the Civil year of the *Siameses* begins in the season that we think it ought to begin according to the Rules of the I. Section, as we shall show in the sequel, it is reasonable to suppose that the meridian to which these Rules have been reduced by the additions mentioned in the VII. and X. Sections, is the meridian of *Siam*; therefore by the calculation which we have made, the new Moon which they have taken for the *Epocha*, must happen at 3 a Clock in the Morning at *Siam*. As the lunar month of this method agrees to near a Second with the lunary month established by all the *European* Astronomers, it may be supposed that this hour of the new Moon of the *Epocha* is very precise, since it may have been deduced from the Observations of the Eclipses of the Moon, which are much more easie to determine than all the other *Phænomena* of the Planets. We may therefore make use of the common Tables to seek the new Moons which happen'd about the seventh Age at three in the morning in the meridian of *Siam*, the difference of which from the meridian of *Paris* is very exactly known to us by several observations of the Eclipses of the Moon, and the *Satellites* of *Jupiter*, which the *Jesuits* sent by the King into the East in quality of his Majesty's Mathematicians have made at *Siam*, and by the Observations of the same Eclipses made at the same time at *Paris* in the Royal Observatory; by the Comparison of which Observations it is found that the difference of the meridians of these two Cities is 6 hours 34 minutes.

To this Character of time we might add the Circumstance of the middle Æquinox of the Spring, which according to the *Hypothesis* of the IV. Section, must happen at 11 hours 11 minutes after the midnight which followed the middle Conjunction of the Moon with the Sun taken for the *Epocha*, according to what has been said on the 5th Article of the IV. Section, where they deduct 373/800 of a day, that is to say, 11 hours and 11 minutes from the days elapsed since the *Epocha*, which distinguishes as much as the *Krommethiapponne*, which we have declared to be the time elapsed from the Suns return to the the point of the *Zodiack*, from whence is taken the motion of the Sun and Moon, which must be the Æquinoxial point of the Spring.

But it must not be pretended that the modern Tables do give the very hour of this Æquinox: for they do not exactly agree together in the Æquinoxes, by reason of the great difficulty which is found to determine them precisely. They agree not with the antient Tables of *Ptolomy* in the middle Æquinoxes, to near 3 or 4 days: wherefore it is sufficient that we found by the modern Tables a new Moon to happen at *Siam* at 3 a Clock in the morning, within a day or two of the middle Æquinox of the Spring found by the modern Tables.

The place of the Suns *Apogæum*, which according to what we have drawn from the Rules of the 2d and 3d Articles of the VIII. Section, was at the time of the Astronomical *Epocha* in the 20th degree of the sign *Gemini*, denotes the Age wherein it is necessary to seek this new Æquinoxial Moon, which according to the modern Tables, was about the seventh after the Nativity of *Jesus Christ*.

It is true that as these Rules give no motion to the Sun's *Apogæum*, it may be doubted, whether it was not in this degree at the time of the *Epocha*, or at the time of the Observations upon which these Rules have been made. But the Age of this *Epocha* is likewise determined by another Character joyned to the former: 'Tis the place of the Moon's *Apogæum*, which according to what we have drawn from the 2d and 3d Articles of the VI. Section, was at the time of the *Epocha* in the 20th degree of *Capricorn*, and to which these Rules do give

 a motion

a motion conformable to that which our Tables do give it; altho they agree not together in the *Epoches* of the *Apogæ*, but to one or two degrees.

In fine, the day of the Week must be a Saturday in the *Epocha*, seeing that according to the 3d Section, the first day after the *Epocha* was a Sunday; and this circumstance joyned to what has been said, that the same day was near the Equinox, gives the last determination to the *Epocha*.

We have therefore sought a new Equinoctial Moon, to which all these Characters do agree; and we have found that they agree to the New Moon, which happened in the 638th year after the Birth of *Jesus Christ*, on the 21 of *March*, according to the *Julian* form, on Saturday at 3 a Clock in the morning, in the Meridian of *Siam*.

This middle conjunction of the Moon with the Sun, according to the *Rudolphine* Tables which are now most used, happen'd on this day at *Siam* on the very same hour, the reduction of the meridians being made according to our Observations: And according to these Tables 'twas 16 hours after the middle Æquinox of the Spring; the Sun's *Apogæum* being at 19 degrees ½ of *Gemini*; the Moon's *Apogæum* 21 degrees ½ of *Capricorne*, and the Node descending from the Moon at 4 degrees of *Aries*: so that this Æquinoxial Conjunction had also this in particular, that it was Eclipsick, being arrived at so little distance from one of the Nodes of the Moon.

This Astronomical *Epocha* of the *Indians* being thus determined by so many Characters, which cannot agree to any other time, by these *Indian* Rules are found the middle Conjunctions of the Moon with the Sun about the time of this *Epocha*, with as much exactness as by the modern Tables, amongst which there are some which for this time do give the same middle distance between the Sun and the Moon, to one or two minutes, the Reduction being made to the same meridian.

But from this *Epocha*, as they remove from it, the middle distances from the Moon to the Sun found by these Rules, do by one minute in twelve years surpass those which the modern Tables do give, as we have before remarked: from whence it may be inferred that if these *Indian* Rules, at the time that they were made, gave the middle distances from the Moon to the Sun more exact than they have given them since, they have been made very near the time of the *Epocha* established by these Rules. Yet they might be established a long time after, on some Observations made very near the time of the *Epocha*, that they would more exactly represent these Observations than those of the other times remote from the *Epocha*: as it ordinarily happens to all the Astronomical Tables, which do more exactly represent the Observations upon which they are founded, than the others made long before and after.

III. *Of the Civil* Epocha *of the* Siameses.

BY the Rules of the first Section I judged, that the Civil *Epocha* which is in use at the East *Indies*, is different from the Astronomical *Epocha* of the *Indian* method which we have explained.

I have at present new assurances by several dates of *Siamese* Letters, which have been communicated to me by Mr. *De La Loubere*, and by other dates of the Letters which Father *Tachard* published in his second Voyage, in the year 1689, by which it appears that the Year 1687, was the 2231th from the *Siamese* civil *Epocha*, which consequently refers to the 544th year before the Birth of *Jesus Christ*; whereas by the 2d and 3d Rules of the 8th Section, and by other Characters of this *Indian* method, it is evident that the Astronomical *Epocha* refers to the 7th Age after the Birth of *Jesus Christ*.

This Civil *Siamese Epocha* is in the time of *Pythagoras*, whose *dogmata* were conformable to those which the *Indians* have at present, and which these people had already in the time of *Alexander* the Great, as *Onesicritus*, sent by *Alexander* himself to treat with the *Indian* Philosophers, testified unto them, according to the report of *Strabo lib.* 15.

The

The Letters which the Ambassadors of *Siam* wrote the 24th of *June* 1687, were dated according to *Mr. de la Loubere*, in the *eighth month, the first day of the increase of the year* Pitolopsoc *of the Æra* 2231. And according to Father *Tachard*, *the eighth month, the second full Moon of the year* Thoh nopasoc *of the Æra* 2231. The full Moon happened not till the day following; and the lunary month which then ran, was the third after the Vernal Equinox; the first after this Equinox beginning the 12th of *April* in the same year, therefore the first month from the Equinox was the sixth month of the Civil year, which must begin the 15th of *November*, 1686.

It appears also that the same year was Leap-year of 13 months, and that there was one which is not put in the number of the others: for the 20th of *October* in the same year they reckon'd *the fifteenth day of the eleventh Moon of the year* 2231, and between the full Moon of *June* and that of *October* there were 4 lunar months. Nevertheless they reckoned only three, seeing that at the full Moon in *June* they reckon'd the eighth month, and at that of *October* they reckon'd only the eleventh; there was therefore in this interval of time a Leap-month which is not reckon'd. This Intercalation is likewise found by comparing the Letter from the Ambassadors with three of the King of *Siam's* Letters, of *December* 22 of the year 1687, recited by Father *Tachard*, page 281, 287, and 407, which are dated *the 3d of the decrease of the first Moon of the year* 2231: and it appears that if the Moon of *June* was the eighth Moon of the Civil year 2231, that of *December* was the fourteenth of the same Civil year, which is reckon'd for the first Moon of the succeeding years, tho the year be yet named 2231, whereas according to the preceding dates, it ought to be named 2232.

Perhaps they chang'd not the name of the Civil year, till it was sufficiently advanced, and had attained the beginning of the Astronomical year: or rather unto this time they do name it after two ways. For another date which Mr. *de la Loubere* communicated unto me, is thus, *the eighth of the increase of the first Moon of the Year* 223$\frac{1}{2}$. which *is the eleventh of December* 1687. It seems that this manner of date denotes that the year may in this month be named either 2231, or 2232: which has relation to the form now used in the Northern Countries, where the dates are frequently set down in two ways, *viz.* according to the *Julian*, and according to the *Gregorian* Calendar; and to the ten first days of the *Gregorian* year, is set a Year more than in the *Julian*.

By comparing the date of *October* 20th which supposes that the first of the Moon was the 6th of this month (which day was also that of the new Moon) with the other date of *December* the eleventh, which supposes that the first of the Moon was the 4th of this month, there are found 59 days in two months, as the motion of the Moon requires. According to these dates the 22d of *December* would be the 19th of the Moon, that is to say, the fourth day of the decrease, which in the King of *Siam's* Letters is set down the 3d of the decrease, the full of the Moon being supposed on the 15th which should denote the intercalation of a day made to the full of the Moon, unless Letters should be antedated one day, or that date is one day wanting in the resemblance which is made thereof to our Calendar.

Amongst the preceding dates, and some others which we have examined, there are only those of *October* 20th and *December* 11th that agree well together, and with the motion of the Moon, and in which they take the very day of the Moon's Conjunction with the Sun by the first day of the month. The other dates differ some days among them; for in those of *June* 24th they take for the first day of the month a day which precedes the Conjunction; on the contrary in the dates of *December* 22d they take for the first day of the month a day which follows the Conjunction. Thus the dates which for the first day of the Month do take the very day of the Conjunction, may be thought, the most regular. We have calculated these Conjunctions, not only by the modern Tables, but also by the *Indian* Rules, after the manner as we shall herein after declare, and we have found that they agree together in the same days of the year.

These *Indian* Rules may therefore serve to regulate the Calendar of the *Siameses*, though they be not at present exactly observed in the dates of the Letters, without a Calendar where the Intercalations of the months and days be regulated according to this method, it would be impossible to make use of these *Indian* Rules in the Calculation of the Planets, without committing the same Error which would be slipp'd into the Calendar; unless that this Error was known by the exact History of the Intercalations, and that regard was thereunto had in the Calculation.

Though by the *Indian* Rules is sought the number of the months elapsed from the *Epocha*, by the means of a Cycle of 228 solar months, supposed equal to 235 lunar months, which is equivalent to the Cycle of our golden number of nineteen years, in the number of our solar and lunar months, which it comprehends: yet it is seen by most of the *Siamese* dates which we have been able to observe, that the first day of their month, even in this age, is hardly distant from the day of the Moons conjunction with the Sun; and that the Calendar of the *Indians* is not run into the Error into which our old Calendar was fallen, where the new Moons were regulated by the Cycle of the golden number, which gives them more slow than they are: so that since they have introduced this Cycle into the Calendar (which was about the fourth Age) to the Age past, the error was amounted to above four days. But the *Indians* have avoided this fault, by making use of the Rules of the I. Section to find the number of the lunar months, and of the Rules of the II. Section, to find the number of the days and hours which are in this number of months; which being founded on the *Hypothesis* of the greatness of the lunar months, which differs not from the real one, a second cannot want above a day in 8000 years; whereas the Ancient Cycle of our golden number supposes that in 235 lunar months there are the number of days and hours which are in 19 *Julian* years, which do exceed 235 lunar months one hour 27′ 33″, which do make 5 days in 1563 years.

It appears also that the Calendar of the *Indians* is very different from that of the *Chineses*, who begin their year with the new Moon nearest the fifteenth of *Aquarius*, according to Father *Martinius*; or the fifth of the same Sign, according to Father *Couplet* (which happen'd out a month and half, before the Vernal Equinox, and who regulate their Intercalations by a Cycle of sixty years; which the *Tunquineses* do likewise, according to the report of Father *Martinius* in his Relations.

IV. *The Method of comparing the* Siamese *dates to the* Indian *Rules.*

TO examine whether the *Siamese* dates agree with the *Indian* Rules, we have found by these Rules the number of the months comprized in the years elapsed from the Astronomical *Epocha*, and the year current and we have thereunto added the month of the year current, which we have begun to compute by the fifth month of the Civil year, for the first date which was of the eighth month before the Intercalation of a month; and for the second date which was of the eleventh month, and after the Intercalation of a month, we have begun to compute the months of the current year, with the fifth of the eleven months which were then computed, which is the same month that they have reckoned for the sixth before the Intercalation of a month, according to the Explication which we have given to the fourth Article of the I. Section.

We have done the same thing for the following dates, having verified that it is necessary to begin to compute from the fifth month, during the residue of the Astronomical year and during that which immediately follows the Intercalation. And having afterwards calculated the number of the days comprized in these sums of months according to the Rules of the II. Section, we have found that the number of the days found by these Rules, agrees with the number of the days comprehended between the Astronomical *Epocha* of the year

638, and the days of the Conjunctions from whence they have taken the beginning of the months in several of these dates, and particularly in those of *October* 20, and of *December* 8, which must have appeared the most regular.

This method, which we have used to compare the *Siamese* dates to the *Indian* Rules, has made known to us the terms in our Calendar, between which must happen the new Moon of the fifth month of the Civil year after the Leap-year, or of the sixth month of the year after a common, whereby they must begin to compute the months according to the 4th *Article* of the I. Section, and which may be considered as the first new Moon of a kind of lunisolar Astronomical year, which we have judged ought to begin after the Vernal Equinox, wherefore it is necessary largely to give an example of this Comparison, which will demonstrate the use of these Rules, and will serve as a demonstration of the Explication that we have made thereof.

EXAMPLE for the I. DATE.

WE have sought what, according to the *Indian* Rules, ought to be the number of the days comprized between the Astronomical *Epocha*, and the middle conjunction of the eighth month of the *Indian* year 2231, in this form.

By the Rules of the I. Section.

FRom the Astronomical *Epocha* of the *Julian* year of *Jesus Christ* 638, to the year 1687, there are 1049 years, which is the *Æra* according to the 1st *Article*; having multiply'd it by 12, according to the 2d *Article*, there are 12588 solar months.

It is necessary to add the months of the current year, *Article* 4; and because the Ambassadors computed the eighth month of the year 2231, before the Intercalation of a month, we have begun to compute from the sixth of these months, according to our Explication; thus to the eighth month, we shall have three months to add to 12588, which will make the sum of 12591.

Multiplying them by 7, *Article* 5thly, the Product will be 88137.

Dividing it by 228, *Article* 6thly, the Quotient will be 386, to add to 12591, *Article* 7thly; and the sum will make 12977 lunar months.

By the Rules of the II. Section.

MUltiplying this number of months by 30, *Article* 2d, the Product will give 389310 artificial days.

Multiplying them by 11, *Article* 4th, the Product will be 4282410.

Dividing this Product by 703, *Article* 6th, the Quotient will be 6091 $\frac{437}{703}$.

Having substracted it from 389310 artificial days, *Article* 8, there remains 383218 $\frac{266}{703}$, which is the number of the natural days elapsed from the Astronomical *Epocha* to the new Moon of the eighth month of the *Indian* year 2231.

The fraction $\frac{266}{703}$ being reduced, gives 9 hours 4', 54'', which this Conjunction happen'd later at *Siam*, according to these Rules, than that of the Astronomical *Epocha* of the year 638.

By the means of our Calendar is found the number of the days elapsed between the twenty first month of the *Julian* year 1638, and *June* 10th of the *Gregorian* year 1687, by this Calculation.

From the year 638, which was the second after the Bissextile 636, to the year 1687, which was the third after the Bissextile 1684, there are 1049 years, amongst

amongst which there were 262 Bissextiles, which give 262 days more than as many common years. In 1049 common years of 365 days, there are 382885 days; and adding thereunto 262 days for the Bissextiles, there will be 383147 days in 1049 years, as well common as Bissextile, between *March* 21st. of the *Julian* year 638, and *March* 21st. of the *Julian* year 1687, which is *March* 31st. of the *Gregorian* year.

From *March* 31 to *June* 10th, there are 71 days, which being added to 383147, do give 383218 days between the 21st. of *March* of the *Julian* year 638, where is the *Indian Epocha* of the new Moons, and the 10th of *June* of the *Gregorian* year 1687, the day of the new Moon of the eighth month of the *Siamese* year 2231. This number of days is the same that we have found between these two new Moons, according to the *Indian* Rules.

To find the same number of days by the one and the other method in the Conjunction of *October* of the same year 1687, after the Intercalation, which appears, by comparing the date of this month with that of the month of *June* foregoing; it is necessary to compute 8 months, beginning with the fifth of of the eleven which were reckon'd. In the Conjunction of *November* are reckon'd 8; and in that of *December*, from whence begins the first month of the year 2232, are computed 9, adding 8 months to those of the current year, to the new Moon of the 31st. of *March* 1688, from whence began the fifth month of the year 2232. They began to reckon from this 5th month during the whole year, which follows the Intercalation, and which was common; and they began to compute from the 6th month only at the new Moon, which happen'd the 19th of *April* of this year 1689. They will also begin to compute from the 6th month, at the new Moon, which shall happen the 9th of *April*, to the Intercalation which shall be made in the same year, after which they will follow the same order as after the preceding Intercalation. We have thought fit distinctly to relate these Examples, thereby the more precisely to determine the 4th *Article* of the I. Section, in which it was possible to err, if it was not illustrated; and it could not be determined without several Calculations made according to the preceding method.

V. *The Terms of the first Months of the* Julian *Years.*

HAving by the same method calculated, according to the *Indian* Rules, the middle Conjunctions of the Moon with the Sun for several years of this and the following Age, we have always found that every one of these Con-junctions fell upon a day whereon the middle Conjunction happen'd according to our Tables, but almost three hours later than by the *Indian* Rules.

By this means we have determined in our Calendar the Terms between which the new Moon must happen, from whence it is necessary to begin to compute the months of the year current, according to the 4th *Article* of the I. Section; and we have found that in this Age this new Moon is that which happen'd between the 28th of *March*, and 27th of *April* of the *Gregorian* year, which are at present the 18th of *March*, and 17th of *April* of the *Julian* year.

We have likewise found that these Terms in the *Gregorian* Calendar, do advance a day in 239 years, and do go back a day in the *Julian* Calendar in 301 years; which it is necessary to know, to be able to make use of these *Indian* Rules amongst us.

To determine in these Calendars the Terms between which the new Moon must happen, from whence the Civil year of the *Siameses* ought to begin according to these Rules, it is necessary to establish a System of common and Bissextile years well digested in the Cycle of 19 years, which System should be such, that the fifth month of the first year after the Bissextile, and the sixth month of the other years, do begin in this Age between *March* 28th, and *April* 27th of the *Gregorian* year.

According to this Rule, the Civil year should begin in this Age before the 12th of *December*. For if it begins the 12th the year following, which would begin, *December* 1, would be after the common year, and according to the Rule they

they would not begin to reckon from the fifth month, which would happen the 19th of *March*, but with the sixth month, which would begin the 18th of *April*, which is contrary to what we have found by the Calculation, that in this Age it is necessary to begin to compute with the month which begins between *March* 19th, and *April* 17th. One might therefore be mistaken in the use of these Rules in the years which would begin after *December* 11th of the *Gregorian* year.

We find likewise by our Calculations, that according to these very Rules, the *Siamese* year should begin on the 12th of *December* in the *Gregorian* year 1700, which will not be Bissextile. This will therefore be the most advanced Term, that must be a whole month distant from the preceding Term. Thus the new Moon, which will happen the Age following between the 12th of *November*, and the 12th of *December*, will be that from whence according to these Rules the Civil year of the *Siamese* ought to begin.

Nevertheless we have lately seen a date of the first of *January* 1684, wherein it is supposed that the beginning of the *Siamese* year was at the new Moon, which happen'd the 18th of *December* 1683. This date being compared with those of the Ambassadors of *Siam*, wherein it is supposed that the beginning of the year 2231, was at the new Moon, which happen'd the 16th of *November* 1686, would shew that the Terms of the first month of the *Siamese* year, according to the usage of these times, are at least 32 days distant from each other, altho' according to the Rules, they ought not to be more than a lunary month, or thirty days distant.

This confirms what we have already remark'd, that in this Age they conform not exactly to these Rules in the dates, altho' they differ not much therefrom. But as these Rules are obscure, and that it is necessary to supply some Circumstances which are not distinctly expressed, it may easily happen that the People be mistaken.

Thus after having determined what should be done according to these Rules, it is necessary to learn from the Relations of Travellers what is actually practised. Mean while we know by the dates which we have seen, that the present Practice is not much different from these Rules.

VI. *Divers Sorts of Solar Years according to the* Indian *Rules.*

is lefs by 9 days, 15 hours, 33 minutes, than that of 292207 days, which are suppofed in the IV. Section, ought to be found in that very number of years. This difference is greater than that which is found between 800 *Julian* years, which confift of 292200 days; and 800 *Gregorian* years, which confift only of 292194 days; the difference of which is 6 days; and in 800 of thefe years, which refult from the Rules of the two firft Sections, there is a furplufage above the *Gregorian* years of 13 days, 8 hours, 24 minutes; whereas 800 years of the IV. Section, do 7 days exceed 800 *Julian* years, and 13 days the like number of *Gregorian*.

As the *Gregorian* is a Tropical year, which confifts in the time that the Sun employs in returning to the fame degree of the Zodiack, which degree is always equally diftant from the points of the Æquinoxes and Solftices; there is no doubt that the year drawn from the Rules of the I. and II. Section, does nearer approach the Tropick, than the year drawn from the Rules of the IV. Section, which, as we have remarked, approaches the Aftral year determined by the return of the Sun to a fixed Star, and the Anomaliftick determined by the Sun's return to its *Apogeum*, which feveral ancient and modern Aftronomers diftinguifh not from the Aftral, no more than the *Indians*, fuppofing that the Sun's *Apogeum* is fixed amongft the fixed Stars, tho' moft of the moderns do attribute a little motion to it.

Neverthelefs, it appears that the *Indians* make ufe of the Solar year of the IV. Section, as we make ufe of the Tropick, when according to the Rules of the VII, VIII, X and XI. Sections, they calculated the place of the Sun and his *Apogeum*, and of the Moon and her *Apogeum*. For the time elapfed from the end of this year called *Kronanthiappanne*, ferves them to find the Signs, Degrees and Minutes of the middle motion of the Sun. They fuppofe then that this year confifts in the Sun's return to the beginning of the Signs of the Zodiack like our Tropical year.

'Tis true, that at prefent the Signs of the Zodiack are taken amongft us in two ways, which were not formerly diftinguifhed. When the Ancients had obferved the tract of the Sun's motion thro' the Zodiack, which they had divided into four equal parts by the points of the Æquinoxes and Solftices; and that they had fubdivided every fourth part into three equal parts, which in all do make the 12 Signs, they obferved the Conftellations formed of a great number of fixed Stars, which fell in every one of thefe Signs, and they gave to the Signs the name of the Conftellations which are there found, not fuppofing then that the fame fixed Stars would ever quit their Signs.

But in the fucceffion of Ages, it is found that the fame fixed Stars were no more in the fame degrees of the Signs, whether that the Stars were advanced towards the Eaft in regard of the points of the Æquinoxes and Solftices, or that thefe very points were removed from the fame fixed Stars towards the Weft; and it is now found that a fixed Star paffes from the beginning of one Sign to the beginning of another in about 2200 years.

Therefore feeing that *Ptolomy* in the fecond Age of *Jefus Chrift*, confirmed this as yet doubtful difcovery, which had been made three Ages before by *Hipparchus*; there is a diftinction made between the Zodiack, which may be called local, which begins from the Æquinoxial point of the Spring, and is divided into 12 Signs, and the Aftral Zodiack compofed of 12 Conftellations, which do ftill retain the fame name, tho' at prefent the Conftellation of *Aries* has paffed into the Sign of *Taurus*, and that the fame thing has happen'd to the other Conftellations which have paffed into the following Signs.

Yet the Aftronomers do ordinarily refer the places and motions of the Planets to the local Zodiack, becaufe it is important to know how they refer to the Æquinoxes and Solftices, on which depends their diftance from the Æquinoxial and Poles, the various magnitude of the Days and Nights, the diverfity of the Seafons, and fome other Circumftances, the knowledg of which is of great ufe.

Copernicus is almoft the fole perfon amongft our Aftronomers, who refers the places and motions of the Planets to the Aftral Zodiack, by reafon that he fup-

pofes

poses that the fixed Stars are immoveable, and that the Anticipation of the Æquinoxes and Solstices, is only an appearance caused by a certain motion of the *Axis* of the Earth. But they who follow his *Hypothesis*, cease not to denote the places of the Planets, in regard of the points of the Æquinoxes in the local Zodiack, by reason of the Consequences of this Situation which we have remarked.

'Twould be an admirable thing that the *Indians* who follow the *Doctrine* of the *Pythagoreans*, should herein conform to the method of *Copernicus*, who is the restorer of the *Hypothesis* of the *Pythagoreans*.

Yet there is no appearance that they designed to refer the places of the Planets rather to any fixed Star, than to the Æquinoxial point of the Spring. For it seems that they would have chosen for this purpose some principal fixed Star, as *Copernicus* has done, who, for the Principle of his Zodiack, has chosen the Point to which refers the Longitude of the first Star of *Aries*, which was found in the first degree of *Aries*, where was the Æquinoctial Point of the Spring, when the Astronomers began to place the fix'd Stars in regard of the Points of the Æquinoxes and Solstices.

But at the place of the Heavens, where the *Indians* place the beginning of the Signs of the Zodiack according to the IV. Section, and the following Sections, there is not any considerable Star; there are only thereabouts some of the smallest and most obscure Stars of the Constellation of *Pisces*; but it is the place where was the Æquinoxial Point at the time of their Astronomical *Epocha*, from whence the fixed Stars advanced afterwards towards the East; so that the Sun, by its annual motion, returns not to the same fixed Star till about 20 minutes after its return to the same Point of the local Zodiack. It was difficult to perceive this little difference in few years to the Ancients, who did not immediately compare the Sun to the fixed Stars, as it is at present compared, and who compared only the Sun to the Moon during the day, and the Moon to the fixed Stars during the night, tho' from the day to the night the Moon changes place amongst the fixt Stars, as well by its own motion, which is quick and irregular, as by its *Parallax*, which was not well known to the Ancients. Wherefore they very lately only perceived the difference that there is between the Tropical year, during which the Sun returns to the Points of the Æquinoxes and the Solstices, and the Astral year during which it returns to the same fixed Stars; and then they had a Solar year of 365 days and a quarter, which is found at present to be the mean between the Tropical and the Astral, and that it surpasses the Tropical by 11 minutes, and is shorter than the Astral by 9 minutes.

VII. *The Determination of the Magnitude of the two sorts of* Indian *Years.*

IT is easie to find the greatness of the year which is supposed in the IV. Section, by dividing 292207 days by 800 years, each of which is found to consist of 365 days, 6 hours, 12′, 36″.

It is a little more difficult to find that which results from the I. and II. Sections, in which it is necessary to supply some Rules which are there wanting, to be able to make this use thereof. For in the I. Section it is supposed that the years are composed of entire lunar months, and that the number of the months which remain, is known besides: And in the II. Section it is supposed that the entire months have been found by the I. Section, and that the number of the days which remain, is known besides; yet a number of solar years, which is not but very rarely composed of entire lunar months, must have not only the number of the months, but also the number of the days determin'd. Indeed, we find that these Rules do tacitly suppose a solar year composed of months, days, hours and minutes, which regulate the luni-solar years.

The way of finding it by these Rules, is to resolve a year into solar and lunar months, by the 3d, 5th, 6th and 7th Rules of the I. Section, and not to neglect the fraction which remains after the division made by the 6th Article of the same Section; but to reduce it into days, hours, minutes and seconds, or into the decimal parts of a month, going to a thousand millions, to prepare it for the operations which must be performed according to the 1st, 2d, 3d, 4th, 6th and 8th rules of the II. Section, as well for that fraction, as for the whole months; and in fine, to reduce after the same manner the fraction called *Avoman* in the II. Section.

After a plainer manner may likewise be found the greatness of this year, by making use of the *Hypotheses*, which we have infolded in these two Sections, to find a period of years, which should be composed of a number of intire lunar months, and likewise of a number of intire days.

By supposing, according to our explication of the *Hypotheses* of the II. Section, that a lunar month is equal to 30 artificial days, and that 703 artificial days are equal to 692 natural days, it will be found that in 703 lunar months there are 20760 natural days; and adding thereunto the *Hypothesis* of the I. Section, according to which the number of 228 solar months which do make 19 years) are equal to 235 lunar months, it will be found that in 13357 solar years there are 165205 entire lunar months, which do make 4878600 natural days, from whence it results that a lunar month, according to these *Hypotheses*, consists of 29 days, 12 hours, 44', 2'', 23''', 23'''', and the solar year of 365 days, 5 hours, 55', 13'', 46''', 5''''.

This *Indian* year conceal'd in the tacit *Hypotheses* of these two Sections, agrees within two seconds with the tropical year of *Hipparchus* and *Ptolomy*, which consists of 365 days, 5 hours, 55', 12''; and to near 13 seconds with that of *Rabbi Adda* an Author of the third Age, which consists of 365 days, 5 hours, 55', 25''. If it could be verified that these years and these months, had been determined by the *Indians* on the Observations of the Sun, independently from the Western Astronomy, this agreement of several Astronomers, of different Nations, so remote one from the other, would serve to prove that the Tropical year has anciently been of this bigness, though at present it is found lesser by 6 minutes, which in 10 years do make an hour, and in 240 years a whole day. But it is probable that this greatness of the year has been determined only by the Observations of the Eclipses and other Moons, and by the *Hypothesis* that Nineteen solar years are equal to Two hundred thirty five lunar months; which *Hypothesis* so nearly approaches the truth, that it was difficult to observe the difference thereof, but in the succession of Ages; which prevented *Hipparchus* and *Ptolomy* from departing therefrom in the determination of the greatness of the solar year.

VIII. *The Antiquity of these two sorts of* Indian *years.*

WE have not a more precise knowledge of the *Indian* years, than that which we have drawn from these Rules. *Scaliger* who has carefully collected all the Memoirs that he could gather from the ancient Authors, from the Patriarch of *Antioch*, from the Missionaries, and different Travellers, and who has inserted them, not only in his work *de Emendatione temporum*, but also in his Commentaries upon *Manilius*, and in his *Isagoge Chronologica*, judging that these Memoirs might please all those that have any curiosity for Learning, establishes nothing thereon which satisfies *Petavius*; and it is certain, that *Scaliger's Indian* year refers neither to the one nor the other of those which we have now found.

But in the Cardinal *de Cusa's* Treatise of the Calendar, there are some *vestigia* of these two sorts of *Indian* years. That which we have drawn from the IV. Section, is there found almost in formal terms; that which we have drawn from the Comparison of the I. and II. Section is found there also, but after a manner so obscure, that the Author himself who relates it has not comprehended it.

This Cardinal says, that according to *Abraham Aven Ezra*, an Astronomer of the Twelfth Age, the *Indians* do add (to the year of 365 days) the fourth part

part of a day, and the fifth part of an hour, when they speak of the year in which the Sun returns to the same Star. This year consists then of 365 days, 6 hours, and 12'; and it agrees to near 36 seconds with the year that we found by the *Hypothesis* of the IV. Section. This Author adds, that they who speak of the year according to which the *Indians* do regulate their Feasts, do alledge that from the fourth part there results a day more in 310 years. *Ex quarta plus 310 annis diem exurgere*: which he explains after a manner which cannot subsist. *This year*, saith he, *is greater than our common year, by one fourth, 23 seconds, and 30 thirds, which in 353 years do make a day.* The means of drawing a tolerable sense from this explication is not evident. For a day divided in three hundred fifty three years gives to each year 4 minutes, 4'', 45'''; and not 23'', 30'''. The true sense of these words, *Ex quarta plus 310 annis diem exurgere*, is, in my opinion, that 310 years of 365 days and a quarter, do by one whole day surpass 310 of these *Indian* years. One day divided in 310 years, gives to each 4 minutes, 30 seconds; which being deducted from 365 and a quarter, do leave 365 days, 5 hours, 55 minutes, and 30 seconds; which will be the greatness of the year, which regulates the *Indian* Feasts. This year exceeds not but by 16 seconds, the greatness of the year, which we have found by the comparison of the *Hypotheses* of the I. and II. Section of the *Indian* Rules: wherefore there is no reason to doubt but it is this which is here treated of.

IX. *The* Epocha *of the Synodical solar years of the* Indians.

THis sort of solar years, drawn from the rules of the two first Sections, may be called Synodical, because that it results from the Equality which is supposed to be between 19 of these solar years, and 235 lunar months, which terminate at the Conjunction of the Moon with the Sun. For the *Epocha* of these years may be taken the day and hour of the middle Conjunction of the Moon with the Sun, which happen'd the very day of the Astronomical *Epocha*, to near a day of the middle Equinox of the Spring; tho some may infer from the 5th, 6th, and 8th Articles of the II. Section, that for the *Epocha* of these years they take the minute which immediately follows this middle Conjunction, at the Meridian to which the rules of this Section were accommodated. Thus in particular calculations, there will be no more need of the Operation prescribed in the 5th Article of the II. Section, which is founded on the difference which was between the instant of this middle Conjunction and the midnight following, at a particular Meridian more occidental than *Siam*; nor of the Operations prescribed in the 8th Article of the VII. Section, and at the 9th Article of the X. Section, which we have judged to denote the minutes of the motion of the Sun and Moon, between the Meridian of *Siam*, and the Meridian to which the rules of the II. Section had been accommodated; and it will suffice to have had regard to these three Articles once for all.

The *Epocha* of these Synodical years will therefore be the 21st of *March* in the 638th year of *Jesus Christ*, at 3 a clock, 2 minutes in the morning at the Meridian of *Siam*.

The greatness of these years, according to the VII. Chapter of these Reflexions, consisting of 365 days, 5 hours, 55', 13'', 46''', 5'''', we shall find the beginning of the following years in the *Julian* years, by the continual addition of 5 hours, 55', 13'', 46''', 5'''', deducting a day from the summ of the days which results from this addition in the Bissextile years; thus we shall find the beginnings of these solar Synodical years, the dates of which we have examin'd as we have here calculated them, at the Meridian of *Siam* with the hours computed after midnight:

		In the Julian Years.		
		Days	H.	M.
	1683	*March* 17	21	57
Biss.	1684	*March* 17	3	52
	1685	*March* 17	9	47
	1686	*March* 17	15	42
	1687	*March* 17	21	38
Biss.	1688	*March* 17	3	33

Astronomical years compleat.	*In the* Gregorian *years.*		
	Days.	H.	M.
1045	*March* 27	21	57
1046	*March* 27	3	52
1047	*March* 27	9	47
1048	*March* 27	15	42
1049	*March* 27	21	38
1050	*March* 27	3	33

These beginnings of years happen a day and a half before the middle Equinoxes of the Spring, according to *Ptolemy*; and five days and a half before the same Equinoxes, according to the moderns: wherefore they may be taken for a kind of middle Equinoxes of the *Indians*. The first new Moon after the beginnings of these solar Synodical years, must be the fifth of the Civil year when the Intercalation precedes these beginnings, as it happen'd in the year 1685 and 1688; and it must be the sixth of the Civil year in the other years.

These are the first new Moons since the Equinoxes of this sort, calculated for the preceding years.

Astronomical years compleat.	Gregorian *years current.*	
1045		1683
1046	Biss.	1684
1047		1685
1048		1686
1049		1687
1050	Biss.	1688

Solar Astronomical years current.	*The first Conjunctions of the Astronomical years current.*		
		Afternoon.	
	Days.	H.	M.
1046	*April* 25	11	41
1047	*April* 14	7	30
1048	*April* 3	16	18
1049	*April* 22	14	50
1050	*April* 11	21	38
1051	*March* 31	7	27

Of the Indian *Period of the* 19 *years.*

To know the first Conjunctions of the solar synodical *Indian* years in our Calendar, it is sufficient to calculate the beginnings of the year from 19 to 19 years after the *Epocha*.

For

For every nineteenth solar synodical year from the *Epocha* ends with the middle Conjunction of the Moon with the Sun, from whence begins the twentieth year. The greatness of this period is found by resolving 19 years into lunar months by the 3^d, 5th, 6th and 7th Articles of the I Section, and by resolving the lunar months into days by the 2^d, 4th, 6th and 8th Articles of the II Section; and in fine, by reducing the fraction of the days called *Avamam*, into hours, minutes, seconds and thirds: and by this means it will be found that the *Indian* period of 19 years, consists of 6939 days, 16 hours, 59 minutes, 21 seconds, 35 thirds.

Tho this *Indian* Period of 19 years agrees in the number of the lunar months, which it comprehends, with the periods of *Numa*, *Meton*, and *Calippus*, and with our Cycle of the Golden number, as we have remarked in the Explication of the I. Section; yet it is different in the number of the hours.

That of *Meto* which contains 6940 days is longer by 7 hours, 30 minutes, 38 seconds, 25 thirds, than the *Indian*. That of *Calippus* and of our golden number which contain 6939 days and 18 hours, are longer by 1 hour, 30 minutes, 38 seconds, 25 thirds, than the *Indian*. That of *Numa* must be of a number of whole days, according to *Titus Livius*, whose words are these: *Ad cursum Lunæ in duodecim menses describit annum, quem (quia tricenos dies singulis mensibus Luna non explet, desuntque dies solido anno, qui solstitiali circumagitur orbe) intercalaribus mensibus interponendis, ita dispensavit, ut vigesimo anno ad metam eandem solis unde orsi essent, plenis annorum omnium spatiis dies congruerent.* In all the Manuscripts that we have seen, it is read *vicesimo anno*, and not *vigesimo quarto*, as in some printed Copies.

The period of 19 years of the *Indians* is therefore more exact than these periods of the Ancients, and than our golden Cycle; and it agrees to 3 minutes, and 5 or 6 seconds with the period of 235 lunar months established by the moderns, which do make it of 6939 days, 16 hours, 53 minutes, 27 seconds.

This is the beginning of the current *Indian* period of 19 years, and of the rest which follow for above an Age in the *Gregorian* Calendar, at the Meridian of *Siam*, with the hours after midnight.

			Days	H.	M.
	1683	*March*	27	21	57
	1702	*March*	28	14	26
	1721	*March*	28	6	56
Biss.	1740	*March*	27	23	25
	1759	*March*	28	15	54
	1778	*March*	28	8	24
	1797	*March*	28	0	53
Biss.	1816	*March*	28	17	22

Of the Indian *Epacts.*

THE *Epact* of the months, is the difference of the time which is between the new Moon, and the end of the solar month current; and the annual *Epact* is the difference of the time, which is between the end of the simple lunar or embolismic year, and the end of the solar year which runs when the lunar year ends.

According to the exposition of the I Section, 228 lunar months, more 7 other lunar months are equal to 228 solar months. Dividing the whole therefore by 228, 1 lunar month more $\frac{7}{228}$ of a lunar month is equal to a solar month.

The *Indian Epact* of the first month, is therefore $\frac{7}{228}$ of a lunar month.

The *Epact* of the second $\frac{14}{228}$ and so of the rest; and the *Epact* of 12 months, which do make a simple lunar year, is $\frac{84}{228}$; the *Epact* of two years $\frac{168}{228}$; the *Epact* of 3 years would be $\frac{252}{228}$ but because that $\frac{228}{228}$ are a month, a month is added to the third year, which is Embolismic, and the rest is the *Epact*. —— $\frac{24}{228}$

Thus the *Epact* of six years, is —————— $\frac{48}{228}$

The *Epact* of 18 years, is —————— $\frac{144}{228}$

And adding thereunto the *Epact* of a year, which is —————— $\frac{84}{228}$

The *Epact* of 19 years would be —————— $\frac{228}{228}$

which do make a lunar month.

To the nineteenth year is added a thirteenth month, to make it Embolismic; thus the *Epact* at the end of the nineteenth year, is 0.

If the lunisolar years are ordered after this manner, they will always end before the synodical Equinox, or in the Equinox it self. But they may be so ordered, that they end always after the synodical Equinox: which will happen, if when the *Epact* is 0, they begin them with the new Moon, which happens a month after the synodical Equinox: and after this manner the first month of the Astronomical year will commence at the beginning of the fifth month of the Civil year after the Embolisme; whereas in the year of the first method, the first month would end at the beginning of the fifth month of the Civil year after the Embolisme.

This *Indian Epact* is a great deal more exact than our vulgar *Epact*, which augments 11 days by the year; so that they deduct 30 days, when it exceeds this number, taking 30 days for a lunar month, and the nineteenth year they substract 29 days to reduce the *Epacta* to nothing at the end of the nineteenth lunisolar year.

The *Indian* Epact of a month, being reduced to hours, consists of 21 hours 45', 33'', 46'''. The *Epact* of a year consists of 10 days, 21 hours, 6', 45''. The *Epact* of 3 years is 3 days, 2 hours, 36 minutes, 13 seconds. The *Epact* of 11 years which is the least of all in the Cycle of 19 years, is 1 day, 13 hours, 18', 7''.

The *Indian Epact* may be consider'd in respect of the *Julian* and *Gregorian* years: and it will serve to find the beginning of the Civil and Astronomical years of the *Indians* in our Calendar, after they shall have established an *Epocha* and denoted the Terms.

From a Common or Bissextile year, to the succeeding common, *Julian* or *Gregorian* year, the *Indian Epact* consists of 10 days, 15 hours, 11', 32''.

From a common year to the following Bissextile year, the *Indian Epact* is 11 days, 15 hours, 11', 32''.

The annual *Epact* must be substracted from the first new Moon of a year, to find the first new Moon of the following year.

But when after the Substraction, the new Moon precedes the Term; they add a month to the year to make it Embolismic. Thus having supposed the first new Moon after the synodical Equinox of the year 1683, as in Chapter IX, on the 25th of *April*, 22 hours, and 41 minutes after noon, that is to say, on the 26th of *April*, at 10 a clock, 41 minutes of the morning in the Meridian of *Siam*: to have the first new Moon of the following year 1684, which is Bissextile, they will substract from this time 11 days, 15 hours, 11 minutes, 32 seconds, and they will have the 14th of *April*, at 19 hours, 29 minutes, 28 seconds of the year 1684: and to have the first new Moon of the solar synodical year, of the year 1685, which is common, they will substract from the preceding days, 10 days, 15 hours, 11 minutes 32 seconds; and they will have the 4th of *April* at 4 hours, 17 minutes, 56 seconds.

In fine, to have the first new Moon of the solar synodical year of the following year 1686, which is common, deducting likewise the same number of days, they will have the 24th of *March*, at 13 hours, 6 minutes, 24 seconds. But because that this day precedes the term of the synodical years, which for this Age hath been found the 27th of *March*; it is necessary to add a lunar month of 29 days, 12 hours, 44 minutes, 3 seconds; thus the year will be Embolismic of 13 Moons, and they will have the first new Moon of the synodical *Indian* year the 23d of *April* at 1 hour, 50 minutes, 27 seconds in the morning at *Siam*, and continuing after the same manner, they will have all the first new Moons of the following years.

In these *Indian* rules the name of an Embolismick or *Athikamat*, agrees to the year which immediately follows the Intercalation.

The lunisolar years may likewise be order'd in such a manner, that the addition of the intercalary month may be made when the Epact exceeds 15, which do make the half of the month; to the end that the term might be as a medium between the several beginnings of the years, some of which commence soon-

er,

er, and others later; as it is practised in our Ecclesiastical years, which begin before the Vernal Equinox, when the Equinox arrives before the 15th of the Moon; and which begin after the Equinox, when the Equinox happens after the 14th of the Moon. But it is more commodious for the Astronomical Calculations to begin the year always before, or always after the Equinox, as it is practised in the Astronomical *Indian* year, according to our Explication.

Nevertheless it is necessary to remark that the point of the *Zodiack*, which the *Indians* do take for the beginning of the signs, according to the Rules of the IV. and following Sections, and which they consider in some sort as the Æquinoxial point of the Spring, is in this Age removed 13 degrees from the Astronomical Term of the years discoursed of In the I. Section; so that the Sun arrives there the fourteenth day after the synodical Æquinox. Wherefore a part of the Astronomical lunisolar years which begin after the Term established by the Rules of the I. Section, will begin in this Age before this sort of Æquinox; and the other part will begin after; so that this sort of Æquinox is as it were in the middle of the several beginnings of the lunisolar years which begin in the fifth and sixth month of the Civil year.

XII. *A Correction of the lunar Months, and of the solar Synodical years of the* Indians.

IT is very easy to accommodate the lunar months of the *Indians* and their solar synodical years to the modern *Hypotheses*.

After having made the calculations according to the *Indian* Rules, it is necessary to divide the number of the years elapsed since the Astronomical *Epocha* by 6 and by 4. The first Quotient will give a number of seconds to substract from the time of the new Moons calculated according to these Rules.

EXAMPLE.

In the year of *Jesus Christ* 1688, the number of the years elapsed from the Astronomical Epocha of the *Indians* is 1050. This number being divided by 6, the Quotient, which is 175, gives 175 minutes, that is to say 2 hours, 55 minutes to add.

This same number being divided by 4, the quotient is 262, which gives 382 seconds, that is to say 6 minutes, 22 seconds to substract; and the Equation will be 2 hours, 48 minutes, 38 seconds. Having added this Equation to the first Conjunction of the solar Synodical year 1051, which, according to these rules, happen'd the 31st of *March*, in the year 1688, at 19 hours, 28 minutes, 24 seconds, after midnight; the middle Conjunction will be the 31st of *March*, at 22 hours, 17 minutes, 2 seconds, at the Meridian of *Siam*. The same Equation serves to the Synodical years which result from the time of 235 lunar months divided into 19 years.

The first division by 6 will suffice, if they take once and a half as many seconds to substract, as there are found minutes to add.

XIII. *The difference between the solar Synodical, and the Tropical years of the* Indians.

IF the *Indians* take for a Tropical year the time which the Sun employs in returning to the beginning of the Signs of the Zodiack, according to the fourth and following Sections; the difference between these years and the Synodical is considerable, as we have already remark'd. According to the Western Astronomy, the beginning of the Signs is the point of the Vernal Equinox, where the ascending demicircle of the Zodiack, terminated by the Tropicks, is intersected fected by the Equinoxial; for they hold no more to the *Hypothesis* of the Ancients, who plac'd the Equinoxes at the eighth parts of the Signs: and the Tropical year is the time that the Sun employs in returning to the same point, whether Equinoxial or Tropical.

The Conjunctions of the Moon with the Sun, which happen in the points of the Equinoxes, return not precisely at the end of the nineteenth Tropical year: for this nineteenth year ends about two hours before the end of the 235th lunar month, which terminates the nineteenth Synodical year.

I say, about two hours: for in this the modern Astronomers agree not among themselves to 9 or 10 minutes, because that the time of the Equinoxes being very difficult to determine exactly, they agree not in the exactness of the Tropical year but to near half a minute; tho they be almost unanimously agreed even to the thirds, in the greatness of the lunar month. Those that do make the greatness of the Tropical year of 365 days, 5 hours, 49 minutes, 4 seconds, and 36 thirds, will have the period of 19 solar Synodical years above two exact hours longer than the period of 19 Tropical years. They that make the Tropical year longer, will have a lesser difference; and they that make the Tropical year shorter, as most of the Astronomers do at present, will have it greater. It may here be supposed that this difference would be 2 hours wanting 3 minutes, seeing that the defect of the lunar *Indian* months in 19 years is 3 minutes; and that the Tropical year would consist of 365 days, 5 hours, 48 minutes, 55 seconds. Thus if at every 19th year from the Astronomical *Epocha* of the *Indians*, they deduct 2 hours from the Equinoxial Term, calculated by the *Indian* rules without the correction; and if they deduct also 14 hours 46 minutes for the time by which it may be supposed that the middle Equinox precedes the *Epocha* of the new Moons, according to the modern *Hypothesis*, they will have the middle Equinox of the Spring of the year proposed since the *Epocha*, conformable to the modern *Hypotheses*.

EXAMPLE.

In the year 1686 the number of the years since the Astronomical *Epocha* of the *Indians* is 1048. This number being divided by 19, the Quotient is 55 $\frac{3}{19}$ which being doubled gives 110 hours, 19 minutes, that is to say, 4 days, 14 hours, 19 minutes; to which having added for the *Epocha* 14 hours, 4 minutes, the summ is 5 days, 5 hours, 5 minutes: and this summ being deducted from the term of the same Synodical year 1048, which has before been found on the 27th of *March*, 1686, at 15 hours, 42 minutes of the evening, there remains the 22d of *March*, 10 hours, 37 minutes of the Evening, at the Meridian of *Siam*, for the middle Equinox of the Spring of the year 1686.

XIV. *An Examination of the great lunisolar period of the* Indians.

IN the VII. Chapter of these Reflexions we have found, that the Period of 13357 years is composed of 165202 entire lunar months, which do make 4878600 whole days, according to the Rules of the II. Section. This Period according to the *Hypothesis* of these Rules, brings back the new Moons which terminate the *Indian* synodical years, to the same hour and to the same minute under the same Meridian.

But having examined it by the method of the XII. Chapter of these Reflexions, it will be found that it is shorter than a period of a like number of lunar months, according to the modern Astronomers, by 1 day and 14 hours, which is almost the Epact of 11 years: and by the method of the XIII. Chapter, it will be found that the Anticipation of the Æquinoxes in regard of this number of synodical years of the *Indians* is 54 days and 5 hours. If they retrench 11 years from this period, there will be one of 13346 years, composed of of 165069 lunar months, or of 4874564 days, which will be more conformable to the modern *Hypotheses*.

XV. *The great lunisolar Equinoxial period, conformable to the preceding corrections.*

BUt instead of correcting the great period foregoing, it is more proper to find out a much shorter, which brings back the new Moons and the Equinoxes to the same hour under the same Meridian, thereby to establish some Astronomical *Epocha's* more near, and to abridge the Calculations which are so much the longer, as the *Epocha's* are more distant from our time.

It is extreamly difficult, or rather it is impossible to find some short and precise periods, which conjunctly reduce the new Moons and the Equinoxes to the same Meridian. *Vieta* proposes one for the *Gregorian* Calendar of 165580000 years, which comprehends 2047930047 lunar months.

It is not possible to verifie the exactness of these periods by the comparison of the Observations that we have, the antientest of which are only of 25 Ages; and these long periods serve not our design, which is to bring the *Epocha's* nearer.

It is better to make use of the shortest, tho less exact periods, and to denote how they want of being exact according to the *Hypotheses* which we follow.

By the rules of the first Section, and by our additions, it is found that 1040 synodical *Indian* years do make 12863 lunar months, and [illegible]; and by the rules of the II. Section it is found that the number of 12863 months without the fraction makes 379851 days, 21 hours, 24 minutes, 14 seconds.

According to the correction made by the method of the XII. Chapter of these Reflexions, to this number of days it is necessary to add 2 hours and 49 minutes, to render it conformable to the *Hypotheses* of the Modern Astronomers; thus in this number of 12863 months, there are 379852 whole days, and 13 minutes, 19 seconds of an hour.

The same number of months, with the fraction according to the Rules of the II. Section, and according to our Additions, makes 379856 days, 13 hours, 16 minutes, 43 seconds; which do make 1040 synodical *Indian* years.

The difference by which these years exceed the Tropical years, by our method of the XIII Chapter of these Reflexions, is found of 4 days, 13 hours, 28 minutes, 25 seconds; and this difference being deducted from 379856 days, 13ʰ, 16', 43", there remains 379851 days, 23 hours, 48 minutes, 18 seconds, for 1040 Tropical years, and to make 379852 whole days, there wants only 11 minutes and 42 seconds, during which the proper motion of the Sun is not sensible.

XVI. *A Modern* Epocha *of the New Moons, extracted from the* Indian Epocha.

HAving added 1040 years to the *Indian Epocha* of the 638ᵗʰ year of *Jesus Christ*, there will be the year 1678 for a new *Epocha*, in which the Conjunction of the Moon with the Sun will happen the day of the middle Equinox, 13 minutes of an hour later in respect of the same Meridian, and 12 minutes later in respect of the middle Equinox; so that the Conjunction happening in the year 638 at *Siam*, at 3 a clock, 2 minutes in the Morning; in the year 1678 it will there happen at 3 a clock, 15 minutes in the Morning.

During this interval the Anticipation of the Equinoxes in the *Julian* Calendar is 8 days, which being deducted from 21, there remains 13; and thus the middle Equinox, which in the year 638 was on the 21 of *March*, is found in the year 1678 on the 13 of *March* of the *Julian* year, which is the 23 of the *Gregorian* year. The middle Conjunction will therefore happen in the year 1678, on the 23 of *March* at 3 a clock, 14 minutes in the morning at the Meridian of *Siam*; that is to ſay, the 22 of *March* at 8 a clock, 42 minutes of the Evening at the Meridian of *Paris*.

XVII. *Modern* Epocha's *of the* Apogæum, *and* Node *of the Moon.*

BEcauſe that in this *Epocha* the new Moons, the *Apogæum*, and Node of the Moon were too remote from the Equinox, we have found an Equinoxial *Epocha* of the *Apogæum*, which precedes by 12 years that of the new Moon; and an *Epocha* of the Nodes, which follows it 14 years.

At the middle Equinox of the Spring, in the year 1666, the *Apogæum* of the Moon was at the Twentieth degree of *Aries*; and at the end of the preſent *Julian* year 1689, the North Node of the Moon will be at the beginning of *Aries*; but at the middle Equinox of the Spring 1690, it will be in the 26 degree and half of *Piſces*, or 3 degrees and half of the Sun.

The *Apogæum* of the Moon performs a revolution according to the ſucceſſion of the Signs in 3232 days, according to the *Indian* Rules; or in 3231 days and a third, according to the modern Aſtronomers. The Nodes of the Moon, of which there is no mention in the *Indian* Rules, do perform a revolution contrary to the ſucceſſion of the Signs in 6798 days⅓.

By theſe Principles there will be found as many *Epocha's* of the *Apogæum* and Nodes, as ſhall be deſired.

XVIII. *An* Epocha *of the new Moons near the* Apogæum, *and the* Nodes *of the* Moon, *and the middle Equinox of the Spring.*

IT is not found that the Equinoxial new Moon ſhould happen nearer our time, and altogether nearer its *Apogæum* and one of its Nodes, than the 17 of *March* in the year of *J. Christ*, 1019. This day at noon, at the Meridian of *Paris*, the middle place of the Sun was in the middle of the firſt degree of *Aries*, at 3 degrees and half from the middle place of the Moon, which joyned with the Sun the Evening of the ſame day.

The *Apogæum* of the Moon preceded the Sun a degree and half; and the deſcending Node of the Moon preceded it a degree, the *Apogæum* of the Sun being in the 26th degree of *Gemini*.

'Twould be needleſs to ſeek out another return of the Moon to its *Apogæum*, to its Node, to the Sun, and to the Vernal Equinox. The concourſe of all theſe circumſtances together being too rare, it is neceſſary to reſt ſatisfied with having ſome *Epocha's* ſeparated at diverſe other times, of which here are three the moſt exact.

The middle conjunction of the Moon with the Sun in the middle Equinox of the Spring, happened in the year of *J. Christ* 1192 on the 15 of *March* about Noon at the Meridian of *Rome*.

The *Apogæum* of the Moon was at the beginning of *Aries*, in the middle Equinox of the Spring, *Anno* 1460, on the 13 of *March*.

The deſcending Node of the Moon was at the beginning of *Aries*, in the middle Equinox of the Spring, *Anno* 1513, on the 14 of *March*.

'Twill not be needleſs to have ſome particular *Epocha's* of the new Moons proper for the *Julian* Calendar, to which moſt of the Chronologers do refer all the times paſt.

Julius Cæſar choſe an *Epocha* of *Julian* years, in which the new Moon happened the firſt day of the year. 'Twas the 45th year before the birth of *Jeſus Chriſt*, which is in the rank of the Biſſextiles, according as this rank was afterwards eſtabliſhed by *Auguſtus*, and as it is ſtill obſerved.

The

The first day of *January* of the same forty fifth year before *Jesus Christ* the middle conjunction of the Moon with the Sun happened at Six a clock in the Evening, at the Meridian of *Rome*.

And the first of *January* in the 32[d] year of *Jesus Christ*, the middle conjunction happened precisely at Noon at the Meridian of *Rome*.

The most commodious of the *Epocha's*, near the middle conjunctions in the *Julian* years, is, that which happened the first of *January*, *Anno* 1500, an hour and half before Noon at the Meridian of *Paris*.

XIX. *An Ancient Astronomical* Epocha *of the* Indians.

IN the III. Chapter of these Reflexions we have remarked, that the *Siameses* in their dates make use of an *Epocha*, which precedes the year of *Jesus Christ* by 544 years, and that after the twelfth or thirteenth month of the years from this *Epocha*, which do now end in *November* or *December*, the first month which follows, and which must be attributed to the following year, is yet attributed to the same year: which has given us ground to conjecture, that they attribute also to the same year, the other months to the beginning of the Astronomical year, which begins at the Vernal Equinox. This conjecture has been confirmed by the report of Mr. *de la Loubere*, who likewise judges that this Ancient *Epocha* must also be an Astronomical *Epocha*.

The extraordinary manner of computing the first and second month of the same year after the twelfth or thirteenth, may cause a belief that the first month of these years, which begins at present in *November* or *December*, began anciently near the Vernal Equinox, and that in process of time, the *Indians*, either thro negligence, or to make use of a Cycle too short, as would be that of 60 years which the *Chineses* do use, have sometimes failed to add a thirteenth month to the year which ought to be Embolismick, whence it has happen'd that the first month has run back into the winter; which having been perceived, the winter months, now called first, second and third, have been attributed to the preceding year, which according to the ancient institution ought not to end but at Spring.

Thus the *Indian* year, which was called 1231, at the end of the year 1687 of *Jesus Christ*, ought not to end, according to the Ancient Institution, till the Spring of the year 1688. Having substracted 1688 from 1231, there remains 543, which is the number of the compleat years from the ancient *Epocha* of the *Indians*, to the year of *Jesus Christ*. This *Epocha* appertains therefore to the current year 544 before *Jesus Christ*, according to the most common way of computing.

In this year the middle conjunction of the Moon happened between the true Equinox, and the middle Equinox of the Spring, at 15 degrees distance from the North Node of the Moon, the 25th of *March*, according to the *Julian* form, a *Saturday*, which is an Astronomical *Epocha* almost like to that of the year 638, which has been chosen, as more modern and more precise than the former.

Between these two *Indian Epocha's* there is a period of 1181 years, which being joyned to a period of 19 years, there are two periods of 600 years, which reduce the new Moons near the Equinoxes.

XX. *The Relation of the Synodical years of the* Indians, *to those of the Cycle of the* Chineses *of* 60 *Years.*

ACcording to the Chronology of *China* which Father *Couplet* published, and according to Father *Martinius* in his History of *China*, the *Chineses* do make use of lunisolar years, and they destribute them into sexagenary Cycles, the 74th of which began in the year of *J. Christ* 1683; so that the first Cycle should have began 2697 years before the birth of *Jesus Christ*.

By the *Indian* Rules of the first Section, in 60 synodical years, there are 720 solar months, and 742 lunar months, and $\frac{14}{124}$. It is necessary to reject this fraction, because that the lunisolar years are composed of entire lunar months. Yet this fraction in 19 sexagenary Cycles, which do make 1140 years, amounts to $\frac{266}{124}$, which do make two months: therefore if the sexagenary Cycles of the *Chineses* are all uniform, 1140 *Chinese* years are shorter by two months, than 1140 synodical years of the *Indians*. Wherefore if the *Indians* have regulated the intercalations of their civil years by uniform sexagenary Cycles, the beginning of the civil year 2232, ought to precede by a little less than four months, the term of their synodical years, which is at present on the 27 of *March* of the *Gregorian* year; as it happened indeed; which confirms what we have conjectured in the foregoing Chapter of the anticipation of the civil years.

To equal the years of the sexagenary Cycle to the synodical years regulated according to the Cycle of 19 years, it would be necessary that among 19 sexagenary Cycles there were 17 of 742 lunar months, and 2 of 743; or rather it would be necessary that after 9 Cycles of 742 months, which do make 540 years, the tenth Cycle following, which would be accomplish'd in the year 600, was of 743 months.

But there is ground to doubt whether they use it thus, seeing that the *Chinese* year has several times had occasion of being reformed, to refer its beginning to the same term; in which nevertheless the modern Relations accord only to 10 degrees: Father *Martinius* denoting it at the 15th degree of *Aquarius*, and Father *Couplet* at the 5th of the same Sign; as if the Term had retreated 10 degrees since the time of Father *Martinius*.

It is unquestionable that a great part of the Eclipses, and of the other Conjunctions which the *Chineses* do give as observed, cannot have happened at the times that they pretend, according to the Calendar regulated after the manner as it is at present, as we have found by the Calculation of a great number of these Eclipses, and even by the sole examination of the Intervals which are remarked between the one and the other: for several of these Intervals are too long, or too short, to be possibly determined by the Eclipses, which do happen only when the Sun is near one of the Nodes of the Moon; where it could not possibly return at the times denoted, if the *Chinese* years had been regulated in the past ages, as they are at present. Father *Couplet* himself doubts of some of these Eclipses, by reason of the Compliment which the *Chinese* Astronomers made to one of their Kings, whom they congratulated, for that an Eclipse, which they had predicted, had not happned; the Heaven, they said, having spared him this misfortune: and this Father has left to Mr. *Thevenot* a Manuscript of the same Eclipses, which he has printed in his Chronology, entituled *Eclipses vere & falsæ*, without distinguishing the one from the other.

But without accusing the *Chineses* of falshood, it may be said, that it may be that the Eclipses set down in the *Chinese* Chronology might happen, and that the contradiction which appears therein may proceed from the Irregularity of their Calendar, on which no Foundation can be laid.

XXI. *A Composition of the lunisolar Periods.*

THE Interval between the two *Epocha's* of the *Indians*, which is 1181 years, is a lunisolar period, which reduces the new Moons near the Equinox, and to the same day of the week.

This period is composed of 61 periods of 19 years, which are longer than 1159 tropical years; and of two periods of 11 years, which are shorter than 22 tropical; the defect of the one, partly recompencing the excess of the others.

As the mixture of the lunisolar years, some longer, others shorter, than the tropical, does more or less recompence the defect of the one by the excess of the other, as far as the Incommensurability which may be between the moti-

ons

ons of the Sun and Moon periods it: It makes the lunisolar periods so much the more precise, as they reduce the new Moons nearer the places of the Zodiack where they arrived at the beginning.

The Antients have first made the use of the little periods, the most famous of which has been that of 8 years, which has been in use not only amongst the ancient *Greeks*, but also amongst the first Christians; as it appears by the Cycle of St. *Hippolytus*, published at the beginning of the third Age.

This period, composed of five ordinary and three Embolismick years, being found too long by a day and half, which in 20 periods do make above a month; they were obliged to retrench a month in the twentieth period. But afterwards the period of 8 years was joyned to another of eleven years, composed of seven ordinary and four Embolismick, which is too short about a day and a half: and thereof was made the period of 19 years, which was supposed at first to be exact, tho it has since had occasion of amendment in the number of the days and hours which it comprehends. The correction of this period was the origine of the period of 76 years, composed of 4 periods of 19 years, corrected by *Calippus*, and of the period of 304 years, composed of 16 periods of 19 years, corrected by *Hipparchus*.

The *Jews* had a period of 84 years, composed of four periods of 19 years, and one of 8 years, which reduces the new Moons near the *Æquinox* on the same day of the week.

But the most famous period of those which have been invented to reduce the new Moons to the same place of the Zodiack, and to the same day of the week, is the *Victorian* of 532 years, composed of 28 periods of 19 years.

Yet the new Moon which should terminate this period, happen'd not till two days after the Sun's return to the same point of the Zodiack, and two other days before the same day of the week, to which the conjunction was arrived at the beginning of the period; and these defects are multiplied in the succession of the times, according to the number of these periods. Nevertheless, after that the defects of this period were known by every one, several famous Chronologers have not ceased to make use thereof, and they terminate it on the same day of the week and on the same day of the *Julian* year, which in this interval of time exceeds the solar tropical year 4 whole days, and the lunisolar year somewhat less than two days.

They do also multiply this period by the Cycle of 15 years, which is that of the Indictions, the origine of which is not more ancient than 13 Ages, to form the *Julian* period of 7980 years, of which they establish the *Epocha* 4713 years before the common *Epocha* of *Jesus Christ*. They prefer this imaginary period, in which the errors of the *Victorian* period are multiplied 15 times, to the true lunisolar periods, and they do likewise prefer this Ideal *Epocha* which they suppose more antient than the World, to the Astronomical and Historical *Epocha's*: even so far that they refer thereto the Historical Acts of the antient times before *Jesus Christ*, and before *Julius Cæsar*; tho the Indictions were not as yet in use, that there was then no Calendar to which this period could serve to regulate the days of the week, and that in fine the Cycle of 19 years extended to this time, demonstrates not the state of the Sun nor of the Moons, which are the three principal things for which these three Cycles which from the *Julian* period, have been invented. Wherefore it gives not so exact an Idea of the ancient times, which were not regulated after this manner, as of those of the thirteen last Ages, which were regulated amongst us according to the *Julian* year.

But the lunisolar periods of 19 years, which in regard of the tropical years are somewhat too long, being joyned to the periods of 11 years which are too short, do form other periods more precise than those which compose them. Among these periods the first of the most precise are those of 334, 353, and 372 years, the last of which is terminated also on the same day of the week, and might be placed in the stead of the *Victorian*.

XXII. *Lunisolar Periods composed of whole Ages.*

THE first lunisolar period composed of whole Ages, is that of 600 years, which is also composed of 31 periods of 19, and one of 11 years. Though the Chronologists speak not of this period, yet it is one of the ancientest that have been invented.

Antiq. Jud. l. 1. c. 3. *Josephus*, speaking of the Patriarchs that lived before the Deluge, says that *God prolonged their Life, as well by reason of their Vertue, as to afford them means to perfect the Sciences of Geometry and Astronomy, which they had invented: which they could not possibly do, if they had lived less than 600 years, because that it is not till after the Revolution of six Ages, that the great year is accomplished.*

This great year which is accomplished after six Ages, whereof not any other Author makes mention, can only be a period of lunisolar years, like to that which the *Jews* always used, and to that which the *Indians* do still make use of. Wherefore we have thought necessary to examine what this great year must be, according to the *Indian* Rules.

By the Rules of the I. Section it is found then, that in 600 years there are 7200 solar months, 7421 lunar months and [illegible]. Here this little fraction must be neglected; because that the lunisolar years do end with the lunar months, being composed of intire lunar months.

It is found by the Rules of the II. Section, that 7421 lunar months do comprehend 219146 days, 11 hours, 57 minutes, 52 seconds: if therefore we compose this period of whole days, it must consist of 219146 days.

600 *Gregorian* years are alternatively of 219145 days, and 219146 days: they agree then to half a day with a lunisolar period of 600 years, calculated according to the *Indian* Rules.

The second lunisolar period composed of Ages, is that of 2300 years, which being joyned to one of 600, makes a more exact period of 2900 years: And two periods of 2300 years, joyned to a period of 600 years do make a lunisolar period of 5200 years, which is the Interval of the time which is reckoned according to *Eusebius* his Chronology, from the Creation of the World to the vulgar *Epocha* of the years of *J. Christ*.

XXIII. *An Astronomical* Epocha *of the years of* Jesus Christ.

THese lunisolar periods, and the two *Epocha's* of the *Indians*, which we have examin'd, do point unto us, as with the finger, the admirable *Epocha* of the years of *J. Christ*, which is removed from the first of these two *Indian Epocha's*, a period of 600 years wanting a period of 19 years, and which precedes the second by a period of 600 years, and two of nineteen years. Thus the year of *Jesus Christ* (which is that of his Incarnation and Birth, according to the Tradition of the Church, and as Father *Grandamy* justifies it in his Christian Chronology, and Father *Riccioli* in his reformed Astronomy) is also an Astronomical *Epocha*, in which, according to the modern Tables, the middle conjunction of the Moon with the Sun happened the 24 of *March*, according to the *Julian* form re-established a little after by *Augustus*, at one a clock and a half in the morning at the Meridian of *Jerusalem*, the very day of the middle Equinox, a *Wednesday*,

De Trin. l. 4. c. 5. which is the day of the Creation of these two Planets.

The day following, *March* 25th, which according to the ancient tradition of the Church reported by St. *Augustine*, was the day of our Lords Incarnation, was likewise the day of the first *Phasis* of the Moon; and consequently it was the first day of the month, according to the usage of the *Hebrews*, and the first day of the sacred year, which by the Divine institution, must begin with the first month of the Spring, and the first day of a great year, the natural *Epocha* of which is the concourse of the middle Equinox, and of the middle Conjunction of the Moon with the Sun.

This

This concourse terminates therefore the lunisolar periods of the preceding Ages, and was an *Epocha* from whence began a new order of Ages, according to the Oracle of the *Sybil*, related by *Virgil* in these words: Eclog. 4.

Magnus ab integro Sæclorum nascitur ordo:
Jam nova progenies Cœlo dimittitur alto.

This Oracle seems to answer the Prophecy of *Isaiah*, *Parvulus natus est nobis*; Isa. 9. v. 6. & 7. where this new-born is called God and Father of future Ages; *Deus fortis, Pater futuri Sæculi.*

The Interpreters do remark in this Prophecy, as a thing mysterious, the extraordinary situation of a *Mem* final (which is the Numerical Character of 600) in this word לםרבה *ad multiplicandum*, where this *Mem* final is in the second place, there being no other example in the whole Text of the Holy Scripture, where ever a final Letter is placed only at the end of the words. This Numerical Character of 600 in this situation might allude to the periods of 600 years of the Patriarchs, which were to terminate at the accomplishment of the Prophecy, which is the *Epocha*, from whence we do at present compute the years of *Jesus Christ*.

XXIV. *The* Epocha *of the Ecclesiastical Equinoxes, and of the vulgar Cycle of the Golden number.*

THe Christians of the first Ages having remarked that the *Jews* of this time had forgot the antient Rules of the *Hebrew* years; so that they celebrated *Easter* twice in one year, as *Constantine* the Great attests in the Letter to the Churches, do borrow the form of the *Julian* years re-established by *Augustus*, which are destributed by periods of 4 years, three of which are common of 365 days, and a Bissextile of 366 days, and do surpass the lunar years by 11 days. (Euseb. de vita Constantini lib. 3. c. 5.) They denote therefore in the *Julian* Calender the day of the Equinox and the days of the Moon with their variation, and they regulate it, some by the Cycle of 8 years, others by the Cycle of 19 years; as it appears by the regulation of the Council of *Cæsarea* in the year of *Christ* 196, and by the Canon of St. *Hippolytus*, and by that of St. *Anatolius*. But afterwards the Council of *Nice*, held in the year 325, having charged the Bishops of *Alexandria*, as the most experienced in Astronomy to determine the time of *Easter*, these Prelates made use of their *Alexandrian* Calendar, where the year began with the 29th of *August*; and for *Epocha* they took the lunar Cycles of 19 years, the first *Egyptian* year of the Empire of *Dioclesian*; because that the last day of the preceding year, which was the 28th of *August*, of the 284th year of *Jesus Christ*, the new Moon happened near Noon at the Meridian of *Alexandria*. By reckoning from this *Epocha* backward the Cycles of 19 years, they come to the 28th of *August* in the year preceding the *Epocha* of *Jesus Christ*; so that the first year of *Jesus Christ* is the second year of one of these Cycles. 'Tis thus that these Cycles are still computed at present, since that *Dionysius* the Less transported the Cycles of the Moon from the *Alexandrian* Calendar to the *Roman*, and that he began to compute the years from the *Epocha* of *Jesus Christ*, instead of computing them from the *Epocha* of *Dioclesian*, denoting the Equinox of the Spring on the 21th, of *March*, as it had been set down in the *Egyptian Epocha*.

For the *Epocha* of the lunar Cycles they might have taken the Equinoxial conjunction of the same year of *Jesus Christ*, rather than the conjunction of the 28th of *August* of the former year, and renew it after 616 years, which reduce the new Moons to the same day of the *Julian* year, and to the same day of the week; which is what they demanded of the *Victorian* period; but they thought only to conform themselves to the rule of the *Alexandrians*, which was the sole method to reconcile the *Eastern* and *Western* Church. Thus these Rules have been followed to the past Age; altho it has been long perceived, that the new Moons thus

thus regulated, according to the Cycle of 19 years, anticipated almost a day in 312 *Julian* years, and that the Equinoxes anticipated about 3 days in 400 of these years.

XXV. *The solar* Gregorian *Period of 400 years.*

ABout the end of the past Age the Anticipation of the Equinoxes since the *Epocha* chosen by the *Alexandrians*, was mounted to 10 days: and that of the new Moons in the same years of the lunar Cycle continued without interruption was mounted to 4 days: wherefore in several Councils there was discourse concerning the manner of correcting these defects; and in fine, Pope *Gregory* XIII. after having communicated his design to the Christian Princes, and to the most famous Universities, and having understood their Advice, deducted 10 days from the year 1582, and reduced the Equinox to the day of the year wherein it had been at the time of the *Epocha*, chosen by the Deputies of the Council of *Nice*.

He established also a period of 400 years, shorter by 3 days than 400 *Julian* years, making common the hundred years for the reserve of each 400, to compute from the year 1600; or which amounts to the same thing, to reckon from the *Epocha* of *Jesus Christ*.

These periods of 400 *Gregorian* years reduce the Sun to the same points of the Zodiac, to the same days of the month, and of the week, and to the same hours under the same Meridian, the greatness of the year being supposed 365 days, 5 hours, 49′, 12″.

According to the modern Observations, in the hundred Bissextiles the middle Equinox happens the 21st of *March*, at 20 hours after noon, at the Meridian of *Rome*; and the 96th after the hundredth Bissextile it happens the 21st of *March*, 1 hours, 43 minutes after noon, which is the Equinox that happens the soonest. But the 303d year after the hundredth Bissextile, the middle Equinox happens the 23d of *March*, at 7 hours, 21 minutes after noon, which is the slowest of all the rest.

By these *Epocha's*, and by this greatness of the year, it is easie perpetually to find the middle Equinoxes of the *Gregorian* Calendar.

XXVI. *The Rule of the* Gregorian Epacts.

IN the *Gregorian* correction they interrupt not the succession of the Cycles of 19 years, drawn from the ancient *Alexandrian Epocha*, as they might have done; but they observe on what day of the Moon the *Gregorian* year ends, at every year of the *Alexandrian* Cycle. This number of the days of the Moon at the end of a year is the *Epact* of the following year. 'Tis found that after the correction of the first year of the Cycle, the *Epact* is 1. Every year it is augmented by 11 days, but after the 19th year it is augmented by 12, always deducting 30 when it surpasses this number, and taking the rest for the *Epact*; which is done in this Age.

They observe also the Variation which the *Epacts* do make from Age to Age in the very years of the Ancient lunar Cycle, and they find that in 2500 *Julian* years they augment 8 days; which supposes the lunar month of 29 days, 12 hours, 44′, 3″, 10‴, 41⁗.

Greg. Calend. c. 1. Explic. Calend. Greg. c. 11. & 14. But to find the *Gregorian Epacts* from Age to Age, they made three different Tables, of which it was judged the Construction could not be clearly explained but in a Book apart, which was not finished till twenty years after the correction. 'Twas thought at first that the whole Variation of the *Gregorian Epacts* was included in a period of 300000 years: But this not being found conformable to the project of the correction, they were forc'd to have recourse to some difficult equations, of which there is not found any determin'd period.

XXVII.

XXVII. *A new lunisolar and Paschal Period.*

TO supply this defect, and to find the *Gregorian Epacts* for future Ages without Tables, we do make use of a lunisolar period of 1600 years, which has for *Epocha* the Equinoxial Conjunction of the year of *Jesus Christ*, and which reduces the new Moons since the correction, to the same day of the *Gregorian* year, to the same day of the week, and almost to the same hour of the day, under the same Meridian. According to this period we give to each period of 400 years since *Jesus Christ* 9 days of Equinoxial *Epact*, by deducting 29 when it surpasses this number: and we add 8 days to the Equinoxial *Epact* since the correction, to have the Civil *Gregorian Epact*, by deducting 30, when the summ surpasses this number.

At every hundredth year, not Bissextile, we diminish the Equinoxial *Epact* 5 days, in respect of the hundredth preceding, and we take every hundredth year for *Epocha* of 5 periods of 19 years, to find the Augmentation of the *Epacts* for an Age at every year of the Cycle, after the accustomed manner.

Thus, to have the Equinoxial *Epact* of the year 1600, which is distant from the *Epocha* of *Jesus Christ* 4 periods of 400 years, multiplying 4 by 9 there is 36; from whence having deducted 29, there remains 7, the Equinoxial *Epact* of the year 1600, which shews that the middle Equinox of the year 1600 happen'd 7 days after the middle Conjunction of the Moon with the Sun: adding thereunto 8 days, there are 15, which is the Civil *Gregorian Epact* of the year 1600, as it is set down in the Table of the Moveable *Gregorian* Feasts. Expl. Cal. p. 410.

It is evident that the Equinoxial *Epact* of the year 11600, which terminates this period, must be 0. But to find it by the same method, since that the year 11600 is removed from the *Epocha* of *Jesus Christ* 29 periods of 400 years, multiplying 29 by 9, and dividing the product by 29, the quotient is 9, and the remainder 0 for the Equinoxial period: Adding 8, there is the Civil *Gregorian Epact* of the year 11600, which will be 8, as *Clavius* had found it by the *Gregorian* Tables, in the 168th page of the Explication of the Calendar; which demonstrates the conformity of the *Epacts* of the future Ages, found by the means of this period, after a method so easie, with the *Gregorian Epacts*, found by the means of three Tables of the *Gregorian* Calendar.

If the hours and minutes of those Equinoxial *Epacts* in the 400 years are also demanded, thereunto shall be always added 8 hours, and besides 1/3 and 1/10 of as many hours as there are whole days in the *Epact*, and a third of as many minutes. Thus for the year 1600, whose Equinoxial *Epact* is 7 days; one third of 7 hours is 2h, 20'; a tenth is 0h, 42'; a third of 7 minutes is 2': the summ added to 7 days 8 hours, makes 7 days, 11h, 4', the Equinoxial *Epact* of the year 1600.

Deducting this *Epact* from the time of the middle Equinox, which in 1600 happened the 21 of *March*, at 20 hours after noon at *Rome*, the middle conjunction preceding will be on the 14th of *March*, at 8h, 56'; adding thereunto half a lunar month, which is 14 days, 18h, 22', the middle opposition will be found on the 29th of *March*, at 3h, 18'. In the Table of the moveable Feasts, where the minutes are neglected, it is set down on the 29th of *March*, at 3 hours. Expl. Cal. p. 410.

To have by hours and minutes the Equinoxial *Epact* in the hundreds, not Bissextiles, from the *Epact* found in the preceding hundredth Bissextile, shall be deducted 5 days, 2h, 12', for the first, double for the second, triple for the third (borrowing a month of 29 days, 12h, 44', if it is required) and you will have the *Epact* in the hundred proposed, which shall be made use of in the preceding example, comparing it with the middle Equinox of the same year.

By this method will be found the middle oppositions in the hundred years, not Bissextile, a day before that they are set down, from the year 1700 to the year 4000 in the Table of the Movable Feasts, which is in the Book of the explication of the Calendar, where they are set down a day later than the *Gregorian* Expl. Cal. p. 484. 581. p. 501. 584.

Mm m *Hypotheses*

Ap. 336. ad p. 509. p. 434. *Hypotheses* require. Which has happened also in the precepts, and in the examples of finding the progresses of the new and full Moons, and in the *Epocha's* of the hundred years not Bissextile, and in all the Calculations which are deduced thence) as is found by comparing together the new Moons calculated in the same Table, the Anticipation whereof, which from one common year to another must always be 10 days, 15 hours, is found sometimes 9 days, 15 hours, as from the year 1699 to the year 1700; sometimes 11 days, 15 hours, as from the year 1700 to 1701; and so likewise in the other hundreds not Bissextile.

Upon this account there were some differences which gave occasion carefully to examine the progress of the new Moon, from one *Gregorian* hundredth to the other; and yet these disputes were not capable of unfolding, at that time, the real differences that there is between several hundred Common and Bissextile years. But as these Calculations of the full Moons have been made only to examine the *Epacts*, which were regulated otherwise, the differences fell only under examination, which being rectified, demonstrates the exactness of these *Gregorian Epacts* much greater, than the very Authors of the Correction supposed it.

Expl. Cal. p. 191. 'Tis a thing worthy of remark, that the Astronomical *Hypotheses* of the *Gregorian* Calendar, are found at present more conformable to the Cœlestial motions, than they were supposed at the time of the correction; for as it appears by the project which Pope *Gregory* XIII. sent to the Christian Princes, in the year 1577, he proposed in the regulation of the years to follow the *Alphonsine* Tables, which were judged to be preferable to the others; but to retrench three days in 400 *Julian* years, he was obliged to suppose the solar year shorter by some seconds than the *Alphonsine*, and to prefer this conveniency to a greater exactness: and yet all the Astronomers, which have since compared the modern observations with the ancient, have found that the Tropical year is indeed somewhat shorter than the *Alphonsine*, altho they be not agreed in the precise difference.

The greatness of the lunar month which results from the *Gregorian Hypothesis* of the Equation of the *Epacts*, which is 8 days in 2500 *Julian* years, is also more conformable to the modern Astronomers, than the lunar month of the *Alphonsine*, and the disposition of the *Gregorian Epacts* and the new and full Moons which result therefrom, are also oftentimes more precise than they which finished the correction pretended.

In fine, the whole system of the *Gregorian* Calendar has some Beauties which have not been known by those who were the Authors thereof, as is that of giving the *Epacts* conformable to those which are found by the great lunisolar period, which has for *Epocha* the same year of *Jesus Christ*, and the very day, which according to the antient tradition, immediately precedes the day of the Incarnation; from whence may be drawn the Equinoxes and new Moons with more facility than from the *Egyptian Epocha* of the Golden number, of which they would in some manner keep the relation.

Expl. Cal. p. 4. 'Twere to be wish'd that, seeing that in the project sent to the Christian Princes and to the Universities, it was proposed to retrench 10 or 12 days from the *Julian* year about the end of the past Age, they had retrenched 12, which is the difference between 1600 *Julian* years and 1600 *Gregorian* years, to place the Equinoxes on the same days of the *Gregorian* year as they were in the *Julian* year, according to the form re-established by *Augustus*, in the *Epocha* of *Jesus Christ*, rather than to restore them to the days whereon they were in the time of the strange *Epocha* chosen by the *Alexandrians* for their particular conveniency; and that instead of regulating the *Epacts* by the defective Cycle of the *Alexandrians*, and of seeking Equations and Corrections for the *Epacts* born by this Cycle, they had also taken heed to the great lunisolar period of 11600 years, that we have proposed, which immediately gives the true days of the *Epacts*; which reduces the new Moons to the same day of the year and of the week, and which has the most august and most memorable *Epocha* amongst the Christians that can be imagined.

I doubt not that if from this time they had found this period which we have proposed, they would have employ'd it not only for the Excellency of its *Epocha*, but also because the greatness of the month which it supposes is as conformable to the *Alphonsine* Tables, as the greatness of the year which they establish to conform themselves to these Tables, the most that the conveniency of the calculation did permit.

For this period is composed of 143472 lunar months, and of 4236813 natural days; and consequently it supposes the lunar month 29 days, 12^h, $44'$, $3''$, $5'''$, $28''''$, $43'''''$, $20''''''$, and the *Alphonsine* Tables do suppose it 29 days, 12^h, $44'$, $3''$, $2'''$, $58''''$, $52'''''$, which is shorter by $2'''$, than that of our period.

According to *Tycho Brahe*, the lunar month is 29 days, 12^h, $44'$, $3''$, $8'''$, $29''''$, $46'''''$, $48''''''$, which exceeds ours by three; thus this month is a mean between that of *Alphonsus*, and that of *Tycho Brahe*.

Therefore this great period composed of a number of these whole months, and of a number of *Gregorian* periods of 400 years, and consequently of entire weeks, and entire days, might be proposed to serve as a Rule to compare all the other periods together, and to relate the times before and after the *Epocha* of *Jesus Christ*, which would be the end of the first of our periods, and the beginning of the second; and as this great period has been invented in the exercises which are perform'd in the Royal Academy of Sciences, and in the Observatory Royal, under the Protection and by the Orders of the King; it seems that if the *Julian* period has taken its name from *Julius Cæsar*, and the *Gregorian* from *Gregory* XIII, this might also justly be named the lunisolar period of ***LOUIS LE GRAND***.

Note, *That what is said at the beginning of Page 189, that in this extract the numbers are written from the top to the bottom, after the manner of the* Chineses, *must be understood, that they place the sum of the minutes under that of the degrees, that of the seconds under that of the minutes, that of the thirds under that of the seconds, and so successively, as we place the sums one under the other, when we would make the Addition thereof; but in every particular sum, whether of degrees, or minutes, seconds, thirds or others, the Cyphers are ranged in this extract according to our manner of ranging them.*

Note, *Also, that the word* Souriat, *which is found Page 193 and elsewhere, is the name of the Sun in the learned Language of* Pallacata, *and that the word* Aatit, *which is found Page 195 is likewise the name of the Sun, but in the* Balie *Tongue and also in the vulgar Language of* Pallacata, *as it has been before remarked in the Chapter of the Names of the days, of the months, and of the years.*

The End.

The Problem of the Magical Squares according to the Indians.

This Problem is thus:

A square being divided into as many little equal squares as shall be desired, it is necessary to fill the little squares with as many numbers given in Arithmetical progression, in such a manner that the numbers of the little squares of each rank, whether from top to bottom, or from right to left, and those of the Diagonals do always make the same sum.

Now to the end that a square might be divided into little equal squares, it is necessary that there are as many ranks of little squares, as there shall be little squares to each rank.

The

The little squares I will call the *cases*, and the rows from top to bottom *upright*, and those from right to left *transverse*; and the word *rank* shall equally denote the upright and transverse.

I have said that the Cases must be filled with numbers in Arithmetical progression, and because that all Arithmetical Progression is indifferent for this Problem, I will take the natural for example, and will take the Unite for the first number of the progression.

Behold then the two first examples, *viz.* the square of nine Cases, and that of 16, filled, the one with the nine first numbers from the unite to nine, and the other with the sixteen first numbers from the unite to 16: So that in the square of 9 Cases, the summ of every upright, and that of every Transverse is 15, and that of each Diagonal 15 also: and that in that of 16 Cases, the summ of every upright, and that of every Transverse is 34, and that of each Diagonal 34 also.

4	9	2
3	5	7
8	1	6

1	15	14	4
12	6	7	9
8	10	11	5
13	3	2	16

This Problem is called Magical Squares, because that *Agrippa* in his second Book *De Occulta Philosophia*, cap. 22. informs us that they were used as Talismans, after having engraved them on plates of diverse metals: the cunning that there is in ranging the numbers after this manner, having appear'd so marvellous to the Ignorant, as to attribute the Invention thereof to Spirits superior to man. *Agrippa* has not only given the two preceding Squares, but five successively, which are those of 25, 36, 49, 64, and 81 Cases; and he reports that these seven squares were consecrated to the seven Planets. The Arithmeticians of these times have looked upon them as an Arithmetical sport, and not as a mystery of Magic: And they have sought out general methods to range them.

The first that I know who laboured therein, was *Gaspar Bachet de Meziriac*, a Mathematician famous for his learned Commentaries on *Diophantus*. He found out an ingenious method for the unequal squares, that is to say, for those that have a number of unequal cases: but for the equal squares he could find none. 'Tis in a Book in *Octavo*, which he has entituled, *Pleasant Problems by numbers*.

Mr. *Vincent*, whom I have so often mentioned in my Relation, seeing me one day in the Ship, during our return, studiously to range the Magical squares after the manner of *Bachet*, informed me that the *Indians* of *Surate* ranged them with much more facility, and taught me their method for the unequal squares only, having, he said, forgot that of the equal.

The first square, which is that of 9 cases, return'd to the square of *Agrippa*, it was only subverted: but the other unequal squares were essentially different from those of *Agrippa*. He ranged the numbers in the cases immediately, and without hesitation; and I hope that it will not be unacceptable that I give the Rules, and the demonstration of this method, which is surprizing for its extream facility to execute a thing, which has appeared difficult to all our Mathematicians.

1. After having divided the total square into its little squares, they place the numbers according to their natural order, I would say by beginning with the unite, and continuing with 2, 3, 4, and all the other numbers successively; and they place the unite, or the first number of the Arithmetical Progression given, in the middle case of the upper transverse.

2. When they have put a number into the highest case of an upright, they place the following number in the lowest case of the upright, which follows towards

towards the right: that is to say, that from the upper transverse they descend immediately to that below.

3. When they have placed a number in the last case of a transverse, the following is put in the first case of the transverse immediately superior, that is to say, that from the last upright, they return immediately to the first upright on the left.

4. In every other occurrence, after having placed a number, they place the following in the cases which follow diametrically or slantingly from the bottom to the top, and from the left to the right, until they come to one of the cases of the upper transverse, or of the last upright to the right.

5. When they find the way stopp'd by any case already filled with any number, then they take the case immediately under that which they have filled, and they continue it as before, diametrically from the bottom to the top, and from the left to the right.

These few Rules, easie to retain, are sufficient to range all the unequal squares in general. An example renders them more intelligible.

17	24	1	8	15
23	5	7	14	16
4	6	13	20	22
10	12	19	21	3
11	18	25	2	9

This square is essentially different from that of *Agrippa*; and the method of *Bachet* is not easily accommodated thereto; and on the contrary, the *Indian* method may easily give the squares of *Agrippa*, by changing it in something.

1. They place the unite in the Case, which is immediately under that of the Center, and they pursue it diametrically from top to bottom, and from the left to the right.

2. From the lowest case of an upright, they pass to the highest case of the upright which follows on the right; and from the last case of a Transverse they return to the left to the first case of the Transverse immediately inferior.

3. When the way is interrupted, they re-assume two cases underneath that which they filled; and if there remains no case underneath, or that there remains but one, the first case of the upright is thought to return in order after the last, as if it was infixed underneath the lowest.

An Example taken from Agrippa.

11	24	7	20	3
4	12	25	8	16
17	5	13	21	9
10	18	1	14	22
23	6	19	2	15

As *Bachet* has not given the demonstration of his method, I have search'd it out, not doubting but it would give me also that of the *Indian* method. But to make my demonstration understood, it is necessary that I give the method of *Bachet*.

1. The square being divided by cases, to be filled with numbers in the Magical order, he augments it before all things by the square sides in this manner. To the upper part of the first transverse, he adds another transverse, but contracted by two cases, viz. one at each end. Over this first transverse contracted he adds a second contracted by two new cases. To the second he adds a third more contracted than the former, to the third a fourth, and so on, if it is necessary, until that the last transverse have but one case. Underneath the last transverse he adds likewise as many transverses more contracted one than the other: And in fine, to the first upright on the left, to the last upright on the right, he adds also as many uprights thus contracted.

EXAMPLES.

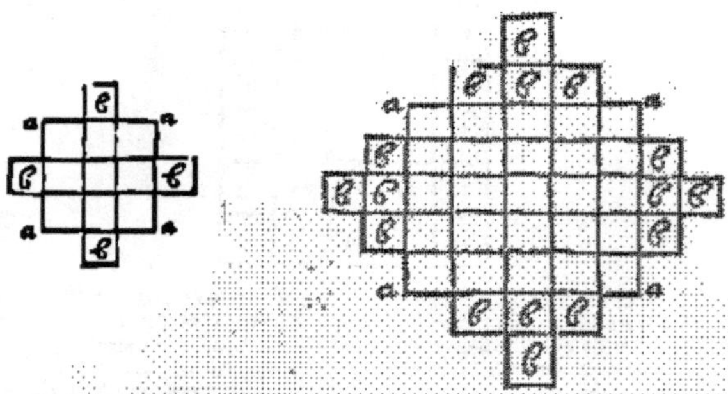

aa are the squares of 9 and 25 cases, *bb* are the cases of Augmentation.

The square being thus augmented, *Bachet* there places the numbers according to the natural order, as well of the numbers as the cases, in the following manner.

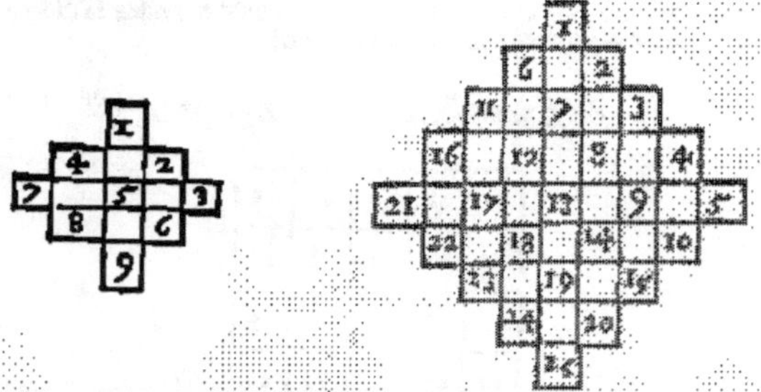

In this disposition it is evident that the cases of the true square are alternately full, and alternately empty, and that its two Diameters are entirely full. Now the full cases receive not any change in the sequel of the operation, and the Diameters remain always such as they are by position in the square augmented: but for the cases of the true square, which are likewise void, they must be filled with the numbers which are in the cases of Augmentation, by transporting the high ones lower, and the low ones higher, each into its upright; those of the right to the left, and those of the left to the right, each into its transverse, and all to as many cases, as there are in the side of the real square. Thus in the square of 9 cases, which has only three in its side, the unite, which is in the case of Augmentation at the top, is removed to the third case below in the same upright; 9, which is in the case of Augmentation below, is removed to the third case above in the same upright; 3, which is in the case of Augmentation on the right, is remov'd toward the left, to the third case in the same transverse; and in fine, 7, which is in the case of Augmentation on the left, is removed towards the right, to the third case in the same transverse.

After the same manner, in the square of 25 cases, which has 5 in its side, the numbers, which are in the cases of Augmentation above, do descend 5 cases below each in its upright. Those of the cases of Augmentation below do ascend five cases above each in its upright. Those of the cases of Augmentation on the right do pass 5 cases to the left, each in its transverse; and those of the cases of Augmentation on the left do pass 5 cases to the right, each also in its transverse. It ought to be the same in all the other squares proportionably, and thereby they will become all Magical.

Definitions.

1. IN the augmented square of *Bachet*, the ranks of Augmentation shall be called *Complements* of the ranks of the true square, into which the numbers of the ranks of Augmentation must be removed; and the ranks which must receive the Complements, shall be called defective ranks. Now as by *Bachet's* method every number of the cases of Augmentation must be removed to as many cases as there are in the side of the true square, it follows that every defective rank is as far distant from its Complement, as there are cases in the side of the true square.

2. Because that the true square, that is to say, that which it is necessary to fill with numbers according to the Magical Order, is always comprehended in the square augmented, I will consider it in the square augmented, and I will call its ranks and its diameters, the ranks and diameters of the true square; but its ranks, whether transverse or upright, shall comprehend the cases, which they have at both ends; because that the numbers which are in the cases of Augmentation, proceed neither from their transverse nor from their upright, when removed into the cases of the true square, according to *Bachet's* method.

3. The diameters of the square augmented are the middle upright, and middle transverse of the true square, and they are the sole ranks which are not defective, and which receive no complement. They neither acquire, nor lose any number in *Bachet's* operation; they suffer only the removal of their numbers from some of their cases into others.

4. As the augmented square has ranks of another construction than are the ranks of the true square, I will call them *Bands* and *Bars*. The *Bands* descend from the left to the right, as that wherein are the numbers 1, 2, 3, 4, 5, in the preceding example, the *Bars* descend from the right to the left, as that, wherein are the numbers 1, 6, 11, 16, 21, in the same example.

Preparation to the Demonstration.

THE Problems of the Magical squares consists in two things.

The first is that every transverse and every upright make the same sum, and the second that every diameter make likewise that same sum. I shall not speak at present of this last condition, no more than if I sought it not. And because that to arrive at the first, it is not necessary that all the numbers, which ought to fill a Magical square, be in Arithmetical proportion continued, but that

that it suffices that the numbers of a *Band* be Arithmetically proportional to those of every other *Band*, I will denote the first numbers of every *Band* by the letters of the Latin Alphabet, and the differences between the numbers of the same *Band* by the letters of the Greek Alphabet: and to the end that the numbers of a *Band* be Arithmetically proportional to the numbers of every other *Band*, I will set down

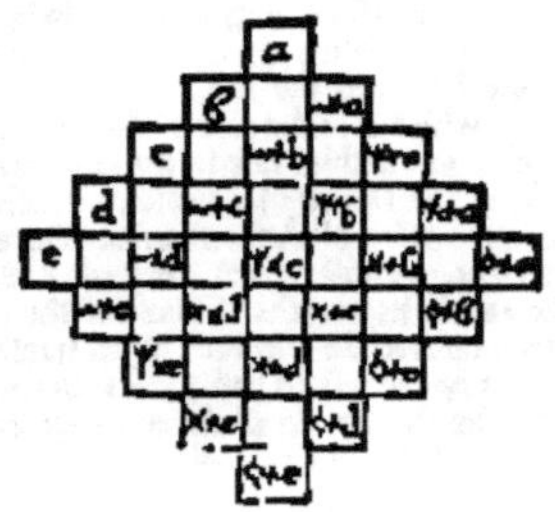

the differences of the numbers of each band by the same *Greek* Letters.

1. Nothing hinders why the Sign —, may not be placed instead of the Sign +, either before all the differences, or before some, provided that the same Sign be before the same difference in each band: for so the Arithmetical proportion will not be altered.

2. The greater a square shall be, the more *Latin* and *Greek* Letters it will have; but every band will never have but one *Latin* Letter, and all the *Greek* Letters, and the *Latin* Letter shall be different in each band. Every bar on the contrary shall have all the *Latin* Letters, and all except the first shall have a *Greek* Letter, which shall be different in every bar.

Demonstration.

From hence it follows. 1. That the diameters of the augmented square have each all the *Latin* and all the *Greek* Letters, because that they have each a case of every band, and a case of every bar, and that the cases of every band do give them all the *Latin* Letters, and the cases of each bar all the *Greek*. The sum then of these two diameters is the same, viz. that of all the Letters, as well *Greek* as *Latin*, taken at once. Now these two diameters do make an upright and a transverse in the Magical square, because that in the operation of *Bachet*, their sum changes not by the loss or acquisition of any number, as I have already remarked.

2. As the ranks of the true square, whether transverse or upright, are as distant from their complements, as there are cases in the side of the true square, it follows that the bands, and the bars, which begin with a complement, or above this complement, touch not, that is to say, have no case at the defective rank of this complement; and that the bands and the bars which begin with a defective rank or above, have no case in its complement: the Letters then of the defective rank, are all different from those of the complements; because that different bands have different *Latin* Letters, and that different bars have different *Greek* Letters. But because that all the bands, and all the bars, have each a case in all the defective ranks, or in their complements: then every defective rank whatever, will have all the Letters, when it shall have received its complement; it will have all the *Latin*, because that all the bands, passing through every defective rank, or through its complement, do there leave all the *Latin* Letters,

Letters ; and it will have all the *Greek*, because that all the bars, passing also through every defective rank, or through its complement, do there leave all the *Greek* Letters. And thus all the defective ranks will make the same sum in the Magical square, and the same sum as the diameters of the square augmented, which are the two sole ranks not defective of the true square.

That this Method cannot agree to even Squares.

THE Demonstration which I have given, agrees to the equal squares, as well as to the unequal, in this that in the augmented equal square, every defective rank and its complement do make the sum, which a range of the Magical square ought to make: But there is this inconvenience to the equal squares, that the numbers of the cases of Augmentation, do find the cases of the true square filled with other numbers, which they ought to fill; because that every case is full, which goes in an equal rank after a full case, and that in the equal squares, the cases of the defective ranks do come in an equal rank, after those of the complements, the defective ranks being as remote from the complements, as the side of the square has cases, and the side of every equal square having its cases in equal number.

Of the Diameters of the unequal Magical Squares.

BY *Bachet's* operation it is clear, that he understands that the diameters are such as they ought to be, by the sole position of the numbers in the augmented square: and this will be always true, provided only that it is supposed, that the number of the case of the middle of each band, be a mean Arithmetic proportion between the other numbers of the same band, taken two by two: a condition, which is naturally included in the ordinary Problem of the Magical squares, wherein it is demanded that all the numbers be in Arithmetical proportion continued. *Alternando* the mean number of each bar, will be also a mean Arithmetic proportional between all the numbers of the same bar taken two by two: and hereby every mean, taken as many times as there are cases in the band, or in the bar, which is all one, will be equal to the total sum of the band, or of the bar. Therefore all the means of the bands, taken as many times as there are cases in every band, or which is all one, in the side of the square, will be equal to the total sum of the square: then taken once only, they will be equal to the sum of one of the ranks of the Magical square; and it will be the same of the means of the bars: and because that the means of the bands do make one diameter, and the means of the bars the other, it is proved that the diameters will be exact by the sole position of the numbers in the augmented square, provided that every mean of a band, be a mean Arithmetic proportional between all the numbers of its band, taken two by two.

In a word, as in the squares there are no augmented pairs, nor *true* square, nor diameters of the *true* square, because that the bands of the equal squares have not a mean number, 'tis likewise a reason, which evinces that this method, cannot be accommodated to the equal squares.

Methods of varying the Magical Squares by Bachet's *Square augmented.*

1. BY varying the order of the numbers in the bands, or in the bars, provided that the order which shall be taken, be the same in all the bands, or the same in all the bars, to the end that in this order the numbers of a band or of a bar, be Arithmetically proportioned to those of every other band or bar: but it is necessary that not any of the diameters loses any of its numbers.

2. Or rather (which will amount to the same) by varying the order of the bars amongst them in the augmented square: for this troubles not the Arithmetical proportion, which is the ground of the preceding demonstration: but it is necessary to remember to leave always in their place the band and the bar, which do make the two diameters.

3. By not putting the first number of each band, in the first case of each band: As for example

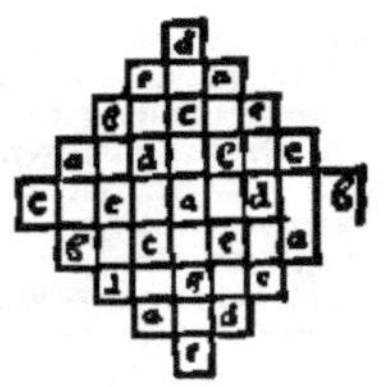

d, *a*, *e*, *c*, *b*, are the five letters of the first band, the order of which is arbitrary, and the letter *d*, which is in the first case of this first band, is not found in the first case of any other band: but in the fourth case of the second band, in the second of the third, in the fifth of the fourth, and in the third of the fifth. Besides the succession or order of the Letters must be the same in every band. But because that in the bands where the Letter *d* is in a case lower than the first, there remains not case enough underneath, to put all the other Letters successively, the first cases of the bands do return in order after the last, and are in this case thought the last cases of their bands. A circumstance which it is necessary carefully to observe.

If then in an augmented square the numbers are disposed in each band, as in the bands of this square I have disposed the Letters *a*, *b*, *c*, *d*, *e*, and which one continues to operate like *Bachet*, that is to say, to remove as he does, the numbers of the cases of Augmentation into the void cases of the real square, the true square will be Magical, at least as to the ranks, whether transverse or upright, for I speak not as yet of the Diameters.

I shall call those capital cases, wherein are found the Letters like to the Letter which is put in the first case of the first band, which I will call the first capital case.

Preparation to the Demonstration.

1. IT is necessary to observe in disposing these Letters, that after having chosen the capital case of the second band, near a Letter of the first band, which I will call the Letter of Indication, so that this second capital case be also the second case of the bar which begins with this Letter of Indication, one may chuse the capital case of the third band, near the Letter of the second band, like to the first Letter of Indication, so that this third capital case be the third of the bar, wherein shall be the second Letter of Indication. After the same manner shall be determin'd the capital case of every band, near the Letter of Indication of the precedent band. From whence it follows, that there are as many capital cases as bands, and no more.

It follows also, that not only the Letter *d* is always under the Letter *e* in the same bar, but that all the other Letters are always under the same Letters in the same bars, and that the Letters have likewise the same order in all the bars, as they have the same in all the bands, though the order of the Letters in the bars, is not the same as the order of the Letters in the bands.

2. The

2. The choice of the capital case of the second band, which determines that of the rest, is not entirely arbitrary. To regulate it 'tis necessary to have regard to the number of the ranks of the true square, which is the number 5 in the preceding example, and which is always the square root of the number, which expresses the multitude of the cases of the true square, and so I will call it the root of the square.

Take then a number at your own choice, provided nevertheless that it be less than the root of the square, and first to this very root, and that by adding two points, it be still first at the same root of the square: 'Twill be by this number, that we shall determine the choice of the second capital case: and we call it the number determining.

The second capital case must not be the second case of the second band, because that this second case is found in the upright diameter of the augmented square, and that there must not be two Letters alike in any of the diameters of the augmented square: and so as the first capital case is already in the upright diameter, the second cannot be there. It is necessary on the contrary, that the case which you shall chuse in the second band, for the second capital, be as far distant from the second case of the upright diameter, as your determining number shall have Unites; and at the same time your second capital shall be removed from the first capital case as many transverses, as your determining number + 2 shall have Unites. Thus in the preceding example, the second capital case, viz. the case of the second band, where is the Letter *d*, is the second case after that, which is in the upright diameter, and it is in the fourth transverse underneath the first capital case, which alone is looked upon as a transverse, and the number 2, which determines this second capital case, is first to 5, which is the root of the square, and 2 + 2 that is to say 4, is likewise first to 5, the third case of the second band is therefore the first, which removes from the upright diameter, and it is with this that it is necessary to begin to compute the distance of the rest: so that the first case of this second band is in this sense the remotest of the second case, though to reckon after a contrary sense it touches it.

You may then in the preceding example, where the root of the square is 5, take either 1 or 2, or 4, which do give you three different cases, of which you may make your second capital case. 1 is first to 5, and 1 will give you the case wherein is *b*, three transverses distant from the first capital case: 2 is first to 5, and 2 + 2 that is to say 4, is also first to 5, and 2 will give you the case wherein is *d*, 4 transverses distant from the first capital case. 3 is also first to 5, but because that 3 + 2, that is to say 5, is not first to 5, 3 can give you in this example only a false capital case. 4 is first to 5, and 4 + 2 that is to say 6, is also first to 5, but from 6 it is necessary to deduct 5 which is the root, and there will remain 1. And 4 will give you the case wherein is *e*, the fourth in distance from the case of the diameter rising, and has a transverse near the first capital. The number 4 will give you then *Bachet's* disposition, who has placed all the capital cases in the first bar: and as often as for a determining number you shall take a less number by an Unite, than the root of the square, you will fall into *Bachet's* disposition.

3. From hence it follows, that the diameter ascending will not have any other capital case than the first, which it has already, and that so it will not have twice the Letter, which shall be in the capital cases. To prove it let us suppose that our bands be sufficiently extended towards the right, to make as many new uprights as we desire: and let us mark the first upright, which shall be as distant from the diameter ascending, as the root of the square has Unites: that is to say, which shall be the fifth on the right of the diameter ascending, if the root of the square is 5. And at a like distance from this first upright marked, let us mark a second, and then a third, and a fourth, always at an equal distance one from the other, until that there are as many uprights marked, as the determining number has Unites. In this case as the determining number and the root of the square are first amongst them, the last upright marked will be the sole one, whose distance to take it from the diameter ascending, would be divisible by the determining number.

Suppose

Suppoſe alſo, that now the bands are long enough, the capital caſes are marked all together, and without ever returning to the firſt caſes of the bands, as it was neceſſary to do, before that the bands were extended, becauſe that then they had not caſes enough after the capital, to receive all the Letters ſucceſſively. I ſay that in theſe ſuppoſitions, none of theſe marked uprights will have a capital caſes except the laſt; becauſe that it is the ſole marked upright, whoſe diſtance from the diameter aſcending unto it, is diviſible by the determining number; for as the uprights, wherein are the capital caſes, are as remote (viz. the firſt from the upright, the ſecond from the firſt, the third from the ſecond, and ſo ſucceſſively) as the determining number has Unites, it follows that no upright has a capital caſe when the diſtance from the upright diameter unto it, is not diviſible by the determing number. 'Tis proved then that no marked upright, except the laſt, will have a capital caſe; and the capital caſe which it ſhall have will be the firſt beyond the number of the caſes neceſſary to your augmented ſquare, becauſe that in counting the firſt capital caſe, there will be as many others before this, as the root of the ſquare has Unites.

Now when you mark the capital caſes in a ſquare augmented, according to the method which I have given, ſo that when you arrive at the laſt caſe of a band, you return to its firſt caſe, as if it was after the laſt, you do no other thing, than ſucceſſively to place all the capital caſes, in reſpect of the diameter aſcending, as in the caſe of the extenſion of the bands, you will place one after the other in regard of all the uprights ſucceſſively marked. And none of your capital caſes, except a firſt ſupernumerary, can fall into your aſcending diameter, as no other, except a firſt ſupernumerary, could fall into your laſt upright marked.

4. But if you conſider the firſt capital caſe, as a tranſverſe, and that you make the ſame ſuppoſitions as before, ſo that there are as many tranſverſes marked, as the determining number † a ſhall have Unites, and as diſtant (viz. the firſt from the firſt capital caſe, the ſecond from the firſt, the third from the ſecond, and ſo ſucceſſively) as the root of the ſquare ſhall have Unites; From this that the root of the ſquare and the determining number ✝ a are firſt amongſt them, and from this that the determining number ✝ a expreſſes the diſtance of the tranſverſes, wherein will be the capital caſes, you will prove that there ſhall be only the laſt tranſverſe marked, which has a capital caſe, which will be the firſt ſupernumerary: and conſequently, that the defective rank, the firſt capital caſe of which is the complement, will have no capital caſe, becauſe that it is the firſt tranſverſe marked; and you will prove alſo that the firſt ſupernumerary capital caſe muſt return to the tranſverſe of the firſt capital caſe, and as it muſt return likewiſe to the upright diameter, it follows that the firſt ſupernumerary caſe, that is to ſay, that which you would mark after the laſt of the neceſſary, is the firſt capital caſe, becauſe there is only this which is common to its tranſverſe, and to the upright diameter.

5. From the order of the letters, alike in all the bands and alike alſo in all the bars, you will prove that all the letters alike, are at the ſame diſtance one from the other, and in the ſame order amongſt them, as the letters of the capital caſes amongſt them, and that ſo all the caſes which contain letters alike may be conſidered as capital, ſo that two letters alike, are never found in the ſame upright, nor in the ſame tranſverſe, nor in a defective rank, nor in its complement. Which needs no other demonſtration.

Demonſtration.

THis ſuppoſed, the demonſtration of the Problem is eaſie, for whereas no letter is twice in any of the diameters of the augmented ſquare, nor in any defective rank and its complement, it follows that every of the two diameters, and every defective rank and its complement have all the letters, and that conſequently they make the ſame ſumms.

of

Of the Diameters.

THe Band which makes one of the diameters being Magical by position, as it ought to be, continues Magical, because that it receives not any new Letter, nor loses any of its own. The bar which makes the other diameter is found Magical by the disposition, and the proof is this.

As far as the bar of the second capital case is removed from the first bar, so much the bar of the third capital case, is removed from the bar of the second, and so successively, the first bars to which you return, being reckon'd in this case as coming after the last. Now the bar of the second capital case is as far distant from the first as there are Unites in the determining number + 1. Therefore if the determining number + 1 is first to the root of the square, the preceding demonstration sufficeth to prove, that not any bar will have two Letters alike, wherefore the bar which shall serve as the diameter, will not have two Letters alike, and so it will have all the Letters once.

But if the determining number + 1 is an *aliquot* part of the root of the square, then each bar will have as many Letters alike, as there shall be Unites in the determining number + 1, and there will be as many different Letters, as there shall be Unites in the other *aliquot* part of the root of the square, which shall be the quotient of the division made from the root by the determining number + 1. These several Letters will be therefore in an odd number, because that this quotient can be only an odd number, being an *aliquot* of an odd number. Of these Letters in an odd number, the one will be the middle of the first band, the others, taken two by two, will be like to the Letters of the first band, which taken also two by two, will be equally remote from the middle, the one towards the head of the band, the other towards the tail; So that if the order of the Letters of the first band, is as the middle by its situation, or middle proportional between all the others, which, taken two by two, shall be equally remote from it, then the bar which shall serve as diameter will be Magical, because that if it has not the middle Letters of all the bands, it will have the power thereof; for the other Letters, which shall not be mean, if being taken two by two, the one is weaker than the middle of its band, the other will be stronger as much as the middle of its own; and thus the two together will countervail the middle of their bands. As for example, in the square of 81 cases, the root of which is 9, if the determining number is 2, as 2 + 1, that is to say, 3 is the *aliquot* part of 9, the corresponding *aliquot* of which, that is to say that, which returns from the division of 9 by 3, is also 3, there will be in each bar three several Letters which will every one be there repeated three times. The first of the different will be the middle of the first band, the two others between the different, will be alike to two of the first band equally distant from the middle. After the same manner in the square of 225 cases, the root of which is 15, if the determining number is likewise 2, as 2 + 1, that is to say, 3 is the *aliquot* part of 15 (of which 5 is the *aliquot* corresponding) it will happen that in every bar there will be 5 several Letters repeated every one three times. The one will be the middle of the first band, the 4 others will be alike to 4 of the first band, which taken two by two will be equidistant from the middle.

The Conclusion is then, that when the determining number + 1, is first to the root of the square, the bar which serves as diameter can only be Magical; but that if the determining number + 1, is *aliquot* of the root of the square, the bar which serves as diameter cannot be Magical; that the middle Letter of the first band, cannot be the middle Arithmetic of all the other Letters of its first band two by two, and that it is not the Letters of its band, which, taken two by two, are at equal distances from it, and the like of which ought to enter into the bar, which shall serve as diameter. After this the order of the Letters of the first band is arbitrary.

In a word, the nearest of these equidistant Letters, shall be each as distant from the middle, as the determining number + 1 shall have Unites, the following shall be as remote from these first, every one from its own, and so successively.

I have said that it is necessary to take the second capital case in the second band, tho it may be taken in such other band as one pleases, provided that the band of the third capital case be as distant from the band of the second case, as this shall be from the first, and that the band of the fourth capital case be at this very distance from the band of the third, and so successively, the first bands returning in order after the last. But besides this, it is necessary that this distance be expressed by a number first to the root of the square, and the thing will return to the same, that is to say, to put a capital case in each band. But if you put the second capital case in a band, whose distance from the first band, was not expressed by a number first to the root of the square, then several capital cases would fall in the first band, which being supposed full of all the different Letters, could not receive the like Letters, which fill the capital cases.

Another way of varying the Magical Squares.

YOU shall double the preceding variations, if you perform in the bars what you did in the bands, and in the bands what you performed in the bars; taking for one of the diameters, a bar which should be Magical by position, and rendring Magical by disposition the band which shall be the other diameter.

From these Principles it follows, that the square of 9 cases is always the same, without being able to receive essential varieties, because that it can have only two for the determining number: and because that the removing of the bands, or of the bars amongst them, makes only a simple subversion, by reason that there are only two bands and two bars subject to transposition, and that the band and the bar which serve as diameters cannot be displaced.

It follows also, that always one of the diameters at least must be Magical by position: and that the greatest and least of the number proposed to fill a Magical square, can never be at the center, because that the center is always filled by one of the numbers of the diameter by position, in which, be it band or bar, the greatest nor smallest number cannot be.

On the contrary, the middle number of the whole square, that is to say, that which by the position is at the center of the augmented square, will remain at the center of the Magical square, as often as the diameter by position shall have the capital case at one of its ends: but in every other case it will go out thence, and yet it will never depart from the diameter by position.

All which things must be understood according to the suppositions above explained. Besides I know that the uneven Magical squares may be varied into a surprizing number of ways, unto which all that I have said would not agree.

In fine, one of the diverse methods, which result from the Principles which I have explained, is *Indian*, as may be proved, by removing into an augmented square the numbers of an *Indian* Magical square, in such a manner, that the cases of Augmentation be full of the Numbers, which they must render to the true square. It will be seen how the numbers shall be ranged in the augmented square, in one of the methods which I have explained.

An Illustration of the Indian *Method.*

AS I had communicated to Mr. *de Malezieu*, Intendant to the Duke of *Mayne*, the *Indian* unequal squares, without saying any thing to him of my Demonstration, which I had not as yet fully cleared, he found out one which has no relation to *Bachet*'s augmented square, and which I will briefly explain, because that the things which I have spoken, will help to make me understood.

Let

Let there be a square which we will call natural, in which the numbers should be placed in their natural order in this manner.

1	2	3	4	5
6	7	8	9	10
11	12	13	14	15
16	17	18	19	20
21	22	23	24	25

The business is to dispose these numbers magically into another square of as many cases and empty.

1. In considering this square, I see that the two diameters, and the middle upright and transverse mean do make the same summ; which Mr. *de Malezieu* thought to have given ground to the Problem, out of a desire of rendering the other transverses and other uprights equal also, without destroying the equality of Diagonals.

2. I see that the first transverse contains all the numbers, from the unite to the root of the square; that the second transverse contains these same numbers and in the same order, but augmented every one with a root; that the third contains also these very numbers in the same order, augmented every one with two roots; that it is the same in every transverse, save that the fourth has every one of these numbers augmented with three roots, that the fifth hath them augmented with four roots, and so in proportion of the other transverses, if there were more.

3. It therefore occurs naturally to my mind to consider another square, where in every transverse I will place the same numbers, which are in the first, that is to say from the unite to the root of the square, without augmenting them with any root in any transverse; and I find presently that the transverses will be equal in their summs, having each the same numbers; and that the uprights of this new square, will have the same surplusage one over the other, as the uprights of the natural square, because that the difference of the uprights in the natural square, proceeds not from the roots affixt to the numbers, but from these numbers which are repeated in every transverse, as it is seen in this example, where the strokes annext to the numbers, do denote the roots wherewith each number is augmented in the natural square.

1	2	3	4	5
$1'$	$2'$	$3'$	$4'$	$5'$
$1''$	$2''$	$3''$	$4''$	$5''$
$1'''$	$2'''$	$3'''$	$4'''$	$5'''$
$1''''$	$2''''$	$3''''$	$4''''$	$5''''$

4. It is evident that in this square all the transverses are equal, in that they have every one the same numbers, and that the uprights are only unequal because that they have not every one all those different numbers which are in every

transverse,

transverse, but on the contrary one alone of these numbers repeated as many times as there are squares in every upright. Therefore I shall render the uprights equal to one another, if I make that not one of these numbers be twice in every upright, but that all be there once. And because that these very numbers do bear every one the same number of roots in the same transverse, I shall also render the transverses equal, if I make that every transverse have not all these several numbers of it self, but that it borrows one of every transverse. Thus the diameters are already equal, because that they have every one the several numbers that it is necessary to have, and that they take one from every transverse, that is to say, one without the root, the other augmented with a root, the other with 2, the other with 3, and so successively.

The true secret then is to dispose all the numbers of every transverse in a diametrical way, that is to say slanting, so that having placed one number, the following will be in another transverse and another upright at the same time, Which cannot be better performed than after the *Indian* manner.

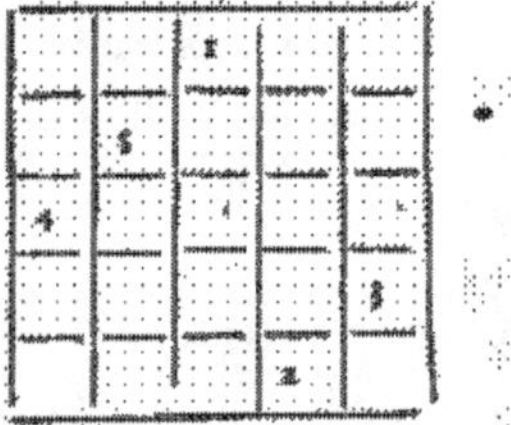

These are the numbers of the first transverse placed slanting ⟶, so that there is not two in the same upright nor in the same transverse. I must therefore dispose the numbers of the second transverse after the same manner, and because that I must avoid placing the first number of this transverse, under the first of the other, I cannot do better than to place it under the last in this manner.

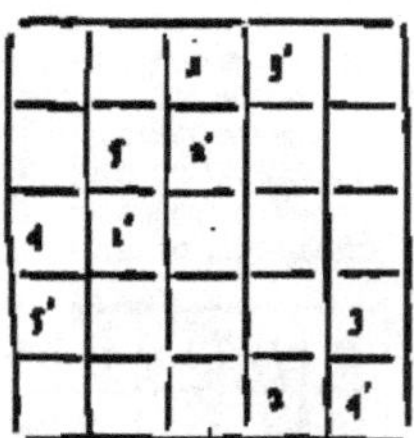

With the same Oeconomy I dispose the other transverses, placing always the first number of the one under the last of the other; and for one of the diameters I put the middle transverse, because that naturally it is Magical.

2‴	4⁗	1	3′	5′
3⁗	5	2′	4″	1‴
4	1′	3″	5‴	2⁗
5′	2′	4‴	1⁗	3
1″	3″	5⁗	2	4′

It is clear that in this disposition not any transverse, nor any upright have two numbers, neither from the same transverse, nor from the same upright of the natural square, and that the diameter which we have not made by position, has also only one number from every transverse, and every upright of the natural square. This is what M. *de Malezieu* thought, without having had the leisure to fathom it further; and it is evidently the Principle, on which the *Indian* Method and that of *Bachet* are grounded, and all the others, of which I have shown, that it is possible to vary the Magical squares. And if care be taken that in a Magical square the ranks parallel to the diameters are defective, and that they have their complements, it will be seen that *Bachet's* augmented square, and the Magical square have opposite proprieties. In the augmented square, the bands which are the true ranks, are not Magical, and its defective ranks augmented with their complements are. On the contrary, in the Magical square the ranks are Magical, and the defective ranks and their complements do contain, every one, what a band of the augmented square contains.

To finish what M. *de Malezieu* has thought, it is necessary only to accommodate what we have said concerning the choice of the capital cases; and because that this is easie to do, I will speak no more of it.

M. *de Malezieu* thought likewise, that this principle might serve to the even squares, and this is true; but here likewise there is found difficulty in the execution, because that in the even squares, the defective ranks and their complements have every one a case in the same diameter, or have none at all, so that by dispersing the numbers from a transverse into a defective rank, and its complement, two numbers of this transverse are put into the same diameter, or else none at all, and the one and the other of these two things is equally bad. Besides there is no transverse in the even squares, which can furnish a diameter by position; and so it would be necessary to remove a little into the even squares, after the *Indian* manner of dispencing the numbers, and to put one into each rank and one into each diameter. But the Method presents not it self immediately: However here is the first example thereof.

8	11	14	1
2	13	12	7
9	6	3	16
15	4	5	10

Of the Indian *Method of the Even Squares.*

I Thought to have divined it from the examples of the squares of 16, 36, and 64 cases, which *Arigga* has given us.

1. As the ranks are in even number in the even squares, they may be considered two by two. Comparing then the first to the last, the second to the last save one, the third to the last but two, and so successively, by equally removing us from the first and the last ranks, we will call them opposite, be they transverse, or upright.

Now because that the numbers of one rank, are arithmetically proportional with those of another rank of the same way, it is clear to those who understand arithmetical proportion, that two opposite ranks do make the same total sum as two other opposite ranks, and that if this sum be divided into two equals, each half will be the sum that a Magical rank ought to make.

2. The opposite numbers are also the first and last of the whole square, the second and last save one, the third and last but two, and so successively, by removing us equally from the first and last numbers: so that the sum of two opposite numbers is always equal to the sum of other opposites.

From hence it is evident, that the numbers opposite to those of one rank, are the numbers which are in the opposite rank, and that to render the sums of two opposite ranks equal, it is necessary only to take the moity of the numbers of one of the ranks, and to exchange them for their opposites, which are in the other. As for Example

1	14	15	4
13	2	3	16

1, 2, 3, 4, do make the first natural rank of the square of 16 cases, and 13, 14, 15, 16, do make the last rank thereof. To render them equal, it is necessary only to take 2 and 3, which are the moity of the numbers of the first, and to exchange them for 14 and 15, their opposites; and so 1, 14, 15, 4, will make the same sum as 13, 2, 3, 16.

The transverses between them, and the uprights between them, may render themselves equal by this Method: but because that the choice of the opposite numbers may be made after several ways, the *Indians* have chosen one, that is easie to retain, which leaves the diameters such as they are in the natural square, because that they are such as they ought to be, and ranges the uprights, when it is intended only to range the transverses. The whole Method consists then in knowing how to range two opposite transverses, and the rules are these.

1. They take the half of the numbers of the upper transverse, and remove them to the lower: and they take their opposite numbers in the lower transverse, and remove them to the upper.

2. The numbers which remain in each rank, do remain there in their natural place, and in their natural order: the transposed do place themselves every one in the case of its opposite, and consequently in a subverted order.

3. The first and the last numbers of every rank do continue in their natural rank, the second and third are transposed, the fourth and the fifth remain, the sixth and the seventh are transposed, and so alternatively two are transposed, and two remain.

EXAMPLE.

1	63	62	4	5	59	58	8
57	7	6	60	61	3	2	64

1, 2, 3, 4, 5, 6, 7, 8, do make the firſt natural rank of the ſquare of 64 caſes; 57, 58, 59, 60, 61, 62, 63, 64, do make the laſt thereof. 1 and 8 the firſt and laſt numbers of the firſt rank remain there, and in their natural place, 57 and 64 the firſt and laſt numbers of the laſt rank do remain there and in their place. Afterwards 2 and 3 are tranſpoſed, 4 and 5 remain, 6 and 7 are tranſpoſed: and after the ſame manner the numbers of the oppoſite rank 58 and 59 are removed, 60 and 61 do remain, 62 and 63 are removed. 1, 4, 5, 8, which remain in the firſt rank, are in their natural caſes, and conſequently in their natural order. 2, 3, 6, 7, which are removed, are in the caſes of their oppoſites, and are in a ſubverted order. After the ſame manner 57, 60, 61, 64, which remain in their rank, are in their natural caſes, and in their natural order. 58, 59, 62, 63, which are removed, are in the caſes of their oppoſites, and in a ſubverted order.

All the oppoſite ranks muſt be ranged according to theſe few rules: but it is not always certain that it may be neceſſary to put the firſt number of the rank in the firſt caſe on the left; for after this manner the firſt and laſt uprights would keep all their natural numbers, and would not be equal. Therefore it is neceſſary to render them equal by the ſame rule as the tranſverſes, by removing half of the numbers of the firſt upright into the caſes of their oppoſites, leaving the firſt and the laſt in their upright, removing the ſecond and the third, leaving the fourth and the fifth, removing the ſixth and the ſeventh, and ſo ſucceſſively according to the rules that we have given for the tranſverſes. The head of every tranſverſe will be then on the right, or on the left, according as its firſt number ſhall be continued or removed, to the firſt or to the laſt upright, to the right or to the left.

An Example of the Square of 64 Caſes.

1	63	62	4	5	59	58	8
56	10	11	53	52	14	15	49
48	18	19	45	44	22	23	41
25	39	38	28	29	35	34	32
33	31	30	36	37	2	26	40
24	42	43	21	20	46	47	17
16	50	51	13	12	54	55	9
57	7	6	60	61	3	2	64

But these rules suffice only to the squares equally even; and there is some particular observation for them unequally even.

Every square unequally even, if you thence deduct a compass (that is to say the first and the last transverses, the first and the last uprights) leaves a square equally even, which must be ranged according to the aforesaid rules with a little alteration, which we will declare. It is necessary therefore to see how the first and last transverses do range themselves, because that the first and last uprights do range themselves after the same manner.

1. The transverses, being of a square unequally even, have each a number of cases unequally even; but if care be not taken about the two middle cases of each transverse, then there will remain in every one a number of cases equally even, which we will call the cases equally even. The first rule is therefore to remove half of the numbers of the cases equally even, and to remove those, which should be chosen for this purpose, into a transverse of a square equally even. Thus the first and the last numbers do remain in their cases, the second and the third are removed, the fourth and the fifth continue, the sixth and the seventh are removed, and so successively: but I speak only of the numbers of the cases equally even, and I only comprehend those in the account which I make, no more than if the middle cases had no numbers.

2. The removed numbers pass not to the cases of their opposites, but into the cases which are against theirs, that is to say in their uprights; and so they are not found in a subverted order in the transverse into which they pass.

An Example taken from the Square of 100 Cases.

1			4			7			10
	2	3					8	9	

I have not set down the numbers 5 and 6 in this example, because that they are those of the two middle cases of the first transverse, and that the number of the two middle cases of the first transverse, in every square unequally even have a particular rule, which I will give. As to the eight other numbers 1, 2, 3, 4, 7, 8, 9, 10, which are those of the cases equally even, they are ranged according to the rules which I have given. 1. The first and last are in their natural cases, then the second and third are removed, the fourth and the fifth remain in their natural cases, the sixth and the seventh are removed. 2. The removed, viz. 2, 3, 8, 9, are in the cases over against theirs, and in their natural order, and not in an inverted order.

3. As to the two middle numbers, the first continues, and the second is removed: but the first remains not in its natural case. It passes to the case of the second, and the second is not removed to the case which is over against its own, but into that of its opposite; because that it is not necessary that the first leaves its natural case to its opposite, which shall be transported into this first transverse, and that the second leaves also to its opposite, the case which is over against its own.

1			4		5	7			10
	2	3		6			8	9	

The numbers 5 and 6 are the middle. 5 remains in its transverse, but it passes to the case of 6, and 6 is removed to the case of its opposite, and not to that which is over against its own.

4. The

4. The numbers of the last transverse are ranged after this manner. The first and the last remain in their cases, the others fill the cases which are vacant, in the two transverses, and it is necessary to place them there successively, but in an Inverted order. After this manner the two transverses become equal, because that they have given one to the other half of the numbers of the cases equally even, and that their middle numbers do make the like sum in every transverse, the opposites being together, and not in different transverses. It is possible if desired to range the second transverse as we have ranked the first, but then 'twould be necessary to rank the first as we have marked the second.

1	99	98	4	96	5	7	93	92	10
91	2	3	97	6	95	94	8	9	100

The numbers 91 and 100, which are the first and the last of the last transverse, do remain in their natural places, the others which are 92, 93, 94, 95, 96, 97, 98, 99, do fill the cases, which remained vacant in the two transverses, and they are there placed successively, but in an Inverted order.

5. The first and the last uprights of the squares unequally even do rank themselves one in relation to the other, as the first and the last transverses; and by this means the whole square unequally even is found Magical, and by a Method easie to retain, and to execute by Memory.

The demonstration thereof is palpable. For to consider the numbers, as we have ranked them in the first and last transverses, it is evident that the opposite numbers, taken two by two, are there placed either diametrically in the first and last cases of every transverse, or directly opposite in the same upright, and because that the opposite numbers taken, thus two by two, do always make equal sums, it follows that these two transverses being at the top and at the bottom of the squares equally even, and interior already Magical, will add equal sums to the diameters, and to the uprights of this interior square equally even; and that so the uprights and diameters of the square unequally, will be equal in their sums. It will be the same of the transverses of the square unequally even, because that its first and its last uprights will likewise add equal sums to the transverses of the interior square equally even. And our demonstration would be compleat, were not the two numbers mean as well of the first, and last transverses, as of the first and last uprights: for these numbers not being placed every right against its opposite, do add unequal sums to the middle transverses and uprights of the interior square equally even. Therefore to repair this inequality, which is only of two points, it is necessary to make a little alteration in the interior square equally even, which will be the last rule of this Method.

6. By ranging the interior square equally even, according to the rules of the Magical squares equally even; it is necessary to invert the order, which according to these rules of the squares equally even, the two middle numbers of the last transverse of the square of 16 cases, which is at the center of all, and the two middle numbers of the last upright of the same square of sixteen cases, ought to have, you will then weaken the first middle upright, and the first middle transverse of the square equally even: forasmuch as in the first transverse of the square of 16 cases the first middle number is always stronger than the second, and that in the last upright of the same square of 16 cases, the middle superior number is stronger than the inferior.

A Square of Thirty six Cases.

1	35	34	3	32	6
30	8	28	27	11	7
24	23	15	16	14	19
3	17	21	22	20	18
12	26	9	10	29	25
31	2	4	33	5	36

This square is that of *Agrippa*, save that I have placed on the right, what he has put on the left, because that he has taken the squares which he gives, after the *Hebrew* Talismans, where the natural order of the numbers is from the right to the left, according to the *Hebrew's* manner of writing.

A Square of 100 Cases.

1	99	98	4	96	5	7	93	92	10
90	12	88	87	15	16	84	83	19	11
80	79	23	24	76	75	27	28	72	21
31	69	33	34	66	65	37	38	62	70
60	42	58	57	45	46	44	53	49	51
41	52	48	47	55	56	54	43	59	50
61	39	63	64	35	36	67	68	32	40
30	29	73	74	26	25	77	78	22	71
20	82	18	17	85	86	14	13	89	81
91	2	3	97	6	95	94	8	9	100

In the square of 36 cases the numbers 9 and 10, which are the middle of the last transverse of the square of 16 cases, which is at the center, are in an order contrary to that which they ought to have, according to the rules of the squares equally even. Than 14 and 20, which are the middle of the last upright of the same square of 16 cases, are in a contrary number, to that which they ought to have by the same rules: for it would be necessary that 10 was before 9, and 14 under 20.

In

In the square of 100 cases at the seventh transverse, the middle numbers 35 and 36 are placed against the very rules of the squares equally even: 36 ought to precede 35 according to the rules: and 44 and 54 which are the middle of the seventh upright are also inversed, because that 44 ought to be under 54.

In every square equally even ranged Magically, according to the rules which I have given, it is infallible that in the transverse, which is immediately under the middle transverses, the two middle numbers should be in an inverted order, that is to say, the strongest precedes the weakest: for either these middle numbers are removed, and consequently in an inverted order, or they are not removed, and they are likewise in an inverted order, because that then their transverse begins at the right: forasmuch as if the middle numbers of each rank are not removed as it is supposed, the middle of the first upright are not, and so the middle transverses begin on the left, therefore the transverse underneath begins on the right. By a like ratiocination it will be proved that according to the rules of the squares equally even, the middle numbers of the upright, which is immediately after the middle uprights, are ranged in such a manner, that the strongest is always above the weakest.

This is *Agrippa's* Method of the even squares, which in my opinion are the *Indian*, the merit of which consists not in giving the sole possible manner of ranging the even squares, but the most easie to execute by memory: For it is to this principally that it seems, that the *Indians* should addict themselves. In a word, the *Indian* even squares are also Magical in the Geometrical Progression.

The *Indians* have two Principles for the Problem of the Magical squares, the one of which they have applied to the uneven squares, and the other to the even. The Mathematicians of this Country, which have laboured herein, have known only one of these two Principles, which is that of the even squares; but they have adapted it likewise to the uneven squares, and moreover they have added a singular condition to this Problem, which is that the Magical square be so ranged, that in deducting its first compass, that is to say its first and its last transverses, its first and its last uprights, the interior square which shall remain is found Magical, after this very kind, that is to say, being able to lose all its compasses one after the other, and to leave always for the rest a Magical square, provided that this residue have at least 9, or 16 cases; because that the square of 4 cases cannot be Magical.

Monsieur *Arnaud* has given the solution of this last Problem at the end of his Elements of Geometry, and before that he had printed it the first time, I had also resolved this Problem in its whole extent, having been proposed to me by the late Monsieur *de Fermat*, Counsellor in the Parliament of *Tholouse*, whose Memory is yet in Veneration amongst the learned; but then I divined not *Agrippa's* Principle of the unequal squares, nor the reason of *Bachet's* Method.

In fine, I am obliged to render this Testimony to Monsieur *Sauveur*, Professor of the Mathematicks at *Paris*, that he found out a Demonstration of the *Indian* uneven squares, which Monsieur *de Meleuse* communicated unto him: and that he has also invented a Method to range the even squares. I leave unto him the care of publishing this, and several other things of his own Invention, because that this Chapter is already too long.

The Care of the Manners amongst the Chineses, *and of the Antiquities of their History.*

CHina is happily situated, having no foreign war to fear. It has no other Neighbours then *Tartary* on the North, and *Tonquin* on the West. Every where else it is bounded either by the Ocean, or with a desart of several days Journey, or with Woods, and Mountains almost impassible. *Tonquin* is a very little state, if compar'd to *China*: and it is seated under those hot climates, from whence it never comes out as Conqueror. The *Tartar* is continu-

ally

ally accustomed only to make incursions on his Enemies, and not wars in form. A wall on the frontiers of *China*, which stops the passages, has sufficed during a long succession of Ages, to stop all the Enterprizes of the *Tartars*.

It is no wonder then if the *Chinese* are little addicted to War, and if the *Tartars*, tho more weak, and otherwise less proper to make Conquests, have yet subdued them twice in the space of three or four thousand years.

But as much as the *Chinese* have ignored war, as much are they experienced in the knowledge of Government. Their good natural wit has made them to improve it with so much care in the repose which their Country has almost continually enjoyed, that next to the Laws which God gave unto *Moses*, there are none perhaps which do make a compleater body of Policy, nor whose parts concur better to the same end, than the *Chinese* Laws. Thus this people is the most numerous that has ever been in the World, except perhaps the people of God: which, in my opinion, is the best sign of an happy Government.

I have sufficiently declared in my relation, how the *Chinese* have suited their Religion to their Policy, by making of the spirit of Heaven, and of the other spirits an invisible Republick like to theirs, of which they suppose that the members have a secret correspondence with the members of theirs, and that they punish the hidden faults of their Kings, of their Magistrates, and of every one of their Citizens in particular.

I have observed likewise how they have provided for the Perpetuity of their Laws, by the dread of their dead Parents, whom they suppose to be provoked in the other life, with the faults which their Children commit in this, and especially with the great want of respect which it would be in the *Chinese* towards their Ancestors, to change the Laws which they have left them. 'Tis not therefore a vain Ceremony that they mourn for three years with an extream Austerity, and separated from all public Employments, which the *Chinese* Laws do order Children to observe at the death of their Father and Mother, and from which they dispence not even their Kings. They cannot too much imprint in their minds this respect, which has always been their greatest support.

But what I most admire in the Laws of *China*, is the care which they have taken to form the Morals, seeing that it is only good manners, which can maintain the Laws, as it is only good Laws that can make good manners. *Plato*, methinks, understood the whole importance of this Maxim, and if my Memory fails me not, he requires in some places of his Laws, that they intermeddle with the privacy of the Oeconomy of his Citizens: and because he feared that this might appear too new to the People, so free as the *Greeks* were in his time, he sought some excuse for the little which he delivered thereof.

The *Chinese*, on the contrary, have not scrupled to give Laws to almost all the Actions of men. One of their most ancient Books regulates not only the Rites, which concern Religion and the Sacrifices, but all the Duties of Children to their Father, and of the Father towards his Children; of the Husband to the Wife, and of the Wife to the Husband; of Brethren and Friends to each other; of the King to his Subjects, and of the Subjects to their King; of the Magistrates to the People, and of the People to the Magistrates. In this Book, which has the Authority of a Law, the old men are considered as the Fathers of all the People, and of the King himself, the Orphans are there considered as his Children, and all the Citizens as Brethren amongst them. Father *Martinius*
[illegible] reports, that there is almost no humane action, how small soever it be, to which this Book prescribes not Laws, even to cause trouble for an exceeding small particular. I doubt not that all the *Europeans* would judge like him, if this Book came to our knowledge, but this is nevertheless a very ancient Testimony, of the extream care which the *Chinese* have continually taken of good manners.

And because they knew the prevalency which the example of Kings has over People, their greatest study has always been to inspire Vertue into their Kings. *The People, they say, is like the Ears of Corn wherewith a field is covered, the Morals of the Prince are like the Wind, which inclines them, where it listeth.*

Their Policy has therefore no particular manners for their Kings, and other manners for the People. Their Kings are obliged to respect old men: they nourish

from the Vertue of his Ancestors, the Magistrates and People growing debauched in their Morals, would forget their fidelity which they owe him, and which is their first duty, and their first Vertue. Examples hereof are frequent in their History: in which they have not better provided for the security of their Master, than all the other Despotic States. According to them it is 4000 years that their Kingdom has continued in these Maxims, which render it the admiration of all its Neighbors. St *Francis Xavier* reports in his Letters that the *Japonese* incessantly objected to him, that the Christian Religion could not be true, seeing that it was not known by the *Chineses*. Yet I know that the *Chineses* have some Vices, but they perhaps sin less against their Moral Law, than we do against ours. How much have our Morals degenerated from those of our Ancestors? and the *Chineses*, more antient than us, do still esteem it a disgrace to violate their Morals in public, and to fail in the respects which they owe to one another, either by any disobedience to their Parents, or by any quarrel with their equals. They are Infidels, say some, in Commerce; but it may be they are only so with Strangers; as the *Hebrews* lent money to usury to Strangers only: and besides, the *Chineses* which have Commerce with Strangers, are those of the Frontiers, whose manners this very foreign Commerce has depraved.

The greatest Vice of the *Chineses* is doubtless an extream Hypocrisy: but besides that it reigns every where, because it is a Vice which is free from the censure of the Laws, it is perhaps a less evil, than a publick corruption.

But if the *Chinese* History may be credited, 'tis Vertue alone that has formed this great Empire: the love of their Laws, which were at first established in a corner of this Country, gradually drew all the Neighbouring Provinces under the same yoke, it not appearing that the *Chineses* have conquered these Provinces by any war. It is true that all these little States, which were at the beginning as so many hereditary Fiefs given usually to the Princes of the Royal Blood, have been reunited to the Crown by Civil Wars, when the Royal race has changed, and that Usurpers have expelled the lawful Kings from the Throne; but it appears that the first subjection of all these little States to the Crown of *China* has been voluntary. They say that 44 Kingdoms, enamoured with the Vertue of *Venvam*, submitted to his Laws. He reigned over the two thirds of *China*, when it was yet divided. However it be, the *Chineses* have been continually Enemies to war, as the principal cause of the corruption of manners, and they have preferred Morality before all the Glory of Conquests, and all the advantages of Commerce with Strangers.

King *Siven*, the ninth of the Race *Hans*, 60 years before the birth of *Jesus Christ*, dreading the consequences of any motion of the *Tartars*, which sometime before had been confined within their Mountains by *Lieanu*, and who were returned to seize on the flat Country, resolved to prevent them, and make war upon them, before they had put themselves in a condition to carry it into *China*. In another Country this Prudence might have been approved, but it was not at *China*, where the care of good manners is the main affair of the State. The History therefore relates, that his Chief Minister disswaded him from this Enterprize by this discourse. *What, Sir, do you think to invade foreign Countrys, when there are such great things to reform in your own. A Prodigy to this time unheard of amongst us! in this year a Son has slain his Father, seven younger Brothers have killed their 25 elder Brethren. These are the fruit of an intolerable boldness, and which presage a very dangerous corruption in our manners. 'Tis what we ought to be alarmed at, it is to what a speedy remedy must be applied; for so long as these Crimes shall not be suffered at* China, China *will have nothing to fear from the* Tartars: *but if they were once permitted, I fear that they would not only extend themselves into all the Territories of the Empire, but even into the Imperial Palace.*

Under *Juen*, the Tenth King of the same race, the Provinces of *Quantong*, and *Quangsi*, and the Isle of *Hainan* revolting, he levied as many forces as it was possible to reduce them to their Obedience: but *Kiafu*, whom he appointed for their General diverted him from this war, by these words. *Anti-*

ently

ously the Kingdom of China, *was bounded on the East by the Ocean, on the West by the Sandy Desarts, and on the South by the River* Kiang: *but by little and little it enlarged its limits less by Arms, than by Vertue. Our Kings do kindly receive under their Empire, those who voluntarily submit themselves out of Love to our Justice and Clemency, and several neighbouring Provinces submitted themselves: not any was compelled by force. 'Tis my advice that you abstain from this war, and that imitating the good Kings which have lived before you, you may make them to revere in your Maxims. The way to reduce a rebellious People to Obedience, is by the allurement of Vertue, and not by the terror of Arms.*

Yet *China* has had some conquering Kings, but two or three at most, if I am not mistaken: though they say, that *Hiavu*, who was one of these, repented of the wars which he had made, and took no care to preserve his Conquests.

Ou Cepe one of the Disciples of *Confucius*, asked him one day what things were necessary to a good Government. *Plenty of Provisions,* replied he, *a sufficient quantity of Souldiers and Ammunition for War, of Vertue in the King and his Subjects. I understand what you tell me,* replied the Disciple, *but if it were necessary to lack one of these three things, which will you quit the first? The Souldiers,* answered the Philosopher. *But if there was a necessity also of lacking Provisions or Vertue, which of these two losses would you chuse? I would chuse,* saith he, *to want Provisions.* He could not better testifie the Contempt of War, and the Love of good Morals. *Plato* would have but a small number of Citizens in his Republic, because that he dreaded the corruption in too great a Multitude; and that he cared not so much as his Republic should last, as that it should be happy, and consequently virtuous, so long as it did last.

In fine, the *Chineses* have never neglected the instruction of the People. Besides that it is easie to know the Laws which are public, and which never alter, they publish every fifteen days, by Proclamation a small number of Precepts, which are the ground of their Moral Law, as the Commandments of God are ours.

They have not neglected Punishments, seeing that the Magistrates do answer for the faults of their Family, the Parents for the faults of their Children, the Superiors for the crimes of their Inferiors; and that they all have a right to punish the faults of those, for whom they answer: but I have already handled these things, and some others in my Relation.

This is what I had to say, concerning the care which the *Chineses* have had to preserve their Morals, the duration of which is doubtless the greatest wonder, that we have seen among men. It may be suspected, that their History is flattering in some things. They can lye, without fearing to be contradicted by their Neighbours: and it is probable that they have not always spoken the Truth, seeing that their History is the work of their policy. The Office of an Historian is amongst them a public Office. The History of a King is written after his death, by the order of his Successor, who sometimes has been his Enemy; and not any History is published, till the Race of the Kings whereof it treats, is extinct, or at least driven from the Throne. It is not lawful for any Historian, to call in question the History already written, nor for any particular person to write History: every one only may make Abridgements of the Histories already published. There is therefore but one single general History, and no particular Memoirs. Yet there is no appearance that they have corrupted the most important of the Events; and the *Roman* Historians cannot perhaps have been more faithful in what they have writ to the Honor of their Country, and to the Shame of their Enemies.

But a particular reason casts a great doubt on the *Chinese* History, from the beginning of their Monarchy to about 200 years before *Jesus Christ*, because that *Xin* the first King of the Race *Cin*, who reigned about 200 years before *Jesus Christ*, burnt as far as it was possible, all the Books of *China*, which treated not of Medicine or Divination. Their History shews that he exercised great cruelties, against those which concealed Books, and that so few escaped his fury, and almost none entirely: A very singular event amongst those who continually destroy the Memorial of things past. This therefore sufficeth in my opinion to doubt, if one will, whether this great Empire could be formed without any war.

Notwith-

Notwithstanding this loss of their Books, the *Chineses* cease not to give a compleat History not only from the beginning of their Monarchy, but from the Origine of Mankind, which they make to re-ascend several thousands of years beyond the Truth. Nevertheless they themselves acknowledge that their History has the semblance of a Fable, in whatever precedes the beginning of their Monarchy; but it has been hitherto difficult to persuade them that they had not had a long succession of Kings before *Jesus Christ*, which remount beyond the time where our common Chronology places the flood: insomuch that several amongst the Missionaries have thought it necessary to have recourse to the Chronology of the *Septuagint*, according to which the Deluge is more ancient by several Ages, than according to the common Chronology. What render'd the *Chinese* History more probable, is, that under every King it records the Eclipses, and other celestial *Phænomena* of his Reign: but *Monsieur Cassini* having examined the time of a Conjunction of the Planets, which they place under their *fifth* King, he has found it above 500 years later than their History makes it; and he proves this very misreckoning of 500 years by another Astronomical remark, referred to the Reign of their *seventh* King. Thus the *Chinese* Monarchy appears less ancient by 500 years than the *Chineses* have thought, and it may be presumed that in this succession of Kings, which they give us, they have put those who have reigned at the same time in diverse Provinces of *China*, when it was divided into several little Feudatary States under the same Lord.

Monsieur Cassini having given me his Reflexions upon this subject, I have thought fit to add them here, and once again to adorn my work with a Chapter after his fancy. And because he has communicated unto me a thought which he had about the situation of the *Taprobane* of the Ancients, I have besought him to give it me; whatever respects the *Indies* being not improper in this Book, and whatever comes from *Monsieur Cassini* being always well received by all.

Reflexions on the Chinese *Chronology*, *by* Monsieur Cassini.

I. *The System of the* Chineses.

THe years of the *Chineses* are lunisolar, some of which are Common of 12 lunar Months, others Embolismick of 13.

The first day of the month is ordinarily the first day after the Conjunction of the Moon with the Sun, so that the Eclipses of the Sun do ordinarily happen the last day of the month, as may be seen in the *Chinese* Chronology of Father *Couplet*.

If the beginnings of the months do remove from this *Epocha* of the Conjunctions, it is easie to restore them after the observation of an Eclipse of the Sun.

The order of the Common and Embolismick years, is regulated by the Cycle of 60 years, in which 22 are Embolismick, and the others Common.

According to Father *Martinius* in his *Chinese* History, the years at the Moons Conjunction with the Sun, the nearest the fifteenth degree of *Aquarius*: that is to say, the point of the Zodiack which is at equal distances from the points of the Winter Solstice, and of the Vernal Equinox; which according to this Author has been observed from the twenty fifth Age before the Birth of *Jesus Christ* to the present Age: tho this beginning has varied according to the will of diverse Emperors, and that they have been obliged sometimes to correct the year, from the Errors which were crept therein.

Their

There may be more error in the *Epocha* of the years, than in the *Epocha* of the months, because that the points of the Zodiack, which determine the first month of the year, are not immediately visible, as the Eclipses of the Sun, which determine the beginnings of the months.

It is certain, as Father *Martinius* remarks, that after a period of 60 lunisolar years, the Conjunctions of the Moon with the Sun return not to the same point of the Zodiack, but that they anticipate three degrees, which the Sun runs through only in three days, which in ten periods of 60 years amount to 30 days. Thus to hinder the beginning of the year from removing above a Sign from the fifteenth degree of *Aquarius*, it would be necessary that the *Chineses* should add to every period of 600 years a month extraordinary, above the 22 months which are added to every period of 60 years. Yet Father *Martinius* relates that they have no need of any intercalation: which I suppose it is necessary to understand of these three days apart, but not of the extraordinary intercalations of the months, when this difference of three days is mounted to a whole month.

II. *Doubts upon the* Chinese *Chronology*.

BUt it is not known whether this be regularly practised, or whether the *Chineses* do add some months extraordinary to their years without rule, when they perceive that the beginning of the year is too remote from the middle of *Aquarius*; and whether the Intercalations of the months, as well ordinary as extraordinary, are made on purpose.

We have reason to doubt of what Father *Couplet*, who has been a long time in *China*, says in his Treatise of the *Chinese* Chronology, that the *Chineses* begin their years at the Conjunction of the Moon with the Sun the nearest the fifth degree of *Aquarius*, which must be so at present: So that from Father *Martinius* to the present *Epocha* of the *Chinese* years, they would have run back 30 degrees.

If the Observation related by Father *Martinius* in his seventh Book of his *History* was true, the beginning of the *Chinese* year would be several Signs distant from the fifteenth degree of *Aquarius*, since the time that this degree has been assign'd for a middle limit of the *Chinese* years; for he says that according to the *Chinese* Historians, whose credit he suspects, the 2514th year before the *Epocha* of *Jesus Christ*, in the beginning of the year, five Planets appeared in the Constellation of *Ching*, which at present extends from the beginning of *Cancer* to the beginning of *Leo*, and then consequently extended from the 4th or 5th of *Gemini* to the same degrees of *Cancer*. It may be seen without any other calculation, that this observation agrees not to the System of the *Chinese* years; for seeing that *Mercury* removes not from the Sun above 28 degrees, nor *Venus* above 48; it is certain that *Venus* could not be in the Constellation *Ching*, before that the Sun had passed half of the Sign *Aries*, which is two whole Signs distant from the middle of *Aquarius*; and that *Mercury* could not appear in this Constellation unless the Sun had passed the beginning of *Taurus*, and because it was necessary that at least one of these two Planets should appear in this Constellation to accomplish the number of five, or both, if the Moon meet not therein; (for the Sun in this *Hypothesis* could not be there) it is certain that the Sun could not be less remote from the middle of *Aquarius* than two whole Signs in the beginning of the year, at which this Conjunction is marked. The *Chinese* History remarks also, that at several times there is found some digressions in the *Chinese* years, which have obliged several Emperors to restore them to the first *Epocha*. These digressions may have happened for having intercalated the months too frequently, or for having neglected the intercalations of the months when it was necessary to make them, and as we have not the History of these intercalations, it is not possible to remove the perplexities which there is, for this cause, in the *Chinese* Chronology.

It is known what has been that of the *Chineses* in this very age: for notwithstanding the Antiquity of their magnificent Observatories, furnished with all sorts of Instruments, and the ample Colledges and Governments of Astronomy, this Nation so very jealous of its own Glory, and an Enemy to Strangers, has been obliged to joyn with its Astronomers for the correction of their Calender, the *Jesuits*, which went thither to introduce a Religion contrary to theirs, and to heap Honors on the Fathers *Licci*, *Schall*, *Verbiest*, and *Grimaldi*, who in the time of his absence in *Italy*, was elected by the Emperor of *China* for President of Astronomy. From whence it may be judged that the *Chineses* had not so certain a method of regulating their years, that they have owned, that they are not capable of regulating them all alone without great Errors.

III. *An ancient Observation of the meeting of the Planets in the Constellation* Xe.

FAther *Martinius* attributes to the fifth Emperor of *China*, whom he reports to have reigned from the year 2513 to the 2435th year before *Jesus Christ*, the rule of beginning the year with the new Moon nearest the 15 of *Aquarius*.

He says that, according to the Author of the *Chinese* History, this Emperor saw five Planets joyned together on the same day of the Conjunction of the Sun and Moon in the Constellation *Xe*, which at present begins about the eighteenth degree of the Sign *Pisces*, and extends to the fourth degree of *Aries*, and that he took this day for the beginning of the year.

He relates not in what year of his Reign the Conjunction of the Planets was: but as this Conjunction is very rare, we may search whether it could happen between the 2513 and 2435th year before *Jesus Christ* in this Constellation of *Xe*.

This research is important, forasmuch as this *Epocha* would be several Ages ancienter than the Deluge, according to the calculation of those who place it about 2300 years between the Deluge and the Birth of *Jesus Christ*.

IV. *Of the* Chinese *Constellations.*

FOR the understanding of this Celestial Character, we have examined the *Chinese* Constellations, of which *Martinius* in his History and in his *Chinese* Atlas gives the Catalogue calculated for the year 1628, after the *European* method, and we have compared them with our Constellations calculated for the same year.

We have found by this comparison, that every *Chinese* Constellation begins ordinarily with some considerable fixed Star, which in the year 1628 is found in *Tycho's* Catalogue almost always in the same minute, as the beginning of the corresponding Constellation in the two Catalogues of Father *Martinius*, except 3 or 4, in which it appears, that there is a mistake of numbers in the two Catalogues, where the distance taken from the point of the Equinox, accords not with the degrees and minutes of the Sign of the Zodiac, to which these Constellations are referred, as it agrees in the other Constellations.

Wherefore we do here insert them after two ways, according to the numbers of Father *Martinius*, and according to our correction.

Con-

Constellationes Sinenses ex P. Martini historia, & ex ejus Atlante Sinico ad annum 1628.

Nomen.			Longitudo.			Gradus.		Signa.
Kio	♃		198	39		18	39	♎
Kang	♀		209	14		29	14	♎
Ti	♄		219	54		9	54	♏
Fang	☉		237	48		27	48	♏
Sing	☽		242	34		8	34	♐
Vi.	♂		250	7		20	7	♐
		corrige	260	7				
Ki	☿		255	43		25	43	♐
Teu	♃		275	3		5	3	♑
Nieu	♀		298	54		28	54	♑
Nio	♄		306	35		6	35	♒
Hiu	☉		318	14		18	14	♒
Guei	☽		318	13		18	13	♒
Xe	♂		346	20		18	20	♓
		corrige	348	20				
Pi	☿		4	8		4	8	♈
Quei	♃		15	32		15	32	♈
Leu	♀		28	46		26	46	♈
					corrige	18	46	♈
Cury	♃		41	46		11	46	♉
Mao	☉		53	37		23	37	♉
Pie	☽		63	16		3	16	♊
Sang	♂		77	14		17	14	♊
Cu	☿		78	35		18	35	♊
Cing	♃		90	8		0	8	♋
Quei	♀		120	33		0	33	♌
Lieu	♄		125	9		5	9	♌
Sing	☉		142	9		22	9	♌
Chang	☽		150	32		0	32	♍
Ye	♂		168	36		18	36	♍
Chin	☿		185	36		5	39	♎

Fixæ ad initia Constellationum Sinensium ex comparatione Tabulæ præcedentis cum Tychonica deductæ Longitudines Tychonicæ ad annum 1628.

Nomina.	Fixæ.	Grad.	Min.	
Kio.	*Spica Virginis*	♎	18	39
Kang.	*Australis in fimbria Virginis*	♎	29	14
Ti.	*Lucida lancis australis*	♏	9	54
Fang.	*Austr. trium in fronte Scorp.*	♏	27	48
Sing.	*Præced. lucent. in corp. Scorp.*	♐	8	34
Vi.	*Dexter humerus Ophiuci.*	♐	20	5
Ki.	*Cuspis Sagittarij*	♐	25	43
Teu.	*Antecedens in jaculo Sagitt.*	♑	5	3
Nieu.	*Austr. in cornu præced. Capr.*	♑	28	54
Nio.	*Antecedens in manu Aquarij*	♒	6	35
Hiu.	*In humero sinistro Aquarij*	♒	18	14
Guei.	*Dexter humerus Aquarij*	♒	18	13
Xe.	*Prima alæ Pegasi.*	♓	18	20

Pi

Pi.	*Extrema alæ Pegasi.*	♈	4	1
Qui.	*In sinistro brachio Andromed.*	♈	15	31
Leu.	*Sequens in cornu austr. Arietis.*	♈	28	46
Guey.	*In femore Arietis.*	♉	11	46
Mao.	*Occid. trium lucid. in Pleiad.*	♉	23	37
Pie.	*Oculus Tauri Borealis.*	♊	3	16
Sang.	*Recedens Balthei Orientis.*	♊	17	14
Cu.	*In extremo cornu austr. Tauri*	♊	19	35
Cing.	*Pes sequens præced. Gemin.*	♋	0	7
Quei.	*Borea præc. in quad. lat. Canc.*	♌	0	33
Lieu.	*Septentrion. in rostro Corv.*	♌	5	30
Sing.	*Cor Hydræ*	♌	22	9
Chang.	*In medio corpore Virginis*	♍	0	37
Te.	*In basi Crateris.*	♍	18	36
Chin.	*Tertia in ala austrina Virg.*	♎	4	59

This agreement of the numbers of these Tables with those of *Tycho*, almost in the same minute, gave me ground to imagine that these Tables have been calculated by the *Jesuites*, who went about an Age since to *China*, and not by the *Chineses*. For what probability is there, that without being drawn from *Tycho's* Tables they should be so conformable thereto? Our Astronomers of this Age find difficulty to agree in the same minute in the place of the fixed Stars: and it is known that between the Catalogues of *Tycho*, and that of the *Landgrave of Hesse*, made at the same time by excellent Astronomers, there is a difference of several minutes. Wherefore it is not very probable that the Observations of the *Chineses*, should agree almost always with the Observations of *Tycho* in the same minute.

V. *The Method of terminating the* Chinese *Constellations at any time.*

FAther *Martinius* remarks, that the *Chineses* do determine the Longitude in the Heaven by the Poles of the World; that is to say by great Circles drawn through the Poles perpendicular to the Equinoxial, where we denote the right ascensions of the Stars. Therefore the stars which are between two Circles, that do pass through the Poles, and through the two fixed Stars which terminate a constellation, relate to that very constellation.

But it appears by the comparison of the two preceding Tables, that the longitudes are not set down differently in the Table of Father *Martinius* from what they are noted in *Tycho's* Table, which reduces the Stars to the Ecliptick, and not to the Equinoxial. They are not therefore set down after the *Chinese* manner; but to reduce them after the *Chinese* method, it is necessary to refer the Stars which are at the beginning of every constellation to the Equinoxial, and to find their right ascensions, and the points of the Zodiack which shall have the same right ascensions, will be at the beginning of these constellations.

When a Star falls in the *Colure* of the Solstices, as the foot of *Gemini* in that Table where begins the constellation Cing, there is no difference between its longitude after our manner, and its right ascension, which is the longitude after the *Chinese*; but as the Stars remove from the *Colure* of the Solstices, the difference of their longitudes and of their right ascensions augments so much more, as the latitudes or declinations of the Stars are greater. And because that the fixed Stars remove continually from one *Colure* and approach the other by a motion parallel to the Ecliptick, and oblique to the Equinoxial, this difference varies continually, and otherwise more constellation than in another: whence it happens that from one Age to the other the same *Chinese* constellation determined by two fixed Stars enlarges, or contracts, and comprehends not always the same number of fixed Stars.

There-

Therefore to know in what *Chinese* constellation a Planet falls at a certain time, it is necessary to find for this time the right ascension of the Planet, and the right ascension of the fixed Stars adjoyning, which determine the beginning and end of the Constellations; which we should not have known without the reflexion which we have made, that every Constellation begins with a certain fixed Star, and without the advice which Father *Martinius* gives us, that the *Chinese* longitudes are taken from the Poles of the world, that is to say, differently from what they are set down in this Table.

It appears by this Table, that the Constellation *Xe* here treated of, begins with the first of the Wing of *Pegasus*, and ends with the last of the same Wing, seeing that according to the second Column of this very Table, this Constellation began in the year 1628, at 18 degrees and 20 minutes of *Pisces*, where we find at the same year the first of the Wing by *Tycho's* Table reduced to the same time; tho the first Column of the *Chinese* Table gives two degrees less, which is doubtless an error of the impression or calculation, which has crept into the two works of Father *Martinius*.

The Originals of the Tables of *Tycho* and *Longimontanus* do likewise give the last of the Wing at 4 degrees and a minute of *Aries*, where ends the Constellation *Xe*, and where begins the following Constellation *Pi*, though the *Rudolphine* and *Philolaick* Tables with those of Father *Riccioles* do show the same Star at 4 degrees of *Pisces*, which certainly is an error of the Transcribers, which is slipt into the works of these Astronomers. As these two Stars have a great Northern longitude, the first being 19 degrees and 26 minutes, the second 12 degrees and 35 minutes; the difference between their longitude and their right ascension, which the *Chineses* take for longitude, is considerable at present, forasmuch as these Stars are near the *Colure* of the Equinoxes, where this difference is greater than elsewhere. But it was not so considerable anciently, when these Stars were near the *Colure* of the Solstices.

VI. *A Determination of the time of the meeting of the five Planets in the Constellation* Xe.

HAving reduced these Stars to the Equinoxial in the twenty fourth and twenty fifth Age before the Birth of *Jesus Christ*, we have not found, that between the Circles of the declinations which pass through these Stars, five Planets could be found joyned together, neither in these Ages, nor in two others before and after, whilst that the Sun was in the sign of *Aquarius*, as the *Chinese* History imports.

But we have found that *Saturn*, *Jupiter*, *Venus*, *Mercury*, and the *Moon* met in that *Chinese* constellation determined by this method, the Sun being in the 20th of *Aquarius*, in the 2012 year before the *Epocha* of *Jesus Christ*, the 26th of *February* according to the *Julian*, the 9th according to the *Gregorian* form, which runs at present, and that the day following 27 of *February* at 6 a Clock in the morning at *China*, happen'd the conjunction of the Moon with the Sun, which may be that which was taken as the *Epocha* of the *Chinese* years.

Then according to the Catalogue of *Tycho*, and the motion which he gives to the fixed Stars, the first of the wing of *Pegasus* from which began the constellation *Xe*, was at 26 degrees 50 minutes of *Capricorn*, and the Circle of its declination cut the Eclíptick at 24 degrees of the same sign.

The last of the wing of *Pegasus* was at 12 degrees and a half of *Aquarius*, and its Circle of Declination cut the Ecliptick, and carry'd it back to the eleventh degree of the same sign.

The Morning of *February* 27 In the *Conjunction* at *China*.

The beginning of the Constellation *Xe* was	♑	24
Saturn,	♑	24
Jupiter,	♑	26
Mercury,	♑	27
Venus,	♒	4

Ii 4 The

The Moon. ♒ 8
The end of the Constellation Xe. ♒ 11
And in 24 hours or thereabouts happened the Conjunction of the Moon with the Sun.

The *Chinese* Chronology places the Conjunction of the Planets between the 2513 and 2435 years before the Birth of *Jesus Christ*. There will be therefore a difference of 5 Ages between the time denoted by this Chronology and the true time. Thus the *Chinese Epocha* will be five Ages later then the *Chinese* Historians suppose it.

VII. *An Ancient Observation of a Winter Solstice made at* China.

THis difference of five Age whereby it appears according to this calculation, that the *Chineses* do make their *Epocha* too antient, is confirmed by another place of Father *Martinius* his History, where this Author reports that under *Yao* the seventh Emperor of the *Chineses*, the Winter Solstice was observed about the first degree of the constellation *Hiu*, which at present begins about the 18th of *Aquarius*, so that since this time the Solstice is removed above 48 degrees from its first place; he refers this Observation to the 20th year of *Yao*, which he reports to have been the 2341 before the Birth of *Jesus Christ*.

It appears by the Table that this constellation *Hiu* began with the Star which is in the left shoulder of *Aquarius*, which in the year 1618 was at 18 degrees, 16 Minutes of *Aquarius*; but the 20th year of *Yao* it was in 29 degrees of *Sagittarius* and some minutes, seeing that the Winter Solstice, which is always at the beginning of *Capricorn*, was at the first of the constellation *Hiu*. The distance between these two places of the Zodiac is 49 degrees 16 minutes, which the fixed Stars according to *Tycho's* Table do make in 3478 years, by reason of 51 seconds *per annum*: from whence having deducted 1625 years at most, which are elapsed from the *Epocha* of *Jesus Christ*, the 20th of *Yao* would be the 1852 year before the Birth of *Jesus Christ*, which Father *Martinius* according to the *Chinese* History placeth in the 2347th year before *Jesus Christ*, making it more antient by about 497 years. Thus there are about 5 Ages difference between this *Epocha* taken from the *Chinese* History, and the same drawn from the motion of the fixed Stars made in this interval of time, as we have found by the Examination of the Observation of the 5 Planets in the Constellation Xe.

According to Father Martinius *in the beginning of his History of* China, *it seems that the* Chineses *do reckon but five Planets,* Saturn, Jupiter, Mars, Venus, *and* Mercury, *and that they suppose at the time of their fifth Emperor, the concourse of these five Planets in the Constellation* Xe, *on the same day that there was a Conjunction of the Moon with the Sun. But if this* Chinese *observation must be thus understood, 'twould be a mere groundless mistake: such a concourse having not happened at the time denoted by the* Chineses, *nor long before it, so that it cannot be known perhaps how to take it.*

The Historians supported with Astronomical Observations, do merit therefore to be examined before that credit be given thereunto. Thus an account of Eclipses, which is at the beginning of Diogenes Laertius, *and which he relates after* Sotion, *is condemned as false by Monsieur* Cassini. Sotion *reckoned 48863 years between* Vulcan *and* Alexander *the* Great, *and in this interval he placed 373 solar Eclipses, and 832 lunar.*

A too ready belief must not likewise be given to an History, because it gives us a well ranged succession of Kings. The Persians *do give us one of this Nature, which we know to be full of falsities; and we have the Genealogies of our Kings from* Adam, *which are yet more spurious. 'Tis not only from a well connected succession, that the Historians which we give credit, do take their certainty, but from that they are confirmed one by the other: All the Nations that can have a knowledge of the same things, relating them after the same manner, at least as to the most important circumstances; so that where there is a diversity of*

ob-

whence we fall into doubt. The History of the Chineses *has neither been contradicted, nor confirmed by their Neighbours: no Authority can be drawn from their silence; and thus all that we have to do, is to believe it true in the gross, especially from about 200 years before Jesus Christ; but not in what oppugnes our Histories, which are better attested than theirs.*

Concerning the Isle Taprobane, *by Monsieur* Cassini.

THE situation of the Isle *Taprobane*, according to *Ptolemy* in the seventh Book of his Geography, was over against the Promontary *Cori*.

This Promontary is placed by *Ptolemy* between the Rivers *Indus* and *Ganges*, nearer *Indus* than the *Ganges*.

This Isle *Taprobane* was divided by the Equinoxial Line into two unequal parts, the greatest of which was in the Northern Hemisphere, extending to 12 or 13 degrees of Northern Latitude. The least part was in the Southern Hemisphere, extending to two degrees and a half of Southern Latitude.

Round about this Island there were 1378 little Isles, among which there were 19 more considerable, the name of which was known in the West.

The Promontory *Cory* could be no other than that, which is at present called *Comori*, or *Comorin*, which is also between the *Indus* and *Ganges*, nearer the *Indus* than the *Ganges*.

Over against this Cape there is not at present so great an Isle as *Taprobane*, which could be divided by the Equinoxial, and environed with 1378 Isles: but there is a multitude of little Isles, called *Maldives*, which the Inhabitants report to be to the number of 12 Thousand. According to the Relation of *Pirard*, who lived there five years, these Isles have a King, who assumes to himself the Title of King of 13 Provinces, and 12 Thousand Isles.

Every one of these thirteen Provinces is an heap of little Isles, each of which is environed with a great bank of Stone, which incloses it all round like a great wall: they are called *Attolons*. They have each Thirty miles in circumference, a little more or less, and are of a figure almost round, or oval. They are end to end one from the other, from the North to the South; and they are separated by Channels of the Sea, some broad, others very narrow. These Stone-banks which environ every *Attolon*, are so high, and the Sea breaks there with such an impetuosity, that they which are in the middle of an *Attolon*, do see these banks all round, with the Waves of the Sea which seem as high as the Houses. The Inclosure of an *Attolon* has but 4 Avenues, two on the North-side, two others on the South-side, one of which is at the East, the other at the West, and the largest of which is 200 paces, the narrowest somewhat less than 30. At the two sides of each of these Avenues there are some Isles, but the Currents and great Tides do daily diminish the number thereof. *Pirard* adds, that to see the inside of one of these *Attolons*, one would say that all these little Isles and the Channels of the Sea, which it incloses, are only a continued plain, and that it was anciently only a single Island, cut and divided afterwards into several. Every where almost is seen the bottom of the Channels which divide them, so shallow they are, except in some places: and when the Sea is low, the water reaches not up to the girdle, but to the middle of the leg almost every where.

There is a violent and perpetual Current, which from the month of *April* to the month of *October* comes impetuously from the West, and causes the continual rains which do there make the Winter; and at the other six months the Winds are fixed from the East, and do bring a great heat, without any rain, which causes their Summer. At the bottom of these Channels, there are great Stones, which the Inhabitants do use to build with, and they are also stored with a kind of Bushes, which resemble Coral; which renders the passage of the Boats through these Channels extreamly difficult.

Linschoten testifies that according to the *Mallabars*, these little Isles have formerly been joyned to the firm Land, and that by the succession of time they have been looſed thence by the Violence of the Sea, by reaſon of the lowneſs of the Land.

'Tis therefore probable that the *Maldives* are a remainder of the great Iſland *Taprobane*, and of the 1378 Iſlands which did encompaſs it, which have been carryed away, or diminiſhed by the Currents, there remaining nothing elſe but theſe Rocks, which muſt formerly be the baſes of the Mountains: and what remains in the incloſure of theſe Rocks, where the Sea daſhes ſo, that it is capable only of dividing, but not of carrying away the Lands which are included within their Circuit.

It is certain that theſe Iſles have the ſame ſituation in regard of the Equinoxial and Promontory, and of the Rivers *Indus* and *Ganges*, that *Ptolomy* alligns to ſeveral places of the Iſle *Taprobane*.

The Lord's Prayer *and the* Ave Mary *in* Siameſe, *with the Interlinary Tranſlation, to be inſerted in* Page 180.

Father our who art in Heaven. The Name of God be glorified in all places
Po raou you ſavang. Sihou Pra hai pra kut tonk lang
by People all offer to God praiſe. The Kingdom of God I pray to find
kon tang tai tonai Pra pon Meuang Pra co hai dai
with us to finiſh conformable to the heart of God in the Kingdom of
ke raou hai leou ning tchai pra Meuang
the Earth even as of Heaven. The Nouriſhment of us of all days I pray
Pen-din ſemo ſavang Ahan raou tonk van co
to find with us in day this I pray to pardon the offences of us even
hai dai ke raou van ni co prot bap raou ſe-
as we pardon perſons who do offences to us do not let us fall into
mo raou prot pon tam bap ke raou. Ta hai raou tok nai
the cauſe of Sin deliver out of evil all.
kouam bap hai poun kiat aucrai tang-poang. *Amen.*

Ave Maria full of Grace God be in the place of you. You juſt-good
Tem ancſong, Pra you leng nang. Nang ſomo-boa
more than all With Sons Womb in the place of you
yingkoua nang tang tai. Teui louk aoierg, leng nang
God the perſon of Jeſus juſt charitable more than all. *Sancta Maria*
pra Onghiao Teſu ſomo-boui ying koua tang tai.
Mother of God aſſiſt by prayer to God for us people of Sin
Me Pra thoai ving van Pra pro raou kon bap
now and in the time of our dying.
tcit-bat-ni te meua raou tcha tai, *Amen.*

E R R A T A.

www.ingramcontent.com/pod-product-compliance
Lightning Source LLC
Chambersburg PA
CBHW020511270326
41926CB00008B/830

* 9 7 8 3 7 4 2 8 1 2 6 7 4 *